Labor Markets and
Human Resource Management

Labor Markets and Human Resource Management

Morris M. Kleiner
University of Minnesota

Robert A. McLean
University of North Carolina at Chapel Hill

George F. Dreher
Indiana University

Scott, Foresman/Little, Brown College Division

Scott, Foresman and Company
Glenview, Illinois   Boston   London

To our families

Library of Congress Cataloging-in-Publication Data
Kleiner, Morris M.
    Labor markets and human resource management/Morris Kleiner,
Robert McLean, George Dreher.
        p.   cm.
    Includes bibliographies and index.
    ISBN 0-673-18342-4
    1. Industrial relations—United States.   2. Personnel management—
United States.   3. Human capital—United States.   I. McLean,
Robert A.   II. Dreher, George F.   III. Title.
    HD8072.5.K56   1988   87-26573
    658.3—dc19   CIP

123456-RRC-929190898887

Preface

Labor Markets and Human Resource Management provides a unique, integrative prospective on labor markets, human resource management, and industrial relations. We think that it is important for general managers to be aware of the role that the economic and social environments have on developing human resource policies, and how these policies, once formulated, are implemented within the organization. Therefore, in this text we combine the major topics of the labor market environment with industrial relations, which forms the basis of strategic policy development in the firm. Next, we integrate that policy with the role that human resource management takes in its detailed implementation. Furthermore, we take a decision-making approach to human resources, which uses cost-benefit analysis in assessing many human resource issues within organizations. Through the integration of the labor market and human resource management, and the use of this decision-making approach, students can analyze an organization's most valuable asset—its human resources—with a more comprehensive perspective.

Labor Markets and Human Resource Management is particularly appropriate for someone who plans to be a generalist within an organization. It is best suited as a first course in human resource management, labor problems, or labor-management relations. It is not intended as a final course in the field for someone who will be a specialist in human resources. The book has been written so that it will be appropriate for juniors and seniors in most colleges and universities, as well as MBA students.

Labor Markets and Human Resource Management includes the major subjects traditionally covered in introductory undergraduate and MBA courses in labor markets, personnel, and labor relations. The first chapter presents the reasons for studying human resources and underlines the importance of the topic within the organization. The decision-making approach is outlined in Chapter 2 and details the importance of cost-benefit analysis in making private and public decisions on labor issues. This chapter presents the importance of knowing firm goals, derives basic present value concepts (with illustrations), develops techniques for the costing-out of labor contracts, and examines the concept of uncertainty in making decisions on labor issues. Most of the remaining chapters in the text have problem sets requiring numerical solutions and their applications to private and public decision-making. The text includes the following major sections: (1) introduction and decision-oriented approach (Chapters 1 and 2), (2) the economics of human resource management (Chapters 3-6), (3) institutional and legal environment of labor (Chapters 7-10), (4) personnel system inputs (Chapters 11 and 12), (5) personnel system interventions (Chapters 13-16), (6) labor relations (Chapters 17-20), and (7) human resource issues in the economy (Chapter 21). A detailed easy-to-follow Instructor's Manual is provided to make the transition from traditional texts to this one relatively easy. It contains Teaching Tips, answers to all questions and problems in the text, and a test bank of approximately twenty true-false and multiple-choice questions per chapter, with answers.

We think this approach and broad coverage integrates human resources into the mainstream of management or business schools and public policy departments in most universities. It is the prospective for faculty who want their students to have an analytic approach to the topic.

In undertaking this project we wish to thank all of our teachers and others who have influenced our careers and prospectives on labor markets, industrial relations, and human resources management. Specifically, we want to thank Hugh Folk, Richard B. Freeman, Anthony L. Redwood, George Hildebrand, Walter Galenson, the late Vladimir Stoikov, Vernon Briggs, Ronald Ehrenberg, Hobart Osburn, and Paul Sparks.

In addition, we want to express our appreciation to the following individuals who have been kind enough to read all or parts of this text. In large part the success to which we are able to present our approach is due to the comments and criticism received from these individuals as well as students at the University of Kansas, who used earlier versions of this text in various courses. The persons who read and commented on this text are:

Dennis A. Ahlburg
University of Minnesota

Trevor Bain
University of Alabama

Brian Becker
State University of New York, Buffalo

John W. Boudreau
Cornell University

Robert Bretz
University of Kansas

Margaret K. Chandler
Columbia University

John Delaney
Columbia University

David Estenson
University of Minnesota

Harry J. Holzer
Michigan State University

Lawrence M. Kahn
University of Illinois, Urbana-Champaign

Douglas M. McCabe
Georgetown University

Michael K. Mount
University of Iowa

Raymond A. Noe
University of Minnesota

Craig Olson
University of Wisconsin, Madison

Richard B. Peterson
University of Washington

Susan Schwochau
State University of New York, Buffalo

Steven Thomas
Western Illinois University

Finally, we want to especially thank our editor at Scott, Foresman, George Lobell, who had the foresight and desire to encourage us to undertake this project. Further, thanks are due to Dorothy J. Jones, who typed the entire manuscript with the patience, accuracy, and the understanding that working with three demanding authors takes.

Morris M. Kleiner
Robert A. McLean
George F. Dreher

Table of Contents

CHAPTER 1

LABOR MARKETS AND HUMAN RESOURCE MANAGEMENT

E ach of us at one time or another has either worked for an organization, been in charge of other people who were paid to accomplish a task, or been the beneficiary of work completed by others. For most individuals in the United States, work is a primary activity. For those persons who do work, more time is spent in that activity than in any other. Understanding what happens at the workplace, and its implications for the success of the organization and the economy is a primary goal of this textbook. For the next several months, you, as a student of labor markets and human resource management, will have an opportunity to investigate and begin to understand the complex circumstances of the employment relationship.

In long-established curricula in management schools, economics departments, and public policy institutes, courses are offered dealing with financial markets or product markets. Why study the labor market in addition to financial or product markets? First, in the U.S. economy, labor costs are currently 75 percent of total national income, and this ratio has remained relatively constant during the past ten years.[1] Further, for most organizations the largest single cost is that related to human resources, and

[1] *Federal Reserve Bulletin,* Vol. 72, No. 2, February 1986, p. A51.

most enterprises consider their people to be their greatest asset.[2] Second, for most individuals money from work is their largest source of income. Third, there are unique aspects of the labor market that distinguish it from other kinds of markets in the economy. These characteristics make the use of solely traditional methods of economic analysis of the price system incomplete in attempting to determine individual or group responses at the workplace, without also knowing more about behavioral relationships.

What are these characteristics of the labor market that distinguish it from other markets in the economy? First, in the labor market, the inputs or people cannot be bought and sold; they can only be rented for specific periods of time.[3] Unlike product or financial markets, the conditions under which these services are rented are often as important as the price. Nonmonetary factors, such as job safety, control over the task, personality of the managers, and flexibility of time, play a much larger role in determining whether transactions are made in labor markets than they do in financial or product markets. Second, there are many more regulations influencing the market behavior of human resources than in most other markets. Regulations affecting the labor market include the Civil Rights Act, the Occupational Safety and Health Act, Minimum Wage legislation, and the National Labor Relations Act. Some of these pieces of legislation place major restrictions on the employers' ability to price labor as well as how human resources will be allocated and treated in an efficient manner.

Characteristics of the Market for Labor

In spite of these restrictions, the conditions under which employers and employees rent labor constitutes a market for labor. This is not as obvious as it may seem to some policymakers. During the late 1960s then Secretary of Labor, Willard Wirtz, following discussions with the AFL-CIO, asked that all references to labor markets be removed from new Department of Labor documents. Although this policy was later overturned, it has not always been apparent that human resources should be classified as operating in a market. However, there are several characteristics which suggest that a market operates for human resources in the United States. First, a price is determined for labor services for the items to be delivered. This price is determined either formally through a labor contract like those obtained in collective bargaining agreements, or implicitly through informal or unwritten agreements that are based on precedents or experience.

---

[2] Henry L. Dahl, Jr., "Is Anybody Measuring Return on Investment in Human Resources?" Upjohn Co., 1979.

[3] Ronald Ehrenberg and R. S. Smith, *Modern Labor Economics, Theory and Public Policy,* Scott, Foresman and Co., Glenview, Illinois, 1985.

The courts, in some recent cases, have ruled that personnel practices are binding and have the weight of a formal contract in setting both wages and the length of employment. These court decisions have modified the longstanding employment-at-will doctrine, which allows employers to fire or dismiss employees at any time. Rulings in California have even given employees punitive damages for "illegal firings" under state law.[4] Second, there are formal institutions established for renters and sellers of labor services to help in the exchange. For example, these transactions in the market for labor occur through help wanted ads, personnel offices, government-sponsored and private employment agencies, and union hiring halls.

In these market exchanges, workers are typically compensated for their time, rather than for what they produce. In most cases this means compensation on an hourly, weekly, monthly, or yearly scale. In the U.S. workforce, most workers are paid to show up for work and follow orders.[5] Under this form of compensation of pay for time worked, employers must give a great deal of attention to the staffing and selection of employees, as well as attention to factors that encourage retention and reduce absenteeism. In the U.S. labor market, the ability to forecast individual differences in motivation and commitment to work can be a major factor in organizational success.

Employers also view the demand for labor services in a way that is different from the way they view transactions in product or financial markets. Employers do not hire labor for the pleasure of having a particular number of employees. For most organizations, workers are hired because they help produce a product or service. This means that the demand for labor is a derived demand; that is, the demand for labor is dependent on the demand for products or other services. Generally, modern methods of production require the simultaneous use of labor, machines, technology, and raw materials. This is called joint demand. If the product is a refrigerator, management must decide how much steel, rubber, and aluminum to use. In deciding how many people to use along with other inputs in production, firms are making a joint demand decision, usually based on current technology and the prices of the other inputs.

Two of the major issues in labor market analysis deal with compensation and productivity. In a competitive market for the products of a firm, two key questions are asked by economists. First, why would one employer choose to pay more to their workers than would another employer? Second, why do not more of those that pay more go out of business?[6] The answer to

[4] R. Michael Smith, "Exceptions to the Employment-at-Will Doctrine," *Labor Law Journal,* December, 1985, pp. 875–891.

[5] Ehrenberg and Smith, *ibid.*

[6] Erica L. Groshen, "Sources of Wage Dispersion: How Much Do Employers Matter?" Ph.D. Thesis, Harvard University, 1986.

the first question of why some firms pay more than others is usually differences in productivity varying across groups of workers and firms, and if this is the case, it also answers the second questions of how these firms can stay in business with higher labor costs.[7] If this is not the answer, then information costs across companies are high in markets for products, or competition does not exist in product markets.

For employers, this implies that a decision must be made on a strategy for wage determination within their organization. For many firms, the decision of what to pay is based on the education and training of their employees. In addition, compensating wage differentials, which are extra pay to attract workers to a job, are based on the fact that some workers perform tasks that are either more unpleasant or hazardous than others.

In other organizations, wages also vary based on the amount of monitoring or supervision needed of other employees. For many blue collar workers and to a large extent in the nonfederal public sector, unions and management determine wages by bargaining. In the private sector, bargained wages are determined based on the economic strength of unions or management with the outcome determining how much should go to workers and how much should be allocated to shareholders of the company. This process assumes that there are profits that can be allocated among the various constituents of the firm. For the most part, these are the market driven factors that influence wage determination by employers in a competitive setting. However, other factors such as race, sex, and market barriers form substantial impediments that also help explain differences in wages across organizations.

Under this view of the market for labor many of the competitive assumptions that influence other kinds of markets are presumed to influence human resources. Both individuals and firms are assumed to be rational, and act in their own self interest in the marketplace. In economics, employers are assumed to make decisions that maximize their long-run wealth position. For workers, they may want to maximize long run satisfaction, or utility, that may or may not involve high income, and may also involve nonmonetary benefits like job safety. In this context, costing out potential opportunities in the labor market forms the basis of decisions for employers and employees. Just as financial market participants attempt to estimate future cash flows, labor markets also take into account long-term wage flows for individuals, or costs for the employer. This includes the importance of knowing that wages today are more valuable than wages in some future period, and the ability to incorporate that assumption in making current decisions.

---

[7] Richard B. Freeman and James L. Medoff, *What Do Unions Do?* Basic Books, New York, 1984.

Internal Labor Markets and Human Resource Management

In contrast to the free market auction that is often assumed to exist in the external market for labor, the market within the organization is often assumed to be dominated by rules and regulations rather than market principles. In their book entitled *Internal Labor Markets and Manpower Analysis,* Peter Doeringer and Michael Piore suggest that

> The internal labor market, governed by administrative rule, is to be distinguished from the external labor market of conventional economic theory where pricing, allocating, and training decisions are controlled directly by economic variables. These two markets are interconnected, however, and movement between them occurs at certain job classifications which constitute ports of entry and exit from the internal labor market. The remainder of jobs within the internal market are filled by the promotion or transfer of workers who have already gained entry. Consequently, these jobs are shielded from the direct influence of competitive forces in the external market.[8]

In their analysis of how labor markets work, Doeringer and Piore suggest that most jobs in firms are largely unaffected by the external market. Their implications for human resource management are that the rules for managing should be set up in a fair manner with little regard for the effect of opportunity costs, that is, other ways of using the funds, on the firm. This approach has been in contrast to much organizational research which suggests relating rewards to performance.[9] The internal labor market approach suggests that workers and unions should pay little heed to the variations in other product or financial markets, because they are protected by the rules and regulations that exist in this internal market.

Although many workers are protected by seniority provisions of labor contracts and implicitly by personnel policies, changes in the product market and the way that the factors of production are used have major effects on how human resources are used over the life cycle of many firms. For example, as Table 1–1 shows, for workers in the U.S. about 27 percent have been with their current employer one year or less, but the percent with little job tenure declines with age. In addition, even among executives and managerial professionals the average tenure with an employer is only eight years. With this amount of mobility, there are extended periods that workers are without the protection of the internal market rules. Also, even

[8] Peter B. Doeringer and Michael J. Piore, *Internal Labor Markets and Manpower Analysis,* Lexington, Mass.: D. C. Heath and Co., 1971.

[9] Herbert G. Heneman, D. P. Schwab, J. A. Fossum, and L. D. Dyer, *Personnel/Human Resource Management,* Richard D. Irwin, Homewood, Ill., 1983.

Age	1 year or less with current employer (percent)
16 years and over	27.3
16 to 24	56.4
25 to 34	30.0
35 to 44	20.0
45 to 54	13.0
55 to 64	9.7
65 years and older	10.2

Occupation	Median years of tenure	
	Men	Women
Executive and managerial	8.1	5.3
Sales	5.8	3.5
Administrative support, including clerical	8.1	5.0
Transportation and material moving	6.5	5.3
Handlers, equipment cleaners, and helpers, and laborers	5.6	5.5

Source: Ellen Sehgal, "Occupational Mobility and Job Tenure in 1983," *Monthly Labor Review,* Vol. 107, No. 10, October 1984, pp. 18–24.

Table 1-1 **Tenure with Current Employer, 1983**

those persons assumed to be protected by the rules and regulations of the internal labor market are subject to real wage cuts or layoffs as product markets become more competitive.

To a much larger extent than during any period following World War II, managers of human resources are applying the techniques that economists and behavioral scientists generally applied to the overall market for labor to internal labor markets. First, the techniques of marginal analysis, or examining the effects of small unit increases or decreases, are being used to a much greater extent than before in human resource practices such as selection procedures for new employees, evaluation of work effort, performance appraisal of individuals and groups of workers, and linking individuals to specific jobs. Second, methods of cost-benefit analysis are being applied to human resource decisions on training and development, which are being treated more like those of a long-term capital expenditure used to analyze capital markets.

One of the major pitfalls of analyzing the role of human resources in organizations has been the treatment of the personnel function as only a cost with little income generating power. However, a number of the major firms, like R. G. Barry, Inc., which manufacturers textiles and employs over 1700 workers, have attempted to cost out the value of various jobs in the firm. In their analysis, they ask the question, what is the dollar investment needed to bring a new employee up to acceptable standards of production within the firm? This company considers both the costs and revenues

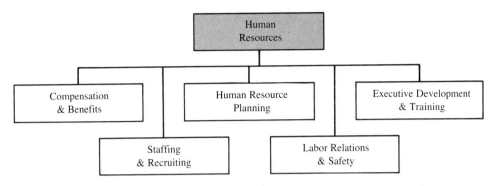

Figure 1-1 **Corporate Human Resources Function**

generated by each job classification. The results for this particular company show wide variations in costs depending on the skill level of the employee. For example, in 1986 dollars it cost $7000 to train and recruit a first line supervisor and over $70,000 to obtain and train a top manager.[10]

The ability and interest of managers in quantifying these costs within the firm has led upper level management to consider labor more as a fixed and less a variable factor of production within the firm. Rather than decisions to immediately lay off or fire people when there is a downturn in business activity, these costs of recruitment, selection, training, and work familiarization are taken into account when human resource costs are going to be reduced because of short-run declines in business activity.

With the increased competition in product markets during the late 1970s and 80s, firms attempting to recruit and retain workers for professional and managerial positions must be more keenly aware of both market wages and variations in individual talents. Certain managerial employees may be able to obtain outside offers well above wage scales that were established on fairness criteria or internal values of the job generated within the organization.[11] The key issue becomes whether top management will decide to follow market forces at the risk of compromising internal wage systems. For management, the decision also hinges upon whether maintaining a system based on internal fairness or one which follows market forces leads to either greater productivity, larger profits, higher market prices of the firm's stock, or greater long-term viability of the enterprise.

---

[10] Eric G. Flamholtz, *Human Resource Accounting,* Jossey-Bass Publishers, San Francisco, 1985.

[11] Edward Lazear, "Raids and Offer Matching," N.B.E.R., 1985.

Figure 1–1 presents the major human resource functions in a major U.S. company. Within this company the range of duties varies from compensation and benefits, recruiting, planning, labor relations, to development and training. The ability of the company to coordinate all of these functions is a major factor in the success of the organization.

Summary and Overview of the Book

This book provides an integrated decision-making approach to deal with the rich issues and varying problems that face persons dealing with human resources. The decision-making approach, which underlies the theme of this book, is detailed in the next chapter and states the importance of cost-benefit analyses in private and public decisions on labor issues. As part of this approach you will be expected to link human resource decisions to those of overall organizational goals. This will involve techniques such as calculating the present value of future income, costing out labor contracts, and understanding the role of uncertainty in making decisions on labor issues. Unlike some other recent textbooks in this field that "do not review theory or research in the labor relations or human resource management field," you will have an opportunity to learn what the current results in economics and behavioral analysis have said about the field you are studying.[12] Also, there are numerous examples throughout this book that will give you a chance to apply the theory and statistical evidence to organizations, unions, individuals and public policy. At the end of many chapters, problems are presented to help you test your mastery of the material.

Following the decision-making approach detailed in the next chapter, the second section of the book details the economics of human resource management (Chapters 3–6). In these chapters the concepts and applications of the supply of labor, and the firm's demand for labor are developed. The third section of the book presents the unique institutional environment in which labor operates, and is one reason that it is different from other commodities in the marketplace (Chapters 7–10). This section details the framework of federal, state, and local regulations and public policies, as well as the development of labor movements. The fourth section of the textbook focuses on models of employee behavior and personnel system inputs (Chapters 11 and 12). The fifth section of the book presents personnel system interventions (Chapters 13–16). These chapters detail the

---

[12] See Michael Beer, Bert Spector, Raul R. Lawrence, D. Quinn Mills, and Richard E. Walton, *Human Resource Management,* The Free Press, 1985 and D. Quinn Mills and Janice McCormick, *Industrial Relations in Transition: Cases and Text,* John Wiley and Sons Inc., New York, 1985.

staffing, training and development, compensation, and performance appraisal functions that personnel systems perform in an organization. The last portion of the text outlines the collective bargaining relationship in the organization (Chapters 17–20). This includes the negotiation and administration of collective bargaining agreements as well as its impact on management. A concluding section (Chapter 21) presents how the aggregate economic environment, which includes international factors, may influence decisions on labor.

PROBLEMS

1. What are the differences among markets for financial instruments, like stocks and bonds; and products; and the labor market?
2. In a competitive market for products why can some employers pay more to their workers than other employers? State additional reasons if there is no competition in product markets.
3. What types of decisions do employers need to make in staffing an enterprise?
4. What type of information would you need to have to analyze the impact of human resources policies on the performance of the firm?

REFERENCES

Cartter, Allan M., *Theory of Wages and Employment,* Richard D. Irwin, Homewood, Ill., 1959.

Dunlop, John T., *Industrial Relations Systems,* Southern Illinois University Press, Carbondale, Ill., 1958.

Freeman, Richard B., *Labor Economics,* Prentice Hall, Englewood Cliffs, N.J., 1979.

Heneman, Herbert G., D. P. Schwab, J. A. Fossum, and L. D. Dyer, *Personnel/Human Resource Management,* Richard D. Irwin, Homewood, Ill., 1983.

Kleiner, Morris M., R. Block, M. Roomkin, and Sidney Salsberg, ed., *Human Resources and the Performance of the Firm,* Industrial Relations Research Association, Madison, Wisc., 1987.

CHAPTER 2

DECISIONS ON LABOR: A COST-BENEFIT APPROACH

T o manage is to make decisions. To manage human resources is to make decisions about the selection and compensation of people in the interest of the employing organization. Too often, both in textbooks and in practice, decisions about human resource management are treated as if they were isolated from the other aspects of the firm's management function. In fact, in investor-owned firms, all aspects of management behavior should be motivated by a desire to maximize shareholder wealth.[1]

Chapter 1 discussed the goal of this textbook: to develop a problem-solving decision-making approach to the management of human resources. This chapter will develop the analytical methods, the frame of mind, that underlies such a decision-making approach. A major component of that framework is cost-benefit analysis, as developed by scholars in managerial economics and finance.

After reading this chapter, you will be able to formulate human resource management problems in cost-benefit terms and to solve a variety of cost-benefit problems.

---

[1] Richard Brealey and Stewart Myers, *Principles of Corporate Finance,* second edition, New York: McGraw-Hill, 1984, ch. 2; and 0. Maurice Joy, *Introduction to Financial Management,* third edition, Homewood, Illinois: Richard D. Irwin, 1983, ch. 1.

The Nature of the Firm

The modern corporation is a recent development, having appeared only in the last century. To understand decision-making as it relates to the management of human resources, one must first understand the nature of the modern corporation and the overall goals which such organizations seek to achieve.

Williamson[2] focused on the reason for the emergence of the modern corporation: the minimization of the costs of contracting for the services of the inputs into production. Under *some* types of production processes, it would be very costly (although possible) to contract in external labor markets for all of the services that go into production. Under an "outside contractor only" arrangement, each participant in the process contracts to do his task without entering into an employment relationship, as is true in much construction activity. Were outside contracting employed in manufacturing, for example, costs of continuous negotiation and, most importantly, of supervising the contracting factors would be high. To reduce those costs, firms are formed, owning capital and hiring labor in an ongoing employment relationship.

Alchain and Demsetz[3] identified the class of production processes for which the formation of firms takes place as those in which team rather than individual output is important. In residential construction, work is done sequentially by earth movers, cement masons, plumbers, electricians, carpenters, and so forth. Coordinating those activities is easily accomplished and contracting, rather than the formation of permanent firms, is the norm. In manufacturing, however, team processes dominate. The output of one type of labor depends on the work input of other types of labor. Each factor must be monitored because the cost of one factor's shirking is not borne by that factor alone, but is also shared by other members of the team.[4] The result is the formation of the firm and the identification of a "residual claimant" (who receives the surplus after other factors have been paid) who has an incentive to monitor and coordinate.

What then are these permanent firms? Jensen and Meckling[5] observe that the firm is nothing more than a focus for contractual relationships among cooperative factors of production. Those contracts are more often

---

[2] Oliver E. Williamson, "The Modern Corporation: Origins, Evolution, Attributes," *Journal of Economic Literature* vol. 19, no. 4 (December 1981): 1537–1565.

[3] Armen A. Alchain and Harold Demsetz, "Production, Information Costs, and Economic Efficiency," *American Economic Review* vol. 62, no. 5 (December 1972): 777–795.

[4] The team includes capital, as well as labor inputs.

[5] Michael C. Jensen and William H. Meckling. "Theory of the Firm: Managerial Behavior, Agency Costs and Ownership Structure," *Journal of Financial Economics* vol. 3, no. 3 (October 1976): 305–360.

implicit than explicit. The residual claimant (the stockholders as a group in a corporation) has an incentive to monitor (or hire agents to monitor) the actions of each cooperating factor in the firm. Human resources hired by the firm have a contractual relationship (often only implicit), working under supervision for some rate of compensation.

The management of human resources, then, has a special place in the modern corporation. The manager must function to insure the continued cooperation of the firm's human resources. Within that constraint, however, the manager acts as an agent of the residual claimant(s), pursuing the goals of that (those) claimant(s).

Thus, human resource management has two goals: to obtain the continued cooperation of labor and to maximize the wealth of shareholders (or to maximize the welfare of some part of the public, for public and not-for-profit organizations). These two goals are equally important, and to neglect either is to engage in poor management practice.

Human Resource Management and Shareholder Wealth Maximization

Decisions about human resource management should be evaluated on the basis of whether or not they add value to the firm. The human resource function is not isolated, but, like marketing, finance, and production, can add value to or subtract value from the firm.

The value of the firm is the market value of all of the shares of stock outstanding (*not the value of the firm's assets recorded in accounting records*). While there remains some controversy on the subject in financial theory, the market value of the firm's shares should be the sum of the discounted future cash flows to the firm. That is, the value of the firm is the value that, if invested today at a known rate of interest, would yield the cash flows that the firm is expected to generate in the future. If each decision on the management of human resources is based on the discounted cash flows attributed to that decision, then those decisions will be tied to their effects on the value of the firm. For that reason, the remainder of this chapter will be devoted to the development of a cost-benefit framework for evaluating human resource management decisions.

Students of labor relations have long ignored the vital connection between their subject of study and the value of the firm. Recently, however, several scholars have identified important links. Becker and Olson; Greer, Martin, and Reusser; and Neumann all found strikes to have at least temporary negative effects on the market value of the firm.[6] Ruback and Zimmerman found union certification elections to have the same effect.[7] Freeman and Medoff report that unionized firms have lower profits than their nonunion counterparts, which has the effect of reducing market values.[8] The connection between specific human resource phenomena and the firm's market value is an area in which more research is greatly needed.

A Note on Union Administration

While most of this chapter is developed from the point of view of the investor-owned firm, the cost-benefit framework can also be applied to decison-making within unions, privately held firms, and public and not-for-profit organizations as well. Atherton and Block studied union decisions on bargaining behavior and internal resource allocation, respectively.[9] If the costs and benefits to the union and its members of a particular decision can be measured, cost-benefit analysis can be employed to compare alternatives and evaluate the desirability of a proposed course of action.

Measuring Costs and Benefits

Any decision-making framework in human resource management must be rooted in several critical factors: incremental cash flows, the time value of money, and a decision rule based on a valid compensation principle (a rule defining the benefits necessary to outweigh the costs of undertaking some action). This section will focus on the measurement of incremental cash flows, while the next section will develop decision rules to apply to them.

The costs and benefits of a course of action by the firm are best measured in terms of the incremental cash flows that result from that course of action.[10] Incremental cash flows are the additional cash inflows and outflows that result from that course of action alone.[11]

 Cash flows, rather than some measure of profit, are used for decision-making for important reasons. Cash is available to meet obligations. The firm can only spend cash. Profits, resulting from applying accounting

[6] Brian E. Becker and Craig A. Olson, "The Consequences of Strikes for Shareholder Wealth," *Industrial and Labor Relations Review* vol. 39, no. 3 (April 1986): 425–438; Charles R. Greer, Stanley A. Martin, and Ted A. Reusser, "The Effects of Strikes on Shareholder Returns," *Journal of Labor Research* vol. 1, no. 2 (Fall 1980): 217–229; and George R. Neumann, "The Predictability of Strikes: Evidence From the Stock Market," *Industrial and Labor Relations Review* vol. 33, no. 4 (July 1980): 515–535.

[7] Richard S. Ruback and Martin B. Zimmerman, "Unionization and Productivity: Evidence From the Capital Market," *Journal of Political Economy* vol. 92, no. 6 (December 1984): 1134–1157.

[8] Richard B. Freeman and James L. Medoff, *What Do Unions Do?* New York: Basic Books, 1984, ch. 12.

[9] Wallace N. Atherton, *Theory of Union Bargaining Goals.* Princeton, New Jersey: Princeton University Press, 1973; and Richard N. Block, "Union Organizing and the Allocation of Union Resources," *Industrial and Labor Relations Review* vol. 34, no. 1 (October 1980): 101–113.

[10] George E. Pinches, *Essentials of Financial Management,* New York: Harper & Row, 1984, ch. 4.

[11] In economic terms, these are the cash flows that are marginal with respect to the decision at hand.

principles to the firm's transactions, are neither unambiguous nor available. Consider a firm with a stable cash inflow of $1,000 per year. Its only expense is depreciation (which involves no cash flow) of a $1000 piece of equipment. If the firm uses straight-line depreciation, over five years, its profits and cash flows for the five years would be as shown in Table 2-1.

Straight-line depreciation takes an equal share of the asset's purchase price as depreciation in each year of the asset's useful life. In the example used here, the tax rate is assumed to be 30 percent. That rate is applied to cash inflows, less depreciation.

In the first year, the firm's $1000 cash inflow is exactly matched by the cash outflow due to purchase of the asset. Depreciation expense on the asset, however, is only $200. Accounting profits before taxes, then are $800 ($1000 − $200). After paying taxes of $240 (30 percent of $800), accounting profits are $560. Net cash flow, however, is −$240, because taxes were due, but no before-tax cash inflow was available.

While the $560 after-tax profit for year 1 is consistent with generally accepted accounting principles, it is not available to pay the bills. Over the full five year life of the hypothetical firm, the total after-tax cash flows equal the total after-tax profits. Note, however, that a real firm buys new equipment more or less continuously. Unlike the example, there is no artificial period over which the cash flow and profit streams must be equal.

The focus on cash inflows (as benefits) and cash outflows (as costs) necessarily implies that the benefits and costs can be quantified and, more narrowly, measured in monetary terms. Some features of contracts cannot, of course, be monetized. How, for example, can one put a monetary value on the loss of managerial discretion that comes from signing a collective bargaining agreement? That one cannot attach a meaningful money value to such a provision does not mean that it is either ephemeral or unimportant. One might use such clauses as "tie-breakers," being deciding factors between two alternatives that are ranked equal on a cost-benefit basis. Note that to allow a non-monetized factor to outweigh a calculated monetary value in decision-making is, implicitly, to assign it a money value greater than the value of the quantifiable factor it outweighs.

Year	Cash inflow	Cash outflow	Depreciation	Tax	Net cash flow after tax	After tax profit
1	1,000	1,000	200.00	240.00	−240.00	560.00
2	1,000	0	200.00	240.00	760.00	560.00
3	1,000	0	200.00	240.00	760.00	560.00
4	1,000	0	200.00	240.00	760.00	560.00
5	1,000	0	200.00	240.00	760.00	560.00

Table 2-1 **Cash Flows Compared to Profits (Assume 30% tax rate) (straight line depreciation)**

Modern financial theory offers another means of dealing with some nonmonetary contractual provisions (although the methods required are, as yet, poorly developed): contingent claims analysis.[12] Suppose one were struggling to assign a value to the loss of discretion that follows signing a collective agreement. One could treat managerial discretion as a set of options (contingent claims), that one might exercise under certain circumstances. The option to discharge employees, for example, could have been exercised when an employee's observed productivity fell below his compensation.

One of the most important developments in financial theory is the derivation of a model for the price of an option to buy a share of common stock.[13] That theory can be modified to determine the value of other types of options, such as the employer's option to discharge his employees. Option pricing theory provides, at least in principle, a way to assign values to the contingent claims surrendered by signing the agreement.

Contingent claims analysis is not well enough developed to be a practical part of cost-benefit calculations in human resource management. It does, however, focus attention on the money values of previously unmonetizable factors in decision making in industrial relations.

Cost-Benefit Analysis[14]

Any system of cost-benefit analysis must be rooted in incremental cash flows, the time value of money, and a decision rule based on a valid compensation principle. The previous section dealt with incremental cash flows. This section will develop decision rules based on compensation principles and the time value of money.

Compensation Criteria

Compensation principles are the theoretical underpinnings of any valid cost-benefit decision rule. Originally developed by scholars in welfare economics (the study of the effects of resource allocation on aggregate

---

[12] Scott P. Mason and Robert C. Merton, "The Role of Contingent Claims Analysis in Corporate Finance," in Edward I. Altman and Marti G. Subrahmanyan (editors), *Recent Advances in Corporate Finance,* Homewood, Illinois: Richard D. Irwin, 1985, pp. 7–54.

[13] Fischer Black and Myron Scholes, "The Pricing of Options and Corporate Liabilities," *Journal of Political Economy* vol. 81, no. 3 (May-June 1973):637–654.

[14] For more nearly complete treatments of cost-benefit analysis (also known as capital budgeting), see Brealey and Myers, *Principles of Corporate Finance* (1984), chs. 5–12; Joy, *Introduction to Financial Management* (1983), chs. 6–8; E. J. Mishan, *Cost-Benefit Analysis,* new and expanded edition, New York: Praeger, 1976; James L. Pappas, Eugene F. Brigham, and Mark Hirschey, *Managerial Economics,* fourth edition, Chicago: Dryden Press, 1983, ch. 13; and Pinches, *Essentials of Financial Management* (1984), chs. 12 and 13.

utility or welfare), they are rules for determining whether or not a reallocation of resources is in society's overall best interest.[15]

The most familiar of the compensation criteria is that attributed to Nicholas Kaldor: make a reallocation if those who gain *could* compensate those who lose and still be better off.[16] The criterion, then, suggests that reallocation (investments, business decisions, public projects) should be undertaken if the total gains exceed the total losses. Of course, in political settings, actual compensation, rather than potential compensation, may be required for a reallocation to take place.

For the business firm, the Kaldor criterion is as applicable as it is for a public policy decision. Decision A should be implemented if the total gain from it exceeds the total costs. The process of cost-benefit analysis (or capital budgeting, as finance students call it) consists of calculating and comparing those total costs and benefits (based, as shown in the previous section, on incremental cash flows).

The Time Value of Money

Consider a dollar (value = V_0) put aside today at a known annual rate of interest r. After one year, the dollar will have grown to a value (V_1) of ($1 + r$1) = $1(1 + r)$. That is, at the end of a year, the depositor would have the original dollar plus one year's interest on the original dollar. If left undisturbed and if the initial year's accrued interest is subject to the same interest rate (the reinvestment rate), at the end of the second year, the account will contain all that it had at the end of the first year plus "r" times the first year's ending balance. In symbols:

$$V_2 = \$1(1 + r) + r\$1(1 + r) = \$1(1 + r)(1 + r) = \$1(1 + r)^2$$

Under the assumption of no withdrawals and a constant reinvestment rate, after n years (where n is any positive number), $V_n = \$1(1 + r)^n$. This simple framework for compound interest is the heart of the time value of money and the calculations for cost-benefit analysis.

Table 2-2 shows the growth of an initial value (or present value) into a future value when money is left undisturbed at a constant reinvestment rate. Note that under the assumptions given, the present value, V_0 ($1 in the previous example), is exactly equivalent to a larger future value, V_5, at the end of five years. The two are exactly equivalent in that the holder of $1 today has a choice (given the assumed fixed reinvestment rate r) of taking the $1 or waiting five years to have $1(1 + r)^5$.

Table 2-3 shows, for several interest rates, the future value of $1 at the end of one through twenty-five years. For initial deposits other than $1,

0	1	2	3	4	5	Time

V_0

$V_1 = V_0(1+r)$

$V_2 = V_1(1+r)$
$= V_0(1+r)^2$

$V_3 = V_2(1+r)$
$= V_0(1+r)^3$

$V_4 = V_3(1+r)$
$= V_0(1+r)^4$

$V_5 = V_4(1+r)$
$V_0(1+r)^5$

$V_5 = V_0(1+r)^5$

$V_0 = V_5/(1+r)^5$

Table 2-2   **Equivalence of Present and Future Values**

simply multiply these compounding factors by the amount of the initial deposit to obtain the resulting future value. For example, if $5 is put aside for ten years at a constant annually compounded rate of 8 percent, the terminal value would be $5(2.1589) = $10.79.

Table 2-3 also demonstrates the fact that a dollar in the future is worth less than a dollar today, even if there is no inflation (which reduces the purchasing power of any fixed amount) in the intervening period. Suppose V_5 is $1 and the reinvestment rate is 10 percent. The present value of the $1 in five years is $1/(1+r)^5$ or approximately $0.62 (that is, $0.62 today, invested at ten percent for five years will compound to $1.00). In this case, the assumed reinvestment rate of 10 percent has been used to "discount" a future value back to the present and is, therefore, called the *discount rate.*

Table 2-4 shows, for several discount rates, the present value of $1 to be received at the end of one through twenty-five years. For future values other than $1, simply multiply the discount factor by the amount of the future value to obtain the equivalent present value.[17] For example, the promise of $10 at the end of 10 years, discounted at 10 percent is $10(0.3855) = $3.85.

---

[15] E. J. Mishan, *Introduction to Normative Economics,* New York: Oxford University Press, 1981, ch. 44; and James M. Henderson and Richard E. Quandt, *Microeconomic Theory: A Mathematical Approach,* second edition, New York: McGraw-Hill, 1971, ch. 7, especially pp. 279–280.

[16] Henderson and Quandt, *Microeconomic Theory* (1971), p. 279.

[17] Another well-known formula is useful in human resource decisions. If a cash flow (CF) is both constant and perpetual, the present value of the series of cash flows is CF/r, where r is the discount rate.

Compounding Rates	5	6	7	8	9
Years					
1	1.0500	1.0600	1.0700	1.0800	1.0900
2	1.1025	1.1236	1.1449	1.1664	1.1881
3	1.1576	1.1910	1.2250	1.2597	1.2950
4	1.2155	1.2625	1.3108	1.3605	1.4116
5	1.2763	1.3382	1.4026	1.4693	1.5386
6	1.3401	1.4185	1.5007	1.5869	1.6771
7	1.4071	1.5036	1.6058	1.7138	1.8280
8	1.4775	1.5938	1.7182	1.8509	1.9926
9	1.5513	1.6895	1.8385	1.9990	2.1719
10	1.6289	1.7908	1.9672	2.1589	2.3674
11	1.7103	1.8983	2.1049	2.3316	2.5804
12	1.7959	2.0122	2.2522	2.5182	2.8127
13	1.8856	2.1329	2.4098	2.7196	3.0658
14	1.9799	2.2609	2.5785	2.9372	3.3417
15	2.0789	2.3966	2.7590	3.1722	3.6425
16	2.1829	2.5404	2.9522	3.4259	3.9703
17	2.2920	2.6928	3.1588	3.7000	4.3276
18	2.4066	2.8543	3.3799	3.9960	4.7171
19	2.5270	3.0256	3.6165	4.3157	5.1417
20	2.6533	3.2071	3.8697	4.6610	5.6044
21	2.7860	3.3996	4.1406	5.0338	6.1088
22	2.9253	3.6035	4.4304	5.4365	6.6586
23	3.0715	3.8197	4.7405	5.8715	7.2579
24	3.2251	4.0489	5.0724	6.3412	7.9111
25	3.3864	4.2919	5.4274	6.8485	8.6231
30	4.3219	5.7435	7.6123	10.0627	13.2677
35	5.5160	7.6861	10.6766	14.7853	20.4140
40	7.0400	10.2857	14.9745	21.7245	31.4094
45	8.9850	13.7646	21.0025	31.9204	48.3273
50	11.4674	18.4202	29.4570	46.9016	74.3575

Table 2–3   **Future Value of $1 Accumulated After N Years Compounded at R Percent**

10	11	12	13	14	15
1.1000	1.1100	1.1200	1.1300	1.1400	1.1500
1.2100	1.2321	1.2544	1.2769	1.2996	1.3225
1.3310	1.3676	1.4049	1.4429	1.4815	1.5209
1.4641	1.5181	1.5735	1.6305	1.6890	1.7490
1.6105	1.6851	1.7623	1.8424	1.9254	2.0114
1.7716	1.8704	1.9738	2.0820	2.1950	2.3131
1.9487	2.0762	2.2107	2.3526	2.5023	2.6600
2.1436	2.3045	2.4760	2.6584	2.8526	3.0590
2.3579	2.5580	2.7731	3.0040	3.2519	3.5179
2.5937	2.8394	3.1058	3.3946	3.7072	4.0456
2.8531	3.1518	3.4785	3.8359	4.2262	4.6524
3.1384	3.4985	3.8960	4.3345	4.8179	5.3503
3.4523	3.8833	4.3635	4.8980	5.4924	6.1528
3.7975	4.3104	4.8871	5.5348	6.2613	7.0757
4.1772	4.7846	5.4736	6.2543	7.1379	8.1371
4.5950	5.3109	6.1304	7.0673	8.1372	9.3576
5.0545	5.8951	6.8660	7.9861	9.2765	10.7613
5.5599	6.5436	7.6900	9.0243	10.5752	12.3755
6.1159	7.2633	8.6128	10.1974	12.0557	14.2318
6.7275	8.0623	9.6463	11.5231	13.7435	16.3665
7.4002	8.9492	10.8038	13.0211	15.6676	18.8215
8.1403	9.9336	12.1003	14.7138	17.8610	21.6447
8.9543	11.0263	13.5523	16.6266	20.3616	24.8915
9.8497	12.2392	15.1786	18.7881	23.2122	28.6252
10.8347	13.5855	17.0001	21.2305	26.4619	32.9190
17.4494	22.8923	29.9599	39.1159	50.9502	66.2118
28.1024	38.5749	52.7996	72.0685	98.1002	133.1755
45.2593	65.0009	93.0510	132.7816	188.8835	267.8635
72.8905	109.5302	163.9876	244.6414	363.6791	538.7693
117.3909	184.5648	289.0022	450.7359	700.2330	1083.6574

Discount Rates	5	6	7	8	9	10
Years						
1	0.9524	0.9434	0.9346	0.9259	0.9174	0.9091
2	0.9070	0.8900	0.8734	0.8573	0.8417	0.8264
3	0.8638	0.8396	0.8163	0.7938	0.7722	0.7513
4	0.8227	0.7921	0.7629	0.7350	0.7084	0.6830
5	0.7835	0.7473	0.7130	0.6806	0.6499	0.6209
6	0.7462	0.7050	0.6663	0.6302	0.5963	0.5645
7	0.7107	0.6651	0.6227	0.5835	0.5470	0.5132
8	0.6768	0.6274	0.5820	0.5403	0.5019	0.4665
9	0.6646	0.5919	0.5439	0.5002	0.4604	0.4241
10	0.6139	0.5584	0.5083	0.4632	0.4224	0.3855
11	0.5847	0.5268	0.4751	0.4289	0.3875	0.3505
12	0.5568	0.4970	0.4440	0.3971	0.3555	0.3186
13	0.5303	0.4688	0.4150	0.3677	0.3262	0.2897
14	0.5051	0.4423	0.3878	0.3405	0.2992	0.2633
15	0.4810	0.4173	0.3624	0.3152	0.2745	0.2394
16	0.4581	0.3936	0.3387	0.2919	0.2519	0.2176
17	0.4363	0.3714	0.3166	0.2703	0.2311	0.1978
18	0.4155	0.3503	0.2959	0.2502	0.2120	0.1799
19	0.3957	0.3305	0.2765	0.2317	0.1945	0.1635
20	0.3769	0.3118	0.2584	0.2145	0.1784	0.1486
21	0.3589	0.2942	0.2415	0.1987	0.1637	0.1351
22	0.3418	0.2775	0.2257	0.1839	0.1502	0.1228
23	0.3256	0.2618	0.2109	0.1703	0.1378	0.1117
24	0.3101	0.2470	0.1971	0.1577	0.1264	0.1015
25	0.2953	0.2330	0.1842	0.1460	0.1160	0.0923
30	0.2314	0.1741	0.1314	0.0994	0.0754	0.0573
35	0.1813	0.1301	0.0937	0.0676	0.0490	0.0356
40	0.1420	0.0972	0.0668	0.0460	0.0318	0.0221
45	0.1113	0.0727	0.0476	0.0313	0.0207	0.0137
50	0.0872	0.0543	0.0339	0.0213	0.0134	0.0085

Table 2-4 **Present Value of $1 Received After N Years Discounted at R Percent**

The compound factors for Table 2-3 and the discount factors for Table 2-4 were both calculated using the "end-of-the-year" convention. That is, it is assumed that all year-one cash flows are received at the end of the first year. This convention is not as limiting as it may seem. Any cash flow at the beginning of year three is equivalent to a cash flow at the end of year two. A mid-year cash flow can be incorporated into the analysis by multiplying the number of periods by two and dividing the interest rate in half.

Discount Rates	11	12	13	14	15
Years					
1	0.9009	0.8929	0.8850	0.8772	0.8696
2	0.8116	0.7972	0.7831	0.7695	0.7561
3	0.7312	0.7118	0.6931	0.6750	0.6575
4	0.6587	0.6355	0.6133	0.5921	0.5718
5	0.5935	0.5674	0.5428	0.5194	0.4972
6	0.5346	0.5066	0.4803	0.4556	0.4323
7	0.4817	0.4523	0.4251	0.3996	0.3759
8	0.4339	0.4039	0.3762	0.3506	0.3269
9	0.3909	0.3606	0.3329	0.3075	0.2843
10	0.3522	0.3220	0.2946	0.2697	0.2472
11	0.3173	0.2875	0.2607	0.2366	0.2149
12	0.2858	0.2567	0.2307	0.2076	0.1869
13	0.2575	0.2292	0.2042	0.1821	0.1625
14	0.2320	0.2046	0.1807	0.1597	0.1413
15	0.2090	0.1827	0.1599	0.1401	0.1229
16	0.1883	0.1631	0.1415	0.1229	0.1069
17	0.1696	0.1456	0.1252	0.1078	0.0929
18	0.1528	0.1300	0.1108	0.0946	0.0808
19	0.1377	0.1161	0.0981	0.0829	0.0703
20	0.1240	0.1037	0.0868	0.0728	0.0611
21	0.1117	0.0926	0.0768	0.0638	0.0531
22	0.1007	0.0826	0.0680	0.0560	0.0462
23	0.0907	0.0738	0.0601	0.0491	0.0402
24	0.0817	0.0659	0.0532	0.0431	0.0349
25	0.0736	0.0588	0.0471	0.0378	0.0304
30	0.0437	0.0334	0.0256	0.0196	0.0151
35	0.0259	0.0189	0.0139	0.0102	0.0075
40	0.0154	0.0107	0.0075	0.0053	0.0037
45	0.0091	0.0061	0.0041	0.0027	0.0019
50	0.0054	0.0035	0.0022	0.0014	0.0009

The costs and benefits of most decisions will be cash flows to the firm over several periods. Recognizing the role of the time value of money, one sees that cash flows in year 5 should not be compared directly to cash flows in year 4. Rather, the present values of cash flows are what ought to be evaluated in making decisions that have multi-period cash flow consequences. The present value of a string of cash flows is simply the sum of the present values of the individual cash flows.

Decision Rules

As the discussions of compensation criteria and of the time value of money suggest, decision rules in cost-benefit analysis are deceptively simple. One merely asks, "is the present value of benefits at least as great as the present value of costs?" If so, the results of the decision will add value to the firm. Among competing alternatives, each of which passes the initial test, one asks, "for which alternative does the present value of benefits exceed the present value of costs to the greatest extent?" That alternative is the one which adds the most value to the firm. This section explores the means of operationalizing those general decision rules.

First, consider the kinds of decisions with which human resource managers are faced. These can be classified into three categories:

1. accept/reject, cash inflows and outflows;
2. mutually exclusive choice, cash inflows and outflows; and
3. mutually exclusive choice, cash outflows only.

Some decisions, whether or not to engage in a new training program, for example, will have cash inflows associated with them, as when the training pays off in enhanced productivity. Other decisions, which of several health insurance plans to select, for example, will involve only cash outflows. While the logic of cost-benefit analysis is quite general, there are subtle differences in the decision rules employed.

An example of the first decision problem, accept/reject with cash inflows and outflows, is the decision to accept a new employee selection method. The use of the new method, a new test procedure, for example, will involve cash outflows, the costs of implementing the test. The manager making the decision believes that the use of the test will generate cash inflows due to higher productivity. The decision problem is to compare those cash inflows and outflows in an appropriate manner. The logic of cost-benefit analysis suggests that one should consider the difference between the present value of cash inflows and the present value of cash outflows. That amount is the *net present value* (NPV) of the decision. It is calculated as follows:

$$\text{NPV} = \sum_{t=0}^{N} \frac{(\text{cash inflow}_t)}{(1 + r)^t} - \sum_{t=0}^{N} \frac{(\text{cash outflow}_t)}{(1 + r)^t}$$

$$\text{NPV} = \sum_{t=0}^{N} \frac{(\text{cash inflow} - \text{cash outflow})_t}{(1 + r)^t}$$

The Greek letter sigma (Σ) with subscript t=0 and superscript N indicates summation. One begins with net cash flow at time $t = 0$, and sums all of the discounted net cash flows through the end of period N. Thus for an employee testing program that will produce cash flows over a five-year period:

$$NPV = \frac{\text{net cash flow}_0}{1} + \frac{\text{net cash flows}_1}{(1 + r)} + \frac{\text{net cash flows}_2}{(1 + r)^2}$$

$$+ \frac{\text{net cash flow}_3}{(1 + r)^3} + \frac{\text{net cash flow}_4}{(1 + r)^4} + \frac{\text{net cash flow}_5}{(1 + r)^5}.^{[18]}$$

The decision rule for accept/reject decisions is: **accept alternatives for which net present value is greater than or equal to zero.** Because net present value is the decision's addition to the net value of the firm, this decision rule means that one should accept projects that enhance the value of the firm.

Sample Decision Problem 2-1 illustrates the calculation of net present value for an accept/reject decision. In this case, insurance premiums occur immediately, at the end of one year and at the end of two years. The cash outlay for safety education occurs only at the present. Because 30 percent of

---

[18] The denominator of the first term is 1, because that is the value of $(1+r)^0$. For any nonzero real number x, $x^0 = 1$.

SAMPLE DECISION PROBLEM 2-1

TO ENGAGE OR NOTE TO ENGAGE IN A SAFETY EDUCATION PROGRAM

Your Workers Compensation insurance company will reduce your premiums by $5,000 per year for three years (beginning with the payment now due) if you conduct a special safety awareness program. World Management Consultants, Inc. will conduct an approved program for $12,500. (If you want to extend the premium reduction, you must repeat the program at the end of three years.) Your marginal tax rate is 30 percent and your after-tax cost of capital is 12 percent.

	Cash Flow Before Taxes	Cash Flow After Taxes
Initially	−$12,500 + 5000	−$5250
One year from now	$5000	$3500
Two years from now	$5000	$3500

Net Present Value
= −$5250 + 3500(0.8929) + 3500(0.7972)
= −$5250 + 3125.15 + 2790.20
= $665.35

the cash flows would be "saved" through tax deductions, only 70 percent of the cash inflows (premium savings) and outflows are cash flows after taxes. The discount factors are obtained from Table 2-4.

In the case illustrated, the net present value of the safety awareness program is greater than zero. Thus, the firm should undertake the program.

One can complicate the analysis of the employee testing process by assuming that, rather than one testing procedure to accept or reject, one is evaluating two or more competing employee selection instruments. This involves evaluating mutually exclusive alternatives involving both cash inflows and cash outflows. In such an analysis, one should **accept the alternative that has the highest positive net present value.** That is, the alternative that adds the most to the value of the firm.

An alternative method is to calculate projects' internal rates of return (the discount rate that sets NPV = 0). That method, however, is not as useful as the use of net present value. Internal rates of return are generally more difficult to calculate than net present values. There are, in some cases, several values that will satisfy the internal rate of return conditions for a single cash flow, and some of those values may be imaginary numbers. The NPV, because it represents the addition to the value of the firm and because it does not suffer the internal rate of return's shortcomings, is the superior measure.[19]

Sample Decision Problem 2-2 illustrates the use of net present value calculations to select between two alternatives. In this case, a second management consultant has offered to conduct the safety awareness program discussed in Sample Decision Problem 2-1. The second firm, International Safety Education requires a different fee schedule. The net present value of working with ISE is $540.26. Because that figure is positive but less than the net present value of working with World Management Consultants, Inc. ($665.35), the firm should contract with World Management Consultants.

The third type of decision problem in human resource management is mutually exclusive choice among alternatives with explicit cash outflows, but no explicit cash inflows. For example, consider the case of a firm selecting among three health insurance plans. Each plan offers the same coverage. Adopting some form of coverage is, in this case, a contractual obligation, but adoption of any one plan over the others will not enhance the firm's cash inflows. Then the firm faces a *cost-only* (cash outflow only) decision problem.

The solution to a cash outflow only choice is straightforward. In such a

---

[19] M. S. Feldstein and J. S. Fleming, "The Problem of Time-Stream Evaluation: Present Value Versus Internal Rate of Return Rules," *Bulletin of the Oxford University Institute of Economics and Statistics* vol. 26 (February 1964): 79–85; Mishan, *Cost-Benefit Analysis* (1976), ch. 29.

SAMPLE DECISION PROBLEM 2.2

WHICH OF TWO SAFETY EDUCATION VENDORS TO SELECT

Review the facts of Sample Decision Problem 2-1. Now another consultant International Safety Education offers an approved program. As payment, ISE demands $10,000 initially and $3,000 one year from now. Your marginal tax rate is 30 percent and your after-tax cost of capital is 12 percent.

As previously calculated, the Net Present Value for purchasing services from World Management Consultants, Inc. is $665.35.

For International Safety Education

	Cash Flow Before Taxes	Cash Flow After Taxes
Initially	−$10,000 + 5000	−$3500
One year from now	−3000 + 5000	$1400
Two years from now	$5000	$3500

Net Present Value
$$= -\$3500 + 1400(0.8929) + 3500(0.7972)$$
$$= -\$3500 + 1250.06 + 2790.20$$
$$= \$540.26$$

case, one compares the present values of the cash outflows of the competing alternatives. **The decision rule is to select the alternative with the smallest present value of cash outflows.** The use of that decision rule, however, presumes that the alternatives are each suitable in meeting the firm's needs.

Sample Decision Problem 2-3 illustrates a cash outflow only decision. A firm has two bids for major medical insurance coverage. Total premiums over a three year contract are the same for the two, but option B requires that more premium is paid initially than does Option A. The payments due at the beginning of Year 2 are discounted for one year (because the beginning of Year 2 is the end of Year 1). Similarly, the premiums due at the beginning of Year 3 are discounted for two years (because the beginning of Year 3 is the end of Year 2). All of the discount factors are taken from Table 2-4. Because Option A has the lower present value of after-tax cash outflows, it is the better option to select.

Cost-benefit analysis can be a tedious process, and it must be based on projections of cash flows that are quite uncertain to materialize. The

SELECTION OF AN INSURANCE CARRIER

Each of two insurance companies (A and B) offers major medical insurance coverage. The difference between the two is the timing of the schedule of required payments. The cost of capital is 10 percent. All figures listed are on an after-tax basis.

	Option A	Option B
Beginning of year 1	$5,000	$10,000
Beginning of year 2	$5,000	$ 2,500
Beginning of year 3	$5,000	$ 2,500

Present Value of After-Tax Cash Outflows

Option A: $5,000 + 5,000(0.9091) + 5,000(0.8264)
= $5,000 + 4,545.50 + 4,132
= $13,677.50

Option B: $10,000 + 2,500(0.9091) + 2,500(0.8264)
= $10,000 + 2,272.75 + 2,066
= $14,338.75

decision rules of cost-benefit analysis, however, are the only valid ways to approach decision-making in attempts to maximize the value of the firm.

Selecting the Discount Rate

To this point, the rate of discount has been taken as given. In fact the rate is an important matter of choice. Looking again at the formula for net present value,

$$\text{NPV} = \sum_{t=0}^{N} \frac{(\text{cash inflow})_t - (\text{cash outflow})_t}{(1 + r)^t},$$

one can see that cost/benefit decisions will be quite sensitive to the rate of discount chosen. Using very high rates of discount, no alternative will have a positive net present value.[20] As rates of discount fall, more and more

---

[20] Hayes and Garvin contend that American firms fail to undertake needed investment precisely because they select unreasonably high rates of discount. Robert H. Hayes and David A. Garvin, "Managing As If Tomorrow Mattered," *Harvard Business Review* vol. 60, no. 3 (May-June 1982): 70–79.

projects and alternatives will pass the net present value test. The sensitivity of net present value to variation in the discount rate is illustrated in Table 2-5. Hypothetical cash flows for five years and their sum and present values of those annual flows and the sums of the annual present values for various discount rates are shown. Because net present value is as sensitive to interest rates as Table 2-5 suggests, the choice of the appropriate discount rate is critical in any cost/benefit-based decision.

Remember how the procedure for discounting future sums was derived? The future value was assumed to have accrued at some interest rate. One can imagine then that the project whose net present value is to be calculated was financed by a loan and that the unpaid principle of the loan is accruing over time. Discounting the periodic net cash flows and comparing the sum of the discounted cash flows to the initial cash outlay (the imaginary loan that financed the project) is the same as asking if future cash flows will be sufficient to repay the accumulating loan balance.

Viewed this way, it is clear that the appropriate discount rate is the firm's after-tax cost of capital (the rate at which an imaginary loan balance would accumulate). The cost of capital is the interest rate at which the firm can acquire funds, either by borrowing or by issuing stock. Such a discount rate, or "hurdle rate," takes account either of the firm's need to acquire funds or of the opportunity cost of using internal financing for this project (rather than loaning the funds to some other firm). Note also that the cash flows in the numerators of the NPV formula should *not* include financing costs (such as interest rates), as those are accounted for by the discounting process itself.

While it is true that the appropriate discount rate (or hurdle rate) for cost-benefit decisions is the after-tax cost of capital, identifying that specific figure is somewhat complex. If the project, or decision, involved is just as risky as the firm as a whole, the firm's weighted average cost of capital is the appropriate figure.[21]

Calculation of the firm's weighted average cost of capital is straightforward. Most firms have more than one source of funds: sale of common

---

[21] Joy, *Introduction to Financial Management* (1981), pp. 221–222.

		Discount Rates				
Year	Net After-Tax Cash Flow	0%	5%	10%	15%	20%
0	−50,000	−50,000	−50,000	−50,000	−50,000	−50,000
1	+15,000	+15,000	+14,286	+13,636	+13,043	+12,500
2	+15,000	+15,000	+13,605	+12,397	+11,342	+10,417
3	+15,000	+15,000	+12,958	+11,270	+9,863	+8,681
4	+15,000	+15,000	+12,341	+10,245	+8,576	+7,234
5	+15,000	+15,000	+11,753	+9,314	+7,458	+6,028
Sum	+25,000	+25,000	+14,943	+6,862	+232	−5,140

Table 2-5 **Sensitivity of Net Present Value to the Choice of Discount Rate**

stock, issuance of bonds, issuance of commercial paper, to name only three. Funds raised from each of those sources, because of different risk characteristics for the providers of funds, require different rates of return, and, therefore, different costs of capital to the firm. The firm's weighted average cost of capital is the average of the costs of capital from each of the firm's sources of funds. In computing that average, the cost of each source of funds is weighted by its share of the *market value* of all of the claims against the firm (see Table 2-6).

Table 2-6 shows the calculation of the weighted average after-tax cost of capital of some representative firm. The firm has three sources of funds (commericial paper, bonds, and common stock). The cost of capital for bonds reflects the interest rate that would be required for a new issue. In computing the after-tax cost of capital, one must bear in mind that interest payments (in this case, on commercial paper and bonds) are tax deductible and, therefore, multiply before-tax interest costs by $(1 - T)$, where T is the firm's marginal tax rate (assumed here to be 30 percent).

That the individual project might be financed entirely by borrowing is irrelevant, the average cost of all sources of funds should be used.[22] Difficulties arise, however, when individual projects have different risk properties than those of the firm as it now stands. These are discussed in the next section.

Dealing with Risk

When projecting the incremental after-tax cash flows that will accrue from a decision, one is, necessarily, making a set of judgments about the future. The future, of course, can seldom be known with certainty. The cash inflows that are inputs into net present value calculations will depend on business conditions. Even cash outflows are only conjectures whose realization will depend on the price level, the possibility of discontinued operation, and other factors that cannot be known with certainty in the present.

The result then is that almost all of the cash flows used to make

Source of Funds	Before Tax Cost of Capital (in percent)	Market Value	Share of Market Value
Commercial Paper	9.5	$100,000,000	.10
Bonds	10.0	$300,000,000	.30
Common Stock	11.0	$600,000,000	.60

Marginal Tax Rate = .30
Weighted Average After-Tax Cost of Capital =
$$= (9.5)(1-.30)(.10) + (10.0)(1-.30)(.30) + (11.0)(.60)$$
$$= .665 + 2.100 + 6.6$$
$$= 9.365 \text{ percent}$$

Table 2-6   **Weighted Average Cost of Capital**

cost-benefit decisions are only *expected* cash flows. The resulting calculations of net present value are, almost always, calculations of expected net present value.

The concept of *expected value* is one of the most basic in statistical analysis. Consider a wager based on a toss of a fair coin (a fair coin has a 50 percent chance of landing heads and a 50 percent chance of landing tails). If the coin lands with heads showing, the bettor receives $1. If the coin lands with tails showing, the bettor receives nothing. The expected outcome of that game is the probability weighted average outcome. In this case, the expected outcome is:

$$\text{Expected Outcome} = \text{(Prob. of Heads)(Payoff for Heads)} +$$
$$\text{(Prob. of Tails)(Payoff for Tails)}$$
$$= (.5)(\$1) + (.5)(0)$$
$$= \$0.50$$

The expected outcome indicates what the outcome would be for a representative trial if the game were repeated over and over again. It does not necessarily indicate what the single most likely outcome would be.

Now consider the problem of determining expected net present value. Suppose that one is evaluating a one-year training program. After-tax costs of the program are known to be $100,000 at the beginning and $50,000 during the year.

Management anticipates that the training program will enhance the productivity of the trainees and, thus, generate some incremental cash flows. These enhanced cash flows will be realized over two years. If overall economic conditions are good, that incremental after-tax cash flow is $90,000. If overall economic conditions are poor, that figure is $60,000. The probability of a good year is .7, while the probability of a poor year is .3. Conditions in year one are assumed not to affect the probabilities of good and bad years for year two.

While the situation described above appears complex, an easily applied tool, the *decision tree,* can be used to sort out the cash flow possibilities.[23] A decision tree for the training program is shown in Figure 2-1.

At the left of the decision tree in Figure 2-1 is the start-up cash outflow of $100,000. From that point, there is a 70 percent chance of a good year for Year 1 and a 30 percent chance of a bad year. If Year 1 is one of good economic performance, the net after-tax cash flow due to the training program will be $40,000 ($90,000 in incremental cash inflows less the $50,000 annual outflow due to program costs). If Year 1 is one of poor

---

[22] Otherwise, one could use the lower after-tax cost of debt to accept poor projects and the higher cost of equity to reject better projects.

[23] John F. Magee, "How to Use Decision Trees in Capital Budgeting," *Harvard Business Review* vol. 42, no. 5 (September-October 1964): 79–96.

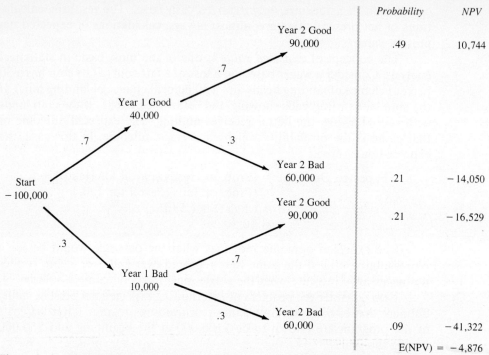

Figure 2-1   **Decision Tree Analysis of a Training Program (Discount rate = 10%)**

economic performance, the net after tax cash flow due to the program is only $10,000 ($60,000 − $50,000).

Given the assumed independence of economic conditions from year to year, Year 2 must be shown as two branches (good economy and bad) from each of the possible Year 1 outcomes. In Year 2, program costs have ceased and the firm realizes only the incremental cash inflows due to higher productivity.

There are, then, for this example, four possible outcomes. Each has its own probability, which is the *product* of the annual probabilities on the branches that led to it. Thus, there is a 49 percent probability (.7 × .7) of good economic performance in both Year 1 and Year 2. If that performance were realized, the net present value of the training program would be

$$NPV = -100,000 + \frac{40,000}{(1.10)} + \frac{90,000}{(1.10)^2}$$

or $10,744 (at the assumed discount rate of 10 percent).

Before the fact, however, one must look at the expected net present value, taking into account all of the branches of the decision tree. That is simply the probability-weighted average of the four possible net present values or:

$$\text{Expected NPV} = (.49)(10,744) + (.21)(-14,050) + (.21)(-16,529) +$$
$$(.09)(-41,322)$$
$$= -\$4876.$$

In this case, the training program should not be undertaken, as its expected net present value is less than zero.

One major problem, however, remains to be solved for the (typical) case of uncertain cash flows. A net present value of $10,000 with certainty is not the equivalent of an expected net present value of $10,000 around which there is possible variation in outcome. One of the most durable facts of economic life is that economic agents (firms, individuals, and households) are *risk-averse*. That is, decision-makers prefer $10,000 with certainty to the expectation of $10,000 with risk. Some means of accounting for the riskiness of cash flows should be incorporated into the cost-benefit calculations.

While there are several such risk adjustment methods available, perhaps the most commonly employed is that of adjusting the discount rate. In the last section, it was shown that if the project under consideration is just as risky as the firm as a whole, the firm's current cost of capital is the appropriate discount rate. To adjust discount rates of differing degrees of risk, one adds a risk premium to the discount rate (for more risky projects) or reduces the firm's overall risk premium (for less risky projects).

Before proceeding, one needs an intuitive feel for project risk. If a project has only one possible cash flow pattern as its outcome, its certain net present value is also expected net present value. There is no dispersion of possible values about the expected net present value and, therefore, no project risk. The project becomes riskier, in the economic not the physical, sense, as the dispersion of possible values about the expected net present value increases. In Figure 2-2, three projects are depicted, each with the same expected net present value [E(NPV)]. For Project I there is no risk. The value of E(NPV) will obtain with certainty, a probability of 1.00. Project II, however is risky in that there is some dispersion of possible outcomes about the expected value. Project II has a 50 percent probability of realizing the expected outcome, but also has the possibility of higher and lower outcomes. Project III displays even more risk, as it has greater dispersion of possible outcomes than does Project II. Indeed, as depicted, Project III has a zero probability of realizing the expected outcome.

The most widely used measure of dispersion for estimating project risk is the variance of possible outcomes. The formula for that variance is:

$$\text{Variance} = \frac{\sum_{i=1}^{N} [\text{NPV}_i - E(\text{NPV})]^2 (\text{Prob}_i)}{N - 1}.$$

That is, the variance is the sum (over N possible outcomes) of the squared

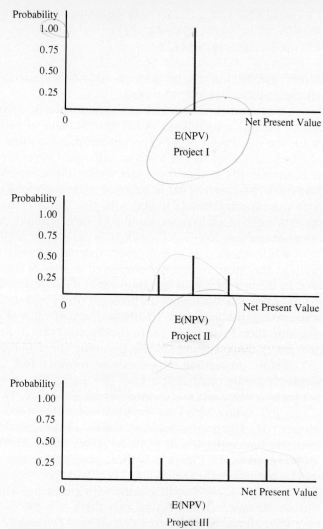

Figure 2-2   **Examples of Varying Project Risk**

difference between the outcome and expected NPV, weighted by the probability of the outcome, divided by one less than the number of possible outcomes.

Because lenders are risk averse, the incremental cost of capital (the cost for a single project in isolation) of a very risky project is higher than that for a risk-free project. Therefore, if a project is completely without risk (like Project I in Figure 2-2), the appropriate rate of discount is the risk-free rate, usually associated with the yield on short-term U.S. Treasury securities. As project risk rises, progressively larger "risk premia" should be added to the discount rate. The procedure for determining those risk premia consists of identifying the risk premia that would be demanded by suppliers of funds, were they financing the individual project in question. The method most often prescribed, employing the Capital Asset Pricing Model, is discussed in detail in most textbooks on financial management, but is beyond the scope of this chapter.[24]

Summary

Cost-benefit analysis provides an objective means of approaching management decisions. Cost-benefit analysis is based on the primacy of cash flows to the firm, recognition of the time-value of money, and decision rules based on the compensation criteria of welfare economics.

The intelligent use of cost-benefit analysis, however, should consider the limitations of cost-benefit analysis, as well as its strengths.[25] Consider, first, the cash flows on which one bases cost-benefit decisions. These are, almost always, uncertain projections of sums to be realized in the future (sometimes quite far into the future). One must, necessarily, work with educated guesses. Further, especially in the realm of human resource management, many of the most important consequences of a decision are not easily converted to monetary units. It is difficult to introduce these important nonmonetary consequences into a cost-benefit framework, except in a tie-breaking capacity.

All cost-benefit calculations are very sensitive to the rate of discount employed. Selection of that rate of discount is difficult, as financial markets don't reveal risk-adjusted costs of capital for individual projects.

A final difficulty in applying cost-benefit analysis to decisions in human resource management lies in organizational politics. Industrial relations practice has often been an atheoretical, nonquantitative arena of management. Convincing practicing managers to adopt cost-benefit criteria in their decisions may prove quite difficult.

Despite all of the limitations of cost-benefit analysis, its application to human resource management can yield enhanced performance for the firm. The balance of the text will explore ways in which these principles can be combined with knowledge of labor economics, collective bargaining, and personnel management to improve the practice of human resource management.

---

[24] See Brealey and Myers, *Principles of Financial Management* (1984), ch. 9; Joy, *Introduction to Financial Management* (1981), pp. 227–232; and Pinches, *Essentials of Financial Management* (1984), ch. 13.

[25] George E. Pinches, "Myopia, Capital Budgeting and Decision Making," *Financial Management* vol. 11, no. 3 (Autumn 1982): 6–19.

PROBLEMS

1. Consider a health insurance contract to cover a group of 300 employees. The before-tax cash outflows for the contract are $400,000 per year, payable at the end of each year of coverage. The contract is to run for 3 years.

   (a) If the firm has a marginal tax rate of .30, what are the after-tax cash flows for each of the three years?

   (b) If the firm's after-tax cost-of-capital is 10 percent, what is the present value of the after-tax cash flows associated with the insurance contract?

   (c) By how much will the present value of after-tax cash outflows change if the $400,000 premiums are due at the beginning of each year of coverage, all else remaining unchanged?

2. Explain why present values, rather than simple totals of cash flows, must be used when comparing streams of cash flows.

3. Spencer Company has one employee. Today is her 64th birthday. Her pension rights guarantee her $20,000 per year on each of her 65th through 70th birthdays. To fully fund that liability, how much money must Spencer have set aside today? Assume the interest rate earned by the pension account is 10 percent.

4. Knapper Corporation is considering two alternatives for its health insurance program. On one hand, Krogh Insurance Company will cover all fifty employees for two years for $1200 per employee per year, payable in advance (a one-time payment of $120,000). Knapper can self-insure, paying the medical bills of its employees. In that case, in each year there is a fifty percent chance of bills of $1800 per employee per year and a fifty percent chance of $800 per employee per year. Compare the expected present value of cost of self-insurance to the one-time payment required by the Krogh Insurance Company. Note that all of the expenses given represent tax-deductible items. Assume a marginal tax rate of 30 percent applies. Assume the cost-of-capital to be 10 percent.

REFERENCES

Black, Fischer, "The Trouble With Econometric Models." *Financial Analysts Journal* (March–April 1982): 29–37.

Freeman, Richard B. and James L. Medoff. *What Do Unions Do?* New York: Basic Books, 1984.

Henderson, James M. and Richard E. Quandt. *Microeconomic Theory: A Mathematical Approach,* second edition. New York: McGraw-Hill, 1971.

Johnston, J. *Econometric Methods,* second edition. New York: McGraw-Hill, 1972.

Magee, John F. "How to Use Decision Trees in Capital Budgeting," *Harvard Business Review,* vol. 42, no. 5 (September–October 1964): 79–96.

Mishan, E. J. *Cost-Benefit Analysis,* new and expanded edition. New York: Praeger, 1976.

Williamson, Oliver E. "The Modern Corporation: Origins, Evolution, Attributes." *Journal of Economic Literature* vol. 19, no. 4 (December 1981): 1537–1565.

INTRODUCTION TO INTERPRETING MULTIPLE REGRESSION RESULTS

Introduction

Often in research, whether academic or practical, one needs to test hypotheses concerning relationships among variables. In particular, researchers in human resource management are concerned about whether or not changes in one or more variables cause changes in another variable. To model and test such causal relationships, statisticians have developed several multivariate statistical techniques. Perhaps the most widely used and most generally applicable of these is multiple regression analysis by the method of ordinary least squares.[26]

Consider a simplified version of a frequently encountered problem in labor economics. A researcher believes that hourly earnings for a large sample of individuals are caused by (or explained by) a set of variables describing those individuals. The causal (independent) variables might include age, level of education (measured by years of school completed), race, and sex. Hourly earnings (the dependent variable), then, are hypothesized to be a function of (to depend upon) those variables. Fischer Black

---

[26] See any textbooks on econometrics. For example Michael D. Intriligator, *Economic Models, Techniques, and Applications,* Englewood Cliffs, New Jersey: Prentice-Hall, 1978; J. Johnston, *Econometric Methods,* second edition, New York: McGraw-Hill, 1972; G. S. Maddala, *Econometrics,* New York: McGraw-Hill, 1977; and Henri Theil, *Principles of Econometrics,* New York: John Wiley & Sons, 1971.

points out that hypotheses about causation are derived from theory and specified in the equation to be estimated. The regression results themselves say nothing about causation. Causation should not be inferred after the fact from estimated relationships.[27]

The investigator's hypotheses can be summarized in functional form as:

$$\text{Hourly earnings} = f(\text{age, education, race, sex}). \qquad (1)$$

Race and sex are zero-one variables, representing assignment to categories. For example, one might make sex = 1 if female, sex = 0 if male. One then needs to specify the functional form of the equation he or she wishes to estimate. While many forms can be specified, the most commonly used is the linear form:

$$\text{Hourly earnings}_i = \beta_0 + \beta_1 \text{Age}_i + \beta_2 \text{Schooling}_i + \beta_3 \text{Race}_i + \beta_4 \text{Sex}_i. \qquad (2)$$

In such a form, the subscript "i" indicates that each observation consists of the hourly earnings, age, education, race, and sex of the "i^{th}" individual. The values β_0, β_1, β_2, β_3, and β_4 are the parameters to be estimated.

An alternative to the linear specification is the multiplicative specification:

$$\text{Hourly earnings}_i = \beta_0 \, \text{Age}_i^{\beta_1} \, \text{Schooling}_i^{\beta_2}. \qquad (3)$$

Such a specification is made linear (and, thus, estimable) by taking the natural logarithm of both sides:

$$\ln(\text{earnings}_i) = \ln\beta_0 + \beta_1 \ln(\text{age}_i) + \beta_2 \ln(\text{schooling}_i). \qquad (4)$$

The variable for race and sex are omitted from the multiplicative specification because of their zero-one nature.[28]

Returning to Equation (2), the coefficient β_1 can be interpreted as the unit change in hourly earnings that can be attributed to a one unit change in age, all other variables held constant. That is, β_1 is the slope of the earnings function with respect to age (see Figure 2-A1). Equation (3) is only slightly more difficult to interpret. In Equation (3), β_1 is the percentage change in hourly earnings attributable to a one percent change in age, all other variables held constant. That is, in a multiplicative specification (which is made estimable by making the equation linear in logarithms), the estimated coefficients are the elasticities of the dependent variable with respect to the associated independent variables.

---

[27] Fischer Black, "The Trouble With Econometric Models," *Financial Analysts Journal* (March–April 1982): 29–37.

[28] Note that if race were included and race = 0, one would predict earnings = 0, no matter what the values of the other variables.

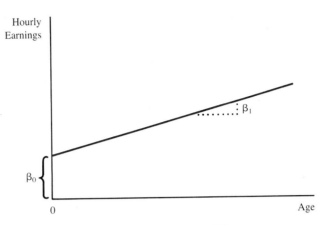

Figure 2–A1   **Coefficients as Slope and Intercept**

As indicators of the estimated direction of change of the dependent variable, given an increase in one of the independent variables, the signs of the estimated coefficients (positive or negative), as well as their magnitudes, are important. That is, a positive estimated value of β_1 in Equation (2) indicates that earnings increase as age increases. A negative estimated value would indicate the opposite.

This discussion has ignored the mathematical problem of estimating the values of β_0, β_1, β_2, β_3, and β_4. Some rule, of course, must be applied to the data (gathered on individuals) that will generate the estimates of those values that are, in some sense, best. The most commonly employed statistical method for estimating linear relationships is the technique of *ordinary least squares.* The logic behind the method is quite simple (although, in the absence of computing equipment and appropriate software, the calculations can be dauntingly tedious). Figure 2-A2 illustrates the least squares method of a single independent variable, years of school completed.

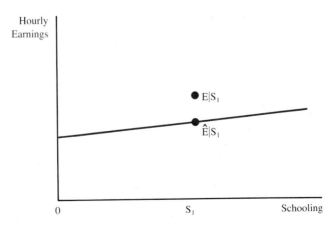

Figure 2–A2   **Least Squares Estimation**

Estimating Technique

One of the individuals in the sample has a level of schooling S_1 and an observed level of earnings E_1, which we can write $E|S_1$ (earnings, given S_1). Any regression function that one might estimate will have an estimated slope with respect to schooling of β_2 and, therefore, a *predicted* earnings level of $\hat{E}|S_1 = \hat{\beta}_0 + \hat{\beta}_2 (S_1)$. There are, of course, an infinite number of possible values of $\hat{E}|S_1$. The best estimators, $\hat{\beta}_0$ and $\hat{\beta}_1$, are those which yield the best estimates, $\hat{E}|S_1$, for all observed values of S_1.

The criterion used to determine the best estimates is that of least squares. Given the observed level of schooling, there is, for each possible regression line, a deviation of prediction from observation, $(E|S_1 - \hat{E}|S_1)$. If we square all of those deviations (so as to work with only positive squared deviations), we want to find the one regression line (values of β_0 and β_1) that minimizes the sum of the squared deviations (hence, the name, least squares).

Computer software, for both mainframe and microcomputers, is available for performing least squares estimations quite quickly. Least squares estimates have been shown to have several desirable statistical properties. In particular, they are relatively impervious to violations of some of the assumptions which underlie their theoretical derivation.

Test Statistics

Given a set of estimates for β_0, β_1, β_2, β_3, and β_4 in Equation (2), two other types of information must be derived: first, are the estimates, whatever their numerical values, statistically significant (significantly different from zero); and, second, to what extent do changes in the independent variables account for changes in the dependent variable (hourly earnings)?

The statistical theory that underlies least squares estimation indicates that the estimated value, $\hat{\beta}_1$, is the mean of a probability distribution that is normal (follows a bell-shaped curve), having a standard error that can be calculated (and is provided as part of the output of almost all OLS software). One can use these facts, then, to test the hypothesis that the true value of β_1 is equal to zero (that there is no relationship between the relevant independent variable and the dependent variable).

The appropriate test for such a hypothesis employs the Students' t-statistic and n-k-l degrees of freedom, where n is the number of observations and k is the number of independent variables. There is a 95 percent probability that the true value of β_1 will fall within a range about the estimated value of $\hat{\beta}_1$ determined by $\hat{\beta}_1 \pm$ (plus or minus) the critical value of student's t for 95 percent confidence (the .05 level) at the appropriate number of degrees of freedom. For large numbers of degrees of freedom that critical value is 1.96 times the standard error of $\hat{\beta}_1$ (see Figure 2-A3).

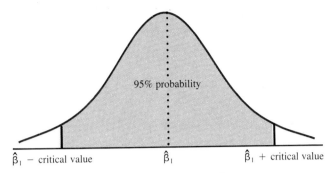

Figure 2–A3 **Confidence Interval For** $\hat{\beta}_1$

The computed t-statistic for each estimated slope coefficient is the estimated coefficient divided by its standard error (β_i/s.e.). One rejects the hypothesis that the true values of β_1 is zero if the computed t-statistic for $\hat{\beta}_1$ exceeds the critical value of the t distribution for the appropriate number of degrees of freedom at the chosen confidence level. Thus, if the number of degrees of freedom is 120 or more and one wishes to test at the 95 percent confidence level, one rejects the null hypothesis that the true value of β_i is zero (that there is no relationship between X_i and the dependent variable) if the computed t-statistic is 1.96 or greater.

Also of interest is the test statistic known as R^2. R^2 is the ratio of the amount of variation in the dependent variable accounted for by the equation estimated to the total variation in the dependent variable. While the purpose of econometric analysis *is not* to find equations with high R^2s, if an estimated relationship has an R^2 close to zero, it has little power to explain movements in the dependent variable. A low value of R^2 suggests that much of the variation in the dependent variable is truly random or that some important independent variables are missing from the equation.

The Problem of Missing Variables

Missing independent variables can cause serious problems in that they might bias the estimated values of the coefficients of the included independent variables (underspecification bias). Suppose a true relationship exists of the form:

$$y = \beta_0 + \beta_1 X_1 + \beta_2 X_2. \tag{5}$$

If an investigator omits X_2 from his specification, he will estimate a relationship

$$y = \hat{\beta}_0 + \hat{\beta}_1 X_1, \tag{6}$$

which is underspecified.

What is wrong with the underspecified estimate, $\hat{\beta}_1$? Rather than the desired unbiased estimator, $E(\hat{\beta}_1) = \beta_1$, the investigator will have an estimate with expected value:

$$E(\hat{\beta}_1) = \beta_1 + \beta_2 \, \text{corr}(X_1 X_2) \tag{7}$$

where $\text{corr}_{1,2}$ is the correlation between independent X_1 and X_2. Thus, missing independent variables exert an influence on estimated coefficients to the extent that missing variables are correlated with included independent variables.

CHAPTER 3

THE LABOR FORCE AND SUPPLY OF LABOR

A fundamental consideration for most employers is the availability of a large and sufficiently trained workforce. Without an adequate number of both unskilled and skilled workers who are willing to provide useful hours of work to an employer, production would cease. The goals of this chapter are to provide you with a basic understanding of the role of the labor force and labor supply concepts in the policy and planning process used nationally and in many organizations. Using these concepts, you should be able to better understand the linkages of external and internal labor markets that influence an enterprise. The chapter will present concepts and information on the labor force and the supply of labor. In order for you to check your understanding of these concepts, several illustrations of applications of labor supply to firms, as well as regional and national public policy analysis are provided.

After reading this chapter you should be able to answer the following questions: How do basic demographic variables such as population, labor force participation and migration assist you in understanding the workings of the aggregate labor market? What are the basic definitions used to define labor force concepts? How does the supply of labor differ in firms, industries, regions, and nationally? Finally, how does knowing labor supply theory assist you in understanding worker choices to work for an organization and the intensity of their work effort?

Labor Supply in Planning

For any major organization, maintaining a sufficient and well-trained workforce is a major objective. Within these public and private organizations, planning targets for human resources are often linked to the "strategic plan" of the enterprise. Once an objective is agreed upon for targets and goals for the firm, it is then the job of the human resource manager, in cooperation with the other major functional parts of the organization such as production, finance, and marketing, to develop strategies on hiring, promoting, and firing for the enterprise. As part of this planning process, some of the key questions that are addressed are the following: Within the market for labor, what kinds of workers are available, and how much in wages, benefits, and work conditions will it take for them to work for my enterprise? What are the internal labor market responses (see Chapter 1) to changes in the external market for labor? That is, as markets become tighter (i.e., the availability of workers decreases) or the market becomes looser (i.e., the availability of workers increases) how will the firm's policies change? Therefore, any type of human resource planning must be linked to the supply of labor.

To illustrate, most staffing or training functions in an organization during the 1970s and 80s have assumed that the supply of labor is greater than the demand for labor. Under these conditions of excess supply, it is important to develop methods of choosing whom of a number of qualified applicants will perform the task in the most cost-effective manner (the methods that larger organizations use to accomplish this will be detailed in Chapters 12 and 13). If there is a decline in the supply of labor for an occupation, the internal firm decisions shift from the selection of persons to the recruitment or further development and training of qualified individuals that are available in the market or in the enterprise.

A further example of how changes in the market for labor can influence recruitment practices is shown in Example 3–1. As a result of greater hiring by other firms in the area, and the changing composition of the workforce, many firms are "struggling to fill vacancies" in traditionally low wage service jobs in many parts of the country. Further, recent public policies have played an important role in low wage jobs. Example 3–2 shows how the recent change in the immigration law has impacted low-wage employers as well as one union's responses.

Although low-wage workers who are needed to fill jobs in other areas are scarce, in some industrial cities with high unemployment rates like Gary, Indiana, jobs are eagerly sought. The policies and practices that firms implement regarding human resources are often dependent on the market for labor external to the firm.

An illustration using labor supply in location decisions is the du Pont Corporation, which attempts to minimize labor costs, subject to maintaining high levels of performance. As part of this policy, they contract out

 **EXAMPLE 3.1**   JOBS GO BEGGING FOR UNSKILLED
WORKERS

On a recent Thursday, Jim Wronski, the director of Chicago's famous Andy Frain Services is frantic. For the coming weekend there will be numerous sports and cultural events. However, he can only find 540 including his office staff, and he needs 600 ushers. In the past there had been lines waiting for the jobs. In the last year a recruiting drive in high schools netted only 60 permanent new hires. Andy Frain has had to really "sell the job" in a new marketing campaign.

Andy Frain Services is not alone. Companies in the low to unskilled services are having the toughest time since the 1960s filling entry-level jobs, that are typically held by teenagers and women. Firms in businesses like fast-food chains, convenience stores, and grocery stores have the most unfilled positions. In addition, businesses like department stores, hotels, and temporary-help stores are also short-handed. The Bureau of National Affairs, a private nonprofit research organization found that 30 percent of fast food stores had been understaffed for a month or more. These factors also reflect the 40-month upturn in the business cycle. However longer-run determinants, that include demographic factors, mean that service industry companies will struggle to fill vacancies for years to come.

Source: *Fortune,* March 17, 1986, pp. 33–35.

much plant construction engineering to small firms who hire engineers and mechanical drafters for short three to six month periods. These small companies then often attempt to find short-term engineers and drafters to work in ample numbers to complete these construction projects with no carryover to employment at du Pont. In order to do this in a timely manner, these small firms open offices in parts of the U.S. where the numbers of technical personnel is the highest with the lowest possible wages. Their decision on location is dependent on the current supply and short-term forecasts of the number of technical personnel within a metropolitan area.

Key Terms to Analyze Labor Supply

In understanding the characteristics of the market for labor, there are certain key definitions that you need to be aware of in order to utilize the information on labor force characteristics. Perhaps the most cited labor force concept is that of unemployment. The basic defintion is that unemployment is the number of persons looking for work who cannot find it. Other key terms in studying the labor market include wage rates, quantity

 2   IMMIGRATION LAW CAUSING SHORTAGES OF
LABOR IN SOME INDUSTRIES

Garth War examines his garment factory and would like to see 150 new employees producing sportswear. Mr. Ward has relied heavily on illegal aliens for his low-wage work force. However, now he cannot find enough new workers to meet a growing demand for his company's products and blames the new immigration law.

The new law places the burden on the employer to show that all new workers have a legal right to work. Many employers, especially small- and medium-sized businesses are complaining that they must hire additional clerical staff to keep track of the paperwork and recordkeeping requirements of the law.

In the textile industry some firms are trying to woo new workers by increasing wages, although they are limited by the prices their customers will pay for finished goods. They add that it is difficult to recruit workers other than immigrants. "The idea of bringing in 'immigrants' is just nonsense to me," said Miguel Machucha, organizing director for the Western states of the International Ladies Garment Workers Union. There is no shortage of workers here in Los Angeles. They just want to exploit people more than they already do."

Source: *New York Times,* June 5, 1987.

of labor, and employment. For each of these terms there exists considerable information through U.S. government and private data collection services.[1]

The definition of each of these terms in the market for labor has been developed by the Department of Labor's Bureau of Labor Statistics. Each month, they administer the Current Population Survey (CPS) to approximately 73,000 households nationally. Using their survey, news commentators, such as Tom Brokaw, confidently state the current month's unemployment rate, change in household earnings, or number employed. A flow chart for the development of the basic concepts in the labor force is presented in Figure 3–1 for 1986. These basic definitions and methods of tabulation in the labor force have remained similar over time.

For example, the CPS definition of employed is all persons aged 16 years and over who answered that they were working or had a job from which they were temporarily absent during the survey week. For quantity of labor, the basic definition is number of hours worked multiplied by the

---

[1] For data on labor supply and definitions see the Bureau of Labor Statistics Handbook of Labor Statistics, U.S. Bureau of the Census's Current Population Survey (CPS), U.S. Department of Labor, Employment and Training Administration, *Employment and Training Report of the President, National Longitudinal Survey,* and the *Panel Study on Income Dynamics.*

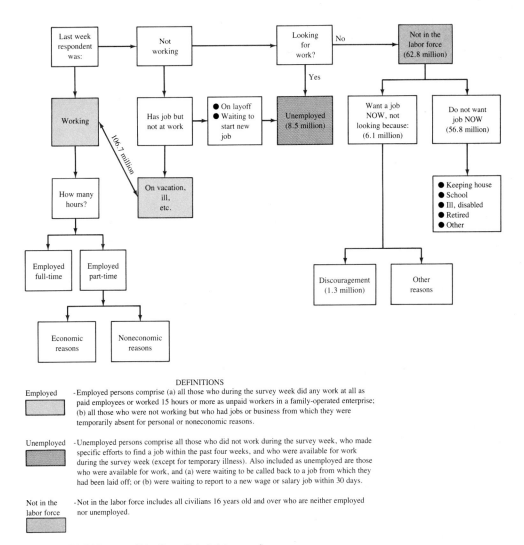

DEFINITIONS

Employed - Employed persons comprise (a) all those who during the survey week did any work at all as paid employees or worked 15 hours or more as unpaid workers in a family-operated enterprise; (b) all those who were not working but who had jobs or business from which they were temporarily absent for personal or noneconomic reasons.

Unemployed - Unemployed persons comprise all those who did not work during the survey week, who made specific efforts to find a job within the past four weeks, and who were available for work during the survey week (except for temporary illness). Also included as unemployed are those who were available for work, and (a) were waiting to be called back to a job from which they had been laid off; or (b) were waiting to report to a new wage or salary job within 30 days.

Not in the labor force - Not in the labor force includes all civilians 16 years old and over who are neither employed nor unemployed.

Source: Report 505, U.S. Department of Labor, Bureau of Labor Statistics

Figure 3-1   **Status of the Labor Force Using the Current Population Survey**

number of people in the labor force. For example, in Figure 3-1, the labor force was 115.2 million (total employed plus unemployed). For a measure of quantity of labor, this figure would be multiplied by the average number of hours worked per week. However, this value does not take into account the quality of labor. For example, a society which has a highly trained, educated, and experienced workforce, will result in output that would be greater than one with a lower quality level of trained and experienced human resources. India has a much larger numerical labor force than the United States, but the educational level and quality is lower than in the U.S.

One of the most important elements in understanding labor supply is the wage rate. The real wage rate is the value of market goods that can be purchased for an hour's work.[2] The wage is such a central item in labor supply because it represents both an inducement to work and a cost to business of hiring labor (the cost of hiring will be discussed more fully in Chapters 5 and 6). Further, a full explanation of wages must also include fringe benefits. Given the growth of fringes to include over 16 percent of worker's compensation, it is a key element that should be included in any complete definition of the wage rate.

Although most information on the aggregate labor market is collected through national surveys such as the CPS, much of the local data is gathered through administrative records such as reports which employers file through the Unemployment Insurance System (U.I.) or the Social Security Administration (SSA).[3] One major concern of analysts of the aggregate labor market has been whether the data collected through surveys or through administrative sources are consistent over time and across various parts of the country.[4] Further, definitions of concepts such as the labor force have changed to include military personnel in the 1980s, but do not include these persons prior to that time. For example, cities with military bases, like Junction City, Kansas, that contain a major army base like Fort Riley, would have a much lower unemployment rate if the military personnel were counted in the local labor force. In this case, the army is not counted in the local labor force statistics, but the military is counted in the determination of the national labor force count. Therefore, in developing an analysis of the labor market for planning or policy purposes, care must be taken to be aware of the different information sources as well as changing definitions in developing labor market concepts.

Characteristics of the Labor Force

The basis for the development of a concept of labor supply is the population. This term can be viewed as a stock much like that of capital equipment at a point in time. The flows into population consist of fertility, and migration; both of these factors have been related to economic

---

[2] Belton M. Fleisher and Thomas J. Kniesner, *Labor Economics: Theory, Evidence and Policy,* Prentice-Hall, Inc. Englewood Cliffs, New Jersey, 3rd ed., 1984.

[3] Morris M. Kleiner, "An Appraisal of New Sources of Employment and Unemployment Statistics," in *Data Collection Processing and Presentation,* Volume 2, National Commission on Employment and Unemployment Statistics, Washington, D.C., 1979, pp. 101–126.

[4] Morris M. Kleiner, "Workforce Entrants and Exits: Some Comparisons of Administrative and Survey Data," *Policy Analysis and Information Systems,* Vol. 5, No. 2, 1981, pp. 139–150.

Year	Both Sexes Percent of non- institutional population	Female Percent of non- institutional population	Male Percent of non- institutional population
1961	60.2	38.1	83.6
1962	59.7	38.0	82.8
1963	59.6	38.3	82.2
1964	59.8	38.7	81.9
1965	59.7	39.3	81.5
1966	60.1	40.3	81.4
1967	60.6	41.2	81.5
1968	60.7	41.6	81.2
1969	61.1	42.7	80.9
1970	61.3	43.4	80.6
1971	61.0	43.4	80.0
1972	61.1	43.9	79.7
1973	61.4	44.8	79.5
1974	61.8	45.7	79.3
1975	61.8	46.4	78.5
1976	62.1	47.4	78.1
1977	62.8	48.5	78.2
1978	63.6	50.0	78.4
1979	64.1	51.0	78.4
1980	64.2	51.6	77.9
1981	64.3	52.2	77.5
1982	64.3	52.7	77.0
1983	64.2	53.0	76.8
1984	64.4	53.7	76.8
1985	64.8	54.5	76.7

Source: *Monthly Labor Review,* May 1986.

Table 3–1   **Labor Force Participation in the U.S. Economy, 1961–1985**

determinants for analysis and forecasting.[5] The flows out of the stock of population are deaths and outmigration. Knowledge of each of these components can be used as the basis for developing human resource planning decisions for an enterprise or region.

The labor force participation rate can be estimated by dividing persons with jobs or seeking work by the population. Estimates of the labor force participation rate are presented in Table 3–1. Perhaps the most striking information is the growth of the participation rates of women and the decline in the rates of participation for men for most age groups and

[5] For examples of the importance of economic determinants on demographic variables see Anthony L. Redwood, "An Economic-Demographic Approach to Forecasting National and Subnational Birth Rates," *SocioEconomic Planning Sciences,* Vol. 17, No. 506, 1983, pp. 355–363, and Morris M. Kleiner and W. T. McWilliams, "Analysis of Alternative Labor Force Population Migration Forecasting Models," *The Annals of Regional Science,* Volume 11, No. 2, 1977, pp. 74–85.

especially older men. This change in the composition of the labor force has had a profound impact on compensation programs to include pensions as well as recruitment and selection procedures of organizations (these issues will be addressed in greater detail in Chapters 12, 13, and 15). For example, the increase in participation rates for married women with children may result in firms providing fringe benefits like child care. This benefit may then increase the quality of the labor force available to the firm.

Another major issue for the economy and labor market is the industrial and occupational composition of the labor force. Table 3–2 shows the shifts that have occurred in major industrial and occupational groups from 1961 to 1981. The table shows some important shifts in the kinds of tasks that people are doing. Specifically, there have been major shifts out of manufacturing industries and out of those occupations that are required in manufacturing. The industries that have been growing relative to the others have been the service industries. Further, agriculture and farm workers have declined greatly during the last twenty-five years. In general, the changing composition of the labor force has required a higher level of skill and training of the labor force. For example, changes have occurred in the economic environment as a result of the shift from production factory jobs to more highly trained service workers in professional and technical occupations.

The information on the labor force that often draws the most attention is the unemployment rate. By definition, the unemployment rate is the number of persons unemployed divided by the labor force. Unlike other measures of vacancies in the economy, like unused plant capacity or unsold homes, people can vote. Further, there is a more limited working life of people relative to machines. Finally, work is the main method that most individuals use as their primary source of income. Therefore, the measure of unused capacity in the labor market, the unemployment rate, is one of the most quoted and important indicators of economic health.

As Table 3–3 shows, there have been wide fluctuations in the unemployment rate during the post World War II period. Some analysts suggest that there is a negative relationship between price changes and unemployment rates; this empirical relationship is called the Phillips Curve, and will be discussed in greater detail in Chapter 21.[6] However, the Table shows that unemployment does not impact all groups in the labor force equally. For example, blacks have consistently had an unemployment rate twice as high as whites. Further, women have generally had higher unemployment rates than men. Although the unemployment rate is often

[6] A. W. Phillips, "The Relationship Between Unemployment and the Rate of Change of Money Wage Rates in the United Kingdom, 1861–1957," *Economica,* 25 (November 1953), pp. 283–299.

used as a measure of how well off the labor market is, it has been criticized as not being a good measure of hardship within the country or in a particular region.[7] However, as a measure of "vacancies" in the labor market, it has generally been widely accepted as being appropriate.[8]

The factor that is most widely used to measure adjustments in the labor market is migration. Movement to a country is typically referred to as immigration. However, in a region or state it is referred to as in or out migration. The factors that influence migration to or away from a geographic area have been studied in considerable detail.[9] Besides amenities of climate and cultural benefits, economic factors such as employment growth and high wages have been shown to influence geographic mobility.[10] As Figure 3–2 shows, there are variations in the mobility patterns of the U.S. population based on age. That is, young adults tend to be much more mobile than persons who are middle aged or older. As a result, they may be more responsive or willing to move in order to advance their careers. Further, immigrants to the U.S. often choose their location based on the numbers of others from the same country that live in the area.[11]

In examining the responsiveness of persons employed in different occupations and industries to move as a result of economic incentives, the results are similar. For example, persons in high wage occupations such as professional and technical workers are more migration responsive to economic incentives than laborers or service workers.[12] Further, workers employed in more highly cyclic industries like manufacturing also tend to be more migration responsive than are workers employed in service oriented industries.[13] In developing firm policies toward the relocation of individuals, the education and training qualities of the workforce should be taken into account in attempting to relocate individuals. These incentives are important in the determination of the types of inducements necessary to get persons to relocate. As these research results show, the age, occupa-

---

[7] Sar A. Levitan and Robert Taggart, "Do Our Statistics Measure the Real Labor Market Hardships?" American Statistical Association, *Proceedings,* 1976.

[8] Glen G. Cain, "Labor Force Concepts and Definitions in View of Their Purposes," *Concepts and Data Needs,* Vol. 1, National Commission on Employment and Unemployment Statistics, Washington, D.C., 1979, pp. 3–45.

[9] Michael J. Greenwood, "Research on Internal Migration in the United States: A Survey," *Journal of Economic Literature,* June 1975, pp. 397–433.

[10] Ibid.

[11] Ann P. Bartel, "Location Decisions of the New Immigrants to the United States," NBER Working Paper #2049, 1986.

[12] Morris M. Kleiner, "Evidence on Occupational Migration: Some New Comparisons," *Growth and Change,* Vol. 13, No. 3, 1982, pp. 43–48.

[13] Morris M. Kleiner, "Metropolitan Area Labor Market Changes: Determinants and Comparisons by Industry," *Regional Studies,* Vol. 19, No. 2, 1985, pp. 131–138.

			White-collar workers				
	Total employed	*Total*	*Professional and technical*	*Managers and administrators, ex. farm*	*Sales workers*	*Clerical workers*	*Total*
Both Sexes							
1961......	100.0	43.9	11.7	10.8	6.4	15.0	36.0
1962......	100.0	44.4	12.0	11.1	6.2	15.1	36.1
1963......	100.0	44.2	12.2	10.8	6.1	15.1	36.6
1964......	100.0	44.5	12.3	10.7	6.1	15.3	36.6
1965......	100.0	44.8	12.5	10.3	6.3	15.7	36.9
1966......	100.0	45.4	12.8	10.2	6.2	16.2	37.0
1967......	100.0	46.0	13.3	10.1	6.1	16.6	36.7
1968......	100.0	46.8	13.6	10.2	6.1	16.9	36.3
1969......	100.0	47.3	13.8	10.2	6.0	17.2	36.2
1970......	100.0	48.3	14.2	10.5	6.2	17.4	35.3
1971......	100.0	48.3	14.0	11.0	6.4	17.0	34.4
1972......	100.0	47.8	14.0	10.8	6.6	17.4	35.0
1973......	100.0	47.8	14.0	10.2	6.4	17.2	34.4
1974......	100.0	48.6	14.4	10.4	6.3	17.5	34.6
1975......	100.0	49.8	15.0	10.5	6.4	17.8	33.0
1976......	100.0	50.0	15.2	10.6	6.3	17.8	33.1
1977......	100.0	49.9	15.1	10.7	6.3	17.8	33.4
1978......	100.0	50.0	15.1	10.7	6.3	17.9	33.4
1979......	100.0	50.9	15.5	10.8	6.4	18.2	33.1
1980......	100.0	52.2	16.1	11.2	6.3	18.6	31.7
1981......	100.0	52.7	16.4	11.5	6.4	18.5	31.1

Occupational Distribution (label for upper table)

						Private	
						Manufacturing	Transportation and public utilities
Year	*Total*	*Total private*	*Mining*	*Construction*	*Total*	*Durable goods* / *Nondurable goods*	
1961......	100.0	84.1	1.2	5.3	30.2	16.8 / 13.4	7.2
1962......	100.0	84.0	1.2	5.3	30.3	17.1 / 13.3	7.0
1963......	100.0	83.7	1.1	5.3	30.0	17.0 / 13.0	6.9
1964......	100.0	83.5	1.1	5.3	29.6	16.8 / 12.8	6.8
1965......	100.0	83.4	1.0	5.3	29.7	17.1 / 12.6	6.6
1966......	100.0	83.1	1.0	5.2	30.1	17.7 / 12.4	6.5
1967......	100.0	82.7	.9	4.9	29.6	17.4 / 12.2	6.5
1968......	100.0	82.6	.9	4.9	29.1	17.1 / 12.0	6.4
1969......	100.0	82.7	.9	5.1	28.7	16.9 / 11.8	6.3
1970......	100.0	82.3	.9	5.1	27.3	15.8 / 11.5	6.4
1971......	100.0	81.9	.9	5.2	26.2	14.9 / 11.2	6.3
1972......	100.0	81.9	.9	5.3	26.0	15.0 / 11.0	6.2
1973......	100.0	82.1	.8	5.3	26.2	15.5 / 10.8	6.1
1974......	100.0	81.9	.9	5.1	25.7	15.2 / 10.4	6.0
1975......	100.0	80.9	1.0	4.6	23.8	13.9 / 9.9	5.9
1976......	100.0	81.3	1.0	4.5	23.9	14.0 / 10.0	5.8
1977......	100.0	81.7	1.0	4.7	23.9	14.1 / 9.8	5.7
1978......	100.0	81.9	1.0	4.9	23.7	14.2 / 9.5	5.7
1979......	100.0	82.2	1.1	5.0	23.4	14.2 / 9.2	5.7
1980......	100.0	82.1	1.1	4.9	22.4	13.5 / 9.0	5.7
1981......	100.0	82.5	1.2	4.7	22.1	13.3 / 8.9	5.6

Industry Distribution (label for lower table)

(a)not available

Source: *Employment and Training Report of the President,* 1981.

Table 3-2   **Percent Occupational and Industry Composition of the U.S. Labor Market, 1961–1981**

		Blue-collar workers					Service workers			Farmworkers	
Craft and kindred workers		Operatives		Non-farm laborers	Total	Private household workers	Other service workers	Total	Farmers and farm managers	Farm laborers and supervisors
	Total	Except transport	Transport equipment								
13.1	17.8	(a)	(a)	5.1	12.6	3.1	9.5	7.5	4.1	3.9
13.0	18.0	(a)	(a)	5.1	12.6	3.0	9.5	6.9	3.9	3.4
13.2	18.4	(a)	(a)	5.0	12.8	3.0	9.8	6.4	3.5	2.3
13.0	18.6	(a)	(a)	5.0	12.8	2.9	9.9	6.1	3.3	2.6
13.0	18.8	(a)	(a)	5.2	12.6	2.8	9.8	6.7	3.1	2.1
13.2	19.0	(a)	(a)	4.8	12.6	2.6	10.0	5.0	2.9	2.0
13.2	18.7	(a)	(a)	4.8	12.5	2.4	10.2	4.8	2.6	2.4
13.2	18.4	(a)	(a)	4.7	12.4	2.3	10.1	4.6	2.5	2.3
13.1	18.4	(a)	(a)	4.7	12.2	2.1	10.1	4.2	2.4	1.5
12.9	17.7	(a)	(a)	4.7	12.4	2.0	10.4	4.0	2.2	1.7
12.9	16.4	(a)	(a)	5.1	13.5	1.9	11.6	3.8	2.1	1.7
13.2	16.6	12.7	3.9	5.2	13.4	1.8	11.7	3.8	2.1	1.7
13.4	16.9	13.0	3.9	5.1	13.2	1.6	11.6	3.6	2.0	1.6
13.4	16.2	12.4	3.8	5.1	13.2	1.4	11.8	3.5	1.9	1.6
12.9	15.2	11.4	3.8	4.9	13.7	1.4	12.4	3.5	1.9	1.6
12.9	15.3	11.5	3.7	4.9	13.7	1.3	12.4	3.2	1.7	1.5
13.1	15.3	11.4	3.8	5.0	13.7	1.3	12.4	3.0	1.6	1.4
13.1	15.3	11.5	3.8	5.0	13.6	1.2	12.4	3.0	1.6	1.4
13.3	15.0	11.3	3.7	4.8	13.2	1.1	12.1	2.8	1.5	1.3
12.9	14.2	10.6	3.6	4.6	13.3	1.1	12.3	2.8	1.5	1.3
12.6	14.0	10.5	3.5	4.6	13.4	1.0	12.3	2.7	1.5	1.3

	Wholesale and retail trade			Finance, insurance, real estate	Services	Government		
	Total	Wholesale	Retail			Total government	Federal[a]	State and local
	21.0	5.8	15.2	5.0	14.1	15.9	4.2	11.7
	20.8	5.8	15.1	5.0	14.4	16.0	4.2	11.8
	20.8	5.7	15.1	5.0	14.6	16.3	4.2	12.1
	20.9	5.7	15.1	5.0	14.9	16.5	4.0	12.4
	20.9	5.7	15.2	4.9	14.9	16.6	3.9	12.7
	20.7	5.6	15.1	4.8	14.9	16.9	4.0	12.9
	20.7	5.6	15.1	4.8	15.3	17.3	4.1	13.2
	20.8	5.6	15.2	4.9	15.6	17.4	4.0	13.4
	20.9	5.6	15.3	5.0	15.9	17.3	3.9	13.4
	21.2	5.6	15.6	5.1	16.3	17.7	3.9	13.9
	21.6	5.6	15.9	5.3	16.6	18.1	3.8	14.3
	21.6	5.6	16.1	5.3	16.7	18.1	3.6	14.5
	21.6	5.6	16.1	5.3	16.7	17.9	3.5	14.4
	21.7	5.7	16.0	5.3	17.2	18.1	3.5	14.6
	22.2	5.7	16.4	5.4	18.1	19.1	3.6	15.5
	22.4	5.7	16.6	5.4	18.3	18.7	3.4	15.3
	22.5	5.7	16.7	5.4	18.6	18.3	3.3	15.0
	22.5	5.7	16.8	5.4	18.7	18.1	3.2	14.9
	22.5	5.8	16.7	5.5	19.1	17.8	3.1	14.7
	22.5	5.8	16.7	5.7	19.8	17.9	3.2	14.8
	22.7	5.8	16.8	5.8	20.3	17.5	3.0	14.5

				Unemployment rate					
				White			Black and Other		
Year	Total	Male	Female	Total	Male	Female	Total	Male	Female
1961	6.7	6.4	7.2	6.0	5.7	6.5	12.2	12.8	11.8
1962	5.5	5.2	6.2	4.9	4.6	5.5	10.9	10.9	11.0
1963	5.7	5.2	6.5	5.0	4.7	5.8	10.8	10.5	11.2
1964	5.2	4.6	6.2	4.6	4.1	5.5	9.6	8.9	10.6
1965	4.5	4.0	5.5	4.1	3.6	5.0	8.1	7.4	9.2
1966	3.8	3.2	4.8	3.3	2.8	4.3	7.3	6.3	8.6
1967	3.8	3.1	5.2	3.4	2.7	4.6	7.4	6.0	9.1
1968	3.5	2.8	4.7	3.1	2.5	4.2	6.4	5.3	7.8
1969	3.5	2.8	4.7	3.1	2.5	4.2	6.4	5.3	7.8
1970	4.9	4.4	5.9	4.5	4.0	5.4	8.2	7.3	9.3
1971	5.9	5.3	6.9	5.4	4.9	6.3	9.9	9.1	10.9
1972	5.6	5.0	6.6	5.1	4.5	5.9	10.0	8.9	11.4
1973	4.9	4.2	6.0	4.3	3.8	5.3	9.0	7.7	10.6
1974	5.6	4.9	6.7	5.0	4.4	6.1	9.9	9.2	10.8
1975	8.5	7.9	9.3	7.8	7.2	8.6	13.8	13.6	13.9
1976	7.7	7.1	8.6	7.0	6.4	7.9	13.1	12.7	13.6
1977	7.1	6.3	8.2	6.2	5.5	7.3	13.1	12.3	13.9
1978	6.1	5.3	7.2	5.2	4.6	6.2	11.9	11.0	13.0
1979	5.8	5.1	6.8	5.1	4.5	5.9	11.3	10.4	12.3
1980	7.1	6.9	7.4	6.3	6.1	6.5	13.1	13.2	13.1
1981	7.6	7.4	7.9	6.7	6.5	6.9	14.2	14.1	14.3
1982	9.7	9.9	9.4	8.6	7.8	7.3	18.9	17.8	15.4
1983	9.6	9.9	9.2	8.4	7.9	6.9	19.5	18.1	16.5
1984	7.5	7.4	7.6	6.5	5.7	5.8	15.9	14.3	13.5
1985	7.2	7.0	7.4	6.2	5.4	5.7	15.1	13.2	13.1

Source: *Employment and Training Report of the President,* 1981. *Monthly Labor Review,* 1986

Table 3-3   **Unemployment Rates by Sex and Race 1961–1985**

tion, and industry of an individual, in part, determines the likelihood that he or she will move at a point in time.

A controversy still exists concerning whether the large amount of migration that occurs in the U.S. is economically beneficial. On one hand, geographic mobility serves to "move labor to where the jobs are." To the extent that it serves this purpose, overall economic efficiency is enhanced. If this is the case, then barriers to geographic mobility like occupational licensing would harm the functioning of the labor market and potentially raise costs to consumers.[14] However, to the extent that these moves involve large transactions costs, learning new jobs, and gaining new friends and support groups, there are losses to both individuals and society.

---

[14] Morris M. Kleiner, Robert Gay, and Karen Greene, "Barriers to Labor Migration: The Case of Occupational Licensing," *Industrial Relations,* Vol. 21, No. 3, 1982, pp. 383–391.

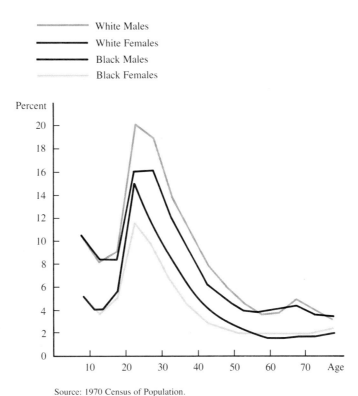

Source: 1970 Census of Population.

Figure 3-2   **Interstate Migration by Demographic Groups**

Supply of Labor

The supply of labor will be discussed from the perspective of the firm, industry, region, and economywide.[15] Following that discussion, we will develop the conceptual foundation for the development of labor/leisure decisions by the individual and firm as well as government responses. Illustrations and examples will be provided showing how labor supply issues at different levels influences human resource decision-making.

   The supply of labor to a firm can be illustrated by Figure 3–3. Along curve S higher wages result in a larger number of workers who are willing to supply labor to the enterprise. This curve is said to be "slightly inelastic." However, the dotted line, S', is "completely elastic" because the firm can have an infinite number of workers at the going wage rate. A movement

---

[15] For a detailed treatment of this segmentation of labor supply, see Gordon F. Bloom and Herbert R. Northrup, *Economics of Labor Relations,* Richard D. Irwin, Inc., Homewood, IL, 1981, pp. 300–306.

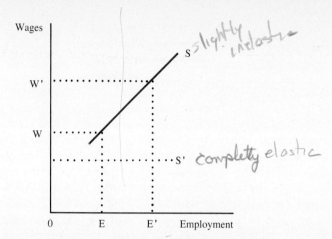

Figure 3-3 **Simple Labor Supply Curve to a Firm**

along curve S states that an increase in wages from W to W′ will bring forth a response in the number of workers willing to work for the firm from E to E′. However, a shift of the curve, that is, a move from S to S′ suggests that there has been either a change in the number of workers available in the market, a change in the number of hours of work, or a change has occurred in efficiency due to the use of either labor or capital in a more productive manner.

In developing the supply curve for a firm, the model that would most likely apply is S′ in Figure 3-3—the supply curve for a firm is generally assumed to be perfectly elastic. However, if the firm employs a significant number of workers in a particular region, like the Caterpillar Tractor Company in Peoria, Illinois, then the supply of workers to the firm in the market may have a positive slope. However, the ability to attract workers to a site may make the difference between an establishment making a profit or a major loss. This is shown in Example 3-3 which presents the Jones and Laughlin Steel Corporation's experience in not accurately estimating how workers would respond to employment opportunities. The result of their not being able to estimate this response was a large loss to the company and state, which had built an infrastructure in the form of roads, with no payback.

In a similar manner, the supply of labor to an industry is highly dependent on the responsiveness of workers to changes in wages and employment opportunities. In large part, this responsiveness is determined by such structural factors as the skill and training needed to move from one industry where there is an ample supply of labor to one where there is a shortage of labor. The efficiency with which such moves are made is often determined by institutional factors like the extent of unionism in the industry, or the conditions under which the people who work in the industry must obtain licenses. If an industry has zero elasticity (or

 **EXAMPLE 3.3   LABOR MARKET MISTAKES**

During the late 1960s the Jones and Laughlin Steel Corporation decided to locate a major steel plant in North Central Illinois. The expectation was that this plant costing over $200 million would turn this part of the state into the "Little Ruhr" valley of the United States. The decision was based largely on excellent transportation provided by a new four lane highway spur built for the Company by the State of Illinois and fine river transportation to major markets. The specific site chosen was Henepin, Illinois, a small farming community with less than 1000 persons and no major source of labor within forty miles. In order for Jones and Laughlin to attract a sufficient number of steel workers from northern and central Illinois cities like Chicago and Peoria, they found that they would have to pay a wage premium over 20 percent above amounts paid in Gary, Indiana and Pittsburgh, Pennsylvania steel plants. Having found this information after the plant was built, it became inefficient from a cost/benefit perspective, and the mill which was already built, never opened as a foundry.

Source: *Peoria Journal Star,* 1979.

responsiveness) additional workers would not be attracted to the industry no matter how high a wage was offered.

Similarly, the supply of labor to a particular location is also affected by the occupational and industrial mix of the area. Migration to an area can be determined by the growth of an area. Conversely, the growth or movement to an area of an enterprise can be affected by the composition of the labor force, which was determined by previous migration.[16] Within a region or large metropolitan area, factors like intraregional mobility patterns, information channels, and the spatial characteristics of a region are of prime importance in understanding the supply characteristics of the labor market.[17]

Finally, issues affecting the national economy include the role that changes in labor supply conditions have on hours of work. Once a decision has been made to perform some market work as was shown in Table 3–1, the next decision involves choosing the desired number of hours of work. As Table 3–4 shows, there has been a dramatic drop in the number of hours worked by individuals in the economy from the turn of this century, although hours worked has remained fairly constant since World War II. In part, this decline has occurred because people have decided to take part of their increased wages during the period in the form of leisure time as

[16] Greenwood, ibid.

[17] Albert Rees and George P. Shultz, *Workers and Wages in an Urban Labor Market,* University of Chicago Press, Chicago, 1970.

1900	62.1	1965	42.0
1905	61.1	1970	40.3
1910	53.5	1975	39.9
1915	58.2	1980	40.1
1920	53.5	1981	40.2
1925	52.2	1982	38.9
1947	40.5	1983	40.1
1950	41.1	1984	40.7
1955	41.3	1985	40.5
1960	40.1		

Source: Belton M. Fleisher and Thomas J. Kneisner, *Labor Economics: Theory, Evidence, and Policy,* Prentice-Hall, Inc., Englewood Cliffs, N.J., 1981 and *Employment and Training Report of the President,* 1981, and the *Monthly Labor Review,* 1986.

Table 3-4   **Average Weekly Hours in Manufacturing 1900–1985 selected years**

opposed to additional income.[18] Therefore, the increases in national labor supply have come from the increase in participation rates of women, but this effect has been modified by the reduction in hours of work, and reduced participation of older men. The net effect has been an aggregate labor supply function that is nearly vertical. Factors that might cause labor supply to shift to the left include any catastrophe such as a war or disease, which reallocates human resources away from private market uses.

Theory of Labor Supply

The discussion in the previous section related how the supply of labor responds at different levels of analysis ranging from the firm to the national economy. However, this section will discuss labor supply as an individual decision. As with most economic analysis, the basic assumption is that individuals are rational. From this perspective, we assume that the individual has a choice in allocating time between working hours and leisure hours. Further, as a result of working an individual receives income. In this analysis any factor that affects the demand for leisure time will result in a reduction or increase in the amount of time allocated toward work. For example, if incomes rises, individuals will allocate more time toward leisure as was shown in Table 3–4 from 1900–1985. This is called the income effect.

However, as wages go up the price of leisure also goes up. For example, as women became more educated their market value increased, and they reduced the amount of time spent on household activities and turned their

---

[18] Thomas Kniesner, "The Full-Time Workweek in the United States, 1900–1970, *Industrial and Labor Relations Review,* 3:1, October 1976, pp. 3–15.

attention to market related ones. Much of their increase in participation can be attributed to this phenomena.[19] When persons forego leisure, and work longer hours as their income goes up, it is called the substitution effect.

In linking these two phenomenon, you should note the following. First, as wages increase, the individual is better off than before because more goods and leisure can be "purchased." Second, if the substitution effect dominates, the individual will work more hours. However, if the income effect dominates, the person will work fewer hours. Based on labor market theory, we cannot say which effect will have greater weight. A more detailed and explicit theoretical presentation of these issues is presented in the Appendix to this chapter.

Some of the implications of the income and substitution effects are presented in Figure 3–4. From a to b in the figure, as wages rise individuals are willing to increase their hours of work—along this part of the curve the substitution effect dominates. However, from points b to c, as wages rise individuals value their leisure time more and are now more likely to reduce their hours of work in the marketplace. Along points b to c, the income effect dominates the substitution effect. It is the lower positive slope and upper negative slope that suggests that this curve should be called the backward bending supply curve of labor.

_____

[19] Rebecca M. Blank, "Simultaneously Modeling the Supply of Weeks and Hours of Work Among Female Household Heads," NBER Working Paper, Princeton University, July 1985.

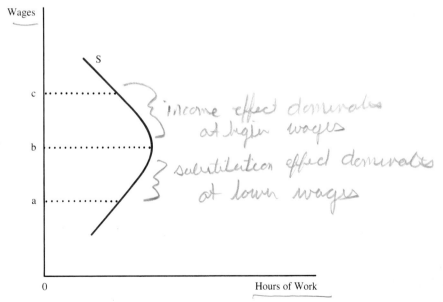

Figure 3–4 **Backward Bending Supply Curve of Labor**

To summarize, the effects of a wage change on the hours of work, one should examine the decision analysis presented in Table 3–5. This Table shows the results of wage changes on hours of work under varying scenarios of the income or substitution effect.[20] Try to relate each of these options to the backward bending supply curve of labor presented in Figure 3–4. For example, along the top portion of the decision tree, when the substitution effect is dominant, an increase in wages increases hours of work, and the supply curve is positive. Now go through the three other scenarios and show the effects of wages on hours of work through a supply curve analysis.

The theory presented in this analysis of the income and substitution effects apply generally to individuals. However, the market supply curve for labor can be derived by the summation of the individual curves and is generally represented as having a positive slope. A key concept for both employers and employees in dealing with the supply curve is the reservation wage. This refers to the lowest wage that a person would choose to work for

---

[20] See Saul D. Hoffman, *Labor Market Economics,* Prentice-Hall Inc., Englewood Cliffs, New Jersey, 1986.

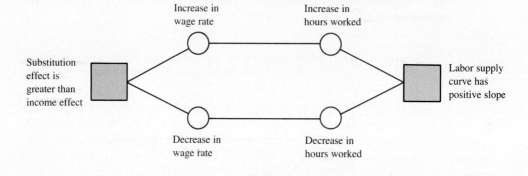

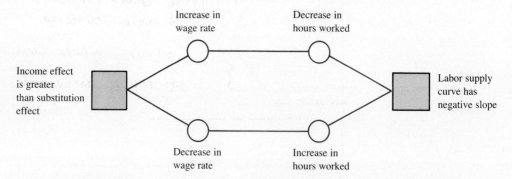

Source: Saul D. Hoffman, *Labor Market Economics,* ©1986, p. 95. Adapted by permission of Prentice-Hall, Inc., Englewood Cliffs, New Jersey.

Table 3–5   **Effects of a Wage Change on Hours Worked: A Decision Approach**

a particular employer. The concept embodies the notion of an opportunity cost or the lowest alternative wage that an employee is willing to work for in that organization.

In using the reservation wage concept, Professor Edward Lazear has developed a model to analyze how employers respond to different wages offered to their nonunion executive personnel.[21] He suggests that only certain types of workers, namely those who are currently underpaid, are raided by outsiders and offered higher wages. Therefore, raids and voluntary turnover are selective of the most productive workers. However, persons who stay with a firm and have their wages increased as a result of being raided by other companies, have the highest productivity related to the specific firm. Lazear suggests that the raiding of top executives helps these people and the organization determine their appropriate reservation wage.

An example of the kind of offers and counteroffers that sometimes determine an appropriate wage for executives is shown in Example 3–4. As this Example shows, for individuals who are viewed as being in short supply, with skills that are viewed as scarce, firms are in some cases willing to enter a bidding war to keep key people. These decisions to engage in counteroffers are based on the costs associated with finding and training a new person.

Statistical Results on Labor Supply

Perhaps the area of labor market analysis where there has been the most empirical research is in analyzing labor supply. As a result of significant expenditures of funds for data to follow the work behavior of individuals over time, economists have been able to examine the impact of changes in wages and nonlabor income on individual's and family's labor market reaction. We cannot cover even a small fraction of these studies in this textbook. However, we will present results of a recent survey which links the income and substitution effects and two studies on how individuals in high and low income groups respond to changes in wages and job opportunities.

In 1985 the Current Population Survey asked persons in the sample the following set of questions. If given a choice of working the same, fewer, or more hours at the same rate of pay would you prefer the same number of hours and earn the same money, fewer hours at the same rate of pay and earn less money, or more hours at the same rate of pay and earn more money? The results by sex and income group are presented in Table 3–6. They show that as earnings rise to higher levels for prime working-age

[21] Edward P. Lazear, "Raids and Offer-Matching," NBER Working Paper Series, No. 1419, August 1984.

 **.4   OFFERS AND COUNTER-OFFERS: THE NEW GAME FOR EXECUTIVES**

Recently, a director of management training at an electronics company in Connecticut accepted a job in Florida that appeared to change his career. His wife supported him in his decision. In addition, he has relatives in the area.

But then his current employers responded, suggesting that the new company was a likely takeover target, and that he would be stuck in a rural city in Florida. Company strategic planners were brought in to give backup to that prediction. The manager was also given an increase in wages and benefits, and additional perks.

The strategy worked. Worried about his career move, the manager reneged on the deal, even though a starting date had been set by his "new employer."

Such reversals, while still rare, reflect changing attitudes by firms in the executive-search game. Companies appear more willing to make counter-offers of substantial amounts to keep their best managers, while waning corporate loyalty due in part to more cost-benefit analysis on executive hiring and turnover leaves those managers receptive to the highest bidder. As a result, turnabouts may be on the rise.

"People who are being wooed are more savvy," say Donald Allerton, president of Allerton, Heinze & Associates, a Chicago search firm. "And companies don't let pride get in the way" when trying to win back good people. Ronald Woods, a vice president at Manufacturers Hanover Trust Co., agrees that "for good players there's more of a tendency to make counter-offers." The cost of finding and training a new person, he says, can far outweigh the increased salary and promotions required to keep a manager.

Source: *Wall Street Journal,* by Larry Reibstein, May 5, 1986, p. 21.

---

adults, smaller proportions want to increase their work weeks and larger fractions prefer to decrease their hours of work.[22] These findings suggest the dominance of the income effect as occurs on the negatively sloped part of the backward-bending supply curve. It also indicates that workers with lower weekly earnings have shorter work weeks and are more likely to want to increase their hours worked. However, even for the highest male income earners, the proportion wanting more hours of work exceeded those wanting fewer hours suggesting the dominance of the substitution effect.

One of the studies that illustrates the use of statistical analysis in analyzing labor markets is Richard Freeman's analysis of the market for college-trained manpower.[23] In his studies, Freeman finds that students

---

[22] Susan E. Shank, "Preferred Hours of Work and Corresponding Earnings," *Monthly Labor Review,* November, 1986, pp. 40–44.

[23] Richard B. Freeman, *The Market for College-Trained Manpower,* Cambridge, Mass., Harvard University Press, 1971.

(Percent distribution)

Weekly earnings	Same hours, same money	Fewer hours, less money	More hours, more money
Men, total........	65.5	6.5	28.0
Less than $150 ..	39.3	3.9	56.7
$150 to $199....	43.9	3.4	52.7
200 to 249....	55.6	4.2	40.2
250 to 299....	60.8	2.9	36.3
300 to 399....	62.6	7.0	30.5
400 to 499....	66.6	6.5	26.9
500 to 599....	71.9	7.9	20.3
600 to 749....	73.0	7.8	19.1
750 and over ...	76.6	8.9	14.5
Women, total	67.2	10.9	21.9
Less than $150 ..	55.6	5.0	39.4
$150 to $199....	66.6	7.4	25.9
200 to 249....	66.6	12.2	21.2
250 to 299....	66.2	14.1	19.7
300 to 399....	72.6	11.9	15.5
400 to 499....	75.7	12.4	11.9
500 to 599....	72.0	15.2	12.8
600 to 749....	73.2	13.9	12.9
750 and over ...	63.6	22.0	14.6

Source: Susan E. Shank, "Preferred Hours of Work and Corresponding Earnings," *Monthly Labor Review,* November, 1986, Vol. 109, No. 11, p. 43.

Table 3-6 **Workweek and Pay Preference of 25- to 54-year-old Wage and Salary Workers, by Sex and Earnings, May 1985, CPS**

have generally good information on the labor market opportunities that exist in other fields, as well as the entry costs of getting into that specialty. Further, he suggests that,

> the supply to high-level occupations is governed by economic incentives. All else being the same, increased wages attract students to a field and add to the supply of specialists several years later. Lags in supply are due primarily to the length of educational programs. Both econometric and survey data indicate rapid response to changes in market conditions.[24]

As a result of the long lead time to produce college graduates (i.e., four years, or three or more years for the specialty training in law), the market follows what he calls a cobweb feedback system. Under this system, the supply of graduates is determined by market forces several years earlier. The results, according to Freeman, are wild fluctuations up and down with shortages turning to surpluses every four or five years.

[24] Freeman, ibid.

One specific test of this model was applied to lawyers.[25] In its simplest form it was estimated as follows:

$$LENT = f(LSAL, ASAL) \tag{1}$$

where in equation 1, LENT was the number of first-year law school enrollees, LSAL was the annual salaries of young attorneys, and ASAL was the average salaries of full-time workers. The salaries of full-time workers represents the opportunity cost of entering the legal profession. The regression estimates (see Chapter 2 Appendix for a methodological explanation) shows that a 1 percent increase in young lawyers' salaries leads to a 2.25 percent increase in law school entrants, holding other salaries constant. Freeman's results show peaks in enrollment followed by troughs every three or four years. This study showed the responsiveness of one group of individuals to labor market changes.

Perhaps the largest funded experiment dealing with issues of labor supply occurred in the late 1960s through the 1970s dealing with the responsiveness of individuals to welfare payments. A large part of the data and analysis was summarized in the Seattle and Denver Income Maintenance Experiments (SIME-DIME). The goal of the negative income tax (NIT), which was analyzed in these experiments, was to reduce poverty while maintaining work incentives. The negative income tax provided welfare payments at a reduced level (50 percent) as income from work went up. This was unlike the existing welfare programs, which resulted in a 100 percent reduction in benefits as income from work increased.[26] The goal of these government funded experiments was to determine the labor supply of selected families who would be eligible to receive NIT support compared to the labor supply of similar families who were members of a statistical control group and received no such aid but technically were eligible. These other families either received no aid or obtained traditional welfare payments.

The results from these experiments showed that these relatively generous income-maintenance programs reduced hours worked of those eligible for the program by less than 10 percent for husbands and about 20 percent for wives.[27] Further, the cost of this kind of program would increase by over 30 percent as a result of these declines in labor supply. The results of this study has been used by members of Congress to stop proposals toward implementing a Negative Income Tax in this country.

---

[25] Richard B. Freeman, "Legal Cobwebs: A Recursive Model of the Market for New Lawyers," *Review of Economics and Statistics,* 57 (May 1975), pp. 171–80.

[26] Michael C. Keeley, *Labor Supply and Public Policy,* New York: Academic Press, 1981.

[27] Robert Moffitt and Kenneth Kehrer, "The Effect of Tax and Transfer Programs on Labor Supply: The Evidence from the Income Maintenance Experiments," in Ronald G. Ehrenberg, ed. *Research in Labor Economics* (Greenwich, Conn., JAI Press, 1981).

Unlike our initial discussion of labor supply, where we could not determine whether individuals would work more or less hours with additional income, the statistical tests on individuals allows us to estimate this impact. Using appropriate research designs gives us the opportunity to answer some of these questions. In two examples of empirical work on labor supply, some of the statistical methodology to analyze the process are presented. In the first example, we saw that individuals are responsive to changes in wages in markets for highly educated individuals. That is, in the long run people chose careers, in part, due to economic opportunities. In the second case, the results showed that for low income individuals the income effect dominates the substitution effect for welfare recipients and that a negative income tax would not be cost effective. These studies show that the impact of income or wage increases/decreases on the willingness of persons to work and the number of hours they are willing to allocate to work versus leisure time activities, can be determined only through data gathering and analysis.

Summary

This chapter has presented basic concepts and definitions underlying the labor force and supply of labor. In developing human resource policies in the organization, a fundamental issue is the availability of a sufficiently large and well-trained workforce. To understand labor supply, key terms in the labor force were developed to include the unemployment rate, labor force participation, and the real wage. During the past twenty-five years numerous changes have occurred in the labor force to include the increased labor force participation of women and the movement from a manufacturing to a service-based economy. Factors that influence the supply of labor for a firm, industry, occupation, and region can have important effects on the organization's effectiveness. Finally, an economic approach to understanding labor/leisure decision-making is discussed as well as some empirical evidence that supports this framework. In the next two chapters you will have an opportunity to examine how firms view the demand for labor and then study how supply and demand interact to determine wage and employment levels.

PROBLEMS

1. Which of the concepts of measuring the labor market would be most useful in determining the availability of less skilled workers in a metropolitan area for your organization?
2. Assume that you have been given the job of determining what your production employees' work/leisure response will be to a 5 percent pay raise. First, how can the workers change hours of work within a traditional

forty-hour work week? Second, what would labor market theory say about the workers' response? Third, what would empirical analysis suggest regarding the workers' labor supply response to this pay raise?

3. If we assume that most geographic moves also involve job changes, using Figure 3.2 estimate the relative costs and benefits of hiring the following two individuals for the Delanny Water Works Inc.

Present value cost of recruitment, selection and training	$10,000
Mr. X—age 20—expected probability of leaving	.20
Present value economic return to company if he stays to retirement	$1,100,000
Ms. Y—age 45—expected probability of leaving	.06
Present value economic return to company if she stays to retirement	$1,000,000

Whom should the company hire in order to maximize profits? Explain.

4. Becker Managerial Services is choosing a metropolitan area for a major chemical company based on the current and near term wage and availability of engineers. Based on other criteria, the following cities were chosen as finalists. You are to make the final selection based on the following human resource criteria. First, no more than 3 percent of the engineering base can be hired without driving wages up by 10 percent in that area in the short run. Your client needs at least 200 engineers. State your site selection, justify your choice, and state potential problems.

	Number of Engineers	*Annual Salary*
Los Angeles, CA	32,000	$30,200
New York, NY	20,000	$31,500
Richmond, VA	2,000	$28,000
St. Louis, MO	7,500	$29,500

REFERENCES

Becker, Gary, "A Theory of the Allocation of Time," *Economic Journal 75* (September 1965), pp. 394–517.

Cebula, Richard J., *The Determinants of Human Migration,* Lexington Books, Lexington, MA, 1979.

Fields, Gary S. and Mitchell, Olivia S., *Retirement, Pensions and Social Security,* Cambridge, Mass.: M.I.T. Press, 1984.

Killingsworth, Mark R., *Labor Supply,* Cambridge, Mass.: Cambridge University Press, 1983.

Werneke, Diane, ed., *Counting the Labor Force,* National Commission on Employment and Unemployment Statistics, Washington, D.C., 1979.

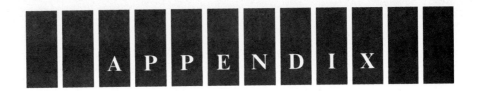

APPENDIX

INDIVIDUAL LABOR SUPPLY DECISIONS: A DEEPER EXAMINATION

In this section we will develop more formally through graphs and algebra how a rational individual might make decisions on work and leisure. By going through this analysis you will be better prepared to make more informed decisions on the economic factors influencing decisions on work, leisure, and nonmarket work.

Assume that an individual's goal is to achieve the most from the amount of resources that are available. The individual's resources are defined by the amount of time available, the value of time, and the individual's ability to purchase market goods when no work is performed (e.g., income from government like social security). The individual's resources can be combined to provide satisfaction through a utility function. This function shows how economic well-being or utility is related to various combinations of market goods and time used in nonmarket activities. The utility function can be written as

$$U = f(M,l)$$

where
U = the level of utility or well-being
M = market goods
l = leisure or nonmarket work

(3–A1)

In equation 3–A1 utility is a mathematical relationship that translates flows of commodities, goods and leisure into utility per unit of time. Figure 3–A1 shows a typical utility function relating economic well-being to the levels of market goods and leisure used by a representative individual. The vertical

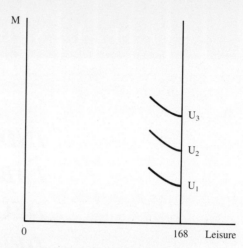

Figure 3-A1   **A Utility Function**

axis measures the consumption of market goods and services per time period. The horizontal axis measures the amount of time an individual can spend in leisure time activities in any week. Each curve in figure 3–A1, U_1, U_2, and U_3, represents a constant level of satisfaction or utility. The further from the origin that a curve is, the higher the level or utility or satisfaction. Along each of these indifference curves, the combinations of hours and goods yield the same level of satisfaction.

The changing slope of the indifference curve reflects what is called the diminishing marginal rate of substitution (MRS). This is defined as the maximum amount of one good that a person is willing to give up to obtain an additional amount of a second good, in a way that the person's utility level remains unchanged. This can be represented as $MRS_{1M} = \frac{\Delta M}{\Delta l}$, which is equal to the slope of the indifference curve. This relationship means that the diminishing marginal rate of substitution is that amount of goods a person is willing to give up to obtain an additional hour of leisure. This amount will be greater when the amount of leisure consumed is small and much less when the amount of leisure is larger. Finally, the shape of the indifference curve may vary from person to person depending on a person's preference for goods compared to leisure.

Persons cannot consume unlimited quantities of goods and hours because only limited amounts of hours and income are available to them. A typical budget constraint is shown in Figure 3–A2 that defines a person's individual consumption opportunities. As in the first figure, consumption is measured along the vertical axis and hours of nonmarket time along the horizontal axis. The absolute value of the slope of the budget constraint in Figure 3–A2 represents the market wage rate.

If it is assumed that a person's preferences are stable, we can analyze how the utility-maximizing labor supply choices change in response to changes in nonlabor income or in the wage rate. The impact of a change in

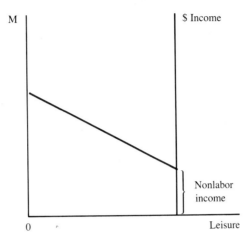

***Figure 3-A2*   Budget Constraint**

non-labor income is shown in Figure 3-A3. The initial budget line m m′ and utility curve (U_1), and utility maximization is at *a*. If there is an increase in nonlabor income (e.g., gift from an estate), the budget line shifts out to m n n′, and if leisure is equivalent to goods (i.e., a normal good), the person will take more leisure and less work. The new utility maximizing curve will lie to the right of *a*, that is point b on figure 3-A3.

The impact of both the income and substitution effects can be shown in Figure 3-A4. In this case the wage rate changes, the budget line pivots around the point on the leisure axis. In this figure there is an increase in the wage rate from budget line m m′ to m n′. The starting point is *A* on indifference curve U_1. This change in the wage rate affects labor in two

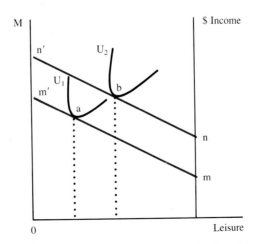

***Figure 3-A3*   Income Impact on the Supply of Labor**

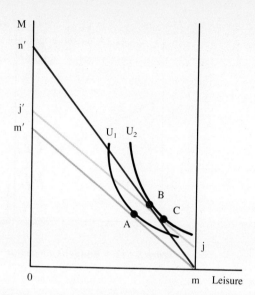

Figure 3–A4   **Income and Substitution Effects of a Wage Increase**

ways: It changes the relative price of goods and leisure and changes the individual's real income.

The shift that occurred as a result of the budget line shift can be broken down into an income increase represented by the line jj′ which is parallel to the original budget line m m′, and tangent to the new indifference curve U_2 at point C. The difference in hours worked between A and C represents the income effect of the wage increase. The shift from the budget line jj′ to mn′ represents a change in the wage rate holding utility constant, because each of these budget lines the tangency point is on the same indifference curve U_2. Consequently, the difference in hours worked between B and C represents the substitution effect of the original wage increase. Therefore, the substitution effect leads to a larger number of hours of work, as long as the indifference curve is concave upward. To assure your understanding of this graphical analysis, go through it showing a decrease in the wage rate. An application of this graphical and algebraic presentation of the income and substitution effects could proceed as follows: Assume your boss is considering increasing wages for employees. Based on this analysis should he/she expect the workers to increase or decrease their hours of work supplied at the workplace? Explain. What kind of additional information or analysis would you want to have to enhance your confidence in the advice you have given?

C H A P T E R 4

THE FIRM, PRODUCTION, AND COST

F | irms employ labor because that labor is an input (or a set of inputs, if more than one type of labor is employed) in the making of the firm's product or service. Firms "mix" labor and other inputs to produce the goods and services that consumers demand. While that fact is quite obvious, it is filled with meaning. It implies that the demand for labor is a *derived demand.* As stated in Chapter 1, the firm's demand for labor is derived from consumers' demand for the firm's product. The statement also implies that the firm's demand for labor depends on the production technology, or the production function, that is employed to make the firm's product or service. The production function employed dictates the firm's ability to substitute capital (the physical, non-human means of production) for labor and to substitute one type of labor for another. The production function also determines the productivity (the output per unit of input) of the labor and capital that the firm employs.

Consider a familiar production process, the typing of manuscripts. Typists are employed because readers demand typed copy. The output per typist per hour depends on the amount and type of physical capital per typist. Consider the output difference between a typist using an old-fashioned upright manual typewriter and the same typist using a modern word-processor. Further, there is room for substitution of capital for labor, even in such a simple process. Again, consider the possibilities inherent in the availability of word processing equipment.

To understand the demand for labor at the level of the firm, we must first understand the elements of production theory. This chapter is a brief non-mathematical introduction to the characteristics of production functions. The relationship of production functions to the firm's cost functions will be explored and some results important to understanding the demand for labor (covered in detail in Chapter 5) will be developed. After reading this chapter, you will understand basic production relations and will be prepared to study the demand for labor.

The Firm Reconsidered

A production function indicates the maximum quantity of output that, at a given level of technological sophistication, can be obtained from given input levels. In its most general form, a production function can be written as:

$$Q = f(K,L),$$

where Q is the quantity of output, K is capital input, L is labor input, and f( ) indicates a functional relationship.[1] In practice, there may be several types of capital and several types of labor involved in production. One could then represent the production function as:

$$Q = f(K_1, \ldots, K_n, L_1, \ldots, L_m),$$

where K_1 through K_n are n types of physical capital and L_1 through L_m are m types of labor.

Chapter 2 discussed the rationale for the formation of firms: minimizing the costs of monitoring the production process. Alchain and Demsetz explain that the monitoring problem is most difficult (and, therefore, firms are most likely to form) when production is done by teams.[2] That is, when the output of labor depends on the nature of the capital it uses, rather than labor and capital contributing independently, firms will be most likely to form and continuous employment relationships to develop. One can represent team production with production functions that are interactive (that is, in which a function of labor input is multiplied by a function of capital inputs).

There is no need for firms to form among carpenters and electricians in residential construction, for example, because each works independently and the effort of each can be observed easily. Sloppy work by carpenters will

---

[1] A function is a mathematical relationship associating each pair of values of the independent variables (K and L) with one and only one value of the dependent variable (Q).

[2] Armen A. Alchain and Harold Demsetz, "Production, Information Costs, and Economic Efficiency," *American Economic Review* vol. 62, no. 5 (December 1972): 777–795.

not reflect badly on electricians. When team production occurs, however, the cost of shirking by one type of labor is borne, not only by that type of labor, but by the providers of capital and of other types of labor as well.

Interactive production functions suggest that possibilities for substitution exist. That is, the same amount of output can be obtained from several different combinations of capital and labor. When such substitution is possible, the firm must select not only the appropriate level of output, but also the appropriate mix of capital and labor inputs.

Chapter 2 argued that the appropriate mix of capital and labor is the one that maximizes the market value of the firm. The value of the firm, if capital markets function properly, will be the present value of all of the firm's expected future cash flows. If each future period is identical to the present, the present value of future cash flows (and the market value of the firm) is maximized by maximizing profit in each period.

Thus, a good approximation of the firm's best allocation of resources across capital and labor is that which maximizes current profit. The remainder of this chapter will examine such allocations over various planning horizons.

Planning Horizons

As a business firm looks to its future, it faces several planning horizons. These differ, not on the basis of calendar time, but on the basis of what variables the firm can change over the horizon.

In the *very short-run* (sometimes called the "market period"), the firm cannot alter either its labor input or its capital input. Thus, the very short-run is a period sufficiently short that only the firm's inventories are variable. The firm's inability to alter the employment of factors of production makes the very short-run of little interest in decision making.

In the *short-run,* some factors of production are variable, while others cannot be altered. Usually, one thinks of labor as being variable in the short-run as hours of work can be varied and workers laid-off or recalled to work quickly. Capital inputs, being difficult to scrap or sell, are usually considered fixed in the short run.

In the *long-run,* all factors of production are variable. The long-run is a sufficiently long time for equipment to be bought or sold, leases signed or canceled, and facilities constructed or abandoned. Even in the long-run, however, the production function itself, the level of technology, is taken as fixed.

The *very long-run* is a planning period sufficiently long to allow a change in the production function itself. Over such a long period, new product lines can be introduced and old ones abandoned. New production functions can be introduced making labor and capital more productive. Indeed, in the very long-run, the nature of the capital stock can change (as, for example, by the introduction of robotic technology in the automobile industry) and the quality of the labor force can improve (as it becomes better educated). The study of the very long-run is the subject of economic growth theory and is beyond the scope of this text.

Production Functions

As discussed above a production function represents the maximum output that can be obtained from a given level of inputs, and is usually written as:

$$Q = f(K,L).$$

Production functions exhibit several important properties that condition the firm's behavior in the labor market.

The rate at which output changes as labor input changes (but capital input is held fixed) is the marginal product (or productivity) of labor (MPL). MPL is the unit change in output that results from the *last* unit (hour) of labor employed, holding the capital input fixed.[3] Most production functions display diminishing MPL as labor input is increased and capital input is held constant.

Consider the task of reshelving books in a library. Assume the library has only one book cart and, initially, only one book shelver. A second reshelver will speed the process, increasing the number of books reshelved. The second shelver allows one worker to push the cart while one places books on the shelf. But two shelvers don't shelve twice as many books as one. Adding a third shelver may not speed the process at all and a fourth may actually impede the process by getting in the others' way. Thus, each additional shelver adds progressively fewer additional books shelved. While the library staff example may be trivial, it demonstrates an *almost* universal feature of production: diminishing marginal productivity of a variable factor of production.

Another important characteristic of production functions is return to scale.[4] If *both* capital and labor input are, for example, doubled, does output more than, less than, or exactly double? If output rises by more than the proportion by which inputs increase, the production function exhibits increasing returns to scale (a happy, but rare occurrence). If output rises by the same proportion as inputs, the production function exhibits constant returns to scale. If output rises by a smaller proportion than inputs, the production function exhibits diminishing return to scale. Unlike the "law" of diminishing returns to a variable factor of production, there is no law of returns to scale, rather returns to scale take many different forms. Two

---

[3] Readers familiar with differential calculus will recognize the marginal product of labor as the first partial derivative of quantity of output with respect to labor input (MPL = $\frac{\delta Q}{\delta L}$).

[4] See James L. Pappas, Eugene F. Brigham, and Mark Hirschey, *Managerial Economics,* 4th edition, Chicago: Dryden Press, 1983, pp. 229–234.

useful classes of production functions (the so-called Cobb-Douglas and Constant Elasticity of Substitution types) show constant returns to scale. That is, when the amounts of all inputs used are doubled, output will exactly double. Many production functions, on the other hand, show the traditional, textbook form of first increasing, then decreasing returns to scale.

Finally, every production function has a degree of substitutability of capital for labor. That degree of substitutability is represented by the elasticity of substitution (σ). The formula for elasticity of substitution is:

$$\sigma = \frac{d \ln (K/L)}{d \ln(MPL/MPK)},$$

where "d" is the first derivative operator (from differential calculus), "ln" is the natural logarithm operator, K is capital input, L is labor input, MPL is the marginal product of labor, and MPK is the marginal product of capital.[5]

The elasticity of substitution, then, is the rate of change of the natural log of K/L as the natural log of MPL/MPK changes. It measures the firm's response to changing productivity ratios. If capital cannot be substituted for labor, the elasticity of substitution is zero. As the degree of substitutability rises, σ moves away from zero. The elasticity of substitution is not (except for Constant Elasticity of Substitution and Cobb-Douglas production functions) a constant, but can change as capital and labor inputs change.

Given a production function and given prices for the factors of production (p_L and p_k), what is the firm's optimal utilization of capital and labor? A firm will use its resources most efficiently when the last dollar spent on capital generates the same additional output as the last dollar spent on labor. Algebraically, that efficiency condition is shown by the equimarginal condition:

$$\frac{MPL}{P_L} = \frac{MPK}{p_k},$$

or, equivalently,

$$\frac{p_L}{p_k} = \frac{MPL}{MPK}.^{6}$$

The equimarginal condition implies that, if the last dollar spent on capital yielded more extra output than the last dollar spent on labor, the firm would benefit from a substitution of capital for labor. That substitution would end when the last dollar spent on capital generated just as much additional output as the last dollar spent on labor. Similarly, if the last

---

[5] James M. Henderson and Richard E. Quant, *Microeconomic Theory: A Mathematical Approach,* second edition, New York: McGraw-Hill, 1971, p. 62.

[6] The equimarginal condition is the result of maximizing the profit function (Profit = Total Revenue − Total Cost).

dollar spent on labor added more additional output than the last dollar spent on capital, the firm should reallocate its spending away from capital and toward labor.

Because the equimarginal condition is the rule for the efficient allocations of labor and capital to production, it represents the basis for determination of the demand for labor in the long run (when labor and capital are both variable). It is, then, easy to see that the long-run demand for labor must depend on input prices and relative marginal productivities.

Total, Average, and Marginal Relations

The decision models developed in Chapter 2 dealt with incremental cash flows. These are the additional cash flows generated by the decision at hand, all else held equal. Economists refer to those cash flows as those that are marginal to the decision. Explicit relationships exist among total, average, and marginal (or incremental) cash flows.

Marginal (incremental) cash flows represent the rate at which total cash flow is changing at any given level of input or output. As long as marginal cash flow from an increase in input is positive, then total cash flow is rising with increasing use of that input. Therefore, total cash flow is maximized with respect to some input when the marginal cash flow with respect to that input is zero. Marginal cash flow is negative if total cash flow is declining.

Average cash flow with respect to some input is total cash flow divided by the level of the input. As long as total cash flow is positive, average cash flow cannot be zero or less. Figure 4-1 shows the relationship that exists among total, marginal, and average cash flows. Total cash flow is maximized where marginal cash flow is zero. If marginal cash flow is above average cash flow, average cash flow must be rising. That is, if the cash flow from the last unit of input is above the average, then that marginal cash flow must be "pulling" the average up. If marginal cash flow is below average, then the average cash flow must be falling. While marginal cash flow can fall below zero, average cash flow can only approach zero as a limit (so long as total cash flow is positive).

Production Decisions in the Short-Run

In the short-run, some factors of production (usually capital) are fixed. Thus, the firm may not be able to achieve efficiency to the full extent implied by the equimarginal condition. In the short-run, one must represent production as a function of the variable factor only:

$$Q = f(L), \text{ K fixed.}$$

Figure 4–1 shows a typical short-run production function and some of its characteristics. Output rises as labor input rises, first at an increasing and then at a decreasing rate. At some level of labor input (L_c), the fixed

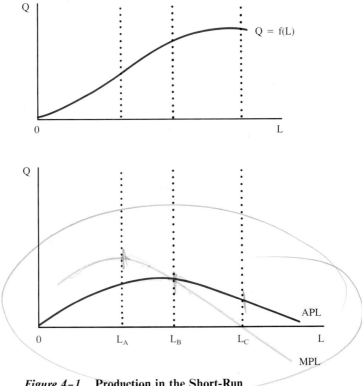

Figure 4–1 **Production in the Short-Run**

capital stock is used so intensively that output is maximized and, were more labor to be added, output would fall.

Graphically, the marginal product of labor is the slope of a straight line tangent to the short-run production function. That slope is zero (the tangent line is horizontal) at L_c, so, at L_c, MPL = O. To the right of L_c, MPL is negative and additional hours of labor actually reduce output. Clearly, no firm would ever want to employ labor to the right of L_c. To do so would be to pay workers to have them reduce total output.

Graphically, the average product of labor (Q/L) is the slope of a ray from the origin to the production function. To see why that is so, first consider the slope of a straight line, vertical distance divided by horizontal distance. For a ray from the origin to the production function, the vertical distance is Q (output) and the horizontal distance is L (labor input). Thus, the slope of such a ray is the average product of labor (Q/L).

Where average product of labor (APL) is maximized, it is equal to MPL, as at L_B. That is, the slope of a ray from the origin to the production is greatest when the ray is also tangent to the production function. Under certain conditions,[7] to the left of L_B, the firm is using so little labor that the

---

[7] These conditions are met when the production function exhibits constant returns to scale. See Pappas, Brigham, and Hirschey, *Managerial Economics*, 1983, pp. 209–211.

marginal product of capital is negative. The range of production from L_B to L_c, then, is the relevant range of production for the firm in the short run. Just where the firm would produce within that relevant range is the subject of Chapter 5.

To the left of L_A, the firm experiences "explosive" returns to labor input. MPL is rising, which means that each unit of labor adds progressively more to total output. If that range exists at all, the firm should immediately exploit such explosive returns, moving to the right of L_A. Hence, the region of production from 0 to L_A is analytically meaningless.

Production in the Long-Run

The long-run is characterized by the firm's ability to vary all factors of production. It is, therefore, in the long-run that the substitution of labor for capital (and vice-versa) is possible. Consider a simple production function:

$$Q = K^{1/2} L^{1/2}.$$

The same level of output is possible with a great number of input combinations, as shown in Table 4–1. The production decision problem in the long-run is to determine, simultaneously, the appropriate level of output and the least-cost combination of inputs to produce that output.

The graphical solution to the long-run production problem is shown in Figure 4–2. All of the input combinations that would produce an output of 100, given the production function $Q = K^{1/2} L^{1/2}$ have been connected. Such a locus of points is called an isoquant (same quantity) line. Each isoquant is a contour line for the long-run production function represented. That is, the isoquant map is a two-dimensional representation of the height of the production function above the plane determined by the K and L axes. Each isoquant connects all of the points of equal altitude on the production function, as represented by the cross-sectional line (Q = 100) in Figure 4–3.

As one moves "northeast" on the isoquant map, one is moving "up" the production surface to higher levels of output. As one moves down and

Q	$Q = K^{1/2} L^{1/2}$ K	L
100.00	100.00	100.00
100.00	81.00	123.46
100.00	64.00	156.25
100.00	49.00	204.08
100.00	123.46	81.00
100.00	156.25	64.00
100.00	204.08	49.00

Table 4–1   **Input Combinations for Constant Output**

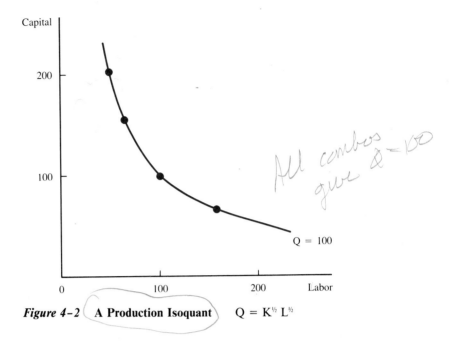

Figure 4-2   **A Production Isoquant** $Q = K^{1/2} L^{1/2}$

to the right along a single isoquant, one is substituting labor for capital, while holding output fixed (see Figure 4–4). The slope of any isoquant is

$$- \frac{MPL}{MPK}.^{8}$$

To determine the appropriate output and the appropriate input ratio, a budget constraint must be imposed on the isoquant map. Consider some (exogenously determined) input prices, p_L and p_K, and a total cost level, TC.

---

[8] The slope is negative because the isoquant slopes down to the right. For a derivation of the formula, see Pappas, Brigham, and Hirschey, *Managerial Economics,* 1983, pp. 217–221.

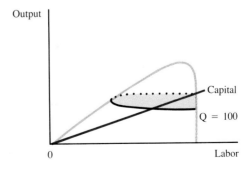

Figure 4-3   **A Production Isoquant as a Contour of a Production Function**

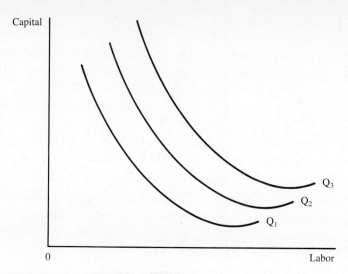

Figure 4-4   **A Family of Isoquants**

If only labor were employed, TC/p_L hours of labor could be purchased. If only capital were employed, TC/p_K units of capital could be obtained.[9] Any combination of labor and capital lying on the straight line connecting TC/p_L units of labor and TC/p_K units of capital can be obtained for the same level of total cost.[10] Such a budget constraint is called an isocost (same cost) line (see Figure 4–5). The slope of the isocost is

$$- \frac{p_L}{p_K}.$$

If prices remain fixed but TC increases, the isocost shifts outward in a parallel fashion. If TC and the price of capital are fixed, but the price of labor rises, the isocost line remains "anchored" at TC/p_K units of capital, but rotates clockwise until it finds its new intercept at TC/p_L', where p_L' is the new, higher, price of labor. If TC and the price of capital are fixed, and the price of labor falls, the isocost line remains anchored at TC/p_K units of capital. In this case, the isocost rotates counterclockwise until it finds its new intercept at TC/p_L'', where p_L'' is the new, lower, price of labor.

---

[9] It is useful to think of P_K as the per-period rental price associated with one unit of physical capital.

[10] If $TC = (K \times P_K) + (L \times P_L)$, then we can solve for K to put the budget constraint in familiar slope-intercept form. The result is:

$$K = \frac{TC}{P_K} - \frac{P_L}{P_K} L.$$

The vertical intercept of the budget line is at $\frac{TC}{P_K}$, and the slope of the budget line is $-\frac{P_L}{P_K}$. Any point on the line connecting those endpoints is also on the budget line.

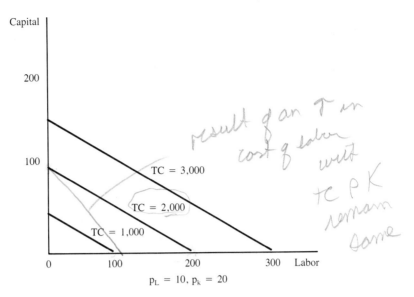

Figure 4-5 **A Family of Isocost Lines**

The firm's profit-maximizing output, given its budget constraint, is shown in Figure 4–6. The firm strives to attain the highest isoquant consistent with the isocost. That is the isoquant that is tangent to the isocost. The point of tangency represents the optimal combination of capital (K*) and labor (L*) to attain the optional output level (Q*).

At such a point of tangency, the slope of the isoquant is equal to the slope of the isocost. Thus, one has

$$-\frac{MPL}{MPK} = -\frac{p_L}{p_K},$$

or, equivalently,

$$\frac{MPL}{p_L} = \frac{MPK}{p_K},$$

which is the equimarginal condition or the long-run profit maximizing solution.

Figure 4–7 shows how capital would be substituted for labor, given an increase in the price of labor. Initially, the firm produces Q_1 using L_1 units of labor and K_1 units of capital at point A. When the price of labor rises, the isocost rotates clockwise. The new optimum position is at point B, where the firm produces Q_2 using L_2 units of labor and K_2 units of capital.

When the price of labor rose, two things happened to the firm. First, it became poorer; it could purchase less of both capital and labor for a given total cost. That is the "income effect." Second, the ratio of input prices changed, forcing the firm to substitute away from the input that is now

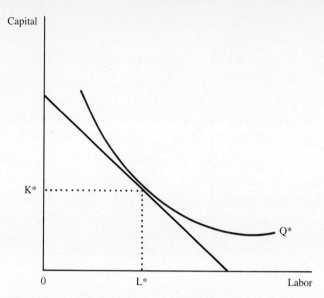

Figure 4-6 **Profit–Maximizing Output**

relatively more expensive (labor) and toward the input that is now relatively less expensive (capital). This second effect is the "substitution effect." As the price of labor rises (falls) both the income effect and the substitution effect indicates the firm should use less (more) labor.

The effect of an increase in the price of labor on the firm's employ-ment of capital is ambiguous in the long-run. It is clearly true that the substitution effect will dictate that the firm use more capital (substitute capital for labor) as the price of labor rises (holding the total cost level and the price of capital fixed). The income effect, however, will operate quite differently. When the price of labor rises, the income effect indicates that the firm has lower purchasing power and will purchase less of both labor and capital. Thus the substitution effect, given an increase in the price of labor, suggests that the firm will use more capital, while the income effect suggests that the firm will use less capital. The net effect on the use of capital depends on whether the income effect or the substitution effect is larger, and it cannot be known without explicit information about the production function.

Cost Functions of the Firm

In the short-run, the firm's cost can be classified as being of two types: fixed and variable. Fixed costs are those that do not vary with the level of output. These include rent for facilities, leasing expenses of equipment (or depreci-ation of purchased equipment), and salaries of management. Fixed costs are incurred even if production is entirely stopped *in the short-run.*

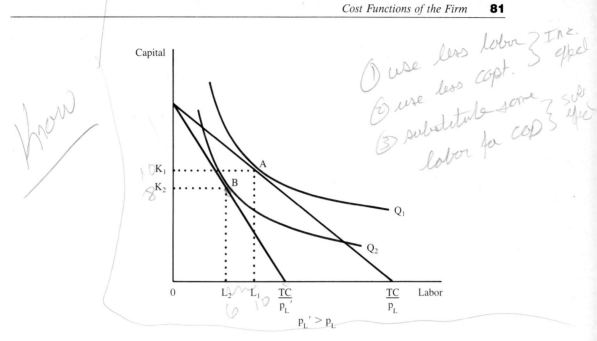

Figure 4-7   **Adjustment to an Increase in the Price of Labor**

For economic analysis (but not for the calculation of accounting costs), an important component of fixed costs is the opportunity cost of capital. An opportunity cost is a foregone benefit. The opportunity cost of reading a chapter in a textbook is the foregone pleasure of watching a televised football game. When one commits, for example, $1,000,000 to some productive activity (i.e., a toy factory), one surrenders the returns that could be obtained by loaning that money through the capital market to an equally risky venture. Should the toy factory offer a rate of return less than the capital market offers (for an equally risky investment), one would, in the long-run, leave the toy manufacturing business. Therefore, in evaluating costs of production, one should consider the return foregone from the best, equally risky alternative. Usually, that opportunity cost is considered to be the capital market (bond) return available from an equally risky investment.

Variable costs are those costs that increase as the level of output increases. These include, but are not limited to, most of the costs of employing workers paid by the hour. As more output is produced, more hourly labor is hired. As output is reduced, hourly workers can be laid off.[11] Marginal costs are the additional (incremental) cash outflows from additional units of output. Because fixed costs do not vary with additional output (*in the short-run*), only variable costs contribute to marginal costs.

---

[11] An important exception, developed in more detail in Chapter 6, is the element of fixed hiring and training cost that is involved in bringing in each hourly worker. See Walter Y. Oi, "Labor as a Quasi-Fixed Factor," *Journal of Political Economy* vol. 70, no. 6 (December 1962): 538–555.

The cost functions of the firm are shown graphically as dollar cost values at various levels of output. These are determined by several factors: the production function (relating input levels to output levels), the prices of inputs, and (in the short-run) the selection of a level of fixed costs (a "scale" or plant size decision). Figure 4–8 shows a typical family of short-run cost functions.

Should there be some technological change that allows more output for a given input level, the cost of producing any given level of output would fall (the cost functions, depicted in Figure 4–8 would shift downward). Should there be an increase in the price of the variable factor of production (for example, an increase in the wage rate), the cost of producing any level of output would rise (the cost functions depicted in Figure 4–8 would shift upward). The behavior of the cost functions when plant size (the scale, or level of fixed cost) is changed is determined by the return to scale of the production function.

In Figure 4–8, average fixed costs (AFC) are declining as quantity of output (Q) increases. This is necessarily the case, as fixed costs (FC) are constant and the formula for AFC is

$$AFC = \frac{FC}{Q}.$$

Average variable costs (AVC) usually fall, as the plant is used progressively more efficiently, and, then, rise as crowding and scheduling bottlenecks become problems at high levels of output. Average Total Costs (ATC) are the sum of Average Variable Costs and Average Fixed Costs.

From the relationship of marginals and averages discussed above, when Average Total Costs are falling, Marginal Costs (MC) are below ATC. When Average Total Costs are rising, Marginal Costs are above ATC. The same is true for the relationship between Average Variable Costs and Marginal Costs.

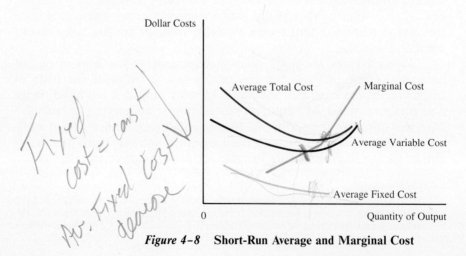

Figure 4-8   **Short-Run Average and Marginal Cost**

In the long-run, the firm can vary its plant size (its fixed costs), and, therefore, select the profit-maximizing capital/labor ratio. If ATC declines as plant size increases (input prices constant), the firm experiences increasing returns to scale (or economies of scale). If ATC rises as plant size increases (input prices constant), the firm experiences decreasing returns to scale (or diseconomies of scale). If ATC is constant as plant size increases, the firm experiences constant returns to scale (neither economies nor diseconomies of scale).

Figure 4–9 depicts a family of short-run Average Total Cost curves, representing the same firm at different plant sizes. In this case, the firm experiences economies of scale in moving from plant size "1" (ATC) to plant size "2" (ATC_2). The firm then experiences diseconomies of scale in moving from plant size "2" (ATC_2) to plant size "3" (ATC_3).

The firm's Long-Run Average Total Cost (LRATC) or the *envelope curve* is defined by the short-run Average Total Cost curves. Graphically, stretch a rubber band around the family of short-run cost curves. The resulting LRATC (the envelope that surrounds all of the short-run average total cost curves) will have as its minimum point the minimum point of one of the short-run ATCs (in this case, ATC). That mimimum LRATC is known as the *point of economic efficiency.* The level of plant size for which minimum ATC is the same as minimum LRATC is known as the optimum scale. While that plant size is optimal in the sense of minimizing LRATC, it is not necessarily the plant size that the firm will actually adopt.

Statistical Cost Estimation

In practice, knowledge of cost functions as numerical relationships, rather than as lines on a page, is very important. While several approaches to arriving at estimates of cost functions are available, they all involve the application of the statistical estimation procedures discussed in the Appendix to Chapter 2.

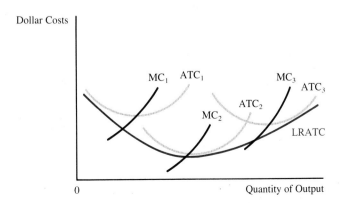

Figure 4–9 **Determination of Long-Run Average Total Cost**

One approach, preferred by economic purists, is to first specify and estimate a production function. Then a cost function is derived by finding, given input prices, the least cost means of producing each level of input. Such *dual* production functions (so called because, in linear programming jargon, the cost function is the dual of the production function[12]) emphasize the role of the production function in determining the cost function, but have the (minor) drawback of assuming that the firm is always on its long-run average total cost function.[13]

A more direct, but less theoretically elegant, approach to estimating cost functions is to estimate them directly from accounting data on costs. One specifies a total cost function such as:

$$TC = \beta_0 + \beta_1 Q + \beta_2 Q^2,$$

which typically follows the U-shaped path. Marginal cost is:

$$MC = \beta_1 + 2\beta_2 Q,$$

which is typically upward sloping.

In a formulation like that above, multiple product types are easily incorporated by allowing for more than one type of output (Q_1 and Q_2) in the total cost specification. For example, one might estimate, for two outputs:

$$TC = \beta_0 + \beta_1 Q_1 + \beta_2 Q_1^2 + \beta_3 Q_2 + \beta_4 Q_2^2.$$

While direct estimation of total cost from accounting data allows the estimation of short-run cost functions, estimation of a single level of fixed cost (β_0) amplifies that the firm was on a single short-run cost function during the whole of the period in which the data were gathered.

Summary

The chapter has developed much of the analytical background that is used in Chapter 5 to derive the firm's demand for labor. Specifically, the concepts of production function and optimal input proportion have been developed. Cost functions have been shown to result from the interactions of production functions and input prices. The basic difference between the

---

[12] In linear programming approaches to optimization, every maximization problem has an equivalent, or dual, minimization problem. The profit maximization problem has a dual represented by cost minimization. See Pappas, Brigham, and Hirschey, *Managerial Economics,* 1983, Ch. 9, especially pp. 340–349.

[13] That assumption is implicit in the dual cost function approach as a consequence of the assumption of substitutability among factors in the production function.

short-run and the long-run has been shown to be that, in the latter, capital and labor can be substituted for one another and, also in the latter, choices among alternative plant sizes are possible.

PROBLEMS

1. Use an isoquant diagram to show that, in the long run, the demand for any factor of production is downward sloping.

2. Cogger Corporation pays $200 per week for each unit of labor and $150 per week for each unit of capital. If MPK is 80 and MPL is 100, should Cogger substitute labor for capital or capital for labor? Why?

3. Davis Hardware has revenues of $1000 per week. Unfortunately for Davis, his costs are $1200 per week. Davis's only fixed cost is his rent (which includes utilities) of $400 per week. His lease won't expire for another six months. Should Davis board up his store now, or keep it open until his lease expires? Why?

REFERENCES

Douglas, Paul H. "Are There Laws of Production?" *American Economic Review* vol. 38, no. 1 (March 1948): 1–41.

Frisch, Ragnar. *Theory of Production,* Chicago: Rand McNally, 1965.

Hildebrand, George H. and T. C. Liu. *Manufacturing Production Functions in the United States, 1957,* Ithaca, New York: Cornell University, New York State School of Industrial and Labor Relations, 1965.

Oi, Walter Y. "Labor As A Quasi-Fixed Factor." *Journal of Political Economy* vol. 70, no. 6 (December 1962): 538–555.

Pappas, James L., Eugene F. Brigham, and Mark Hirschey. *Managerial Economics,* 4th edition, Chicago: The Dryden Press, 1983. Chs. 6–8.

C H A P T E R 5

THE DEMAND FOR LABOR

C hapter 4 introduced the production process and argued that the firm pays employees (demands their labor) because those employees' labor is an important element in the production of goods or services. This chapter develops the production system one step further to explain the firm's best hiring decisions at various prices of labor. We develop these demand for labor functions both for the short-run and for the long-run. After reading this chapter, you will understand the interrelationships among production functions, output prices, input prices, and employment decisions.

The demand for labor is defined as the quantity of labor that would be purchased, at various prices of labor (wage rates), holding all other things equal.[1] Thus, the demand for labor, like the demand for a product or service, is a schedule relating quantities purchased to prices (wages). In the case of the demand for labor, the "other things" that must be held unchanged include the production function, the demand function for the firm's output, and the prices of other inputs, including the prices of any other types of labor that the firm might employ.

One can look, then, at the demand for labor from three different perspectives. First, there is a demand for labor in the aggregate. That is, at various levels of some overall wage index, how many hours of labor will the

---

[1] "Holding all other things equal" is the economist's so-called *ceteris paribus* assumption.

economy as a whole employ? This is the problem of job-creation that looms so large in macroeconomic policy.

Second, one can examine the demand for labor by a particular firm. Such an analysis depends on principles of profit-maximization and has important implications for the labor costs of the firm and for the wages received by the firm's employees.

Third, either in the macroeconomic sense or from the perspective of the individual firm, one can look at the demand for a particular type of labor. For example, one might be interested in variations over time in the demand for chemical engineers in the aggregate, or in Exxon Corporation's demand for chemical engineers at any one point in time. It is with the latter two perspectives, the demand for labor by the firm and the demand for a particular type of labor, that this chapter deals.

The firm's demand for labor is derived from consumers' demand for the output that labor produces.[2] That is, it is to the consumers' demand for various types of goods and services that the firm is responding when it hires labor. An accounting firm's demand for hours of labor from income tax accountants is derived from consumers' desire to have expert assistance in preparing income tax returns. As was demonstrated in Chapter 4, labor's role in the production function (especially the degree to which labor can be substituted for other factors) is one important determinant of the derived demand for labor. Another important determinant of the firm's derived demand for labor is the nature of consumers' demand for the final product. Is that demand great or small? Is that demand price elastic or inelastic?[3] These factors are reflected in the shape of the firm's demand for labor.[4]

The firm's demand for labor, just discussed, is the amount of a particular type of labor—usually measured in person-hours—that the firm would purchase at various prices of labor, holding all other things equal. It is, then, a plot of quantities of labor against the price of labor, as in Figure 5–1. In Figure 5–1, the quantity of labor hired is a function of (depends upon) the price of labor.

The price of labor as shown in Figure 5–1 requires some explanation. The price of labor to the firm is, naively, thought to be the money wage rate, or, for salaried employees, the salary per period divided by some standard number of hours worked per period. Such a notion of the price of labor is only a crude approximation of the true price the firm pays. Much of the compensation that employees receive is not in the form of wages or salary,

---

[2] The most readable treatment of the theory of derived demand is Milton Friedman, *Price Theory, A Provisional Text,* Chicago: Aldine, 1962, ch. 7.

[3] Price elasticity of demand is the percentage change in quantity demanded for a one percent change in price.

[4] See Alfred Marshall, *Principles of Economics,* eighth edition, London: Macmillan, 1927, pp. 381–387; and J.R. Hicks, *The Theory of Wages,* second edition, London: Macmillan, 1963, pp. 241–247.

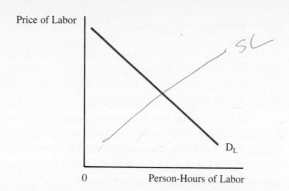

Figure 5-1 **A Typical Firm's Demand for Labor**

but non-wage benefits.[5] These include vacation and holidays, life and health insurance, and employers' contributions to pension plans. The value of these fringe benefits must be included in the price of an hour of labor to the firm.[6]

An item that should not be included in the price of an hour of labor is any fixed costs associated with administering the human resource management function. Those costs are not variable with respect to the number of hours worked, and to allocate them to specific hours worked can lead to faulty conclusions. The price of an hour of labor should include the average incremental cost incurred per unit of labor.

Finally, for some purposes, it is the after-tax cash flows associated with an hour of labor that matter for decision making. It may be necessary to adjust the prices of various types of labor and of capital to account for differential tax treatments.

The Demand for Labor in the Short-Run

The short run, as discussed in Chapter 4, is a period in which some factor or factors of production are fixed, but at least one factor's input can be varied. Usually capital inputs and some labor inputs (especially management input) are fixed and non-management labor is considered variable in the short run.

The firm's demand for variable labor in the short run, then, is the result of maximizing profit, taking product demand, production technology, the price of capital, and the quantity of capital used as fixed. The result

---

[5] Such fringe benefits account for almost 18 percent of total compensation. See U.S. Department of Labor, Bureau of Labor Statistics, *Handbook of Labor Statistics,* 1980, Washington, D.C.: U.S. Government Printing Office, 1980, p. 320.

[6] Chapter 18 discusses the methods for determining the cost of such items.

is that the firm should hire labor up to the point that the last unit of labor adds just as much to total revenue as it does to total cost.[7] Algebraically,

$$MR \times MPL = MCL.$$

The expression on the left-hand side of the equation is marginal revenue multiplied by the marginal product of labor. Marginal revenue is the additional revenue generated by the last unit of output. The marginal product of labor is the additional output added by the last unit of labor hired. The product of these two quantities, known as the marginal revenue product of labor (MRPL) is the additional cash inflow generated by the last unit of labor. That quantity (MRPL) is the short-run demand for labor.

The term on the right-hand side of the equation, marginal cost of labor, is the additional cash outflow generated by hiring one more unit of labor. If the firm is able to hire all of the labor it wants at a single value of MCL, then that value of MCL is the all-inclusive "wage" discussed in the previous section. Figure 5–2 shows the demand for labor and the firm's employment decision (L^*) under the assumption of a constant MCL.

In Figure 5–2, the demand for labor is shown as downward sloping. This is typically the case because, as argued in Chapter 4, in the relevant range, the marginal product of labor (MPL) is almost always downward sloping. MRPL fulfills the requirements of the definition of the demand for labor. If the price of labor (the all-inclusive "wage") is taken by the firm to be w_1, then the intersection of w_1 with MRPL indicates the number of hours of labor that the firm would hire. Thus, a higher MCL will, in most instances, cause a lower level of employment.[8]

Note one thing that the demand for labor is not: It is not the marginal product of labor times price of output. That measure (the so-called Value of Marginal Product) is often confused with the demand for labor (MRPL), but is relevant only in the rare circumstances in which it is equal to MRPL. For Value of Marginal Product to be equivalent to the demand for labor (MRPL), price must equal marginal revenue, which requires perfect competition in the product market.

Consider the situation depicted in Figure 5–3. The firm can hire all of the labor it wants at a fixed "wage," w_1. The MRPL is as depicted. Were the firm to hire L_1 hours of labor per period, management might, given the

---

[7] The reader who is familiar with differential calculus can derive the profit-maximizing condition:

$$MR \times MPL = MCL$$

by maximizing the profit (π) function:

$$\pi = Q \cdot P - P_K K - P_L L$$

with respect to labor input (L).

[8] The one exception is discussed in Chapter 6.

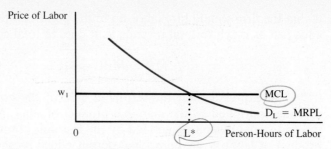

Figure 5-2   **The Demand for Labor and the Firm's Decision Under Constant MCL**

necessary information, reason that the last hour of labor hired generates more additional revenue than it generates in additional costs. Thus, that last hour of labor is a producer of net cash inflow. That is good for the firm. Indeed, it is so good for the firm that the firm would want to hire another hour of labor just like it. The firm would want to continue hiring until the last hour of labor generated no net cash flow (at point L^*).

If, on the other hand, the firm in Figure 5–3 were hiring L_2 hours of labor per period, management could see that the *last* hour of labor hired generates more additional costs than it generates in additional revenues. That's bad for the firm. The firm would want to reduce its employment of labor until the last hour of labor hired no longer generated negative cash flow (at point L^*).

Table 5–1 shows the derivation of the firm's short-run demand for labor, given a fixed production function, price of capital, and stock of capital employed. The firm is assumed, for simplicity, to face a horizontal marginal revenue function.[9] By application of differential calculus, the

---

[9] That is, the firm is assumed to be in a perfectly competitive market, taking the market price as given.

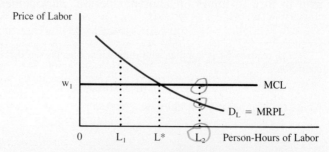

Figure 5-3   **Selecting the Optimal Employment Level**

Let Q = f(K,L)
   Q = $20K^{\frac{1}{2}} L^{\frac{1}{2}}$
   p_k = 50 (assumed fixed)
   K = 100 (assumed fixed)

Product demand indicates Marginal Revenue (MR) = 100
From application of differential calculus:

MPL = $10K^{\frac{1}{2}} L^{-\frac{1}{2}}$
MPL = $10(100)^{\frac{1}{2}} L^{-\frac{1}{2}}$
MPL = $10(10) L^{-\frac{1}{2}}$
MPL = $100L^{-\frac{1}{2}}$

Demand for labor is Marginal Revenue Product of Labor.
MRPL = MR × MPL
MRPL = $100 \times 100 L^{-\frac{1}{2}}$

In equilibrium:

MCL = MRPL
p_L = $100 \times 100 L^{-\frac{1}{2}}$
p_L = $10{,}000 L^{-\frac{1}{2}}$
$L^{-\frac{1}{2}}$ = $P_L/10{,}000$
$L^{\frac{1}{2}}$ = $10{,}000/p_L$
L = $100{,}000{,}000/p_L^2$

Table 5-1   **The Short-Run Demand for Labor**

marginal product of labor, and, thus, the marginal revenue product of labor are obtained.

The logic of the demand for labor dictates that the firm will hire labor up to the point that the marginal revenue product of labor is equal to the marginal cost of labor. If the firm faces a constant marginal cost of labor (equal to the price of labor), then the firm should set the expression for MRPL equal to the price of labor:

$$P_L = 10{,}000 L^{-\frac{1}{2}}.$$

Rearranging terms to solve for L (the quantity of labor that the firm will employ at various prices of labor), yields the short-run demand for labor.

Figure 5–4 illustrates an important point that is poorly understood, even by many decision makers. An increase in demand for the firm's final output will increase the additional revenue that the firm receives from the last unit sold (marginal revenue) and, therefore, will increase labor's marginal revenue product (MRPL = D_L). The result of that shift in the demand for labor is to increase the firm's level of hiring at any given price of labor.

What is not well understood is that the same result is achieved if, through some technological improvement, labor's marginal product rises.

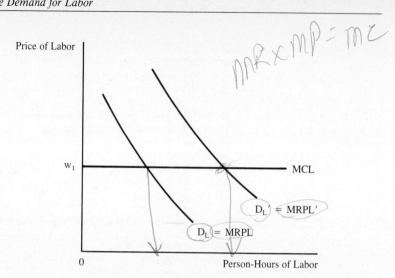

Figure 5-4   **Effect of a Change in Productivity or Product Demand**

Many believe that if labor becomes more productive, the same output would be generated by fewer hours of labor and total hours of labor hired would be reduced. In fact, that is not the case. An increase in the firm's labor productivity gives the firm a cost advantage over its competitors. The result is an increase in sales, and, therefore, output and employment.

The Demand for Labor in the Long-Run

One can develop the demand for labor in the long run from several perspectives. Some texts view the long-run demand for labor as being determined by a string of observations, each taken from a different short-run demand for labor (see Figure 5–5).[10] At one time, conditions are such that demand for labor is observed to be at point A in Figure 5–5. Over time, the demand for labor shifts (perhaps due to an increase in productivity). Later, the demand for labor is observed to be at point B. Connecting points A and B yields a long-run demand for labor. While that approach is both technically correct and intuitively appealing, it doesn't capture the essential distinction between the firm's planning in the short run and in the long run.

The demand for labor in the long run is derived from the firm's long-run production process. As developed in Chapter 4, management, in making decisions about the long run, must recognize the possibility of

[10] An excellent example of this treatment is F. Ray Marshall, Vernon M. Briggs, Jr., and Allan G. King, *Labor Economics,* fifth edition, Homewood, Illinois: Richard D. Irwin, 1984, p. 303.

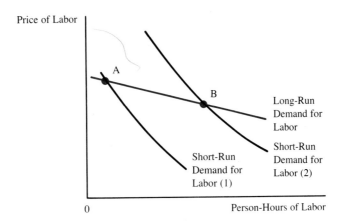

Figure 5-5   **The Long-Run Demand for Labor, First Approach**

substituting labor for capital or capital for labor to attain the best mix of inputs. In this section, then, the long-run demand for labor will be developed taking explicit account of those possibilities of substitution between labor and capital.[11]

Figure 5–6 shows how the firm would establish its long-run demand for labor, recognizing the substitutability of labor and capital in the long-run demand for labor, recognizing the substitutability of labor and capital in the long run. The upper panel of Figure 5–6 shows a family of isoquants, representing a production function of the form:

$$Q = f(K,L).$$

The firm has a fixed production function ($Q = f(\cdot)$), a fixed level of total cost (TC), and a fixed price of capital (p_k). That price of capital is the price to lease one unit of physical capital per period. Because we are considering the long run, both labor and capital are variable inputs.

The demand for labor, over any planning horizon, is the quantity of labor hired per period, at various prices of labor, all other things being equal. Holding $f(\cdot)$, TC, and p_k fixed, let the price of labor vary. In Figure 5–6, the price of labor starts at a low level (p_L), rises to a higher level (P_L'), and then rises to yet a higher level (P_L''). As the price of labor rises, the isocost line rotates clockwise, indicating that, at higher prices of labor, the firm is able to hire less labor per period.

Under each isocost regime, the firm would, in the long-run, adjust its

---

[11] For simplicity, assume there is only one type of labor and only one type of capital. The more complex case, allowing substitution among different types of labor, is a straightforward extension of the simplified analysis.

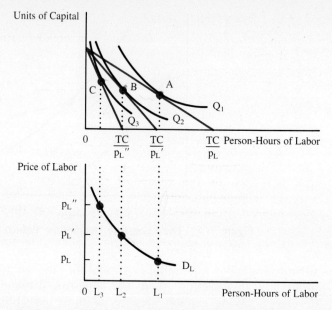

Figure 5-6 **The Long-Run Demand for Labor, Second Approach**

use of labor and capital to fulfill the equimarginal condition derived in Chapter 4:

$$-\frac{P_L}{P_k} = -\frac{MPL}{MPK},$$

which implies

$$\frac{MPL}{P_L} = \frac{MPK}{P_k}.$$

Thus, at each price of labor, all else equal, the firm will employ labor and capital in the proportions indicated at the points of tangency between the isocost lines and the isoquants (points A, B, and C in the upper panel of Figure 5-6).[12]

The lower panel of Figure 5-6 conveys the same information as the upper panel, but in the familiar price/quantity framework. Because the horizontal axes of the two panels are the same (person-hours of labor employed), one can project those numbers of hours down from the upper to the lower panel. Under the lowest price of labor considered (P_L), the firm

---

[12] For detailed algebraic and geometric deviations, see Ronald G. Ehrenberg and Robert S. Smith, *Modern Labor Economics,* second edition, Glenview, Illinois: Scott, Foresman and Company, 1985, pp. 82–89.

would choose to operate at Point A, employing L_1 hours of labor. On the lower panel, that level of employment is associated with the corresponding price of labor.

Each price of labor (p_L, p_L', and p_L'') can be associated with the employment level that the firm would select at that price, after making full, required, substitution of capital for labor. This has been done in the lower panel of Figure 5–6. The line traced out by the resulting points is the firm's long-run demand for labor.

That the firm's long-run demand for labor is downward sloping (less labor will be employed at higher wage levels than at lower wage levels) is all but guaranteed by the nature of the income and substitution effects involved (income and substitution effects due to a change in the price of a factor of production were discussed in Chapter 4). When the price of labor rises, the income effect dictates that the firm can purchase less labor and less capital. The substitution effect dictates that the firm should substitute capital for labor. Thus, the two effects are mutually reinforcing in their results on the quantity of labor employed: as the price of labor rises the quantity of labor employed falls.

Because in the long run the firm has a substitution effect (between labor and capital) that it does not in the short run, the firm's response to rising wages is stronger in the long run than in the short run. One measure of the firm's response is the elasticity of demand for labor with respect to the wage.[13]

The elasticity of demand for labor with respect to the wage rate (E_w^L) is defined as the percentage change in the number of hours of labor hired per period for a one percent change in the wage rate. That is:

$$E_w^L = \frac{\Delta L/L}{\Delta w/w}$$

or, equivalently:

$$E_w^L = \left(\frac{\Delta L}{\Delta w}\right) \times \left(\frac{w}{L}\right).[14]$$

The downward slope of the demand for labor guarantees that this elasticity will be negative.

The absolute value of the elasticity of demand for labor is greater in the long run than in the short run (the demand for labor is "more elastic" in the long run than in the short run). The difference in elasticities is

---

[13] Again, where "wage" is understood to include all variable costs of employment.

[14] Those readers who have studied calculus will be more familiar with the "instantaneous" form:

$$E_w^L = \frac{\partial L}{\partial w} \cdot \frac{w}{L}.$$

demonstrated graphically in Figure 5–5. Point A in Figure 5–5 is a point on both long-run and short-run demand curves. Thus at Point A, the value of (w/L) is the same for both long-run and short-run demand functions. However, the absolute value of the inverse of the slope of the long-run demand function $\frac{\Delta L}{\Delta w}$ is much greater than is that of the short-run demand function.[15]

In the long run, management is more sensitive to changing wage rates than in the short run. In the long run, when substitution is possible, management has more options for reactions. Table 5–2 shows the derivation of a long-run demand for labor from certain assumed conditions. The firm will seek to meet the equimarginal condition, which will indicate the appropriate ratio of labor to capital. Given an assumed level of total costs, the derivation of the demand for labor is a straightforward exercise in algebra.

Some Evidence

Empirical estimates of the demand for labor are usually performed for large samples of the population, with the analysis of some public policy proposal as the goal, rather than for a single firm. Some empirical results useful at the level of the firm, however, have been produced.

In virtually all statistical analyses the demand for labor has been shown to be downward sloping. Hammermesh shows that some of that downward slope is due to the firm's ability to substitute between labor and other factors.[16] Also in his review of research on the demand for labor, Hammermesh found a great deal of consistency in the estimates of the elasticity of demand for labor. In particular, the elasticity of demand for labor in the aggregate is quite low, around −.15 (meaning that for a one percent increase in the wage level, all else equal, employment falls about .15 percent).

Complication from Real Life

While the theory of the demand for labor presumes easy substitution and no constraints on hiring and firing, experience imposes limitations on the firm's ability to make profit-maximizing adjustments.

One of the most familiar limitations on many firms' abilities to

---

[15] In calculating elasticities, one must look at the inverse of the geometric slope of the demand functions. Economists long ago developed the unfortunate habit of putting the dependent variables on the horizontal, rather than on the vertical, axes of their graphs.

[16] Daniel S. Hammermesh, "Econometric Studies of Labor Demand and Their Application to Policy Analysis," *Journal of Human Resources* vol. 11, no. 4 (Fall 1976): 507–525.

Let Q = f(K,L)
Q = 20 K$^{1/2}$ L$^{1/2}$
p_K = 50 (assumed fixed)
p_L = 100 (initially)

Total cost per period is $5,000 (assumed fixed)
From application of differential calculus:

MPK = 10 K$^{-1/2}$ L$^{1/2}$
MPL = 10 K$^{1/2}$ L$^{-1/2}$

$$\frac{MPL}{p_L} = \frac{MPK}{p_K}$$

Substituting: $$\frac{10\ K^{1/2}\ L^{-1/2}}{100} = \frac{10\ K^{-1/2}\ L^{1/2}}{50}$$

Simplifying: $$\frac{K^{1/2}}{10\ L^{1/2}} = \frac{L^{1/2}}{5\ K^{1/2}}$$

$$\frac{K}{100\ L} = \frac{L}{25\ K}$$

Cross-multiplying: $\quad$ 100 L^2 = 25 K^2

Simplifying again: $\quad$ K = 2L

Substituting into
the total cost function: $\quad$ TC = p_k K + p_L L

Simplifying and solving: $\quad$ 5,000 = 50(2L) + p_L L
$\qquad\qquad\qquad\qquad\quad$ 5,000 = 100 L + p_L L
$\qquad\qquad\qquad\qquad\quad$ 5,000 = L (100 + p_L)
$\qquad\qquad\qquad\qquad\quad$ L = 5,000/(100 + p_L)

Table 5-2 **The Long-Run Demand for Labor**

substitute capital for labor is the licensing of occupations by the states. All states license the members of some occupations. Physicians, attorneys, nurses, dentists, and optometrists, for example, must be licensed in every state in which they wish to practice. Some occupations (fortune-telling, for example) are licensed in some states, but not in others.

Most of the literature on occupational licensing focuses, as does Chapter 3, on its effect on reducing the supply of labor to the licensed occupation. There is, however, another effect from licensing. The firm that employs licensed professionals (nurses, for example) has much more limited ability to adjust its demand for labor in the long-run (through substituting the work of other professionals for that of nurses) than would otherwise be the case. Licensing, then, limits the ability of firms to make necessary adjustments in their demands for labor, reduces profits in the current period, and reduces the market value of the firm.

Another complication in the firm's demand for labor is the possible presence of a fixed cost component in labor cost.[17] Walter Oi introduced the possibility of hiring and training cost to the firm's decision. Those costs are incurred at the time of hiring and are then fixed for the duration of the employee's tenure with the firm. A competitive firm would only hire an employee under such circumstances if

$$w \leq \text{MRPL} + \text{(one year's share of hiring and training costs)},$$

assuming w (the wage) and MRPL to be constant over the employee's tenure. Thus, in Oi's framework,

$$w \leq \text{MRPL},$$

quite unlike the rule for hiring labor discussed earlier in this chapter.

In times of recession, when sales and, therefore MRPL, fall, Oi's analysis has interesting implications. The hiring and training costs are fixed and, therefore, irrelevant for future decisions (they are not incremental cash flows for any decision after the hiring decision). If MRPL falls, the employee is not immediately laid off. As long as

$$w \leq \text{MRPL},$$

the profit maximizing competitive firm should retain the employee. For an employee under such conditions, then, MRPL can vary without layoffs taking place.

Ehrenberg analyzed similar sources of fixed employment costs in the context of whether to add new employees (incurring more fixed costs) or whether to require incumbent employees to work overtime (incurring an overtime premium).[18] In such a case, substitution is complicated by the different nature of the costs over the two classes of workers. The solution lies in amending the decision calculus to account for the different natures of the employment costs.

Summary

This chapter has developed the demand for labor, using tools from production theory developed in Chapter 4. The demand for labor shows the appropriate number of hours to hire at various wage rates, all other things equal.

The demand for labor depends on labor's productivity and on consumers' demand for the products that labor produces. In the long-run, the demand for labor also depends on the firm's ability to substitute other

---

[17]See Walter Y. Oi, "Labor As A Quasi-Fixed Factor," *Journal of Political Economy* vol. 70, no. 6 (December 1962): 538–555; and Ronald G. Ehrenberg, "Heterogeneous Labor, the Internal Labor Market, and the Dynamics of the Employment-Hours Decision," *Journal of Economic Theory* vol. 3, no. 1 (March 1971): 85–104.

[18]*Ibid.*

EXAMPLE 5.1   QUASI-FIXED LABOR COSTS IN ACTION

"Worksharing" is a means of dealing with layoffs that allows firms to retain those in whom they have invested hiring and training costs. Oi's theory of quasi-fixed labor costs (discussed elsewhere in this chapter) suggest that, when productivity falls, workers will not be laid off until productivity falls below the wage rate. The higher each period's share of amortized hiring and training costs is, the greater the permissible decline in productivity.

In the late 1970s and early 1980s, some firms developed worksharing as a way to keep employees from moving on it times of recession (and, therefore, of low marginal revenue product). Under worksharing, each employee works a four-day week and collects unemployment benefits on the fifth day. While the firm's unemployment insurance tax rises, many believe that the long-run savings labor cost more than off-set the tax increase.

After initial opposition from both labor and the National Association of Manufacturers, worksharing has gained some support, including an AFL-CIO endorsement. Even in the states that have endorsed the idea, however, only about 1 percent of employees have adopted worksharing.

Source: Kim Watford, "Shorter Workweeks: An Alternative to Layoffs," *Business Week*, April 14, 1986, pp. 77–78.

factors of production for labor. The next chapter will bring together the concepts of the supply of labor and of the demand for labor to evaluate wage and employment outcomes under different market structures.

PROBLEMS

1. Houston Corporation faces a marginal revenue of $50 per unit. The marginal product of its manufacturing operatives, in the short-run, is MPL $= 10L^{-1/2}$. Houston can hire all of the operatives it wants for $10 per hour. In the short-run, how many hours of operatives' labor should Houston hire?
2. Bossert and Company experiences the following: MPL = $150, MPK = $100, p_L = $10, p_k = $15. Should Bossert substitute labor for capital or capital for labor? Why?
3. Explain the adjustment that the firm should make if it discovers that MRPL > "wage."
4. Graphically, derive the effect on the long-run demand for labor of an increase in the extent of health insurance coverage.

REFERENCES

Hicks, J. R. *The Theory of Wages,* second edition, London: Macmillan, 1963.
Rosen, Sherwin and M. Ishaq Nadiri. *A Disequilibrium Model of Demand for Factors of Production,* New York: Columbia University Press for the National Bureau of Economic Research, 1974.

CHAPTER 6

WAGE AND EMPLOYMENT OUTCOMES

T he last three chapters have developed the tools necessary to understand and analyze the supply of and the demand for labor. This chapter completes the section on labor markets by describing the process of their equilibration and by developing some approaches to decision-making in that market framework. After reading this chapter, you should have an understanding of how labor markets value employees' characteristics and how those values can be used by the firm in developing compensation schemes (the subject of Chapter 15).

The process by which labor markets generate wage and employment outcomes is a constraint on a firm's or a union's ability to make decisions and take initiatives in its own interest. That is, the firm cannot recruit the type of labor it desires at wages less than those for which such labor is offered. A union cannot, except within a narrowly defined range, negotiate a higher wage without suffering a loss of employment. A firm that wishes to have employees perform dirty or dangerous work is faced with the need either to redesign the work or pay higher wages.

Four Models of Short-Run Equilibrium

The starting point for the study of market-determined wage and employment outcomes is the construction of a set of models under highly simplifying assumptions. These four basic models all assume that labor is perfectly homogeneous, that firms are very efficient processors of information, and that there is no involuntary unemployment.

While these are highly restrictive models, they capture some essential features of wage determination. Among those features are the interaction of the firm's demand for labor with the supply of labor to the firm, and the role of market wages and prices as constraints on the firm.

Equilibrium outcomes for any firm depend on the competitive structures of the markets in which the firm operates. Competition, in this sense, does not mean the extent of rivalry (advertising, price promotion) in which the firms in the market engage. Rather, competition refers to the structure of the market: the number of firms in the market, the distribution of their market shares, and, as a result, the degree to which each firm takes the market price for its product as given.

In the extreme (and unrealistic) case of pure competition, there are an infinite number of firms in the market, each with an infinitesimally small market share. In such a market, each firm believes itself to have no price-setting power, and it accepts the market price as being fixed. At the other extreme is pure monopoly. In such markets, there is only one seller, which has the power to set the market price at the level that will maximize its own profits. Most markets have structures that combine elements of monopoly and elements of competition.

While one usually thinks of the firm as being a competitor or a monopolist in the market for its products, the firm also participates in one or more labor markets. The firm might be such a small part of a labor market that it takes the price of labor in that market as given (e.g., a single insurance agency in the secretarial labor market in a large metropolitan area). The firm would then be facing a competitive (albeit imperfectly competitive) labor market.

Similarly a firm could be the only employer (or one of very few employers) of a given type of labor in an area (a large university in the computer programmers' labor market in an isolated college town). In such a case, there is only one employer, a *monopsonist* (from the Greek for "one buyer"), and the labor market is said to be monopsonistic.

There are, then, in the short-run, four distinct cases for the firm's equilibrium wage and employment position. As shown in Figure 6–1, the product market can be characterized by a greater degree of competition or by a greater degree of monopoly. Also, the labor market can be characterized by a greater degree of competition or by a greater degree of monopsony. The firm might find itself in any of the four cells of Figure 6–1. It is not the case that monopoly power in the product market is automatically associated with monopsony power in the labor market.

Chapter 3 indicated that the supply of labor to the firm depends on the firm's position in the labor market. Chapter 5 argued that the demand for labor depends on the firm's marginal revenue product curve, and, therefore, on its position in the product market. The firm's equilibrium wage and employment decision is a function of its labor market and its product market position.

The case depicted in Figure 6–2 is that of a firm which is a perfect

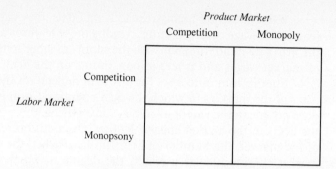

Figure 6-1 **Characteristics of Short-Run Equilibrium, Product and Labor Markets**

competitor in both the product market and the labor market. A perfect competitor in the product market believes it can sell all of its output at a price determined by the market.[1] Such a firm also believes that it cannot alter that market price. Therefore that firm takes the demand for its output to be horizontal at the market-determined price. When price does not fall as quantity produced rises, price is equal to marginal revenue.

The firm's demand for labor (D_L) as in all cases, is its Marginal Revenue Product of Labor (MRPL).[2] Because of the perceived equivalence of price and marginal revenue, the firm's MRPL (MRPL = MR · MPL) is also its Value of Marginal Product of Labor (VMPL = p · MPL).

The firm in Figure 6-2 is also a competitor in the labor market (it believes that it can hire all the labor it desires at a market-determined wage). Because labor is supplied to the firm at that wage (w^*), the supply of labor to the firm is horizontal at w^*. The Average Cost of Labor is w^* and, because ACL is constant, w^* is also the firm's Marginal Cost of Labor (review the average-marginal relationship from Chapter 4).

The firm in Figure 6-2 equates its MCL with its MRPL, to hire L^* hours of labor. The wage, set not by the firm, but by the market, is w^*.

The firm depicted in Figure 6-3 is in a somewhat different position from that described in Figure 6-2. While this firm is also a price-taking competitor in the product market, it has some degree of monopsony power in the labor market. The firm is like the coal mine in an isolated Appalachian community, selling its coal in a market in which it has little (if any) monopoly power, but having great monopsony power in the local labor market.

If there is no involuntary unemployment in the labor market in which

---

[1] For a thorough discussion of industries under varying degrees of competition, see James L. Pappas, Eugene F. Brigham, and Mark Hirschey, *Managerial Economics,* 4th edition, Chicago: Dryden Press, 1983, Ch. 10.

[2] See Chapter 5, above.

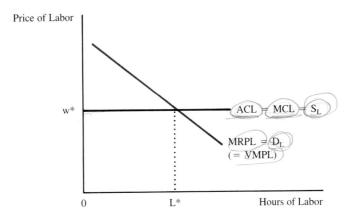

Figure 6-2 **Wage and Employment Outcomes, Competitive Product Market/Competitive Labor Market**

the firm participates, the firm must entice workers away from other labor markets or induce non-participants to enter the labor market if it is to increase its employment.[3] If it is either to induce outsiders to move in or to entice workers from other firms, the firm must raise its wage. Thus, the supply of labor to the firm (the Average Cost of Labor Curve) is upward sloping. To hire more labor, the wage rate must rise. Because the ACL is upward sloping, the MCL must lie above it, as drawn in Figure 6-3.[4]

The product market competitor/labor market monopsonist, like any other profit-maximizing firm, will equate MCL and MRPL, as at point A in Figure 6-3. That intersection indicates the appropriate number of hours of labor to hire (L*). Labor is paid, however, not its marginal cost, but its average cost. The firm will then pay the lowest wage necessary to induce L* hours of labor to be offered. That wage (w*) is found at L* on the supply of labor (ACL) curve.

The difference (w_A - w*) between labor's marginal revenue product and the wage rate is often called monopsony exploitation. It is part of labor's marginal product captured by the employer because of the presence of the monopsonistic labor market.

Suppose an employer offered each of L* hours a payment of w_A per hour, the marginal revenue product of labor at L*. At w_A, L_B hours of labor would be offered to the employer. Needing some way to ration L* hours of work among the L_B hours offered, the employer would begin to lower his wage offer, reducing the number of hours of labor offered, until the hours demanded and hours supplied were equal. That equilibrium

---

[3] Conditions of the supply of labor are developed in Chapter 3, above.

[4] Again, see the average-marginal relationship is described in detail in Chapter 4.

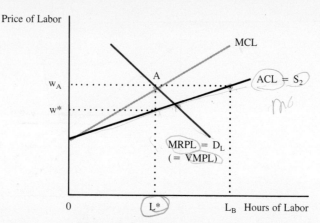

Figure 6-3   Wage and Employment Outcomes, Competitive Product Market/Monopsonistic Labor Market

would be at (L^*, w^*). Monopsony exploitation, then, is not due to the actions of a rapacious monopsonist, but to the market structure of monopsony.

Figure 6–4 depicts the case in which the firm has some degree of monopoly power in the product market, but is a competitor in the labor market. A large pharmaceutical manufacturer has monopoly power in drug markets in which it holds patents or in which it has strong brand-name identification. If the headquarters of such a firm is in New York City, however, that firm would be a nearly perfect competitor in the market for clerical employees.

As a competitor in the market for labor, the firm in Figure 6–4 takes the market-determined wage (w^*) as given, believing that it can hire all of the hours of labor it wants at that wage. The horizontal line at w^* then becomes the supply of labor to the firm and the average and marginal cost of labor curves.

Under normal assumptions (as described above) the firm will have a downward sloping MRPL, which is the firm's demand for labor. Lying above the MRPL is the Value of Marginal Product of Labor (VMPL). Just as the MRPL is marginal revenue multiplied by marginal physical product, VMPL is price (value in older terminology) multiplied by marginal physical product. Under conditions of monopoly, price is greater than marginal revenue. Therefore, VMPL must be above MRPL.

The firm sets MRPL equal to MCL, to find an equilibrium level of employment of labor at L^*. The market-determined wage rate, w^*, is the equilibrium wage outcome for the firm. The VMPL, for all of the attention it sometimes receives, is irrelevant for decision-making.

Finally, Figure 6–5 depicts the case of the firm with some degree of monopoly power in the product market and with some degree of monopsony power in the labor market. Like the firms in each of the other three cases, this firm sets its MRPL equal to its MCL. The firm's optimal employment

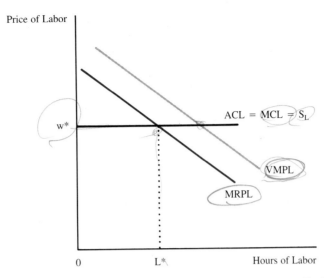

Figure 6-4 **Wage and Employment Outcomes, Monopolistic Product Market/Competitive Labor Market**

of labor, then, is L*. As the firm has monopoly power, its VMPL is greater than its MRPL. The difference between these two curves at L* ($w_B - w_A$) is sometimes called monopoly exploitation. Similarly, the difference between MCL and ACL at L* ($w_A - w^*$) represents monopsony exploitation. While monopoly exploitation is lost to the worker, one effect of collective bargaining is to recapture some of monopsony exploitation.

Figure 6-6 shows how a union can effect the recapture of monopsony exploitation. The firm depicted in Figure 6-6 has monopsony power in the labor market. Like the case in Figure 6-3, the firm equates MCL to MRPL, for an optimal wage/employment decision of w*/L*. Now let a union impose a wage of w_u. At w_u, the firm can hire all of the labor it wants out to the intersection of w_u with ACL (that is, every hour of labor that would be offered to the firm at a wage below w_u would be offered at w_u).

The firm now believes that the supply of labor it faces is horizontal at w_u and that w_u has become its MCL.[5] Equating MCL and MRPL now results in a level of employment at the higher union wage of L_u, which is greater than the original level, L*. The highest union wage for which the firm's optimal employment level is not lower than w* is w_A. That fact led Hicks to call the area from w* to w_A the "bargaining range."[6] That is the range within which the union is recapturing monopsony exploitation and generates no employment loss.

---

[5] The reader may wish to review the average-marginal relationship in Chapter 4 once again.

[6] J. R. Hicks, *Theory of Wages,* second edition, London: Macmillan, 1963.

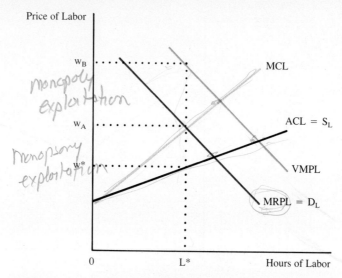

Figure 6-5 **Wage and Employment Outcomes, Monopolistic Product Market/Monopsonistic Labor Market**

Human Capital and Compensating Wage Differentials: Individual Characteristics

The models just developed share a common simplifying assumption. In each, the firm's labor inputs are assumed to be homogeneous. Each hour of labor is assumed to be just like every other hour of labor. In reality, each worker is unique and each hour worked by an individual is unlike any other hour worked by that individual. Each employee has his or her own special set of characteristics. Some of those (race, sex, and religious beliefs, for example) are unrelated to the employee's contribution to the firm's cash flows. Other individual characteristics, however, influence productivity, make employees attractive to other employers, and, therefore, influence compensation.[7]

Human capital is the term applied to all forms of productive power embodied in individuals.[8] Although many writers use human capital to mean "years of school completed," it is, in fact, quite different. First, human capital includes more attributes than education alone. Health status, acquired on-the-job training, and, in some occupations, physical strength all constitute forms of human capital. Further, while human capital is usually measured by years of schooling, it is actually the enhanced

---

[7] How firms incorporate employee and job characteristics into compensation systems is the subject of Chapter 15.

[8] Gary S. Becker, *Human Capital,* second edition, New York: Columbia University Press for the National Bureau of Economic Research, 1975.

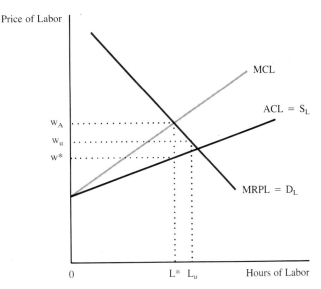

Figure 6-6   **Recapture of Monopsony Exploitation Through Collective Bargaining**

productive capacity that is the result of schooling, rather than the schooling itself.

Employers' demands for educated workers have been credited with some of the observed differences between union and non-union wages in some industries.[9] Consider the union that succeeds in increasing the wages of the workers it represents. Given that it now pays higher-than-market wages, the employing firm will, over time, be able to recruit more-able-than-average workers. Those workers should have higher than average productivities, meriting the wages the union originally won. The union wage effect becomes, in part, a wage differential due to individual differences (see Example 6-1).

The evidence on the wage effects of schooling is voluminous and compelling.[10] Firms that seek to hire more workers who are more highly skilled than average will need to adjust their pay scales upward to do so. Firms that are willing to settle for less than average skill levels can reduce the wage levels they offer. The characteristics that determine skill are, then, *compensable factors,* because the labor market puts a price on them. Failure of the firm to offer a wage premium for an individual characteristic to which the labor market attaches a price will mean that the firm is unable to attract employees having that characteristic.

---

[9] Lawrence M. Kahn, "Unionism and Relative Wages: Direct and Indirect Effects," *Industrial and Labor Relations Review* vol. 32, no. 4 (July 1979): 520–532.

[10] See, for example, Sherwin Rosen, "The Earnings Effect of Human Capital: A Survey of Empirical Evidence," in Ronald G. Ehrenberg (editor), *Research in Labor Economics, Volume 1,* Greenwich, Connecticut: JAI Press, 1977, pp. 3–39.

EXAMPLE 6.1   HIGHER EFFICIENCY MEANS HIGHER PAY

Great Atlantic and Pacific Tea Company had a powerful weapon in its 1982 negotiations with store employees in Philadelphia: the threat to close stores that were losing money. In response, members of the United Food and Commercial Workers (UFCW), accepted a cut in pay in return for a promise of bonus of 1 percent of sales if they kept labor costs below 10 percent of sales.

The effect of the agreement was to tie the wage directly to productivity. The effect, according to A&P officials, was to contribute in a major way to A&P's 81 percent increase in operating profits since 1984.

Officials of the UFCW are pleased with the plan's having kept stores open and rewarding workers with higher earnings. The union's only objection is that it subjects part of wages to risk. That risk may limit such plans to areas in which A&P faces the greatest degree of competition.

Source: *Business Week,* December 22, 1986, p. 44

Conversely, it is never in the firm's interest to offer a premium for a characteristic that the labor market does not value. Consider the employee who has special knowledge of how to process paperwork more quickly through the bureaucracy of General Electric Corporation. That knowledge is of no use in any other firm. Therefore, no other firm would be willing to offer any wage premium for such G.E.-specific knowledge. As no other firm is willing to pay a premium for such skill, G.E. should also refrain from paying such a premium. To pay such a premium is to offer the employee an economic rent, a payment above what is necessary to keep him employed at G.E.[11]

Compensating Wage Differentials: Job Characteristics

Not only must individuals be compensated to induce them to acquire special productive characteristics, they must also be compensated to accept odious employment conditions. Employers offering particularly pleasant working conditions can, conversely, offer negative wage differentials and

---

[11] The general training/specific training argument was originally made by Becker. Note that, because he receives no earnings enhancement for firm-specific training, no employee would be willing to bear its cost, either through direct payment or through reduced wages. Employees will only be willing to pay for training that enhances their own earnings (training sufficiently general to be valued by the labor market).

still recruit employees. Adam Smith, in his *Wealth of Nations,* was the first to observe this feature of labor markets and compensation:

> The whole of the advantages and disadvantages of the different employments of labor and stock must, in the same neighborhood, be either perfectly equal or continually tending to equality. If in the same neighborhood, there was (sic) any employment evidently either more or less advantageous than the rest, so many people would crowd into it in the one case, and so many would desert it in the other, that its advantages would soon return to the level of other employments.[12]

Positive wage differentials have been estimated statistically for occupational death rates, absence of schedule flexibility, and physically unpleasant surroundings. While controversy remains on the exact nature of these differentials, the support for their existence is strong enough that employers need to be aware of their possible need to offer such wage premiums.[13]

The logic suggesting that employers need to offer compensating wage differentials for work hazards is most easily demonstrated in the case of the differential for industrial accidents. Potential employees are concerned about the losses that might be suffered by their families and by themselves in the case of an accident. Some of those costs (pain and suffering, for example) would be uncompensated, even in the presence of Workers' Compensation. Therefore, employees demand a wage premium that compensates, before the fact, for the expected uncompensated loss in each period.[14]

The size of such a premium is determined by factors of supply and demand in the labor market. Workers, by offering more services in hazardous settings, depress such premiums, and, by withholding their services, force such premiums up. Some workers will be willing to accept hazardous work for a lower compensating differential than will others. Such workers will tend to find employment in the most hazardous firms and occupations.

There is no reason to expect any compensating wage differential to remain constant over time. As unemployment rates rise, for example, one would expect the compensating differential for hazardous work to fall.

---

[12] Adam Smith, *An Inquiry into the Nature and Causes of the Wealth of Nations,* London: 1776 (Modern Library Edition, 1937), p. 99.

[13] For a review of evidence supportive of the existence of compensating wage differentials, see Robert S. Smith, "Compensating Wage Differentials and Public Policy: A Review," *Industrial and Labor Relations Review* vol. 32, no. 3 (April 1979): 339–352. For a skeptical view, see Charles Brown, "Equalizing Differences in the Labor Market," *Quarterly Journal of Economics* vol. 94, no. 1 (February 1980): 113–134.

[14] Expected uncompensated loss in each period in the product of the probability of an accident in the period and the average magnitude of uncompensated loss, should an accident occur.

Unemployed workers with few alternative opportunities might be willing to offer their services in hazardous workplaces for a lower wage premium than in times of full employment and abundant opportunity.

Compensating Wage Differentials and the Evaluation of Job Characteristics: A Cost-Benefit Approach

Review for a moment the effects of compensating wage differentials. Employers who offer dirty, dangerous, or unpleasant jobs will need to pay a wage premium to attract employees, to the extent that information about those job characteristics are known among potential workers. Employers, then, face a choice: to spend resources to make work cleaner, safer, and more pleasant; or to spend resources to pay compensating wage differentials. Such a choice invites the application of cost-benefit analysis.[15]

The redesign of workplaces involves cash outflows in the current period over time for increased maintenance, higher energy costs for ventilation, or greater employment to redesign jobs. The payment of wage premiums involves higher cash outflows for employment over extended periods of time. The methods developed in Chapter 2 suggest that the appropriate comparison is between the present value of cash outflows from redesign of the job and the workplace and the present value of incremental cash outflows for the payment of wage premiums.[16]

Consider a firm that attracts laborers at only $10.00 per hour, while the locally prevailing wage is $9.00. The differences between the firm in question and others in the area is the (widely discussed) heat emanating from an open hearth furnace on the premises. The firm has 50 full-time (2080 hours per year) laborers and uses no overtime. The current situation is expected to continue indefinitely. The firm's tax rate is 0.30.

One option for the firm is to enclose the furnace, install automatic controls, and let the laborers work in isolation of the heat source. That installation would involve a one-time after-tax cash outflow of $250,000 and yearly after-tax maintenance expenses of $50,000 in perpetuity. Which option should the firm follow? The after-tax cost of capital is ten percent.

The present value [17] of cash outflows for redesign is

$$\text{P.V.} = 250,000 + \frac{50,000}{.10}$$

$$\text{P.V.} = 250,000 + 500,000$$
$$\text{P.V.} = 750,000.$$

Without redesign, the firm's hourly incremental after-tax cash outflows per year are:

Cash flow after taxes (CFAT) = ($1 per hour) × (50 employees) × (2080 hours per year) × (1 − tax rate).

CFAT = 72,800 (outflow) per year

Taking the present value,

$$P.V. = \frac{72,800}{.10}$$

$$P.V. = 728,000$$

In this case, the present value of the firm's after-tax incremental cash outflows from redesign ($750,000) is greater than the present value of the firm's after-tax incremental cash outflow due to unpleasant working conditions. The firm should not invest in the enclosure of the furnace.

Labor Contracts: Explicit and Implicit

Employees represented by labor organizations seek explicit, written contracts to govern the terms and conditions of their employment. Those contracts usually provide certain protective rights to the employees they cover. Among those rights are layoff based on seniority, rights to due process, and often union participation in pension plan administration.

An important recent line of analysis by economists suggests that nonunion workers have protection of a sort provided by unwritten (but very real) implicit contracts.[18] The implicit contract literature suggests that workers are willing to give up some of the market-determined wage for enhanced job security. Firms are willing to offer that enhanced job security, in the form of an implicit contract, because they are more willing to bear risks than the average employee.

While implicit contract theory does not explain wage rigidity, it does explain much of the employment stability that is observed in American labor markets. The theory has managerial significance in that it suggests that features of employment contracts (whether explicit or implicit) that

---

[15] Such cost-benefit analysis may be constrained by regulation.

[16] This is equivalent to a net present value problem, in which each period's net cash flow is wage saving less cash outflow for redesign.

[17] Recall from Chapter 2 that the present value of an annual sum (s) in perpetuity is s/r, where r is the rate of discount.

[18] Sherwin Rosen, "Implicit Contracts," *Journal of Economic Literature* vol. 23, no. 3 (September 1985): 1144–1175.

reduce employees' risks of layoff can be used to reduce the wages that those employees demand. Thus, features like layoff/recall seniority rights offering growing protection from layoffs, whose implementation is of low cost to the firm, can be substituted for money wages, and the firm will continue to attract employees. Interestingly, implicit contract theory suggests that the nature of the compensation mix affects the type of employees the firm attracts. Very risk averse employees will gravitate to firms offering a great deal of employment stability, but relatively low wages. Less risk averse employees will seek positions offering higher wages, but less employment stability.

Summary

The theory of equilibrium in labor markets is a theory of relative wages. It does not account for the absolute level of compensation, which also depends on the level of real national income and on the price level. A theory of equilibrium wages is, however, an important part of a manager's "kit of tools."

Wages are determined in markets. Even when based on a strict internal wage schedule, firms cannot ignore the external market factors that drive compensation. Understanding the sources of market wages is important for the manager who would understand his/her compensation system.

Further, managers must be able to justify compensation levels to curious (and often disgruntled) subordinates. Knowledge of the functioning of labor markets is essential to being able to make such an explanation.

PROBLEMS

1. Explain how a union-induced wage increase can be "justified" by a change in the workforce.
2. Should an employer ever offer a wage premium for a skill that no other employer values? Explain.
3. Heartsill Corp. is considering an employee tuition assistance program. The program would pay college tuition for up to six hours per semester for any employee with one year or more of service. On what grounds is such a program justified?
4. Noftz and Company operates warehouses in Texas, Oklahoma, and New Mexico. Clerical workers in the warehouses have complained that the heat in their offices is unbearable in the summer months. Air conditioning the offices is difficult, as they are in the interiors of the buildings. Currently, and for the foreseeable future, Noftz must pay 75 cents per hour more than other employers for skilled clericals. Noftz has a marginal tax rate of 30 percent and an after-tax cost of capital of 10 percent. To air condition a warehouse office would require an initial after-tax cash outflow of $5000

and would involve annual before-tax cash outflows of $1000 in perpetuity. Each office has two clerical employees, working 2080 hours per year. Should Noftz air condition its offices?

REFERENCES

Becker, Gary S. *Human Capital,* second edition, New York: Columbia University Press for the National Bureau of Economic Research, 1975.

Ehrenberg, Ronald G. and Robert S. Smith. *Modern Labor Economics,* third edition, Glenview, Illinois: Scott, Foresman and Company, 1988.

Hicks, J. R. *The Theory of Wages,* second edition, London: Macmillan, 1963.

Rosen, Sherwin. "Implicit Contracts" *Journal of Economic Literature* vol. 23, no. 3 (September 1985): 1144–1175.

THE LOGIC OF REGULATORY INTERVENTION

H uman resource management does not take place in a vacuum. The last section described how labor market conditions affect decision-making on employment and compensation. This section will describe how social institutions, especially government and labor organizations, influence human resource management and limit the firm's scope of decision-making.

Government, defined broadly to include all branches and all levels of government, is always an important participant in the human resource management function. Government imposes taxes which, if tied to wage levels (like the Social Security tax in the United States), alter the variable cost of labor. Government is a direct employer of labor, and government is, through its use of private contractors, an indirect employer of even more labor.

In most settings, however, one of government's most important roles in human resource management is as a regulator of the terms of the employment relationship. This chapter and the next will discuss decision-making under various forms of regulation. The purpose of this chapter is to describe the rationale behind government's regulatory intervention. After reading it, you will better understand why regulations are enforced and how firms can react to them.

Heterogeneous Regulation

Regulation is a term covering a broad range of activities (discussed below). As used here, regulation includes all of government's efforts to alter the outcomes of market processes or to order employers to use resources in ways other than they otherwise would. Thus, in the human resource management arena, regulation includes, among other things, minimum wage laws, rules governing collective bargaining, rules guaranteeing equal employment opportunity, and rules on the allocation of resources to the promotion of a safe workplace. There is not a clear distinction between regulation and government's other functions. Government regulates human resource management with respect to its own employees. Some taxing activities (Social Security taxation, for example) exist to support quasi-regulatory activities.

Certainly, the activities that one can classify as regulation are heterogeneous. Some deal with wages, some with procedures for selecting representation in collective bargaining, and some deal with the criteria employers may (and may not) use to select employees. No blanket advocacy of regulation or deregulation can be applied to such a broad range of interventions.

Just as government regulations are heterogeneous, so are the government's regulators. The United States is governed by a federal system. Some regulation is accomplished at the state level, while most human resource regulations are imposed by the national government. States, for example, have jurisdiction to regulate collective bargaining on the part of their own employees and on the part of employees of the local governments within their borders. The federal government, acting under a broad interpretation of the Commerce Clause of the Constitution, has the authority to regulate in most other arenas of human resource management.[1]

Just as there is a hierarchy of jurisdictions, so there is a hierarchy of laws at the federal level. The U.S. Constitution is the "supreme law of the land." The U.S. Congress cannot pass legislation (laws and treaties) that is inconsistent with the Constitution. Acts of Congress (statutory law), whether signed by the president or passed by two-thirds vote of each house of Congress over his veto, supercede decisions made by federal regulatory agencies (administrative law). Also superceding administrative law is the system of legal precedents embodied in common law.

Standing outside the general hierarchy of federal law is the president's ability to issue executive orders. The president's authority to issue such orders derives from tradition, being nowhere mentioned in the Constitu-

---

[1] The Commerce Clause (Article I, Section 8, paragraph 3) of the United States Constitution reads as follows: "[The Congress shall have power] to regulate commerce with foreign nations, and among the several states, and with the Indian tribes."

tion or in statutory law. Executive orders govern the administration of the executive branch and are in force until modified by an act of Congress or by a subsequent executive order. In the human resource arena, executive orders have assumed some prominence, governing affirmative action programs (rules for the granting of federal contracts) and, for a time, collective bargaining by federal employees.

Theories of Regulation

Why does government (at any level) intervene in the labor market and in firms' management of human resources? Three major theories attempt to explain why regulation takes place. In fact, some cases may appropriately be described by each of the three.

The *public interest theory of regulation* suggests that government intervenes in market processes in the interest of the public at large.[2] There are cases in which markets do not generate socially optimal outcomes (such cases are known as market failures).[3] For example, provision of safety inputs in the workplace (hard hats, guard rails, information, and training) generates benefits for employees and employers. Labor markets, by generating compensating wage differentials for hazardous work, provide some incentive for firms to provide safety inputs.[4] However, there may be parties who benefit from safe work places whose preferences cannot be expressed through the labor market. The taxpayer who wants to reduce his contribution to public hospital support or the child who benefits from having a healthy parent does not participate in the labor market. Government may, then, intervene in the labor market to subsidize safety inputs or to tax accidents or unsafe conditions to represent those non-market participants and to achieve a socially optimal outcome.

Many scholars, even the most politically conservative, approve of government intervention when it is justified by such cases of *market failure*. There are cases, however, in which government intervention has other motivation than to serve the public interest. The close associations between some regulatory agencies and the industries they regulate led some scholars to advance the *capture theory of regulation*. Proponents of the capture theory argue that regulatory bodies (the National Labor Relations Board,

---

[2] Theories of regulation are summarized and discussed in Richard A. Posner, "Theories of Economic Regulation," *Bell Journal of Economics and Management Science* vol. 5, no. 2 (Autumn 1974): 335–58.

[3] F. M. Bator, "The Anatomy of Market Failure," *Quarterly Journal of Economics* vol. 72, no. 3 (August 1958): 351–79.

[4] Regulation of industrial safety is discussed in detail in the next chapter. For a discussion of management's incentives to provide safety inputs, see Robert S. Smith, "Compensating Wage Differentials and Public Policy: A Review," *Industrial and Labor Relations Review* vol. 32, no. 3 (April 1979): 339–352, especially pages 340–41.

the Occupational Safety and Health Administration, or, in a different context, the Securities and Exchange Commission) are so securely under the control of those they are meant to regulate (the AFL-CIO, firms in high-injury rate industries, or, in a different context, major brokerage and investment banking firms) that they will, unfailingly, act in the interest of the regulated parties.

The capture theory, based on anecdotal evidence, has great appeal for some observers. It appears consistent with the minimum freight rates once set by the Interstate Commerce Commission, with the Federal Communication Commission's early opposition to the establishment of cable television systems (a development also opposed by the major television networks), and with the compositions of most state professional licensing boards (physicians license physicians, attorneys license attorneys). The capture theory does not, however, square with the objections of many business people to the "burdensome" level of government regulation. It also fails to explain how a "captured" National Labor Relations Board, which regulates labor relations, could shift support from the AFL-CIO to employers as easily as many allege it to have done.

A theory of regulation that permits a broader range of behavior by regulators is the *political economy theory of regulation.* The political economy theory begins with the proposition that regulators act, neither in the interest of the public nor in the interest of the regulated industries, but in their own self-interest.

Consider the issue of an employer's right to discourage unionization of employees. For most of the public, such an issue is not a significant matter. For the AFL-CIO and its constituent unions, however, the issue is of great importance. Members of the National Labor Relations Board, the regulating body having jurisdiction over such a case, will act, according to the political economy theory of regulation, in their own self-interest. Their self-interest is served when they act so as to maximize support for their remaining in office. That support will be greatest for members who act in the interest of the AFL-CIO (or, in a different climate, in the interest of organized employer groups), rather than in the interest of the largely uninterested public. Single-issue political groups, then, have distinct advantages over the public at-large in gaining support from regulatory bodies. Like the capture theory the political economy theory suggests that regulatory authorities will *usually* act in the interest of those they regulate.

Regulation Can Restore Competitive Market Outcomes

While every individual firm (and the members of every occupation) has a set of regulations it would like to see enacted and enforced, from society's point of view, the only desirable regulations are those that are genuinely in the public interest. That is, if one could momentarily forget his or her own station in life, the only regulations he or she would approve would be those that are unambiguously in the interest of all.[5]

There are circumstances in which unregulated markets (including labor markets) generate outcomes that do not fully reflect social preferences.[6] In such cases regulation is often imposed, either to establish competition or to replace competition with some set of administrative rules.

The most commonly discussed case in which regulation can be in the public interest is that in which *spillover effects* are present. That is, some benefit or harm falls on some party other than those who are directly involved in the transaction. When (as is usually the case) there is no market in which these affected third parties can express their preferences, some type of interventions may be necessary.

The Preamble to the National Labor Relations Act of 1935 justified the Act with a spillover effect argument. Labor disputes, the authors of the Act wrote, caused harm to persons other than the firms and managements involved by disrupting interstate commerce.

Figure 7–1 depicts a possible justification for regulation of industrial safety. The *marginal* benefit of safety inputs is declining because, as more safety inputs are added (as one proceeds from training to guardrails to informational posters, for example), the *last* unit of input adds progressively fewer benefits. The *marginal* cost of safety inputs rises because, typically, the least expensive inputs are imposed first, with progressively more costly inputs added later. The decision to provide safety inputs (training, protective gear, and workplace enhancements) is made by the employer. These inputs impose costs on the employer, but also confer benefits (reduced wage premiums, lower insurance costs, reduced turnover). Employers will equate their own marginal benefits to marginal costs, providing S_1 in safety inputs.

There are also, however, benefits (reduced pain and suffering, greater social product, reduced medical costs) accruing to employees, to their families, and to those who, through insurance plans, would participate in paying employees' medical bills. Thus, social marginal benefits exceed private marginal benefits, and society as a whole would prefer to have S_2 in safety inputs.

Such a situation, in which benefits from an employer's decision spill over to others, calls for intervention. To achieve the socially optimal level of safety input provision, a subsidy (whose cost would be borne by the community, which also receives the benefits) could be paid to the employer. That subsidy would be equal to the difference between the marginal social benefit and the marginal private benefit, raising the employer's benefit to the level of the social benefit.

---

[5] John Rawls, *A Theory of Justice,* Cambridge, Massachusetts: Harvard University Press, 1971, especially pages 17–22.

[6] F. M. Bator, "The Anatomy of a Market Failure" (1958).

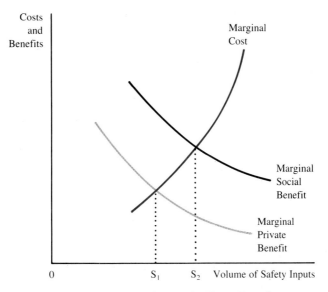

Figure 7-1 **Subsidy Justified by Spillover Benefit**

Costs and Unintended Consequences of Regulation

Regulation, even in the public interest, is not without costs. One can classify the costs of regulation along two dimensions: private or social, and static or dynamic. Private costs are the concern of the regulated firm while social costs are of concern to society as a whole. Static costs occur in the current period, while dynamic costs are due to potential declines in the rate of growth of the economy (see Figure 7-2).

In some cases, the very purpose of regulation is to impose costs on corporate shareholders. For example, one purpose of the Occupational Safety and Health Act of 1970 (OSHA) was to shift costs from injured workers to corporate shareholders (who would now have to pay for safety inputs). The private, static costs of OSHA, then, are the reductions in shareholder wealth (due to lower expected net cash flows) that compliance generates. Private, dynamic costs arise if firms reduce their growth rates as a result of complying with OSHA. A good management team will attempt to keep the costs due to compliance as low as possible.

If private costs to firms are merely the result of shifting costs away from affected employees and consumers to firms, then the social costs of the regulation are zero. If, on the other hand, total output falls due to the imposition of the regulation, the reduction in total output is a cost to society as a whole. It is that cost, plus the direct cost of implementing the regulation, that should be weighed against the expected benefits of the regulation (see the Appendix to this chapter).

	Private Costs	Social Costs
Static Costs	Current period's reduction in shareholder wealth due to regulation	Total lost output in the current period
Dynamic Costs	Present value of lost shareholder wealth in all future periods due to reduction in product innovation activity and growth	Lost output in all future periods due to reduced rates of innovation and growth

Figure 7-2   **The Costs of Regulation**

Charles Wolf has raised a different set of questions about regulatory interventions.[7] There may be incentives and goals for regulators that prevent regulations from achieving their goals. If, for example, those setting safety standards under OSHA have a bias toward the adoption of newly developed safety technologies, the cost of complying with OSHA will rise. That is, if OSHA officials believe that every new safety and health innovation should be adopted, regardless of cost, higher cost regulations will be adopted. If the regulators' bias is sufficiently strong, that increase in costs may not be merited by reduced numbers of accidents in the workplace.

Forms of Regulation

Regulation is of two principal types: regulation to supplant the workings of a competitive market, and regulation to restore the workings of a competitive market. Both types of regulation affect the work of the human resource manager.

As discussed above, regulation to supplant the market is adopted when market failure is so severe that, for the good of the public or of some interested group, market outcomes must be abandoned entirely. In such cases, regulation can be adopted either to determine prices or to determine allocations.

---

[7] Charles Wolf, Jr., "A Theory of Nonmarket Failure: Framework for Implementation Analysis," *Journal of Law and Economics* vol. 22, no. 1 (April 1979): 107–39.

EXAMPLE 7.1

DEREGULATION HAS UNINTENDED SIDE-EFFECTS TOO

The late 1970s and early 1980s saw a wave of deregulation. Recognizing that regulation was not always in the public interest, price regulations were lifted in several industries (trucking, airlines, railroads, and long-distance telephone service) that had been controlled for decades. The intent was to encourage price competition, but that was not always what happened.

An unintended consequence was to encourage mergers that increased the degrees of concentration (the percentage of industry revenues received by the four largest firms in the industry) in these industries. That increased concentration may be causing reduced competition and rising prices (where deregulation was intended to allow prices to fall).

To be sure, there are differences of opinion as to whether or not such a reduction in competition is occurring. Top officials in the U.S. Department of Transportation believe there is an unprecedented degree of competition in newly deregulated industries. Alfred E. Kahn, the Robert Julius Thorne Professor of Economics at Cornell University disagrees. Kahn calls the possibility of increasing concentration, "a critical issue we're going to have to confront increasingly in the months ahead."

Source: Chris Welles, Seth Payne, Frances Seghers, and Tom Ichniowski, "Is Deregulation Working?" *Business Week*, December 22, 1986, pp. 50–55.

Minimum wage legislation (under the Fair Labor Standards Act of 1937) is a case of supplanting the workings of the market in favor of regulatory determination of prices. For reasons discussed in the next chapter, Congress has decided that an unimpeded labor market will reward some employees at unacceptably low levels. To remedy that situation, a wage of $3.35 per hour (as of 1987) has been determined to be the minimum allowable for covered employees.

Safety regulation, as conducted under the Occupational Safety and Health Act of 1970, is a case of supplanting the workings of the market in favor of regulatory determination of resource allocations, rather than through price-setting. Congress decided that no market incentive would be sufficient to induce employers to provide adequate safety inputs. Therefore the Act provides that regulators will determine what resources must be allocated to safety in every covered workplace. Employers no longer have the choice of unprotected walkways or railings. Rather railings are mandated, as are their physical specifications.

Quite a different form of regulation is that which accepts market determined outcomes, but seeks to alter the "rules" within which those outcomes are determined. In the case of the anti-trust laws, such regulation seeks, explicitly, to restore competition to the workplace. In human resource management, the National Labor Relations Act has a similar purpose.

The Act accepts the legitimacy of wages as determined either by market forces or by collective bargaining. The Act, however, establishes a framework within which employees may select whether or not to be represented by a union in collective bargaining. If employees select such representation, the Act establishes a framework within which collective bargaining, and the determination of the rules of the workplace, will be conducted.

Management Response to Regulation

Management, in the interest of maximizing shareholder wealth, should seek to comply with regulation in the least costly manner possible. This does not mean, the authors believe, that management should refuse to comply. Rather, given that compliance is a constraint, the least costly means of achieving compliance should be adopted. The methods explained in Chapter 2 are applicable to the decision as to choice of method of compliance.

Consider a problem analyzed by Ehrenberg (and discussed in Chapter 5).[8] A firm needs more hours of labor for the next month. Overtime regulations in place (under the Fair Labor Standards Act of 1937) require that, if current employees work more than forty hours per week, they be paid one-and-one-half times their base wage; the base plus the overtime premium. On the other hand, hiring temporary employees to work forty or fewer hours per week requires the expenditure of hiring and, perhaps, training costs. Given the need to comply with overtime premium rules, which is the least costly way to acquire additional hours of work?

The decision methods of Chapter 2 suggest the use of a present value of incremental cash outflows. Evaluate the present value of incremental cash outflows for each alternative (hiring on new workers and paying an overtime premium to current employees). Then select the alternative with the lower present value of incremental cash outflows.[9]

If the expected penalty for non-compliance is less than the current cash outflow required to comply with a regulation, many managements will fail to comply.[10] An early criticism of the enforcement of OSHA was that just such a situation existed.[11] The expected penalty was the average fine multiplied by the probability of inspection. Such expected penalties were

---

[8] Ronald G. Ehrenberg, "The Impact of the Overtime Premium on Employment and Hours in U.S. Industry," *Western Economic Journal* vol. 9, no. 2 (June 1971): 199–207.

[9] For one-month decision problems, discounting is rarely important. The discount factor, $(1 + r)^{-1/12}$, is always very small.

[10] Again, the authors do not advocate non-compliance.

[11] Robert Stewart Smith, *The Occupational Safety and Health Act,* Washington, D. C.: American Enterprise Institute, 1976, pp. 60–62.

seen, by many observers and by some employers, as less than the out-of-pocket costs of compliance. The incentives to comply, then, were weakened and the potential effects of the Act were reduced.

Views of Regulation

There are, then, several ways to view government's regulatory intervention in the economy. Citizens should ask whether a specific intervention is in the interest of the public or of some private interest. Regulators should ask whether or not the enforcement of the policy invites non-compliance. Managements should ask what constitutes the least costly action, given their obligation to comply.

Each of these questions can only be answered on a case-by-case basis. There is no single answer to the question of the desirability of regulation. There is no single-most cost-effective way for management to deal with regulation. The methods of cost-benefit analysis, however, give management a means by which to make a decision as to how to deal with their regulatory environments.

Summary

Government intervenes in labor markets in a variety of ways and for a variety of reasons. As argued in the chapter, how one reacts to any specific intervention depends, in part, on one's economic incentives. Regulation can either enhance or impair both the equity of labor market outcomes and the efficiency of labor market processes. Regulation can also redistribute costs and benefits among labor market participants.

Chapter 8 will discuss several important government interventions. Those examples will illustrate the controversies that surround the issue of regulation in general: controversies as to the public's interest, and controversies based on opposing economic incentives.

PROBLEMS

1. Guenther-Brust Manufacturing Company estimates it will need 10,000 additional hours of labor over the next year. Its current production workers could supply that labor as overtime, or it could hire 5 new employees. Hiring and training costs are $7500 per employee. Production workers earn $10 an hour. Should the new employees be hired, or should current employees be paid an overtime premium? The firm's cost of capital is 8 percent.
2. What are the types of benefits that might result from the introduction of state laws forbidding the possession of alcohol in all workplaces? Which are measurable and which are not? To what extent do firms have incentives to enforce "no alcohol" rules in the absence of government regulations? Against what costs should the benefits of such a regulation be compared?

REFERENCES

Ashenfelter, Orley and James Blum. *Evaluating the Labor-Market Effects of Social Programs.* Princeton, New Jersey: Industrial Relations Section, Department of Economics, Princeton University, 1976.

Mishan, E. J. *Cost-Benefit Analysis,* new and expanded edition. New York: Praeger, 1976.

Mishan, E. J. *Introduction to Normative Economics.* New York: Oxford University Press, 1981.

Wolf, Charles, Jr. "A Theory of Nonmarket Failure: Framework for Implementation Analysis." *Journal of Law and Economics* vol. 22, no. 1 (April 1979): 107–39.

COST-BENEFIT ANALYSIS OF REGULATION: DECISION-MAKING IN THE PUBLIC INTEREST

Just as firms can employ cost-benefit analysis in their human resource management decisions, so public officials can and, sometimes, do use cost-benefit analysis in their decisions on regulatory intervention. In making public policy choices, there are two distinct roles for cost-benefit analysis. *Prospectively,* cost-benefit analysis can be used to ask whether or not a particular regulation should be introduced. *Retrospectively,* cost-benefit analysis can be used to determine whether or not the observed results of the regulation were worth its social costs.

Society's resources, including those resources managed by government, have alternative uses. Those who make non-market decisions about the allocations of those resources should, therefore, be concerned that their decisions put resources to effective use and that regulations don't impose costs on society without at least equal benefits. Prospective cost-benefit analysis addresses just that concern. The goal of prospective cost-benefit analysis is to determine whether a proposed intervention or public investment will pay. That is, will the present value of the total social benefits outweigh the present value of the total social costs? This question is derived from the compensation principle discussed in Chapter 2.

The preferred analytical method, then, for prospective cost-benefit analysis is net present value.[12] One attempts to quantify future social

---

[12] E. J. Mishan, *Cost-Benefit Analysis,* new and expanded edition, New York: Praeger, 1976, ch. 29.

benefits and costs and treats these as if they were the cash flows in the net present value formula. In practice such a task is difficult indeed.

Many of the projected benefits of public policy intervention are not easily quantified. How, for example, does one value a life saved by an industrial safety law?[13] Further, projected benefits of some regulations are, by their very nature, not subject to the cost-benefit calculus. One of the purposes of minimum wage legislation, for example, is to achieve greater equity in the distribution of incomes. Cost-benefit analysis does not address distributional issues.

If intended benefits are difficult to quantify, the nature of social costs cannot, in many cases, be known before the fact. The magnitude of lost output due to regulation can seldom be assessed and potential unintended effects cannot be identified until they appear.[14]

There is, further, a problem in the selection of the discount rate for public initiatives. Mishan argues that, for public action, the appropriate rate of discount is the social rate of time preference, which may not be the same as any interest rate observable in financial markets.[15] The social rate of time preference is the rate at which society as a whole would exchange consumption (not dollars) today for consumption one year hence. It is, then, a rate of interest without adjustment for risk of any kind and without adjustment for expected inflation. For projects and programs whose anticipated lives cover non-overlapping generations, even greater logical problems exist.[16] Future generations, who take early costs of intervention as a gift would like the current generation to use a zero rate of discount, to make benefits during those future lives valuable in a present value model. The logic of cost-benefit analysis, however, forces decisions to be made in the interest of currently living generations.

Retrospective cost-benefit analysis proceeds in two steps. First, the direction and magnitude of effects due to the regulation or investment must be determined. Typically, one estimates a regression equation over time, the dependent variable of which is the level of (or change in) the variable that the policy was meant to affect.[17] That the target variable actually changed is not, by itself, evidence that the policy intervention caused the change.[18] Rather, the independent variables in the regression model should

---

[13] For discussion of the valuation of life, see E. J. Mishan, "Evaluation of Life and Limb: A Theoretical Analysis," *Journal of Political Economy* vol. 79, no. 4 (July/August 1971): 687–705; and Steven E. Rhoades, "How Much Should We Spend to Save a Life?" *The Public Interest* no. 51 (Spring 1978): 74–92.

[14] Wolf, "A Theory of Nonmarket Failure" (1979).

[15] Mishan, *Cost-Benefit Analysis* (1976), chs. 31–33.

[16] E. J. Mishan, *Introduction to Normative Economics,* New York: Oxford University Press, 1981, ch. 67.

[17] See the Appendix to Chapter 2.

[18] Donald T. Campbell and Julian C. Stanley, *Experimental and Quasi-Experimental Designs for Research,* Chicago: Rand McNally, 1963, especially ch. 3.

include both a dichotomous variable for the presence or absence of the policy and a set of variables to control for *all* of the other factors that might influence the target variable in the absence of the policy. A statistically significant coefficient of the desired sign for the policy variable, then, is evidence of a desired result due to the policy intervention. If the intervention was intended, for example, to reduce the rate of industrial accidents and the estimated effect of the intervention was to increase the accident rate, one needs to reconsider one's policy. The coefficient of the desired sign also indicates the amount of the change in the target variable due to the policy intervention.

The second step is to determine whether or not that change due to the policy intervention was worth the costs involved. From society's point of view, those costs should include both the cost of administering the program and the (often immeasurable) costs of lost output due to the policy. These are used as if they were cash inflows and outflows in a net present value calculation.

While this Appendix has emphasized the problems involved in social cost-benefit calculations, the practice of cost-benefit analysis of regulation is still important. As is the case for decision-making within the firm, cost-benefit analysis provides a way of thinking about decisions that affect the way society allocates its limited resources. Government regulation can strongly affect the way firms (and, therefore, society as a whole) allocate and manage human resources. Regulatory decisions on human resource management issues, then, ought to be subjected, however imperfectly, to the cost-benefit calculus.

CHAPTER 8

PUBLIC POLICY AND THE CONDITIONS OF EMPLOYMENT

T he impact of federal regulation on managerial action has been dramatic over the past twenty years. Almost any management practice that relates to hiring, promoting, compensating, firing, training, or protecting employees faces the potential for federal or state regulation. This chapter attempts to introduce readers to regulations designed to solve social problems. The focus will be in areas such as equal employment opportunity, job safety, and compensation practice. These topics regularly concern all managers, and management responses to these forms of regulation have clear implications for firm performance. In the previous chapter we suggested that management should seek to comply with regulation in the least costly manner. In this chapter we develop in more detail the process of cost-effective regulatory environment management. As will be noted, compliance in the least costly manner represents an over simplification of managerial responsibility. There are both costs and benefits at the level of the individual firm that result from activities initiated out of concern for government intervention. Managers need to think in cost-benefit terms (this requires an understanding of what current regulations say a manager can or cannot do) and to predict future changes in the external environment. Therefore, a second goal will be to focus on the process of regulation, not just the content. Managers need to realize that there are principles of regulation that can guide their actions and that there is some degree of predictability associated with the regulatory process. In this chapter we review public policies that relate to the staffing process, compensation practices, and employee health and safety. The regulation of union-management relations is omitted from this chapter because of its extensive coverage in subsequent sections of the text. The material is organized such that key federal laws are described and interpreted. Within each major section we then comment on appropriate managerial action and response.

Public Policies on Hiring, Firing, and Promotion

Equal Employment Opportunity

In the United States, norms demand that individuals be given the opportunity to succeed regardless of origins. The norm implies that ability, hard work, and perseverance serve as the dominant criteria for advancement and attainment. Unfortunately, a conflicting norm allows outcomes to be unequal. James Rosenbaum,[1] in a detailed treatment of corporate mobility patterns, describes the situation as follows: "Since outcomes at any period become inputs at the next, a perplexing dilemma arises: To what extent do early selections to unequal positions curtail subsequent advancement opportunities? (p. 1)." The problem, of course, is that we live in a highly stratified society. For example, at the time major civil rights legislation was enacted in the 1960s, there was dramatic economic inequality between blacks and whites. Black unemployment was nearly double white unemployment, the average black family had only half the average white family income, and whites were much more likely than blacks to be employed in professional or managerial jobs.[2] These inequalities are difficult to account for, but to many seem to be tied to past segregation. Segregation was commonplace in schools and job classifications. Since educational attainment and work experience (early career outcomes) are related to subsequent career attainment, early career inequality is likely to have lasting negative consequences for those not receiving sponsorship and attention early in life.[3] This issue relates to a variety of other groups (e.g., women) and is at the heart of legislation and executive orders that regulate employment (staffing) practices. For a recent editorial comment on this issue see Example 8–1.

We now turn our attention to some key federal laws and regulations that prohibit employment discrimination. While our coverage will not be complete, it will include the more significant sources of federal prohibition. Both nondiscrimination laws and executive orders will be summarized. While public and private employers, employment agencies, and unions are

---

[1] James E. Rosenbaum, *Career Mobility in a Corporate Hierarchy,* New York: Academic Press, Inc., 1984.

[2] James Ledvinka, *Federal Regulation of Personnel and Human Resource Management,* Boston: Kent Publishing Company, 1982, pp. 33–36.

[3] Ledvinka, *Ibid.*

EXAMPLE 8.1   A HAVE AND HAVE-NOT AMERICA

Using multiple sources of information, Hodding Carter III argued (in a recent Wall Street Journal editorial) that the "America of assimilation, of upward mobility and of equalization of opportunity over time is becoming a thing of the past." For example, he cited a Census Bureau report that found that the net worth of the median white household was 12 times more than that of the typical black household and eight times higher than the typical Hispanic household. The data reviewed support the conclusion that the wealth gap between whites and blacks and between whites and Hispanics is widening.

The essence of the argument focuses on wealth (or the value of a family's assets) versus income. This issue received further attention in another 1986 Wall Street Journal article whose headline said: "Rich get richer in U.S., Congressional study finds." According to the study, the richest U.S. citizens amassed an even greater share of the nation's total household wealth during the last 20 year period.

Source: Hodding Carter III, Have and Have-not America," *Wall Street Journal*, July 24, 1986, p. 19; *Wall Street Journal*, July 28, 1986, p. 3.

subject to nondiscrimination laws, many organizations also are subject to executive orders given their role as government subcontractors.

United States Constitution[4] While Courts prefer to defer to existing statutory law (laws enacted by Congress speak directly to specific subjects), the First, Fifth, and Fourteenth Amendments relate to certain forms of employment discrimination. The First Amendment restricts Congress from enacting laws that would deprive individuals of employment rights on the basis of religious preference. The Fifth and Fourteenth Amendments prohibit the federal and state/local governments respectively from depriving individuals of employment rights without due process of law.

Civil Rights Acts of 1866 and 1871[5] While these laws do not directly address private sector employment discrimination, they do provide a federal remedy against discrimination on the basis of race. They accomplish this by giving all citizens the right to make and enforce contracts for employment and to sue if these rights have been deprived. Section 1981 of

---

[4] There are several excellent sources for detailed review and interpretation of key fair employment practice laws and regulations. For example, see Benjamin J. Taylor and Fred Witney, *Labor Relations Law*, Englewood Cliffs, New Jersey: Prentice-Hall, Inc., 1983, chapter 22; Ledvinka, *Ibid.*

[5] Ledvinka, *Ibid.*, pp. 27, 73, 81, 85–86, 175–76, 253–54.

the Civil Rights Act of 1866 speaks directly to race discrimination by granting all citizens:

> the same right in every state and territory to make and enforce contracts, to sue, be parties, give evidence, and to the full and equal benefit for all laws and proceedings for the security of persons and property as is enjoyed by white citizens.

Title VII, Civil Rights Act of 1964 (as amended in 1972)[6]   The Civil Rights Act of 1964 is multi-faceted, covering several areas of discrimination. For the purposes of this text we will review key aspects of title VII. Title VII forbids employment discrimination on the basis of race, color, religion, sex, and national origin. It is the major federal law in the area of fair employment practice and contains the following critical sections:

> *Section 703(a)* – It shall be an unlawful employment practice for an employer
>
> 1. to fail or to refuse to hire or to discharge any individual, or otherwise to discriminate against any individual with respect to his compensation, terms, conditions, or privileges of employment, because of such individual's race, color, religion, sex, or national origin; or
> 2. to limit, segregate, or classify his employees or applicants for employment in any way which would deprive or tend to deprive any individual of employment opportunities or otherwise adversely affect his status as an employee, because of such individual's race, color, religion, sex, or national origin.
>
> *Section 703(b)* – (Title VII forbids) discrimination against any individual because of his race, color, religion, sex, or national origin in admission to, or employment in, any program established to provide apprenticeship or other training.

As the language implies, Title VII coverage is quite broad. Most employment practices can potentially be regulated by Title VII. As amended in 1972, the Act covers 1) public and private employers with 15 or more employees, 2) labor unions with 15 or more members, and 3) public and private employment agencies. Congress established the Equal Employment Opportunity Commission (EEOC) to ensure compliance with the Act and provided for a number of remedies, including backpay awards (limited to two years in Title VII cases).

Age Discrimination in Employment Act of 1967 (as amended in 1978)
While there are differences, the Age Discrimination in Employment Act (ADEA) mirrors the major provisions of Title VII. The Act essentially

---

[6] Taylor and Whitney, *Ibid.*, chapter 22; Ledvinka, *Ibid.*, pp. 25, 27, 33–43.

creates a new protected group (The prohibitions in this Act shall be limited to individuals who are at least 40 years of age but less than 70 years of age—Section 12). Many of the EEO principles governing age are similar to those governing other classifications. However, there are some features of the ADEA that require comment.[7] First, there is only one protected group (people age 40 through 69). Reverse discrimination is not possible. Under the provisions of Title VII, it is illegal to use such factors as race or sex when making employment decisions. Note that Title VII provides protection for minorities and whites or for men and women. ADEA only outlaws discrimination against older people. Second, ADEA specifically regulates retirement. Most employees cannot be forced to retire before age seventy. Finally, ADEA allows employers to differentiate among employees where:

> age is a bona fide occupational qualification reasonably necessary to the normal operation of the particular business, or where the differentiation is based on reasonable factors other than age.   Section 4(f)(1)

The "reasonable factors" provision leads some to reason that ADEA is more permissive than Title VII, even though EEOC regulations seem to suggest that practices having an adverse impact on the protected age group require a demonstration of job-relatedness similar to that required under Title VII.[8]

Vocational Rehabilitation Act of 1973 In 1973 Congress enacted the Vocational Rehabilitation Act to address discrimination against handicapped people. The Act applies only to government contractors and includes an affirmative action requirement. Two important excerpts from the Act are the following:

> Subject to the second sentence of this subparagraph, the term "handicapped individual" means, for purposes of titles IV and V of this Act, any person who (i) has a physical or mental impairment which substantially limits one or more of such person's major life activities, (ii) has a record of such an impairment, or (iii) is regarded as having such an impairment. For purposes of sections 503 and 504 as such sections relate to employment, such term does not include any individual who is an alcoholic or drug abuser whose current use of alcohol or drugs prevents such individual from performing the duties of the job in question or whose employment, by reason of such current alcohol or drug abuse, would constitute a direct threat to property or the safety of others. Section 7(6)(b)
>
> Any contract [or subcontract] in excess of $2,500 entered into by any Federal department or agency for the procurement of personal property and nonpersonal services (including construction) for the United States shall contain a provision requiring that, in employing persons to carry out such contract the

---

[7] Ledvinka, *Ibid.,* pp. 75–77.

[8] Ledvinka, *Ibid.,* p. 76.

party contracting with the United States shall take affirmative action to employ and advance in employment qualified handicapped individuals as defined in section 7(7).   Section 503(a)

The affirmative action obligation is discussed by Department of Labor guidelines that say:

> A contractor must make a reasonable accommodation to the physical and mental limitations of an employee or applicant unless the contractor can demonstrate that such an accommodation would impose an undue hardship on the conduct of the contractor's business. In determining the extent of a contractor's accommodations, the following factors among others may be considered: (1) business necessity and (2) financial cost and expenses.[9]

Executive Orders 11246, 11375, and 11478   Presidential executive orders are directed at federal contractors and subcontractors. Executive Order 11246, as signed by President Johnson in 1965, prohibits discrimination on the basis of race, color, religion, or national origin. Executive Order 11375 prohibits sex-based discrimination and Executive Order 11478 supersedes certain parts of 11246. Taken as a unit these orders provide requirements that are similar to those of Title VII. They differ from Title VII in that they explicitly require covered employers to initiate affirmative action plans (the topic of affirmative action will receive special attention in a subsequent section of this chapter).

Sexual Harassment (as a violation of Title VII)   Government agencies (e.g., the Equal Employment Opportunity Commission), in their role to monitor compliance with federal law, issue a variety of interpretive guidelines. These guidelines help employers understand the terms and conditions of the law and provide strategies for compliance. One recent and controversial issue deals with what is termed "sexual harassment." In 1980 the EEOC published, in the Federal Register, guidelines directed toward this form of sex discrimination. Section 1604.11 of these guidelines reads as follows:

> (a) Harassment on the basis of sex is a violation of Sec. 703 of Title VII. Unwelcome sexual advances, requests for sexual favors, and other verbal or physical conduct of a sexual nature constitute sexual harassment when (1) submission to such conduct is made either explicitly or implicitly a term or condition of an individual's employment. (2) submission to or rejection of such conduct by an individual is used as the basis for employment decisions affecting such individual, or (3) such conduct has the purpose or effect of substantially interfering with an individual's work performance or creating an intimidating, hostile, or offensive working environment.
> (b) In determining whether alleged conduct constitutes sexual harassment, the Commission will look at the record as a whole and at the totality of the circumstances, such as the nature of the sexual advances and the context in

---

[9] Ledvinka, *Ibid.,* p. 87.

which the alleged incidents occurred. The determination of the legality of a particular action will be made from the facts, on a case by case basis.

(c) Applying general Title VII principles, an employer, employment agency, joint apprenticeship committee or labor organization (hereinafter collectively referred to as "employer") is responsible for its acts and those of its agents and supervisory employees with respect to sexual harassment regardless of whether the specific acts complained of were authorized or even forbidden by the employer and regardless of whether the employer knew or should have known of their occurrence. The Commission will examine the circumstances of the particular employment relationship and the job functions performed by the individual in determining whether an individual acts in either a supervisory or agency capacity.

(d) With respect to persons other than those mentioned in paragraph (c) of this section, an employer is responsible for acts of sexual harassment in the workplace where the employer, or its agents or supervisory employees, knows or should have known of the conduct. An employer may rebut apparent liability for such acts by showing that it took immediate and appropriate corrective action.

(e) Prevention is the best tool for the elimination of sexual harassment. An employer should take all steps necessary to prevent sexual harassment from occurring, such as affirmatively raising the subject, expressing strong disapproval, developing appropriate sanctions, informing employees of their right to raise and how to raise the issue of harassment under Title VII, and developing methods to sensitize all concerned.[10]

For some firms' specific examples of how companies are addressing this issue see Example 8–2.

Employment-at-Will While the employment-at-will doctrine receives more detailed treatment in the chapter devoted to the internal staffing process, we will briefly comment on it here. This doctrine relates to the employer's right to dismiss employees at will. This concept does not come from any particular statute. Rather, it is based on a body of common law.[11] While a variety of laws specifically prohibit dismissals based on such factors as sex, race, or being in the 40–70 age group, the employment-at-will doctrine has historically provided that employees may quit or be dismissed at will, for no cause. As noted in the internal staffing chapter, employers generally can terminate employees at will. However, exceptions to this doctrine have increased over the years as a result of legislative and court decisions. Also, employees covered by collective bargaining agreements, written employment contracts, or public employees, represent major exceptions to the employment-at-will doctrine.

---

[10] *Federal Register,* Vol. 45, No. 72, Friday, April 11, 1980, p. 25024.

[11] Daniel J. Koys, Steven Briggs, and Jay E. Grenig, "The Employment-At-Will Doctrine: A Proposal," *Loyola University of Chicago Law Journal, 17,* 1986, pp. 259–274.

EXAMPLE 8.2 — FIRMS CRACK DOWN ON SEXUAL HARASSMENT

A recent Supreme Court decision made it clear that sexual harassment is becoming a particularly complex issue for employers. The Court said that unwanted sexual advances can violate Title VII even if the loss of a job or promotion isn't involved. The key seems to be whether or not such behavior creates a hostile, intimidating, or offensive working environment. Since it is possible for a company to be held liable in such cases, even if management isn't aware of the problem, firms are taking proactive steps to reduce the likelihood of complaints and their associated negative consequences.

* * *

Du Pont has invested approximately $500,000 in a wide-ranging anti-harassment program. The program offers employees practical advise on dealing with harassment and provides skills training in the areas of personal safety, rape and harassment prevention, and assertiveness. In addition, Du Pont threatens harassers with disciplinary action that includes discharge and the company encourages open communication with neutral managers if problems develop.

Philip Morris U.S.A. focuses on harassment prevention by requiring employees to participate in a series of sexual harassment work shops. The program consists of group discussions and a video called "Shades of Gray."

Merck & Co. has adopted an extensive training program that incorporates video dramatization, questionnaries, group exercises, and discussion sessions. Nearly 5,000 employees have completed the program (that lasts from two to three hours) to date.

* * *

Generally, companies are recommended to follow four basic steps when dealing with sexual harassment:

—Prohibit sexual harassment in the workplace by issuing a specific anti-harassment policy.
—Design and implement an internal complaint proceduure.
—Develop employee education programs that encourage people to come forward if they have been harassed.
—Move quickly to investigate and resolve complaints.

Source: Cathy Trost, "With problem more visible, firms crack down on sexual harassment," *Wall Street Journal,* August 28, 1986, p. 17.

Employment Discrimination

Title VII of the Civil Rights Act of 1964 forbids discrimination on the basis of race, color, religion, sex, or national origin (other laws forbid discrimination on the basis of other factors). We have used the term "discrimination" repeatedly, and yet the concept has multiple meanings and leads to considerable confusion when applied to the employment process. For most employment situations, three basic types of illegal discrimination can occur:[12]

1. *Evil intent.* This refers to blatant discrimination in which an employer explicitly refuses to consider members of a protected class for employment opportunities. For example, explicit statements that women or minorities need not apply for a position are clearly illegal.

2. *Differential treatment.* This refers to the application of different employment standards to members of protected classes. For example, conducting race or sex specific reference checks or asking unique interview questions to women represents inappropriate behavior on the part of management.

3. *Adverse impact and a lack of business necessity.* Employment practices that exclude members of a protected class at a higher rate than their counterparts (e.g., 20 percent of the female job applicants are hired while 30 percent of the male applicants are hired) can lead to illegal discrimination if the employer is not able to show that the employment practice is job-related and of business necessity. This important principle is the result of the 1971 Supreme Court decision in *Griggs* v. *Duke Power Company.* This case dealt with the issue of whether discriminatory intent had to be shown in Title VII cases. Given the significance of this case we have reprinted a description of it as it appeared in a 1971 issue of the *Monthly Labor Review.*

Griggs v. *Duke Power Company*[13]

In its Dan River steam station at Draper, N.C., the Duke Power Co. maintained a hiring and promotion requirement of high school diploma for all its employees except those in the lowest paying "labor department," which was virtually reserved for blacks. When the Civil Rights Act went into effect in 1965, the company added another requirement to its criteria—a satisfactory score on two professionally designed tests, one measuring general intelligence, the other mechanical aptitude. The management claimed that these criteria were not intended for discrimination against Negroes, that they were applied to whites as well as to blacks, and that their purpose was, generally, to "improve the overall quality of the work force." (Court's language.) All of this might have been true, but the unavoidable fact was that these standards also discriminated against Negroes. . . . A Federal district court ruled that the company's policy had ceased to be discriminatory when the 1964 law went into effect, and that the impact of past inequities could not be remedied under Title VII because the law was intended for a "prospective" application only. An appeals court agreed that there had been no intentional discrimination, but disagreed as to the law's

---

[12] George F. Dreher and Paul R. Sackett, *Perspectives on Employee Staffing and Selection,* Homewood, Ill: Richard D. Irwin, Inc., 1983, pp. 99–102.

[13] Eugene Skotzo, "Significant Decisions in Labor Cases—*Griggs* v. *Duke Power Company, Monthly Labor Review,* June, 1971, pp. 79–81.

prospective application; residual discrimination resulting from past practices was not beyond the law's remedy, it held.

In the Supreme Court, Chief Justice Burger, who delivered the Court's opinion, phrased the question brought before the bar as being "whether an employer is prohibited by the Civil Rights Act of 1964, Title VII, from requiring high school education or passing of a standardized general intelligence test as a condition of employment in or transfer to jobs when (a) neither standard is shown to be significantly related to successful job performance, (b) both requirements operate to disqualify Negroes at a substantially higher rate than white applicants, and (c) the job in question formerly had been filled only by white employees as part of a longstanding practice of giving preference to whites." The Court's answer was a definite "yes."

Does Title VII prohibit testing of job applicants? No, it does not; educational requirements as well as test scores may be essential to determine whether a man gets the right kind of job and vice versa. And indeed, the Supreme Court said here, "Nothing in the act precludes the use of testing or measuring procedures; obviously, they are useful. . . ." But such tests and other criteria part company with propriety and legality when their avowed purpose is but a sham.

Section 703(h) of the act provides that, "Notwithstanding any other provision of [Title VII], it shall not be an unlawful employment practice for an employer . . . to give and to act upon the results of any professionally developed ability test provided that such test, its administration or action upon the results is not designed, intended, or used to discriminate because of race, color, religion, sex or national origin. . . ." There is no absolute prohibition of ability tests here, there is only the condition that they not be used for purposes of discrimination. Yet this somewhat involuted and negative phraseology of a conditional approval does not deprive the statutory provision of its potential for a positive function in preventing discrimination, as has been demonstrated in this case.

"What Congress has prohibited," said the High Court, "is giving these [testing] devices and mechanisms controlling force unless they are demonstrably a reasonable measure of job performance. Congress has not commanded that the less qualified be preferred over the better qualified simply because of minority origins. Far from disparaging job qualifications as such, Congress has made such qualifications the controlling factor, so that race, religion, nationality, and sex become irrelevant. . . ." Obviously, then, "The touchstone is business necessity. If an employment practice which operates to exclude Negroes cannot be shown to be related to job performance, the practice is prohibited."

There may, however, be a situation where—as the employer claimed to be true in this case—a test or other criterion is not exactly job-related, nor is the employer's motive improper. What then? Is the standard proscribed?

The Court concerned itself with this type of situation, and its answer was somewhat in line with the old saying that good intentions may, and often do, pave the road to hell. It said, "good intent or absence of discriminatory intent does not redeem employment procedures or testing mechanics that operate as 'built-in headwinds' for minority groups and are unrelated to measuring job capability." And, "Under the act, practices, procedures, or tests neutral on their face, and even neutral in terms of intent, cannot be maintained if they operate to 'freeze' that status quo of prior discriminatory employment practices.

As already mentioned, the employer sought refuge in the fact that its hiring and promotion criteria applied equally to whites and blacks. Chief Justice Burger, who delivered the opinion of the Court, referred to the petitioners' "inferior education [received] in the segregated schools" and cited Aesop's fable about the fox, the stork, and a shallow dish of milk before them: ". . . Congress has . . . provided that tests or criteria for employment or promotion may not provide equality of opportunity only in the sense of the fabled offer of milk to the stork and the fox. On the contrary, Congress has . . . required that the posture and condition of the job-seeker be taken into account. It has—to resort again to the fable—provided that the vessel in which the milk is preferred be one all seekers can use. The act proscribes not only overt discrimination but also practices that are fair in form, but discriminatory in operation. . . ."

The Court stressed more than once that "Congress did not intend by Title VII . . . to guarantee a job to every person regardless of qualifications. . . . Discriminatory preference for any group, minority or majority, is precisely and only what Congress has proscribed. What is required by Congress is the removal of artificial, arbitrary, and unnecessary barriers of employment when the barriers operate invidiously to discriminate on the basis of racial or other impermissible classifications." The appellate court's holding that the practices complained of had no purpose or intent of racial discrimination was overruled.

At this point, most of our attention has been directed at the concept of equal employment opportunity. The essence of this concept is that inappropriate employment barriers should be removed. Irrelevant information (e.g., race, sex) should not be considered when making staffing decisions. Each person should be considered for employment opportunities solely on the basis of his or her qualifications. However, recall the dilemma discussed by James Rosenbaum. If we allow unequal outcomes to serve as inputs in subsequent rounds of competition for jobs, can barrier-free employment practices in these subsequent rounds of competition ever fully compensate for past segregation and inequality of opportunity? It is to this issue we now turn our attention by commenting on the concept of "affirmative action."

Affirmative Action

Many people argue that the intent of Title VII (and related laws and executive orders) was to provide more than "equal opportunity." This goal was to increase the representation of minority groups and women in job categories traditionally staffed by white men (resulting in "equal" or "proportional" employment). The time it will take to increase minority and female representation will likely be a function of a variety of factors. Multiple roles are available for employers. Seligman[14] has outlined four

---

[14] D. Seligman, "How Equal Opportunity Turned into Employment Quotas," *Fortune,* March, 1973, 160–168.

approaches to addressing employment discrimination that serve to clarify the differences between equal opportunity and affirmative action.

1. *Passive nondiscrimination.* This represents an equal opportunity stance. Over time, the elimination of irrelevant employment barriers should increase minority representation in the work force. However, since discrimination is still prevalent in other areas (e.g., the quality and availability of educational and training experiences), increases in minority representation will likely come very slowly.

2. *Active recruiting.* This represents the first step in taking an affirmative action stance. Applicants for job openings are evaluated solely on the basis of job-related qualifications. The affirmative action takes place by attempting to increase the pool of qualified minority applicants. Minority conscious recruiting (taking exceptional steps to notify protected class members of job openings) should increase the number of qualified minority applicants, resulting in an increase in minority employment.

3. *Minority preference.* This represents a major philosophical shift from the previous approaches. Group membership is explicitly recognized as a potential factor in making employment decisions. The most conservative strategy is to use group membership as a factor only when all other things are essentially equal. For example, given two equally qualified job candidates, preference would be given to the minority applicant.

4. *Proportional hiring.* The most extreme position is represented by a quota approach to employment decision making. A fixed numerical hiring objective is set and a fixed proportion of openings is reserved for protected class members. This represents the fastest way to increase minority representation in the work force.

The last three approaches all represent forms of affirmative action. The degree to which an employer can use group membership as a factor in reaching employment decisions is, of course, very controversial. The legal environment in this area always has been uncertain. A landmark Supreme Court case in this area was *Steelworkers* v. *Weber.* The controversy is clearly depicted in a summary of the case that appeared in the *Monthly Labor Review* not long after the Court reached a decision. That summary is reproduced below.

Steelworkers v. Weber[15]

Voluntary affirmative action programs that utilize quotas to eliminate racial imbalances in "traditionally segregated job categories" are permissible under Title VII in the 1964 Civil Rights Act. . . .A 5-to-2 majority rejected arguments that the law prohibited such programs because, by using quotas, they discriminate on the basis of race. Instead, the Court reasoned that the legislative history of Title VII and the historical context in which the act arose "make clear that an interpretation . . . that forbade all race-conscious affirmative action would

---

[15] Gregory J. Mounts, "Significant Decisions in Labor Cases – *Steelworkers* v. *Weber,*" *Monthly Labor Review,* August 1979, pp. 56–57.

'bring about an end completely at variance with the purpose of the statute' and must be rejected. . . ."

The voluntary plan in question designed in 1974 by the United Steelworkers and Kaiser Aluminum, provided that half of all entrants in a craft training program be black. The plan was to remain in effect until the percentage of black craftworkers (1.83 percent in 1974) approximated the percentage of blacks in the local labor market (39 percent in 1974). During 1974, seven blacks and six whites were selected as craft trainees. The most junior black selected had less seniority than several white production workers not selected; one of these workers, Brian Weber, filed suit claiming a violation of Title VII.

Writing for the Court, Justice William Brennan emphasized the narrowness of the case: "The only question before us is the narrow statutory issue of whether Title VII forbids private employers and unions from voluntarily agreeing upon bona fide affirmative action plans that accord racial preferences in the manner and for the purpose provided in the Kaiser—USWA plan."

Subsections 703(a) and (d) of Title VII make it unlawful to "discriminate . . . because of . . . race" in hiring and in the selection of apprentices for training programs. Weber claimed that this language, read in the context of a 1976 Supreme Court ruling that "Title VII protects whites as well as blacks from certain forms of racial discrimination," prohibited the Kaiser-USWA plan.

Brennan acknowledged that Weber's argument "is not without force. But," he continued, "it overlooks the significance of the fact that the Kaiser—USWA plan is an affirmative action plan voluntarily adopted by private parties to eliminate traditional patterns of racial segregation. In this context, respondent's reliance upon a literal construction of Section 703(a) and (d) and upon [our earlier ruling] is misplaced. It is a 'familiar rule that a thing may be within the letter of the statute and yet not within the statute, because not within its spirit, nor within the intention of its makers.' "

Brennan turned to the legislative history and found that "Congress' primary concern" in enacting the prohibition against racial discrimination in Title VII was with "the plight of the Negro in our economy." He cited the House Report which suggested that the law ". . . will create an atmosphere conducive to voluntary or local resolution of other forms of discrimination." He concluded that Congress "did not intend wholly to prohibit private and voluntary affirmative action efforts. . . ."

Brennan also found support for his view in the language and history of Section 703(j) of Title VII. Congress wrote that nothing contained in Title VII "shall be interpreted to require any employer . . . to grant preferential treatment . . . to any group because of the race . . . of such . . . group." Brennan reasoned that the lawmakers could have substituted *permit* for *require* if they had intended to outlaw all voluntary race-conscious affirmative action.

Although the Court's decision removed much of the uncertainty surrounding the use of racial goals and quotas in voluntary affirmative action plans, the majority declined to expand its ruling:

> We need not today define in detail the line of demarcation between permissible and impermissible affirmative action plans. It suffices to hold that the challenged Kaiser—USWA affirmative action plan falls on the permissible side of the line. The purposes of the plan mirror those of the statute. Both were designed to break down old patterns of racial segrega-

tion and hierarchy. Both were structured to "open employment opportunities for Negroes in occupations which have traditionally been closed to them."

In dissent, Chief Justice Warren Burger complained that the majority ruling, through "intellectually dishonest means," does "precisely what both . . . sponsors and opponents agreed that the statute was not intended to do." It illustrates, Burger noted, the old adage that "hard cases make bad law."

Justice William Rehnquist, also in dissent, scored the "Orwellian" tone of the ruling:

> Whether described as "benign discrimination" or "affirmative action," the racial quota is nonetheless a creator of castes, a two-edged sword that must demean one in order to prefer another. In passing Title VII, Congress outlawed all discrimination, recognizing that no discrimination based on race is benign, that no action disadvantaging a person because of his color is affirmative. With today's holding, the Court introduces into Title VII a tolerance for the very evil that the law was intended to eradicate, without offering a clue as to what the limits on that tolerance may be. We are simply told that Kaiser's racially discriminatory admission quota "falls on the permissible side of the line." By going not merely beyond, but directly against Title VII's language and legislative history, the Court has sown the wind. Later courts will face the impossible task of reaping the whirlwind.

While *Steelworkers* v. *Weber* represents a rather narrow ruling, the Supreme Court reaffirmed its support for the concept of affirmative action in two recent decisions.[16] The first case involved firefighters in Cleveland where the city and minority firefighters agreed (in a plan to settle a lawsuit) to promote whites and minorities on a 1-to-1 ratio. In a 6–3 decision the Supreme Court said the agreement resembled the voluntary affirmative action plan approved by the Court in the steelworkers' case and was not a violation of federal civil rights law. In a second case the Court upheld a ruling against the Sheet Metal Workers' union in New York. The union was sued for excluding minorities from membership and was under a court order to achieve a goal of 29 percent minority membership and provide training assistance to minority workers. The Court endorsed the idea that affirmative steps may be appropriate when dealing with persistent patterns of discrimination even for those workers who were not direct victims of bias. While the limits to preferential treatment are not yet fully defined, it is clear that certain forms of affirmative action do not violate Title VII or related laws. One principle that seems to be emerging is that, under certain conditions, affirmative action is allowable if it does not go too far in creating undue hardships for the majority. For example, a procedure that deprives a majority person of a promotion or an opportunity to participate in training is more likely to be acceptable than a layoff resulting from affirmative action. See Example 8–3 for a recent example of this principle.

---

[16] Andy Pasztor and Stephen Wermiel, "Supreme Court Reaffirms its Support for Affirmative Action in Employment," *Wall Street Journal,* July 3, 1986, p. 3.

EXAMPLE 8.3   THE COURT FAVORS SENIORITY OVER
MINORITY

In 1980 a court-approved affirmative action plan required that at least 50 percent
of all new Memphis fire fighters be black
until two-fifths of the department was
black. The plan had increased the proportion of black fire fighters from 4 percent
in 1974 to over 11 percent in 1980. Then,
as a result of a 1981 budget crisis, the city
followed the seniority system negotiated
with the union and started laying off employees (including many new black fire
fighters).

The Supreme Court ruled in favor of
the city and against Carl Stotts (the black
fire fighter who brought the original suit).
Writing for the court, Justice White found
that Title VII of the Civil Rights Act of
1964 "protects bona fide seniority systems" unless found to be intentionally discriminatory.

Source: *Time,* June 25, 1984, p. 63.

Let us stress, however, that you should be alert to court decisions reached
since the publication of this text.

Managerial Response

Managers are confronted with a vast array of federal and state laws and
regulations that affect employment decisions. There are two general strategies management can follow to comply with this area of regulation. One is
to make employment decisions that do not adversely affect protected class
members. The focus here is on removing adverse impact from all staffing
systems. The second approach is to use the most job-related procedure
available when making employment decisions. There is a cost here.
However, as developed in subsequent chapters, the introduction of job-
related selection techniques often represents a very cost-effective way to
increase productivity. We believe a good case can be made for the use of
such systems. The benefits often outweigh the costs (resulting in sound
management decision-making) and job-relatedness serves as a defense if
protected class members are adversely affected by the practice. We therefore recommend following the guidelines provided by regulatory agencies
(taking into account new knowledge and professional standards) when
designing and implementing staffing systems. In particular, employers
should review the Uniform Guidelines on Employee Selection Procedures.[17] These guidelines describe acceptable methods for establishing the

---

[17] Uniform Guidelines on Employee Selection Procedures, *Federal Register,* Vol. 43, no.
166, August 25, 1978, pp. 38295–38309.

job-relatedness of procedures used for such things as hiring and promoting employees. It usually will be to the advantage of the firm to follow an equal employment opportunity stance and focus on job-related employment criteria. The degree to which affirmative action works to the advantage of the firm represents a more complex issue. As suggested in Figure 7–1 (Chapter 7), there can be marginal societal benefits that do not provide immediate returns to the firm associated with certain inputs (in this case the initiation of an affirmative action plan).

Regulation Affecting Wages

Government regulation can dictate prices, dictate allocations of resources, or determine the rules by which prices and allocations are set. The previous section (on regulations on hiring and promotion) discussed regulations that set rules under which labor is allocated and priced. The next section (on health and safety regulations) will discuss regulations that dictate allocations of resources. This section will discuss regulations that dictate prices. As will be discussed, regulation of prices usually generates incentives to alter resource allocations.

Wage regulation is introduced when it appears that wage outcomes, in the absence of regulations, are unfair or otherwise inappropriate. Thus, minimum wage legislation has been enforced in the belief that it will ameliorate poverty among the working poor and anti-wage discrimination legislation is enforced in the belief that to offer differentially low wages on the basis of race or sex is unfair.

Some wage regulations, those that prohibit wage differentials based on non-productivity-related characteristics, for example, are passed in the interest of society as a whole. To eliminate such wage differentials restores efficiency to labor markets. Other wage regulations, such as those requiring the payment of the union wage scale to non-union workers in certain cases, are passed largely in the interests of union laborers and of their employers. In those cases, union members no longer need fear competition from lower-paid non-union substitutes and employers of union labor no longer need fear competition from employers who, by virtue of their non-union status, have lower labor costs.

Equal Wage Regulation

A large body of statute law dictates that employers may not pay lower wages to certain employees because of their race, sex, religion, national origin, age, or disabled status. The Equal Pay Act of 1963 requires that employers pay the same wage to women as to men when the two perform the same work. Title VII of the Civil Rights Act of 1964 forbade, for all but the smallest employers, discrimination in pay (as well as in hiring and promotion) on the basis of race, sex, religion, or national origin. The Equal

Employment Opportunity Act of 1972 reinforced that rule. The Age Discrimination in Employment Act of 1967 and the Rehabilitation Act of 1973 forbid unequal treatment on other bases.

Economists have long grappled with the reason why wealth-maximizing firms would pay some workers more (or less) than others who perform equally well.[18] Becker's theory that employers have a taste for discrimination (or that employers pander to other employees' tastes for discrimination) leads to the conclusion that the least racist and/or sexist employer could, by hiring only the disadvantaged, lower his labor costs and gain a competitive advantage over all others.[19]

Phelps' argument, that employers pay some groups less because they are unable to obtain reliable predictors of that group's productivity, has been a subject of some controversy.[20] Aigner and Cain were critical of the theory as originally stated, but found the notion of cheap but unreliable information to be useful in building a model in which wages were unequal between groups.[21] Smith used the Phelps approach as a starting point to construct a complex model in which unequal wages were the necessary result of differences in the reliability of productivity predictors across groups.[22] Whatever may be the source of wage discrimination, the elimination of unequal pay for equal work would make labor markets function more efficiently.[23]

The effect of the regulations outlawing wage discrimination is difficult to assess. Several scholars have found salutary effects attributable to the enactment and enforcement of equal pay laws.[24] Other scholars have sounded more pessimistic notes. Lazear suggested that, while entry level wages of blacks have risen, they may have done so at the expense of lower wages in later years.[25] Lower entry level wages for blacks, Lazear argued,

---

[18] For a survey of the early literature, see Ray Marshall, "The Economics of Racial Discrimination: A Survey," *Journal of Economic Literature* vol. 12, no. 3 (September 1974): 849–871.

[19] Gary S. Becker, *The Economics of Discrimination,* second edition, Chicago: University of Chicago Press, 1971.

[20] Edmund S. Phelps, "The Statistical Theory of Racism and Sexism," *American Economic Review* vol. 62, no. 4 (September 1972): 659–661.

[21] Dennis J. Aigner and Glen G. Cain, "Statistical Theories of Discrimination in Labor Markets," *Industrial and Labor Relations Review* vol. 30, no. 2 (January 1977): 175–187.

[22] Marvin M. Smith, "Towards a General Equilibrium Theory of Racial Wage Discrimination," *Southern Economic Journal* vol. 45, no. 2 (October 1978): 458–568.

[23] The more controversial topics of affirmative action and equal pay for *comparable* worth are discussed above.

[24] See, for example, Robert J. Flanagan, "Actual Versus Potential Impact of Government Antidiscrimination Programs," *Industrial and Labor Relations Review* vol. 29, no. 4 (July 1976): 486–507; and Richard B. Freeman, "Changes in the Labor Market for Black Americans, 1948–72," *Brookings Papers on Economic Activity* (1: 1973): 67–131.

[25] Edward Lazear, "The Narrowing of Black-White Wage Differentials Is Illusory," *American Economic Review* vol. 69, no. 4 (September 1979): 553–564.

permitted early training (the wage differential's being the price of the training), which led to higher earnings (returns to training) later in working life. The absence of the entry level wage differential will, then, according to Lazear, deny those training opportunities to young blacks and their earnings will not rise as much as they otherwise would.

Andrea Beller developed an even more interesting theory of the effect of equal pay regulations.[26] Employers, Beller argued, perceive differences between whites and non-whites and between men and women. Whether or not those differences affect productivity is irrelevant, as long as employers believe that they do. Enforcement of equal pay regulations, then, raises the pay of non-whites relative to whites and of women relative to men. One would expect, then, a substitution effect due to the changing relative wage. As, for example, women's wages rise relative to those of men, Beller predicted a substitution of men for women on firms' payrolls. Beller, finding some empirical support for her prediction, argued then that anti-wage discrimination regulation weakens the effects of antiemployment discrimination regulation.

Minimum Wage Legislation

Among the most controversial forms of wage regulation is the imposition of a minimum wage in most private establishments and, after 1985, in much of state and local government.[27] The Fair Labor Standards Act of 1938 guarantees a minimum wage ($3.35 per hour as of 1987) to all employees in interstate commerce, other than in a small number of specified circumstances. The FLSA also mandates that overtime premiums be paid to hourly-rated employees for work in excess of forty hours per week.[28]

The controversy over the minimum wage (see Example 8–4) is over whether the wage reduces the incidence of poverty (by raising wages) or increases unemployment among the least skilled (by requiring that employers pay labor more than it is worth.) Secondary issues relate to whether the wage reduces the amount of on-the-job training available (if employers cannot reduce wages during training periods, they may be unwilling to provide that training) and whether or not the minimum wage has differen-

---

[26] Andrea H. Beller, "The Economics of Enforcement of Title VII of the Civil Rights Act of 1964," University of Wisconsin-Madison, Institute for Research on Poverty, Working Paper No. 313–75, October 1975.

[27] See Finis Welch, "Minimum Wage Legislation in the United States," *Economic Inquiry* Vol. 12, no. 3 (September 1974): 285–318; and William E. Brock, "The Application of the FLSA to State and Local Governments," *Labor Law Journal* vol. 36, no. 10 (October 1985): 739–743.

[28] Managerial response to the overtime premium is discussed in Chapter 5, above. See Ronald G. Ehrenberg, "Heterogeneous Labor, the Internal Labor Market, and the Dynamics of the Employment-Hours Decision," *Journal of Economic Theory* vol. 3, no. 1 (March 1971): 85–104; and Ronald G. Ehrenberg, "The Impact of the Overtime Premium on Employment and Hours in U.S. Industry," *Western Economic Journal* vol. 9, no. 2 (June 1971): 199–207.

EXAMPLE 8.4 THE MINIMUM WAGE DEBATE "THE
WORKING POOR DESERVE A RAISE"
BY SAR A. LEVITAN AND ISAAC SHAPIRO

Economists are predicting continued economic growth and prosperity for the foreseeable future, and that is good news. Unfortunately, the millions of Americans who work for the minimum wage are not sharing this prosperity. The real value of the minimum—which was designed to protect the working poor by placing a floor under their meager earnings—is now at its lowest level since 1955.

At $3.35 an hour, the minimum wage is still at the same level it was in January 1981. In that same time, the cost of living has risen by 26 percent, so that a full-time, year-round minimum wage worker currently earns income equivalent to only 76 percent of the poverty level for a family of three.

* * *

An adequate minimum wage reinforces the work ethic. A worker earning a reasonable minimum not only gains economic independence but also moves his family above the poverty level. Greater work effort also boosts productivity and cuts the welfare rolls.

* * *

The minimum wage may indeed cause some job loss, but its posititive income and work-incentive effects outweigh this loss. The current challenge is for Congress to establish a minimum wage that strikes the right balance between loss in employment and a rise in earnings. The minimum wage is now so low that we could raise the minimum substantially without significant job loss.

* * *

A youth sub-minimum would encourage employers to hire teenagers instead of adults, and would lower the earnings of employable youths. Also, it would be of least help to the youngsters who need the most help—disadvantaged youths do not live in the areas where new jobs might be created. Moreover, many of these young people, lacking job skills, need training before employers will hire them.

* * *

The purchasing power of the minimum wage should be raised by modest annual increments—say, 5 percent annually—until it is equivalent to its traditional level of half the average hourly earnings in private industry. In current dollars, the target level is $4.36 an hour. The minimum wage is now 38 percent of the average hourly wage, its lowest level by this measure since 1949.

In the absence of Congressional action, the minimum wage will continue to wither. The notion that state action will supplant Federal policy is false. Only three states have a minimum higher than the Federal standard.

Congress should raise the minimum wage to assist the working poor and other minimum-wage earners. This would be the surest way to increase their income without raising the Federal deficit. More working Americans would then share in the benefits of continued economic growth.

THE MINIMUM WAGE DEBATE (CONTINUED) "AN INCREASE WOULD HURT TEENAGERS" BY MARVIN H. KOSTERS

Is it time once again to raise the minimum wage? It has indeed fallen since it was last raised in 1981, after adjustment for inflation and relative to average wages. But we should look carefully at the consequences of raising the minimum.

The most obvious effect is that some workers would get higher wages. If this were the whole story, raising the minimum wage would be a very promising strategy and there would be no reason to settle for a small increase. Since this is only part of the story, it is essential to consider the other, less direct effects.

First, research on previous increases has established that the argument is no longer about whether but about how much a rise in the minimum wage reduces employment.

* * *

But the story does not end here. When fewer jobs are available, teenagers face difficulties in developing valuable work experience. In addition, minimum wages encourage employers to emphasize work that contributes to their revenues and to skimp on on-the-job training.

* * *

Curiously, the same people who would raise the minimum wage think nothing of subsidizing education and, at the post-secondary level, paying hefty tuition fees along with the "work" that schooling entails. Some young people, however, choose work instead of schooling. Why should these workers willing to "pay"—in the form of lower current earnings for jobs with more training content

—be prevented by the minimum wage from making such arrangements?

* * *

Regrettably, data on how many poor families might benefit from a higher minimum wage are scant. Estimates show that only about 6 percent of household heads work for wages at or below the minimum, and about 10 percent of households with poverty-level incomes may include a year-round full-time worker.

* * *

Despite data limitations, certain generalizations are possible. First, the principal reasons for low incomes are not low wages but the absence of work for those who are employable and the absence of transfer payments for those who are not. Second, income from sources other than earnings, especially transfers, is so broadly distributed today that the link between earnings and levels of living has been greatly weakened. Most analysts agree that raising minimum wages is a remarkably ineffectual policy for reducing poverty or reducing income inequality.

* * *

Both the detailed examination of the effects of minimum wages on particular groups and general performance in the economy point to a simple conclusion: however well intentioned, boosting the minimum wage is not a policy that deserves support.

tial effects on some groups, especially women and the very young.[29] While the argument over the minimum wage has raged hot and heavy, the percentage of the labor force affected directly is rather small, given the relatively low level at which the minimum wage is set.[30]

The argument about whether the labor force as a whole is made better or worse off by the minimum wage is, essentially, an argument about the overall elasticity of demand for labor. The elasticity of demand for labor is the percentage change in quantity of labor demanded for a one percent change in the wage rate (defined broadly to include fringe benefits as well as money wages). If the elasticity of demand for labor is between 0 and −1 an increase in the minimum wage will increase the total income of the labor force. If the elasticity of demand for labor is between −1 and negative infinity, an increase in the minimum wage will decrease the total income of the labor force, although increasing the earnings of those low-wage workers who keep their jobs.

Gramlich found the minimum wage to have little effect on the earnings of adult men, but to have significant effects on other groups.[31] In particular, higher minimum wages generate a substitution of adult women for teenagers. Gramlich also found that the minimum wage did little to redistribute income toward low income households.

Wage Regulation for Government Contractors

Those employers who elect to bid for government contracts face yet another form of wage regulation. The Davis-Bacon Act of 1931 mandates that firms engaging in construction work under U.S. Government contracts pay the locally prevailing wage, usually interpreted to be the local union wage rate. Ostensibly to prevent the exploitation of construction workers by government contractors, the Act also protects union construction workers and their employers from being under-bid by non-union firms.

The Walsh-Healey Act of 1937 mandates that government contractors outside construction pay a minimum wage; such mimima to be set for specific industries by the Secretary of Labor. Davis-Bacon and Walsh-Healey wage regulations have been subjected to substantial criticism on the grounds that they erode economic efficiency by government contractors.[32]

---

[29] See Sherwin Rosen, "Learning and Experience in the Labor Market," *Journal of Human Resources* vol. 7, no. 3 (Summer 1972): 326–342; and Marvin Kosters and Finis Welch, "The Effects of Minimum Wages on the Distribution of Changes in Aggregate Employment," *American Economic Review* vol. 62, no. 3 (June 1972): 323–332.

[30] Edward M. Gramlich, "Impact of Minimum Wages on Other Wages, Employment, and Family Incomes," *Brookings Papers on Economic Activity* (2, 1976), pp. 421–423.

[31] Gramlich, "Impact of Minimum Wages" (1976), pp. 409–462.

[32] See, for example, Robert S. Goldfarb and John F. Morrall III, "The Davis-Bacon Act: An Appraisal of Recent Studies," *Industrial and Labor Relations Review* vol. 34, no. 2 (January 1981): 191–206.

From a public policy perspective, the efficiency costs of Davis-Bacon and Walsh-Healey must be weighed against the benefits of enforcement of the Acts. Those benefits may include the (difficult to monetize) effects of preventing jobs from moving to those contractors who offer the lowest wages to the least skilled employees; and preventing the federal government from becoming an (indirect) employer at substandard wages.

From the standpoint of the firm, Davis-Bacon and Walsh-Healey should be evaluated from a different perspective. Consider a small manufacturer of machine tool products. Acceptance of a federal contract to supply fasteners could provide higly desired stable cash flows. Such acceptance, however, comes at the expense of Walsh-Healey wage regulation. Will the firm be required to raise the wages of all employees in some classification in order to accept a contract that might constitute only a fraction of its revenues? Further, acceptance of a federal contract would subject the firm to affirmative action regulation, with its own costs.

For most types of regulation, the relevant question for employers is, "How can I comply at minimum cost?" For Davis-Bacon and Walsh-Healey regulation, the relevant question for employers is, "Do I want to be subject to such wage controls at all?"

Public Policies on Health and Safety in the Workplace

An area that has come under intense regulatory scrutiny is the physical safety of the workplace. Students of industrial safety use the term "industrial safety" to refer to freedom from accidents and the term "industrial health" to refer to freedom from workplace related disease. Health and safety, although different in many ways, are covered by the same items of legislation.

To a great extent, the safety of the workplace is beyond the control of either managers or regulators. First, many accidents are caused by nonrecurring conditions (bad weather) or by employee carelessness. Neither of those can be directly controlled. Second, there are inherent risks in life. Some occupations (fire-fighting) and some industries (non-residential construction) are innately riskier than other occupations (university teaching) and other industries (banking).

Further, Smith has demonstrated that as unemployment rates fall (and firms begin to hire less experienced employees) occupational injury rates rise.[33] Falling accident rates, sometimes offered as evidence of successful regulation, are often the result of recession and rising unemployment.

---

[33] Robert S. Smith, "Intertemporal Changes in Work Injury Rates," *Proceedings of the Annual Meeting of the Industrial Relations Research Association,* 1972, pp. 167–174.

There is, however, considerable scope for managerial influence of the rate of industrial accidents. Indeed, the prevalence of safety departments, often staffed by graduate engineers, in many manufacturing and public utility firms is but one indication of private concern over the costs of industrial accidents. Managements have several sorts of incentives to control accidents in their workplaces. First, industrial accidents impose direct costs on the firm. Accidents generate downtime. Higher accident rates lead to higher Workers' Compensation premia. Severe accidents lead to the need to replace injured staff, thus imposing hiring and training costs.

As was argued in Chapter 6, the firm with higher-than-average accident rates incurs other costs as well. It must pay a compensating wage differential to attract workers. The higher the accident rate (and, therefore, the higher the *ex ante* expected loss to the employee), the higher will be the compensating wage differential required by the employee. Managements, then, have incentives to seek the optimal trade-off between the costs of accidents and the costs of providing a safe workplace. The myth of callous management ignoring physical danger to its employees is not descriptive of any but a small, short-sighted minority of firms.

Table 8–1 illustrates the relative safety of most American workplaces. While there is rather a lot of interindustry variation in injury rates, most American workers have a low probability of injury on the job.

While it is in the interest of the firm's residual claimants to control (but not to minimize) the rate of accident, there are costs of accidents not borne by the firm. Principle among these is the pain and suffering of the victim. As discussed in Chapter 7, such "spillover" costs suggest that some form of regulation is appropriate. Figure 8–1 reproduces the spillover analysis that was depicted in Figure 7–1.

Because there are social costs of accidents not borne by the firm, there are social benefits from the use of safety inputs not received by the firm. The

	United States Total Cases	Lost Work-Day Care
1972	10.9	3.3
1973	11.0	3.4
1974	10.4	3.5
1975	9.1	3.3
1976	9.2	3.5
1977	9.3	3.8
1978	9.4	4.1
1979	9.5	4.3
1980	8.7	4.0
1981	8.3	3.8
1982	7.7	3.5

Source: U.S. Department of Labor, Bureau of Labor Statistics, *Handbook of Labor Statistics, 1985,* Washington, D.C.: U.S. Government Printing Office, 1985, p. 412.

Table 8–1   **Occupational Injury and Illness Rates Incidents Per 100 Full-Time Workers Per Year**

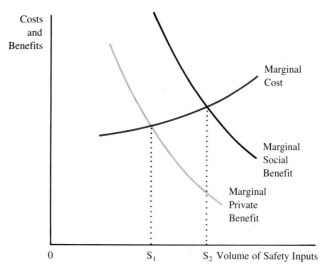

Figure 8-1   **Intervention Justified by Spillover Effects**

firm, left to its own private decision calculus, would provide too few safety inputs (S_1, rather than S_2). One way to induce firms to provide a level of safety inputs closer to the social optimal is to make firms bear the costs of accidents whether or not they are at fault and to charge higher insurance premia for firms with higher accident rates.

"Liability without fault" and "experience rating" are two of the cornerstones of the Workers' Compensation system. While Workers' Compensation was intended to be an income maintenance program, providing income support and medical payments to injured workers one of its unintended consequences has been to generate stronger incentives for accident control than would otherwise have been the case.

In the late 1960s, national concern focused on what were viewed as unacceptably high levels of industrial accidents and dangerously high rates of exposure to toxic substances in many workplaces. The response of Congress was to pass the Williams-Steiger Occupational Safety and Health Act of 1970, popularly known as OSHA.[34] OSHA covers all but the smallest of private workplaces in the United States.

The approach to safety regulation taken by OSHA does not rely on incentives, but mandates that every firm adhere to safety and health (toxic substance exposure) standards promulgated by the Occupational Safety and Health Administration (also known as OSHA), part of the U.S. Department of Labor. Research on safety and health standards is to be conducted by the National Institute on Occupational Safety and Health (NIOSH), part

---

[34] See Robert S. Smith, *The Occupational Safety and Health Act,* Washington, D.C.: American Enterprise Institute, 1976.

of the U.S. Department of Health and Human Services. Workplaces are to be inspected for violations, with fines for violations to be set by the Occupational Safety and Health Review Board.

Debates over OSHA began even before the law became effective in April 1971. One area of debate was over the appropriateness of standard-setting as a means of controlling accidents. Note that OSHA imposes no penalties for accidents, only for violation of standards. Some felt that a better approach was to impose accident penalties and then to allow firms to find the best way to control accidents.[35]

Unfortunately, reasoned opposition to OSHA and to the standard-setting approach to safety regulation has often been confused with lack of concern for safe workplaces. As Northrup, Rowan, and Perry pointed out, however, major criticism of OSHA has sometimes come from safety professionals who found their safety priorities usurped by the mandates of OSHA.[36] Some of these professionals believed that they knew their own industries and workplaces and should be left alone to improve safety outcomes as they saw fit.

Another interesting and controversial feature of OSHA is its absolutist approach to standard-setting and enforcement. Standards are to be set and enforced without regard to cost-benefit calculations. No firm can challenge a standard or appeal a fine on the basis that the violated standard is not a cost-effective accident deterrent.

The debate over the effectiveness of OSHA as an accident-reducing regulation can never be resolved. One of the mandates of the legislation itself was a new manner of collecting accident data. The pre-OSHA accident data collection program of the U.S. Bureau of Labor Statistics (a division of the U.S. Department of Labor) was terminated. As the two data series are inconsistent, no one has been able to perform a fully discriminating test on the effect of OSHA on accident rates. Smith, however, found that the experience of an OSHA inspection resulted in a reduced accident rate.[37]

Whatever has been the effectiveness of OSHA in reducing accidents, it remains the law of the land. Managements must develop an optimal way of living with OSHA standards. Several approaches are possible. Originally, inspections were so infrequent and fines so low that expected penalties for violations of standards were almost trivially small.[38] As first offense

---

[35] See, for example, Robert S. Smith, "The Feasibility of an 'Injury Tax' Approach to Occupational Safety," *Law and Contemporary Problems* vol. 38, no. 3 (Summer-Autumn 1974): 730–744; or Albert L. Nichols and Richard Zechkauser, "Government Comes to the Workplace: An Assessment of OSHA," *The Public Interest* vol. 49 (Fall 1977): 39–69.

[36] Herbert R. Northrup, Richard L. Rowan, and Charles R. Perry, *The Impact of OSHA,* Philadelphia: Industrial Research Unit, The Wharton School, University of Pennsylvania, 1978, p. 47.

[37] Robert S. Smith, "The Impact of OSHA Inspections on Manufacturing Injury Rates," *Journal of Human Resources* vol. 14, no. 2 (Spring 1979): 145–170.

[38] Robert S. Smith, *The Occupational Safety and Health Act* (1976), pp. 61–64.

violations carried such small expected penalties, many firms found an optimal response in ignoring OSHA standards until found in violation. Possible criminal penalties for failure to comply with standards after being found in violation make later compliance important.

Northrup, Rowan, and Perry report one firm's use of a more sophisticated response.[39] The firm's safety staff divided the violations into four categories. The most critical (category A) were those in which the standard violation constituted a real danger to employees. The least critical (category D) were those believed to be trivial or believed to be based on safety standards about to be changed by OSHA. Category A violations received immediate attention, while category D violations were noted with no response planned.

An interesting and important issue concerns what to do about violations in categories B and C (where immediate danger is not present, but in which the standard is unlikely to be repealed). For such cases, the firm's rule might be to consider the present value of the cash outflows due to conviction. These can be compared to the present value of the cash outflow saved due to correction. The cash outflow savings include future fines that need not be paid, (possible) compensating wage differentials saved, and (possible) production down-time avoided.

While OSHA is the most widely discussed industrial safety and health program in the United States, the discussion here would be incomplete without mention of the Workers' Compensation laws.[40] Workers' Compensation laws are state laws that evolved beginning in 1895. Prior to the enactment of these laws, employers who were sued for damages due to industrial accidents could rely on any or all of three defenses: the "fellow-worker" defense (it was another worker, not the firm, that was responsible); "contributory negligence" (the worker was responsible for his own injury); and the "doctrine of the assumption of risk" (the worker knew the risks inherent in his job and assumed them voluntarily).

Workers' Compensation laws set up insurance plans under which the employer provided compensation for damages, whether or not he was at fault. While some firms "self-insure," most firms find it appropriate to carry commercial insurance for Workers' Compensation. To the extent that Workers' Compensation insurance premiums depend on the firm's own accident rate ("experience rating"), the firm has additional incentives to control that accident rate.

Accidents are costly to firms. They generate higher wage expenses, higher insurance expenses, higher training costs, and costly interruptions of production. Unfortunately, accident prevention is expensive also. In an unregulated environment the firm should balance the present value of

---

[39] Northrup, Rowan, and Perry, *The Impact of OSHA* (1978), p. 53.

[40] For details, see F. Ray Marshall, Vernon M. Briggs, Jr. and Allan G. King, *Labor Economics,* Fifth edition, Homewood, Illinois: Richard D. Irwin, 1984, pp. 526–529.

marginal accident costs to the present value of marginal accident prevention costs.[41] Because of the spillover effects of industrial accidents, choices about safety inputs are not unregulated. Firms must find ways of dealing with OSHA and with Workers' Compensation that minimize the cost of compliance.

Summary

This chapter has discussed several important areas of labor market regulation in the United States: guarantees of equal employment opportunity, equal wage regulation, minimum wage regulation, and industrial health and safety regulation. These represent all three types of regulation discussed in Chapter 7: calling prices (minimum wage), calling allocations (health and safety regulation), and determining the rules by which markets will function (equal employment opportunity). Each of these is an interesting case study in the controversy over regulation.

In each case, some labor market participants lobbied for the passage of regulations. In each case, other labor market participants argued that the regulation adopted did not represent the best approach, or, in the case of the minimum wage, that no regulation at all was appropriate. Further, in each case, there is controversy over the efficacy of the regulation in carrying out its purpose.

Employers' responses to these regulations have varied from law to law and from employer to employer; from full acceptance to outright non-compliance. A few of these regulations, Davis-Bacon wage rules, for example, offer employers the choice of whether or not to be affected. In those cases, the appropriate decision criterion is the net present value of expected future incremental cash flows.

PROBLEMS

1. Discuss the differences between a staffing system that maintains an "equal employment opportunity" stance and a system that focuses on "affirmative action." What are the costs and benefits associated with each orientation?

2. The Equal Pay Act of 1963 requires that employers pay the same wage to women as to men when the two perform jobs that are essentially the same (require equal skill, effort, and responsibility and which are performed under similar working conditions). What other wage and salary practices conceivably could violate federal antidiscrimination laws?

3. D. J. Jones and Company produces lightweight clothing. The firm is considering acceptance of a contract to produce 100,000 pairs of khaki trousers for the Department of the Navy. Payment for the trousers would be

---

[41] See Guido Calabresi, *The Costs of Accidents,* New Haven: Yale University Press, 1970.

at the time of delivery, one year from today. Wages to employees are paid at the end of each month. The next such payment is one month from today. The firm's cost of capital is one percent per month. The delivery price for the trousers is $2,000,000. To produce the trousers on time, at Walsh-Healey wages, the firm will have cash outflows of $157,697.57 per month. Ignore all tax effects.

(a) Acceptance of the contract would subject the firm to what other sorts of regulations?

(b) Based on the information provided, should D. J. Jones accept the contract?

Number of Periods	Discount Factor at 1%
1	0.9901
2	0.9803
3	0.9706
4	0.9610
5	0.9515
6	0.9405
7	0.9327
8	0.9235
9	0.9143
10	0.9053
11	0.8963
12	0.8874

4. The Jeter Products Company's fire extinguishers are mounted two inches higher on the wall than the maximum allowed by OSHA. In Jeter's plant, there are 600 extinguishers. To remount *each* would require $25. Jeter's chief safety engineer estimates the likelihood of inspection in any given year to be ten percent. If inspected and found in violation the firm would face a total fine of $1,000 and be required to remount all of the extinguishers. The plant will be scrapped in three years. Should the firm remount the fire extinguishers today? The cost of capital is 10 percent.

REFERENCES

Ashford, Nicholas Askounnes. *Crisis in the Workplace: Occupational Disease and Injury.* Cambridge, Massachusetts: The MIT Press, 1976.

Jones, James E., William P. Murphy, and Robert Belton. *Discrimination in Employment,* fifth edition. St. Paul, Minnesota: West Publishing Company, 1987.

Welch, Finis. "Minimum Wage Legislation in the United States." *Economic Inquiry,* vol. 12, no. 3 (September 1974): 285–318.

CHAPTER 9

THE NATURE OF MODERN LABOR MOVEMENTS

T he decision-maker in a unionized firm bargains, negotiates, and deals, not with individual employees, but with representatives of one or more complex organizations. Unions have histories, organizational cultures, ideologies, and programs for action, just as firms do. While the manager need not know the histories of the unions he faces in rich detail, he or she must, to be effective, understand their agendas and their ideologies. Failing to do so, he or she may misinterpret union motives and actions and aggravate, rather than relieve, the tensions in the workplace.

The answers to several questions must be understood if the manager is to make sense of the unionized environment. Why did unions evolve? Why is trade unionism a ubiquitous (if not always a majority) phenomenon in democratic societies? How did the ideologies of particular labor organizations evolve? What sorts of demands, initiatives, and cooperative efforts can one expect from the labor organizations with which he or she must deal?

This chapter will first discuss the evolution of labor organizations in the contexts of industrial relations systems. Then, the American labor movement will be discussed in some detail. Finally, some examples of the rich diversity of modern labor movements will be sketched. After reading this chapter, you will understand the role of unions in the American industrial relations system and will have a basic knowledge of how American unions compare to some of their foreign counterparts.

Labor Movements and Industrial Relations Systems

Writing in the late 1950s, John T. Dunlop was the first to elaborate the concept of an industrial relations system.[1] An industrial relations system is not something that one can see, but is a subset of the overall social system. It overlaps the economic and political systems, but is not a subset of either (see Figure 9–1).

    The output of the industrial relations system is what Dunlop called the "web of rules" governing the workplace. Some of those rules, especially those governing compensation, are also outputs of the economic system. Others, especially those governing the rights of employees in the workplace, are also outputs of the political system. It is with the determination of that "web of rules" that all industrial relations activity, whether in a unionized setting or not, is concerned. As shown in Figure 9–2, an industrial relations system (whether national or industrial) exists in a particular environment. That environment has four important dimensions.

---

[1] John T. Dunlop, *Industrial Relations Systems,* Carbondale, Illinois: Southern Illinois University Press, 1970 (originally published in 1958), especially Chapter 1.

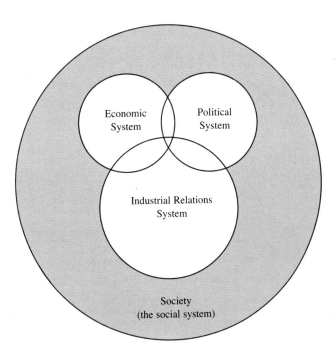

Figure 9–1   **Adapted from John T. Dunlop,** *Industrial Relations Systems,* Carbondale, Illinois: Southern Illinois University Press, 1970 (originally published in 1958), pp. 3-7.

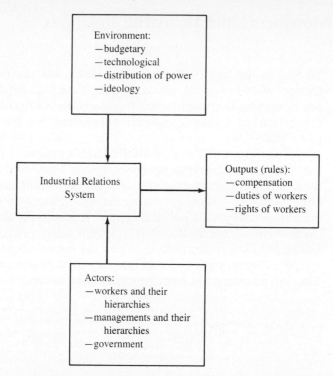

Figure 9-2   **Adapted from John T. Dunlop,** *Industrial Relations Systems,*
Carbondale, Illinois: Southern Illinois University Press, 1970
(originally published in 1958), pp. 7-18.

The first of those is the budgetary or economic dimension. This
dimension includes the organization of the economy (whether capitalist or
other) and the aggregate level of economic activity (for a national industrial
relations system) or the economic health of the relevant industry (for an
industry-specific industrial relations system).

The second dimension of the industrial relations system's environment is the technological dimension. This dimension refers to such
questions as: how is work organized? and what is the prevailing capital/
labor ratio? The third dimension of Dunlop's framework is the distribution
of power in society at large. Rule-making activity will be quite different in a
society in which power is highly centralized (as in the Soviet Union) from
its form in a society where power is widely diffused (as in the United States
or Canada).

The final dimension of the industrial relations environment is the
ideology of the system. When all of the actors in the system share a
common ideology (a common set of beliefs as to the appropriate roles of the
actors in the rule-making process), industrial conflicts are minimized.

Also as shown in Figure 9–2, every industrial relations system has
three sorts of actors. The first of these three is composed of workers and the
hierarchies (organizations) that they form. In some cases, white collar work,

for example, those organizations may be quite weak, and the individual employee participates in rule-making on his own. In other industrial relations systems, throughout Sweden for example, worker hierarchies may be so strong as to attenuate any form of individual rule-making participation.

The second actor consists of managements and their hierarchies. In the American industrial relations system, individual managements usually participate in rule-making alone. Management, however, is not homogeneous. The various levels and functions of management within one firm may form a complex hierarchy. In underground coal mining, however, a management hierarchy, the Bituminous Coal Operators Association, negotiates a master agreement on behalf of all of its members. In Sweden, industry-wide employers' associations play a much more important role than in the United States.

The third actor in any industrial relations system is government. Government may serve (in various circumstances) as a maker of rules for the workplace, as an enforcer of rules made by the other two parties, and as a regulator of the environment in which the rules of the workplace are made. Chapters 7, 8, and 10 discuss the role of government in the American industrial relations system in detail.

Much of the conflict in any industrial relations system deals with the relative roles of labor, management, and government in the rule-making process. A major element in the evolution of any industrial relations system is the change that occurs in those roles over time. Indeed, the most basic conflict in any industrial relations system is not over the rules themselves, but over how rule-making authority is shared.

As the elements of the industrial relations environment evolve, so does the industrial relations system (the rule-making process) and the actors in that system. Worker organizations and rule-making are quite different in the developing countries of Africa from those one observes in Western Europe. As each nation's economic, technological, power distribution, and ideological environments have evolved along unique paths, so has each modern labor movement taken on its own character. The manager who deals with a Swedish union faces a different type of organization than does the manager in the United States. To function with minimal conflict, the manager must understand and accept the ideology of the industrial relations system in which he or she works.

The Origins of Labor Movements

The first trade unions evolved in England as its industrial relations system responded to the changing technological environment of the industrial revolution.[2] Prior to the introduction of power-driven machinery and

---

[2] Allan Flanders, *Trade Unions,* seventh edition, London: Hutchinson University Library, 1968, Chapter 1.

interchangeable parts, every employed tradesman (journeyman) could realistically aspire to become an employer (master). The geographic market served by each weaver's or shoemaker's shop was quite small. Thus, a great many such shops were called for. Further, the capital required of each master, in the pre-industrial era, was small.

The industrial revolution altered the journeymen's perceptions. With power-driven machinery, one weaver's shop could serve a wider market and the number of such shops (or mills, as they became known) that could survive was reduced. Also, the capital requirements for establishing a mechanized shop increased. The use of interchangeable parts and, in the shoe industry, standard sizes, meant that journeymen were in competition with less skilled workers.

Thus, in the last quarter of the eighteenth century, a class of journeymen evolved who perceived their status as employees to be permanent and who perceived a threat of loss of opportunity to those outside their traditional crafts. The "journeymen's societies" that those permanent wage earners formed, first in Great Britain and later in the United States, became the first trade unions.

Selig Perlman, in his *Theory of the Labor Movement,* wrote that all unions, like the original journeymen's societies, are motivated by a perception of scarcity of opportunity.[3] To ration opportunities among themselves and to gain a role in the rule-making process, most visibly in making the compensation rule, remain among the principal goals of modern trade unions.

The American Case[4]

This section will discuss the origins of the American labor movement. The unique features of organized labor in the United States, especially its pragmatic, job-oriented approach to rule making, are the results of adaptation to the evolution of the American industrial relations system.

The Beginning

American labor unions had their origins in Great Britain. British journeymen, immigrating to North America, brought their concerns, and their journeymen's societies, with them. These organizations were formed to

---

[3] Selig Perlman, *The Theory of the Labor Movement,* New York: Augustus M. Kelley, 1968 (originally published in 1928), p. 6.

[4] Several comprehensive histories of the American labor movement are available. See Foster Rhea Dulles, *Labor in America,* New York: Thomas Y. Crowell, 1949; Martin Estey, *The Unions: Structure, Development, and Management,* third edition, New York: Harcourt Brace Jovanovich, 1981; George H. Hildebrand, *American Unionism: An Historical and Analytical Survey,* Reading, Massachusetts: Addison-Wesley, 1979; Harry A. Millis and Royal E. Montgomery, *Organized Labor (The Economics of Labor, Volume III),* New York: McGraw-Hill, 1945; Henry Pelling, *American Labor,* Chicago: University of Chicago Press, 1960; Joseph G. Rayback, *A History of American Labor,* New York: The Free Press, 1966; and Philip Taft, *Organized Labor in American History,* New York: Harper and Row, 1964.

protect the positions of their members in the workplace and were not political organizations. American trade unions, from the very beginning, were not established for political purposes or with political ties.

Three characteristics of early American labor organizations are particularly important. These organizations were composed almost exclusively of skilled craftsmen, they were local in scope, and they were organized as fraternal societies.

That these unions were composed of members of the skilled trades —most importantly, shoemakers—reflects their origins as journeymen's societies. It also reflects the fact that, as discussed later in Chapter 17, skilled craftsmen, because of the difficulty of substituting other factors of production for their labor, have great bargaining power. Not until the 1930s did the mainstream of the American labor movement include semi-skilled and unskilled workers.

The absence of any level of organization other than the local reflected the economic, or budgetary, context of the industrial relations system. Transportation was poor in the early days of the Republic and American industry had yet to realize any great economies of scale. Thus, production was for local markets. Cordwainers (shoemakers) in Baltimore, for example, were not in competition with cordwainers in Boston. There was neither the need for national organization, nor the communications network to coordinate a national organization.

That the organizations were established as fraternal bodies was both a quaint feature of American labor history and a means of solidifying support for those organizations among their members. The members of these early local unions came predominately from Great Britain and had a tradition of membership in fraternal societies. Establishment of unions as "lodges" with initiation fees and rituals was a means, perhaps unintended, of building loyalty among the membership. A charming, if anachronistic, remnant of that early organizational form is preserved in modern unions which cling to fraternal titles (such as the International Brotherhood of Electrical Workers) and to their practice of addressing their members as "brother."

These labor organizations didn't conduct contract negotiations as we know them. Hildebrand calls the unions' approach, agreeing among the membership not to work for less than a specified rate, "take it or leave it."[5] Strikes, refusals to work at less than the union's rate, were not uncommon.

The "take it or leave it" approach of these early unions, of course, required that they have the economic power to make their demands effective. That need for economic power restricted effective unionization to the crafts and required that the unions oppose the introduction of less skilled workers (who would accept lower rates of pay) into their industries. That opposition was often justified as being necessary to protect the quality of the product.

---

[5] George H. Hildebrand, *American Unionism*, p.2.

Economic power was required because employers and the courts were uniformly hostile to union wage setting demands (another feature of the early American industrial system imported from Great Britain). The first major court case to test the status of union demands was the Philadelphia Cordwainers Case (*Commonwealth* v. *Pullis*) of 1806. The court ruled that the union, the Journeyman Cordwainders of Philadelphia, had conspired (a key word) not to work at less than a specified rate. In this case, the union sought, through a conspiracy, to benefit its members and to harm their employers. Both the benefit and the harm were ruled illegal.

The precedent set by *Commonwealth* v. *Pullis* was observed throughout the United States for many years. Some courts, however, took a modified position. In 1842, a Massachusetts state court ruled, in *Commonwealth* v. *Hunt,* that if a union employed legal means to seek a legal end, no violation of the law was involved. To induce all members of a craft to join a union was not considered an unlawful end, even if an employer's profits were reduced. *Commonwealth* v. *Hunt,* however, was not a binding precedent on courts in other states and, even where cited, was open to a great deal of interpretation. Throughout the nineteenth century, and well into the twentieth, the state and federal courts were, on the whole, hostile to trade union formation and activity.

National Organizations

One of the most significant developments in the history of the American industrial relations system was the evolution of a genuinely national economy in the last half of the nineteenth century. Prior to 1850, inter-regional trade in the United States was difficult, shipment by water being the only economical way to move large quantities of goods.

From 1860 to 1900, the total track mileage of railroads in the United States was multiplied almost sevenfold. While the great age of the railroads is an interesting story in itself,[6] one aspect of the completion of the rail system is of concern here: it created a national marketplace for manufactured goods. By 1875, for example, shoes manufactured in Milwaukee (at that time a major center of boot and shoe production) could be marketed in New York or Boston. By 1890, farm machinery from Chicago could be shipped for sale throughout the nation.

One result of the rise of national markets was that the products of workers in Baltimore and Boston competed with those of workers in Milwaukee and Minneapolis. The craft union perception of the need to ration opportunities required that workers within crafts coordinate their demands and expectations on a national basis.

The National Labor Union was organized in 1866, with its roots in organizations dating to the 1830s. It was the first national federation of

---

[6] Jonathan Hughes, *American Economic History,* Glenview, Illinois: Scott, Foresman and Company, 1983, Chapter 14.

unions but its program was quite different from that of later federations. The NLU was a social reform organization from its beginnings.[7] It sought to recruit members around a political agenda and ran an unsuccessful presidential campaign in 1872. Not recognizing the great heterogeneity of the American labor force, the NLU was, in a sense, doomed to failure.

One of the most colorful of the early national trade union groups, and, like the National Labor Union, one that planted the seeds of its own death through advocacy of social reform, was the Noble and Holy Order of the Knights of Labor.[8] The Knights began as a fraternal organization of tailors in Philadelphia in 1869. By the mid-1870s, its membership had spread throughout the East Coast. In 1879, Terrence V. Powderly assumed the position of Grand Master Workman and, more than any other individual, was responsible for the Knights' subsequent success.

Powderly was able to convince officials of the Roman Catholic Church that the Knights' secret ritual was not offensive to Church doctrine, opening membership to the immigrant groups then entering the United States. For an organization that would admit all working people, except "lawyers, bankers, gamblers, liquor dealers, and Pinkerton detectives," such an opening was crucial.

The Knights were phenomenally successful in attracting members during Powderly's term in office. Dulles assessed the Knights' membership at over 700,000 by 1886.[9] The program of the Knights, while not well defined, called for social reform and general improvement in the life of American workers. Such a philosophy, however, could not hold membership in the face of losses of major strikes in the mid-1880s. Craft unions, more concerned with direct benefits to members than with social reform, were drawn away from the Knights by a new organization, the American Federation of Labor.

The AFL and Business Unionism

In 1881, a group of craft union representatives met in Pittsburgh to form the Federation of Organized Trades and Labor Unions. These unions, dissatisfied with the Knights of Labor, desired a better forum for the representation of unions of skilled workers. In 1886, the F.O.T.L.U. turned its treasury over to a new body, the American Federation of Labor (AFL), whose first president and principal strategist was New York cigarmaker Samuel Gompers.[10]

---

[7] Foster Rhea Dulles, *Labor in America,* Chapter 6.

[8] Foster Rhea Dulles, *Labor in America,* Chapter 8; and Philip Taft, *Organized Labor in American History,* Chapter 7.

[9] Foster Rhea Dulles, *Labor in America,* p. 141.

[10] Dulles reports that the F.O.T.L.U. and the AFL were distinct bodies. The AFL-CIO, however, dates its birth from that of the F.O.T.L.U. in 1881. See Foster Rhea Dulles, *Labor in America,* p. 161.

Gompers, as a young immigrant from England, had rejected social-ism. As a member of the Knights of Labor, he had grown dissatisfied both with social reform as a trade union goal and with all-inclusive unionism. Apparently, he had also come to understand the degree of political, religious, and cultural diversity among American workers. The union philosophy that Gompers developed, to become known as "business unionism," became the hallmark of the AFL and with some modifications remains the operating strategy of the American labor movement.

Because of the pluralism of the labor force, the main arena in which workers share common interests is the workplace. The outstanding feature of business unionism is its focus on what happens in the workplace (the business) and, as Gompers articulated the philosophy, its relative neglect of broader social and political issues. Having rejected socialism himself, Gompers sought (successfully after 1895) to rid his new Federation of socialist influences. The major operating rules of the business unionism approach are quite simple:

- the AFL would consist of strong, independent unions, each conducting its own affairs;
- union activity would focus on the workplace;
- unions chartered by the AFL would consist of skilled craftsmen only;
- each constituent union would charge high dues in order to be able to provide a high level of benefits to its members;
- the AFL and its member unions would avoid reliance on legislation to accomplish their goals, nor would they become involved in politics; and
- the goals of the AFL and of its members would be short-term in nature. Asked once what it was he wanted, Gompers responded, simply, "More."

Except for 1894–1895, Gompers was president of the AFL until his death in 1924. His long tenure in office and the dominance of his personality made Gompers' approach to union strategy the dominant one for the American labor movement.

While trade union membership was only a small fraction of the American labor force at the end of the nineteenth century, the new AFL succeeded in drawing virtually all of the craft unions away from the Knights of Labor. By the end of the 1890s, the Knights were gone and the AFL, with its pragmatic philosophy, dominated the American labor movement.

The New Deal and Transformation

While the AFL under Gompers had established the philosophical basis for the modern American labor movement, union membership remained a small minority of the labor force. Government, in the form of the federal and state courts, remained hostile to unionization.

One of the most common tactics of employers in union resistance was the use of the injunction. In the face of an impending strike, an employer could find a cooperative judge who was convinced that such a strike would constitute a restraint of interstate commerce in violation of the antitrust laws. The judge would then issue an injunction against the strike. While the injunction was in force, the employer could discharge the union leaders. Courts were also willing to enforce so-called yellow-dog contracts. Under such a contract, a newly hired employee agreed not to join a union, under threat of discharge.

The role of government in the industrial relations system began to change, and the labor movement began to adapt to that change in the 1930s. In 1932, Congress passed and President Herbert Hoover signed the Norris-LaGuardia Anti-Injunction Act. The purpose of Norris-LaGuardia (whose content is discussed in detail in Chapter 10) was not to promote union activity, but to remove the federal government from participation in labor-management relations. By restricting federal courts from issuing injunctions in any case arising from labor disputes or from enforcing yellow-dog contracts, however, the Norris-LaGuardia Act tended to strengthen unions' position vis-a-vis employers.

The election of November 1932 created a Democratic majority in both houses of Congress and placed Franklin D. Roosevelt in the White House in March 1933. Roosevelt's mandate was to end the Depression, which he sought to do through a plethora of legislation. Particularly important was the National Recovery Act of 1933 which established both industry councils to regulate wages and prices and a National Labor Board to settle labor-management disputes. The logic of the National Recovery Act was to prevent wages and prices from falling, thus maintaining corporate and consumer purchasing power. The National Recovery Act was quickly declared unconstitutional, along with such other New Deal legislation as the Agricultural Adjustment Act and the Public Works Act.

The Roosevelt Administration and the congressional leadership remained convinced that collective bargaining, by preventing wages from falling, was a weapon for fighting the Depression. Thus, in 1935, the National Labor Relations Act (NLRA), better known as the Wagner-Connery Act (or, later, simply as the Wagner Act) became law. The Wagner Act made note of the Supreme Court's objection to the earlier legislation, claiming that NLRA was intended to stop labor disputes which might impede interstate commerce (thus falling within Congress's constitutional jurisdiction).

Much of the early New Deal legislation had been declared unconstitutional by the Supreme Court by 5 to 4 majorities. Justice Roberts, who had voted against the first round of New Deal legislation, altered his position on the Commerce Clause in 1936, agreeing that regulation of manufacturing and promotion of economic prosperity could fall under the rubric of "commerce." Thus, a second round of legislation survived Supreme Court review, often by 5 to 4 vote. The Wagner Act was one of those statutes whose constitutionality was upheld, in *NLRB* v. *Jones and Laughlin Steel Corporation*[11] in 1937.

Whatever the intent of the Wagner Act, its result was to encourage the growth of the American labor movement. With a legal guarantee of the right to organize and a duty on the part of employers to bargain in good faith, union membership exploded. Government's role in the industrial relations system had made a dramatic change. From an anti-union stance prior to 1932, to a hands-off position from 1932 to 1935, government now moved to the position of encouraging union formation and collective bargaining under the Wagner Act. The responses of the labor movement were quick: rapid growth; the expansion of collective bargaining as it is now understood; and, with the birth of the C.I.O., recruitment of unskilled workers in emerging mass-production industries.

The CIO and Rapid Expansion[12]

Prior to passage of the Wagner Act and the implementation of the substantive and procedural rights that the Act guaranteed (these are discussed in detail in Chapter 10), winning collective bargaining rights depended on a union's ability to exert economic pressure on the employer. Unskilled and semi-skilled workers had little such power, as they were easily replaced, especially in times of high unemployment. The Wagner Act opened the possibility of effective organizing and collective bargaining by the less skilled.

John L. Lewis became president of the United Mine Workers in 1933. The UMW was (and is) an industrial union, organizing all of the workers in a mine, regardless of craft. The UMW was one of the very few such unions in the craft-dominated AFL. Lewis was both a dedicated believer in the importance of aggressive organizing and a personally ambitious man.

Lewis's demands that the AFL take action to organize along industry, rather than craft, lines in mass-production industries were first brought to the AFL's Convention in 1935. Rebuffed there, Lewis and a few like-minded union leaders formed the Committee on Industrial Organizations. Their success in establishing the Steel Workers Organizing Committee and the Autoworkers Organizing Committee was ignored by the AFL, which refused to issue charters to the new bodies. By 1938, the CIO had become the Congress of the Industrial Organizations, its members no longer affiliated with the AFL, and a new era of union growth, with two national federations was underway.

Spurred by the CIO's success in organizing industrial unions, the AFL decided after 1939 to enter the fray, establishing its own competing industrial groups. For a time, employees in automobile assembly plants

---

[11] 301 U.S. 1 (1937).

[12] See Walter Galenson, *The C.I.O. Challenge to the A.F.L.*, Cambridge, Massachusetts: Harvard University Press, 1960.

were offered the choice of representation by the United Automobile Workers-CIO (which survives as the United Automobile, Aerospace, and Agricultural Implement Workers-AFL-CIO) and the United Automobile Workers-AFL (which survives as the Allied Industrial Workers-AFL-CIO). The strengths of the CIO's effort and of the AFL's "rival unionism" response were among the factors leading to the rapid growth of trade union membership after 1935 (see Table 9–1).

Public Policy Intervention and Merger

In the years following World War II, government's role in the industrial relations system was modified once again, and the labor movement responded to that change. Members of Congress found several faults with the Wagner Act as originally written. There were no limitations on union behavior in the Act. Employers, but not unions, could commit unfair labor practices under the Act. Employers complained that the Act violated their freedom of speech during union representation campaigns. There was no mechanism to end strikes in cases of national emergency. A wave of highly visible strikes in strategically important industries shortly after World War II highlighted, in the minds of Congress and much of the public, these perceived problems.

Year	Membership (000)	Percent of Non-Agricultural Employment
1930	3,980.6	12.7
1935	3,793.6	13.5
1940	7,523.7	22.5
1945	12,728	30.4
1960	16,584	28.6
1970	22,349	29.6
1971	22,099	29.1
1972	22,640	28.8
1973	23,371	28.5
1974	23,661	28.3
1975	23,701	28.9
1976	23,686	27.9
1977	23,178	26.2
1978	23,353	25.1
1979	23,672	24.5
1980	22,556	23.2
1981	22,204	22.6
1982	21,131	21.9
1983	20,185	20.7
1984*	19,930	19.4

*preliminary

Source: Leo Troy and Neil Sheflin, *Union Sourcebook,* West Orange, New Jersey: Industrial Relations Data and Information Services, 1985, pp. 3–10 and Appendix A. Reprinted by permission.

Table 9–1 **Union Membership in the United States and Canada**

In 1947, Congress passed, over President Truman's veto, the Labor-Management Relations (Taft-Hartley) Act, rewriting the NLRA of 1935. The thrust of the Taft-Hartley Act (which is covered in detail in Chapter 10) was: (a) to establish a better balance between the rights of labor and management in collective bargaining; (b) to remedy some procedural shortcomings of the Wagner Act; (c) to regulate union activities, particularly by establishing unfair labor practices on the part of unions; and (d) to establish a procedure for halting strikes which represent national emergencies.

Both the AFL and the CIO (and their affiliated unions) found the Taft-Hartley Act to be an anathema. The passage of Taft-Hartley demonstrated both the federations' need to influence national legislation (in contrast to Gomper's policy of ignoring Congress) and the need for a single voice for the American labor movement.

William Green had become the president of the AFL in 1924 and Philip Murray had become president of the CIO in 1940 (Lewis supported Murray's election, but withdrew the United Mine Workers from membership in the CIO in 1942). Green and Murray shared no common vision, making merger between the two federations unlikely.

Green and Murray both died in 1952, bringing George Meany to the presidency of the AFL and Walter Reuther to the leadership of the CIO. Merger negotiations began almost immediately, with formal merger into a single federation, the AFL-CIO, finalized in 1955.

The last major act of modern, national labor legislation, the Labor-Management Reporting and Disclosure Act of 1959 (better known as the Landrum-Griffin Act) was passed shortly after the AFL-CIO merger. During the 1950s, Congress held a series of hearings on allegations of influence by organized crime and by the Communist Party in the internal affairs of labor organizations. Evidence of isolated, but serious, abuse of power was uncovered, leading to the formation of the Senate Select Committee on Improper Activities in the Labor or Management Field (known popularly as the McClellan Committee, after its chairman John L. McClellan of Arkansas). The result of the McClellan Committee's investigation was the proposal of the Landrum-Griffin Act.[13]

The AFL-CIO opposed passage of the Landrum-Griffin Act, preferring not to have federal intervention in internal union affairs. To counter its deteriorating image, the Federation conducted its own investigation, resulting in the expulsion of the Teamsters from the AFL-CIO. The Landrum-Griffin Act did, however, become law, incorporating a Bill of Rights for Members of Labor Organizations and regulation of union conduct and finances, as well as making minor amendments to the basic labor law embodied in the Taft-Hartley Act.

---

[13] For a popularized account, see John Hutchinson, *The Imperfect Union,* New York: E.P. Dutton, 1972.

The merger of the AFL and the CIO and passage of the Landrum-Griffin Act established American trade unionism in its modern form. The AFL-CIO includes the overwhelming majority of American unions, representing a vast majority of union members. In large part, the AFL-CIO and its member unions adhere to the strategy laid down by Gompers in 1886. The focus of concern is on the workplace, although much more attention is paid to legislation today than earlier in this century. There is no formal affiliation between the AFL-CIO and any political party, and, while many of the leadership of the federation affiliate with the Democratic Party, there is no effective union discipline over the vote of the rank-and-file member.

Interestingly, the American labor movement, both within and without the AFL-CIO, is strongly non-socialist. Walter Galenson, explaining this almost uniquely American phenomenon, pointed to four factors in the evolution of the American industrial relations system: the high standard of living of American workers; the high rate of economic growth throughout American history; the barrier to the formation of a viable socialist party that the strong two-party system represents; and the emergence of collective bargaining, rather than political action, as the chief means of expressing the demands of union members in the workplace.[14]

Modern Union Structure

The labor movement that has emerged in the United States is diverse in the extreme. On one hand is the AFL-CIO, governed by a biannual convention, and in the interim, by an Executive Board (see Figure 9–3). The AFL-CIO is composed of international unions (so called both out of courtesy and because of the Canadian districts of some of the unions) and a few Directly Affiliated Local Unions.

The internationals each have their own organizational charts, the basis of which is the local union. In some industries—residential construction, for example—bargaining is conducted at the local level and, as a result, the local unions are quite powerful. In other industries, automobile manufacturing, for example, national bargaining has made the local union a less important organization.

Outside the AFL-CIO are some independent internationals, including the largest American union—the International Brotherhood of Teamsters, Chauffeurs, Warehousemen, and Helpers.* Some of these independent organizations are outside the AFL-CIO by choice, others because of expulsion. Also outside the AFL-CIO are several professional associations that, although not calling themselves unions, represent some of their members in collective bargaining. Among these are the National Educational Association (by far the largest), the American Nurses Association, and the American Association of University Professors.

---

[14] Walter Galenson, "Why the American Labor Movement Is Not Socialist," *American Review* vol. 1, no. 2 (winter 1961): 1–19.

*The teamsters rejoined the AFL-CIO in October 1987.

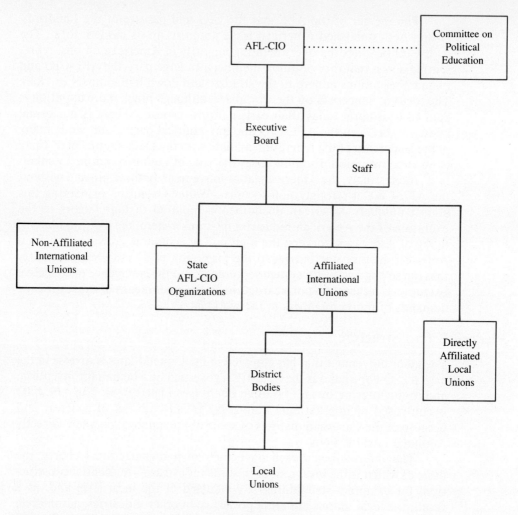

Figure 9-3   **Structure of the American Labor Movement**

Decline and the Search for a Response

The recent history of the American labor movement has been one of secular decline. Table 9-1 shows the decline in union members for recent years. While organizing activities in the public sector, in education, among service workers, and in health care have received substantial attention in the press, these membership gains have not been sufficient to offset overall declines in the percentage of all workers organized and, recently, in the absolute number of union members.[15]

Table 9-2 shows, for twelve of the largest American unions, recent

---

[15] For recent union membership figures by industry, occupation, and location, see Edward C. Kokkelenberg and Donna R. Sockell, "Union Membership in the United States, 1973 –1981," *Industrial and Labor Relations Review* vol. 38, no. 4 (July 1985): 497–543.

	United Auto Workers	Carpenters and Joiners	Communications Workers
1950	908.4	716.9	201.1
1955	1,328.5	804.8	244.8
1960	1,136.1	756.6	269.1
1965	1,326.1	728.6	323.1
1970	1,485.6	777.0	363.5
1975	1,356.7	788.7	466.7
1980	1,357.1	715.6	525.9
1983	1,025.7	678.1	577.8

	Electrical Workers (IBEW)	Electrical Workers (IUE)	Ladies Garment Workers
1950	478.1	159.9	385.4
1955	601.1	284.2	386.6
1960	689.8	271.7	393.1
1965	735.7	291.5	397.4
1970	831.1	309.0	394.1
1975	909.4	278.1	341.2
1980	939.9	224.5	358.9
1983	869.2	172.3	303.4

	Machinists	Oil, Chemical, & Atomic	State, County, & Municipal
1950	562.1	67.8	83.7
1955	700.1	169.8	103.5
1960	686.8	159.8	195.1
1965	728.2	151.2	253.9
1970	842.3	161.1	339.8
1975	764.2	161.3	584.4
1980	754.4	124.1	926.5
1983	539.7	116.0	955.3

	Steelworkers	Am. Fed. Teachers	Teamsters
1950	867.6	41.4	1,057.4
1955	1,015.8	46.0	1,291.1
1960	944.7	55.7	1,480.6
1965	1,035.4	106.5	1,540.2
1970	1,091.0	188.3	1,893.5
1975	1,256.4	379.7	1,923.8
1980	966.1	392.9	1,915.1
1983	693.6	456.6	1,616.4

Source: Leo Troy and Neil Sheflin, *Union Sourcebook,* West Orange, New Jersey: Industrial Relations Data and Information Services, 1985, pp. Appendix B. Reprinted by permission.

Table 9–2 **Membership in Selected Unions, United States and Canada (thousands)**

trends in membership. Substantial membership losses have been recorded in some of the established manufacturing unions. Indeed, the United Steelworkers have lost nearly half of their peak membership. Losses by construction unions (the Carpenters and the IBEW, for example) have not been so heavy, while some unions representing "high-tech" workers (the Communications Workers of America) and public employees (the State, County, and Municipal Employees) have shown continued growth.

Many writers have suggested reasons for these declines. Some argue that unions have become unnecessary as economic growth and public policy intervention have improved working conditions.[16] While that argument contains an element of truth—that the wages and working conditions have improved in both union and nonunion sectors over the past fifty years—it ignores the desire for collective control of job opportunities that was the original motivation for union formation.

Others argue that union membership has declined because of shifts in employment from industries of traditional union strength, like manufacturing, to service industries and from the Northeast to the South and Southwest. While those employment shifts have certainly occurred, their role in declining union membership is subject to question. Dickens and Leonard found that secular change in industry composition was not a significant factor in declining union membership, but that an overall decline in workers' willingness to vote for union representation was.[17] Kochan found Southern blue-collar workers to be as likely to vote for certification as were their Northern counterparts.[18]

Difficult to document but often cited is employers' increased willingness to resist unionization. In part, such resistance is motivated by a desire to maintain managerial discretion, and, in part, it is motivated by increasing realization that unionization results in reduced profitability.[19] Such resistance may have been given added momentum by the perception of an increasingly pro-management orientation of the National Labor Relations Board and by the emergence of a successful "management consulting" (union resisting) profession.

Whatever the causes of the decline in trade union power in the United States, the effects have been significant. The proportion of representation elections resulting in union certification is now well below half and the proportion of the civilian, nonagricultural labor force belonging to unions is the lowest since before World War II. (Those who claim the figure is at "an all-time low" have very short memories.)

The response of union leadership to this decline in membership has taken four forms.[20] First, there has been a significant increase in the rate of mergers among international unions. These mergers allow reductions in administrative expenses and are a reasonable response to declining membership. At the federation level, the United Automobile Workers' reentry to

---

[16] Robert Schrank, "Are Unions An Anachronism?" *Harvard Business Review* vol. 57, no. 5 (September–October 1979): 228–235.

[17] William T. Dickens and Jonathan S. Leonard, "Accounting for Decline in Union Membership, 1950–1980," *Industrial and Labor Relations Review* vol. 38, no. 3 (April 1985): 323–334.

[18] Thomas A. Kochan, "How American Workers View Labor Unions," *Monthly Labor Review* vol. 102, no. 4 (April 1979): 23–31.

[19] Richard B. Freeman and James L. Medoff, *What Do Unions Do?* New York: Basic Books, 1984.

[20] For a thoughtful discussion, see A.H. Rankin, "Labor's Grand Illusion," *New York Times Magazine* Sunday, February 10, 1985, pp. 52–68.

the AFL-CIO in 1980 may have been motivated, in part, by such cost-cutting desires.

Mergers among international unions can save money, but they don't alter the decline in membership. On a second front, unions have sought to recruit among new groups of workers. While organizing activity is a lower priority today than in the 1930s, recruiting among public sector employees, service workers (especially in the health care industry), and school teachers has been vigorous in the 1970s and 1980s. Indeed, some view the recruitment of young workers in these industries as the most important means of assuring the labor movement's survival.[21]

A third form of union response has been in the political arena. To an unprecedented extent, the AFL-CIO's leadership has sought to influence public policy in the 1980s. The endorsement of presidential candidate Walter Mondale before the Democratic Party's nomination in 1984 is an example both of the AFL-CIO's desire for increased political strength and of its frustration in achieving it. (Until the 1970s, the endorsement of any presidential candidate by the AFL-CIO was quite rare.)

A fourth form of union response has been to seek greater cooperation with management. Willingness to engage in *concession bargaining,* willingness (in the case of the UAW vis-a-vis the Chrysler Corporation) to accept a seat on the board of directors in return for reduced compensation and willingness to engage in activities that promote the health of the enterprise are emblematic of this response. Willingness to sacrifice on the part of union members is not, however, as widespread as some believe and may be only a means of insuring jobs when plant closing is threatened.[22] A related response has been union efforts to be participants in corporate merger negotiations.[23]

As the industrial relations system changes, as the labor force becomes better educated, and as the role of government evolves, the labor movement must adjust. The managers who work with organized workers must remain sensitive to those adjustments and adapt their human resource management strategies accordingly.

Labor Movements in Diverse Industrial Relations Systems

The American labor movement is only an example of the wide variety that labor organizations have taken as their industrial relations systems evolved. Table 9–3 illustrates one dimension of that variety, the great variation in

---

[21] See Steven Greenhouse, "Reshaping Labor to Woo the Young, *"New York Times,* Sunday, September 1, 1985, sec. 3, pp. 1 and 6.

[22] Peter Cappelli, "Plant Level Concession Bargaining," *Industrial and Labor Relations Review* vol. 39, no. 1 (October 1985): 90–104.

[23] Nell Henderson, "The Union's Heavyweight Deal-Maker," *Washington Post* Sunday, September 22, 1985, sec. F, pp. 1 and 7.

EXAMPLE 9.1   A UNION RESPONSE TO A CHANGING ENVIRONMENT

As firms merge, close, or "downside," some centers of union strength cease to exist. One possible union response is to become involved directly in the negotiations resulting in the acquisition of the employer.

When United Press International was a takeover candidate, the Wire Service Guild hired Brian M. Freeman to represent its interest in the ensuing negotiation. Freeman's job was to insist on "a return" for the union members in the form of stock or profit sharing. Freeman said, "These are just deals, not a social program, not an ideology."

Freeman has acted as an "investment banker" to several unions in the past. In some cases, the unions have left the experience disgruntled. One colleague of Freeman's suggested that the unions themselves need better planning and more experience to take full advantage of Freeman's services.

Source: Nell Henderson, "The Unions' Heavyweight Deal-Maker," *Washington Post,* September 22, 1985, sec. F, pp. 1 and 6.

strike-proneness across countries. Some understanding of other national labor movements is useful, not only for the manager who will serve abroad and encounter those labor movements firsthand, but also for the domestic manager who needs to gain a broader perspective on his or her own situation. A few, brief examples will highlight the differences between the American labor movement and its counterparts abroad.

Sweden[24]

Europeans refer to national coordinating federations of unions as *national centers.* The AFL-CIO is, thus, the American national center. In surveying the Swedish labor movement, we must look first to its five, strong, noncompeting national centers. By far the largest of these is the Swedish Trade Union Confederation (L.O.). Most Swedish wage earners belong to unions affiliated with the L.O. Other national centers are the Central Organization of Salaried Employees (T.C.O.), the Confederation of Professional Association (S.A.C.O.), the National Federation of Civil Servants (S.R.), and the Central Organization of Workers (S.A.C.).

---

[24] For detailed discussions see Bo Carlson, *Trade Unions in Sweden,* Stockholm: Tidens Fonlag, 1969; and Gunnar Hogburg, "Recent Trends in Collective Bargaining in Sweden," in International Labour Office, *Collective Bargaining in Industrialized Market Economics,* Geneva: International Labour Organization, 1974, pp. 337–352.

Country	Working Days Lost (thousands)	Working Days Lost per 1000 workers
Australia	1256.20	174.1
Austria	22.752	6.8
Canada	3188.7	252.3
Denmark	2332.7	847.3
France	726.7	304.3**
Germany (Federal Rep.)	34.4	1.2**
Italy	3830.8	164.0
Japan	264.05	4.4
Norway	66.473	32.2
Sweden	504.21	114.0
United Kingdom	6402	245.9
United States	7079.1	60.4

N.A.: not available
*: Based on 1981 labor force
**: Based on 1984 labor force

Source: International Labour Office. *Year Book of Labour Statistics, 1986.* Geneva, Switzerland: I.L.O., 1986, pp 13–44 and 923–961. Copyright 1986, International Labour Organisation, Geneva. Reprinted by permission.

Table 9–3 **Industrial Disputes in Selected Countries 1985**

The Swedish labor movement is distinguished from the American not only by its much greater percentage of the workforce unionized (about 90 percent for Sweden compared to less than 20 percent for the United States), but also by the much greater authority held by the L.O. over its member unions compared to that of the AFL-CIO over its member unions. The Swedish industrial relations system offers only a limited role for government. The basic framework for collective bargaining is not a statute (such as the Labor-Management Relations Act of 1947 in the United States), but is the *Basic Agreement* of 1938 between the L.O. and the Swedish Employers Federation (S.A.F.). Rather than relying on detailed labor laws, the Swedish federation and employers' associations have worked out a voluntary framework for the conduct of collective bargaining.

Collective bargaining is conducted, in Sweden, at two levels. First, for wage earners, the L.O. and the S.A.F. negotiate a central agreement. Only then are wage levels and work rules negotiated at the industry level. All industry agreements must reflect the wage settlement in the central agreement. There is virtually no scope for local or plant-level negotiations.

This centralized procedure is possible because of several features unique to Sweden. The philosophy of the L.O. is one of democratic socialism. Wage equality among all wage earners is highly valued. Further, the strong majority of wage earners represented by L.O. unions makes control by the L.O. over industry settlements possible.

A manager in a Swedish firm would find that he has little, if any, direct control over the content of the firm's labor contract (and he would, in the overwhelming majority of cases, find that there were formal contracts covering all of the firm's wage and salary earners). He faces a labor organization that, at once, espouses a socialist philosophy and is highly disciplined. Both of these features of the labor movement, as well as the relative absence of direct government regulation, are unlike the situations facing the manager in the United States.

The United Kingdom[25]

As in the Swedish industrial relations system, collective bargaining in Great Britain relied very little on government intervention before 1970. Since 1970, however, the British have passed a series of laws that make government an active participant in collective bargaining, its chief role being to curtail union power.

The Industrial Relations Act of 1971 was an anathema to the British labor movement. The widespread resentment and noncompliance with the Act (formally called for by the British national center, the Trades Union Congress) was one of the factors leading to the election of a Labour Party majority in Parliament in 1974. The 1971 Act was replaced by the Trade Union and Labour Act of 1974 and the Employment Protection Act of 1975. The Conservative government elected in 1979, however, has moved to restrict union power through the Employment Acts of 1980 and 1982. Roberts argues that these regulatory actions, quite novel in the British context, were deemed necessary, as the British economic system had been handicapped to such an extent that it could not meet the demands of Britain's (previously) strong, unregulated labor movement.[26]

The labor organizations facing a manager in Britain have several interesting features. The ideology they profess is socialist. It was the Labour Party, formed by union representatives, and in whose leadership the Trades Union Congress (TUC) is guaranteed participation, that led the post-World War II nationalization of key industries and the establishment of the welfare state. Socialist ideology is reinforced by very strong working class identification. That identification has proven strong enough to keep roughly 50 percent of the British labor force enrolled in the labor movement.[27]

In the workplace, unions compete directly for members. There are seldom any established jurisdictional boundaries and workers may join any

[25] For extended discussions, see Allan Flanders, *Trade Unions,* seventh edition; B. C. Roberts and Sheila Rothwell, "Recent Trends in Collective Bargaining in the United Kingdom," in International Labour Office, *Collective Bargaining in Industrialized Market Economics,* pp. 353–382; and B. C. Roberts, "Recent Trends in Collective Bargaining in the United Kingdom," *International Labour Review* vol. 123, no. 3 (May-June 1984): 287–306.

[26] B. C. Roberts, "Recent Trends in Collective Bargaining in the United Kingdom" (1984).

[27] B. C. Roberts, "Recent Trends in Collective Bargaining in the United Kingdom" (1984), pp. 288–289.

of the unions in the workplace they choose. Each union, then, represents only its own members in contract negotiations. Thus, within a single establishment, where most contract negotiations now take place, management might be required to deal with ten or more unions. In most cases, all of the unions in an establishment sign a single master agreement.

In contract administration, management must deal with a Shop Stewards Committee, consisting of representatives chosen by each of the unions present. The American idea of exclusive representation, where all of the employees in a bargaining unit are represented by a single union, is not shared by the British.

While some British unions organize only within single crafts or industries, the largest of the British unions are *general unions,* which organize and represent any workers willing to join, regardless of craft or industry. The Transport and General Workers Union is the largest of these.

The presence of a multiplicity of highly politicized unions in a British establishment, coupled with an industrial relations ideology that demands that there be little government intervention, is a stark contrast to the American experience.

Japan[28]

Japanese trade unionism did not so much evolve as spring to life during the post-World War II period of American occupation. With the encouragement of the American Army of Occupation, a group of industrial unions was established. What evolved from that official model, however, was a unique form of organization known as *enterprise unionism.* In each unionized firm, an enterprise union emerged, its membership the same as the permanent work force of the establishment. It is at the level of these enterprise unions that industrial relations activity takes place. There are national labor organizations, organized along industry lines, but their functions are quite limited. There are also several competing national centers, the largest of which are Sohyo (General Council of Trade Unions of Japan) and Domei (Japanese Trade Union Congress), but their principal activities involve their linkages to political parties (although Sohyo coordinates an annual spring wage offensive).

The enterprise union model is consistent with the Japanese model of lifetime employment. Once designated as permanent employees, workers

---

[28] For extended discussions, see Robert E. Cole, *Japanese Blue Collar,* Berkeley, University of California Press, 1971; Alice H. Cook, *An Introduction to Japanese Trade Unionism,* Ithaca, New York: Cornell University, New York State School of Industrial and Labor Relations, 1966; Tadash, Mitsufuji and Kiyohiko Hagisawa, "Recent Trends in Collective Bargaining in Japan," in International Labour Office, *Collective Bargaining in Industrial Market Economics,* pp. 295–314; and Taishiro Shirai, "Recent Trends in Collective Bargaining in Japan," *International Labour Review,* vol. 123, no. 3 (May–June 1984): 307–318.

tend to remain employed within that firm until retirement (indeed, after retirement, such workers may remain with the firm as temporary employees). Wage adjustments come with seniority, a practice the enterprise unions have endorsed. Thus, the permanent employee's fortunes are tied closely to the firm in which he works and the need to be part of an independent labor organization is quite small. While the rigorous discipline of the lifetime employment system has broken down somewhat in recent years, and many workers never become permanent employees, the model remains typical of the Japanese industrial relations system.

The paternal style of Japanese management, the fact that white collar as well as blue collar employees are members of the enterprise unions, and the nature of the lifetime employment relationship make Japanese unions identify closely with their firms. As shown in Table 9–3, one of the consequences of that identification is the very low rate of strike activity by Japanese unions. Robert Cole wrote that the Japanese unions which he observed had very little role in the day-to-day functioning of the workplace.[29] More recently, Shirai cites joint consulation between management and lower-level employees within firms both as a means of solving problems and as a partial substitute for collective bargaining.[30]

Summary

Labor movements evolve within the context of industrial relations systems. Their goals are both economic (conflict over the rules of the workplace) and more basic (conflict over the degree to which rule-making is shared). To deal with a union successfully, a manager must understand the character of the specific union with which he deals and the nature of the industrial relations system in which it has evolved.

PROBLEMS

1. How might the American labor movement be different today had a socialist, rather than Samuel Gompers, played the dominant role in the establishment of the AFL?

2. What changes in union conduct and demands would a manager encounter in moving from a unionized plant in the United States to one in Great Britain? In Japan?

3. Is there a possibility of the American labor movement's evolving into a smaller, but socialist, movement? Explain.

---

[29] Robert E. Cole, *Japanese Blue Collar*, pp. 229–234.

[30] Taishiro Shirai, "Recent Trends in Collecting Bargaining in Japan," (1984), pp. 315–316.

REFERENCES

Dulles, Foster Rhea. *Labor in America.* New York: Thomas Y. Crowell, 1949.

Dunlop, John T. *Industrial Relations Systems.* Carbondale, Illinois: Southern Illinois University Press, 1970 (originally published in 1958).

Freeman, Richard B. and James L. Medoff. *What Do Unions Do?* New York: Basic Books, 1984.

International Labour Office. *Collective Bargaining in Industrialized Market Economies.* Geneva, Switzerland: International Labour Organization, 1974.

Juris, Hurvey, Mark Thompson, and Wilbur Daniels. *Industrial Relations in a Decade of Economic Change.* Madison, Wisconsin: Industrial Relations Research Association, 1985.

Perlman, Selig. *The Theory of the Labor Movement.* New York: Augustus M. Kelley, 1968 (originally published in 1928).

Taft, Philip. *Organized Labor in American History.* New York: Harper and Row, 1964.

LABOR RELATIONS LAW AND APPLICATIONS

T he controversy surrounding the National Labor Relations Act is illustrated by the following two comments.

> Nearly 50 years of experience under this legislation have taught the American labor movement that the original promises of the Act are often little more than a cruel hoax. The basic right to engage in concerted activity has little meaning to a fired union activist who must wait three or more years to get his or her job back. Nor does the token sanction of posting a notice on a bulletin board make an employer think twice before flaunting its legal responsibilities. The very bodies charged with enforcing the Act have instead distorted fundamental employee rights beyond recognition.
>
> > Richard L. Trunka, President International Union, United Mine Workers of America, 1984, Testimony before Subcommittee on Labor-Management Relations, U.S. House of Representatives

> If this hysterical climate leads this Congress to injure or destroy the National Labor Relation Board (NLRB) or cut short appropriations or take any action of that kind, I think that would also be tragic. The NLRB is a valuable institution. It should be respected. It should be preserved.
>
> > Edward B. Miller, Former Chairman, NLRB, and Management Attorney, 1984, Testimony before Subcommittee on Labor-Management Relations, U.S. House of Representatives

As these statements suggest, the National Labor Relations Act has proven to be one of the most controversial and contested pieces of New

Deal legislation receiving both support and condemnation from the groups affected by it. In this chapter we will present the basic provisions of labor relations law and its application across the private and public sector. The laws and applications to be covered in this chapter include the National Labor Relations Act (as amended), the Railway Labor Act, and the various Federal and State Laws affecting Public Sector Employees. In reading and examining these statutes you should understand how knowing these laws and procedures will make you a more effective manager of human resources.

In the previous chapter we developed the background of the environment that influenced current public policies influencing labor-management relations. It should now be evident that over different periods of U.S. history, government policies and procedures toward unions and collective bargaining have differed, with important effects on the union movement. In this chapter we will present the current status of these public policies affecting labor relations, and you should be able to answer the following questions: What direction is public policy toward collective bargaining taking? How do private and public sector managers respond to current public policies regarding labor relations? How do union leaders respond to the current public policy environment facing them?

Development of the Provisions of the National Labor Relations Act

With the economic dislocation of workers during the Great Depression of the 1930s, and the growing influence of the AFL in Presidential and Congressional politics, two major pieces of legislation were passed dealing with labor relations in the private sector.[1] The first was the Norris-LaGuardia Act passed in 1932, which restricted the availability of injunctions in labor disputes. Also, as discussed in Chapter 9, the Act made contracts unenforceable in which employers required employees to sign agreements to refrain from union activities or membership (called *Yellow Dog Contracts*). The second piece of legislation was the National Labor Relations Act (or Wagner Act) in 1935. The purpose of this Act, as stated in Section 7, was to give employees the right of "self organization to join or assist labor organizations to bargain collectively through representatives of their own choosing and to engage in concerted activities for the purpose of collective bargaining or other mutual aid or protection."

Following World War II, workers who had in large part restrained their wage demands during the conflict engaged in a number of long and highly visible strikes in key industries like autos and steel. Management found considerable support in Congress to amend the Wagner Act. In 1947, Congress enacted the Taft-Hartley Act which balanced the NLRA to

[1] See James A. Gross, *The Making of the National Labor Relations Board,* State University of New York Press, Albany, New York, 1974.

include union unfair labor practices. In addition, Section 7 of the Act was amended to recognize the employees' rights to refrain from engaging in concerted activity. The Taft-Hartley Amendments also made illegal closed shop agreements, which stipulated that employers could agree to provisions in a labor contract that they hire only union members. It did permit "union shops" under which employees could be required to pay dues as a condition of employment. This usually occurred after a 30 to 60 day trial employment period. Another highly controversial section of these amendments was section 14b, which permitted States to outlaw even these "union shop" provisions. States which passed these provisions became known as right-to-work states. Currently, there are 21 States that have taken advantage of these provisions of the Taft-Hartley Act and passed statutes outlawing the "union shop" provision in their states for covered workers.[2]

In further developing a national labor relations policy the Taft-Hartley Act provided for presidential power to limit strikes in National Emergency situations, and for special third party mediation in strikes through the creation of the Federal Mediation and Conciliation Service. Finally, provisions were included which legitimized the enforcement of labor agreements by the Federal Courts under Section 301 of the Act. This provision became an unwritten federal law enforcing collective bargaining agreements, and it encouraged arbitration as a means to resolve labor disputes.

During the next decade trade union membership leveled off, and public attention regarding the trade union movement focused on labor corruption. Perhaps the archtypical example of union corruption that was discussed in Congressional Hearings was the portrayal of unions in the 1950s Hollywood film "On the Waterfront." This movie portrayed unions as undemocratic and involved with underworld activities and corruption. In 1959, Congress, after numerous well-publicized hearings, enacted the Landrum-Griffin Act which regulated internal union affairs. Union members' rights of free speech and protest were explicitly protected, and union officials were required to be elected in a democratic manner under the protection of a special division of the Department of Labor.

Provisions and Consequences of the National Labor Relations Act

The current National Labor Relations Act consists of the Wagner Act, the Taft-Hartley Act, and some provisions in the Landrum-Griffin Act. The NLRA is limited to covering workers in private nonagricultural employment engaged in interstate commerce. In effect, the NLRA covers slightly more than 50 percent of the workforce.[3] Various sectors such as agricultural

---

[2] See John T. Delaney, David Lewin, and Donna Sockell, "The NLRA at Fifty: A Research Appraisal and Agenda, *Industrial and Labor Relations Review,* Vol. 39, No. 1 (October 1985) pp. 46–75.

[3] See Robert J. Rosenthal, "Exclusions of Employees Under the Taft-Hartley Act, *"Industrial and Labor Relations Review,* 4, (July 1951) 556–570.

laborers, independent contractors, supervisors, transportation workers, and government employees were excluded for either political reasons or other statutes applied in their case. The basic provisions of the Act were implemented to define and protect the rights of employees and employers.

In order to implement the intent of the Act, two sets of procedures were established. First, a procedure was established for certifying or decertifying unions in elections conducted by the National Labor Relations Board (NLRB), the federal agency that was established to administer the NLRA. Second, the Act limited the types of tactics that employers could use in dealing with employees who desired to use concerted activities in collective bargaining. Table 10–1 lists the various sections of the Act, the provisions of each section, stated penalties for violating the provision, and, where available, average monetary penalities for violating that portion of the Act.[4] The NLRB was the administrative agency empowered to obtain compliance with these provisions of the Act.

Although the kinds of limitations placed on employers in Table 10–1 appear significant, the net monetary costs are not high, if the benefits include thwarting unions through the use of these unfair labor practices.[5] In addition, the political nature of the NLRB can have major effects on how the Board treats unfair labor practices and union election conduct.[6] However, these political swings can be partially offset by the stability of the Federal bureaucracy at the 38 regional offices around the country, who initially investigate charges of unfair labor practices. Although these short term monetary penalties shown in Table 10–1 are factors that many managers may consider, the long term reputation capital or *good will* in the community, in accounting terms, may carry greater weight. If firms only considered short term costs, violations would likely be even higher. However, the negative publicity associated with breaking a federal statute or "flouting the law" often receives greater weight than the short term gains associated with violating a particular section of the NLRA. Certainly, for the greater part of American industry this perspective of adhering to the law is the dominant managerial style.

Sections 8(a)(1) and 8(b)(1) are parallel provisions stating that neither unions nor management can coerce employees into joining or not joining a union. These provisions are generally cited when there are also other potential violations of the Act. Similarly, Sections 8(a)(5) and 8(b)(3) both state that the parties in collective bargaining must attempt to reach agreement in "good faith." For example, the rule of conduct for manage-

[4] Studies listing potential penalties for the NLRA include Paul Weiler, "Promises to Keep: Securing Workers' Rights to Self-Organization Under the NLRA," *Harvard Law Review,* 96 (June 1983): 1769–1827 and Morris M. Kleiner, "Unionism and Employer Discrimination: Analysis of 8(a)(3) Violations," *Industrial Relations* 23 (Spring, 1984): 234–243.

[5] Richard B. Freeman and James L. Medoff, *What Do Unions Do?,* Basic Books, New York, 1984.

[6] William N. Cook and Frederick A. Gautschi, "Political Bias in NLRB Unfair Labor Practice Decisions," *Industrial and Labor Relations Review,* 35 (July 1982): 539–549.

Unfair Labor Practice for Employers Section	Penalty, if guilty
8(a)(1): To interfere with, restrain, or coerce employees in exercise of their rights to join or refrain from joining a union	No specific fine, but cited in conjunction with other 8(a) provisions
8(a)(2): To dominate or interfere with the formation or administration of a labor organization or contribute financial or other support to it	Employer must cease assisting union; union can be decertified or labor contract voided; average penalty is reimbursement of union dues paid by members
8(a)(3): To discriminate in regard to hire or tenure of employment to encourage or discourage membership in any labor organization	Backpay plus interest minus earned income (average range $11,000 – 16,000 per violation)
8(a)(4): To discharge or otherwise discriminate against employees because they have given testimony under the Act	Backpay plus interest minus earned income (about the same as 8(a)(3) violations)
8(a)(5): To refuse to bargain collectively with representatives of its employees	Firm ordered to bargain in good faith, no explicit monetary penalties

Unfair Labor Practices for Labor Organizations	
8(b)(1): To restrain or coerce employees in the exercise of their rights to join or refrain from joining a labor organization	No specific fine, but cited in conjunction with other 8(b) provisions
8(b)(2): To cause or attempt to cause an employer to discriminate against an employee	Backpay plus interest minus earned income (similar to 8(a)(3) violations)
8(b)(3): To refuse to bargain collectively with an employer	Union ordered to bargain in good faith, no monetary penalties
8(b)(4): To engage or encourage a secondary boycott	Liability damages and injunction in a civil lawsuit
8(b)(5): To require of employees the payment of excessive or discriminatory fees for membership	Backpay of fees plus interest (generally under $100)
8(b)(6): To cause an employer to pay for services not performed (feather-bedding)	Liability damages and court injunction (rarely used)
8(b)(7): Force employer to recognize union through picketing or to recognize a union without an election	Decertify union and conduct an NLRB election

Unfair Labor Practice for both Union and Management	
8(e) To refuse to handle any product of any other employer (hot cargo)	Liability damages and court injunction for both union and employer

Table 10-1   **Unfair Labor Practices Provisions and Penalties Under the National Labor Relations Act**

ment has been made explicit by the courts, who stated that the employer must deal "with the Union through the employees rather than with the employees through the Union."[7] Further, the courts have stated that there must be evidence of "give and take" in the bargaining process for the parties to be considered as bargaining in good faith. Therefore, an initial proposal no matter how scientifically derived must be subjected to the process of bargaining.[8] However, this does not mean that "no" is an illegal response to an offer or demand by unions or management to any of the terms and conditions or the items discussed. However, as Table 10–1 shows, there are no significant monetary remedies for these kinds of unfair labor practices.

Similarly, sections 8(a)(3) and 8(b)(2) deal with discrimination against employees by the employer and union. Examples of 8(a)(3) violations would include discharging or threatening to discharge an employee, demoting a union member in violation of seniority provisions, or refusing to reinstate a laid-off union employee. In a like manner, as a result of 8(b)(2), unions cannot put pressure on management to discriminate against an employee for not being a good union member, except where the member refused to pay dues where a union shop agreement exists. In the court deliberations on these issues their effectiveness has been partially nullified by emphasizing the motivation of employers in discriminating actions against employees.[9]

The provisions of the NLRA provide substantial potential penalties on unions and employees engaged in activities that may harm the efficiency of the economy. Specifically, 8(b)(4), 8(b)(5), 8(b)(6), 8(b)(7), and 8(e) provide for Court intervention where unions or employers, in the case of 8(e), are found to be guilty of infringing on the efficiency of interstate commerce. These sections, which were part of the Taft-Hartley Act, state that acts where "unions might engage or encourage any concerted stoppage or slow-down to force the employer or any other person to stop dealing in the products of another employer or to stop doing business with any other person are illegal."[10] If a union is found guilty of any of these violations, they can be held liable for damages to anyone whose business or property was injured, and the NLRB must seek an injunction if it has reasonable cause to believe that the charge was true. These actual and potential penalties on unions have appeared to serve as a real deterrent to these types of actions in this area. When a strike occurs, employers can legally replace striking employees under the NLRA, when it occurs for economic reasons,

---

[7] NLRB v. General Electric Co., 418 F.2d 736 (2nd Circuit, 1969).

[8] NLRB v. Wooster Division of Borg-Warner Corp., 356 U.S. 342 (1958).

[9] Thomas G. S. Christensen and Andrea H. Svanoe, "Motive and Intent in the Commission of Unfair Labor Practices: The Supreme Court and Fictive Formality," *The Yale Law Journal* 77 (June 1968): 1269–1332.

[10] *A Guide to Basic Law and Procedures Under the National Labor Relations Act,* U.S. Government Printing Office, Washington, 1976.

and when the employer bargains in "good faith."[11] The newly hired employees become members of the bargaining unit and are represented by the striking union. When a new contract is negotiated the new workers can lose their jobs if they are temporary replacements for striking employees. Also, strikers may get their jobs back when they return before the strike is over, or after a strike, if the position is open. Furthermore, they are given preference for rehiring when jobs open.[12] However, if the strike involves an unfair labor practice, strikers retain their right to jobs as long as the strike is unsettled.

The Legal Environment of Union Certification and Decertification

The NLRA, in Section 9 of the Act, provides a procedure for unions to become both the sole representatives of employees in a particular work unit, as well as to lose the right to be certified as the sole representatives of the employees. In order to become the authorized agent for collective bargaining for the employees under the NLRA, the steps presented in the flow chart in Figure 10–1 must be followed. During the decision to organize, the union must obtain sufficient support in one of two ways. First, the union must obtain a sufficient number of authorization cards (which is a signed card signifying union membership at the workplace) for the appropriate work unit. The employer can then recognize the union at this point (that happens in approximately 2 percent of all cases) or it can petition the NLRB, questioning the appropriateness of the unit (called an RC election). In a second case, the union must obtain at least 30 percent of the unit to sign these authorization cards for the NLRB to conduct an election. Once the NLRB, through a hearing process, determines an appropriate bargaining unit and settles whether there is a sufficient showing of interest by a tally of these cards, an election is conducted. If the tally by the bargaining unit showed that the union obtained 50 percent plus one vote of all ballots cast, it is declared the bargaining agent for the employees.[13] Specifically, the Act states in Section 9(a) that "representatives designated or selected for the purpose of collective bargaining by the majority of the employees in a unit appropriate for such purposes shall be the exclusive representatives of all the employees."

A major issue under the NLRA has been the type of actions that are deemed to be appropriate behavior by the parties during these elections. Specifically, one of the major issues has been the extent to which free speech protects the expression of antiunion opinions by employers. Early

---

[11] NLRB v. MacKay Radio and Telegraph, 304 U.S. 333 (1938).

[12] NLRB v. Fleetwood Trailer Co., Inc., 389 U.S. 375 (1967).

[13] Dennis Ahlburg, "Majority Voting Rules and the Union Success Rate in National Labor Relations Board Elections," *Journal of Labor Research,* Summer 1984, pp. 229–236.

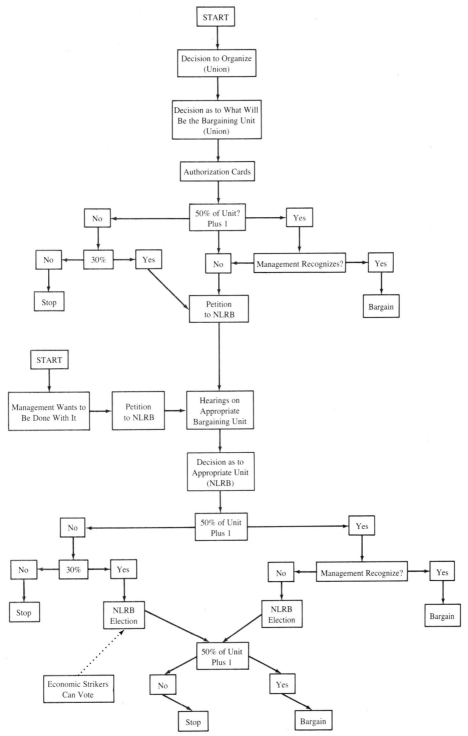

Figure 10-1 **Alternative Steps in Gaining Bargaining Recognition Under the NLRA**

NLRB restrictions of employer speech generated Congressional opposition such that the Taft-Hartley Amendments section 8(c) was added to the Act protecting noncoercive free speech. The use of various behaviorally oriented research studies by Getman, Goldberg, and Herman, which was cited in a major court decision entitled the *Shopping Kart* case, have broadened free speech rights by suggesting that employer conduct has little effect on the outcome of the election.[14] However, a reexamination of the same data by Professor William Dickens finds that in close elections employer threats may make the difference between a union loss or win.[15] In recent years the courts have broadened employer free speech rights. In contrast, free speech guarantees have not been an effective defense for union charges of unfair labor practices particularly in the area of picketing an establishment that may not be directly involved in a labor dispute.

The NLRA also gives employees the right to decertify a union. The procedure is similar to the one presented for certification in Figure 10-1. (You may want to trace through a decertification procedure using the Figure.) If a majority of workers in the bargaining unit vote to not have the union represent them, the union is declared to no longer represent the employees in the bargaining unit. There has been an increase in the number of decertification elections in recent years. As a percent of all NLRB elections they were only 2 percent in 1950 and were 10.8 percent in 1980. Unions won 33 percent in 1950 but only 27 percent of these types of elections in 1980.[16]

The Role of the National Labor Relations Board

The National Labor Relations Board (NLRB) was established as an independent regulatory agency to administer the NLRA. Its primary purposes are to determine whether employees want union representation and whether unions or employers have committed unfair labor practices. In addition to having jurisdiction over most profit-making institutions, it also covers private nonprofit hospitals, and the U.S. Postal Service. The Board is somewhat unusual in that it serves both prosecutional and judicial functions within the same agency. In order to handle both functions, two

---

[14] Shopping Kart Food Market Inc., 228 NLRB 1311 (1977) and Julius G. Getman, Stephen B. Goldberg, and Jeanne B. Herman, *Union Representation Elections: Law and Reality.* New York: Russell Sage, 1976; Joseph Pichler and H. Gordon Fitch, "And Women Must Weep: The NLRB as Film Critic," *Industrial and Labor Relations Review,* Vol. 28, No. 3, April 1975, pp. 395–410.

[15] William T. Dickens, "The Effect of Company Campaigns on Certification Elections: Law and Reality Once Again." *Industrial and Labor Relations Review,* Vol. 36, No. 4, July 1983, pp. 560–575.

[16] Dennis A. Ahlburg and James B. Dworkin, "The Influence of Macro Economic Variables on the Probability of Union Decertification," *Journal of Labor Research,* Winter 1984 pp. 13–28.

separate parts of the Board were organized. The General Counsel's office investigates alleged violations of the NLRA by unions and management. However, the members of the Board and their staff make judicial decisions on the cases challenged by unions and management through the General Counsel's office. Cases appealed by either party go directly to the Federal Appellate Courts for enforcement. NLRB members are appointed by the president for a five-year renewable term with confirmation by the Senate.

The vast majority of all cases that the Board receives are unfair labor practices called (C) cases (approximately 80 percent of total workload), while the remainder are named (R) cases or elections. During the last thirty years there has been a dramatic increase in the number of charges filed with the NLRB for violations of unfair labor practices. For example, in 1950 there were 3213, 8(a)(3) unfair labor practice charges filed against management and by 1983 the number had climbed to 17,526. Similarly, the number of "Good Faith Bargaining" charges against management had risen from 1309 in 1950 to 9866 in 1980. Further, the number of charges to findings of merit by the Directors of the Regional offices of the NLRB has remained relatively constant.[17] The major increase in union violations has occurred in 8(b)(4) secondary boycott charges against unions. The number of these violations has risen from 341 in 1950 to 2987 in 1980, an increase of over 800 percent. No other type of unfair labor practices charge against unions by employees or employers has exceeded 2000 per year during the 1950 to 1980 period.[18]

The other major function of the NLRB is to conduct elections on the certification or decertification of unions. As Table 10–2 shows there has been a downward trend in union success in obtaining certification (RC petitions) under NLRB procedures over the long run (1936–1981). Among the reasons given for this long-term decline has been the lack of access to employees by unions through NLRB rulings, long time delays in the processing time of elections, employer resistance to unions, and the lack of union effectiveness in organizing workers.[19] The Board does have the power to issue a cease-and-desist order and set aside elections results when it thinks that a new election would be affected by past unfair labor practices. In this case the board may certify the union as representatives of the employees and order the employer to bargain. This is done only if over one-half of the employees signed authorization cards (see Figure 10–1).[20] A similar procedure would apply in decertification called (RD) elections under the Board's rules.

---

[17] Paul Weiler, "Striking a New Balance: Freedom of Contract and the Prospects for Union Representation," *Harvard Law Review,* December 1984, pp. 351–421.

[18] Annual Reports of the National Labor Relations Board.

[19] Myron N. Roomkin and Richard N. Block, "Case Processing Time and the Outcome of Representation Elections: Some Empirical Evidence," *Illinois Law Review,* Vol. 75, No. 1, 1981 pp. 75–97.

[20] Gourmet Foods Inc., 270 NLRB No. 113 (1982).

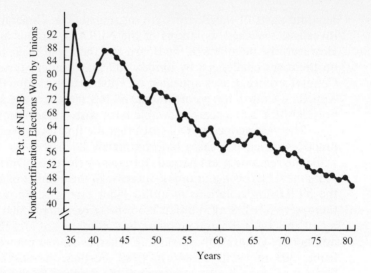

Source: NLRB Annual Reports, 1936–81

Table 10-2   **Percentage of NLRB Nondecertification Representation Elections Won by Unions, Fiscal 1936 - Fiscal 1981**

Managerial Responses to the NLRA

Management and union responses to the NLRA can be analyzed based on the costs and benefits of the various provisions of the law.[21] For management, abiding by the letter of NLRA could mean a higher probability of becoming organized and added labor costs, reduced managerial flexibility, and resulting lower firm profits and market valuation of the firm's stock. In a similar manner, unions may view a larger number of members in an organizing drive as a benefit, or the appearance of weakness in negotiations as a high cost of adherring to the Act. The fact that there is real conflict between the objectives of unions and management, and the goals of the law, also can create important ethical issues for both parties. You may want to examine the impact on society of behaving in this manner by both labor and management.

However, within this cost/benefit framework, firms may make decisions regarding NLRB compliance. Analysis by Greer and Martin suggests that under certain conditons it is economically feasible for employers to

---

[21] Richard A. Posner, *Economic Analysis of Law,* Little Brown and Company, Boston, second edition, 1977.

secure economic gains by violating the NLRA.[22] One procedure illustrating how firms may cost out union organizing under NLRB election procedures is presented in Example 10–1. From this procedure it is apparent that if the union has little economic strength through the use of strikes or work slow-downs, public policy restrictions on costs imposed by the NLRB currently are relatively small deterents to violations, relative to the potential for lost profits of labor law compliance.

Statistical evidence of actions by employers to reduce union organizing has been presented by Professors Freeman and Medoff.[23] They calculate a one-in-twenty ratio of the number of workers ordered reinstated by the NLRB due to 8(a)(3) violations in 1980 divided by the number of workers who voted for unions in that year's election. Freeman and Medoff argue that this is a rough indicator of the risk facing a pro-union worker. Further, they present regression results that from 1950 to 1980 the estimated impact of a 10 percent increase in unfair labor practices per election reduced the proportion of workers newly organized in NLRB elections by 3.4 percent. They conclude that due to the increased cost of unionization to firms because of rising differences in union/nonunion wages, companies have been more willing to use unfair labor practices to stop organizing. Freeman and Medoff say that the U.S. is in the process of de-unionization, and that contributing to this is the use of the NLRB election process to discourage organizing.

Once a union wins an NLRB election, the next step is the negotiation of a labor contract. However, employers may further use the NLRA procedures to avoid a first contract, if the union has little economic power. William Cooke, in a study of first labor contracts, found that discriminatory discharges of union activists and unnecessary delays associated with NLRB resolution of employer objections and challenges to lost elections and employers' refusal to bargain, 8(a)(5), have substantial negative effects on the probability that agreements will be reached.[24] Firms may perceive compliance with the law as the costs of committing an 8(a)(5) violation to be relatively small in comparison to the costs of higher wages, benefits, and potential work rules that unions may bring with them through collective bargaining.

A decision rule that firms may use in deciding whether to violate the law, without taking into account economic power, is presented in Figure 10–2. A company may make a decision to bargain in good faith based on the expected financial outcomes. If a firm wins the court case, along the middle branch of the decision tree, then there are only economic gains as a

---

[22] Charles R. Greer and Stanley A. Martin, "Calculative Strategy Decision during Union Organization Campaigns," *Sloan Management Review,* Winter 1978, pp. 61–74.

[23] Richard B. Freeman and James Medoff, ibid.

[24] William N. Cooke, "Failure to Negotiate First Contracts: Determinants and Policy Implications, *Industrial and Labor Relations Review,* January 1985, Vol. 38, No. 2, pp. 163–178.

PROFIT MAXIMIZATION AND UNION ORGANIZING UNDER THE NLRA

EXAMPLE 10.1

How firms oppose unions under NLRA procedures can be illustrated through the adaptation of a firm bargaining model developed by Ashenfelter and Johnson. Assume that a firm is faced with a potential union that may be certified under NLRA mandated election procedures and that the union will stay for an indefinite length of time if it is voted as the bargaining agent. Taking output, capital, and labor as fixed (see Chapters 4 and 5) during each period, firm profits per period are

$$\pi_t = R_t - (W_t \cdot L_t) - F, \qquad (1)$$

where π_t = profit during period t, F = fixed cost (assumed constant), W_t = wage rate during period t, L_t = labor input during period t, R_t = total sales during revenue during period t.

The firm is not concerned with profit during any given period, but rather with the present value of profits over its existence. This means that the firm seeks to maximize

$$PV(\pi) = \sum_{t=0}^{T} \frac{\pi_t}{(1+r)^t}, \qquad (2)$$

where $PV(\pi)$ = present value of profit stream, r = (constant) rate of discount, T = terminal period.

The linkage between unionism and $PV(\pi)$ is clearer if we rewrite equation (2) using equation (1):

$$PV(\pi)_{nu} = \sum_{t=0}^{T} \frac{R_t - W_{tnu} L_t}{(1+r)^t} - \sum_{t=0}^{T} \frac{F}{(1+r)^t}, \qquad (3)$$

where nu = nonunion and

$$PV(\pi)_u = \sum_{t=0}^{T} \frac{R_t - W_{tu} L_t}{(1+r)^t} - \sum_{t=0}^{T} \frac{F}{(1+r)^t}, \qquad (4)$$

where u = union.

From our discussion of the production function in Chapters 4 and 5, fixed costs are the same in each period, the only items affecting $PV(\pi)$ are W_{tnu} and W_{tu} and the number of periods in which production occurs. Therefore, the value of a threat of a union would be a function of the wage differences

$$PV(\pi_{nu}) - PV(\pi_u) = \sum_{t=0}^{T} \frac{L_t(W_{tu} - W_{tnu})}{(1+r)^t}$$
$$= f(W_{tu} - W_{tnu}).$$

The firm would be willing to either increase wages and benefits or pay the costs associated with unfair labor practice charges up to the value of the function $f(W_{tu} - W_{tnu})$ during an NLRA election. With an NLRB election, wages may increase up to the level that would stop future organizing drives.

Sources: Ashenfelter, O. and G. E. Johnson, "Bargaining Theory, Trade Unions, and Industrial Strike Activity," *American Economic Review,* 59 (March 1969) pp. 35–42. Freeman, R. B. and M. M. Kleiner, "Firm Behavior Under NLRB Election Campaigns," Report to the National Science Foundation, 1988.

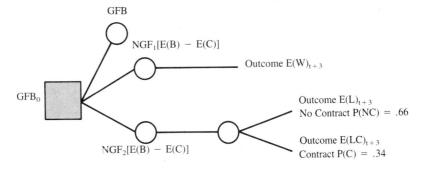

GFB = good faith bargaining
NGF = nongood faith bargaining
E(W) = expected value of winning the court case
E(L) = expected value of losing the court case
E(LC) = expected value of losing the court case and having a negotiated agreement
E(B) = expected benefits
E(C) = expected costs
P(NC) = probability of no contract
P(C) = probability of a contract

Source: Morris M. Kleiner and M. Schliebs, "Good Faith Collective Bargaining: The Decision to Comply" in James A. Anderson, Melvin Dubnick and Alan R. Gittelson, eds. *Public Policy and Economic Institutions,* Greenwich, Ct. J.A.I. Press 1987. Reprinted by permission.

Figure 10-2 **Simulated Firm Decisions under the Good Faith Bargaining Process**

result of not bargaining in "good faith," based on the lower wages they can pay their employees relative to a union environment minus legal fees. Following the lower branch of the decision tree, the employer may lose when testing the limits of the law. In this case an Appellate court may order the firm to bargain in good faith. However, only about one-third of employers have a union present following the average three year time delay after filing. Analyses by Kleiner and Schliebs on closely matched competitor firms find that there are no differences between the value of labor contracts reached following a court order to bargain in good faith, and those who decided to bargain in good faith initially.[25] They argue that the firms not bargaining in good faith may have gained economic advantages by not complying with the NLRA.

A numerical example using the approach presented in Figure 10-2 in the following manner is shown in Example 10-2. If a company bargains in good faith now, its present value labor costs will be $1,500,000. However, if it refuses to bargain it has a .5 profitability of winning before the NLRB or federal courts. If it wins, the present value labor costs are $1,250,000.

---

[25] Morris M. Kleiner and M. Schliebs, "Good Faith Collective Bargaining: The Decision to Comply," in James A. Anderson, Melvin Dubnick and Alan R. Gittelson, eds., *Public Policy and Economic Institutions,* Greenwich, CT., JAI Press, 1987.

EXAMPLE 10.2   COSTING GOOD FAITH BARGAINING

1. If firm bargains in good faith P.V.
   labor costs are $1,500,000
2. If firm "tests the limits of the law"
   using probabilities found in Figure
   10–2, P.V. labor costs are $1,250,000
   if no contract is reached.

If found not guilty	P(X) − No union (.5)(.66) = .33	P(X) − union (.5)(.34) = .17

$1,292,500 = .5 · ($1,250,000) + .33 · ($1,250,000) + .17 · ($1,500,000)

How high would the firm value
"goodwill" or legal fees to make the firm
indifferent with respect to following policy
I versus 2?

Furthermore, even if it loses there is a .66 probability that the union will have lost in the intervening 3 year period, through a potential decertification election and the present value labor costs would then be $1,250,000. If the union is present when the firm is found guilty of not bargaining in good faith the impact is a present value labor cost of $1,500,000. Therefore, the firm would be better off not bargaining in "good faith" under the conditions posed if the present value legal fees were less than $207,500 (see Example 10–2). If this is the case, then why do over 60 percent of all union NLRB victories end in labor contracts and generally stable labor relations?

In part as a public policy response to the perceived benefits that management received under the NLRA, the Labor Law Reform Act of 1977 was proposed to Congress. The major concerns of the legislation were to first provide speedier election proceedings. Second, it would have added members to the Board to provide faster decisions. Third, it provided remedies for violations to be increased so that employers found guilty of willful unfair labor practices would be barred from federal contracts. A worker fired for union activities would be eligible for double backpay in addition to any earned income. Further, if an employer refused to bargain for a first contract, the NLRB could have made the "employees whole" by ordering that they be paid wages equal to the average union wage scale in their area. The Bill passed the U.S. House by a 58 percent margin but was tabled to committee in the Senate as a result of a filibuster. (Analyze the impact that this bill might have had on firm behavior toward organizing and collective bargaining in the context of Examples 10–1, 10–2, and Figure 10–2.)

For labor organizations several parts of the NLRA are viewed as having few costs. In markets where unions are able to organize a high percent of the workforce, and there are few labor substitutes, unions may be able to set wages without bargaining in good faith in violation of section 8(b)(3). Just as with 8(a)(5) violations, union presidents, or bargaining agents would have few economic incentives to bargain in good faith based on legal penalties. However, there are major penalties for union violations of secondary boycott provisions 8(b)(4) as stated in Table 10–1. The issuance of an injunction in this case forces the union to stop a boycott under a contempt of court order. Further, the company may sue the union for any damages for lost income as a result of the boycott. In part as a result of these heavy potential penalties union violations have been about 10 percent of total violations of the NLRA.

Based on these differences in the costs and benefits of management and labor unions violations of the NLRA, it is not surprising that AFL-CIO President Lane Kirkland has proposed repealing the NLRA (see Example 10–3). However, many union officials disagree, stating that state laws regulating labor-management relations would be implemented in place of the NLRA and would impose even greater costs on unions for activities in restraint of trade. Further, some unions are boycotting the NLRB process even when potential violations occur, stating that recent rulings favor management and that the time delays and time spent in the process are not worth the potential benefits. Although many other factors have contributed to the decline in the trade union movement, some of which were discussed in Chapter 9, union officials in particular contribute a large part of the decline to the calculative strategy decisions of management under the NLRA.

Legal Environment of the Noncovered Sectors

The major group of private sector workers not covered by the NLRA are railway workers and airline employees. These employees are covered by the Railway Labor Act (RLA) which was passed in 1926 with major amendments in 1934, 1936, and 1951. The purposes of the Act are as follows:

1. Avoid interruption of commerce
2. Forbid limitations on employees association to join a union
3. Provide for the independence of employee's with respect to unionization
4. Provide for the prompt and orderly settlement of pay and working condition disputes
5. Provide for prompt and orderly settlement of grievances

Unlike the NLRA remedies, the potential penalties for violations of the Railway Labor Act are potentially more stringent. For example, a willful

EXAMPLE 10.3   ## AFL-CIO PRESIDENT SUGGESTS THAT THE NLRA SHOULD BE REPEALED

Recently AFL-CIO President Lane Kirkland suggested repealing the nation's labor laws and letting business and labor battle it out "mano a mano."

Since he publicly presented the idea in August 1984, in an interview with *The Wall Street Journal,* this idea has become the subject of a growing national debate. Union and management lawyers have discussed the suggestion with seriousness on both sides, and there has been some congressional interest as well.

Labor unions argue there is currently antiunion bias in the NLRA and with Reagan appointments. Some labor officials want Congress to repeal or revise the 41 pages of federal laws and 272 volumes of rulings that give workers the right to strike, organize, join unions and bargain collectively—but that also restrict certain union activities like secondary boycotts.

Overall, "we'd be better off with the law and the National Labor Relations Board scrapped." James Kane, president of the United Electrical, Radio and Machine Workers union, told a House subcommittee recently. Says Robert Pleasure, a lawyer for the United Brotherhood of Carpenters: "We are living in the law of the jungle right now, except that unions are living in a cage and the employers are well armed."

Generally business does not think much of the idea, even though many management consultants say it would do well if the laws were repealed. Some argue that the ultimate losers would be individual workers.

Unions feel particularly hampered by a 1947 labor law amendment that outlaws secondary boycotts. This means that if one union has a impasse with an employer, another sympathetic union is not legally able to join the dispute by ordering its members to refuse to handle materials headed to the targeted employer.

The secondary boycott law, part of the Taft-Hartley amendments that unions fought, prompted John L. Lewis, the former president of the United Mine Workers, to boycott the NLRB altogether for several years following its passage. Management says that before the amendments were enacted, boycotts and other labor actions created problems in the economy and whipsawed one employer against another.

Doing away with the current labor laws would allow unions to organize workers more rapidly, Mr. Kirkland says. But many other union officials question whether repeal is the answer. "Unions are in a legalistic mind-set," says Bill Patterson of the Amalgamated Clothing and Textile Workers. Mr. Patterson, who says laws aren't the only way for labor to organize, adds: "We're just starting to look at new forms of leverage." Further, Charles Jones, President of the Boilermakers Union, fears that some states would pass even more anti-union legislation.

Based on the material presented in this chapter do you think unions would expand or contract if the NLRA were repealed?

Source: *Wall Street Journal,* "Kirkland's Call to Void Labor Laws Ignites a Growing National Debate," Leonard M. Apcar, November 6, 1984.

violation of the major provisions of the RLA is a "misdemeanor, and upon conviction . . . the carrier, officer or agent shall be subject to a fine of not less than $1000, nor more than $20,000 or imprisonment for not more than six months."[26] However, there has been only one trial for unfair labor practices, and no one has been found guilty of violating this section of the Act. Other important elements of the law are detailed provisions for union security provisions recognizing the union as the sole bargaining agent, and the submission of disputes to arbitration, where the process is paid for by the government rather than the parties.

A highly controversial section of this Railway Labor Act has been its provisions on collective bargaining, where the potential exists for strikes by labor. The RLA states that if a major dispute between a carrier and workers in the view of the National Mediation Board threatens to disrupt interstate commerce in any part of the country, the Board shall, following notification of the President, investigate the dispute. Neither management nor the employees can engage in a strike or lockout or affect the rates of pay for thirty days. One major impact of this procedure is to make the parties engage in nonserious collective bargaining until after the Mediation Board makes its recommendations. Following this period, labor and management are free to use their economic weapons. Under partial deregulation in 1980 many railroads have taken a tougher stand toward unions in bargaining. This stance is illustrated through Example 10–4. Given the political nature of the RLA there is considerable room for Presidential political action into labor management disputes, which has resulted in complaints from management, as illustrated in Example 10–4.

The use of these RLA-type provisions for emergency disputes found its way into the Taft-Hartley Act. The NLRA provides that whenever the President thinks that a labor dispute imperils the national health or safety he may appoint a board of inquiry to find facts but make no recommendation. The President can then seek an injunction ordering the employees back to work, or precluding a stoppage for eighty days. Following a secret ballot vote of the employees on the last offer of the employer, the injunction is dissolved. The law provides no restraint on the strike or lockout after the eighty day period. These provisions of the Taft-Hartley Act have been used sparingly and with limited success.[27]

Public Policy Toward Public Sector Employees

The largest single group of employees not covered under the NLRA are public sector employees. Originally these workers were excluded from coverage under the Act because of the sovereignty doctrine which stated

---

[26] Charles M. Rehmus ed. *The Railway Labor Act at Fifty: Collective Bargaining in the Railroad and Airline Industries.* Washington, D.C. Government Printing Office, 1977.

[27] John A. Ackerman, "The Impact of the Coal Strike of 1977–78," *Industrial and Labor Relations Review* Vol. 32 (January 1979) pp. 175–188.

EXAMPLE 10.4   BIG RAILROADS WATCH AS REGIONAL LINE TRIES TO OVERPOWER UNION

Recently, David Fink, a railroad executive, was greeted by his effigy swinging from a gallows tree when he walked past strikers at a freight yard in Portland, Maine.

As chairman of the railroad unit of Guilford Transportation Industries Inc., he found the events to his liking—so much so that he ordered an enlarged photo of the scene for his office wall. The mock hanging "showed the frustration of the people out there," he says. "Hell, yes, I enjoyed it."

While other railroad executives move slowly to overcome work rules that have hampered management for most of this century, Mr. Fink is aggressive. In March he refused track workers' demands for job guarantees, causing them to strike. He put supervisors and nonunion employees to work running the trains, with smaller crews and without work rules. The result was cutting labor costs in half.

There have also been public policy setbacks for Mr. Fink. For example, President Reagan's appointment of an emergency board to look into the strike. The order forced Guilford to take back some of the 3,500 striking freight workers for 60 days.

Although Guilford is only the nation's 16th-largest railroad and isn't publicly owned, the outcome of its showdown with the unions is a matter of keen interest to the larger railroads, truckers and shippers. The strike is intensifying debate in the railroad industry about how to tackle work-rules that cost $4 billion a year by some estimates and make the rails increasingly uncompetitive with trucks, and other shippers.

Railroad leaders are increasingly critical of past settlements under the Railroad Labor Act, which has brought a political rather than an economic resolution of rail labor impasses. "The act was written to impede confrontation because railroads were considered an essential part of the economy," says Frank Wilner, an assistant vice president of the Association of American Railroads, a trade group. "But most attempts to increase efficiency have been prevented because the Act allows Congress to impose a politically acceptable solution."

Source: *Wall Street Journal,* May 30, 1986.

that, since the government represented the sovereign or government, it should be the only one who could set the terms and conditions of employment for its employees. With the passage of the Lloyd-Lafollette Act in 1912 some rights were given to public sector workers in the federal government. However, it was not until 1962 with the issuance of the Executive Order 10988 by President Kennedy that a specific policy was specified for federal public sector workers.

The Executive Order developed three types of recognition. The first type was exclusive recognition where employees received majority support from employees. The second type provided for informal recognition where unions represented up to 10 percent of the members in a bargaining unit. The third type provided formal recognition for unions representing between 10 to 50 percent of the employees in a bargaining unit, which enabled them to be advised on managerial changes in employment policy.

In contrast to liberal recognition provisions, bargaining for federal workers was restricted and did not include wages and benefits. This was established by Congress using the Federal Pay Comparability Act of 1970. This legislation tied wages for white-collar federal workers to that of wages of similar workers in the private sector which over time resulted in paying federal workers more than their private sector counterparts.[28] A further modification of federal policy toward unionization occurred in 1969 with President Nixon's executive order 11491. It stated that federal employees were only eligible for exclusive representation based on majority rule. It also established varying types of unfair labor practices and standards of union conduct based in large part on the NLRA.

Beginning in 1979, the executive orders were superceded by the Federal Service Labor-Management Relations Statute. Under the provisions of this statute, Federal workers had the right to organize under statute rather than executive order. This Act created the Federal Labor Relations Authority (FLRA), which was similar to the NLRB, to administer the Act. Although wage issues were not negotiable and strikes were forbidden, this Act allowed for grievance procedures with binding arbitration. Further, the FLRA can stop unfair labor practices by issuing orders requiring backpay for unfairly discharged workers. Given the additional pressure that may be brought on public sector managers through the political process, there may be greater pressure to follow the Federal Labor Relations Statute than the costs and benefits of violations that apply in the private sector. There has been considerable comment from federal managers that, given the structure of the legislation, federal unions have increased the number of work rules in the federal service so that the suspension and dismissal of workers are more difficult. You may want to compare to what extent employee rights in the federal service are comparable to those of private sector workers.

Unlike the uniform national statutes that apply to workers in most of the private sector, and for federal employees, there are a wide range of statutes facing state and local workers. These laws vary greatly by state and have changed dramatically during the past thirty years. For example, in the 1950s only a small minority of public sector workers were organized and almost no states had laws permitting collective bargaining for public employees. Furthermore, strikes were prohibited.[29] In contrast, estimates derived from the Current Population Survey for 1984 showed that about 44

---

[28] See Sharon Smith, "Pay Differentials Between Federal Government and Private Sector Workers. *"Industrial and Labor Relations Review,* Vol. 29, 1976, pp. 179–197 and Steven F. Venti, "Wages in the Federal and Private Sectors" NBER Working Paper No. 1641, June 1985.

[29] Richard B. Freeman, "Unionism Comes to the Public Sector," *Journal of Economic Literature,* March 1986, pp. 41–86.

percent of government employees were represented by labor organizations, over three-quarters of the states had legislation authorizing collective bargaining by public employees, and nine states permitted strikes by some public workers.[30]

Table 10–3 illustrates further the changes that have occurred in state laws regulating public sector unions. For example, in 1959 only one state had a "bargaining required" statute, but this had increased to 34 in 1984. This type of law obligates public managers to negotiate the terms and conditions of employment with representatives of the employees. Meet and confer statutes required public sector managers to discuss employment conditions with employees. This type of statute has increased from 6 to 8 from 1959 to 1984.

Studies using regression analysis of the growth in public sector unionism show that the changes in these laws were a major factor in their expansion.[31] In general, more favorable laws toward unions resulted in a greater growth rate of unionization, and states that did not enact such laws had little or no growth. Unlike their private sector counterparts, public officials are more likely to be dismissed or demoted for breaking the law, which usually means they are less likely to strictly oppose unionization through the use of unfair labor practices. The greater public scrutiny of public sector managers appears to reduce their likelihood of committing these violations.

There are several reasons why the new laws at the state level may have induced the growth spurt in public sector unionization. First, the various state public employee labor laws established mechanisms, much like the NLRA, for workers to vote in collective representation elections. Second, the laws required some form of bargaining with representatives of the employees. Third, public managers reduced their opposition to unionization, which they had justified by the sovereignty doctrine, following the enactment of these laws.

One of the effects of the laws encouraging public sector unionism has been organizational efforts to further enhance their members' welfare. A major direction of these efforts has been toward political lobbying to increase expenditures on the outputs of public goods. Another has been attempts at adding requirements to restrict entry for occupations, like teachers, that are mainly employed in the public sector.[32]

Some recent analyses on public sector bargaining found that departments in cities that have bargaining have higher expenditures than those

---

[30] Freeman, *ibid.*

[31] W. J. Moore, "An Analysis of Teacher Union Growth," *Industrial Relations,* Vol. 17(2), 1978, pp. 204–215.

[32] Morris M. Kleiner and Daniel Petree, "Unionism and Licensing of Public School Teachers: Impacts on Wages and Output Quality," in *The Public Sector Look of American Unions,* ed. Richard B. Freeman and Casey Ichniowski, NBER and University of Chicago Press, 1988.

	1959	*1969*	*1984*
No Law	40	17	11
Prohibit Collective Bargaining	4	6	4
Bargaining that Permits "Meet and Confer"	6	15	8
Bargaining Required	1	18	34

Source: Richard Freeman, "Unionism Comes to the Public Sector," *Journal of Economic Literature,* (March 1986) pp. 41–86.

Table 10-3   **Changes in State Laws Regulating Public Sector Unionism**

without it. Further, municipal unions are associated with higher overall expenditures in a city. However, municipal unionism does not change community property values.[33]

The area of public sector unionism that often receives the most attention is strike activity and public policy responses. It is sometimes suggested that the strike or some legal substitute (e.g., binding arbitration of the issues disputed) forces management to take union demands seriously. The growth of public sector unionism also has resulted in the growth of public sector work stoppages from 32 per year in the 1960–64 period to 500 per year during the 1976–80 period.[34] This occurred despite the fact that strikes are outlawed and have heavy penalties in many jurisdictions as Table 10–4 shows. Recently, Illinois and Ohio have permitted certain strikes and Michigan will enjoin public sector strikes only when there is a clear danger to public health and safety thereby creating a de facto strike right for some public employees. However studies of the impact of these statutes on the frequency or duration of strike activity in the public sector is not clearcut.[35]

One technique that has been used to curb strikes in the public sector is the use of compulsory arbitration. Under this procedure, if the parties fail to negotiate the terms and conditions of employment, the unresolved issues are submitted to a third party who is deemed to be acceptable to both labor and management. This type of arbitration typically takes two forms: a) conventional (where the arbitrator has great latitude in determining the settlement) and b) final offer (where the arbitrator must choose either labor or management's final offer as the settlement). As of 1981, eighteen states had some form of binding arbitration, eight of whom used conventional arbitration and ten used some form of final offer arbitration.[36] In an extensive study of the New Jersey compulsory arbitration system, Ashen-

---

[33] Robert G. Valletta, "The Impact of Unionism on Municipal Finances: Who Claims the Residual?" Ph.D. Thesis, Harvard University, 1987.

[34] Freeman, *ibid.*

[35] John L. Burton and Charles E. Krider, "The Incidence of Strikes in Public Employment," in *Labor in Public and Nonprofit Sectors,* D. S. Hamermesh ed., New Jersey: Princeton University Press, 1975.

[36] U.S. Department of Labor, Labor Management Services Administration. Summary of Public Sector Labor Relations Policies, 1981.

Strikes are legal for some public sector workers (9 states)

Alaska	Oregon
Hawaii	Pennsylvania
Idaho	Vermont
Minnesota	Wisconsin
Montana	

Strikes of some public sector workers not treated in law but regarded as illegal by courts (11 states)

Arizona	
Colorado	None
Illinois	Strikes are illegal and striking employees may be fired.
Louisiana	Police officers can't strike; labor organizations violating may be fined $500; otherwise silent
Mississippi	None
New Mexico	Silent; state employees prohibited and may lose deduction privileges and certification
North Carolina	Silent
South Carolina	Silent
Utah	None
West Virginia	None
Wyoming	Silent

Strikes prohibited, with no sanction or with no specific penalties provided (16 states)

Alabama	Prohibited
Arkansas	Prohibited
California	Prohibited
Connecticut	Prohibited
D.C.	Prohibited
Kansas	Prohibited
Kentucky	Prohibited

felter and Bloom found that unions tend to win about two-thirds of all decisions. They state that the reason for this is that their offers tend to be more realistic. In addition, they find that final offer arbitration produces smaller settlements than conventional arbitration because union leaders tend to be more risk-averse than public sector officials.[37]

Public sector policies toward employees have been a rapidly changing set of rules and procedures. Starting from the sovereignty doctrine, these procedures in most states have moved to models similar to those in the private sector. Unions in this sector have been active in attempting to increase public expenditures in general as a way of increasing the demand for public sector employees. Further, there have been cases of attempts at restricting supply for some public sector employees in education. The unique environment of public employees has led to the implementation of

---

[37] Orley Ashenfelter and David Bloom, "Models of Arbitration Behavior: Theory and Evidence," *American Economic Review,* Vol. 74, No. 1, March 1984 pp. 111–124.

Maine	Prohibited
Massachusetts	Prohibited
Michigan	Prohibited
Missouri	Prohibited
North Dakota	Prohibited
New Hampshire	Prohibited
New Jersey	Prohibited
Rhode Island	Prohibited
Washington	Prohibited; uniformed employees fined up to $250 per day.

Heavy penalties

Delaware
Florida
Georgia
Indiana
Iowa
Maryland
Nebraska
Nevada
New York
Ohio
Oklahoma
South Dakota
Tennessee
Texas
Virginia

Source: Richard B. Freeman, "Unionism Comes to the Public Sector," *Journal of Economic Literature,* March 1986, pp. 68–69.

Table 10-4   Statutory and Case Law Regulation of Public Sector Strikes by State, 1979

legal means of settlement of disputes different from those in the private sector: for example, various methods of binding arbitration. However, one of the major differences between public and private sector labor relations has been management opposition to unionism. In the private sector, management violations of the NLRA has been growing in part as an indication of the growth of opposition to unionization. In contrast, as a result of the greater importance of following stated public policies in the public sector, managers have been much more reluctant to engage in unfair labor practices to stop organizing or oppose unionization. However, when federal employees strike in violation of the law, elected public officials have fired striking employees. This is illustrated by President Reagan's action in firing Professional Air Traffic Controller members who struck the Federal Air Traffic Control System in 1981 in violation of the Federal Service Labor-Management Relations Statute. However, in 1987 the Air Traffic Controllers voted to form a bargaining unit because of alleged deteriorating work conditions. The development of both public and private sector legislation and policies during the next decade should be one of the more important areas of public policy. These changes may alter current costs and benefits of managerial decision making toward human resources policies. However, it is important to recognize that taking into account only the short term costs and benefits of the law on an organization fails to account for the "good-will" generated by being a socially responsible member of the community.

Summary

This chapter has presented many of the basic provisions of U.S. labor relations law and their applications across a variety of managerial decisions. Initially, the development of the National Labor Relations Act was presented. Next, the provisions of the Act were described. These provisions were presented in the context of managerial decisions to test the "limits of the law." The implications of firm good-will and the ethical issues of such a policy were discussed. Numerical examples were presented that showed how firms can gain short run economic advantages if they choose to not follow certain provisions of the NLRA.

The basic provisions covering railway and airline employees were discussed. In this sector there are greater roles for public policy in settling labor-management disputes. The area which has experienced the greatest change in labor relations law is the public sector. Generally, the provisions have favored increasing the rights of employees in the public sector to organize and engage in collective bargaining. Several states have even given public sector employees the limited right to strike. Several studies suggest that these changes in the legal environment have been important in the growth of public sector unionism during the past twenty years. Unlike their private sector counterparts, public sector managers seem less likely to use unfair labor practices to stop union organizing.

PROBLEMS

1. The Whitman Manufacturing Company is a profit maximizing firm facing a union organizing drive, which it estimates will increase wages and benefits of the bargaining unit by 15 percent if successful. The company can either recognize the union or use the following strategies to stop the organizing campaign.

   Financial Data for Whitman Manufacturing Co.

Total revenue	$1,500,000
Total labor costs	750,000
Total bargaining unit costs	500,000

   a. First the company can use unfair labor practices such as firing the two major organizers, which it thinks may result in two $11,000 fines plus $10,000 in legal fees. The company thinks this strategy has a .8 probability of success. Evaluate this strategy over a one year period, using the expected value of profits as your criteria.

b. Now evaluate two additional policies. First, a strategy the company may use is to immediately increase wages and benefits for the potential bargaining unit by 10 percent and maintain this wage, which it is certain will result in the defeat of the union campaign. In a second case Whitman can recognize the union and negotiate the union wage increase that would not go into effect until next year, but would remain constant during the contract. Assuming a 10 percent discount rate and four year labor contract time horizon wages paid and revenues received at the beginning of the year, which of these two strategies should Whitman choose?

c. If both strategies outlined in (a) and (b) are seen as testing the "limits of the law," is it appropriate for firms to use these quasi-legal approaches? What might be the long term effects of being found guilty of violating a federal statute?

2. Assume you are the International Representative of the Boilermakers Union and the only way you can put real economic pressure on your employer is through a boycott of the purchases of their manufactured furnaces. Develop a strategy to maximize net total wages to your members, assuming that they would also pay any fines or monetary judgments for illegal actions.

Boilermaker Union Data

Total members	250
Average annual wages and benefits per member	$40,500
Dues per year per member	$500

a. The expected effect of a successful two-week boycott of building construction contractors of boilers would be to increase the average annual salary by 10 percent. Assume it takes the NLRB two weeks to investigate and issue a cease and desist order. What would be the expected total dollar pay increase to your members, if no strike occurred?

b. Now assume the company can sue your union for lost sales of $1,500,000 due to a secondary boycott. Calculate potential benefits and costs of this strategy by the union using the above information.

c. Should the union consider the ethical implications of testing the "limits of the law" in this case? What might be the long-term effects of being found guilty of violating the law on the union and its membership?

3. Assume you are a public administrator for the Smallville Public School District and the school teachers are in the process of organizing and demanding a collective bargaining contract. Based on data from neighboring districts you expect an overall wage increase of 8 percent with no noticeable increase in student performance. State the tactics you might use to stop the organizing drive. Would you be as likely to test the "limits of the law" as your private sector counterpart in management? Why?

REFERENCES

Freeman, Richard B. and James Medoff. *What Do Unions Do?* Basic Books, New York, 1984, Chapter 15.

Getman, Julius, and John Blackburn. *Labor Relations: Law, Practice, and Policy,* The Foundation Press, Inc. 1983.

Guide to Basic Law and Procedures Under the National Labor Relations Act, U.S. Government Printing Office, Washington, 1976.

"Has Labor Law Failed?" Subcommittee on Labor-Management Relations, Committee on Government Operations, 98th Congress, 1985.

Rehmus, Charles M. ed. *The Railway Labor Act at Fifty: Collective Bargaining in the Railroad and Airline Industries,* Washington, D.C. Government Printing Office, 1977.

ANALYZING PERSONS AND JOBS: MOVING FROM THE LABOR MARKET TO THE FIRM

T his is the first of a series of chapters designed to introduce certain personnel concepts and techniques that have relevance for the practicing manager. One focus of this chapter will be to provide multiple frameworks used in classifying and describing the characteristics of jobs and individuals. The extent to which the aptitudes, abilities, skills, preferences, and personality characteristics of persons who comprise the labor force match the requirements and other characteristics of jobs is the key issue for this chapter.

We are moving from an analysis of the aggregate labor market to an analysis based on the links between labor market characteristics, personnel programs and practices, employee behavior, and outcomes at the level of the individual firm. The relative usefulness of various personnel/human resource management activities depends, to a large degree, on factors that influence the demand for and supply of labor. Early in this chapter we will provide an illustration of this interplay between the external environment and personnel/human resource strategy. This will be followed by a basic review of certain models found useful in understanding and predicting the behavior of persons in organizations. Each model serves to emphasize the concept of person-job attribute matching. It is important to recall, however, that in the chapters to follow we emphasize the use of decision-making methods that estimate the economic returns associated with personnel programs and interventions. Estimating the relative dollar value of different personnel activities and the financial impact of behavior in organizations should become a more central managerial activity. The person-job attribute models represent a critical intermediate step in this process. For managers to allocate their human resource expenditures efficiently, they need to be able to determine the likely causes and consequences of employee behavior. The degree to which behavior can be influenced by a personnel practice is an important issue, but the usefulness or utility of the personnel practice also depends on such things as the cost of the program and the dollar value associated with the behavioral outcome.

The chapter will conclude with a review of certain taxonomic orientations and procedures used to characterize jobs and individuals. Being able to make these characterizations represents an important managerial ability that serves as a basis for sound personnel/human resources decision making. Most personnel practices seek to create additional congruence between person and job attributes. This chapter provides the building blocks for such an approach. In subsequent chapters we will focus on the relative worth of different personnel programs, given the costs and benefits of each. While these costs and benefits will be shown to vary as a function of the external environment, much of what follows will emphasize how to implement a firm's personnel/human resources strategy.

After studying this chapter you should be knowledgeable about a general framework for describing persons and jobs. This will assist you in addressing questions of the following variety: What are the determinants of key behavioral job outcomes, such as job performance, absenteeism, and turnover? What are the consequences of and the interrelationships among these job outcomes? How can knowledge about job analysis methods be used by line managers to enhance organizational effectiveness? How do various personnel/human resources interventions affect employee behavior?

A Brief Illustration

There are many programs, actions, and interventions available to practicing managers that affect the behavior of organization members and ultimately firm performance. Staffing practices, development activities, the design and implementation of reward systems, and a wide variety of other managerial activities all play a role in meeting a firm's human resources needs. While certain activities are more likely to be linked to certain goals, managers must often select—from a set of alternative practices—the one most appropriate given the goals, costs, and characteristics of the organizational and external environments surrounding the specified problem.

For a brief illustration concerning the interplay between the supply of and demand for labor, and the directions firms take in meeting human resource needs, consider the changing labor market for middle managers. In a 1966 Wall Street Journal article, it was argued that due to expanding business activity and a shortage of qualified people in the prime managerial age range of thirty-five to forty-five, more and more managerial jobs were going unfilled.[1] In fact, as early as the 1950s, organizations were making projections that due to the lower birth rates of the depression years and disruptions resulting from World War II and the Korean War, serious shortages of qualified middle managers would develop in the late 1960s and early 1970s.[2] For many companies, the solution to this problem came in the form of utilizing a *sponsored mobility* orientation to meet managerial staffing needs.[3] The sponsored mobility approach stresses efficiency and the early identification of managerial talent. Firms following this norm attempt to benefit from the efficiencies of specialized training and socialization by providing high potential employees with challenging assignments and other opportunities believed to be conducive to managerial development. Promotional opportunity is curtailed for persons not assigned to these so-called "fast-track" programs. Sponsored mobility firms attempt to identify high potential individuals early and then devote resources to the training and development of these individuals. These firms are characterized by a promotion from within approach to staffing.

At the other extreme (note that no firm completely represents either of these idealized forms) firms may follow a form of *contest mobility*.[4] Here selection, not training and development, dominates the staffing system. The focus is on identifying individuals with proven achievement records. Late career mobility is permitted and both internal and external candidates can compete for a particular opening. These firms attempt to minimize selection error (potential is more difficult to identify than proven achievement or performance) and emphasize the continuing possibility that hard work, education, training, and perseverance will lead to valued rewards.

The decision to follow a sponsored versus contest mobility approach to staffing in many ways is a function of the labor market. The contest approach works best when there are large numbers of highly qualified applicants available at each organization level. An accurate selection system is most useful when the firm can be highly selective. In a subsequent chapter we will develop the idea that selection system usefulness is in part a function of what is called a selection ratio. Selection ratios are small when there are many applicants for a small number of job openings. The sponsored approach may be a useful alternative when selection ratios are large (i.e., when there is a talent shortage).

One company that predicted a shortage of qualified middle managers for the late 1960s and early 1970s was what was then the Standard Oil

---

[1] G. Melloan, "Young men move into executive suite faster at many companies." *The Wall Street Journal,* Aug. 26, 1966.

[2] John P. Campbell, Marvin D. Dunnette, Edward E. Lawler, and Karl E. Weick, *Mangerial Behavior, Performance, and Effectiveness.* New York: McGraw-Hill, 1970, 1.

[3] Ralph Turner, "Modes of social ascent through education: Sponsored and contest mobility," *American Sociological Review,* 1960, *25,* 855–867; Rosenbaum, J. E. *Career Mobility in a Corporate Hierarchy.* London: Academic Press, 1984, 16–23.

[4] Ibid.

Company of New Jersey. In 1955, this company initiated a well known Early Identification of Managerial Potential program (EIMP) to help meet future managerial needs.[5] They believed that the traditional selection process—trial, evaluation, and promotion—was unlikely to meet the demand. During this same time period other companies acted in a similar manner. For example, AT&T initiated a large scale program to identify managerial potential using what is known as a managerial assessment center.[6] Details of the operation of an assessment center are reserved for chapters 12 and 13.

The labor market for middle managers has changed dramatically since the 1970s. This can be illustrated by considering the phenomenon of the "baby-boom" generation. This group is usually defined as including persons born between 1946 and 1964. The fertility rate in the United States (the number of children born to the average woman in her lifetime) increased to 3.8 during the mid-1950s. This compares to a fertility rate of 2.1 during the 1930s and a rate of 1.76 by 1976. This group of relatively well educated individuals will face high levels of competition for middle-level managerial jobs. A 1981 Wall Street Journal article describes Bureau of Labor Statistics projections showing the number of jobs for managers and administrators to increase from 8.8 million to 10.5 million during the decade of the 1980s, an increase of 19 percent.[7] This is contrasted with an increase in the number of persons aged 35–44 (prime middle management years) from 25.4 million in 1980 to 36.1 million in 1990, a 42 percent increase. This is shown graphically in Figure 11–1.

It may be that the contest mobility orientation will be more relevant to many firm's making middle management staffing decisions in the late 1980s and early 1990s. Selection ratios are likely to be much smaller at middle management levels during this time period. Continuing competition for advancement is likely to affect post baby boom generation labor force entrants as this huge group which preceded them will remain in place for some time.

In summary, the size and composition of the labor force along with the skill/attribute requirements of jobs in the economy, affect how firms choose between alternative personnel policies and programs. As we move from the level of the labor market to the level of the individual firm, the process of matching the attributes of persons with the requirements of jobs continues to take on a high level of importance. To emphasize this point we

---

[5] C. Paul Sparks, "Paper-and-pencil measures of potential," In G. F. Dreher, and P. R. Sackett (Eds.), *Perspectives on Employee Staffing and Selection.* Homewood, Ill: Richard D. Irwin, 1983, 349–368.

[6] Douglas W. Bray, "The management progress study," *American Psychologist,* 1964, *19,* 419–420.

[7] E. C. Gottschalk, Promotions grow few as baby boom group eyes managers jobs. *The Wall Street Journal,* Oct. 22, 1981, 1; 24.

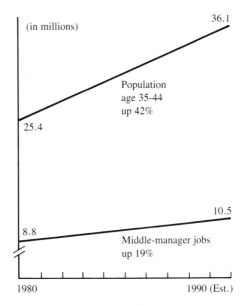

Figure 11–1   **The Likely Surplus of Middle-Managers**

now move to selected models of employee behavior. The attempt is to illustrate that the characteristics of persons and the characteristics of jobs are almost always simultaneously taken into account in conceptualizations of employee behavior. What follows only samples from the domain of organizational behavior models. Our goal is not to provide a detailed review of each but to continue to focus on the importance of person/job characteristic interactions.

The Importance of Matching Individuals with Jobs

A General Framework

Many writers have been guided by the notion that employee behavior is a function of ability, motivation, and opportunity.[8] Figure 11–2 was originally presented in a text devoted to understanding managerial behavior, but it serves to illustrate some basic concepts.[9]

There are many forms of employee behavior that personnel programs

---

[8] Norman R. Maier, *Psychology in Industry.* Boston: Houghton Mifflin, 1955.
[9] Campbell, et al. *Managerial Behavior, Performance, and Effectiveness.*

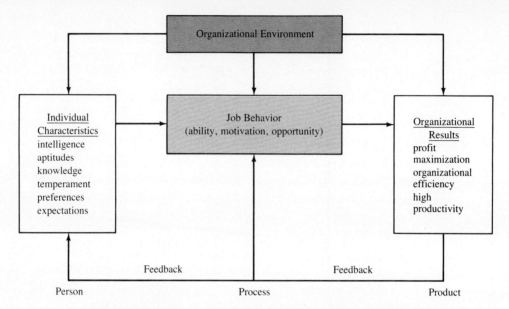

From J. P. Campbell, M. D. Dunnette, E. E. Lawler, and K. E. Weick, *Managerial Behavior, Performance, and Effectiveness.* Copyright 1970 by McGraw-Hill, Inc. Reprinted by permission of the publisher and authors.

Figure 11-2 **A General Model of Employee Behavior**

and practices attempt to predict and influence. The traditional behaviors that are targeted include job choice, job performance, attendance, and voluntary turnover. Figure 11-2 can be used to address each of these behavioral outcomes, but for ease of presentation we will focus on job performance as this general framework is discussed. The primary statement coming from this figure is that the organizational environment and individual characteristics must be simultaneously taken into account when attempting to predict, explain, or modify employee behavior.

Job performance will be influenced by a variety of factors. Given a particular pattern of person-centered attributes, the individual is faced with the task demands and reward system associated with the job. High performance will be most likely when the person's temperament, preferences, and expectations are congruent with the organization's reward system. This is essentially a form of person-job matching that influences motivation to perform. However, at least two additional ingredients are necessary to translate effort or motivation into high performance. First, required job knowledge, skills, and aptitudes must be present. This must also be accompanied by the opportunity to perform. For example, a number of situational constraints on performance have been identified, including 1) the lack of information to do the job; 2) lack of tools, equipment, materials, or supplies needed to do the job; 3) the help needed from coworkers to do the job; 4) the time needed to do the job; and 5) a physical work environment which restricts job performance due to such factors as heat, cold, or noise.[10] While not shown in the diagram, a high degree of role clarity also is a likely requirement for high levels of job performance. The individual must know where to direct attention and effort.

Finally, Figure 11–2 makes the important point that desired job behavior only translates into outcomes at the level of the firm (e.g., profits, productivity, and growth) under certain conditions. While a personnel program or practice may influence employee behavior, organizational results depend on the value of the behavior change in relation to the costs associated with the program. The administrative and labor costs associated with a particular personnel program may be too high to justify its continued use.

While it is well beyond the scope of this text, a careful review of current models of employee motivation to perform would provide considerable evidence that performance motivation is very dependent on a high degree of congruence between person and job characteristics.[11] This along with the obvious requirement that high level performers must possess job-related knowledge, skills, and aptitudes, builds a sufficient case for the emphasis on person-job matching models in the area of job performance enhancement.

Employee Attendance

While it is possible that certain forms and degrees of employee absenteeism may serve useful purposes (e.g., by providing temporary escape from stressful situations and thereby potentially contributing to the mental health of employees) most people agree that, in general, absenteeism is very costly to individual companies and the economy as a whole.[12] The control of absenteeism represents a complex managerial responsibility. One primary reason for this complexity is that some forms of absenteeism are caused by factors largely outside the area of managerial action. Certain obvious situational constraints (e.g., poor health, family responsibilities) can interfere with an employee's desire to come to work. (See Example 11–1 for a company specific example of how to deal with one aspect of this problem.) Therefore, the major influences of employee attendance behavior depicted in Figure 11–3 include certain factors that are under managerial

---

[10] Lawarence H. Peters, and Edward J. O'Connor, "Situational constraints and work outcomes: The influence of a frequently overlooked construct," *Academy of Management Review,* 1980, *5,* 391–397.

[11] Edward E. Lawler, *Motivation in Work Organizations.* Monterey, Cal: Brook-Cole, 1973.

[12] Richard R. Steers, and Susan R. Rhodes, "Major influences on employee attendance: A process model," *Journal of Applied Psychology,* 1978, *63,* 391–407.

EXAMPLE 11.1 TRANSAMERICA LIFE SUPPORTS "SUPERCARE FOR KIDS"

Transamerica Life Companies estimated that employees' absences and incidents of tardiness due to children's illness was costing the company $150,000 annually. The company joined forces with a local medical center facility to provide employees with a day care facility for children suffering from minor ailments such as colds, earaches, or the flu. Transamerica employees will pay a subsidized rate of $10 a day for the service on the first day and $5 for subsequent consecutive visits. The company also operates a child care resource and referral center.

Source: *Employee Benefit Plan Review,* July 1986, p. 12.

control (e.g., incentive/reward system) and other factors largely beyond managerial control (e.g., illness, transportation problems). This framework attempts to explain both voluntary and involuntary absenteeism.

The primary influence on attendance (assuming the ability to attend) is the employee's motivation to come to work. The model is consistent with a large literature contending that the characteristics of employees (e.g., values, job expectations) interact with characteristics of the job situation (e.g., leader style, job level) to influence satisfaction with the job. This, along with other factors (e.g., incentives and rewards associated with attending work, economic conditions, work group norms) affect actual attendance. The model suggests a variety of ways to control absenteeism, depending on the reason for the problem in a particular case. For example, for some employees, a modification of task processes may serve a useful purpose. For others, with greater financial needs, a reward system modification may prove appropriate. Or, over time, a selection system change may be useful to select persons displaying values and job expectations that are congruent with the job situation. The fundamental premise of this and other models of employee behavior rests on the importance of job and person characteristic interactions.

Voluntary Turnover

Another behavioral outcome that represents a complex management problem is voluntary turnover. In most organizations the complete elimination of voluntary turnover is not the objective. The appropriate approach is to manage the turnover process to generate positive results at the level of the firm. There are a variety of costs (e.g., replacement costs, disruption to existing work groups) that must be compared with certain gains (e.g., new promotional opportunities for lower level employees, external replace-

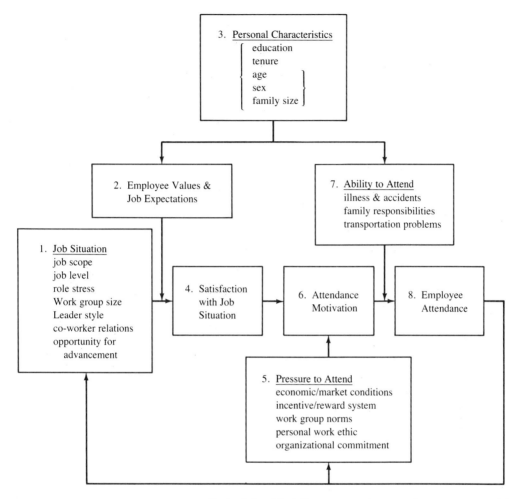

From Steers, R. M., and Rhodes, S. R. Major influences on employee attendance: A process model. *Journal of Applied Psychology,* 1978, *63,* 391–407. Reprinted by permission of the publisher and authors.

Figure 11–3   **Major Influences on Employee Attendance**

ments possessing innovative ideas, lower wage rates for less experienced replacements) achieved by voluntary resignations.[13] This cost-benefit analysis will be particularly sensitive to the performance levels of the leavers.

Voluntary turnover has historically been viewed as a function of two general constructs, the perceived *desirability of movement* and the per-

---

[13] George F. Dreher, "The role of performance in the turnover process," *Academy of Management Jouornal,* 1982, *25,* 137–147; John W. Boudreau, and Chris J. Berger, "Decision-theoretic utility analysis applied to employee separations and acquisitions," *Journal of Applied Psychology Monograph,* 1985, *70,* 581–612.

ceived *ease of movement*.[14] A more recent view of the turnover process is partially based on this earlier work.[15] As shown in Figure 11–4, employee turnover is influenced by two perceptions: 1) the expected utility of the present job (desirability of movement using the March and Simon framework), and 2) the expected utility of alternative jobs (the ease of movement according to March and Simon). It is the balance between the attraction and expected rewards associated with the present job and the attraction and expected rewards associated with other jobs that determines whether an individual will remain or leave. The model predicts that dissatisfied employees with good external job opportunities are more likely to leave than are counterparts with poorer opportunities.

The primary reason for this representation of the turnover process is to once again emphasize the importance of simultaneously taking individual differences and job characteristics into account when predicting or explaining employee behavior. In addition to this basic point, this approach emphasizes the centrality of labor market perceptions to the decision-making process.

A Comment on Outcomes

So far we have emphasized person-situation interactions, or at least the importance of taking both classes of variables simultaneously into account when attempting to understand the determinants of employee behavior. The identified models were sampled from a larger domain but represent the current state of knowledge based on various programs of research. Other behavioral or affective outcomes could also be characterized in the same way. For example, various models of job choice exist that provide guidance when we attempt to explain how individuals choose between multiple job offers or search until an acceptable job is found.[16] These models have practical implications related to the design of recruiting and selection programs and also relate to reward and job design aspects of the firm. Also, frameworks for understanding affective responses like job satisfaction could be discussed in considerable detail.[17] The scope of this text will not permit this kind of development, but if additional models were discussed, the same general point would be made. Being able to characterize and

---

[14] James G. March, and Herbert Simon, *Organizations.* New York: Wiley, 1958.

[15] W. H. Mobley, H. H. Griffeth, H. H. Hand, B. M. Meglino, "Review and conceptual analysis of the employee turnover process," *Psychological Bulletin,* 1979, *86,* 493–522.

[16] William F. Glueck, "Decision making: Organization choice," *Personnel Psychology,* 1974, *27,* 77–93; Schwab, D. P. Recruiting and organizational participation. In K. M. Rowland and G. R. Ferris (Eds.), *Personnel Management.* Boston, Allyn and Bacon, 1982, 103–128.

[17] Edwin A. Locke, "The nature and causes of job satisfaction," In M. D. Dunnette (Ed.), *Handbook of Industrial and Organizational Psychology.* Chicago: Rand McNally, 1976, 1297–1349.

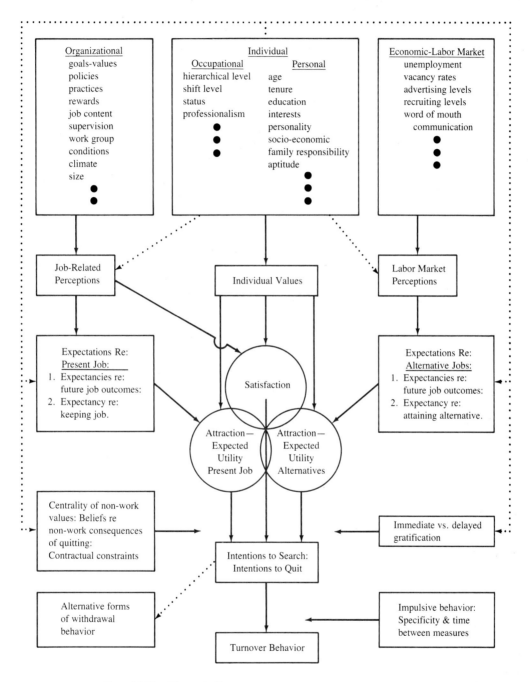

From Mobley, W. H., Griffeth, H. H., Hand, H. H., and Meglino, B. M. Review and conceptual analysis of the employee turnover process. *Psychological Bulletin,* 1979, *86,* 493–522. Reprinted by permission of the publisher and authors.

Figure 11-4   **A Schematic Representation of the Primary Variables and Process of Employee Turnover.**

measure the attributes of people and jobs represents an important managerial role. Individual and job measurement will be the topic for the final two sections of the chapter. This will begin to provide knowledge that can be directly applied in a managerial setting.

However, one more basic point needs to be made before moving directly to the measurement oriented material. While personnel programs attempt to impact employee behavior (e.g., job choice, job performance, turnover, and absenteeism) it must be recognized that the particular determinants of specific behavioral or affective outcomes may be unique to that outcome. It also may be that one outcome serves as a determinant of another so-called outcome variable. This suggests that the relationships among this class of variables are complex. For example, a program to reduce absenteeism may have no effect on performance, or may even serve to reduce the performance level of certain employees.[18] The relationships between the traditional outcome variables are not fully understood and may be moderated by other variables.

Recent evidence suggests that performance and turnover are related only under certain conditions. For example, turnover was negatively related to job performance among managerial and professional employees of a large oil company.[19] For this sample, high job performance was associated with a decreased likelihood that an individual would voluntarily resign. However, it was suggested that this relationship should only occur for companies that relate pay and other rewards (such as promotional opportunity) to job performance. Also, it is likely that the turnover-performance relationship depends on how visible an individual is to external firms.[20]

Another example of the complexity surrounding relationships between traditional outcome variables focuses on absenteeism.[21] In an empirical study based on the tradition of person-environment interactionism, the performance-absenteeism relationship depended on whether the job was congruent with individual needs. When there was person-job congruence, there was a negative correlation between performance and absenteeism. When the job was inconsistent with individual needs there was a positive correlation between absenteeism and performance. The researchers reasoned that absenteeism may serve a maintenance function by increasing the ability of an individual to cope with a job that does not meet important needs. Obviously, too much absenteeism will have a negative effect on job performance. But for certain employees, a particular level of absenteeism may serve a useful purpose.

[18] Barry Staw, and Gregg R. Oldham, "Reconsidering our dependent variables: A critique and empirical study," *Academy of Management Journal,* 1978, *21,* 439–559.

[19] George F. Dreher, The role of performance in the turnover process.

[20] Ibid.

[21] Barry M. Staw, and Gregg R. Oldham, "Reconsidering our dependent variables: A critique and empirical study."

Characteristics of Jobs

Basic Units of Analysis

Describing the properties of jobs and identifying the knowledge, skills, and abilities required for satisfactory job performance serves a supporting role in the management of human resources. Staffing, employee training and development, compensation, labor relations, and job design are among the managerial activities that utilize the results of the job analysis process.[22] A job analysis is a procedure that subdivides a job into components or elements and then describes these elements. The results are specific to the method used in analyzing jobs. Various units or levels of analysis (i.e., components or elements that become the focus of study) can be emphasized depending on the user's purpose or goal. Before discussing the purposes served or the methods available for collecting job information, a further consideration of the level of analysis issue should prove useful.

One basic unit of analysis is the job *task.* Figure 11–5 provides a general framework for defining the level of specificity associated with a job task. *Tasks* can be clustered to form *positions;* positions within the same company can be clustered to describe a *job;* jobs across companies can be clustered to form job types or *occupations;* and occupations can be clustered to define *job families.*

While not shown in Figure 11–5, tasks can be subdivided into *person-oriented* units. The knowledge, skills, abilities, aptitudes, and attributes of individual employees required to successfully perform job tasks are described at this level. For example, task 3 in Figure 11–5 (calculate employee wages from timecards) requires a certain level of mathematical reasoning. When mental processes are described we are performing a *person-oriented* analysis.

To this point we have been discussing possible levels of aggregation, or units of analysis. Traditional job analysis methods are usually directed at the task and/or person-oriented level. These serve as basic elements for further analysis. We now turn to various purposes served by this information base.

Uses of Job Information

The job analysis literature provides many examples of how job-based information is used. [23] The following list of uses summarizes much of this work, but only focuses on the most fundamental applications of job-based information.

---

[22] Herbert G. Heneman, Donald P. Schwab, John A. Fossum, and Lee D. Dyer, *Personnel/Human Resource Management.* Homewood, Ill.: Richard D. Irwin, 1983, 75–87.

[23] Ronald A. Ash, "Job analysis in the world of work," In S. Gael (Ed.) *Job Analysis Handbook.* New York: Wiley and Sons, in press.

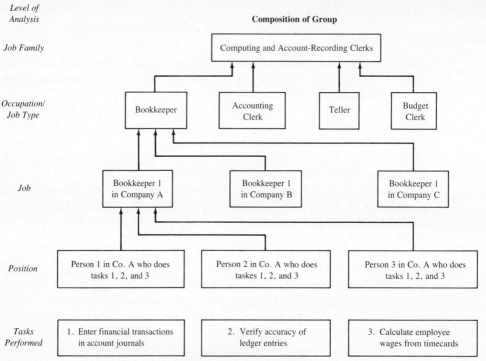

From Pearlman, K. Job families: A review and discussion of their implications for personnel selection. *Psychological Bulletin,* 1980, *87,* 1–28.

Figure 11–5   **Example of Different Types of Job Groupings at Different Levels of Analysis**

1. *Human Resources Planning.* Human resource planning is a process that forecasts human resource needs, and leads to the development and implementation of personnel programs to meet future staffing requirements.[24] Needs forescasting includes estimating future demand for labor and comparing these estimates to labor supply predictions. The usual approach is to determine, for specified jobs or job types within a firm, the degree to which there is likely to be either a labor surplus or labor shortage. Depending on the outcome of this analysis, various personnel programs can be evaluated to determine the most useful way to prepare for the predicted outcome.

A firm's future human resource requirements (demand for labor) depend on a variety of factors including the firm's business plans and budgets, management policies and philosophy, technological advances, and affirmative action goals and timetables. Future human resources availability (supply of labor) is determined by internal and external factors. Within the firm, factors such as the current inventory of talent, forecasted attrition,

---

[24] James W. Walker, *Human Resource Planning.* New York: McGraw-Hill, 1980.

forecasted movement and development, and the effects of past human resource programs, must be considered. The analysis of external conditions focuses on the composition and size of the labor force, and employment opportunities created by competing firms.[25]

Job analysis information plays an important role in the planning process. For example, creating job families by clustering positions, jobs, and job types is useful in planning rational lines of succession. Identifying the jobs that constitute the most likely internal labor supply for jobs at higher levels requires clustering jobs on the basis of either task or person-oriented traits and attributes. Or consider the linkages between external sources of employment data and information specific to the firm. Job-based information is used to match internal jobs or job types to appropriate counterparts in these external data bases.

2. *Personnel Recruitment.* Recruitment is the process of creating an applicant pool of qualified individuals who are likely to accept a job offer. The term recruitment usually is applied to searches for external job candidates, but can be applied whether the search is conducted inside or outside an organization. The goal is to create a sufficiently large pool of applicants so that the firm can efficiently meet its staffing needs. The optimal size of the applicant pool depends on a variety of as yet to be described factors. Job-based information serves two primary purposes related to the recruitment process.

First, through the use of the traditional *job description* and *job specification,* candidates are able to learn about the essential requirements of a job.[26] The job description lists the major tasks and responsibilities of a job. The job specification lists the knowledge, skills, abilities, and other required person-oriented attributes associated with a job. Taken together, these sources of information allow the job candidate to preview the position and make judgments about job interest and qualifications. A form of self selection or self screening can occur at this stage. The second application relates to initial screening decisions made by the firm. Since basic employment standards can be determined through job analysis, employers can make initial screening decisions by systematically comparing position requirements with information presented by the applicant (usually in the form of a resume or job application).

3. *Selection.* A variety of purposes are served by job-based information as applied to the selection process. There are two basic approaches to making selection decisions. One is to identify applicants who already possess the required attributes for the job. These applicants can perform most aspects of the job at the time of selection. Here, past achievement, training, and experience are stressed in the selection process. The ideal selection technique for this type of problem is to give the applicant a work

---

[25] Ibid.

[26] John P. Wanous, *Organizational Entry: Recruitment, Selection, and Socialization of Newcomers.* Reading, Mass.: Addison-Wesley, 1980.

trial or work sample that represents actual work content. By putting the applicant in a situation that resembles the actual job and observing performance directly, accurate estimates of actual job performance are possible. Task-oriented job analysis information is required to construct these testing environments.

The second approach to employee selection is to identify candidates who possess the potential to become high performing job incumbents. In this situation new employees are trained and therefore selection techniques must focus on the measurement of potential to learn. Person-oriented job analysis information is useful here. After identifying the relevant person-oriented attributes (e.g., inductive reasoning, perceptual speed, spatial aptitude, manual dexterity), decisions can be made concerning the appropriate ways to measure these qualities.

Finally, job-based information is used to compare work settings for the purpose of generalizing research results. If a selection procedure has been shown to be useful for certain jobs in one firm, and a job analysis has determined that there is a high degree of job similarity between this firm and a second firm, it may be possible to use the selection procedure in the second firm. For this purpose, task-oriented job information is useful, particularly when the analysis method covers standard (not position-specific) dimensions of the job.

4. *Training and Development.* Training and development refers to a planned program that facilitates the learning of job-related behavior. Training techniques are applied when it is determined that a performance deficiency is the result of insufficient knowledge, skills, or abilities. If the performance problem is a function of low motivation or environmental constraints (e.g., lack of equipment or poor working conditions) training will not serve a useful purpose. One fundamental purpose of job-based information relates to the identification of training needs. The first step in the design and implementation of a training progam is to determine specific training needs. A variety of techniques are available for identifying training needs, but all make comparisons between the attributes required to perform the job and attributes possessed by individuals. The job analysis process (usually a form that focuses on person-oriented attributes) identifies what is required for successful job performance.

Also, the transfer of learning to the actual work setting is likely to be maximized when there is a high degree of similarity between the training situation and the job situation.[27] Task-oriented job analysis information, and information about the context within which the work is performed, help in the design of realistic training experiences.

5. *Compensation.* Two fundamental issues faced when designing a

---

[27] Kenneth N. Wexley, and Gary P. Latham, *Developing and Training Human Resources in Organizations.* Glenview, Ill.: Scott, Foresman and Company, 1981.

compensation system require complete, high quality job-based information. The first issue focuses on *external equity*. External equity refers to pay relationships among companies. Companies need to determine how their pay rates compare to competitors.[28] Paying below market rates is likely to adversely affect a firm's ability to attract and retain employees. Paying well above the market rate can result in unsatisfactory labor costs. The primary way firms collect information about market pay rates is through the use of market surveys. When making comparisons it is critical that the external job is essentially the same as the target job. Job titles are not sufficient for making decisions about job similarity. A systems analyst in one company may perform a variety of tasks not performed by a systems analyst in another company. The market survey process, therefore, includes the exchange of job analysis information. This helps guarantee that equivalent jobs are being compared.

The second fundamental pay administration issue concerns *internal equity*. Internal equity refers to pay relationships among jobs within the same firm.[29] The essential problem is to rank jobs or job classes in an equitable manner. A common way to address internal equity is to conduct a *job evaluation*. Job descriptions serve as input into the job evaluation process. The job descriptions are reviewed and a formal weighting or classification system can be used to estimate the relative worth of jobs within the firm. The development of internal pay structures will be discussed in more detail in Chapter 15. The point to be made here is that this process begins with a thorough job analysis.

6. *Performance Appraisal.* The systematic evaluation of employee performance serves multiple roles in organizations. The development of job-related measurement procedures begins with a job analysis. For a performance appraisal system to be job-related it needs to measure the critical or important job duties, work behaviors, or work outcomes associated with the job. If it measures person-oriented attributes, these must be shown to be directly linked to critical work behaviors. Determining the measurement dimensions begins with a review of job information. The job analysis information also serves as a check to make sure critical aspects of the job are not ignored or that trivial aspects of the job are not given too much weight. Most forms of job analysis provide a way to determine which aspects of the job are critical or important.

There are many other uses for job analysis information. Job design and restructuring, career counseling, and career development are illustrative activities that rely heavily on the results of a job analysis. Also, there are a variety of legal requirements that regulate the management of human

---

[28] George T. Milkovich, and Jerry M. Newman, *Compensation.* Plano, Texas: Business Publications, Inc., 1984.

[29] *Ibid.*

resources. Showing that selection and promotion systems, compensation systems, and training interventions are job-related and bias free depends on a job analysis framework. There are even guidelines established by regulatory agencies that specify the appropriate form of a job analysis.[30] These issues will be given additional coverage when we begin our discussion of specific personnel programs and practices. For now however, we turn to a description of some widely used methods of job analysis.

Job Analysis Methods

Job analysis methods can vary in numerous ways.[31] We have emphasized differences in the types of elements used to describe a job. Our focus has been on the distinction between *task-oriented* and *person-oriented* analysis. But there are other dimensions along which job analysis methods can be compared. A second distinction is the way job information is collected. Data collection methods include direct observations, individual interviews, group interviews, and the use of structured questionnaires and checklists. Methods also differ with regard to the source of job information. The source may be the incumbent, supervisory or managerial personnel, a job analyst, available documents (e.g., technical reports, training manuals), or a mixed approach using multiple sources. Finally, job analysis methods can vary along a standardization continuum.[32] Some methods result in information about a specific job and may produce unique descriptive categories. Other methods are standardized and allow comparisons to be made across different jobs. Standardized methods use the same descriptive categories and rating formats for all jobs.

With the exception of the personnel specialist, the general manager does not need to become an expert job analyst. What is useful is knowledge about the types of situations and problems requiring job analysis results and knowledge about which method best serves a particular need. By knowing the purposes served by job-based information and having knowledge about the kind of information that is available, managers can develop specific job analysis strategies as required. This often includes interacting with personnel/human resource specialists. What follows only samples from the domain of job analysis methods. This only serves to illustrate possibilities. Additional knowledge can be gained by reviewing the section's

---

[30] Equal Employment Opportunity Commission, Civil Service Commission, Department of Labor, and Department of Justice. Adoption by four agencies of uniform guidelines on employee selection procedures. *Federal Register,* 1978, *43,* 38290–38315.

[31] Ronald A. Ash, Job analysis in the world of work.

[32] P. M. Wright, and Kenneth N. Wexley, How to choose the kind of job analysis you really need. *Personnel,* May, 1985, 51–55.

references.[33] We will conclude the material on traditional job analysis procedures with a comment on method/purpose congruence.

1. *Job Element Method.* The Job Element Method (JEM)[34] represents a person-oriented approach to job analysis. The procedure begins with the identification of subject matter experts (SMEs) who serve as panel members for data collection purposes. SMEs usually are experienced workers or supervisors of job incumbents. First, the panel members generate elements required to perform the job. An element can include a knowledge, a skill, an ability, a willingness to perform a task, an interest, or a personal characteristic, such as reliability or dependability. The second phase of the analysis consists of rating each job element on four scales. Ratings indicate the degree of relationship between elements and job success. The approach focuses on differentiating between superior and barely acceptable workers. The JEM results in a person-oriented analysis that is job specific. While the rating scales create some uniformity, the identified elements are unique to a particular job (or at least include a unique mix of elements).

2. *Functional Job Analysis (FJA).* The FJA method represents a generalized approach that can serve multiple purposes.[35] This results from a task-oriented primary analysis that is supplemented by a variety of task specific ratings. Task statements describe what workers do (worker actions) and the immediate result of each action. Each task is then analyzed according to several scales. For example, the *People Scale* describes the nature of worker interaction with other people when performing a particular task (ranging from taking instructions to mentoring). In addition to contextual description (tasks performed in the context of data, people, and things), the FJA provides person-oriented ratings of each task. Tasks are rated in terms of the level of general reasoning ability, mathematical sophistication, and language development required for successful completion.

3. *Position Analysis Questionnaire (PAQ).* The PAQ is a structured job analysis questionnaire that can be used to analyze virtually any position or

---

[33] Ernest J. McCormick, "Job and task analysis," In M. D. Dunnette (Ed.), *Handbook of Industrial and Organizational Psychology.* Chicago: Rand McNally, 1976, 651–696; Gael, S. *Job Analysis: A Guide to Assessing Work Activities.* San Francisco: Jossey-Bass, 1983; Ron A. Ash, E. L. Levine, and Frank Sistrunk, "The role of jobs and job-based methods in personnel and human resources management," In K. M. Rowland, and G. R. Ferris (Eds.). *Research in Personnel and Human Resources Management: A Research Annual (Vol. I).* Greenwich, Conn.: JAI Press, 1983, 45–84; E. L. Levine, *Everything You Always Wanted to Know about Job Analysis and More: A Job Analysis Primer.* Tampa, Florida: Mariner Publishing Company, 1983.

[34] E. S. Primoff, *How to Prepare and Conduct Job Element Examinations.* Washington, D.C.: U.S. Government Printing Office, 1975.

[35] S. Fine, and W. Wiley. *An Introduction to Functional Job Analysis Methods for Manpower Analysis.* Kalamazoo, Mich.: Upjohn Institute for Employment Research, 1971.

job.[36] It is a standardized measurement approach that describes a job in terms of 194 common job elements or items. The questionnaire's items focus on sources of job information, job required mental processes, behaviors involved in performing the work, the interpersonal activities of the job, the work environment, and other job characteristics. Computerized data analysis procedures lead to the statistical derivation of job dimension scores that reflect a job profile. From ratings on the 194 common items, jobs are profiled in terms of 32 job dimensions. Dimensions such as *Decision Making, Information Processing, Physical Coordination, Using Machines/Tools/and Equipment,* and *Job-Related Communication,* are used to describe each job. From the basic analysis a variety of derived scores can be generated. For example, scores can be provided on dimensions of human attributes needed to perform the work. In addition, the system can supply scores on special indexes such as the amount of education required to perform the job, and an occupational prestige indicator.

Although the PAQ is one of the most useful and thoroughly researched methods available, it is lengthy and time consuming to use, and requires well trained analysts. Data collection usually requires individual interviews with job incumbents. During the interview the analyst rates each of the 194 items on such things as applicability, importance to the job, and extent of use. Each interview can last up to three hours. Multiple interviews are required to analyze each job.

4. *Critical Incident Technique.* This technique results in job specific descriptions that are behavioral in orientation.[37] Subject matter experts describe situations that they have observed that characterize various performance levels. Critical incidents usually are recorded as brief scenarios or episodes of employee behavior. Each describes what led up to the incident, what the employee did, and the consequences of the critical behavior. The critical incidents are then examined and grouped according to some underlying theme. The resulting categories or dimensions form a composite picture of the job. The categories can then be rated and fully described in terms of importance to the overall job or the incidents can be used separately to serve other purposes. For example, the incidents are the basic elements in certain performance appraisal systems.

5. *Exxon's Position Description Inventory.* Early in the 1980s the Personnel Research Group in Exxon U.S.A. initiated a company-wide study of executive, managerial, professional, and technical job positions.

---

[36] Ernest J. McCormick, Paul R. Jeanneret, and Robert C. Mecham, "A study of job characteristics and job dimensions as based on the Position Analysis Questionnaire (PAQ)," *Journal of Applied Psychology,* 1972, *56,* 347–368; Ernest J. McCormick, Paul R. Jeanneret, and Robert C. Mecham, *Position Analysis Questionnaire: Manuals and Related Materials.* West Lafayette, Indiana: Purdue Research Foundation, 1977.

[37] J. C. Flanagan, "The critical incident technique," *Psychological Bulletin,* 1954, *51,* 327–358.

The objective of the project was to modify the company's performance and promotability rating system. The company appropriately desired to base the new performance appraisal system on specific job requirements and the context in which jobs are performed. The first step was to construct a questionnaire or inventory that would be completed by job incumbents and their immediate superiors. The inventory was divided into three sections. Section I listed 175 job activities. Each activity was then rated. If the activity was judged to be part of the job, it was rated in terms of importance and the amount of time spent on the activity. Section II listed 57 abilities potentially related to performing the job. The abilities were then rated on a usefulness scale indicating the degree to which the ability affected job performance. Finally, the third section listed 53 environmental, contextual, or personal characteristics. Each also was rated in terms of its relation to the job being analyzed. Representative material from Sections I and II is displayed in Figure 11–6.

After the inventories were completed, the information was subjected to statistical analyses designed to organize the various elements (i.e., the individual activity, ability, and job characteristic items) into meaningful categories. These categories then become the basis for further analysis and evaluation. In Chapter 16, one result of the Exxon job analysis will be described in detail.

The Exxon inventory is presented because it represents the use of a sophisticated job-based method that was uniquely designed to meet the needs of a particular company. The approach uses both a person- and task-oriented methodology to meet the company's objectives. Also, it represents what is possible when a company sets out to develop a personnel system supported by a thorough program of research.

Method/Purpose Congruence

There are many other methods that could have been described in the previous section.[38] The five selected methods represent high quality, but dissimilar approaches to job analysis. They were presented to illustrate and clarify a critical point. There is no one best job analysis method. The appropriate method depends on the purpose it serves.

Ultimately, systematic research will provide the necessary evidence needed to select the job analysis method most useful given a particular organization problem. Currently, expert opinion provides perhaps the best guidance regarding method/purpose congruences.[39] Based on this form of evidence, it is clear that certain methods possess a clear relative advantage

[38] E. L. Levine, R. A. Ash, H. Hall, and F. Sistrunk, "Evaluation of job analysis methods by experienced job analysts," *Academy of Management Journal,* 1983, *26,* 339–348.
[39] *Ibid.*

Activity

	Part		Importance					Time Spent				
	Not Part	Part	Unimportant	Limited Importance	Important	Very Important	Essential	Much Less	Less	Average	More	Much More
031 Compare actual performance with forecasts, schedules and/or budgets	N	P	1	2	3	4	5	1	2	3	4	5
032 Write regular work/logs or other summaries of work activities	N	P	1	2	3	4	5	1	2	3	4	5
033 Consolidate data and/or information from numerous sources	N	P	1	2	3	4	5	1	2	3	4	5
034 Prepare speeches, briefings, or presentations	N	P	1	2	3	4	5	1	2	3	4	5
035 Schedule/coordinate events or visits (e.g., briefings, conferences, interviews)	N	P	1	2	3	4	5	1	2	3	4	5
036 Brief others on the content of reports, letters, etc.	N	P	1	2	3	4	5	1	2	3	4	5
037 Prepare agenda for and conduct meetings	N	P	1	2	3	4	5	1	2	3	4	5
038 Interpret and organize complicated information in order to write reports, briefs or memoranda to summarize the information	N	P	1	2	3	4	5	1	2	3	4	5
039 Keep track of proposed and existing legislations, court interpretations and agency regulations that might affect the company	N	P	1	2	3	4	5	1	2	3	4	5
040 Monitor the compliance of company practices with local, state and federal laws, regulations, and guidelines	N	P	1	2	3	4	5	1	2	3	4	5
041 Study and interpret government rulings and/or directives	N	P	1	2	3	4	5	1	2	3	4	5
042 Work outside the company in the drafting and discussion of legislation and agency regulations that might affect the company	N	P	1	2	3	4	5	1	2	3	4	5
043 Represent the company in litigation—testify and/or answer questions before courts, regulatory agencies, or legislative committees	N	P	1	2	3	4	5	1	2	3	4	5
044 Explain company policies and procedures to outsiders	N	P	1	2	3	4	5	1	2	3	4	5
045 Write articles, news releases or other such material	N	P	1	2	3	4	5	1	2	3	4	5

Ability
(Please do not skip any of these items)

	Time Spent				
	Much Less	Less	Average	More	Much More
176 Ability to write with clarity and precision	1	2	3	4	5
177 Ability to check grammar, spelling and punctuation in written material	1	2	3	4	5
178 Ability to express one's self orally with clarity and precision	1	2	3	4	5
179 Ability to make speeches or presentations before groups of varying sizes	1	2	3	4	5
180 Ability to explain technical materials to others who are not familiar with the pertinent technical terms	1	2	3	4	5
181 Ability to listen effectively (hear accurately and confirm understanding)	1	2	3	4	5
182 Ability to comprehend new material that has been read, heard or observed	1	2	3	4	5
183 Ability to perform quantitative operations rapidly and accurately	1	2	3	4	5
184 Ability to reason abstractly using quantitative concepts and symbols	1	2	3	4	5
185 Ability to manipulate mentally visual images in two or three dimensions	1	2	3	4	5
186 Ability to perceive pertinent detail which has been presented in a complex form (chart, drawing, report, article, etc.)	1	2	3	4	5
187 Ability to perform clerical functions (checking, coding, etc.)	1	2	3	4	5
188 Ability to handle confidential information appropriately and to exercise care in safeguarding proprietary information	1	2	3	4	5
189 Ability to remember pertinent information and selectively recall at a later time	1	2	3	4	5
190 Ability to sell an idea or proposal to others (higher management, customers, store operators, etc.)	1	2	3	4	5

Figure 11-6   **Sample Items from Exxon's Position Description Inventory**

over other methods given a particular goal. For example, the Position Analysis Questionnaire possesses a relative advantage over many techniques when used as input into the job evaluation process. Job evaluation requires a standardized approach since different jobs need to be compared across a common set of job dimensions or factors. The Job Element Method, as a second example, is well suited to aid in the identification of training needs, since it focuses on job specific knowledge, skills, and abilities that would become the target of a training intervention. These are the kinds of issues that need to be addressed before initiating the collection of job-based information. For firms that develop one general strategy for the collection of job analysis data, the method will need to serve multiple purposes. In this case the method should include an anlysis of important work behaviors (along with a rationale for this determination) and the resulting products and services. It is upon this base that person-oriented information must be linked.

Task Characteristics

In recent years there has been considerable attention paid to the design of jobs. Many theorists have argued that internal work motivation is central to sustain high levels of employee performance.[40] Internal or intrinsic motivation is thought to be directly linked to the task properties of a job. The experienced meaningfulness and responsibility associated with a job, along with knowledge of results, apparently relates to high internal motivational states. For example, modifying a pure assembly line task so that employees take part in planning, assembly, and inspection activities is believed to enhance the experienced meaningfulness of work.

Companies that are engaged in job design activities find it useful to measure task characteristics both before and after a modification has taken place. Currently most task design studies use one of two measurement instruments created to assess employee perceptions of task properties. This type of measurement also serves as a useful supplement to a traditional job analysis for companies not directly engaged in job redesign efforts.

The first instrument is referred to as the Job Diagnostic Survey or JDS.[41] A manger who administers the JDS can focus on five key job design dimensions. Taken together they are used to describe the motivating potential of a job. The dimensions include *skill variety, task identity, task significance, autonomy,* and *feedback.* Variety refers to the number of different activities required by the job. Task identity relates to whether or not the output of work is an identifiable whole or the degree to which the

---

[40] Ricky W. Griffin, *Task Design: A Integrative Approach.* Glenview, Ill.: Scott, Foresman and Company, 1982.

[41] J. Richard Hackman, and Gregg. G. Oldham, "Development of the Job Diaagnostic Survey," *Journal of Applied Psychology,* 1975, *60,* 159–170.

job requires completion of an identifiable piece of work. Task significance is the degree to which the job has a substantial impact on the lives or work of other people. Autonomy refers to individual freedom and discretion in completing assignments, while feedback is the degree to which job activities provide clear and direct information about the effectiveness of performance. The JDS provides scores on these core job dimensions, a method for combining these dimensions into an overall job rating, and other related summaries.

The second measurement instrument is the Job Characteristics Inventory or JCI.[42] The JCI, like the JDS, measures skill variety, task identity, autonomy, and feedback, but does not measure task significance. Also, the JCI includes two measurement dimensions referring to interpersonal relations with co-workers.

Dimensions of Individual Differences

Given that the characteristics of jobs and the characteristics of individuals need to be simultaneously taken into account when designing a personnel program, it follows that we now turn our attention to ways of describing individual differences. This section will concentrate on frameworks for describing differences between people. It will not focus on the available technology for measuring individual differences. Therefore, this section will be brief in comparison to the discussion of job-based information. This is intentional, since the measurement of individual differences is so central to many personnel practices that detailed information about measurement issues will follow in subsequent chapters as we focus on staffing and developmental activities.

Aptitudes, Abilities, and Skills

There is considerable overlap, confusion, and unnecessary complexity associated with definitions of human attributes. We will follow one generally accepted orientation and use the following definitions of aptitudes, abilities, and skills.[43] *Aptitude* refers to a relatively stable person-centered attribute that indicates a general pattern of performance. *Abilities* develop as a result of specialized training and the possession of required aptitudes. Therefore, a person may possess many aptitudes which, when nurtured through education, will lead to a set of abilities. As used here, aptitudes and

---

[42] Henry P. Sims, Andrew D. Szilogyi, and R. T. Keller, "The measurement of job characteristics," *Academy of Management Journal,* 1976, *19,* 195–212.

[43] Marvin D. Dunnette, "Basic attributes of individuals in relation to behavior in organizations," In M. D. Dunnette (Ed.), *Handbook of Industrial and Organizational Psychology.* Chicago: Rand McNally, 1976, 469–520.

abilities both designate cognitive processes. *Skill* is used to designate physical and motor processes. These can be stable or can be modified through training.

The distinction between an aptitude and an ability is important to much of what follows. Certain personnel practices are designed to identify people with potential and to develop these individuals through training and education. Other practices rely on past records of achievement and identify people who are ready to perform job duties with minimal training and development. The identification of potential relies on aptitude measurement while achievement based approaches rely on ability measurement.

There are many taxonomies available for classifying human aptitudes. According to Dunnette,[44] the following are frequently included as independent groupings of aptitudes. *Verbal comprehension* relates to understanding the meaning of words and their relations to each other, such as displayed when playing anagrams. *Number aptitude* focuses on a facility for numerical reasoning (e.g., to be speedy and accurate in making arithmetic calculations). *Inductive reasoning* is an aptitude for discovering a rule or principle and applying it to solving a problem. *Rote memory* is the aptitude for being able to recall paired words, lists of numbers, and so forth. *Spatial aptitude* relates to being able to visualize objects in space and to perceive their properties and spatial relations with other objects if changed in position. Finally, *perceptual speed* is an attribute related to being able to perceive visual details—similarities and differences—quickly and accurately.

Relatively stable motor and physical skills also have been identified. While cognitive aptitudes are presumed to be important for understanding the elements in our environment, motor skills relate to the capacity to physically manipulate objects in the environment. Fleishman[45] concluded that there are eleven independent motor skills. These include such skills as *manual dexterity, arm-hand steadiness, finger dexterity, reaction time,* and *multi-level coordination.*

So far, we have discussed the organization of cognitive aptitudes and motor skills. These are the attributes that form a composite view of human potential. This potential can only be realized through appropriate training, experience, and education. The ability to successfully perform on the job is therefore a function of aptitude, skill, experience, and opportunity. However, job behavior also depends on a willingness to perform. There are other person-centered attributes that relate to motivation. Personality, needs, and vocational interests are important to this aspect of classifying differences in individuals. It is to these attributes that we now turn our attention.

---

[44] *Ibid.*

[45] Edwin A. Fleishman, "The description and prediction of perceptualmotor skill learning," In R. Glaser (Ed.), *Training Research and Education.* Pittsburgh: University of Pittsburgh Press, 1962.

Personality, Needs, and Interests

Classifications that organize people according to dispositions to act in certain ways are numerous. It is common to observe speech, dress, manner, and modes of reaction and infer a degree of behavioral predictability. People seem to display a level of individuality that characterizes how they will behave in a particular setting. The perceived consistency of behavior that seems to differentiate one person from another is central to what is meant by the concept of personality.[46] Personality, needs, and interests are concepts that are closely related. The goal is not to make fine distinctions between these constructs, but to briefly introduce or survey certain concepts that seem to have relevance for understanding work behavior. We simply sample from a rather large domain to illustrate possibilities.

McClelland's Learned Needs

McClelland has proposed a theory of motivation that focuses on learned needs.[47] Three of these are the need for achievement (n Ach), the need for affiliation (n Aff), and the need for power (n Power). High n Ach is characterized by people who desire accomplishment. These individuals seek situations in which it is possible to take personal responsibility and get personal credit for a successful outcome. They attempt to achieve success through their own efforts and abilities, prefer tasks characterized by intermediate levels of difficulty and risk, and seek situations that provide knowledge of results within a reasonable time. Individuals with high n Power seek to control their environments and influence the behavior of others, while n Aff is associated with a need to develop friendships and to be sociable and caring of others.

McClelland views power motivation as an essential attribute for explaining managerial effectiveness in large corporations. A strong need for affiliation, however, may interfere with effective managerial performance. Perhaps the greatest attention has been paid to the need for achievement. There is evidence that n Ach is related to a variety of work roles but is most often associated with entrepreneurial success.

Work Orientation

A variety of attributes relate to what has been termed *work orientation*.[48] Work orientation is characterized by high personal work standards. Irrespective of task type, high work oriented people are described as industri-

---

[46] H. Gough, Personality and personality assessment. In M. D. Dunnette (Ed.), *Handbook of Industrial and Organizational Psychology.* Chicago: Rand McNally, 1976, 571–607.

[47] D. C. McClelland, *The Achievement Motive.* New York. Appleton-Century-Crofts, 1953; McClelland, D. C., and Burnham, D. Power is the great motivator. *Harvard Business Review,* March-April, 1976, 100–111.

[48] Harrison G. Gough, "A work orientation scale for the California Psychological Inventory," *Journal of Applied Psychology,* 1985, *70,* 505–513.

ous, conscientious, responsible, and persevering. The concept resembles what has historically been termed the Protestant work ethic. There are likely to be many occupations and work settings that require people who set high work standards but who do not necessarily strive for advancement and status.

Locus of Control

There are a variety of traits that relate to an individual's cognitive style or the way information is processed and interpreted. Locus of control refers to such a trait. Individuals who believe that they control their environments or that what happens to them is caused by their own actions are classified as having an *internal* locus of control. Individuals classified as having an *external* locus of control tend to see the external environment as less controllable and predictable than do internals. Externals are more likely to believe that what happens to them is a function of luck, chance, or some autonomous external agent. Locus of control has been shown to relate to a number of work relevant issues. For example, internals are more likely to be satisfied when working under a participative management system while externals appear to prefer a more directive leadership style.[49]

Managerial Motivation

Based on a comprehensive program of research, Miner has developed a measure of the motivation to manage.[50] It appears to be a stable, multidimensional personal trait that relates to managerial role performance. Individuals possessing high levels of managerial motivation desire to engage in competitive activities, desire to behave in an active and assertive manner, desire to influence others, desire to assume highly visible and distinctive positions, and are willing to take on administrative tasks.

Vocational Interests

There has been a tremendous amount of research concerned with the concept of vocational interest.[51] When people are asked to express their interest in such things as occupations, school subjects, amusements, and usual activities, stable interest profiles appear. Most measures of vocational interest cluster respondents in terms of interest similarities with people actually working in given occupational groups. Research evidence shows that there is a high degree of interest profile permanence. The evidence also suggests that early interests are predictive of later occupational choice. As

---

[49] T. R. Mitchell, C. M. Smyser, and S. E. Weed, "Locus of control: Supervision and work satisfaction," *Academy of Management Journal,* 1975, *18,* 623–630.

[50] John B. Miner, "Twenty years of research on role-motivation theory of managerial effectiveness," *Personnel Psychology,* 1978, *31,* 739–760.

[51] Robert M. Guion, *Personnel Testing.* New York: McGraw-Hill, 1965, 307–312.

EXAMPLE 11.2   SURVEY SHOWS MAJOR INTEREST AND VALUE SHIFTS AMONG COLLEGE STUDENTS

A record 24 percent of college freshman recently participating in the 21st annual survey by the University of California, Los Angeles, and the American Council on Education said they were headed for careers in business, up from 12 percent in 1968. This represents only one of many signs indicating that the values and interests of current college students differ substantially from the students of the late 1960s and early 1970s. Perhaps the most significant finding is that 73 percent of the current students listed "being very well-off financially" as a top goal while only 39 percent felt that way in 1970.

Source: Christopher Connell (AP education writer), "Survey of college freshman shows interest rising in business, dropping in computers," *Lawrence Journal World,* January 11, 1987, p. 8a.

depicted in Example 11–2, interests and values can vary dramatically across cohorts of new entrants into the labor market.

Summary

This chapter has set the stage for what is to follow. Describing the properties of jobs and identifying the knowledge, skills, abilities, and other attributes required for satisfactory job behavior serves a supporting role in the management of human resources. In following chapters we will describe and evaluate key human resource management activities. Staffing, development, and compensation practices will be discussed in terms of their impact on behavior and ultimately in terms of their usefulness or effect on firm performance.

In this chapter we have argued that for managers to efficiently allocate their human resources expenditures they need to be able to determine the likely causes and consequences of employee behavior. Therefore certain frameworks have been reviewed that illustrate the importance of taking the attributes of people and the properties of jobs simultaneously into account when designing human resource programs. These frameworks illustrate the importance of creating congruence between person and job attributes.

The final sections of the chapter provided information on how jobs and individuals can be described. The purposes served by job-based information and the methods available for collecting information were reviewed along with general frameworks for describing differences between people. These processes serve as input into a variety of managerial practices. It is to these key decision making and human resource management activities that we now turn our attention.

PROBLEMS

1. You are a unit manager in a large retailing organization. After reviewing annual absenteeism records you are convinced that your unit's absenteeism rate must be reduced. How would you approach this problem? How do you know a problem exists? What are the determinants of absenteeism? What do we know about the relationship between absenteeism and other important outcome variables (e.g., job performance)?
2. How does a firm's regional (and national) labor market affect:
   a. decisions about the use of various personnel interventions (e.g., improving productivity via the use of a staffing strategy versus a training and development strategy versus a compensation strategy)?
   b. its strategic business plan?
3. Describe the various methods used by firms to create congruence between person and job attributes.
4. How has the "baby-boom" generation affected the management of human resources?
5. Why is it useful for line managers to possess knowledge about the job analysis process and the various methods currently available for meeting a firms job-based information needs?
6. Employees can differ on many dimensions (abilities, skills, needs, interests, values, etc.). Discuss the costs and benefits associated with a heterogeneous group of employees. That is, at the level of operating departments, consider how employees with different personal attributes can work to the advantage and disadvantage of the firm.

REFERENCES

Gael, S. *Job Analysis Handbook.* New York: Wiley and Sons, in press.

Goodman, Paul S. and Atking, Robert S. *Absenteeism.* San Francisco: Jossey-Bass, 1984.

March, James G. and Simon, Herbert. *Organizations.* New York: Wiley, 1958.

Pinder, Craig C. *Work Motivation: Theory, Issues, and Applications.* Glenview, Il.: Scott, Foresman and Company, 1984.

Tyler, Leona E. *The Psychology of Human Differences.* New York: Appleton-Century-Crofts, 1965.

Vroom, Victor H. *Work and Motivation.* New York: John Wiley and Sons, 1964.

CHAPTER 12

ORGANIZATIONAL ENTRY

T his chapter is about meeting organizational staffing needs through the external hiring process. The mechanisms controlling external labor markets and the roles these markets play in formulating human resource policy decisions at the level of the firm were outlined in Chapter 3. The concepts and practices described in this chapter relate to identifying people who will be able and willing to do a job well within the context of a particular organization.[1] An idealized version of this process would begin with the identification of human resource needs through a systematic analysis of a firm's demand for and supply of labor. As a practical matter, demand for labor within the firm often depends on such things as a firm's business plans and budgets, management philosophy, and technological advances. Similarly, the supply of labor to an enterprise varies as a function of many internal and external factors such as a company's current talent inventory, attrition and internal employee movement, the effects of past training and compensation programs, the composition and type of the external labor force, and employment opportunities created by competing firms. As discussed in the chapter on labor supply, if a personnel shortage is predicted, a variety of firm policy approaches could be used to meet this need. An external hiring program represents one such alternative and will be our focus here. Once a shortage has been predicted, recruiting activities

---

[1] Benjamin Schneider, *Staffing Organizations,* Scott, Foresman and Co., Glenview, Illinois.

236

generate applicants for target jobs, and selection decisions must then be made that attempt to choose the subset of applicants, or the applicant, most likely to succeed.

This chapter has four primary objectives. First, various methods of selection will be described. These are the techniques used by companies when making job offer decisions. This section will be descriptive, not evaluative, and will provide a general framework for classifying procedures. The second objective will focus on ways organizations go about showing that a selection procedure is valid (i.e., showing that a selection procedure samples job performance or is predictive of subsequent performance or other relevant job behaviors). Third, a general cost-benefit approach to making hiring decisions will be developed. This is a critical section since it serves to develop the underlying principles used for making cost-benefit estimates as they relate to a variety of personnel practices and interventions. These underlying principles are essentially the same as those developed earlier in the text, but since they were developed by personnel researchers they address unique operational issues. Also, these ideas are described here since employee selection represents the first area where a true cost-benefit approach to personnel decision making emerged in the 1940s.[2] Finally, the chapter will make some evaluative statements regarding the various selection methods. These statements will be based on the published research literature that addresses employee selection. After completing this chapter you should be better prepared to: 1) identify and design selection procedures that will meet specified objectives (e.g., the identification of job candidates possessing job knowledge versus the identification of candidates possessing a willingness to perform and remain with the firm); 2) demonstrate the job relatedness of various selection procedures; 3) critically evaluate alternative selection procedures in terms of costs and benefits to the firm; and 4) identify selection procedures that have a history of providing relatively accurate predictions of employee behavior.

Methods of Selection

Being willing is not the same as being able to perform a job. In characterizing the various methods of selection this simple distinction will be used to classify typical approaches. First, we will describe common methods used to measure ability or capacity to perform. Then, measures of motivation will be discussed. Unfortunately, many hiring procedures cannnot be classified without first considering intended use. Therefore, it will be necessary to describe a variety of common hiring methods in a situation specific manner. These we will refer to as specially derived measures.

---

[2] H. D. Brogden, "When Testing Pays Off," *Personnel Psychology,* 2, 1949, pp. 171–185.

Measures of Capacity

Many procedures are available to help firms identify individuals who currently possess the knowledge, skills, and abilities (KSA's) required to perform a job, or individuals who possess the aptitudes required to acquire the necessary KSA's through training and experience. Seven general forms of measurement are described in what follows.

1. *Aptitude Tests.* One common approach that addresses the potential to learn job-related KSA's is the use of standardized occupational aptitude tests. Descriptions of these tests are available from many sources. Information can be found in test reviews, such as those reported in the series of Mental Measurements Yearbooks,[3] from test publisher catalogs and manuals, and from text books and articles devoted to this topic.[4] Aptitude tests range from measures of general intelligence, to multidimensional test batteries, to measures of specific aptitudes believed to be relevant for specific jobs (e.g., clerical aptitude tests or computer programmer aptitude tests). They cover cognitive, sensory, and psychomotor capacities. For example, tests of vision, dexerity, flexibility, balance, and coordination are used in specific industrial settings.

2. *Academic Performance.* Performance in academic settings is regarded as an important hiring standard by many employers. The most convenient and frequently used measures of performance in high school, college, or graduate school are average grades (GPA) or class rank. While these would seemingly measure cognitive factors, some employers may use academic performance as an indicator or sign of other attributes. For example, some may infer that a bachelor's degree indicates commitment to particular goals and values. Therefore, classifying academic performance as an indicator of capacity is problematic. Also, academic performance can be thought of as a sample (an A in an accounting class may indicate a required level of job knowledge) or as a sign (being able to learn accounting principles indicates the capacity to learn). This further complicates these forms of measurement.

3. *Trainability Tests.* Trainability tests are used to select personnel for training rather than to choose people who are already able to perform the job.[5] Here, training content is sampled and the job applicant experiences a structured and controlled period of learning. Applicants receive training on a sample of job tasks and are evaluated on their ability to perform the tasks. These tests are job specific and must be redesigned as the target job changes. The essential process is to obtain a sample of the applicants' training behavior as a basis for prediction. The degree to which the applicant is able to acquire job-related knowledge during the trial training session is taken to be a measure of job specific learning ability.

[3] James V. Mitchell, Jr. (Ed.), *The Ninth Mental Measurements Yearbook,* Buros Institute of Mental Measurements, Lincoln, Nebraska, 1985.

[4] Schneider. *Ibid.*

[5] A. D. Siegel, "Miniature Job Training and Evaluation as a Selection/Classification Device," *Human Factors,* 20, 1978, pp. 189–200.

4. *Job Knowledge Tests.* There are many hiring situations that call for the identification of trained personnel for positions that require technical knowledge and skill. Companies that hire such individuals, rather than develop them through training programs, often rely on job specific knowledge tests. When developed properly, these tests include questions that represent the entire knowledge domain of the job and often weight knowledge areas by considering how critical they are to total job performance. These tests are of the paper-and-pencil variety and often use a multiple choice response format. They are developed by persons knowledgeable about the target job, such as current incumbents and their supervisors. These tests are most commonly used in craft (e.g., for hiring machinists, electricians, electronic technicians) and other technical positions. At another level, many licensing procedures require the passing of a knowledge test designed to cover key concepts needed to practice a particular profession.

5. *Work Sample Tests.* Work sample tests are based on the principle that miniature replicas of on-the-job behavior serve as particularly good estimates of subsequent on-the-job behavior. One of the best examples of a hiring system based on work sample tests was reported by Campion,[6] who developed a series of work samples to hire fully trained maintenance mechanics. He developed a four-hour work sample that required the completion of four tasks: installing pulleys and belts, disassembling and repairing a gearbox, installing and aligning a motor, and pressing a bushing into a sprocket and reaming it to fit a shaft. Performance on these work samples was judged by using a carefully constructed checklist evaluation form. For most work samples it is possible to evaluate both the final result and the steps followed in completing the assigned task.

Work sample tests have been used in many settings and can include both motor and cognitive components. Most are developed specifically for a target job. A few examples from a review article by Asher and Sciarrino[7] serve to illustrate possibilities and include:

- a vehicle repair test
- a test for the inspection of electronic defects
- a drivers test
- a map reading test
- a programming test
- a technical magazine editor's test which involves writing skill, the choice of picture headlines, layout, story organization, and design
- an oral fact-finding test for communications consultants
- a skill in writing business letters test
- a role playing test that simulates telephone contact with customers

[6] James E. Campion, "Work Sampling for Personnel Selection," *Journal of Applied Psychology,* 56, 1972, pp. 40–44.

[7] James J. Asher and James A. Sciarrino, "Realistic Work Sample Tests: A Review," *Personnel Psychology,* 27, 1974, pp. 519–533.

6. *Assessment Centers.* Assessment centers represent a special form of the work sample technique. Their primary use in major U.S. companies has been in the area of supervisory and managerial selection. In an assessment center, job candidates participate in multiple exercises designed to simulate managerial work. Performance is observed and evaluated by a team of trained assessors. This assessor group can be and often is made up of higher-level managers of the hiring company. After the observation of behavior in a variety of exercises, assessors evaluate the extent to which candidates possess each of a series of personal characteristics. These often include dimensions such as leadership, decision making, stress tolerance, management control, initiative, oral communication, and planning and organizing. These evaluations of candidates' standing on the various dimensions are then combined to form an overall assessment of managerial potential. Common simulations include in-basket exercises, analysis problems, group discussions, role play exercises, and oral and written communication exercises. These are all designed to realistically simulate various aspects of managerial work.

7. *Training and Experience Evaluations.* In most hiring situations applicants provide information via application forms, questionnaires, resumes, and other written documents. The likelihood of success in the job under consideration is then evaluated by making judgments about the applicants' past experiences. These judgments often focus on past work and educational experiences. What actually is being measured when purely subjective judgments are made is difficult to determine, since past experiences could be used to make inferences about required knowledge, skills, and abilities or about motivational states. The name for formal procedures for collecting and scoring information of this type is Training and Experience Evaluation (T&E).[8] Formal T&E systems are most commonly found in the public sector where judgments about candidates' backgrounds are translated into scores and then used for ranking purposes. Multiple T&E evaluation methods currently are available for making employment decisions.

Measures of Motivation

Here our attention will focus on ways of measuring the "will do" component in a selection system. It is possible that highly qualified people (i.e., they possess needed KSA's) will not use their qualifications. The general orientation is to attempt to measure either motives, needs, and values or relatively stable behavior patterns or styles (usually called personality traits). There is great variety associated with this form of assessment but we will follow convention and consider both so-called personality tests and interest inventories.

---

[8] Ronald A. Ash and Edward L. Levine, "Job Applicant Training and Work Experience Evaluation: An Empirical Comparison of Four Methods," *Journal of Applied Psychology,* 70, 1985, pp. 572–576.

EXAMPLE 12.1   MORE FIRMS USE PERSONALITY TESTS FOR ENTRY-LEVEL JOBS

There is evidence that companies are increasing their use of personality and other tests designed to measure the motivational states of potential employees. This trend seems most prevalent at companies using participative approaches to management and for jobs requiring an overall "motivation to please others." When technical and production employees are organized into semi-autonomous work teams, some employers now screen applicants by considering personality dimensions (e.g., "people orientation") considered to be required for high job performance and satisfaction. For example, a Midwest food-products company considers how candidates for blue-collar technician and maintenance jobs work in groups. The company also attempts to gauge candidates' flexibility. One company official credits the hiring process for low turnover and absenteeism and improved productivity.

Other companies say that personality testing can help them hire better clerical and customer-service employees. This trend seems to be developing in financial service and insurance firms where competition requires improved customer service.

Source: Larry Reibstein, "More firms use personality tests for entry-level, blue-collar jobs." *Wall Street Journal,* January 16, 1986, p. 31.

1. *Personality Tests.* The most common form of personality testing in industry is the paper-and-pencil, self-descriptive inventory. There are many tests available and as in the case of aptitude testing, information about these tests can be readily found in publishers' catalogs and manuals, texts devoted to personnel testing,[9] and sources that publish reviews of various tests.

Among the criticisms lodged against standardized, self-report inventories is the concern that applicants will be motivated to give the answers an employer might want to hear rather than an accurate self description. For this and other reasons, projective techniques have been used in industry. These are tests like the Rorschach inkblot test.[10] These tests offer unrestricted response possibilities and apparently are resistant to faking and response bias.

Personality assessment can take many forms. Inferences about personality dimensions are probably central to the standard practice of interviewing job candidates and are even made by observing samples of handwriting. A recent *Wall Street Journal* article suggests that handwriting analysis for employment purposes may be rather widespread.[11] Handwriting analysis or

---

[9] Schneider, *Ibid.*

[10] David Rapaport, Merton M. Gill and Roy Shafer, *Diagnostic Psychological Testing,* International Universities Press, New York, 1968, pp. 268–463.

[11] Roger U. Ricklip, "To Land a Position in Paris, Penmanship Can be Paramount," *Wall Street Journal,* September 3, 1985.

graphology seems to focus on possible linkages between handwriting and personality/motivational tendencies. Some examples of how personality tests are used in industry are provided in Example 12–1.

2. *Measures of Interest.* Interests are defined as attitudes toward activities.[12] The general concept here is that interests are motivating; people do things that interest them and perhaps even do the things that interest them well. There are certain tests used in career counseling that have received limited attention in the hiring context.[13] Also, other approaches are being developed specifically for making hiring and placement decisions. For example, Ash, Levine, and Edgell[14] have developed a measurement strategy that matches applicant preferences with job conditions. Applicants are asked to indicate which tasks and job conditions they most like and dislike. These are then matched against the attributes of specific jobs. This general approach can be very job specific and is often based on detailed information coming from a job analysis.

Specially Derived Measures

The collection of information about job applicants can take many forms. This information then must be evaluated and used in the hiring process. Certain techniques are clear with regard to the underlying constructs we are attempting to measure. For example, aptitude tests usually address learning ability while work samples are used to measure KSA levels previously acquired through training and education. Other methods, however, can be used for multiple purposes, depending on the stated goals of decision makers. Also, certain selection procedures apparently work (i.e., generate accurate estimates of future job behaviors or outcomes) but the rationale for their usefulness is not well known. It is this general class of selection procedures that we will characterize next.

1. *Employment Interview.* The typical employment interview represents a complex form of information gathering and processing that leads to judgments about prospective job holders. An interview is a social event in which applicant and interviewer characteristics mutually influence the final result.[15] Research has made it clear that many factors influence an interviewer's impressions about the applicant and the final hiring decision.

---

[12] Robert M. Guion, *Personnel Testing,* McGraw-Hill, New York, 1965, pp. 307–314.

[13] John L. Holland, "Vocational Preferences," In M. D. Dunnette (Ed.), *Handbook of Industrial and Organizational Psychology,* Rand McNally, Chicago, 1976, pp. 521–570.

[14] Ronald A. Ash, Edward L. Levine, and Steven L. Edgell, "Exploratory Study of a Matching Approach to Personnel Selection: The Impact of Ethnicity," *Journal of Applied Psychology,* 64, 1979, pp. 35–41.

[15] Richard D. Arvey and James E. Campion, "The Employment Interview: A Summary and Review of Recent Research," *Personnel Psychology,* 35, 1982, pp. 281–322.

As mentioned earlier, the interview can attempt to measure relevant KSA's by addressing past training and educational experiences and by focusing on previous jobs held by the applicant. However, it is common for interviews to address applicant needs, values, and motivational tendencies. It is not uncommon for interviewers to ask about interests, career plans and expectations, and probing questions about why an applicant is considering a position with the hiring company.

Another form of interview may serve as a type of work sample test. For positions that require verbal interaction and communication skills, the interview can provide a direct behavior sample. Finally, a form of interviewing that relies on the assumption that intentions are related to actual behavior is called the situational interview.[16] During a situational interview applicants describe how they would handle a variety of job-specific problems if given the chance. In the best instances these interviews are based on careful job analysis results. Here, both KSA's and motivation to do and stay on the job can potentially be measured.

2. *Biographical Data.* Biographical data or "bio" data have a long and controversial history in personnel selection.[17] Research about bio data already was appearing in the 1920s when life insurance companies were trying this technique to predict the success of life insurance agents.[18] While the use of biographical or life history data to predict job success is a common part of many selection processes (e.g., reference checks, subjective reviews of application blanks), our purpose here is to describe biographical data that is systematically scored. One approach, the weighted application blank (WAB), is based on empirically scoring the items on a company's application blank to determine which items are indicative of success. The other basic approach involves a formal biographical information blank (BIB). Here, hundreds of questions about past experiences can be asked and again the BIB is scored based on how each question correlates with a measure of job success. The kinds of questions found on a BIB can be of great variety.[19] A few sample bio items include:

1. Did you ever build a model airplane that flew?
2. Before you were 12 years old, did you ever try to perform a chemistry experiment at home?

---

[16] Gary P. Latham, Lise M. Saari, Elliott D. Pursell and Michael A. Campion, "The Situational Interview," *Journal of Applied Psychology,* 65, 1980, pp. 422–427.

[17] George F. Dreher and Paul R. Sackett, *Perspectives on Employee Staffing and Selection,* Richard D. Irwin, Homewood, Illinois, 1983, Chapter 9.

[18] Paul W. Thayer, "Somethings Old, Somethings New," *Personnel Psychology,* 30, 1977, pp. 513–524.

[19] James J. Asher, "The Biographical Item: Can it be Improved?" *Personnel Psychology,* 25, 1972, pp. 251–269.

3. By the time I had graduated from high school, I had been: (the person selects all that apply from a list including such things as editor of the school paper, captain of an athletic team, etc.).

4. When I first went alone on a trip of over 100 miles, my age was:

5. The undergraduate college I attended for the longest period of time was: (the person responds to the appropriate multiple choice alternative).

6. List your three best subjects in high school.

7. As a child did you collect stamps?

This represents only a brief example. Bio data items can cover past achievements, past developmental influences, socioeconomic origins, and a wide variety of other activities and interests.

3. Reference Checking. There are essentially two approaches to reference checking.[20] First, a new employer may contact past employers to verify self-reports of an applicant's previous work history. The other form is more general and is associated with letters of reference written by people selected by the job applicant. In both instances, reference checking and letters of reference, the assumption is that past behavior and performance, as observed by the reference given, is a good predictor of future performance.

4. Honesty and Polygraph Testing. There is extensive and growing interest in using the polygraph and other physical indicators of stress and paper and pencil tests as mechanisms for detecting employee deception.[21] The polygraph (or so-called lie detector) is used for pre-employment screening, in periodic surveys of employee honesty, and for investigating specific thefts or other forms of undesirable behavior. Apparently, these techniques most often are used by commercial banks and retailers.[22] Also, there is a large industry supplying paper and pencil honesty tests for employment use.[23] Some tests used to predict honesty are undisguised and inquire into an applicant's attitudes and beliefs about theft. Others claim to be disguised, and include standard personality items in an attempt to differentiate between so-called honest and dishonest individuals.

---

[20] Richard R. Reilly and Georgia T. Chao, "Validity and Fairness of Some Alternative Employee Selection Procedures," *Personnel Psychology,* 35, 1982, pp. 1–62.

[21] Paul R. Sackett and Phillip J. Decker, "Detection of Deception in the Employment Context: A Review and Critical Analysis," *Personnel Psychology,* 32, 1979, pp. 487–506; Paul R. Sackett and Michael M. Harris, "Honesty Testing for Personnel Selection: A Review and Critique," *Personnel Psychology,* 37, 1984, pp. 221–245.

[22] J. A. Belt and P. B. Holden, "Polygraph Usage Among Major U.S. Corporations," *Personnel Journal,* 57, 1978, pp. 80–86.

[23] Sackett and Harris, *Ibid.*

The Validation Process

A central issue in the area of personnel selection is the validation of selection and promotion systems. Demonstrating the job-relatedness of a selection procedure is critical from at least two vantage points. First, as we will demonstrate in the next section, even slight increases in predictability can (under certain conditions) translate into substantial benefits for the hiring company. Sound management practice, therefore, often dictates the introduction of more valid selection procedures. The second reason for stressing the use of job-related selection techniques is that such procedures help meet state and federal equal employment opportunity requirements. Decision making in both instances requires accurate estimates of validity.

Selection specialists have relied most on two broad classes of validation evidence (criterion-related validation and content validation). Each will be described and illustrated in what follows. Criterion-related evidence is most useful when the goal is to predict future employee behavior. Evidence based on the content validation process represents an atempt to directly sample job behavior. It is most useful when the goal is to identify individuals already possessing the KSA's required to perform the job.

Criterion-Related Validity

This type of validation evidence relies on actually comparing how well individuals perform on some type of selection procedure with some important outcome variable like job performance, promotional success, or turnover. That is, the observed relationship between scores on the selection procedure and one or more independent criteria provides evidence concerning the degree to which the selection device is job-related. The convention is to report this relationship in the form of a correlation coefficient. This statistic summarizes the degree of linear association between two variables. This general analytic approach also is used because making predictions about subsequent behavior is central to making staffing decisions. Regression equations which were discussed in the Appendix to Chapter 2 (i.e., equations for lines that represent the best "fit" to the data) are based on the same assumption of linearity used for this purpose.[24]

In Figure 12–1, we represent the concept of a correlation in scattergram form. Consider a situation in which job applicants complete an

---

[24] For a brief review of statistical concepts as applied to validation principles see Richard D. Arvey, *Fairness in Selecting Employees,* Addison-Wesley, Reading, Massachusetts, 1979, Chapter 2.

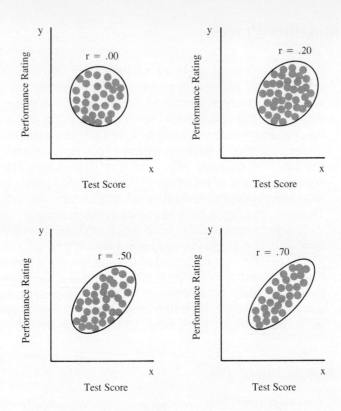

Figure 12-1 **Several Types of Correlational Relationships Represented by Ellipse Diagrams (r = the value of the correlation coefficient)**

aptitude test as part of a company's experimental hiring system. That is, as part of the normal information gathering process, applicants complete employment tests only for the purpose of providing test scores for empirical study (for this round of hiring the scores will not be used for decision-making purposes). A subset of the applicants are then hired on the basis of the company's traditional employment interview. Some time after being hired, the new employees are rated by their immediate supervisor on their overall job performance. Each point indicates a single individual with the test score represented on the x axis and the corresponding performance rating represented on the y axis. Note that when there is essentially no correlation between the two variables the scattergram can be represented by a circle. When the correlation increases we can represent this by using ellipse diagrams of the appropriate shape. These ellipse diagrams will be used in subsequent sections to illustrate certain key points.

Correlation coefficients of sufficient size to be useful to the firm become the primary form of evidence that the selection procedure is job-related. While the research design (method of collecting information) can vary, the essence of the argument focuses on the observed relationship between scores on the selection procedure and scores on an appropriate job outcome measure.[25] The results of the validity study are then used to estimate how job-related and useful the selection procedure would be if used in subsequent rounds of hiring.

Content Validity

The content oriented strategy is a rational, judgmental process that can appropriately be applied only in certain employment contexts. Selection procedures developed in this way should be used to sample from a person's current repertoire of job-related behaviors. Also, it is possible to infer current knowledge, skills, and ability levels using this approach. It is not appropriate to use content validation when the goal is to justify the use of a selection procedure that measures capacity to learn new skills after being hired. Thus, the approach is not applicable for many entry-level jobs.

In conducting a content validity study a job analysis is completed so that a relevant job-content domain can be defined. This includes a description of job tasks, knowledge, skills, and abilities. The selection procedure is then developed by sampling from this domain. The steps followed in sampling and the processes used in evaluating performance on the selection device need to be carefully documented. The most defensible sampling strategies often result in selection procedures that are miniature replicas of certain job components or even the job as a whole. Selection procedures of the work sample variety can appropriately be justified based on the logic of content validation.

Some Illustrations

1. *A Criterion-Related Study.* Previously we described a particular form of employment interview called a situational interview. A validation study focusing on this technique will serve as a useful illustration. Recall that a study of this type is used by the hiring organization to determine the job relatedness of the selection procedure. The results are then used, along with appropriate cost/benefit data, by decision makers to determine whether or not the selection procedure should be used for future rounds of hiring. In this particular case, the job relatedness of the situational interview, when used to hire entry-level workers in a wood products mill, was investigated using a criterion-related validity study.[26]

---

[25] For a description of various research design possibilities along with a discussion of their strengths and weaknesses, see Robert M. Guion and C. J. Cranny, "A Note on Concurrent and Predictive Validity Designs: A Critical Reanalysis," *Journal of Applied Psychology,* 67, 1982, pp. 239–244.

[26] Latham et al., *Ibid.*

The first step in conducting the study was to perform a job analysis using the critical-incident technique.[27] Based on this analysis a measure of job performance (in this case a procedure based on ratings made by supervisors) was developed that addressed key job factors. The job analysis data also were used to construct the interview questions. The questions were in the form of realistic, job-specific situations. Each applicant was asked to describe what they would do if confronted with such a situation. A scoring procedure was established such that the responses to the interview questions could be quantified. The interview (the same set of questions for all applicants) was administered to 56 applicants for the entry-level mill jobs, and all were subsequently hired. The employees' job performance was evaluated by their immediate supervisors after they had been on the job for one year. The evaluating supervisors were not aware of how well any employees had performed in the interview. The correlation between performance in the interview and performance on the job 12 months later was .33 for all 56 employees and .39 for 30 female employees. These correlations were statistically significant at the .05 level and served as evidence of job relatedness. These correlations are usually referred to as validity coefficients. Deciding whether or not the firm should introduce the situational interview as a regular hiring procedure ideally should be determined only after conducting a cost/benefit or utility analysis. In the next section we will develop the concepts needed to integrate selection procedure validity into the standard cost/benefit framework.

2. *A Content-Oriented Study.* The use of content validity to demonstrate the job-relatedness of a series of tests used by a small business to hire a construction superintendent was reported by Robinson.[28] The business is a privately held general contracting firm which builds single- and multi-family houses. The company estimates building costs given land and architectural requirements, invites subcontractor bids, and supervises construction. The properties are then sold or retained for investment. The construction superintendent has general responsibilities for overseeing the entire construction process.

The first step in designing the selection system was to conduct a detailed job analysis. The needed information was collected by bringing together a panel consisting of the president of the company, the production vice president, the financial vice president and the incumbent construction superintendent. Four work sample tests and one structured interview (i.e., the same questions were asked of each interviewee) were developed based on the job analysis results. Careful attention was paid to scoring procedures such that various performance levels on the work samples and interview

---

[27] J. C. Flanagan, "The Critical Incident Technique," *Psychological Bulletin,* 51, 1954, pp. 327–358.

[28] David D. Robinson, "Content-Oriented Personnel Selection in a Small Business Setting," *Personnel Psychology,* 34, 1981, pp. 77–87.

were specified. A multiple-hurdle selection strategy was used (applicants had to pass each test sequentially; failing one test resulted in rejection, and subsequent tests were not then taken). This approach was used since the knowledge and skills required to pass each test were considered critical to successful job performance. This procedure also results in considerable cost savings since work sample tests can be costly to administer.

One excellent example of a job-related work sample test was what Robinson called the "Construction Error Recognition Test." The job analysis results identified the need to be able to find construction errors. Correcting these errors was costly and there was the need to closely follow building codes. The job analysis panel and a number of subcontractors generated a list of 25 common and expensive construction errors. Then, an 8' by 12' shed was constructed such that it incorporated these errors. Applicants were given unlimited time to inspect the building and to list identified errors on a piece of paper. Applicants were given one point for each identified error.

This procedure captures the essence of content validation. Based on job analysis results, a test was developed that represented a critical aspect of the job. In fact, this test was a miniature replica of the actual job setting. Applicants were given the opportunity to demonstrate their knowledge and skill in a realistic way and objective scoring procedures were utilized. This clearly is an instance of the appropriate use of content validation to demonstrate the job-relatedness of a selection test.

Decision Theory and Personnel Selection[29]

Decision theory offers a framework for determining if selection/staffing system modifications are in the best interest of the firm. Using this framework we can move from understanding the behavioral consequences of a selection system change to understanding consequences at the level of the firm such as organizational costs and the value of goods and services produced. This is a very important transition in thinking about the usefulness of personnel programs and practices. This kind of thinking is relatively new and will be presented to take into account the evolving nature of decision theory contributions to the area of personnel selection. The goal will be to develop more than a set of techniques or tools. Possessing an intuitive grasp of the material is important. Therefore, certain preliminary concepts will be reviewed as background and will set the stage for presenting the standard utility model.

---

[29] For a review of the history and development of selection utility models see Frank L. Schmidt, John E. Hunter, Robert C. McKenzie, and Tressie W. Muldrow, "Impact of Valid Selection Procedures on Work-Force Productivity," *Journal of Applied Psychology,* 64, 1979, pp. 609–626.

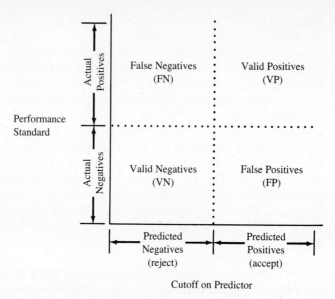

Figure 12-2 **Classification of Predictions Based on Selection Procedure Results by Actual Outcomes**

Classifying Predictions by Outcomes

In simplified form we can say that one of four possible outcomes can result from a personnel selection decision.[30] When success is predicted (e.g., applicants pass a selection test or an interviewer determines that certain applicants should be hired) and success results (after being hired the individuals perform at or above the minimum standard set by the firm), we refer to these individuals as valid positives (VP). When success is predicted and the hired individuals subsequently fail to perform at the minimum standard, we refer to these individuals as false positives (FP). When failure is predicted and failure would occur (we correctly reject applicants), we classify these individuals as valid negatives (VN). Finally, when individuals are predicted to fail or are rejected for employment but succeed when given the chance (e.g., an applicant is hired by a competitor and performs at or above an acceptable level), we classify these individuals as false negatives (FN). This is graphically represented in Figure 12-2.

---

[30] Jerry S. Wiggins, *Personality and Prediction: Principles of Personality Assessment,* Addison-Wesley, Reading, Massachusetts, 1973, Chapter 6.

In most situations the goal is to minimize selection errors (FP and FNs) and maximize correct decisions (VPs and VNs), since there is positive return to the firm associated with hiring above standard performers and negative returns associated with both forms of error. False positives can cost more than they are worth, disrupt the performance of others, damage equipment and supplies, and cause injury to others while FNs represent an opportunity cost.

Validity, Base Rates, and Selection Ratios

The usefulness or utility of a selection procedure depends on multiple factors. One of these factors is the association between scores on the predictor or selection device and scores on an important outcome variable like job-performance (the validity of the predictor). In addition to predictor validity, the context within which the predictor is used must be captured in the analysis. Two primary factors are 1) the base rate (BR), and 2) the selection ratio (SR). The base rate refers to the proportion of the total applicant group or pool that would perform at or above the minimum standard if given the chance. The BR will vary as a function of labor market characteristics, the recruiting strategies used by the firm, and the level of performance considered acceptable to the organization. The selection ratio represents the proportion of the total applicant pool actually selected by the hiring firm. These individuals are predicted to succeed (i.e., they meet the firm's hiring standard). The SR is influenced by labor market characteristics and a variety of decisions affecting selectivity. As the number of applicants increases in relation to the number of openings, the firm can become more selective. One way to do this is by raising the hiring standard.

Recall that one goal usually is to decrease the number of selection errors (FPs and FNs) and to increase the occurrence of correct decisions (VPs and VNs). This can be accomplished in multiple ways by operating on validities, BRs and SRs. This will be illustrated in what follows.

Consider the following hypothetical situation. A firm plans to hire 50 new employees for a particular job classification. One hundred applicants respond to a recruitment advertisement. Approximately 50 percent of these individuals have the capacity and motivation to perform the target job at or above the company's minimum standard. The jobs all must be filled and the company's personnel director personally interviews all 100 applicants. Unfortunately, the personnel director is not a competent interviewer and his decisions are not better than chance (i.e., random selection would work just as well). The interviewer is not aware of his lack of interviewing ability and ranks the 100 applicants in terms of his judgments. This also could be

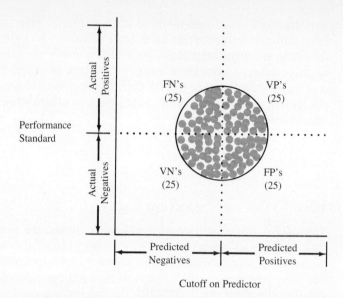

Cutoff on Predictor

Figure 12-3 **Outcomes When r = .00, BR = .50, and SR = .50 (values in parentheses represent the number of individuals per cell)**

accomplished by setting a minimum passing score that would separate the applicants at the median. This situation is represented in Figure 12–3.

Note that random selection is the same as using a selection procedure with a validity of 0 (r = .00). In this illustration the BR = .50 and the SR = .50. If 50 applicants are randomly selected and 25 are expected to meet the minimum performance standard, we have a situation in which there will be 25 VPs and 25 FPs. Since the same logic can be applied to the rejected applicants, the results here would be 25 FNs and 25 VNs.

Now consider what would happen if, instead of using the judgment of the personnel director, the company uses a valid selection test (a work sample test). Assume that the validity of the work sample test is .50 (r = .50). This change is represented in Figure 12–4. By introducing the work sample test the number of correct decisions (VPs and VNs) has increased and the number of errors (FPs and FNs) has been reduced.

Likewise, changes in either the BR or SR will affect the proportion of VPs, FPs, VNs, and FNs. Figure 12–5 represents what would happen if the quality of the applicant pool improved (i.e., a larger proportion of the applicant pool would succeed if given the chance). In this illustration we have retained a validity of .50.

Finally, what if the company only needed to hire 25 new employees. With 100 applicants the company can become more selective and raise the

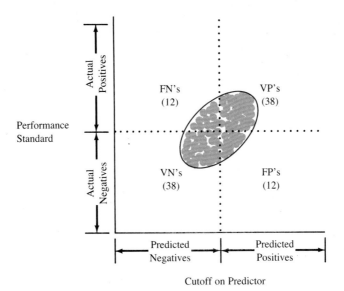

Figure 12-4 **Outcomes When r = .50, BR = .50, and SR = .50 (values in parentheses represent the number of individuals per cell)**

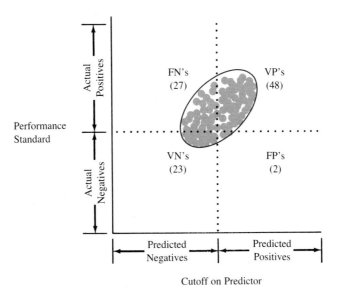

Figure 12-5 **Outcomes When r = 50, BR = .75, and SR = .50 (values in parentheses represent the number of individuals per cell)**

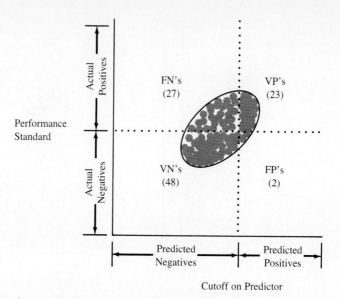

Figure 12-6   **Outcomes When r = .50, BR = .50, and SR = .25 (values in
parentheses represent the number of individuals per cell)**

passing point on the work sample test. As shown in Figure 12–6, a change
in the SR results in a different outcome pattern.

Since VPs, FPs, VNs, and FNs represent different benefit or cost levels
to the firm, it is the case that changing any of the three key parameters (r,
SR, BR) will affect the usefulness of the selection procedure. Taking all
three simultaneously into account can help clarify many selection decisions. These concepts serve as a base for understanding the standard utility
model. This model takes a different form and introduces other needed
components, but still incorporates much of the logic of the previous
discussion.

The Standard Utility Model[31]

The utility or net benefit derived from improved selection procedures is
based on the following utility equation:[32]

$$\Delta \overline{U}/\text{selectee} = (r_{xy})(SD_y)(\overline{Z}_x) - C/p. \tag{1}$$

[31] Schmidt et al., *Ibid.*
[32] H. E. Brogden, "When Testing Pays Off," *Personnel Psychology,* 2, 1949, pp. 171–185.

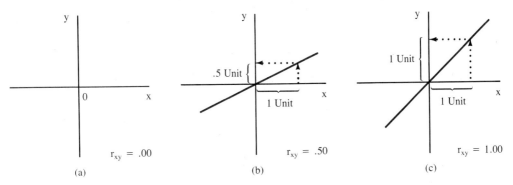

Figure 12-7 **Regression Lines at Difference Values of r_{xy} When x and y Are in Standard or Z Score Form**

where:

$\Delta\overline{U}$/selectee = the average gain in dollar-value payoff per selectee that results from using selection procedure x instead of selecting randomly.

r_{xy} = the correlation coefficient between predictor scores (x) and dollar-value payoff among prescreened applicants.

SD_y = the standard deviation of dollar-value payoff in the group of prescreened applicants.

$\overline{Z}_x$ = the average standardized predictor score for the selected group.

C = the cost of using the selection procedure per applicant screened.

p = the selection ratio (ratio of selectees to applicants).

We now turn to how each component of the model affects utility.

The Role of r_{xy}.   When a regression equation is cast in standard score form, the correlation coefficient is the slope of regression line.[33] One interpretation of the correlation coefficient, therefore, is that it states the amount of increase in y which accompanies a unit increase in x when both measures are expressed in standard score or Z score units. A Z score states how many standard deviations the score lies above or below the mean of the distribution. Following our previous discussion, assume that we are able to estimate the correlation between scores on a selection procedure (x) and a measure of job performance for prescreened applicants. If both units of measurement are in Z score form, the correlation coefficient is the slope of the regression line. In Figure 12–7 we illustrate what happens when the correlation increases.

[33] Edward W. Minium, *Statistical Reasoning in Psychology and Education,* John Wiley & Sons, New York, 1970, pp. 174–177.

Since the regression line is a horizontal line passing through the origin (0,0), when $r_{xy} = .0$ the best estimate of performance (y) at any value of x is the mean of y in standard score form or 0. As the correlation increases from .0 to .5, as shown in Figure 12–7(b), the predicted level of y increases .5 units. If we could hire a group scoring, on average, one standard deviation above the mean predictor score for the entire applicant group, we would predict a .5 standard deviation improvement in mean performance for these individuals. Likewise, a perfect predictor would result in a one standard deviation improvement in performance as represented in Figure 12–7(c).

SD_y. This represents the value of one standard deviation difference in performance among job applicants cast in dollar terms. Most applications and our current treatment will define SD_y in terms of "service value" or the dollar value of products and services. SD_y captures the differences between average performers and superior performers (or average and poor performers) and will vary as a function of labor market characteristics and job type. For example, SD_y is likely to be much larger for systems analysts than for janitors. However, in any given situation, a very homogeneous group of systems analysts will result in lower SD_y estimates than for an applicant population consisting of analysts with varying degrees of capacity and desire to perform.

Detailed procedures for estimating SD_y will be presented in Chapter 16. Current research suggests that rational estimates of SD_y are sufficient for many applications, thus it is not necessary (and often not possible) to rely on complex cost accounting procedures when making SD_y estimates. The standard estimation method was developed by Schmidt, Hunter, McKenzie, and Muldrow[34] and is based on the assumption that job performance is a normally distributed variable. If this is the case, the differences between the value of products and services produced by the average employee (50th percentile performer) and those produced by a superior employee (85th percentile performer) will equal SD_y. (Recall that for normally distributed variables, approximately 85 percent of the cases have values less than the value that lies one standard deviation above the mean.) Data are collected from persons knowledgeable about the target job (usually supervisors) using questionnaires. They estimate the value to their organization of the products and services produced by average, 85th percentile, and 15th percentile performers. When making these judgments, respondents are asked to consider what the cost would be of having an outside firm produce these products and services. Multiple judges are used and their estimates averaged to minimize idiosyncratic tendencies, biases, and random errors. The difference between the average value assigned to the 85th percentile performer and the average value assigned to the 50th percentile performer (or between the 15th and 50th percentile performers)

---

[34] Schmidt et al., *Ibid.*

is used as SD_y. Also, as described in Chapter 16, other methods for estimating SD_y have been proposed. For example, there is some evidence that SD_y equals about 40 to 60 percent of the average salary received by employees in the target job. Thus, some very inexpensive and relatively easy to use procedures exist for making SD_y estimates.

$\overline{Z}_x$. This is the average predictor score (in standard score form) for the group of hired individuals. This will increase as the firm sets higher employment standards. If we assume that the predictor scores are normally distributed, then $\overline{Z}_x$ for the selected group may be computed by the formula λ/p, where λ is the height of the normal curve at the point of cut (normal curve ordinate at a given predictor cutoff value in Z score form), and p is the selection ratio. Table 12–1 provides values of λ and λ/p for selected values of p. In some situations it is possible to compute $\overline{Z}_x$ directly. However, in most instances, we assume that predictor scores are normally distributed and estimate $\overline{Z}_x$ by substituting λ/p since p (the selection ratio) can be readily determined. This substitution will be used in all subsequent versions of equation 1. When r_{xy} is multipled by $\overline{Z}_x$ we estimate the performance gain to be expected from using predictor x instead of hiring randomly. When we multiply this term by SD_y we are able to estimate the improvement in service value since we are simply translating improvement in Z score form into dollar form.

C/p. C is the cost of using the predictor per applicant. The C/p term represents the increased cost associated with using a predictor with a validity of r_{xy} in place of random selection. We set the cost of random selction at \$0. As the number of applicants goes up in relation to the number finally hired, costs will increase. These increased costs must be subtracted from the increased service value associated with hiring better performers to arrive at an estimate of net benefit.

p (selection ratio)	λ (normal curve ordinate)	λ/p (estimate of $\overline{Z}_x$)
.05	.1023	2.05
.10	.1758	1.75
.20	.2803	1.40
.30	.3485	1.16
.40	.3867	.96
.50	.3989	.80
.60	.3867	.65
.70	.3485	.50
.80	.2803	.35
.90	.1758	.20
.95	.1023	.11

[1]For a complete set of tabled values see: Cascio, W. F. *Costing Human Resources: The Financial Impact of Behavior in Organizations.* Boston: Kent, 1982.

Table 12–1   **A Table for Estimating $\overline{Z}_x$[1]**

In its current form, equation 1 is incomplete and deficient. In what follows we will systematically modify equation 1 taking these concerns into account. The final form of this equation will be used to illustrate how this approach can be applied in the context of employee selection. These modifications will result in what appears to be a cumbersome, unwieldly model. The examples that follow this developmental material will demonstrate, however, that in practice the various model components can be estimated and used to make informed decisions.

Some Operational Adjustments

The standard utility model (Equation 1) has received considerable recent attention. In 1979, Schmidt, Hunter, McKenzie, and Muldrow,[35] published a very influential paper that reviewed the historical development of selection utility models and applied these ideas, in modified form, to estimate the impact of using a valid aptitude test for hiring computer programmers. Two adjustments described in the Schmidt et al. paper will be made to Equation 1.

Adjusting for Existing Alternatives. Using Equation 1, the benefits from using a new selection procedure, per selectee, instead of selecting randomly can be estimated. Since SD_y is usually measured in terms of annual employee contribution, we are estimating the net benefit resulting from the better-selected employee working for one year. Equation 1 is based on the assumption that the existing selection procedure, since it operates at the level of chance, is essentially cost free. In most situations, however, a decision maker is attempting to determine if a new selection procedure should be introduced instead of continuing to use an existing procedure that works better than chance (i.e., $r > .00$). In this case the existing procedure will incur costs. Equation 1 must be modified to reflect this situation.

Adjusting for Number Hired. We usually are interested in the net benefit associated with hiring more than one individual. Equation 1 can be modified to reflect this by simply multiplying both the service value term and the cost term by the number of persons hired in a given year.

Taking both operational issues simultaneously into account results in

$$\Delta U = (N)(r_1 - r_2)(SD_y)(\lambda/p) - (N)(C_1 - C_2)/p. \qquad (2)$$

where: ΔU = the increase in dollar payoff (realized at the end of one year) that results from selecting N employees using a new selection procedure instead of the existing procedure.

N = the number selected in a given year.

r_1 = the validity of the new selection procedure.

---

[35] Schmidt et al., *Ibid.*

r_2 = the validity of the existing selection procedure.

SD_y = the standard deviation of dollar-value payoff, estimated in terms of annual contribution.

λ/p = the estimated $\overline{Z}_x$.

C_1 = the cost per applicant of using the new procedure.

C_2 = the cost per applicant of using the existing procedure.

p = the selection ratio.

Adjustments Based on Economic Concepts

Boudreau,[36] noting that investments in personnel programs must be evaluated like other investment options, incorporated three economic concepts into the basic utility framework. His contributions will be discussed and a version of his adjusted utility model will be presented. We will then use this framework to provide some illustrations.

Adjusting for Variable Costs. There are many potential variable costs associated with higher-performing employees. For example, better-selected, higher-performing employees generate increased sales revenue but may demand higher levels of compensation. The most obvious case is in the area of sales where a bonus or commission is often associated with higher sales volume. In addition, higher-producing people in many jobs may demand higher levels of compensation to prevent them from resigning or may increase costs by requiring additional material and staff support. The dominate variable costs for many products will be material and processing costs. Conversely, it is possible, in certain jobs, for high performers to save costs. For example, high performers may save material and maintenance costs by creating less waste and by properly using equipment. If these costs are proportional to sales value, Boudreau[37] has shown that certain adjustments are appropriate.

Adjusting for Taxes. For many organizations, taxes produce a proportional reduction in both revenue and costs. Boudreau[38] has argued that the marginal tax rate should be used to make this adjustment.

Discounting. As noted throughout this text, the principles of discounting are relevant to personnel program utility since benefits, and sometimes costs, accrue over time. For example, when a new hiring procedure is used to select employees, the benefits received are spread out over the tenure of the new employee group. Better-selected employees will continue to make contributions throughout the duration of employment. These gains in future time periods must take into account different opportunity costs.

---

[36] John W. Boudreau, "Economic Considerations in Estimating the Utility of Human Resource Productivity Improvement Programs," *Personnel Psychology,"* 36, 1983, pp. 551–576.

[37] Boudreau, *Ibid.*

[38] Boudreau, *Ibid.*

Boudreau[39] provides the needed adjustments for dealing with a series of discounted yearly payoffs. For ease of presentation we will assume that certain model components are constant over time (e.g., variable costs, taxes).

The final form of the utility equation takes all three of Boudreau's adjustments into account and assumes that the costs of selection occur only at the beginning and therefore are not subject to discounting.

$$\Delta U = (N) \times \left\{ \sum_{t=1}^{T} [1/(1+i)^t](r_1 - r_2)(SD_y)(\lambda/p)(1 + V)(1 - TAX) \right\}$$
$$- [(N)(C_1 - C_2)/P][1 - TAX] \qquad (3)$$

where: ΔU = the increase in dollar payoff (realized over the tenure of the new employees) that results from selecting N employees using a new selection procedure instead of the existing procedure.

$\quad\quad$ N = the number of employees selected

$\quad\quad$ t = the time period in which the benefit occurs.

$\quad\quad$ i = the discount rate.

$\quad\quad r_1$ = the validity of the new selection procedure.

$\quad\quad r_2$ = the validity of the existing selection procedure.

$\quad SD_y$ = the standard deviation of dollar-value payoff, estimated in terms of annual contribution.

$\quad \lambda/p$ = the estimated $\overline{Z}_x$.

$\quad\quad$ T = average tenure of new employees.

$\quad\quad C_1$ = the cost per applicant of using the new procedure.

$\quad\quad C_2$ = the cost per applicant of using the existing procedure.

$\quad\quad$ V = the proportion of service value (attributable to improved selection) represented by variable costs (will take on a negative value when costs increase with increased revenue and will take on a positive value when costs decrease with increased revenue).

$\quad$ TAX = the marginal tax rate.

$\quad\quad$ p = the selection ratio.

Some Illustrations

Assume that a medium-sized food products manufacturing firm expects to hire 10 new salespersons during the next year. Experience indicates that the average tenure of persons in these occupations is two years. The yearly sales value difference between a superior and average performing salesperson is expected to be $9500. This value is used to estimate the standard deviation of annual dollar-value payoff. As noted earlier, these estimation procedures will be discussed in detail in the chapter devoted to performance measurement and appraisal. For our purposes, it is sufficient to say that the yearly

---

[39] Boudreau, *Ibid.*

sales value generated by a high performing salesperson (an 85th percentile performer) is compared to the yearly sales value generated by an average salesperson (a 50th percentile performer). Also, assume that variable costs represent a large proportion of the sales price for the company's products. Material costs, sales commissions, distribution costs, and other processing costs that increase as a function of improved selection comprise 45 percent of sales revenue. A discount rate of 10 percent also is appropriate for this company as is a 30 percent marginal tax rate. The company foresees a stable labor market and expects approximately five applicants for every two positions.

The question before the company's budget committee is whether or not to implement a new hiring procedure in the sales area. The personnel director has reviewed a variety of alternative selection procedures and, based on published validity studies, estimates that a half-day assessment center would result in better predictions of subsequent salesperson performance. The estimated validity (correlation between assessment center ratings and job performance) is .35. Currently the company uses a hiring procedure requiring multiple interviews per applicant with an estimated validity of .15. The per-applicant cost of the interview is $75 while the assessment center will cost approximately $250 per applicant.

To assist in answering the question, Equation (3) is used in the following form:

$$\Delta U = (10) \times \left\{ \sum_{t=1}^{2} [1/(1+.10)^t](.35 - .15)(9{,}500)(.39/.40)(1 - .45)(1 - .30) \right\} - [(10)(250 - 75)/.40][1 - .30] = 9347.40.$$

Under these circumstances, the net benefit of using the assessment center instead of the interview for hiring 10 new salespersons would be $9347.40. This represents the gain realized over the tenure of the new employees. Given these results, the decision would normally be to implement the assessment center.

This same company also expects to hire approximately 15 sales route drivers over the next year. These individuals serve retail distributors by making deliveries over established routes. They do not solicit new business but do provide other direct customer services by stocking shelves and vending machines and by setting up merchandise and sales promotion displays. Their performance directly influences sales revenue but at a level far below that of the district salesperson. For example, late deliveries or low quality display maintenance can influence customer preferences for products. The labor market also does not reflect great individual differences in the capacity or motivation to perform jobs of this type. The company estimates the yearly sales value difference between superior and average performing route drivers to be $1500. The annual tenure for route drivers is again two years. Also, assume that costs which vary with increases in sales value resulting from better selection will comprise 40 percent of sales value. The route drivers do not receive merit or bonus pay. As in the previous case, the discount rate is 10 percent and the marginal tax rate is 30 percent. The labor market is stable and a constant recruiting cost generates many more applicants than positions. Essentially, the company can make decisions regarding how many applicants to process (i.e., the company can set the selection ratio).

Once again, the question before the company's budget committee is whether or not to implement a new hiring procedure. Currently the company uses an inexpensive hiring procedure consisting of a resumé review and reference check with previous employers. Based on data collected during the past five years the company has been able to estimate the procedure's validity. While the current procedure displays some predictive power ($r = .20$) there is growing evidence that more valid alternatives are available. In particular, a competitor is using a highly structured, situational interview with a reported validity of .45. However, the new procedure is expensive, costing nearly $95 per applicant. This compares with a $12 per applicant cost for the existing procedure. While the essential question relates to picking the most useful selection procedure, a second issue relates to determining the appropriate selection ratio (i.e., how many applicants should be accepted before the round of recruiting closes?).

Applying Equation 3 and using a range of selection ratios provide useful information for the budget committee. This information is displayed in Table 12–2.

As indicated in Table 12–2, decisions regarding the use of the new selection procedure depend on the number of applicants interviewed or the selection ratio (SR). The new procedure would almost always be judged to be more useful, but, of the SRs included in the table, SR = .30 would result in the greatest net benefit. Note that at very low selection ratios (e.g., SR = .05) the cost of using the new interview exceeds the benefits gained.

Table 12–2 also illustrates a very important point. The technology now exists that allows managers to ask "what if" questions and to quickly see the impact of changing the values of utility model variables. Table 12–2 presents estimates for a range of selection ratios. When operating with anything but very low selection ratios the decision is always to use the situational interview. Spreadsheet software and the availability of micro-computers provides an environment in which managers can compute net benefit estimates while varying critical model components. This allows the decision maker to set the conditions, in the form of boundaries, that must be met before selecting one alternative over another.

Validity Evidence

In this final section of the chapter we will briefly comment on the existing literature devoted to the validity of various selection methods. One of the most interesting features of this literature is that for certain commonly used approaches to screening and selection almost no systematic research exists regarding job-relatedness. For other selection procedures the literature is vast and often difficult to summarize. For any given selection problem, the

SR	Number interviewed	Total gain	Increased cost of interview	Net benefit
.05	300	$8,405	$17,430	−$9,025
.10	150	7,175	8,715	−1,539
.20	75	5,740	4,357	1,383
.30	50	4,756	2,905	1,851
.40	37	3,936	2,179	1,757
.60	25	2,665	1,453	1,212

Table 12-2 **Estimated Net Benefit Associated with Using the Situational Interview to Hire Sales Route Drivers**

relevant literature should be thoroughly reviewed. What follows simply serves as an introduction to this information source. Also, we saved these comments for last because, without proper concern for cost-benefit or utility concepts, it is easy to mistakenly interpret validity in terms of usefulness.

Measures of Capacity

Standardized tests designed to measure aptitude have been found to be related to various criterion measures in many settings. In a classic review of the literature, Ghiselli[40] concluded that validity coefficients were "quite respectable" for training criteria and "somewhat less so" for predicting proficiency or job performance criteria. This is to be expected since aptitude testing focuses on capacity to acquire new knowledge, skills, and abilities. Thus, there should be a closer correspondence between aptitude and success in training programs than between aptitude and general measures of job proficiency. When identifying the best test per occupation, average validities in Ghiselli's review were in the mid .40s for training criteria and the mid .30s for proficiency criteria. Most recent reviews substantiate the finding that standardized aptitude tests are valid for many selection purposes.[41]

Job samples of the work sample and assessment center variety have received considerable research attention. Asher[42] summarized the early literature and observed that 78 percent of the validity coefficients associated with motor work samples (work samples with a clear physical skill component) were equal to or greater than .30 when job proficiency was a criterion. The percentage of validity coefficients equal to or greater than .30 for verbal work samples (language or people oriented work samples) was 60 percent. The validity evidence for managerial assessment centers is some-

[40] Edwin E. Ghiselli, "The Validity of Aptitude Tests in Personnel Selection," *Personnel Psychology,* 26, 1973, pp. 461–477.

[41] Reilly and Chao, *Ibid:* Neal Schmitt and Michael Kirsch, "Metaanalyses of Validity Studies Published Between 1964 and 1982 and the Investigation of Study Characteristics," *Personnel Psychology,* 37, 1984, pp. 407–422.

[42] James J. Asher and James A. Sciarrino, "Realistic Work Sample Tests: A Review," *Personnel Psychology,* 27, 1974, pp. 519–533.

what more complex. While there have been many empirical studies focusing on the assessment center process, only a few studies have used uncontaminated criterion variables.[43] Unfortunately, much of the research in this area uses data from operational assessment centers. Here, the results of assessment are made available to the job candidates' superiors or others involved in making hiring or promotion decisions. Thus, criteria like "promotion success" are often contaminated. The result of this contamination is an overestimate of what the validity would be if assessment results were not used to make promotion decisions. Given this limitation, a recent review reported that assessment center validities in the low .40s are common.[44]

The results of a large number of studies investigating the relationship between academic performance and job/career success are not very promising.[45] The degree to which GPA or class standing predicts rated job performance is particularly low with validity estimates rarely exceeding .20. One potential reason for these disappointing results is that these measures take on different meanings per applicant depending on such factors as school quality, grading standards, and subject difficulty.

Some form of training and experience (T & E) evaluation is perhaps the most commonly used screening device. Almost all employers use some form of application blank or resumé review for collecting information about job candidates. Interestingly, little empirical evidence exists regarding job-relatedness. Many employers use a content validity approach to justify the use of T & E requirements. This may be appropriate when very specific requirements, as identified through a job analysis, are the focus of attention (e.g., the specification of certain college course requirements due to their content). The logic of content validity becomes less convincing when general requirements (e.g., the possession of a high school diploma) are the focus of attention. Similarly, trainability tests and job knowledge tests are commonly defended on content validity grounds.

Measures of Motivation

Personality testing and, to a lesser degree, interest testing has dominated standardized attempts to measure motivation and use this information to make hiring decisions. Most reviews of this literature conclude that personality and interest inventories have produced disappointing results when used to make employment predictions.[46] The noted exception involves certain managerial and sales occupations, where the results seem

---

[43] Paul R. Sackett, "A Critical Look at Some Common Beliefs About Assessment Centers," *Public Personnel Management,* 11, 1982, pp. 140–147.

[44] Schmitt and Kirsch, *Ibid.*

[45] Reilly and Chao, *Ibid.*

[46] Herbert G. Heneman III, Donald P. Schwab, John A. Fossum, and Lee D. Dyer, *Personnel/Human Resources Management,* Richard D. Irwin, Homewood, Illinois, 1983, p. 285.

more promising. Of all the predictors recently examined in a review of validity studies published between 1964 and 1982, personality tests consistently generated comparatively low validity estimates.[47] The average validity coefficient across all job and criterion variables for personality tests was .15. A similar review of recent studies using projective measures of personality reached the same conclusion.[48]

Part of the problem here may be that tests originally designed for clinical and counseling purposes have been inappropriately used in the employment context. It may be that personality-like measurement, when designed to address key aspects of work behavior, will produce more favorable results. For example, there is evidence that *achievement motivation* relates to success in starting a small business.[49] The link between entrepreneurial success and the need for achievement represents one promising area in which personality testing may play a useful role.

Specially Derived Measures

The employment interview is perhaps the most commonly used selection technique; and yet there is research literature showing the interview to be a particularly poor predictor of job success.[50] This literature focuses on the typical, unstructured employment interview and attributes (in part) the problem of low validity to low levels of inter-rater reliability. Multiple interviewers, each gathering and processing information from the same interviewee, often disagree about the candidate's potential or ability to perform the target job.

This literature not only documents the lack of validity and reliability associated with the interview, but also includes many studies of the interviewing process. The logic being that these "process" studies will provide insight into why the typical interview is not particularly useful. Some of the findings from these studies include:[51]

1. Material is not covered consistently in unstructured interviews.
2. Interviewers are likely to weight the same information differently when making final decisions.
3. Structured interviews are likely to display higher inter-rater reliability.
4. Interviewers make decisions quite early in the unstructured interview.
5. Interviewers are influenced more by unfavorable information than favorable information.

---

[47] Schmitt and Kirsch, *Ibid.*

[48] Reilly and Chao, *Ibid.*

[49] John B. Miner, *Theories of Organizational Behavior,* Dryden Press, Hinsdale, Illinois, 1980, p. 60.

[50] Arvey and Campion, *Ibid;* Heneman et al., *Ibid.*

[51] Arvey and Campion, *Ibid.*

6. Nonverbal sources of information are quite important.
7. Inter-rater reliability increases when interviewers receive or already possess detailed information about the target job.
8. The form of the evaluation may be linked to interview validity (e.g., when interviewers rate job candidates on specific and relevant job dimensions, accuracy is enhanced).
9. Contrast-effects, or how a given candidate compares to previous interviewees, may influence absolute judgments.

In summary, interviewer judgments are influenced by a variety of potentially irrelevant factors when conducting the typical, unstructured interview. On the positive side, however, certain steps are likely to favorably influence the interviewing process. These include providing more structure, job information, and task relevant rating scales. Also, the *situational interview,* as previously discussed, has produced some promising results. Finally, there are likely to be hiring situations that require skills that can be displayed directly during the interview (e.g., jobs requiring interpersonal comunication skills). For this situation, interviews become work sample tests and are likely to be useful.

Empirically scored biographical data seem to work, but require very careful development and maintenance. A sophisticated program of research is required to develop and score biographical instruments. In a recent review by Reilly and Chao[52] the mean validity coefficient, across 44 studies was .35, with results indicating success in predicting multiple criteria, including tenure (mean r = .32), performance in training (mean r = .39), job performance (mean r = .36), productivity (mean r = .46), and salary progress (mean r = .34). While these are favorable results, it needs to be emphasized that most employers will not have sufficient resources to develop a selection system dependent upon this type of predictor. Also, the question of why biographical data works is largely unanswered. Many argue that empirical evidence is not sufficient to warrant use and that a rational justification for the inclusion of questions is necessary.[53]

Some form of reference checking often plays a role in the screening and selection process and yet this is another area in which there is little empirical research. Based on this limited research, most reviews conclude that reference checking has relatively low validity in the employment context.[54] Low reliability, leniency, and poor response rates are associated with these conclusions. The most common complaint is that references and recommendations all tend to be favorable and therefore are not very useful in differentiating between job candidates.[55] Simply consider the process

---

[52] Reilly and Chao, *Ibid.*

[53] L. A. Pace and L. F. Schoenfeldt, "Legal Concerns in the Use of Weighted Applications," *Personnel Psychology,* 30, 1977, pp. 159–166.

[54] Reilly and Chao, *Ibid.*

[55] Heneman et al., *Ibid,* p. 287.

used by job candidates when they select reference persons, and part of the problem becomes obvious.

Finally, we will conclude our review of the validity evidence by commenting on procedures used to detect deception in employment settings. This is a very controversial area. For example, eleven states prohibit the use of polygraphs and another twenty-one states provide that the polygraph is to be voluntary.[56] While all of the selection procedures discussed in this chapter should be used in such a way as to comply with employment laws, no other direct legal exclusion exists. Two thorough reviews of the literature have been published.[57] These reviews discuss the problems of conducting research on this topic and, due to their complexity, should be studied in depth by prospective users. At this point there does not seem to be sufficient evidence to draw firm conclusions. In both reviews the authors conclude that more research is urgently needed, given the widespread use of these procedures in industry, if we are to understand when and where these procedures can be appropriately applied.

Summary

In this chapter we have discussed alternative courses of action that can be taken when there is a current or predicted labor shortage and the initiation of a hiring program, as compared to other P/HR activites (e.g., training, compensation, or job design), is judged to be appropriate. We described various methods of selection, discussed the procedures used by firms to show the job-relatedness of these procedures, provided a general utility or decision-theoretic framework, and briefly reviewed the validity evidence associated with these procedures. This was intended to preview managerial options and provide a general, structured approach to personnel decision making. To determine the "usefulness" of a particular approach to staffing, the approach cannot be evaluated in the abstract. It must be compared to alternatives with regard to benefits, costs, and compliance with state and federal employment laws. Here we have emphasized costs and benefits. In chapter 8 we emphasized the legal context within which these decisions must be made. Certainly, if a selection procedure results in adverse impact against a protected group, there is a greater need to show that the procedure is job-related and of business necessity. It is important to note however, that the steps we take to make sound hiring decisions (as defined by our utility models) are often steps that simultaneously comply with the standards set by regulatory agencies. Thus, the employment concepts discussed in this chapter represent an area in which sound managerial practice and legal compliance usually do not lead to contradictory courses of action.

---

[56] William E. Hartsfield, "Polygraphs," *Labor Law Journal,* 36, 1985, pp. 817–834.
[57] Sackett and Decker, *Ibid;* Sackett and Harris, *Ibid.*

PROBLEMS

1. Your consulting firm has been hired by a large state university to develop standards to be used when hiring new faculty members. For a variety of reasons the university must be able to demonstrate that the hiring system is job-related. They intend to rely on a content-oriented approach to making this demonstration. What steps need to be followed in designing a "content valid" selection system? What kinds of selection procedures would you recommend? Is this an appropriate selection problem for the application of content-oriented validation procedures?

2. Recall the illustration of a food products firm and the question before the company's budget committee regarding the implementation of a new hiring procedure for district salespersons. If the assessment center only had an estimated validity of .25, what would the likely decision be concerning its implementation? What if the validity of the assessment center was .40? Holding other conditions constant, how expensive could the assessment center become before it would no longer be to the company's advantage to use it in place of the existing hiring procedure?

3. Why does screening on the basis of college grades (particularly when using overall GPA) pose problems for company's hiring recent college graduates? What would these firms need to do to increase the likelihood that information taken from a college transcript is job-related?

4. You are a real estate broker and have, on average, 20 sales associates working for you. You have experienced great difficulty in hiring new associates. Many are non-productive and eventually leave the industry. They simply are not capable of selling. A recent article in a real estate trade journal, written by the president and vice-president of a test publishing company, described the use of a personality test specially developed to select "top producing" sales associates. You are considering the use of this test. Outline the questions you would ask the test publisher before deciding to purchase this service.

5. What is known about the validity of 1) aptitude tests, 2) personality tests, 3) work sample tests, 4) letters of reference, and 5) assessment centers, when used to select employees?

6. Discuss the affects of the labor market on decision making about alternative practices designed to alleviate an employee shortage within the context of a single firm. Also, how are labor market conditions represented in the standard utility model described in this chapter?

REFERENCES

Cascio, W. F. *Costing human resources: The financial impact of behavior in organizations* (second edition), Boston, Kent Publishing Company, 1987.

Gatewood, R. D., and Field, H. S. *Human resource selection,* New York: The Dryden Press, 1987.

Schneider, B., and Schmitt, N. *Staffing organizations,* (second edition), Glenview, IL: Scott, Foresman and Company, 1986.

CHAPTER 13

INTERNAL STAFFING

I n the previous chapter the process of acquiring new employees was examined. The predicted imbalance in a firm's workforce (in that case a talent shortage) led to decisions to acquire new employees. Particular attention was paid to the utility of adding these new employees to the existing workforce. In reality, however, firms must be concerned with managing an intricate system of employee flows.[1] In this chapter we will extend our discussion of the staffing function to include the movement of employees within and out of the organization's internal labor market.

During periods of projected employee surpluses, internal staffing programs can take on many forms. Depending on the circumstances, firms use such things as hiring freezes, layoffs, early retirement incentives, and employee transfer and promotion policy modifications to manage employee flows. For example, as shown in Example 13–1, an early retirement program was used by IBM to reduce staff size.

Likewise, in the case of predicted employee shortages, firms can initiate a variety of personnel programs that do not focus on external hiring. Methods for identifying and training promising employees, coupled with effective promotion systems are central to meeting internal staffing needs. To manage such a system, the quality of incoming employees must be compared with the quality of exiting employees. An organization that uses highly valid selection and promotion systems will not maximize its returns unless it simultaneously retains the most valued members of its workforce.

---

[1] John W. Boudreau, "Effects of employee flows on utility analysis of human resources productivity improvement programs," *Journal of Applied Psychology,* 68, 1983, pp. 396–407; John W. Boudreau and Chris J. Berger, "Decision-theoretic utility analysis applied to employee separations and acquisitions," *Journal of Applied Psychology,* 70, 1985, pp. 581–612.

EXAMPLE 13.1   IBM SETS PLAN OF INCENTIVES TO TRIM STAFF

In anticipation of sluggish computer demand, International Business Machines Corp. recently announced a program designed to cut several thousand employees from its U.S. workforce. The early retirement offer is expected to save the company more than $100 million annually.

The plan is strictly voluntary as stressed in a written message to U.S. employees by John F. Akers, chairman and chief executive officer. In the message Akers states that the plan will make IBM "leaner, stronger" and still "help us preserve the tradition of full employment."

IBM has had a long tradition of not laying off workers.

The early retirement program creates an incentive to retire by increasing benefits. For example, five years of service and five years of age are added to IBM's basic formula for calculating retirement benefits. This would increase the yearly pension received of a 55-year-old employee who earns $40,000 annually from $12,621 to $16,361.

Source: Dennis Kneale, "IBM sets plan of incentives to trim staff," *Wall Street Journal*, September 15, 1986.

The goal, over time, is to systematically improve overall workforce quality. Of course, the benefits of such an improvement need to be greater than the associated program costs.

This chapter has two fundamental goals. The first is to introduce the reader to some basic notions about career systems. Here we pay particular attention to how employers make internal staffing decisions. The second is to focus on organizational exit. The costs and benefits associated with voluntary turnover are given special attention. Finally, we will discuss constraints to managerial action that affect employee separations. The emerging exceptions to the employment-at-will doctrine will be discussed in the final section of the chapter. After completing this chapter you should be better prepared to 1) design and implement internal staffing systems that are congruent with the external labor market and the mission/goals of the organizational unit of interest; 2) develop and implement strategies for making promotion and separation decisions; and 3) protect your firm from claims of unlawful discharge.

Managing Career Systems

Understanding and exercising direction over a company's career system is, to understate the issue, a complex managerial responsibility. For an illustration we direct your attention to a classic paper written by Mason Haire.[2] He created a hypothetical organization as represented in Figure 13–1. This organization has five levels of management with level I repre-

---

[2] Mason Haire, "Approach to an integrated personnel policy," *Industrial Relations*, 7, 1968, pp. 107–117.

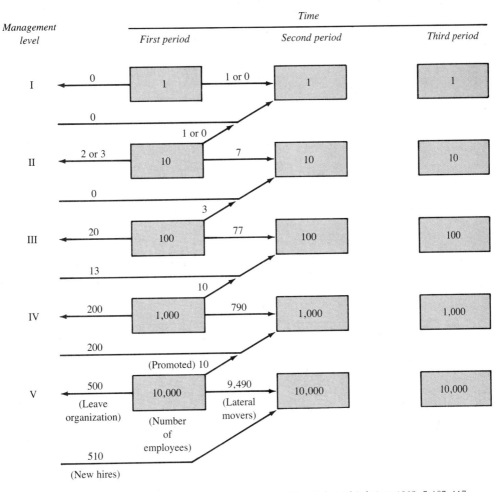

From Haire, M. Approach to an integrated personnel policy. *Industrial Relations,* 1968, *7,* 107–117. Reprinted by permission.

Figure 13-1 **Schematic Diagram of Personnel Movement Over Time**

senting the chief executive. For the sake of simplicity, each level has .10 times as many managers as the level immediately below it, individuals can only move up one level at a time (no one may skip a level), certain promotion probabilities are assumed, individuals may leave the system (certain turnover probabilities are assumed), lateral movement is allowed, and finally, over time the numbers of managers at each level are constant.

The primary goals of the system are 1) to produce goods and services efficiently, and 2) to maintain an optimal pool of promotable managers for the next and eventually higher levels of responsibility (note that under certain circumstances these goals may be in conflict). If the promotion system is performance-based and top performers at level V are promoted to level IV, and so on, maintaining overall system quality depends on many interrelated factors. For example, if the best are promoted out of level V, the remaining employees, on average, will be less good than the original group. If new hires are equal in average quality to the original level V group (i.e., recruiting success is constant over time) and performance is not related to turnover, the average quality of level V employees will be reduced. The only way to maintain original level V quality is to either improve recruiting success or manage the turnover process such that below average performers leave at a higher rate than above average performers. At higher levels the same processes operate with an additional concern being the relative quality of those promoted from below. If an above average group is promoted into higher management and turnover is among higher performing members of the original group, it is quite difficult to maintain the quality of the original group. To do so would require above average external hires and above average performance from those promoted from below. The point here is that a systems perspective is required. Personnel practices must be considered in terms of their simultaneous effects on employee separation, acquisition, and internal movement patterns.

Archetype Career Systems

To complicate the situation further, the most appropriate career system is likely to be a function of additional factors not yet discussed. Theorists are beginning to speculate about the possibility that staffing systems are congruent with organizational characteristics such as structure, size, and business strategy, in high performing companies.[3] Under this view, there needs to be congruence between the organization and its staffing decisions or staffing patterns. Such things as a) executive values and philosophical orientation, b) organization strategies, design, and type, and c) organization life cycle, are thought to influence the choice of appropriate staffing and succession patterns. The premise is that congruence between organization and staffing strategy should affect organization-wide outcomes.

Following the work of Miles and Snow,[4] Olian and Rynes[5] suggest a variety of possible linkages between staffing systems and firm type. A few of these possibilities are illustrated in what follows. Two of the firm types identified by Miles and Snow,[6] defender and prospector firms, will be used to highlight this theoretical work.

Defender companies face relatively stable environments. They strive to become more efficient in producing and or distributing their current products and services. They face strong competition and rely on a continuous process of improving upon what they currently do as a means to enhance firm performance. Prospector companies, on the other hand, face

---

[3] Judy D. Olian and Sara L. Rynes, "Organizational staffing: Integrating practice with strategy," *Industrial Relations, 23*, 1984, pp. 170–183.

[4] Raymond E. Miles and Charles C. Snow, *Organizational Strategy, Structure and Process,* New York: McGraw-Hill, 1978.

[5] Olian and Rynes, *Ibid.*

[6] Miles and Snow, *Ibid.*

Firm Type

Prospector	Defender
To be able to move quickly into new businesses, managerial/profession/technical talent is often acquired from outside the organization.	Individuals tend to enter at low levels, receive considerable on-the-job training and steady promotions if they are of high potential. This is possible due to more highly centralized organizational structure and functional orientation. Managers tend to have narrow specialized skills. This is appropriate since the overall emphasis is on the development of efficient technology and production.
More likely to be more decentralized and organized along divisional or product lines. Employees likely to face relatively frequent changes in duties and assignments due to changing strategic direction.	
Upper-level hiring decisions focus on selection criteria related to proven achievement and specified levels of knowledge, skills and ability.	Selection criteria give minor weight to past achievements and instead focus on future aptitude and potential.
Less likely to formalize selection criteria since job requirements are revised with changes in strategic direction.	Due to stability, types and levels of job qualifications are clearly articulated. Selection and promotion criteria are formalized.
Individuals with a preference for risk taking and unstructured environments best suited for this organization type.	Individuals with high needs for security and structure and low tolerance for change and ambiguity best suited for this organization type.
General reliance on external sources of managerial talent.	Managers tend to be promoted from within. General reliance on internal versus external recruits.
Increased need to use external search and recruiting agencies.	Reduced need to use outside search and recruiting agencies.
More likely to use selection devices that emphasize work history.	More likely to use selection devices that assess applicants' future aptitudes and potential promotability.

[1]This view of strategy-staffing practice linkages comes from Olian, J. D., and Rynes, S. L. "Organizational staffing: Integrating practice with strategy." *Industrial Relations,* 1984, *23,* 170–183. Reprinted by permission.

Table 13-1   **Firm Characteristics and Staffing Systems**[1]

rapidly changing environments. Their strategy is to enhance firm performance by identifying and exploiting new product and market opportunities. Innovation and adaptability characterize these companies. As represented in Table 13–1, the appropriateness of different staffing practices would seem to be a function of firm type.

Another interesting way to characterize career systems is to use the framework originally proposed by Turner[7] and subsequently refined by

---

[7]Ralph Turner, "Sponsored and contest mobility and the school system," *American Sociological Review,* 25, 1960, pp. 855–867.

Rosenbaum.[8] Rosenbaum was able to dimensionalize career and succession systems in terms of sponsored versus contest mobility norms. These represent normative patterns that have potential for clarifying the relationship between a firm's corporate strategy and its guiding staffing principles.

As summarized in Table 13–2, the sponsored mobility approach stresses the early identification of talent. Firms following this norm attempt to benefit from the efficiencies of specialized training and socialization by providing high potential employees with challenging assignments and other opportunities believed to be conducive to employee development. Promotional opportunity is curtailed for persons not assigned to these so-called "fast-track" programs. Sponsored mobility firms attempt to identify high potential individuals early and devote resources to the training and development of these individuals. These firms are characterized by a promotion-from-within approach to staffing.

At the other extreme firms follow a form of contest mobility. Here selection, not training and development, dominates the staffing system. The focus is on identifying individuals with proven achievement records. Late career mobility is permitted and both internal and external candidates can compete for a particular opening. These firms attempt to minimize selection error (potential is more difficult to identify than proven achievement or performance) and emphasize the continuing possibility that hard work, education, training, and perseverance will lead to valued rewards. Of course, no firms follow either succession pattern exclusively. These patterns may be considered as archetypes, and firms may be visualized as approaching one archetype or the other. Even a cursory review of Tables 13–1 and 13–2 suggests that the staffing/succession patterns proposed for prospector firms are very consistent with the guiding principles associated with the contest mobility norm. In like manner, defender firms are shown to require a staffing orientation that is congruent with the principles of sponsored mobility.

Factors Influencing Promotion Decisions

We now turn to factors that influence staffing decisions. For illustrative purposes the focus will be on promotion decisions, but these same processes can usefully be applied to other staffing issues. The goal is to describe a general framework within which the primary factors can be defined. To accomplish this we use a conceptual scheme provided by Stumpf and London.[9] Their approach has a managerial orientation but, for the purpose at hand, does not have to be restricted to this occupational group. As noted in Figure 13–2, the decision process is most directly

---

[8] James E. Rosenbaum, *Career Mobility in a Corporate Hierarchy*, New York: Academic Press, 1984.

[9] Stephen A. Stumpf and Manuel London, "Management promotions: Individual and organizational factors influencing the decision process," *Academy of Management Review*, 6, 1981, pp. 539–549.

Staffing Patterns

Contest Mobility	Sponsored Mobility
Contest mobility is a system (organizing norms) in which successful upward mobility is the prize in an open contest.	Sponsored mobility favors a controlled selection process. Mobility is a process of sponsored induction into the elite.
Contest mobility is like a sporting event in which many compete for a few positions. The contest is judged to be fair only if all participants compete on an equal footing.	The governing objective of sponsored mobility is to make the best use of the talents in society by sorting persons into their proper niches. The norm focuses on efficiency.
The governing objective of contest mobility is to give elite status to those who earn it. The norm focuses on equal opportunity. Contest mobility disapproves of premature judgments and special advantage to those ahead at any point in the competition.	Fairly early selection of the number of persons necessary to fill elite positions is desirable. Early selection allows time to prepare recruits for elite positions.
Contest mobility tends to delay the final award as long as possible to permit a fair race.	Aptitudes and inherent attributes are stressed since elitists take the initiative in training. Early recruitment is important since it insures control over selection and training.
By permitting late mobility, a contest system helps maintain motivation and morale by holding out the possibility that continued effort will pay off.	Selection for ultimate career occurs early. Those selected for elite status are separated from others and given specialized training and socialization.
By focusing on achievement, not potential, a contest system minimizes the chances of selection error.	The sponsored norm stresses efficiency. This is possible due to the efficiencies associated with early selection of a few and specialized training and socialization.
The internal labor market is characterized as offering open opportunity. Attainment is largely a function of continued effort, ability, and the accumulation of human capital.	After assignment to entry jobs, subsequent careers are largely determined since early placements lead to predetermined progression systems.

The terms *sponsored* and *contest* mobility were originally used by Turner (Turner, R. H. Sponsored and contest mobility and the school system. *American Sociological Review,* 1960, *25,* 855–867) and subsequently by Rosenbaum (Rosenbaum, J. E. *Career mobility in a corporate hierarchy.* New York: Academic Press, 1984). Entries in the table are concepts abstracted from both sources.

Table 13-2   **Contest Versus Sponsored Mobility and Organizational Staffing**

influenced by who the decision makers are and the various policies and rules that govern a given situation. For employees represented by a union, the collective bargaining agreement represents a formal set of personnel policies that influence most decisions regarding promotions, layoffs, recalls, and transfers. In other situations the personnel policies are not specifically articulated in written documents. Stumpf and London suggest that decision

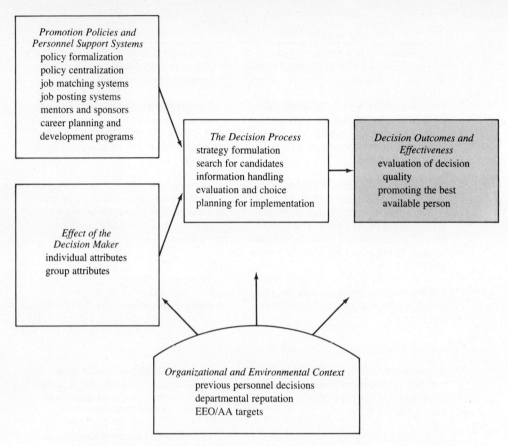

From Stumpf, S. A., and London, M. Management promotions: Individual and organizational factors influencing the decision process. *Academy of Management Review,* 1981, *6,* 539–549. Reprinted by permission.

Figure 13-2   **Factors Influencing Management Promotion Decisions**

maker attributes have the strongest effect on ultimate decisions when personnel policies and rules are not clearly delineated. Thus, when there is concern about decision maker bias and favoritism, formalized policies should help to control these tendencies.

The decision process, as affected by company rules and policies, decision maker attributes, and other contextual factors (e.g., Equal Employment Opportunity and Affirmative Action targets), involves strategy formulation, searching for candidates, processing information, evaluating and choosing between candidates, and planning for implementation.

Strategy formulation represents the extent to which decision makers plan ahead. For example, some managers approach staffing decisions informally, reacting to needs as they arise. Others tend to develop detailed plans in advance of vacancies and create a priori specifications of promotion criteria.

EXAMPLE 13.2 COMPUTERS HELP FIRMS DECIDE WHOM TO PROMOTE

With the advent of software designed to monitor executive talent, computerized career-tracking systems are being used in the personnel planning process. For example, Dallas-based Southland Corporation has computerized its search for fast-trackers. Managers file reports on the promotability of their subordinates and these are consolidated using the new technology. Blake Frank, Southland's manager of personnel research, says that the system is used to "find out whether there will be a deficit of people coming up through the ranks." Among other companies using computerized personnel planning systems are Aetna Life and Casualty Co., Northern Telecom Inc., and Security Pacific National Bank.

Generally, these systems provide rapid means of organizing and retrieving information that already exists in less readily available form (e.g., the employee's resumé). Computerized files are essentially re-coded resumés that include information on salary and performance histories, training and experience records, and employee preferences and expectations.

Source: William M. Bulkeley, "The fast track: Computers help firms decide whom to promote," *Wall Street Journal,* September 18, 1985.

The search process is shown to be a function of both the individual decision maker and the situation. Certainly, explicit company policies specifying such things as formal posting and job matching systems will influence search behavior. However, informal procedures (such as asking others to recommend candidates) play a role of varying importance, depending on the individual characteristics of the decision maker.

How information is collected and combined represents another stage in the decision-making process. There are likely to be individual differences in how much information is collected, the degree to which information is checked for accuracy, and how multiple sources of information are weighted to reach a final decision. Thus, information handling processes are central to understanding how staffing decisions are made. The growing sophistication of companies in being able to collect and process information is depicted in Example 13–2.

Evaluating and choosing between candidates and initiating the process of getting a decision implemented are the final two stages developed in the Stumpf and London framework. Final decisions will depend heavily on the type of information used in judging candidates. In what follows we will discuss commonly used procedures or information gathering techniques. Conceptually, this information is used to predict subsequent success. While all of the *methods of selection* (e.g., assessment centers, reference checking, biographical data, aptitude and personality testing) discussed in the previous chapter can and are used for making internal staffing decisions, we will comment on the use of measures designed and/or used specifically for this purpose. These will include: 1) measures of past performance, 2) seniority systems, 3) the staff analysis method, and 4) the review-board method.

Past Performance. There is a natural tendency to assume that performance in lower level jobs will be predictive of performance in successively higher level jobs. Therefore, using existing performance appraisal systems, past performance is often given some weight when making promotion and transfer decisions. In certain situations, using past performance as a predictor of success in higher level jobs is appropriate. However, in other organizational settings this practice is likely to lead to errors in judgment. To clarify this point we direct you back to Figure 13–1. Recall that this hypothetical organization attempts to: 1) produce goods and services efficiently, and 2) maintain an optimal pool of promotable managers for the next and eventually higher levels of responsibility. If past performance is used as a heavily weighted predictor, both organizational goals will be met only if the system, using Haire's[10] term, is transitive. That is, we must assume that top performers in level V positions will be top performers in level IV positions and that the best at level IV also have the greatest potential for performance at levels III and above. This assumes a set of transportable abilities and characteristics that are equally important at all levels. There are likely to be many situations in which the assumption is inappropriate. Thus, using past performance as a predictor of success in higher level positions is a conceptually sound practice only under a limited set of circumstances. Finally, to date little empirical evidence exists about when and where past performance represents a useful predictor. This will ultimately depend on organizational characteristics (e.g., the degree to which the system is transitive versus intransitive) and the quality of the performance appraisal system. The use of past performance as a deciding factor when making promotion decisions requires a reliable and valid performance appraisal system and appropriate organizational characteristics.

Seniority. While there is some controversy regarding the relative weights managers give to seniority and ability when selecting persons for promotion, employees often are advanced because of their greater length of service.[11] While the empirical evidence concerning whether or not seniority has a worthwhile influence on either individual or company-wide performance is rather sparse, a variety of arguments have been forwarded regarding this issue. A few of the most common are as follows.[12]

---

[10] Haire, *Ibid.*

[11] Katharine G. Abraham and James L. Medoff, "Length of service and promotions in union and nonunion work groups," *Industrial and Labor Relations Review,* 38, 1985, pp. 408–420; D. Quinn Miles, "Seniority versus ability in promotion decisions," *Industrial and Labor Relations Review,* 38, 1985, pp. 421–425.

[12] Michael E. Gordon and William A. Johnson, "Seniority: A review of its legal and scientific standing," *Personnel Psychology,* 35, 1982, pp. 255–280.

1. *Seniority ▓▓▓▓rmance.* While the historical writing on the topic proposed a na▓▓▓▓d positive correlation between productivity and experience, Gordon ▓▓▓Johnson,[13] after reviewing the available literature, concluded that "there is little evidence that workers with longer tenure are more productive either in present or higher level jobs" (p. 266). A summary of their review is presented in Table 13–3.

Specifically, seniority-job performance relationships will likely depend on many complicating factors. These include such things as the time required to acquire job specific knowledge and skills and the relationship between length of service and employee obsolescence.

2. *Seniority and Fairness.* Since seniority can be accurately and reliably assessed, its use should lead to fair decisions. This is a reasonable argument when seniority provisions eliminate staffing decisions based upon favoritism, but it becomes less convincing when the alternative is a staffing system based upon valid predictors of future performance.[14] Also note that definitions and perceptions of "fairness" are likely to vary across subgroups of employees. For example, women and minorities, since they are relative newcomers to many positions traditionally held by white men, may perceive seniority as a mechanism that inhibits movement into higher paying jobs. Thus, certain employees may conclude that seniority provisions are unfair since they simply perpetuate past discrimination against certain groups.

3. *Seniority and Training.* Some labor economists reason that for certain jobs, seniority based promotions work to the advantage of the organization. If knowledge and skills are acquired on the job, there are potential training implications associated with the seniority based approach. Brown and Medoff make the following argument:[15]

> Since promotions and other rewards are not dependent in any clear-cut way on their productivity, seniority can greatly weaken the feeling of rivalry among workers. This can increase the amount of informal training and assistance that workers are willing to provide others (p. 358).

---

[13] The studies reviewed by Gordon and Johnson and displayed in Table 13–3 are as follows: M. E. Gordon and W. J. Fitzgibbons, "Empirical test of the validity of seniority as a factor in staffing decisions," *Journal of Applied Psychology,* 67, 1982, pp. 311–319; M. E. Gordon and S. L. Cohen, "Training behavior as a predictor of trainability," *Personnel Psychology,* 26, 1973, pp. 261–272; J. L. Medoff and K. G. Abraham, "Experience, performance, and earnings," *The Quarterly Journal of Economics,* 95, 1980, 703–736; J. L. Medoff and K. G. Abraham, "Are those paid more really more productive? The case of experience," *The Journal of Human Resources,* 16, 1981, pp. 186–216; W. W. Ronan, "Evaluation of three criteria of management performance," *Journal of Industrial Psychology,* 5, 1970, pp. 18–28; A. F. Siepert, "Promoting our best managerial potentials," *Personnel Administration,* 34, 1971, pp. 8–21; J. Tiffin and E. J. McCormick, *Industrial Psychology* (5th edition), Englewood Cliffs, N.J.: Prentice-Hall, 1965; J. W. Walker, F. Luthans and R. M. Hodgetts, "Who really are the promotables?" *Personnel Journal,* 49, 1970, 123–127.

[14] Gordon and Johnson, *Ibid.*

[15] C. Brown and J. Medoff, "Trade unions in the production process," *Journal of Political Economy,* 86, 1978, 355–378.

Author(s)	Manner in Which Seniority Is Defined		
Gordon & Fitzgibbons (1982)	Time with company prior to assuming current job	162 sewing m̲. operators	...ncantly (p ...performance as mea... ᴜy a quarterly index of production efficiency in higher level organizational roles.
Gordon & Fitzgibbons (1982)	Time in previous job	162 sewing machine operators	Seniority was not significantly ($p > .10$) related to performance as measured by a quarterly index of production efficiency in higher level organizational roles.
Gordon & Fitzgibbons (1982)	Time in job	162 sewing machine operators	$r = .15$ ($p < .05$) between tenure and productivity as measured by a quarterly index of performance.
Gordon (Ref. Note 2)	Time in non-managerial positions within the company	Approx. 1000 managers in a large insurance company (sub-divided by professional specialty)	The shorter the time required to reach management level, the better job performance as measured by promotion rate as a manager ($F = -.30$, $p < .01$).
Gordon & Cohen (1973)	Time required to complete the first standarized segment of a welding training program	3 groups of disadvantaged trainees ($N = 18$ thru 21)	The shorter the time spent in completing the first segment, the shorter the time required to complete the remaining portions of the program ($\bar{r} = .87$).
Medoff & Abraham (1980)	Time within grade	Managerial and professional employees in two major U.S. corporations ($N = 4,788$ and $2,841$)	There is either no association between tenure and ratings of performance
Medoff & Abraham (1981)	Time within grade	Managerial and professional	Cross-sectional and longitudinal analyses revealed that

Therefore, there are few reasons for more experienced employees to withhold information or training from less experienced employees.

4. *Seniority and Turnover.* There is evidence that turnover rates are higher in nonunion organizations than in union establishments.[16] Since the weight assigned seniority in decision making is usually greater in union than in nonunion settings, seniority provisions are generally thought to reduce turnover and save costs. However, even a low rate of turnover can be dysfunctional if competent, high performing employees leave. Seniority provisions may lead to attrition of this sort if advancement opportunities are low among high performers with low seniority standing.[17] To date, there are no studies comparing performance-turnover relationships between companies with and without seniority-based promotion systems.

---

[16] R. B. Freeman, "Individual mobility and union voice in the labor market," *American Economic Review,* 66, 1976, pp. 361–368; R. N. Block, "The impact of seniority provisions on manufacturing quit rate," *Industrial and Labor Relations Review,* 32, 1978, pp. 474–488.

[17] Gordon and Johnson, *Ibid.*

Author(s)	Manner in Which Seniority Is Defined	Sample	Results
Renan (1970)	Time in non-managerial positions within the company	employees of a large U.S. manufacturing firm ($N > 7,000$) Stratified sample of managers from various functional areas of a major corporation ($N = 100$)	performance ratings remained constant or fell with passage of time Seniority was not significantly related to performance ($p > .10$) as measured by a corporate rating and a plant rating
Siepert (1971)	Time in grade for G. S. levels 7 thru 14	115 G. S. -15 and 217 G. S. -14 managerial personnel at Kennedy Space Center	Employees rated highest in terms of promotability advanced through non-managerial levels significantly faster ($p < .003$) than employees considered least qualified for promotion.
Tiffin & McCormick (1965)	Years of service on present job	Approx. 9000 steel workers in unspecified jobs from a single plant	The shorter the seniority the higher the rating of performance
Tiffin & McCormick (1965)	Years of service in plant	Approx. 9000 steel workers in unspecified jobs from a single plant	There was no marked or systematic change in the ratings with total plant service
Walker, Luthans, & Hodgetts (1970)	Time with company	3202 employees in the marketing department of a large petroleum company	Employees rated "immediately promotable" had significantly less years of company service ($p < .01$) then those judged "not promotable"
Walker, Luthans, & Hodgetts (1970)	Time in current job	3202 employees in the marketing department of a large petroleum company	Employees rated "immediately promotable" had significantly less time in their present job ($p < .01$) than those judged "not promotable"

From Gordon, M. E., and Johnson, W. A. Seniority: A review of its legal and scientific standing. *Personnel Psychology,* 1982, *35,* 255–280. Reprinted by permission of the publisher and authors.

Table 13-3   **Summary of Empirical Evidence on the Relationship of Seniority to Job Performance**

Staff Analysis. The process of identifying managerial potential can take many forms. As described in the previous chapter, judgments can be based on assessment center results, biographical reviews, and such things as test batteries. The staff analysis method represents a formal attempt at combining information. As described by Odiorne,[18] staff analysis by a staff psychologist, a director of management development, or similar professional, is practiced in many companies. It also is possible to use external consulting services for this purpose. In either case, professional staff analysts, who are trained in the evaluation of human behavior, make judgments about managerial potential.

---

[18] George S. Odiorne, *Strategic Management of Human Resources,* San Francisco: Jossey-Bass, 1984.

An example of a company using a formal assessment program is the NCR Corporation of Dayton, Ohio. As described in a *Wall Street Journal* article,[19] the company reviewed the records of 4000 young white-collar employees to identify 828 high performers. This group then received biographical questionnaires and interest inventories. One goal was to see whether the employees' background and interests resembled those of successful NCR managers. The company eventually identified 24 high-potential employees from the field of 828. The company then made an effort to broaden the experience of these individuals by moving them through a series of managerial jobs.

Review-Boards. Odiorne[20] describes the review board method as a widely used way to assess potential. Here, top managers review the qualifications of lower level managers. Often, extensive files are compiled containing performance reviews, work histories, and other information about personal qualifications. This is also called the dossier approach. A dossier is compiled on each manager. These reports can even include interview results gathered by talking with subordinates, peers, and superiors. Little empirical information is available regarding the accuracy or usefulness of this approach.

Managing Organizational Exit

Recall that to effectively manage the movement of employees, the quality of newcomers must be compared with the quality of existing employees. Over time, the goal is to improve overall workforce quality at a cost that results in a net benefit to the firm. Therefore, processes that relate to employee retention are just as important as processes that relate to employee acquisition. We therefore turn our attention to the costs and benefits of turnover.

The Costs of Turnover

While few hold the view that all organizational turnover is dysfunctional, there are clear costs associated with the loss of employees. To introduce procedures for identifying and measuring turnover costs, we will review the approach originally developed by Smith and Watkins and later refined by Cascio.[21] This approach places costs into three major categories: separation costs, replacement costs, and training costs. Each will be briefly discussed. The usual practice is to compute these costs at a yearly rate for subunits of an organization.

[19] Bernard Wysocki, Talent hunt: More companies try to spot leaders early, guide them to the top, *Wall Street Journal,* Wednesday, February, 25, 1981.
[20] Odiorne, *Ibid.*
[21] H. L. Smith and Watkins, L. E. "Managing manpower turnover costs," *The Personnel Administrator,* 23, 1978, pp. 46–50.

Separation Costs. When employees are terminated or voluntarily resign there are many costs associated with such things as

- conducting exit interviews
- administrative time required to delete employees from active status
- separation pay
- unemployment tax rate changes in states where unemployment tax rates are based upon employer's history of claims

Replacement Costs. The basic cost elements include

- recruiting costs
- administrative costs associated with collecting applicant information
- time required to design and conduct selection interviews
- staff time required to process applicant information and make selection decisions
- postemployment administrative costs
- preemployment medical examination

Training Costs. While training costs will be discussed in greater detail in a subsequent chapter, consider

- providing informational material and company orientation programs
- formal training via structured, off-the-job training programs
- on-the-job training costs associated with using existing employees as trainers

For each of the three cost categories the general approach is to estimate the time and material requirements. Time estimates are then multiplied by the average wage rates of persons directly involved with the particular activity.[22]

In addition to the general framework just provided, other potential costs include[23]

- productivity loss for leavers during time of alternative job search
- disruption of social and communication patterns among stayers
- decreased job satisfaction among stayers
- increased work load for stayers during and immediately after search for replacement

---

[22] For a complete discussion of these steps see Wayne F. Cascio, *Costing Human Resources: The Financial Impact of Behavior in Organizations,* Boston: Kent Publishing Company, 1982.

[23] William H. Mobley, "Some unanswered questions in turnover and withdrawal research," *Academy of Management Review,* 7, 1982, pp. 111–116.

The Benefits of Turnover

There is growing evidence that certain forms of turnover, at appropriate rates, increase, not decrease, organizational effectiveness.[24] Turnover does not represent a simple dichotomous variable. Dalton, Todor, and Krackhardt[25] provided the taxonomy displayed in Figure 13–3 to define the notion of functional turnover. Graphic 1 illustrates the traditional approach to measuring and reporting turnover while graphic 2 makes explicit the possibility that the voluntary turnover of marginal employees may be functional.

In addition to the displacement of poor performers, other possible positive consequences of turnover include[26]

- infusion of new ideas, technology, and knowledge via replacements
- stimulation of needed changes in policy and strategic direction of the firm
- increased promotional and internal mobility opportunities for stayers
- possible cost reductions due to consolidation
- payroll savings associated with replacing individual at top pay in a wage schedule with an entry level new hire
- the possibility that new entrants will be better performers than leavers (e.g., possess needed KSA's and motivation levels to a higher degree than leavers)

Optimal Turnover Rate

As previously noted, turnover results in costs associated with the separation of incumbent employees plus the costs associated with searching for and training new employees. However, personnel programs designed to reduce turnover can have major cost consequences of their own. To reduce turnover, employers may choose to increase wages, redesign jobs, or modify selection systems to better identify individuals who will not resign. These retention costs must be compared with turnover costs to properly manage a firm's turnover rate.

The concept of an optimal turnover rate was described by Abelson and Baysinger[27] as "the rate that minimizes the sum of the costs of turnover

---

[24] Dan R. Dalton and William D. Todor, "Turnover turned over: An expanded and positive perspective," *Academy of Management Review,* 4, 1979, pp. 225–235; Mobley, *Ibid;* Dan R. Dalton, William D. Todor and David M. Krackhardt, "Turnover overstated: The functional taxonomy," *Academy of Management Review,* 7, 1982, pp. 117–123.

[25] Dalton et al., *Ibid.*

[26] Mobley, *Ibid;* Dan R. Dalton and William D. Todor, "Turnover: A lucrative hard dollar phenomenon," *Academy of Management Review,* 7, 1982, 212–218.

[27] Michael A. Abelson and Barry D. Baysinger, "Optimal and dysfunctional turnover: Toward an organizational level model," *Academy of Management Review,* 9, 1984, pp. 331–341.

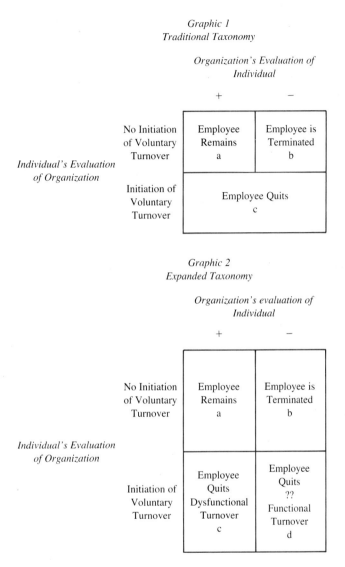

From Dalton, D. R., Todor, W. D., and Krackhardt, D. M. Turnover overstated: The functional taxonomy. *Academy of Management Review,* 1982, *7,* 117–123. Reprinted by permission.

Figure 13–3 **A Comparison of Turnover Taxonomies**

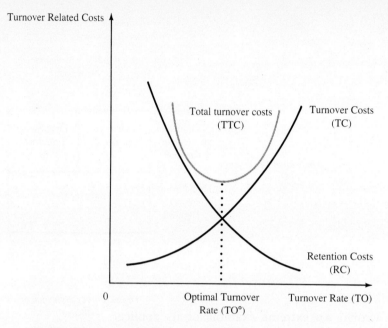

From Abelson, M. A., and Baysinger, B. D. Optimal and dysfunctional turnover: Toward an organizational level model. *Academy of Management Review,* 1984, *9,* 331–341. Reprinted by permission.

Figure 13-4 **Optimal Organizational Turnover**

plus the costs associated with reducing it" (p. 333). They provided the material in Figure 13–4 to illustrate this concept. The costs associated with the separation and replacement of employees are labeled TC (turnover costs). The costs associated with programs to retain employees are labeled RC (retention costs). As noted in Figure 13–4, as firms spend more on programs to retain employees, turnover rates are decreased as are turnover costs. At high rates of turnover, retention costs are likely to be low, while turnover costs are likely to be high. At low rates of turnover, retention costs are likely to be high, while turnover costs are likely to be low. The optimal rate of turnover occurs at the point where total turnover costs (TC + RC) are at their lowest level. This approach focuses on the optimal rate of organizational turnover. The point is basic; employees should be allowed to leave if the cost to retain exceeds the cost to replace. Be careful to note, however, that turnover costs (TC) ultimately must reflect the balance between separation and replacement costs and the benefits of turnover previously described.[28]

---

[28] Boudreau and Burger, *Ibid.*

Managerial Constraints on Terminating Employees

While many legal constraints operate to limit employers' freedom to hire, promote, and terminate employees (for a general discussion of these issues see chapter 8), the right to terminate an employee is currently receiving renewed attention. Historically, under a century-old common law rule, *at-will employees* (employees who agree to work for an employer but receive no specification of how long the employment is to last) may be terminated at the will of their employers. At-will employees have a similar right to leave their jobs, at any time and without notice.[29] Since managing employee flows depends on regulating both who enters and who leaves an organization, further discussion of the "right to terminate" seems appropriate, particularly as the legal environment in this area undergoes modification.

Employment At-Will Doctrine

The essence of the employment at-will doctrine is that employees may quit or be dismissed at will, for no cause or even for causes that are morally wrong. An extreme example of its application comes from a decision reached by the Supreme Court of Alabama in 1938.[30] In this case an employment at-will employee, Mr. J. C. Comerford, had worked for the International Harvester Company for many years. The following restates the allegations of Mr. Comerford's complaint. In 1936, Mr. Comerford alleged that his supervisor, Mr. J. B. Dawson, attempted to "alienate the affections" of his wife. According to Mr. Comerford, the attempt was not successful, and because of his failure, Mr. Dawson wrongfully reported that Mr. Comerford's work was no longer satisfactory. Mr. Dawson's report resulted in the dismissal of Mr. Comerford. The Supreme Court of Alabama agreed with the trial court that held that actions of this type did not violate Alabama's common law of employment relations. Even if the firing was malicious and done for improper reasons, it was not illegal. While current legal developments, if applied to this case, may have resulted in a different result, the case highlights the nature of the employment at-will concept.

While the employment at-will doctrine still stands; not all employees are "at-will" employees and the effects of the doctrine have been curtailed over the years by legislative and court decisions.[31] Employees covered by

---

[29] Lawrence Z. Lorber, J. Robert Kirk, Kenneth H. Kirschner and Charlene R. Handorf, *Fear of Firing: A Legal and Personnel Analysis of Employment-at-will,* Alexandria, Virginia: The ASPA Foundation, 1984.

[30] Lorber et al., *Ibid.*

[31] Lorber et al., *Ibid.*

Law	Major Provisions
Railway Labor Act (1962)	Prohibits dismissals of railroad employees engaged in labor relations activity (e.g., choosing collective bargaining representatives).
National Labor Relations Act (1935)	Prohibits dismissals that interfere with employee's rights to do such things as organize, bargain collectively, and to strike, as specified by the Act.
Energy Reorganization Act of 1974	Prohibits dismissals of nuclear industry employees based on their participation in proceedings to enforce the act or the Atomic Energy Act of 1954.
Federal Water and Pollution Control Act (1948)	Protects employee activity in support of enforcing the Act.
Air Pollution Prevention and Control Act (1977 amendment)	Protects employee activity in support of enforcing the Act.
Occupational Health and Safety Act (1970)	Protects employee activity in support of enforcing the Act.
Coal Mine Health and Safety Act (1969)	Protects employee activity in support of enforcing the Act.
Railroad Safety Act (1975)	Protects employee activity in support of enforcing the Act or against dismissals for refusing to work under conditions where there are good reasons to believe a serious injury could occur.
Jury System Improvement Act of 1978	Prohibits dismissals for performing jury duty in a federal court.
Title VII of the Civil Rights Act of 1964	Prohibits dismissals based on race, color, religion, sex or national origin.
Age Discrimination in Employment Act (1967)	Prohibits dismissals on the basis of age for certain age groups.
Fair Labor Standards Act (1938)	Protects employee activity in support of enforcing the Act.
Veteran's Employment Act (1976)	Prohibits dismissal of verterans without cause for a specified period following discharge.
Employee Retirement Income Security Act (1974)	Protects employee exercising rights provided by the Act (e.g., attainment of benefits from a pension plan covered by the Act).
Consumer Credit Protection Act (1968)	Prohibits dismissals because wages have been subject to garnishment.
Civil Service Act (1978)	Federal employees can be dismissed only for performance reasons or for a reason that will promote efficiency of the federal government.

Source: Lorber, L. Z., Kirk, J. R., Kirschner, K. H., and Handorf, C. R. Fear of firing: A legal and personnel analysis of employment-at-will. Alexandria, Virginia: The ASPA Foundation, 1984.

Table 13-4 **Laws Limiting the Rights of Employers to Terminate Employees**

collective bargaining agreements, written employment contracts, or public employees, represent major exceptions to the employment at-will doctrine. Also, a variety of laws limit the rights of employers to terminate employees. These are shown in Table 13–4.

Finally, some courts have begun to interpret laws in ways that extend certain protections to at-will employees. These usually relate to instances such as: 1) firing individuals who refuse to commit illegal acts for an employer, 2) firing individuals who have entered into implied contracts with an employer, and 3) firing in bad faith or for a reason that is malicious.[32] There also are state laws protecting employees from certain dismissal practices.

These developments have served to make employers review and revise termination policies and practices. The following represent the areas requiring attention when attempting to protect against exceptions to the employment at-will doctrine.

Recruitment.   The issue here is to ensure that a company's recruitment techniques, such as advertisements or brochures, do not imply permanent employment or specify a term of employment. The general rule is to remove words that establish a fixed duration of employment since they have the potential to be taken as implied agreements.[33]

Interviewing.   The employment interview serves two primary purposes. It is used as a selection device and it is used to "sell" the organization to qualified prospective employees. Oral statements during the interview may constitute enforceable contracts.[34] Interviewers need to be trained. They need to be aware of inappropriate questions and need to exercise caution when describing the benefits of employment with the hiring company. Structured interviews and trained interviewers also increase the likelihood of making valid decisions and decrease the likelihood of employment discrimination.

Applications, Handbooks, and Manuals.   Company documents that are read by applicants or current employees should be reviewed to ensure that they do not imply other than at-will employment. Statements about job security, or permanent employment should generally be deleted. Also, statements that dismissals will only be based on "just and sufficient cause" can create an exception to the employment at-will principle.[35]

Performance Evaluation.   Being able to dismiss incompetent employees is best handled when a well-designed, well-managed system of performance

---

[32] Lorber et al., *Ibid.*
[33] Lorber et al., *Ibid.*
[34] Lorber et al., *Ibid.*
[35] Lorber et al., *Ibid.*

appraisal exists. A system that measures only job-related dimensions of performance and provides the employee with notice of performance problems will give the employer a documented basis for dismissal. A progressive discipline program also is advisable. These usually include a four step process beginning with an oral warning, followed by a written warning, followed by a suspension, finally resulting in a dismissal if performance does not improve.

Summary

In this chapter we were concerned with staffing decisions that relate to the movement of employees within and out of the organization's workforce. The general goal, over time, is to improve workforce quality while controlling costs. This represents a complex managerial responsibility since multiple factors account for workforce quality at any given point in time. Such things as the validity of selection and promotion decisions, organizational characteristics and strategy, the quality and size of external applicant pools, and the degree to which competent employees desire to leave and have external opportunities, influence and regulate employee flows. In addition to complexity, many issues central to decision making in this area have not received systematic research attention. For example, the consequences of seniority systems, both at the level of the individual and the organization, are not well understood. Also, the importance of establishing a staffing system that is congruent with firm type is not well documented, and few data exist that specify the costs or consequences associated with programs designed to retain top performers. It is our hope, however, that we have defined the relevant issues and have convinced the reader that a systems perspective is essential. The flow of employees into, within, and out of the company's workforce must simultaneously be taken into account along with the associated acquisition and retention costs. Finally, programs designed to influence the knowledge, skills, abilities, and motivation levels of employees are not independent of a firm's approach to staffing. It is to these programs and practices that we now turn our attention.

PROBLEMS

1. There are a variety of potential payroll savings associated with employee turnover. Consider an organization that staffs a job classification that has six pay steps, reached on the basis of seniority. The entry level pay is $6.50 per hour and the final pay step is $9.75. The pay schedule is as follows:

Full pay	$9.75
5th year	$9.06
4th year	$8.43
3rd year	$7.84
2nd year	$7.29
Entry level	$6.50

Assume that 120 employees are evenly distributed across the six pay steps at time one. Now consider annual payroll costs for the period beginning in two years. What degree of payroll savings results from a 20 percent turnover rate? Assume that the turnover is evenly distributed among the pay steps, that the organization makes a 7 percent pension plan contribution that is fully vested after 5 years of service, and that the company is responsible for a 7.15 percent FICA contribution that applies to the first $39,000 of employee income. Also, discuss other costs and benefits associated with this rate of turnover.

2. How would one go about incorporating the concept of "employee flows" into the standard utility model described in chapter 12?

3. What are some negative consequences associated with the use of a staffing system based on the principle of "sponsored mobility"?

4. Discuss the kinds of questions potentially asked during an employment interview that could create an employment at-will exception.

5. Under what set of circumstances would a seniority based reward system likely work to the advantage of the firm?

6. Under what set of circumstances will a firm most likely be able to retain top performers?

REFERENCES

Greenhaus, J. H. *Career management,* New York: The Dryden Press, 1987.
Sorcher, M. *Predicting executive success,* New York: John Wiley & Sons, 1985.
Walker, J. W. *Human resources planning,* New York: McGraw-Hill, 1980.

CHAPTER 14

EMPLOYEE TRAINING AND DEVELOPMENT

U nder certain circumstances training represents a preferred solution to meeting a firm's personnel needs. Labor market conditions, a firm's business plans and strategies, the central task processes, the effects of other personnel practices on employee behavior, and the costs of alternative courses of action are among the factors that play a role in evaluating the relative benefits associated with the initiation of a training program. While training can influence various aspects of employee behavior, it is usually defined as a process intended to increase learning among organization members. This learning, in idealized situations, should alter the behavior of organization members in a way that contributes to organizational effectiveness.[1] Most training specialists view behavior in the broadest sense, and see training as a process intended to modify the knowledge, skills, and abilities of employees. Thus, training applies to a wide range of person-centered qualities, including motor, cognitive, and interpersonal attributes. While training can influence such things as needs, values, and attitudes, the traditional approach to training is to focus on employee ability to perform more than employee willingness to perform.

Our goal in this chapter is to introduce the reader to the field of personnel training. The chapter is organized around three major themes. First, we will argue that training in industry, as a formal or informal

---

[1] John R. Hinricks, "Personnel training," In M. D. Dunnette (Ed.), *Handbook of Industrial and Organizational Psychology,* Chicago: Rand McNally, 1976, pp. 829–860.

process, is widespread and very costly. Throughout this chapter be alert to when and where evidence exists supporting this level of expenditure. That is, is there evidence that the benefits of various training practices outweigh the costs? This, of course, needs to be considered in relation to the returns associated with alternatives to training. The second theme will address the various components of well designed training systems. For decades, firms have been advised to think about their training and development efforts using a systems perspective. We will follow tradition and make similar arguments. The processes associated with the assessment of training needs, the determination of training objectives, program content and form, and program evaluation will be described. Finally, we will provide an extended utility framework for evaluating the impact of training on outcomes at the level of the firm. Here, the standard utility model described in Chapter 12 (this section of the chapter assumes that the reader possesses a thorough understanding of the utility concepts described in Chapter 12) will be presented in a form that is useful for evaluating the economic effect of any personnel program or practice. After completing this chapter you should be in a better position to evaluate the usefulness of a firm's training programs and practices. Usefulness refers to the likelihood that the training is needed, that training is the preferred solution (as compared to other personnel interventions), and that the particular form of training represents the most cost-effective approach.

Practices and Costs

While there are numerous conditions that signal a need for training (e.g., a low base rate coupled with a need to hire a large proportion of the applicant pool, selection systems that produce many selection errors, and firm specific knowledge and skills that only can be acquired via on-the-job training), the rapidly changing business environment has produced a new awareness of the importance of training. International competition, technological advances, and deregulation have increased the pace of job change. As job functions and their required knowledge, skills, and abilities undergo rapid change, the training function takes on increased importance. Evidence suggests that U.S. employers are increasing training expenditures and that nearly all firms engage in employee development. The range of activities is immense as depicted in Table 14–1.

Estimates of the annual collective cost of training for U.S. employers have exceeded 100 billion dollars.[2] Some companies (IBM, Xerox, AT&T,

---

[2] W. J. McKeon, "How to determine off-site meeting costs," *Training and Development Journal*, 35, 1981, pp. 116–122.

Type of training	Sample providing
1 Supervisory skills	77.1
2 New employee orientation	71.2
3 Management skills and development	67.3
4 Communication skills training (reading, writing, listening, etc.)	58.2
5 Technical skills and knowledge updating	58.2
6 Time management	51.2
7 Safety	50.4
8 New equipment orientation	47.4
9 Productivity improvement	46.0
10 New methods and/or procedures	46.0
11 Customer relations and/or customer service	46.6
12 Mandated programs (EEO, OSHA, etc.)	43.0
13 Clerical and/or secretarial skills	42.3
14 Personal growth	38.6
15 Employee (nonsales) motivation/incentive/recognition programs	36.7
16 Sales skills	36.3
17 Labor relations	35.7
18 Information management (word processing, MIS, etc.)	35.0
19 Data processing	32.6
20 Team building	32.5
21 Disease prevention and health promotion (stress, nutrition, exercise, etc.)	29.2
22 Organization development	28.5
23 Product knowledge	27.2
24 Career planning	22.8
25 Outplacement and/or retirement	17.2
26 Customer education	17.0
27 Foreign language and/or cross-cultural skills	8.5

Reprinted with permission from the U.S. Training Census & Trends Report, Oct. 1982 issue of *Training,* the Magazine of Human Resources Development. Copyright 1982, Lakewood Publications, Inc., Minneapolis, MN (612) 333-0471. All rights reserved.

***Table 14–1* Types of Training Most Frequently Provided**

GE, GM, Wang, and Motorola) are operating what amount to internal universities with enrollments and expenditures that rival public and private institutions of higher education.[3] A recent *U.S. News and World Report* article provides an example of the use of corporate schools. Excerpts from this article are presented in Example 14–1.

While aggregate estimates are of some interest, perhaps the best way to consider training costs is to outline various cost elements. For example, consider McKeon's[4] framework for determining off-site meeting costs. The cost categories for a typical program include the following:

---

[3] Herbert G. Heneman III, Donald P. Schwab, John A. Fossum, and Lee D. Dyer, *Personnel/Human Resources Management,* Homewood, Ill.: Richard D. Irwin, Inc., 1986, p. 386.

[4] McKeon, *Ibid.*

EXAMPLE 14.1 BUSINESS SPENDS BILLIONS ON PROGRAMS THAT COMPETE WITH UNIVERSITIES AND COLLEGES

It is now possible for General Electric employees to earn master's degrees in electrical engineering without ever leaving the company's offices. GE and many other companies invest huge sums of money to educate their employees. Most of the money is spent inside the firms on courses designed by corporate officials and taught by corporate trainers. These programs are designed by individuals whose main areas of expertise and knowledge can be focused on specific company needs.

The impact of this form of education is moving beyond corporate walls. For example, the American Council on Education (ACE), has approved more than 3000 courses offered by industry. The ACE has recommended to universities and colleges that these courses be accepted for credit. Many corporate programs have been accredited to award the bachelor's, master's, and doctoral degree (many of these degrees were once considered the sole province of traditional universities).

Two reasons business likes to do its own educating include:

● Employees have difficulty adjusting to the "academic rhythm"—September to May day classes.
● Universities emphasize theory, while businesses want theory more firmly grounded in specific job applications.

Source: *U.S. News and World Report*, February 10, 1986, pp. 50–51.

A. Program development
  1. Training department overhead
  2. Training staff salaries
  3. Outside consultants
  4. Equipment and materials
B. Participant costs
  1. Salaries
  2. Benefits
C. Program support costs
  1. Facility costs
    a. Sleeping rooms
    b. Meals
    c. Coffee breaks
    d. Misc. (telephone services, etc.)
    e. Reception costs
  2. Meeting charges
    a. Room rental
    b. Secretarial services
    c. A/V rental
  3. Transportation costs

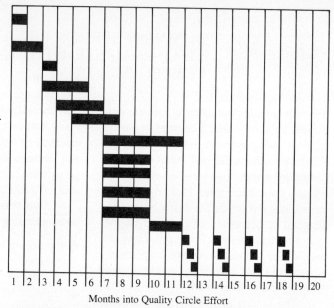

Investigate quality circle in other organizations or through consultant.
Obtain management understanding and approval, involve the union.
Institutionalize sponsorship.
Organize quality circle office and hire staff.
Determine installation strategy.
Train staff—send to outside courses.
Purchase or develop training materials and prepare courses.
Set up incentives program.
Set up technical support system.
Set up proposal implementation system.
Set up measurements system.
Codify rules.
Train managers.
Train supervisors.
Train employees.

Months into Quality Circle Effort

From *Quality Circles: How to Make Them Work* by P. C. Thompson, p.173 © 1982 by P. S. Thompson. Published by AMACOM Book Division, American Management Association. All rights reserved. Reprinted by permission of the author.

Figure 14–1   **Startup Pattern for a Quality-Circles Program**

Specific training cost estimates are available from many sources. One interesting example can be drawn from reviewing the program catalogs published by leading consulting firms and universities. These organizations provide many services, including general management development programs that attract participants from multiple firms. Topics such as business writing, stress management, effective time use, motivation and leadership, collective bargaining, and effective performance appraisals are commonly covered. While the costs vary, current tuition for the standard two day workshop rarely falls below the $400 per trainee level. These costs, of course, do not cover such things as transportation and housing accommodations. Week long management programs at leading universities commonly average in the $1500 to $2000 per participant range.

Training and development programs conducted internally also incur substantial costs. To illustrate the time, commitment, planning, and therefore costs associated with an organization intervention, consider the startup activities and planning processes associated with a quality circles program. Quality circles currently are popular in the manufacturing sector. Lockheed imported such a program (quality circles were first extensively used in Japan) in the mid 1970s to become one of the first U.S. companies to experiment with this form of participative management.[5] As the name implies, the goal is to improve quality. Employees are encouraged to volunteer to work in small groups (usually no more than 15) for the purpose of identifying and solving problems associated with the manufacturing process. Regular meetings are held and group members identify and prioritize problems. Possible solutions are proposed and evaluated by the entire team. Solutions are then presented to management and if judged to be of merit the recommended changes are implemented. Training is one major aspect of a quality circles program. Participants receive extensive training in problem diagnosis and solving skills. The process of meeting and presenting solutions to management also is designed to enhance interpersonal and communication skills. The process of developing and implementing such a program is depicted in Figure 14–1. Many other in-house training programs require a similar planning horizon. The comprehensiveness of in-house training for certain companies is characterized in Example 14–2.

---

[5] John B. Miner and Mary Green Miner, *Personnel and Industrial Relations,* New York: Macmillan, 1985, p. 415.

EXAMPLE 14.2 PILLSBURY'S HOLISTIC APPROACH TO EMPLOYEE DEVELOPMENT

In 1985 Pillsbury Co. unveiled a 18,400-square foot training and development facility called the Pillsbury Learning and Health Center. A full office floor in the company's corporate headquarters in Minneapolis is devoted to human resource development. Seventy-five percent of Pillsbury's 3000 headquarters-based employees used the facility in 1985. The company believes that an entire floor dedicated to employee development relates well to the Pillsbury mission to "Be the Best."

One part of the Center emphasizes computer-based learning and self-development. Included are individual study carrels, tape and video cassette players, a library, and computer/courseware resources. The fitness facility focuses on the physical well-being of headquarters employees. Fitness classes, individual attention, and feedback and progress reports are provided.

Among the benefits associated with this approach to employee development two are emphasized by management:

● A facility dedicated to health and/or learning represents a tangible statement of concern for employees.
● The Center serves as a powerful recruiting device.

Source: Diana Doshan, "Pillsbury's learning and health center. A holistic approach to employee development," *Personnel Administrator,* April 1986, pp. 133–134, 136–141.

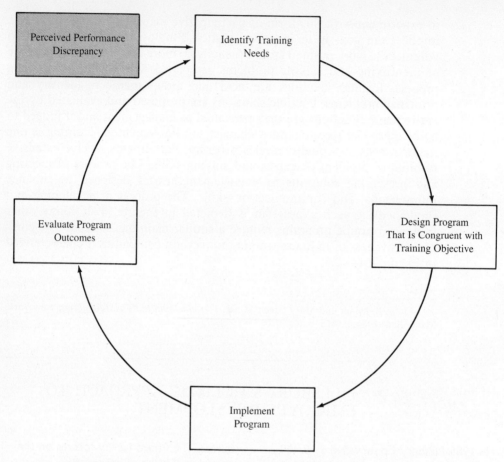

Figure 14-2 **The Training Process as a Form of Organizational Experimentation**

The Training and Development System

In his widely read book, Goldstein[6] presented a model of an instructional system. His analysis, taking into account multiple interacting systems, will serve as an organizing framework for this section of the chapter. However, before we summarize Goldstein's approach, consider Figure 14-2. Here we simply point out that organizational training represents one area of managerial activity that is ideally suited for experimentation, or learning how well things work by trying them out and observing the consequences. This bias for experimentation will continue throughout the chapter. While this may appear to require costly and sophisticated evaluation techniques,

---

[6] Irwin L. Goldstein, *Training: Program Development and Evaluation,* Monterey, Calif.: Brooks/Cole, 1974; Irwin L. Goldstein, *Training in Organizations: Needs Assessment, Development, and Evaluation,* Monterey, Calif.: Brooks/Cole, 1986.

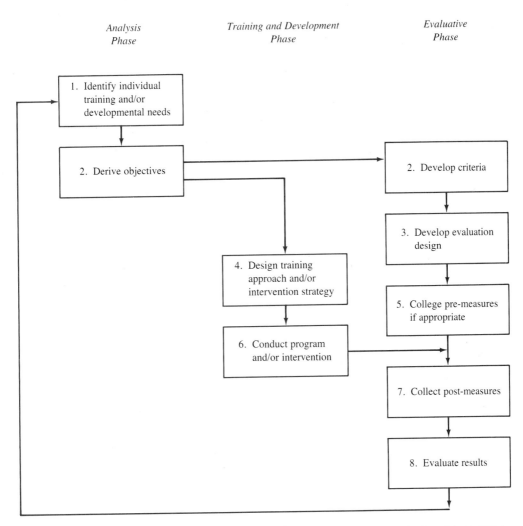

From *Training: Program Development and Evaluation*, by I. I. Goldstein. Copyright © 1974 by Wadsworth Publishing Company, Inc. Reprinted by permission of Brooks/Cole Publishing Company, Pacific Grove, California 93950.

Figure 14-3 **Training and Development System**

this need not be the case. We only want to emphasize that managers should think systematically about the causes of perceived performance discrepancies, should design and implement training interventions that are rational given the available theoretical and empirical evidence, and should monitor the results of their interventions so that ineffective programs are not repeated.

A modified version of the Goldstein training and development system is depicted in Figure 14–3. The three phases are shown to operate in sequence with the evaluative phase serving to provide input into subsequent rounds of needs assessment. We will follow this form and discuss each phase separately. It is important to point out however, that specific activities ideally should occur as represented by the numbers associated with each activity. That is, while it is common practice to complete the analysis phase first, certain evaluative phase activities should be conducted before the design and implementation of the training intervention (i.e., operational definitions of the various criteria and the method of collecting evaluative data need to be in place before designing or conducting the training program).

Analysis Phase

The analysis phase, or the process of identifying individual training needs, begins with a perceived performance discrepancy. Performance is broadly defined to include outcomes at the level of the firm, work group, or individual. The recognition of a problem results from some perceived deviation between actual and expected or desirable outcomes. This perceived discrepancy can be attributed to many causes. If it seems likely that the discrepancy is based on a knowledge, skill, or ability deficiency, a systematic assessment of individual training and development needs may be appropriate. Note that one key source of information is provided by an ongoing evaluation of the degree to which current training programs are meeting stated objectives.

Organizational Analysis. Before illustrating the specific activities associated with individual needs assessment, recall that training is simply one of many possible personnel practices from which to choose. Therefore, the first step in conducting a training needs analysis is to consider the broader organizational context. For any training program to be useful it needs to affect outcomes that are congruent with the short- and long-term goals of the organization. It also must receive sufficient resources and support from high level decision makers and must make conceptual sense given the organization's environment. For example, when companies face very turbulent environments (frequent scientific discoveries, technical innovations, and changes in market conditions) they confront perplexing alternatives. Change can mean that training will be continuously required to maintain skilled employees. However, when the rate of change is very fast, often there is not sufficient time to develop current employees. At some point external hiring may be a preferred solution. Talent simply must be purchased when there is not time to develop it internally. Finally, it is important to remember that many performance discrepancies do not result from KSA deficiencies. Nontraining factors such as poor organization and work design, low wages, and poor physical working conditions can be the prime contributors to an observed performance problem.[7]

---

[7] Kenneth N. Wexley and Gary P. Latham, *Developing and Training Human Resources in Organizations,* Glenview, Ill.: Scott, Foresman and Company, 1981, p. 30.

Job Attribute Analysis. Once it has been determined that training represents a workable alternative, the formal needs analysis begins with the collection of job-based information via a job analysis. Recall that the various methods of job analysis were described in Chapter 11 and that an analysis focusing on person-oriented attributes is often useful when identifying training needs. Task-oriented job information is helpful when designing realistic training experiences that enhance the transfer of learning to actual work settings. Thus, a comprehensive job analysis program is ideally suited for supporting a training needs assessment. When such a support system is not available it is possible to estimate training needs while job-based information is being collected. This common practice will be illustrated in what follows.

Person Analysis. Training needs assessment requires that comparisons be made between the attributes needed to perform the job and attributes possessed by job incumbents. This can be accomplished in a variety of ways. Individuals can be evaluated by using existing systems or by using measurement procedures designed specifically for the purpose at hand. For example, a well designed performance appraisal system (see Chapter 16) can provide useful evidence when determining if a training need exists. Also, direct testing can be used to estimate employee proficiency across key KSA's. Job knowledge tests, work sample tests, and even managerial assessment centers can be used to evaluate employee skill levels.

Perhaps the most widely used formal approach to needs assessment is to survey incumbents and their immediate supervisors. To illustrate, consider the form displayed in Figure 14–4. In Chapter 11 we described a position description inventory designed for use at Exxon U.S.A. That inventory was used to analyze executive, managerial, and professional positions within the company. One section of the inventory was person-centered and focused on abilities needed to perform important tasks. We have selected illustrative ability elements and have constructed an abbreviated needs assessment survey. Data of this type can be collected from large numbers of respondents and allows for the simultaneous determination of important KSA's and KSA deficiencies.

Training Objectives. If a true KSA deficiency is observed and training (when compared with other solutions) represents a cost-effective means of correcting the performance discrepancy, training objectives need to be operationally defined. Training objectives serve as the standard against which the training program can be evaluated. They also serve a useful purpose when training content and the method of training is determined.

Formal training objectives usually take one or more of the following five forms:[8]

---

[8] Heneman et al., *Ibid.*

Individual Needs Assessment

This survey provides for an evaluation of the extent to which various abilities are useful in performing your (your subordinates') job. These abilities are job-related when relative presence or absence can affect the job performance of the job incumbent. Use the scales provided below to rate the degree to which the ability is useful when performing job responsibilities and the degree to which you perceive a need for training on each ability element.

Ability Element	Not useful	Slightly useful	Moderately useful	Very useful	Extremely useful	Low need		Moderate need		High need
	1	2	3	4	5	1	2	3	4	5
1. Ability to express one's self orally with clarity and precision	1	2	3	4	5	1	2	3	4	5
2. Ability to make speeches or presentations before groups of varying sizes	1	2	3	4	5	1	2	3	4	5
3. Ability to sell an idea or proposal to others (higher management, customers)	1	2	3	4	5	1	2	3	4	5
4. Ability to represent the company in activities with individuals from outside the company	1	2	3	4	5	1	2	3	4	5
5. Ability to persuade others to accept a point of view	1	2	3	4	5	1	2	3	4	5
6. Ability to use effective interpersonal skills when working with others	1	2	3	4	5	1	2	3	4	5
7. Ability to evaluate the quality of ideas introduced as potentially profit making	1	2	3	4	5	1	2	3	4	5
8. Ability to evaluate the quality of ideas introduced as potentially cost reducing	1	2	3	4	5	1	2	3	4	5

Figure 14-4   **An Illustrative Needs Assessment Survey**

1. **Knowledge objectives**   These objectives refer to knowledge acquired during training. It is normal practice to set some minimum standard necessary for adequate performance of job duties.
2. **Attitudinal objectives**   Based on the belief that attitudes influence behavior, it is common for training programs to target job attitudes for modification. By attitudes we do not mean attitudes toward training program content or the instructor. Ideally, attitudes should be of the variety that influence desired job behaviors.
3. **Skill objectives**   The term skill refers to physical and motor processes. As applied to the training literature, skill objectives describe the behaviors training program participants should display when still experiencing the training environment. They have a behavioral orientation but reflect the degree to which participants have acquired skills and abilities judged to influence on-the-job behavior.
4. **Job behavior objectives**   Here, attention focuses on the extent to which knowledge, skills, and abilities acquired during training generalize or transfer to real work settings.
5. **Results-oriented objectives**   As stressed throughout the text, understanding and influencing employee behavior should affect firm or work group performance. Revenue and costs should be, in part, a function of employee behavior. Results-oriented objectives are formulated to address the consequences of employee behavior.

Training and Development Phase

The design and implementation of a training program should follow the assessment of training needs and the determination of training objectives. The fundamental goal is to design a program that: (1) provides representative content coverage, and (2) utilizes a method of instruction that is most likely to meet the stated objectives. Representative content coverage can be achieved by systematically covering the KSA categories identified as being critical to successful job performance and possessed below acceptable levels by job incumbents.

The proper method of training represents a more difficult problem. While billions of dollars are spent each year on training program design and implementation, little systematic knowledge has been accumulated that provides decision makers with comparative evidence by which to evaluate the relative advantages of various training technologies. A recent article by Burke and Day provides an exception to this statement as it relates to managerial training.[9] Interested readers are urged to review this high quality, thorough review of the managerial training literature. Even here, however, the authors conclude that a great deal more empirical research is needed if firm conclusions are to be reached. Before commenting further on this point, consider a sample of the possibilities. For a full discussion of each (and other techniques) refer to one of the many texts devoted to this topic.[10] For our purposes note that training techniques can be classified in a variety of ways. Some distinguish between on-the-job training techniques (the most widely used training method probably involves simply assigning new employees to experienced workers) and off-site training methods.[11] Others tend to focus on whether the training actively involves the participant (e.g., information processing techniques or simulation techniques) or represents a passive experience (e.g., information presentation techniques of the lecture or observing a film variety).[12] In providing our sample we make no attempt at classification. Our goal is simply to preview the possibilities.

1. *Lecture.* The standard lecture is familiar to anyone who has experienced a U.S.-based university. It represents the standard technology used to transfer knowledge. It can take on many forms (e.g., it can be live, video-taped, audio recorded, or even transcribed).

2. *Programmed Instruction.* This technique is based on key principles of learning. The material to be learned is presented (usually in printed form) in a series of frames. The learning is of the self-instructional variety permitting the learner to progress at his/her own rate. Material is broken into discrete frames or steps. Each frame (or unit of information) usually is

---

[9] Michael J. Burke and Russell R. Day, "A cumulative study of the effectiveness of managerial training," *Journal of Applied Psychology,* 71, 1986, pp. 232–245.

[10] Goldstein, 1986, *Ibid;* Wexley and Latham, *Ibid.*

[11] Wexley and Latham, *Ibid.*

[12] Heneman et al., *Ibid.*

followed by a question requiring a response. The learner receives immediate feedback regarding the correctness of the response and will either proceed to learn new material or will be directed back through previously presented material. Recent developments in this area now rely on various forms of computer-assisted instruction. The trainee interacts directly with a computer that continuously monitors progress and presents material to fit the trainee's particular needs.

3. *Case Study.* The usual format is to present a real or at least realistic organizational situation/problem to a group of learners. They then discuss the situation and attempt to reach a conclusion regarding appropriate courses of action. This technique is similar to what is termed the "conference" method.

4. *Sensitivity Training.* Here a group meets to discuss the behavior of group members. The content for discussion is derived by observing such things as interaction patterns, the display of interpersonal skills, and other dynamics of member behavior. The process is very unstructured and emphasizes open communication among participants regarding their perceptions and "feelings" about each other.

5. *Simulation Techniques.* Facsimiles of actual work situations are created so that the learner can experience and react to realistic job demands without generating costly errors associated with equipment, other employees, or the firm's financial resources. The possibilities are unlimited. Managerial work can be simulated by using such things as business games, role play exercises, and in-basket exercises. At the other extreme, complex equipment simulators (e.g., fight simulators, power plant control room simulations, etc.) are used in many industries.

6. *Apprenticeship Training.* The typical apprenticeship program is utilized in the skilled crafts. Apprenticeship programs usually last from two to five years and combine on-the-job training (provided by a skilled journeyman) and formal classroom training.

7. *Coaching.* This is basically a form of on-the-job training. The coach provides needed job information and can act as a role model for the learner. Coaching takes many forms and can become quite comprehensive. The most comprehensive form is characterized by formal mentoring programs as applied to managerial careers.[13]

8. *Job Rotation.* Trainees are systematically assigned to a series of positions that familiarize them with the key functional or product divisions of the company. The concept is to provide the trainee with an overall organizational perspective that emphasizes the interrelationships among divisions or departments.

---

[13] Robert D. Bretz and George F. Dreher, "Sponsored versus contest mobility: The role of mentoring in managerial careers." In R. S. Shuler and S. A. Youngblood (Eds.) *Readings in Personnel and Human Resource Management,* Third Edition, St. Paul, Minn.: West Publishing Company, Forthcoming.

9. *Behavior Modeling.* Recently, considerable attention has been paid to using the principles of social learning theory when designing training programs. Skills are developed by following the steps outlined by Albert Bandura;[14] these include:

- The presentation, by a role model (this can be live or via film/video recordings), of the correct way to complete a task.
- Group discussion of the model's approach and effectiveness.
- Actual practice (role-playing) in front of the training class.
- Feedback regarding trainee effectiveness, with possible further rounds of role-playing and feedback as necessary to reach desired behaviors.

The approach seems particularly well suited for skill development among first-line supervisory personnel.

We now return to the problem of selecting an appropriate instructional technique. Given the present state of the evaluation research literature, firm recommendations cannot be made. A well integrated evaluation literature does not exist to the extent that it does in other areas of personnel practice (e.g., the literature pertaining to employee selection procedures). Therefore, organizations will have to review the available evidence, focusing on a particular problem or training issue, and take an experimental stance. One indication of this state of affairs is that surveys of expert opinion regularly appear in published form. Here, training and development experts are asked to rank order training methods in relation to a variety of training objectives. As noted in Table 14–2, opinion remained

---

[14] Albert Bandura, *Social Learning Theory,* Englewood Cliffs, New Jersey: Prentice-Hall, 1977.

Training Method	Knowledge Acquisition 1972	Knowledge Acquisition 1981	Changing Attitudes 1972	Changing Attitudes 1981	Problem Solving Skills 1972	Problem Solving Skills 1981	Interpersonal Skills 1972*	Interpersonal Skills 1981	Participant Acceptance 1972	Participant Acceptance 1981	Knowledge Retention 1972	Knowledge Retention 1981
Case Study	2	4	4	4	1	1	4	5	2	2	2	4
Conference	3	3	3	3	4	3	3	3	1	1	5	3
Lecture	9	2	8	6	9	5	8	6	8	3	8	6
Business Games	6	8	5	5	2	2	5	4	3	4	6	5
Movie Films	4	7	6	7	7	8	6	7	5	6	7	7
Programmed Instruction	1	1	7	9	6	6	7	9	7	7	1	2
Role Playing	7	5	2	1	3	4	2	1	4	5	4	1
Sensitivity Training	8	9	1	2	5	7	1	2	6	9	3	8
TV Lecture	5	6	9	8	8	9	9	8	9	8	9	9

*The 1972 rankings are from Carroll, S. J., Paine, F. T., Ivancevich, J. J., "The relative effectiveness of training methods —expert opinion and research," *Personnel Psychology,* 495–509

Source: L. Neider, "Training effectiveness: Changing attitudes," *Training and Development Journal,* December, 1981, p. 25. Copyright 1981 American Society for Training and Development. All rights reserved. Reprinted with permission.

Table 14–2 **Rankings of Training Directors of Effectiveness of Alternative Methods for Various Training Objectives**

relatively stable across the decade of the 1970s. The noted exception is that the lecture method received higher rankings in a 1981 survey than it did in a 1972 survey. This improvement was constant across all training objectives. We can offer no clear explanation for this change. The major trends suggest that knowledge acquisition and retention can best be achieved by programmed instruction (empirical research on programmed instruction suggests that its primary advantage is to reduce learning time[15]) and that skill acquisition requires an instructional technique that makes the learner an active participant in the process (e.g., situational exercise, case studies).

Evaluative Phase

The evaluative phase includes multiple activities associated with gathering evidence that the training intervention influenced or changed the learners. The standard approach is to determine if the training influenced employee behavior (e.g., job performance). In the final section of this chapter we will take the analysis to its final step and consider the cost effectiveness of the training intervention. A thorough discussion of research design and methodology is well beyond the scope of this text. The interested reader should examine one of the many excellent books devoted to this topic.[16]

The classic treatment of experimental and quasi-experimental research designs is that of Campbell and Stanley.[17] There are two primary problems associated with evaluating a change program. These are the problems of internal and external validity. Questions of internal validity address whether an observed change in behavior is attributable to a specified personnel practice (in this case a training program) or to some rival explanation. Campbell and Stanley identified a variety of factors that could account for change over time. When these factors (e.g., the natural maturation of employees, informal on-the-job training, or becoming aware of a training need and pursuing a course of self-study) co-vary with a formal training program, the evaluator can falsely conclude that the change was brought about by the training intervention. The ideal solution to this problem is to conduct a true experiment where employees randomly are assigned to either a training group or a control group that does not receive instruction. This can be difficult and costly to implement. Therefore, a variety of quasi-experimental research designs offer useful alternatives.

The problem of external validity is essentially a problem of generalizability. Once it is determined that training is responsible for the improve-

---

[15] A. N. Nash, J. P. Muczyk, and F. L. Vettori, "The relative practical effectiveness of programmed instruction," *Personnel Psychology,* 24, 1971, pp. 397–418.

[16] Donald T. Campbell and Julian C. Stanley, *Experimental and Quasi-Experimental Designs for Research,* Chicago: Rand McNally, 1963; Thomas D. Cook and Donald T. Campbell, *Quasi-Experimentation: Design and Analysis Issues for Field Settings,* Chicago: Rand McNally, 1979.

[17] Campbell and Stanley, *Ibid.*

ment in performance, we ask if this same form of training will work in other settings, with other trainees, and in future time periods. Often we are concerned with the transfer of learning to actual job settings. While it is possible to acquire skills in a protected learning environment it is sometimes difficult to use these new skills in a non-supportive workplace.

While true experimentation is the ideal, let us point out that there are likely to be instances when evidence of this type is not essential. For example, there are certain positions that require extensive knowledge that only can be acquired through experience provided by the employing firm (i.e., company specific technical and operating information). It can be assumed that new employees do not possess this knowledge. While it may be useful to use experimental procedures to evaluate the relative effects of alternative training techniques, comparing post training performance to some standard is likely to provide sufficient evidence that the training program worked.

An Extended Utility Framework

Thus far our primary attention has focused on training and development at the level of individual behavior. While the degree to which behavior can be influenced by training is an important issue, managerial decisions must simultaneously take into account the costs of training and the estimated dollar value associated with a behavioral change. We therefore will present an extended treatment of the utility concepts described in Chapter 12.

Recall that the standard single cohort utility equation from Chapter 12 was of the following form:[18]

$$\Delta U = (N) \, x \left\{ \sum_{t=1}^{T} [1/(1 + i)^t](r_1 - r_2)(SD_y)(^\lambda/_p)(1 + V)(1 - TAX) \right\} \\ -[(N)(C_1 - C_2)/p][1 - TAX] \tag{1}$$

where ΔU represented the marginal utility of using a new selection procedure to hire N new employees instead of using the existing procedure. This payoff was realized over the tenure of the average new employee (T). ΔU represents a series of discounted yearly payoffs that are adjusted for variable costs and taxes. The equation includes the term $[(r_1 - r_2) \, (\lambda/p)]$ which simply represents the expected (average) improvement in job performance (in standard score form) of the group hired using the new procedure (compared to the average performance of a group hired using the existing procedure).

---

[18] In chapter 12 the utility framework described is based on the extensions provided by John W. Boudreau, "Economic considerations in estimating the utility of human resource productivity improvement programs," *Personnel Psychology,* 36, 1983, pp. 551–576. Before reviewing this section of the chapter the reader should be familiar with the coverage provided in chapter 12 or the original articles by Boudreau.

Since we are interested in the utility associated with many different forms of personnel interventions (e.g., training, goal setting programs, incentive systems) the utility equations described in Chapter 12 need to be modified. The procedure for doing so was provided by Schmidt, Hunter, and Pearlman[19] in an article that extended the standard utility equation to allow for any type of personnel program modification. Essentially, this is accomplished by replacing $[(r_1 - r_2)(\lambda/p)]$ with a general term representing the difference in job performance between the average treated (e.g., trained) and untreated (e.g., untrained) employee in standard deviation units (d). Thus, Equation (1) is rewritten as:

$$\Delta U = (N) \times \left\{ \sum_{t=1}^{T} [1/(1 + i)^t](d)(SD_y)(1 + V)(1 - TAX) \right\} - (N)(C)(1 - TAX) \tag{2}$$

where: ΔU = the increase in utility (realized over the duration of the training effect) resulting from treating (training) one cohort of N employees.

N = the number of employees trained.

T = the number of years duration of the training effect on job performance.

t = the time period in which the benefit occurs.

i = the discount rate.

d = the true difference in job performance between the average trained and untrained employee in standard deviation units.

SD_y = the dollar value of a one standard deviation difference in job performance.

V = the proportion of service value (attributable to increased performance) represented by variable costs.

TAX = the marginal tax rate.

C = the cost of training per trainee.

Some Variations[20]

There are instances when an intervention must be readministered (applied regularly each year) to maintain the performance improvement. Certain forms of training and interventions such as incentive salary plans may require this type of action. Here, program costs are incurred every year and are subject to opportunity costs of time. To account for this the cost term would be multiplied by the discount factor:

$$\sum_{t=1}^{T} [1/(1 + i)^{t-1}].$$

The discount factor for costs reflects that training takes place one time period before receiving the benefits. (These discount factors are presented in Table 2-4.)

Following from Chapter 12, there also may be instances when decision makers must choose between two (or more) different personnel interventions. When two alternatives are being compared $(d_1 - d_2)$ and $(c_1 - c_2)$ are substituted for d and C respectively.

Finally, many personnel programs are applied over and over again to multiple cohorts. For example, it is common for employees promoted to first level supervisory jobs to receive training. Over time many groups of employees are trained. The utility models presented here are termed single-cohort models. These models fail to account for the effects of applying personnel programs to future cohorts and therefore may understate long-term consequences. Boudreau[21] has provided the necessary modifications to reflect the period-to-period changes in the number of treated employees in the workforce. These models take into account the number of employees treated in previous periods and their expected tenure. They also can reflect the fact that program costs vary over time (e.g., some training programs have high startup and development costs).[22]

An Illustration

The following illustration was first used by Schmidt, Hunter, and Pearlman[23] in the article that extended standard utility models to cover essentially any personnel intervention. We modify it to take into account the various economic factors introduced by Boudreau.[24]

Suppose a company employs 200 computer programmers and 100 are assigned randomly to a training course and the other 100 receive no training. The company is attempting to conduct a true experiment. If the training proves to be useful, the company will train the remaining 100 programmers and all new programmers once hired. Here we only are interested in the effects of training this single cohort of 100 programmers. The training is held at night and supervisors are not informed of who was selected to receive training. The cost of training is $500 per trainee, the appropriate parameter for the variable cost estimate is $-.05$ (there are few

---

[19] Frank L. Schmidt, John E. Hunter, and Kenneth Pearlman, "Assessing the economic impact of personnel programs on workforce productivity," *Personnel Psychology,* 35, 1982, pp. 333–347.

[20] For a detailed presentation see John W. Boudreau, "Effects of employee flows on utility analysis of human resources productivity improvement programs," *Journal of Applied Psychology,* 68, 1983, pp. 396–406; Schmidt et al., *Ibid.*

[21] Boudreau, *Ibid.*

[22] To fully appreciate the effects of employee flows in utility measurement the interested reader should review: Boudreau, 1983, *Ibid;* John W. Boudreau and Chris J. Berger, "Decision-theoretic utility analysis applied to employee separations and acquisitions," *Journal of Applied Psychology Monograph,* 70, 1985, pp. 581–612.

[23] Schmidt et al., *Ibid.*

[24] Boudreau, *Ibid.*

additional costs associated with high performing programmers), the marginal tax rate is .45, and the discount rate is .10. The estimated standard deviation of the value of services produced (SD_y) is $10,413 and the trained programmers receive higher performance rating than the untrained programmers (for a full discussion of procedures used to rate job performance and to estimate SD_y refer to chapter 16). The estimated true difference in rated job performance between the average trained and untrained programmer is .65 (in standard deviation units). This value of d was computed by subtracting the average performance rating received by untrained programmers from the average rating received by trained programmers and then dividing by the standard deviation associated with the performance ratings. The value of d also was adjusted for unreliability in the ratings.[25] It simply reflects the observation that average trained programmers receive supervisory ratings of performance that are .65 standard deviations higher than the untrained programmers. We now have all the information we need to estimate the dollar value of the training program except for T. For our purpose, assume the training effect is constant over time but that the average job tenure of programmers is only two years. Thus our estimate of T is two years.

The value of the training program, as applied to 100 programmers, is computed by using Equation (2) in the following form:

$$\Delta U = (100) \times \left\{ \sum_{t=1}^{2} [1/(1 + .10)^t](.65)(10,413)(1-.05)(1-.45) \right\} - (100)(500)(1 - .45) = 587,854$$

Under these circumstances, the expected value of the training program for the 100 programmers, compared to no training, is nearly $600,000. This represents the gain realized over the tenure of the trained programmers.

Summary

This chapter prescribes an orientation toward organizational training that includes (1) a thorough assessment of training needs, (2) the design and implementation of training interventions that are congruent with organizational realities and trainee needs, and (3) a bias for experimentation. While the costs of training are high, there is too little empirical evidence showing

---

[25] For a complete discussion of procedures for estimating d, refer to Schmidt et al., *Ibid.* The procedure for adjusting d due to the unreliability of performance ratings (the adjustment reflects disagreement between raters—interrater reliability) is as follows:

$$d_{adjusted} = d/\sqrt{r_{xx}} ,$$

where: $d = \dfrac{\overline{X}_{trained} - \overline{X}_{untrained}}{SD_x}$

r_{xx} = estimate of interrater reliability

that certain forms of training make much of a difference to either individuals or entire organizations. It is critical that practicing managers become skillful at evaluating the potential usefulness of the many available training practices. We suggest that the greatest degree of skepticism should be reserved for general training programs that are advertised as being appropriate and necessary for large numbers of job classifications across multiple firms. Search for evidence that the training modifies critical job behaviors and think systematically about costs versus benefits. Certain types of training experiences clearly are important and contribute greatly to firm performance. Successful managers will be able to make reasoned decisions about when to implement a costly training program and when to rely on an alternative course of action.

PROBLEMS

1. In this chapter we illustrated the use of a utility analysis in evaluating the value of a training program, as applied to 100 programmers. Re-analyze this case by assuming:
   a. that the average post training tenure of a programmer is four years (not two).
   b. that the training program must be repeated every year (the training effect diminishes and programmers must be re-trained annually).
   c. The cost of training is $1000 (not $500) per trainee per year.
   Should the training program be implemented?
2. You have been given the responsibility to design, implement, and evaluate a company-wide training program. The goal of the program is to improve the company's selection interviewing process. Currently, interviews are used throughout the company as a final selection hurdle. Describe the steps you would take in designing, implementing, and evaluating such a system.
3. You work for a large natural gas pipeline company. There are approximately 100 middle-level managers. The company's president wants to initiate a management training program for this group. How would you go about assessing training needs and setting training objectives? Generate a list of possible training needs that could result from this analysis.
4. Many corporate training departments teach a basic module with a title like "Effective Time Management." These modules focus on helping managers prioritize and organize activities. They also often include a series of prescriptions about how to better utilize and manage a schedule. Spend some time in the library to:
   a. see how many books on this topic have been published in the last ten years.
   b. determine if there is evidence that such a training experience is related to managerial success or firm performance.
5. Assume that a firm projects a future talent shortage in a middle-level technical job family. Under what set of circumstances would training represent a more viable alternative than a solution based on an external hiring strategy?

REFERENCES

Goldstein, I. L. *Training in Organizations: Needs Assessment, Development, and Evaluation,* Monterey, Calif.: Brooks/Cole Publishing Company, 1986.

CHAPTER 15

COMPENSATION PRACTICE

M any of the earlier chapters (the chapters devoted to the economic environment) reviewed the major theories of wage determination. Chapter 3 considered methods of analyzing the supply of labor and emphasized determinates of individual decisions to participate in the labor market based on income and leisure trade-offs. Chapters 4 and 5 focused on the demand for labor and reasoned that the worth of a job is the marginal revenue product it generates. Chapter 6 addressed the economic argument that a job is worth the exchange rate clearing in the market (i.e., wage levels are determined where labor demand and labor supply intersect) and also developed concepts suggesting that wages represent, in part, a return on the investments made to develop human capital. Taken together these and other factors (e.g., collective bargaining and government regulation) were used to explain the observed variation in wages and salaries. These explanations become quite complex given the existence of large wage differences across industries for similar job classifications.[1] Managers need to understand this theoretical emperical work in order to explain current wage rates, to adjust wage rates for unique positions, and to predict future wage rates. While it is possible to determine wages directly from financial and labor market data, this process is rarely followed. What we will emphasize in this chapter is a discussion of current compensation practice.

---

[1] J. Dunlop, "Industrial relations and economics: The common frontier of wage determination," *IRRA Proceedings 1984,* 1985.

Practice refers to the general steps followed when determining wage and salary ranges for firm-specific job classifications and the decision rules used in allocating pay to individuals within each of these job classes. Again, let us emphasize that, for certain jobs, wage levels can be directly estimated from accounting data and knowledge of the supply/demand characteristics of the labor market. However, this approach does not represent common practice. Most firms determine wage levels for each classification by conducting or purchasing compensation surveys of industrial competitors. These rates can be adjusted to take into account unique firm characteristics by using reasoned judgment (i.e., the technology of job evaluation) and considering other factors related to compensation strategy (e.g., ability to pay, long-range business plans, and firm success in attracting, motivating, and retaining employees). The job evaluation process also is used to set wage rates for jobs that do not have clear market comparisons. Setting wages is a process that assumes similarity of product, technology, raw material costs, and product prices among competitors.[2] While setting wages to reflect the levels paid by competitors has a basis in economic analysis, the actual steps followed rely on a technology that requires only minimal training in labor economics. It is this technology that will be emphasized in this chapter. This, of course, is necessary because it is to this technology that managers most often will be exposed early in their careers.

This chapter also differs from previous chapters that focused on compensation issues in that our orientation is to consider employee compensation as it affects other related phenomena. While economic analysis often attempts to explain or predict a wage rate, here we begin with a market rate and ask questions about how that rate (as adjusted by decision makers within a given firm) affects key employee behaviors. This difference in orientation was clearly described by Mahoney[3] in his text devoted to compensation and reward systems. Figure 15–1 considers employee compensation as both cause and effect of important outcome variables.

In summary, this chapter will consider compensation practice as it affects firm performance through its influence on employee choice and behavior. We will review basic pay setting practices, discuss non-monetary compensation (benefits) and comment on reward system utility. This material should enhance your ability to (1) make reasoned decisions about pay plan policy and implementation alternatives, (2) predict the behavioral consequences of modifications to a reward system (along with knowledge acquired in earlier chapters), and (3) provide subordinates with rational explanations about why certain standard compensation plan components are necessary.

---

[2] Thomas A. Mahoney, *Compensation and Reward Perspectives,* Homewood, Illinois: Richard D. Irwin, Inc., 1979.

[3] Mahoney, *Ibid.*

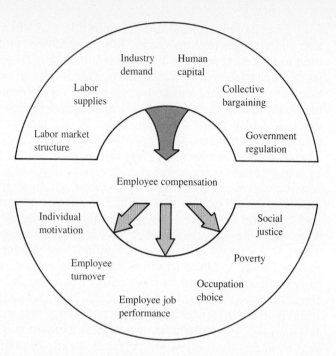

Industry demand   Human capital

Labor supplies   Collective bargaining

Labor market structure   Government regulation

Employee compensation

Individual motivation   Social justice

Employee turnover   Poverty

Occupation choice

Employee job performance

Source: From Thomas A. Mahoney, *Compensation and Reward Perspectives,* Copyright © Richard D. Irwin, Inc., 1979. Reprinted by permission of the publisher and author.

Figure 15-1 **Employee Compensation Considered as both Cause and Effect of Related Phenomena**

Finally, we would like to point out that compensation management will likely represent one of your greatest managerial challenges. While this chapter will review common wage setting practices, we believe effective management will depend on an understanding of the economic concepts developed earlier in this text. One key managerial role is to provide logical explanations for a company's personnel practices and policies. For example, consider Table 15–1. This represents average salaries across different areas for full time faculty members at the University of Kansas. These salaries were for the 1986/1987 academic year.

In this chapter we will emphasize the wage setting process as practiced in most organizations. This does not provide the necessary answers to a disgruntled employee who questions the results of such practices. While recommended steps were taken in establishing the salaries shown in Table 15–1, the effective manager will need to provide an explanation for this outcome. Why would an organization follow established procedures that lead to the differentials shown in the table? Assistant professors from the departments of economics, chemistry, and English have made investments in human capital that equal their School of Business counterparts and they perform similar job duties. Why they receive (and apparently accept) from almost $10,000 to over $17,000 less for a nine month appointment requires an explanation based on economic analysis, not reference to established

Academic area	Full professors	Associate professors	Assistant professors
Business	$51,450	$37,903	$42,996
Chemistry	48,729	32,185	26,992
Economics	47,994	35,542	33,125
English	39,344	28,505	25,922

Source: The University of Kansas Budget (fiscal year ending June 30, 1987).

Table 15–1 **Average Salaries for a Nine Month Appointment for Faculty Members in Selected Disciplines**

practice. The effective manager also will be able to predict the behavioral consequences of such a reward system.

Compensation Objectives

The Sequence of Pay-Related Behaviors

Compensation theorist Thomas Mahoney argues that the overall supply of labor services can be analyzed in terms of individual behavior models.[4] He sees compensation practices affecting a sequence of individual decisions and choices. Individual employers have little control over the first two dimensions but exercise considerable control over the last three. As indicated in Figure 15–2, individuals make decisions about entering the

---

[4] Mahoney, *Ibid.*

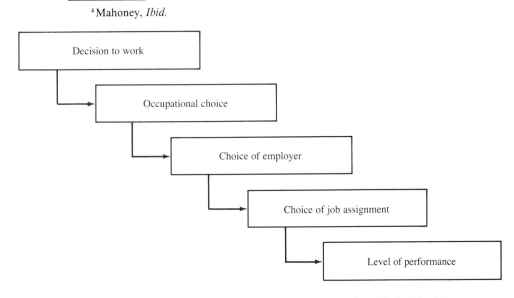

Source: From Thomas A. Mahoney, *Compensation and Reward Perspectives,* Copyright © Richard D. Irwin, Inc., 1979. Reprinted by permission of the publisher and author.

Figure 15–2 **Behavioral Dimensions of Supply of Labor Services**

labor market, about choosing a particular occupation, about selecting a firm or employer, about accepting job assignments and whether or not to remain with an employer, and, as suggested by many contemporary theories of motivation, about providing various levels of performance.

Employers attempt to influence employee behavior and simultaneously control costs such that compensation practices contribute to the profitability of the firm. While employers attempt to (1) attract high quality applicants, (2) retain high performing employees, (3) create environments that lead to employee cooperation and information exchange (e.g., on-the-job training), and (4) stimulate and sustain high levels of effort, each compensation objective must be analyzed from a cost-benefit perspective. The realization of profit requires that the cost of labor be constrained. This point is summarized by Mahoney[5] who states that the "realization of profit from production dictates that the average cost of labor be constrained to a level less than the average revenue product of labor minus all costs other than labor" (p. 369). For our purposes, compensation objectives at the level of the individual firm will include the attraction and retention of high quality employees, the enhancement of effort expenditure and cooperation among employees, cost containment, and finally, regulatory compliance.

External, Internal, and Employee Equity

Compensation practice confronts three primary issues when valuing labor at the level of the firm. Most compensation theorists see these issues as being represented by a set of equity questions.[6] The term equity, as used in the compensation literature, takes on a unique meaning that is not equivalent to the term as used by many labor economists. Traditional economic theory often uses the terms equity and efficiency to distinguish between reward allocation practices based on equality versus contribution. Equity based allocation rules are best characterized by seniority systems (individuals doing the same job and possessing equal service records will receive the same wage) while efficiency based allocation rules are best characterized by bonus and piece-rate systems (individuals performing a common job receive a wage that reflects their contribution). Throughout this chapter the term equity will take on a very different meaning. This meaning is reflected in the social comparison process. Many so-called equity theories of employee motivation argue that individuals seek fairness in their exchange relationships.[7] For a compensation system to meet its

---

[5] Mahoney, *Ibid.*

[6] George T. Milkovich and Terry M. Newman, *Compensation,* Plano, Texas: Business Publications, Inc., 1984.

[7] J. S. Adams, "Wage inequities, productivity and work quality," *Industrial Relations,* 3, 1963, pp. 9–16.

objectives it needs to reflect this concept. Equity and social comparison theories suggest that employees analyze their job inputs (e.g., time, effort, and experience) and what they receive in return (e.g., outcomes such as money, praise, and interesting job assignments). They then compare their input/output ratio to their perceptions of what they think the ratio is for similar others. When these ratios are unequal, an attempt will be made to bring them back into equilibrium. It is this desire for equity that drives many employee behaviors.

The primary equity questions addressed by compensation theorists are defined by Milkovich[8] in the following way:

> External equity refers to pay relationships among organizations and focuses attention on the competitive positions reflected in these relationships (p. 192).
>
> Internal equity refers to the pay relationships among jobs within a single organization and focuses attention on employee acceptance of those relationships (p. 24).
>
> Employee equity refers to pay relationships between individuals within the same job and organization (p. 268).

External equity generally requires the employer to pay wage rates determined by labor demand (what employers are willing to pay) and supply (what employees are willing to accept). Internal equity requires the employer to set wages that correspond to internal norms of job worth (e.g., a job is worth the revenue it generates, its characteristics, and the human capital required for adequate performance). Employee equity requires the employer to pay wages that allow distinctions to be made among individual employees reflecting valued job inputs such as effort, training, or seniority.

Since this chapter will review compensation practice, it is useful to note that each form of equity is addressed using different techniques. Questions of external equity are often resolved by conducting market wage and salary surveys. Internal equity is studied via the job evaluation process. Establishing employee equity depends on judgments about how to best distribute outcomes to employees within a given job classification (e.g., seniority versus merit).

Maintaining all three forms of equity represents a critical managerial challenge. This results from the observation that in certain instances a focus on establishing one type of equity can disrupt other equity perceptions. A fundamental managerial issue is to decide when to emphasize one form of equity versus another. This essentially requires an analysis of practice and compensation objective congruence. To illustrate this concept consider Figure 15–3. The form of equity requiring emphasis is likely to be a function of the most central compensation objective facing the firm. The

---

[8] Milkovich and Newman, *Ibid.*

Forms of Equity Comparison		Compensation Objectives			
		Attraction	Retention	Cooperation/OJT	Effort
Position Equity	External	●	●		
	Internal			●	●
Employee Equity	Seniority		●	●	
	Performance	●			●

Figure 15-3 **Forms of Pay Equity Required to Meet Various Compensation Objectives**

prescriptions displayed in Figure 15–3 are somewhat speculative at this time. They are simply presented to stimulate discussion about the need for congruence. If attraction and retention are the dominant compensation objectives, the firm will need to focus on market forces. If jobs require a great deal of information exchange and cooperation among incumbents, internal equity and non-competitive employee pay policies are likely to be required (e.g., seniority rules). If a high level of individual effort is required, more competitive individual pay policies are likely to be needed (e.g., individual bonus and incentive rules).

We now turn our attention to a review of specific practices. This discussion should help clarify issues and expose the reader to techniques that are regularly used in many organizations. Both line and staff managers play a role in this process. Line managers along with compensation specialists put these systems in operation. Also, a primary managerial role is to explain and justify compensation practice to subordinates. Knowledge of how theory is translated into practice is essential.

Establishing Pay Rates

The Labor Market and External Comparisons

Employers typically estimate the so-called market wage for a given job classification by conducting, participating in, or purchasing wage and salary surveys. Many see the market rate as a given, as an inherently job-related estimate of job worth. Economic theories of the wage determination process often are translated into economic principles that guide decision makers. Many people reason that the results of a wage and salary survey represent an unambiguous, objective estimate of job worth. Recently, Rynes and Milkovich[9] have challenged the use of the conventional wage

---

[9] Sara L. Rynes and George T. Milkovich, "Wage Surveys: Dispelling some Myths about the Market Wage," *Personnel Psychology,* 39, 1986, pp. 71–90.

survey by arguing that both the construct and measurement of the market wage are far from unambiguous and objective. First, they argue that while there are many theoretical assertions, little is actually known about relationships between wage levels and a firm's ability to attract and retain high quality employees. They state that "precious little is known about the actual relationships beween wages, attraction, and labor quality in the real world of imperfect information, discrimination, and imperfect competition. For example, no reserach at the employer unit of analysis has systematically examined the relationships between changes in wage levels and changes in the quantity, and quality, of applicants for positions" (p. 87). They also argue that the measurement process is highly judgmental. They point out that decisions need to be made regarding (1) the appropriate labor market to be surveyed, (2) the number of surveys to be used, (3) the ways in which data are collected, analyzed, and reported, (4) the target job in a competitor's organization (i.e., the process of matching jobs across organizations), (5) the measurement of total pay, or how to account for indirect pay (benefits), and (6) choosing a pay policy (pay at, below, or above the market wage). Thus, collecting, summarizing, and interpreting survey data requires the multiple judgments of many people.

Wage and Salary Surveys. Since our goal is to emphasize the role of the line manager, not the role of the personnel staff specialist, we only seek to familiarize the reader with some minimum standards associated with the survey process. Quality wage and salary surveys (whether or not they are purchased or conducted in-house) need to reflect the following attributes:

1. There needs to be a rationale for selecting the appropriate labor market. This represents a very complex issue that requires a thorough examination of the firm's recruiting practices and other relevant information. Not only does recruiting in specified labor markets need to contribute to the firm's attraction and retention goals, but it must not result in excessive labor costs. The definition of the appropriate labor market is further complicated by the likelihood that the markets differ for different occupations.[10]

2. The survey process needs to include a thorough exchange of job-based information or information resulting from a comprehensive job analysis. As discussed in Chapter 11, when making wage comparisons it is critical that the external job is essentially the same as the target job. Job titles are not sufficient for making decisions about job similarity. It simply is not appropriate to use a market survey that does not include complete job descriptions.

3. The context within which pay is distributed in a competitor's firm must be described in the survey. Interpreting a wage structure is not

---

[10] Rynes and Milkovich, *Ibid.*

Organization	Annual Base Pay	Relative Value of Total Annual Compensation
A	$23,148 (67)[1]	$28,435 (42)[1]
B	24,456 (89)	31,784 (72)
C	21,913 (56)	31,903 (78)
D	23,835 (81)	33,128 (83)
E	23,387 (75)	27,834 (36)
F	30,812 (100)	37,728 (94)
G	19,859 (22)	33,034 (81)
H	21,351 (47)	28,567 (44)
I	21,864 (50)	30,466 (61)
J	21,307 (42)	20,592 (3)
K	15,729 (3)	20,657 (6)
L	21,126 (39)	26,104 (22)
M	21,329 (44)	27,474 (33)
N	22,704 (61)	28,873 (50)
O	20,267 (31)	28,697 (47)
P	27,690 (97)	34,315 (89)
Q	22,763 (64)	31,595 (67)
R	23,886 (83)	28,244 (39)
S	20,628 (33)	26,498 (25)
T	23,761 (78)	36,510 (92)
U	19,866 (25)	24,369 (14)
V	18,158 (11)	23,375 (11)
W	22,412 (58)	28,994 (53)
X	16,625 (6)	23,221 (8)
Y	18,692 (17)	25,445 (19)
Z	17,170 (8)	24,552 (17)
A1	24,948 (94)	33,300 (86)
B1	23,256 (72)	29,922 (58)
C1	20,770 (36)	31,598 (69)
D1	18,174 (14)	26,552 (28)
E1	23,983 (86)	30,490 (64)
F1	23,238 (69)	38,751 (97)
G1	24,917 (92)	39,884 (100)
H1	19,925 (28)	29,465 (56)
I1	18,990 (19)	26,807 (31)
J1	21,890 (53)	31,861 (75)

[1]Percentile scores, or the percentage of the 36 agencies that the organization in question pays equal to or better than.

Source: Ash, R. A., Dreher, G. F., and Krider, C. E. *Compensation Package Survey: A Study for the Kansas Highway Patrol.* Lawrence, Kansas: Institute for Economic and Business Research, 1985.

***Table 15-2*   Base Pay and the Relative Value of Total Compensation for the "Typical Trooper"**

possible in the abstract. For example, a competing firm may pay a below average direct salary, but follow the compensatory practice of providing a leading benefits package.

4. It follows from the previous item that the survey needs to include a mechanism for estimating the total compensation provided competitor's employees. For example, in a recent compensation survey

of law enforcement agencies, an index of the relative value of total compensation was derived by applying a combination of 13 pay policy and benefits rules.[11] The profile of the typical trooper (the entry level position for uniformed officers) was determined through an examination of demographic and survey data. The result of this procedure is shown in Table 15–2. Note that the relative position of each of the 36 agencies can change dramatically when total compensation is taken into account. For example, organization G pays a base wage equal to or better than only 22 percent of the reporting agencies. However, the total relative annual compensation (taking into account such things as compensation for days not worked, the employees' contribution into insurance and pension plans, clothing allowances, and educational and shift differentials) places this agency at the 81st percentile.

5. The survey needs to report not only official wage ranges, but also actual rates. Two organizations may have a similar pay structure but actual expenditures may differ as a function of the number of individuals below, at, or above a specified midpoint. Many surveys address this issue by providing maturity curves based on a scatter-plot of wages as a function of years of experience.

6. If an extended labor market is used, the survey needs to be adjusted for regional living cost differences. At the level of the individual employee, pay is not evaluated in the abstract. Many firms make explicit pay adjustments that reflect regional differences.[12]

Finally, for the reader interested in a more technical description of the wage and salary survey process, many excellent texts are currently available.[13] These references also describe the many surveys that can be obtained from public and private sources.

Developing Internal Pay Structures

An alternative, supplementary, and/or complementary method for estimating job worth is to utilize the results of job evaluation procedures. Originally, job evaluation systems were developed to allow firms to rank order jobs (based on some judgment of job worth) that were unique or firm specific. Many jobs that require company-specific knowledge and skills do not have market comparisons. Most job evaluation plans were designed to

---

[11] Ron A. Ash, George F. Dreher, and Charles E. Krider, *Compensation Package Survey: A Study for the Kansas Highway Patrol.* Lawrence, Kansas: Institute for Economic and Business Research, 1985.

[12] George F. Dreher, "Salary satisfaction and community costs," *Industrial Relations,* 19, 1980, pp. 340–344.

[13] Milton L. Rock (Ed.), *Handbook of Wage and Salary Administration,* New York: McGraw-Hill, 1984; Milkovich and Newman, *Ibid.*

slot these jobs into an existing pay structure comprised of so-called benchmark or key jobs (i.e., jobs that serve as reference points by having stable content and are common across employers in a given industry). Recently, however, the job evaluation methodology has been proposed as an alternative to using market wages as the indicator of job worth. Thus, firms must make choices concerning the relative weights given to market versus job evaluation evidence when constructing pay structures.

The Job Evaluation Process. The job evaluation process includes a series of judgmental steps that result in an estimate of job worth based on some internal standard or value system. Common steps include the following:

1. Job analysis information is collected for jobs within a firm defining relevant tasks, KSA's, and working conditions. Job descriptions are the result of this process.

2. A job evaluation method is purchased or internally developed. These methods range from simple rank ordering procedures to more complex "point" systems. The typical point system includes a set of rules for evaluating job worth. So-called "compensable factors" are defined that reflect the skill, responsibility, effort, and working conditions associated with the various jobs. The compensable factors are weighted to indicate their relative importance and the levels of each factor are defined (some examples will follow).

3. A job evaluation committee is formed to apply the rating rules to each job. The committee reviews the job descriptions and makes judgments about the degree to which the jobs possess varying degrees of each compensable factor. This leads to the assignment of points that allow the committee to rank order positions within the firm. When there are discrepancies between raters, common practice is to let the raters discuss their differences and reach a consensus rating for each factor.

4. The final step is to review the relationship between job points and some current wage index. Benchmark and portal jobs (jobs that serve as entry or exit points for the organization) are priced by examining market rates. The remaining jobs can then be priced by being slotted into the pay structure using the job evaluation points as a guide.

Before providing some illustrations, let us again emphasize that the job evaluation process is highly judgmental. Every step includes subjective decisions that reflect the value system of the decision maker. The potential for bias in job evaluation procedures is an issue receiving considerable attention.[14]

---

[14] Richard D. Arvey, "Sex bias in job evaluation procedures," *Personnel Psychology,* 39, 1986, pp. 315–335.

Skill	Effort	Responsibility (for)	Working Conditions
Education or trade knowledge	Physical demands	Safety of others	Exposure to hazardous materials
Previous experience	Monotony of work	Machinery and equipment	Exposure to dangerous machinery
Time required for training	Fatigue	Protection of materials	Temperature extremes
Human relations skills	Concentration	Contact with public	Exposure to high noise levels levels
Analytical ability	Visual alertness	Records	Mobility requirements
Manual/motor skills	Attention to detail	Monetary responsibility	Flexibility of hours
Creative ability	Stress	Work of others	Physical isolation

Table 15-3   **Potential Factors for Point Systems of Job Evaluation**

Some Potential Compensable Factors. Job evaluation systems often include from three to fifteen compensable factors. These factors can be supply-side in orientation (capture the KSA's and person-centered attributes required to perform a given job) or demand-side in orientation (reflect the content and working conditions of a given job). Some potential compensable factors are shown in Table 15–3. The factors are organized around the common skill, effort, responsibility, and working condition dimensions.

Defining Factor Levels. After the importance of a compensable factor has been determined (by allocating a specified number of points) the various levels of the factor are defined. This is what is compared to a job description (on a factor by factor basis) to arrive at a total value (the points allocated to each factor usually are summed to estimate total job worth). The levels for the factor "visual alertness" are illustrated below (a total of 25 points has been allocated to this factor):

Degree	Points	Degree Assignment Guides
1	5	Little need for vigilance or visual monitoring
2	10	Intermittent visual monitoring of easily observable stimuli (close examination not required)
3	15	Intermittent monitoring of stimuli which are difficult to observe (close attention or examination is required)
4	20	Continuous visual monitoring of easily observable stimuli
5	25	Continuous visual monitoring of stimuli which are difficult to observe

Common Job Evaluation Systems. There are many commonly used systems. For example, the Hay Guide Chart-Profile Method of job evaluation is used by many firms, particularly in the area of managerial compensation. Descriptions of this and other methods are available in a number of sources devoted to wage and salary administration practices.[15]

---

[15] Rock, *Ibid;* Milkovich and Newman, *Ibid.*

Establishing Individual Pay Rates

A variety of approaches can be taken when allocating pay among members of the same job classification. To illustrate, consider the following.

1. *Job-based* pay approaches this issue by paying employees within a given job classification the same wage. Job content, not individual contribution, is used as the allocation rule.

2. *Seniority-based* pay systems are associated with regular pay increases that depend on length of service.

3. *Individual-merit* systems link wage and salary increases to some measure of individual performance or contribution. These increases become part of the employees' base pay. Often, merit is used to allocate pay within a job classification only to the extent that the integrity of the salary structure can be maintained. For example, as individuals reach the upper limit of a salary range their percentage increases are constrained irrespective of rated performance.

4. *Skill-based* pay systems are described by Lawler[16] as plans that increase pay to individuals as new jobs are mastered. While individuals will perform only one job at a time, they will reach the top rate when they have learned all the jobs included in the production process. The goal is to communicate to employees the importance of skill development and to create highly flexible work teams.

5. *Gain-sharing* plans are based on paying a bonus to all employees as a function of operating results at the level of the firm or some division within the business unit. These plans take on many forms, with some merely representing an economic incentive (e.g., the typical profit-sharing plan) while others include the modification of a variety of managerial practices (e.g., the Scanlon Plan).[17]

As suggested earlier in this chapter, the most appropriate allocation rule is likely to depend on multiple factors. For example, Lawler[18] suggests that certain conditions favor gain-sharing plans. These conditions include such things as relatively small work units (less than 500 employees), participative management styles, clear financial measures of firm performance, and a high to moderate degree of work floor interdependence. On the other hand, something like an individual-merit plan is likely to work best when jobs are highly independent, job performance standards can be objectively measured at a reasonable cost, and individual effort will have a clear impact on work results. For whatever the reason, there does seem to be a return by many companies to productivity-based allocation rules (see Example 15–1).

---

[16] Edward E. Lawler, III, *Pay and Organization Development*, Reading, Massachusetts: Addison-Wesley, 1981, p. 65.

[17] Lawler, *Ibid*, p. 133.

[18] Lawler, *Ibid*, p. 144.

EXAMPLE 15.1 BACK TO PIECEWORK: MANY COMPANIES NOW BASE WORKERS' RAISES ON THEIR PRODUCTIVITY

Two recent surveys of companys' compensation practices (a survey of 600 companies by Hay Management Consultants and another by Hewitt Associates) found that many firms are using pay-for-performance procedures when establishing individual pay rates. The Hay survey suggests that there is a movement to use pay-for-performance principles at all organization levels. Under such plans middle and lower-level workers, like their executive counterparts, receive raises, bonuses, or prizes for excelling on a wide variety of performance indexes.

For example, General Motors Corp. placed all 110,000 of its North American salaried staff on pay-for-performance status, abandoning the past practice of considering cost-of-living when adjusting salaries. With this change GM has joined other U.S. corporations (e.g., TRW Inc., Honeywell Inc., and Hewlett-Packard Co.) in using entirely merit-based pay. The need to remain competitive in a changing international economy is usually cited as the central factor in making changes to existing pay practices. This is captured by recent comments from the director of executive compensation for Honeywell Inc. "When you're vying in a world market, you have to get as much out of your reward system as possible. Nearly 50 percent of revenues go toward compensation. It's a waste of resources not to use pay as a tool to motivate people."

Source: Carrie Dolan, "Back to piecework: Many companies now base worker's raises on their productivity," *Wall Street Journal,* November 15, 1985, pp. 1, 19.

Comparable Worth

Now that we have examined the three equity-based issues faced when designing and administering a salary program, it is appropriate to comment on the potential for sex bias in such systems. As most readers are aware, the concept of comparable worth has generated considerable debate and a reanalysis of the wage setting process. As discussed in Chapter 8, the Equal Pay Act requires that men and women receive equal pay for equal work. The Act sets very specific standards against which to judge whether a male/female wage difference is illegal. Sex-based differentials are illegal if men and women are performing jobs within the same establishment, are performing jobs requiring similar skills, efforts, and responsibilities, and are performing jobs under similar working conditions. There are four affirmative defenses that permit pay inequalities, these include pay differences caused by seniority rules, pay differences based on merit or production inequalities, and pay differences resulting from some factor other than sex.

The comparable worth controversy centers on jobs that differ in terms of content or working conditions but that are of similar "worth" to the employer.[19] Comparable worth claims are based on the provisions of Title VII, not the Equal Pay Act. These claims usually revolve around cases in which female-dominated jobs (e.g., clerical employees) have lower wages than similarly evaluated male-dominated jobs (e.g., physical plant maintenance workers). These claims often emerge when the results of a market survey do not correspond with the results produced after conducting a job evaluation. A typical finding is that the regression line (a line of best fit characterizing the relationship between job evaluation points and average pay levels for assorted job classifications) for female-dominated jobs falls below the line for male-dominated jobs. The organization's internal standard of job worth is not congruent with some market driven estimate of job worth. Many employers argue that, in order to attract and retain employees, they must give more weight to market factors. Thus, under this set of circumstances, women receive less pay even though their jobs are shown to be of similar worth to those held by men.

Even though the legal environment is still rather uncertain, managers need to be well aware of the comparable worth issue. While one court has ordered wage adjustments to correct differentials of the sort just described,[20] managers need to realize that this is becoming a social issue of considerable consequence. State legislatures are enacting comparable worth laws (e.g., Minnesota), comparable worth principles are receiving attention in the collective bargaining process, and some companies already are considering the implications of the comparable worth debate (Example 15–2, from a recent Business Week article, makes this point in very clear terms).

In summary, women in the workforce are aware of female/male pay differences and are knowledgeable about pay setting practices. The result is that these practices will be receiving continued scrutiny. Whether a firm uses market wages or job evaluation procedures to estimate job worth, the potential for sex bias exists.[21] The successful manager will likely take a proactive stance on this issue.

Benefits

Employee benefits are a form of indirect compensation and currently account for a large share of total labor costs. The growth in total benefit-related compensation has been dramatic over the past fifty years with expenditures on benefits for full-time employees often exceeding 30 percent

---

[19] Donald J. Treiman and Heidi J. Hartmann (Eds.), *Women, Work and Wages: Equal Pay for Jobs of Equal Value,* Washington, D.C.: National Academy Press, 1981.

[20] AFSCME v. State of Washington, USDS Washington, No. C82-455T (December 14, 1983).

[21] Rynes and Milkovich, *Ibid;* Arvey, *Ibid.*

EXAMPLE 15.2   COMPARABLE WORTH: IT'S ALREADY HAPPENING—COMPANIES ARE QUIETLY EVENING UP PAY SCALES

Business Week reports that many companies are quietly trying forms of comparable worth. Major companies such as AT&T, BankAmerica, Chase Manhattan, IBM, Motorola, and Tektronix are experimenting with procedures designed to raise women's pay. One management consultant is quoted as saying: "In 10 years we'll probably have comparable worth, even though businesses will still be saying we won't." In order to make so-called comparable worth adjustments some companies have started to adhere more closely to internal comparisons, even if this requires paying more than the market demands for certain jobs.

Source: *Business Week,* April 28, 1986.

of direct compensation costs.[22] While many benefits are mandated by the federal government, growth in other areas can be attributed to such things as favorable Internal Revenue Code treatment, union preferences for benefit provisions, cost effectiveness associated with "group" coverage, and the belief that benefit program expenditures help to attract and retain employees.

The components and levels of benefit packages vary across firms within a given industry and across industries (for example the petroleum industry has historically been a leader in terms of the percent of total payroll devoted to benefits). Wallace and Fay[23] provide a useful summary by organizing the major components of the benefit package into three areas: security and health benefits; pay for time not worked; and services provided by the organization at reduced or no cost. For a detailed discussion of these components see Wallace and Fay[24] or the chapters devoted to this topic in texts like Rock's *Handbook of Wage and Salary Administration.*[25]

Benefits administration is complex given the wide range of alternatives and changes that take place in the tax codes, in the legal environment, and in employee preferences. It is beyond the scope of this text to examine these issues in detail. However, we do want to point out that there is little empirical evidence showing that additional expenditures on employee benefits lead to valued outcomes. We find this curious given the large sums of money expended on employee benefits.[26] There is some evidence that

---

[22] Employee Benefits 1983, Washington, D.C.: U.S. Chamber of Commerce, 1984, p. 30.

[23] Marc J. Wallace and Charles H. Fay, *Compensation Theory and Practice,* Boston: Kent Publishing Company, 1983.

[24] Wallace and Fay, *Ibid.*

[25] Rock, *Ibid.*

[26] In 1983 the U.S. Chamber of Commerce estimated total benefit payments of over 500 billion dollars.

benefits influence employee job satisfaction,[27] but almost no empirical evidence at the employer level of analysis showing benefit expenditures to influence outcomes such as retention, attendance, attraction, and job performance. Since benefits are rarely provided at different levels depending on differences in employee performance, there are few theoretical arguments linking benefits to this important outcome variable. This lack of information seriously limits decision makers in their ability to make informed judgments based on costs versus returns. While there is an emerging literature that examines fringe benefit/labor mobility linkages, much remains to be done.[28] This literature suggests that employer-sponsored pensions deter the probability of job change. Other fringe benefits do not seem to have a very strong effect on turnover. After reviewing the relevant literature, Milkovich and Newman[29] concluded that "there is at best only anecdotal evidence that employee benefits are cost justified" (p. 366). Much of the problem potentially can be attributed to the finding that employees do not have accurate perceptions regarding their benefits. The problem for employers is that employees seem to under-value the benefits provided by their companies.[30]

A Comment on Reward System Utility

Pay systems are designed to influence employee behaviors and attitudes at a cost that contributes to the objectives of the organization. Pay systems are particularly central to the management of human resources given their pervasive nature. Pay system design can contribute to the ability to attract and retain high performing employees, sustain continued work effort, and create a work climate that encourages cooperation and on-the-job training. Over time, reward systems must play a dominant role in determining whether or not overall employee quality is enhanced, remains constant, or declines. The consequences of inequitable pay structures and inappropriate rules for allocating pay to individuals have received considerable research attention. For example, inequitable situations lead to employee dissatisfaction and the negative behavioral consequences of pay dissatisfaction have been well documented.[31] Also, moving from job-based to individual merit and incentive systems often has resulted in improved employee performance. One major review of field studies concluded that individual

---

[27] Chris J. Berger, "The effects of fringe benefits on satisfaction," Paper presented at the National Academy of Management Meetings, Dallas, August, 1983; George F. Dreher, "Predicting the salary satisfaction of exempt employees," *Personnel Psychology,* 34, 1981, pp. 579–589.

[28] Olivia S. Mitchell, "Fringe benefits and labor mobility," *The Journal of Human Resources,* 17, 1982, pp. 286–298.

[29] Milkovich and Newman, *Ibid.*

[30] Richard Huseman, John Hatfield and Richard Robinson, "The MBA and fringe benefits," *Personnel Administration,* 23, 1978, pp. 57–60.

[31] H. G. Heneman, III, "Pay satisfaction," in *Research in Personnel and Human Resources Management* (3rd ed.), K. Rowland and G. Ferris (Eds.), Greenwich, Conn.: JAI Press, 1985.

monetary incentives produced the greatest improvement in job performance when compared to other employee motivation techniques (e.g., goal setting, job enrichment).[32] The median performance improvement after the introduction of individual pay incentives was 30 percent while group incentives resulted in 20 percent improvements. Of course, improved performance is not expected to be universal. As noted earlier, individual merit and incentive plans are not likely to be effective when performance/contribution is very difficult to measure objectively, when jobs are interdependent, and when firms lack the ability to link performance to sufficiently large pay increases.

While there has been considerable research attention devoted to the behavioral consequences of pay system modifications, the degree to which these modifications add value to the firm is not well known. Some studies have attempted to take increased pay system costs into account when reaching conclusions about the benefits of a system modification,[33] but there is a clear need to conduct discounted cash flow analyses when evaluating pay system interventions. Since pay system modifications can be treated like any other intervention (e.g., introducing improved training or selection techniques) the utility framework provided in previous chapters can be used for this purpose. Recall, however, that compensation objectives (e.g., attraction, retention, cooperation, and effort/motivation) are interrelated in complicated ways. It can be very difficult to simultaneously accomplish multiple goals. For example, a strategy to attract newcomers (high entry level wages) can interfere with perceptions of employee equity when the firm is simultaneously attempting to constrain overall labor costs.

Summary

In this chapter we have discussed alternative methods used to value jobs (i.e., job evaluation techniques and the procedures followed in conducting wage and salary surveys). In both instances we have stressed that determining the value of a job is far from an unambiguous and objective process. Also, we have reviewed alternative strategies for allocating pay and benefits to individuals within job classifications. Throughout, our focus has been on compensation practice and the technology of wage and salary adminstration. The goal has been to consider compensation practice as it affects firm performance through its influence on employee choice and behavior.

Our basic argument in this and other chapters is that what constitutes sound management practice depends on the unique characteristics of the situation at hand. While compensation practice can be viewed from a

---

[32] E. A. Locke, D. B. Feren, V. M. McCaleb, K. N. Shaw, and A. T. Denny, "The relative effectiveness of four methods of motivating employee performance," in *Changes in Working Life,* K. D. Duncan, M. M. Gruneberg, and D. Wallis (Eds.), New York: John Wiley and Sons, 1980, pp. 363–388.

[33] Gary P. Latham and Dennis L. Dossett, "Designing incentive plans for unionized employees: A comparison of continuous and variable ratio reinforcement schedules," *Personnel Psychology,* 31, 1978, pp. 47–62.

cost/benefit perspective, we also want to suggest that compensation practice represents an opportunity to communicate to employees the firm's overall strategy or philosophy regarding the management of human resources. For firms that attempt to maximize organizational performance by increasing employee commitment and concern for the goals of the entire enterprise, linking individual rewards to organizational performance represents an appropriate approach. Thus, profit sharing, stock options, and other forms of gain-sharing (at all organizational levels) are congruent with other approaches that attempt to foster organizational loyalty. Tying pay to individual performance signals a different managerial approach. Since compensation practices are particularly visible, a systems view is necessary.

PROBLEMS

1. Pay systems need to be equitably administered. One form of equity is termed *internal* equity and is concerned with the relative value or contribution of jobs within a given company. This "relative worth" of jobs is often determined using formal job evaluation methods (e.g., point systems). A second form of equity (*external* equity) focuses on comparing a firm's wage rates with the rates being paid by other organizations. This is often determined by conducting salary surveys. The balance or relative emphasis given to these two forms of equity represents a key compensation strategy decision. If job evaluation studies and salary surveys disagree regarding the relative worth of a firm's jobs, when does it make sense to emphasize internal equity? When does it make sense to emphasize external equity?

2. Personnel specialists are increasingly becoming concerned with the costs versus benefits associated with personnel interventions and practices. Describe a general strategy for determining whether or not a pay system modification will add value to the firm.

3. When would each of the following approaches to establishing *employee equity* likely result in a positive return to the firm?
   a. an individual merit system
   b. reward allocation rules based on employee seniority
   c. a plant wide incentive plan (e.g., a Scanlon Plan)

4. Discuss why training in traditional labor economics (e.g., the wage determination process) is useful to the practicing line manager.

5. How might an organization administer employee benefits to increase the likelihood that these expenditures will make a positive contribution to firm performance?

6. What are the likely determinants of pay satisfaction?

REFERENCES

Ehrenberg, R. G., and Milkovich, G. T., "Compensation and firm performance," In M. Kleiner, R. Block, M. Roomkin, and S. Salsburg (Eds.), 1987 Research Volume of the Industrial Relations Research Association (entitled—*Human Resources and the Performance of the Firm*).

Milkovich, G.T., and Newman, J. M. *Compensation,* Plano, Texas: Business Publications, 1984.

ASSESSING
EMPLOYEE
PERFORMANCE

M anagerial work is multidimensional. In his widely read Harvard Business Review article, Mintzberg described ten roles that formed an overall picture of managerial behavior.[1] Two key roles, the *leader* and *resource allocator,* depend heavily on the availability of high quality information about the job performance of individual employees. In particular, managers need performance data when hiring, training, motivating, and terminating subordinates. They also need to make resource allocation decisions that add value to the firm. Thinking in utility or cost-benefit terms requires an analysis of both the costs and returns associated with a personnel practice. Ultimately, some measure of performance effectiveness is required to carry out the cost-benefit studies discussed in this part of the text. Therefore, while performance measurement only supports the leader and resource allocator roles, it represents an important managerial activity that all managers (line and staff) engage in throughout their careers.

The goals of this chapter are to introduce you to basic concepts. We want to make it clear that effective management largely depends on the availability of high quality estimates of employee performance. Therefore, we will begin by describing the many uses of performance data. We will then survey a representative sample of performance appraisal methods. One sub-goal will be to emphasize the need to use a measurement strategy that best meets a stated objective. That is, we will stress the point that no one form of measurement will simultaneously meet the multiple objectives set for a performance appraisal system. Effective managers will modify

[1] Henry Mintzberg, "The manager's job: Folklore and fact," *Harvard Business Review,* July-August, 1975, pp. 49–61.

their measurement strategy as unique needs develop. Since utility and cost-benefit models underpin much of this text, we will devote one section of this chapter to the problem of estimating the dollar value associated with observed differences in employee performance. The utility framework used in the personnel practice chapters depends on being able to translate performance differences into dollar terms. These models require estimating the dollar value associated with a one standard deviation improvement in job performance. That is, what sales or service value differences exist between average performers and above average performers (those performing better than approximately 85 percent of their peers). Finally, we will comment on the legal issues surrounding performance appraisal systems. Since many personnel decisions are based on alleged performance differences among employees, performance appraisal systems often receive critical examination by the courts.

After completing this chapter you should (1) better understand the centrality of performance measurement to many managerial activities (and therefore be motivated to devote time and resources to the performance appraisal process), (2) be able to make reasoned judgments about the appropriate form of performance measurement given a unique requirement, (3) be familiar with the problems associated with translating differences in job performance into dollar terms, and (4) be prepared to design and implement job-related performance measurement systems.

Using Performance Data

Managers use performance data to enhance the quality of decision making, to evaluate the usefulness of personnel programs and practices, and to encourage high levels of effort expenditure from subordinates. Our treatment will be necessarily brief. For a full discussion we suggest the appropriate chapters from Landy and Farr's text devoted to the measurement of work performance.[2] We draw from their work in what follows. First, we will describe what Landy and Farr call administrative uses of performance data, then we will summarize certain research oriented uses, and finally we will comment on performance feedback as a motivational strategy.

Promotion/Lateral Movement

As developed in the chapter addressing the movement of employees within the organization's internal labor market (internal staffing), past job performance often is given weight when making promotion decisions. This, of course, is based on the assumption that performance in lower level jobs will be predictive of performance in successively higher level jobs. For this

---

[2] Frank J. Landy and James L. Farr, *The Measurement of Work Performance,* New York: Academic Press, Inc., 1983, chapters 6 and 7.

strategy to be useful, common performance components or knowledge/skill requirements must exist across organizational levels and various candidates for a given position must be compared against a common performance standard. Unfortunately, when these conditions are not met and when low quality performance estimates are used, much can go wrong when using past performance to predict future performance in a higher level job. These same issues apply when making decisions about the lateral movement of employees.

Training Needs Analysis

Managers commonly work with individual employees or study aggregate performance records to identify knowledge/skill deficiencies that can be alleviated via training and development experiences. For this purpose, a performance appraisal system that rates employees over person-centered attributes (e.g., knowledge, skill, and ability dimensions) is most useful.

Access to Training

Another administrative decision relates to the identification of individuals who will be given additional training, sponsorship, or challenging job assignments. Access to these opportunities can, in part, be based on past performance records. When this strategy is used future opportunities can be thought of as rewards for past achievements. The goal is to identify individuals with the most "potential." In fact, many firms use managerial rating systems that directly ask for an estimate of potential.

Salary Decisions

Many theories of employee motivation make it clear that effective managers are able to link valued rewards to employee contribution and performance. Many firms, particularly for managerial positions, use so-called merit salary systems. The idea is to allocate salary to persons performing the same job on the basis of contribution. To accomplish this, estimates of individual performance and contribution must be available. In practice, most merit systems include other allocation rules that, along with performance information, are used in making salary adjustments (e.g., position within a job grade, seniority, and such things as cost of living adjustments). While there may be appropriate situations for the application of performance-based pay allocations, there also are situations that call for the use of other allocation rules. One requirement for a useful merit pay system is that valid performance information must exist at a reasonable cost.

Termination/Layoff Decision

Individuals can be fired for cause and organizations may need to reduce workforce size to cope with unfavorable product market conditions. While alternatives to employee layoffs are sometimes available and desirable from a cost-benefit standpoint, layoff decisions based on job performance represent one possible strategy for dealing with an over supply of labor in the organization.

Selection System Evaluation

One approach to demonstrating that a selection procedure is job-related is to provide evidence that scores on the selection procedure (e.g., aptitude test scores, interview ratings) correlate with some independent measure of job performance. That is, the observed relationship between applicant performance on the selection device and subsequent performance on the job serves as evidence of job relatedness. Measures of job performance are essentially the dependent variables in evaluative studies of selection system effectiveness.

Training Evaluation

To determine whether or not training and development activities (or any personnel intervention) influence or change employee behavior, some form of evaluation is required. The typical strategy is to compare trained employees with employees that have not yet received instruction. The dependent variable in such a comparison often is some measure of job performance. The general point here is that measures of individual job performance or job output can serve as dependent or criterion variables whenever we attempt to evaluate the impact of a personnel program or intervention. Interventions, ranging from changes in selection techniques to the modification of reward and pay systems, first need to be judged based on their behavioral consequences. If there is a behavioral consequence we then attempt to determine its contribution to firm value (i.e., conduct a cost-benefit or utility analysis).

Cost-Benefit Analysis

As will be developed in a subsequent section, the cost-benefit or utility models used to evaluate personnel practices depend on being able to translate individual differences in job performance into dollar terms. Most estimation procedures rely on a manager's ability to at least rank order employees in terms of their job performance. Conducting a utility analysis is another form of research that depends on high quality performance data. Of course, the costs associated with performance measurement must be included in our utility estimates.

Feedback

There is evidence that performance feedback can influence employee motivation and satisfaction. Feedback provides information about goal accomplishment, effort-performance linkages, and training needs. While performance feedback can be a natural result of completing certain job tasks (the activity itself provides clear and direct information about the effectiveness of performance) knowing where you stand on many jobs requires an external performance evaluation. The performance review process itself can take many forms and its usefulness is apparently affected by a wide variety of variables. Such things as supervisory style (e.g., autocratic versus participative, degree of openness and supportiveness, etc.), subordinate preparation, and feedback specificity and frequency can influence how subordinates will react to evaluation. For a thorough review of this area we refer you to the appropriate section (Chapter 7) of Carroll and Schneier's text.[3]

Performance Appraisal Methods

There are many approaches from which to select an appropriate measurement strategy. One simple framework for classifying methods is shown in Figure 16–1. First, some methods focus on results, not on how the results are achieved. Results-oriented measurement concentrates on the amount of output produced, the amount of time required to reach a production target, or outcomes such as sales revenue. New computer technology now is being used by some firms to monitor what might be termed "micro-level" results.[4] For example, the number of pages typed or the number of keystrokes per minute represent this form of measurement (see Example 16–1). Other measurement systems attempt to evaluate employee performance in terms of either the behaviors exhibited or the person-centered attributes required for successful job performance. In addition to these three levels of analysis, it is possible to use absolute rating standards or comparative standards. In

---

[3] Stephen J. Carroll and Craig E. Schneier, *Performance Appraisal and Review Systems: The Identification, Measurement, and Development of Performance in Organizations,* Glenview, Ill.: Scott, Foresman and Company, 1982, pp. 160–189.

[4] M. W. Miller, "Productivity spies: Computers keep eye on workers and see if they perform well," *Wall Street Journal,* June 3, 1985, pp. 1 and 15.

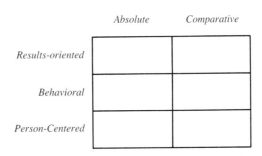

Figure 16–1   **A Framework for Classifying Performance Appraisal Methods**

EXAMPLE 16.1

COMPUTERS ARE WATCHING OVER EMPLOYEES AND MONITORING PRODUCTIVITY

Results-oriented performance measurement is now becoming increasingly popular given new technology that makes the practice less costly. For example, Leprino Foods Co. in Denver monitors truck drivers by outfitting its trucks with portable computers that record truck speed, engine and transmission data, and when the truck stops. The system is used to keep trucks under 60 miles per hour. Truckers who drive too fast put strain on engines and increase fuel costs.

The use of computers also is becoming popular among managers of clerical employees and machine operators. Sophisticated systems keep track of such things as number of pages typed, key-strokes pro-

duced per minute, number of customer calls answered, how long each call takes, and a variety of other indexes of operating speed and efficiency.

While many managers view these systems in very favorable terms, a growing number of labor experts believe such practices create stress and dehumanize employees. Thus, there is an emerging debate about the long-term effects of electronic performance measurement. Many believe this type of monitoring degrades the quality of work life and can have a negative impact on productivity.

Source: Michael W. Miller, "Productivity spies: Computers keep eye on workers and see if they perform well," *Wall Street Journal*, June 3, 1985.

absolute systems, employees are compared to some standard of performance. All employees within a given job classification are compared to the same standard. Therefore, it is possible for all or many employees to meet, fall below, or exceed the predetermined level of performance. Comparative procedures judge performance in relation to others. An individual's relative standing among other similar employees is used in the measurement process. This framework suggests that there are at least six possible general categories depicting performance measurement systems.

While the possibilities are many, the following illustrations should clarify our previous statements. To simplify we have created or reproduced sample rating formats that all address managerial/supervisory performance dimensions. Also to be concise, our samples include only a few dimensions. Note that while it is possible to make overall evaluations, most contemporary performance appraisal systems are dimensionalized. This increases the likelihood that the essential aspects of the job are considered, and allows for rating composites that uniquely cover job specific content.

Our first example (Figure 16–2) represents a form of result-oriented measurement that sets absolute performance standards. Note that the major job objectives are listed, weighted for importance, and defined in terms of a performance standard. Ultimately, the rated individual is judged to have performed at, below, or above each target. These ratings can then be

Prepared by manager	Date	*General manager* Position title	Progress reviews 1st _____ 2nd _____
Reviewed by supervisor	Date	*Production* Position title	3rd _____ Date

Major job objectives	% WT	Measures of results	Std. of perf.	Results Target	Actual	Dates Target	Actual
1. Product delivery (May be broken down by products)	25%	a. Percent of on-schedule delivery	94%	Increase to 98%		8/31	
		b. Number of customer complaints as a % of monthly purchase orders	4%	Decrease to 3%		9/30	
2. Product quality (May be broken down by products)	30%	a. Percent of rejects per total monthly volume	6%	Decrease to 4%		7/31	
		b. Ratio of factory repair time to total production hours/month.	7%	Decrease to 4%		9/31	
		c. Number of units service free during warranty period	73%	Increase to 86%		10/31	
3. Operating efficiency	25%	a. Cost per unit of output per month	$35.75/ unit	Reduce to $35.50/unit		2/1	
		b. Equipment utilization time as a % of monthly available hours	86%	Increase to 95%		11/15	
4. Other key objectives	20%						

Source: R. W. Beatty and C. E. Schneier, *Personnel Administration: An Experimental Skill-Building Approach,* p. 156, Reading, Mass.: Addison-Wesley Publishing Co. Reprinted with permission.

Figure 16-2   **Results-Oriented Performance Measurement**

summarized, by taking importance weights into account, to create an overall statement about job performance.

Figures 16-3 and 16-4 depict two strategies that rely on a behavioral

PERFORMANCE WORK SHEET

NAME (LAST, FIRST, MIDDLE)

PART 1-ACTIVITIES

Before making any assessments, determine for each dimension whether it is a major part of the employee's job, a relatively minor part of the job, or is not applicable. Check as appropriate under "Job Profile."

For all dimensions where the Major or Minor columns are checked, assess the employee according to the scale definitions.

	JOB PROFILE PART OF JOB								COMMENTS (Where appropriate, give specific examples.)
	Major	Minor	Not Applicable	Exceptional	Generally Exceeds Requirements	Generally Meets Requirements	Needs Improvement	Unsatisfactory	
Acquiring and Maintaining Job and Professional Knowledge. Includes staying abreast of the latest technology, knowledge, and other developments in the employee's area of professional competence. Also includes acquiring and applying knowledge of the assignment, as well as related knowledge of the organization.	☐	☐	☐	☐	☐	☐	☐	☐	
Planning and Organizing Own Work. Includes planning own work schedule, setting and monitoring personal performance goals, and taking initiative to accomplish those goals.	☐	☐	☐	☐	☐	☐	☐	☐	
Planning, Objective-Setting, Developing Strategy, and Stewardship. Includes the business management cycle of planning material, staffing, etc., needed to accomplish business objectives; setting business objectives; developing strategies and methods for accomplishing objectives; measuring results against plans. Does not include personal work planning.									
Designing, Implementing, Analyzing, and Reporting Studies or Investigations. Includes research or study of a particular topic; aspects include designing and planning the study; implementing it through data or information collection; analysis of the data or information; and reporting the results of the study.	☐	☐	☐	☐	☐	☐	☐	☐	

Preparing and Making Briefings and Presentations. Includes the preparation and delivery of briefings, speeches, proposals, and presentations; may be written or oral; may involve negotiating or persuading others to adopt a position or accept a proposal; may involve translating complex or technical information to a form appropriate to the audience.

Economic, Financial or Business Analysis and Forecasting. Includes aspects of economic, financial or business analysis and forecasting, such as return on investment analysis, capital expenditure recommendations, analysis of economic trends, analysis of competitors, and analysis of business areas in which the Company is, or might be, engaged.

Development and Delivery of Training Programs and Materials. Includes the design, preparation, presentation, and evaluation of the effectiveness of training programs or materials.

Supervisor's Performance Assessment	Definition
Exceptional	Performance that consistently exceeds the requirements of the position.
Generally Exceeds Requirements	Performance that generally exceeds the requirements of the position.
Generally Meets Requirements	Performance that generally meets the requirements of the position.
Needs Improvement	Performance that is generally below what is normally expected of the position and requires improvement.
Unsatisfactory	Performance that does not meet the minimum requirements of the position and the necessary improvements have not been forthcoming. Employee is to be informed and appropriate action taken.

Source: Behavioral/Task-Oriented Performance Measurement. Copyright 1984 by Exxon Corporation. Reprinted with permission.

Figure 16–3 **Behavioral/Task-Oriented Performance Measurement**

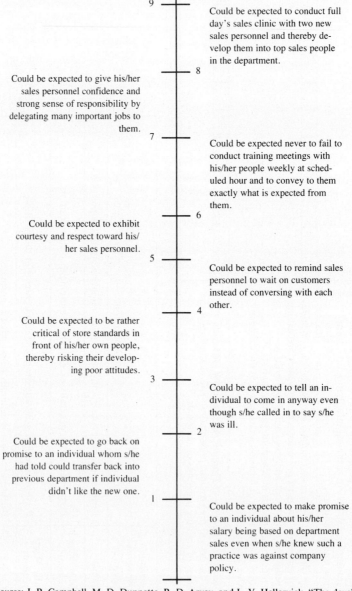

Supervising Sales Personnel

Gives sales personnel a clear idea of their job duties and responsibilities; exercises tact and consideration in working with subordinates; handles work scheduling efficiently and equitably; supplements formal training with his/her own ''coaching''; keeps informed of what the salespeople are doing on the job; and follows company policy in agreements with subordinates.

9

Could be expected to conduct full day's sales clinic with two new sales personnel and thereby develop them into top sales people in the department.

8

Could be expected to give his/her sales personnel confidence and strong sense of responsibility by delegating many important jobs to them.

7

Could be expected never to fail to conduct training meetings with his/her people weekly at scheduled hour and to convey to them exactly what is expected from them.

6

Could be expected to exhibit courtesy and respect toward his/her sales personnel.

5

Could be expected to remind sales personnel to wait on customers instead of conversing with each other.

4

Could be expected to be rather critical of store standards in front of his/her own people, thereby risking their developing poor attitudes.

3

Could be expected to tell an individual to come in anyway even though s/he called in to say s/he was ill.

2

Could be expected to go back on promise to an individual whom s/he had told could transfer back into previous department if individual didn't like the new one.

1

Could be expected to make promise to an individual about his/her salary being based on department sales even when s/he knew such a practice was against company policy.

Source: J. P. Campbell, M. D. Dunnette, R. D. Arvey, and L. V. Hellervick, "The development and evaluation of behaviorally based rating scales," *Journal of Applied Psychology*, 1973, *57,* 15–22. Reprinted by permission.

Figure 16–4 **Behaviorally Anchored Rating Scale (BARS)**

orientation. The first represents segments of a performance appraisal system that was developed by creating rating dimensions derived from a thorough job analysis. The assessment of each applicable performance category is made using the corresponding five-point scale. Absolute or comparative rating standards (absolute are shown here) are possible when using this approach. The second is an example of a rating dimension from a behaviorally anchored rating scale (BARS). In practice, a separate scale is generated for each important job dimension. BARS usually anchor each level of performance with an absolute, not a comparative standard.

Person-centered or trait-oriented measurement is illustrated in Figure 16–5. Here, two factors are usually considered in making ratings: (1) the extent the incumbent possesses a particular job-related knowledge, skill or ability, and (2) the degree the individual applies the KSA when performing the job.

These illustrations only serve to highlight some of the possibilities. Performance appraisal methods have received considerable research attention and the variety of approaches almost is unlimited. The research literature is characterized by a concern for measurement quality. The reliability and validity of the various methods and formats have been studied at great length along with the degree to which a method resists constant rating errors.[5] Before developing or implementing a performance appraisal system a current text devoted to this topic should be consulted. Finally, to restate an earlier point, appraisal methods need to be evaluated not only in terms of their measurement properties but also in terms of other criteria. There needs to be congruence between method and the objective being served. For example, results-oriented approaches can be very useful for allocating scarce resources (e.g., merit salary increases) or in establishing targets and goals. However, if our objective is to counsel a poor performing employee, a behaviorally-oriented or person-oriented approach is likely to be appropriate. In this instance we need to provide guidance regarding why a particular performance standard is not being met. Other criteria for evaluating rating methods include user acceptance, perceived fairness, compliance with fair employment practice legislation, and costs (including the costs associated with designing, implementing, and maintaining the system). Some hypothesized linkages between evaluation method and common objectives are shown in Figure 16–6. Others have provided similar ratings of method effectiveness.[6] These typically rely on expert judgment. The judges that make these ratings are knowledgeable about the existing research evidence, but additional research focusing on method/objective congruence is necessary before clear decision rules become available. All that we hope to highlight in Figure 16–6 is that managers

---

[5] H. John Bernardin and Richard W. Beatty, *Performance Appraisal: Assessing Human Behavior at Work,* Boston: Kent Publishing Company, 1984; Stephen J. Carroll and Craig E. Schneier, *Performance Appraisal and Review Systems,* Glenview, Ill.: Scott, Foresman and Company, 1982.

[6] Bernardin and Beatty, *Ibid;* Carroll and Schneier, *Ibid.*

PERFORMANCE WORK SHEET

NAME (LAST, FIRST, MIDDLE)

PART 2-ABILITIES In making your assessments in Part 2, you should consider the degree to which the employee demonstrates each ability by applying it to the performance of the job.	*JOB PROFILE* *PART OF JOB* *Major*	*Minor*	*Not Applicable*	*Exceptional*	*Generally Exceeds Requirements*	*Generally Meets Requirements*	*Needs Improvement*	*Unsatisfactory*	*COMMENTS* (Where appropriate, give specific examples.)
Adaptability to Time Pressures and Changing Priorities. Includes effectively adapting to tight deadlines, heavy workloads, and sudden or frequent changes in priorities, in order to accomplish objectives.									
Interpersonal Abilities. Includes interacting effectively with others; relating appropriately to persons at higher, same, and lower levels in the organization; exhibiting appropriate behavior, particularly in difficult situations; responding productively to constructive criticism; maintaining motivation even in the face of reversal or disappointment.									
Coordination Abilities. Includes working with and coordinating the activities of persons over whom the employee may have no direct authority; coordinating activities of employees from more than one work group, unit, or organization.									

Comprehension, Reasoning, and Analytical Abilities. Includes applying comprehension, reasoning, and analytical abilities to accomplish job objectives; comprehending and using pertinent aspects of data or information; comprehending written or spoken information; generating creative ideas, solutions, or techniques having useful application.

Communicative Abilities. Includes writing and speaking clearly, concisely, and persuasively.

Decision-Making Abilities. Includes weighing risks and advantages; showing initiative and taking appropriate risks to make decisions; making judgments which are timely, decisive, and effective; tailoring decisions for unusual or ambiguous situations.

Business Judgment. Includes identifying and evaluating ways for improving Company performance (for example, cost reductions, more effective use of resources, new profit-making opportunities, monitoring customer requirements, etc.).

Source: Person-Centered Rating Scale. Copyright 1984 by Exxon Corporation. Reprinted with permission.

Figure 16–5 **Person-Centered Rating Scale**

Objective	Results-oriented		Behavioral		Person-Centered	
	Absolute	Comparative	Absolute	Comparative	Absolute	Comparative
Promotion decisions		●				●
Training needs					●	
Access to training		●				●
Termination decisions	●					
Selection evaluation			●			
Training evaluation			●		●	
Feedback/ counseling			●		●	
User acceptance	●		●			
EEO compliance	●		●			
Costs	This will likely vary as a function of unique setting and problem characteristics					

Figure 16-6 **Hypothesized Linkages Between Performance Evaluation Method and Various Objectives (● denotes congruence)**

must first be clear about what they hope to achieve. They then can make reasoned decisions about the type of evaluation system to design and implement.

Estimating the Dollar Value of Performance

In the chapters devoted to the basic personnel functions (staffing, development, and compensation), cost-benefit or utility models are developed and illustrated. The organizational entry chapter, in particular, reviews the history of these utility models and presents a general strategy that can be used to estimate the net benefit associated with any personnel/human resource intervention. These models depend on being able to estimate the standard deviation of individuals' dollar contribution to the organization (SD_y). We need to estimate the institutional benefits associated with a one standard deviation improvement in job performance. While complex cost accounting procedures could be used for this purpose, many previous attempts resulted in the conclusion that most human performance differences defied the cost accounting approach. For example, Cascio and Ramos,[7] working with a team of certified public accountants in a Bell operating company, concluded (like others before them) that the cost accounting approach will not produce meaningful results in many situations. They state that they "abandoned a cost accounting approach and focused instead on the development of a user-friendly, behaviorally based method that would still permit reliable measurement . . ." (p. 20).

In 1979, Schmidt, Hunter, McKenzie, and Muldrow[8] reported on the use of a procedure for obtaining rational estimates of SD_y. This paper was very influential and encouraged the application of utility models in a wide variety of settings. Essentially, Schmidt et al. used the following reasoning: "If job performance in dollar terms is normally distributed, then the difference between the value to the organization of products and services produced by the average employee and those produced by an employee at the 85th percentile in performance is equal to SD_y" (p. 619). After pilot testing the procedure for a budget analyst position, estimates of SD_y were provided by experienced supervisors of computer programmers in the federal government. These supervisors provided the necessary estimates by completing the questionnaire reproduced in Figure 16–7. Estimates for average, low, and superior performing programmers were computed by averaging the corresponding values supplied by 105 supervisors. The hope was to minimize idiosyncratic tendencies, biases, and random errors by using a large number of judges. In this particular instance, SD_y was estimated to be $10,413.

Since the publication of the Schmidt et al. article, other methods for estimating SD_y have been proposed. Cascio and Ramos[9] have developed and tested a method that sets the benchmark value of labor equal to the cost of labor (average salary) and uses rated deviations from this benchmark to provide a dollar-valued index of variability in job performance. For a variety of reasons this approach almost always will underestimate the value of labor and therefore lead to conservative estimates when used in conjunction with the standard utility models presented in this text. Also, since the publication of the 1979 paper, Schmidt and Hunter[10] have provided evidence that their rational estimates of SD_y are usually about 40 to 60 percent of the average salary received by employees. Thus, they recommend

---

[7] Wayne F. Cascio and Robert A. Ramos, "Development and application of a new method for assessing job performance in behavior/economic terms," *Journal of Applied Psychology,* 71, 1986, pp. 20–28.

[8] Frank L. Schmidt, John E. Hunter, Robert C. McKenzie, and Tressie M. Muldrow, "Impact of valid selection procedures on work-force productivity," *Journal of Applied Psychology,* 64, 1979, pp. 609–626.

[9] Cascio and Ramos, *Ibid.*

[10] Frank L. Schmidt and John E. Hunter, "Individual differences in productivity: An empirical test of estimates derived from studies of selection procedure utility," *Journal of Applied Psychology,* 68, 1983, pp. 407–414.

The instructions to the supervisors were as follows:

The dollar utility estimates we are asking you to make are critical in estimating the relative dollar value to the government of different selection methods. In answering these questions, you will have to make some very difficult judgments. We realize they are difficult and that they are judgments or estimates. You will have to ponder for some time before giving each estimate, and there is probably no way you can be absolutely certain your estimate is accurate when you do reach a decision. But keep in mind three things:

1. The alternative to estimates of this kind is application of cost accounting procedures to the evaluation of job performance. Such applications are usually prohibitively expensive. And in the end, they produce only imperfect estimates, like this estimation procedure.

2. Your estimates will be averaged in with those of other supervisors of computer programmers. Thus errors produced by too high and too low estimates will tend to be averaged out, providing more accurate final estimates.

3. The decisions that must be made about selection methods do not require that all estimates be accurate down to the last dollar. Substantially accurate estimates will lead to the same decisions as perfectly accurate estimates.

Based on your experience with agency programmers, we would like for you to estimate the yearly value to your agency of the products and services produced by the average GS 9–11 computer programmer. Consider the quality and quantity of output typical of the average programmer and the value of this output. In placing an overall dollar value on this output, it may help to consider what the cost would be of having an outside firm provide these products and services.

Source: From Schmidt, Hunter, McKenzie, and Muldrow. Impact of Valid Selection Procedures on Work-Force Productivity, *Journal of Applied Psychology*, 1979, *64*, 621. Copyright © 1979 by the American Psychological Association. Reprinted by permission of the author.

Figure 16-7 **Instructions for the Estimation of SD$_y$**

that 40 percent of salary be used as a conservative estimate of SD$_y$ when it is not possible to use their full estimation procedure. While there are a variety of reservations about the Schmidt et al. estimation procedure,[11] similar methods have been used in the application of decision-theoretic principles to many complex questions. In many applications it is not critical that SD$_y$ estimates be accurate down to the last dollar.

Appraisal System Utility

The costs associated with system design, rater training, and the time commitment associated with the ongoing appraisal process can be very high.[12] While performance appraisal serves to support many personnel functions, the feedback process has the potential to directly affect employee contribution. The research literature suggests that feedback may result in increases in performance varying from 10 to 30 percent.[13] Using a standard utility framework, Landy et al. provided a demonstration showing the gains

Based on my experience, I estimate the value to my agency of the average GS 9–11 computer programmer at _____ dollars per year.

We would now like for you to consider the "superior" programmer. Let us define a superior programmer as a programmer who is at the 85th percentile. That is, his or her performance is better than that of 85 percent of his or her fellow GS 9–11 programmers, and only 15 percent turn in better performances. Consider the quality and quantity of the output typical of the superior programmer. Then estimate the value of these products and services. In placing an overall dollar value on this output, it may again help to consider what the cost would be of having an outside firm provide these products and services.

Based on my experience, I estimate the value to my agency of a superior GS 9–11 computer programmer at _____ dollars per year.

Finally, we would like you to consider the "low-performing" computer programmer. Let us define a low-performing programmer as one who is at the 15th percentile. That is, 85 percent of all GS 9–11 computer programmers turn in performances better than the low-performing programmer, and only 15 percent turn in worse performances. Consider the quality and quantity of the output typical of the low-performing programmer. Then estimate the value of these products and services. In placing an overall dollar value on this output, it may again help to consider what the cost would be of having an outside firm provide these products and services.

Based on my experience, I estimate the value to my agency of the low-performing GS 9–11 computer programmer at _____ dollars per year.

associated with a formal feedback program to far outweigh the costs. In making their calculations they considered the costs of developing the performance appraisal system, the costs associated with training supervisors in the evaluation and feedback process, and the time required to actually evaluate performance and conduct the feedback sessions. Thus, while performance data are required to conduct utility studies, these systems also can be thought of as direct interventions. In this context, raters need to possess the ability and willingness to provide feedback. While there are many obstacles associated with conducting an effective performance appraisal interview, few research-based prescriptions exist. For a review of this literature and a tentative set of prescriptions we suggest Bernardin and Beatty's book devoted to the performance appraisal process.[14]

[11] George F. Dreher and Paul R. Sackett, *Perspectives on Employee Staffing and Selection,* Homewood, Ill.: Richard D. Irwin, Inc., 1983, pp. 91–95.

[12] Bernardin and Beatty, *Ibid,* pp. 208–211.

[13] Frank J. Landy, James L. Farr, and Rick R. Jacobs, "Utility concepts in performance measurement," *Organizational Behavior and Human Performance,* 30, 1982, pp. 15–40.

[14] Bernardin and Beatty, *Ibid.*

Legal Issues in Appraising Performance

Many employment decisions are made using job performance as at least a partial factor in reaching a conclusion. As discussed in Chapter 8, if an employment practice which operates to exclude persons covered by the provisions of Title VII (or other related laws) cannot be shown to be related to job performance (or of business necessity), the practice is prohibited. While this can become somewhat circular, measures of job performance must be job-related if their use in the decision making process generates adverse impact against a protected group (e.g., women, minorities). One of the most-often cited cases in this area is *Rowe* v. *General Motors*.[15] In this case, promotion decisions were based on foremen's subjective evaluations of hourly employees. Judgments regarding such things as ability, merit, and capacity were used in a process that resulted in adverse impact against blacks (a smaller proportion of qualified black employees were promoted than majority employees). Foremen received no formal training in the evaluation process, the standards were vague and subjective, and the links between the so-called standards and subsequent job performance had not been verified. In summarizing the decision, the court stated that:

> All we do today is recognize that promotion/transfer decisions which depend almost entirely upon the subjective evaluation and favorable recommendation of the immediate foreman are a ready mechanism for discrimination against blacks, much of which can be covertly concealed. . . .

Other cases make it clear that performance appraisal systems can be successfully challenged under the provisions of federal and state fair employment practice legislation. Under such circumstances, employers must determine the characteristics of a defensible performance appraisal system. One useful guide was provided by Feild and Holley[16] after they examined empirically the effects of thirteen appraisal system characteristics on the verdicts rendered in sixty-six employment discrimination cases. Certain characteristics were found to differentiate between judgments for the plaintiffs and the defendants. Their review is summarized in Table 16–1.

To interpret the table look for appraisal system characteristics that result in a p value less than .05. This indicates that the characteristic identifies a pattern where either plaintiffs or defendants (employers) most often prevail. For example, consider the type of appraisal system used

---

[15] Rowe v. General Motors, 4 FEP 445, 1972.

[16] Hubert S. Feild and William H. Holley, "The relationship of performance appraisal system characteristics to verdicts in selected employment discrimination cases," *Academy of Management Journal*, 25, 1982, pp. 392–406.

(behavioral versus trait-oriented). Trait-oriented refers to a system that focuses on person-centered attributes like knowledge, skills, abilities, and personality dimensions. Of the forty-eight cases reviewed, plaintiffs generally won when trait-oriented systems were used while defendants were most successful when the appraisal system had a behavioral orientation. Using Table 16–1 as a guide, we will describe some important characteristics of a defensible performance appraisal system.

1. Appraisal systems should be based on an analysis of job requirements. For a performance appraisal system to be job-related it needs to measure the critical or important job duties, work behaviors, or work outcomes associated with the job. Employees should be evaluated on each specific job dimension identified in the job analysis. Also, it may be appropriate to assign weights to the various rating dimensions that correspond to the job analysis results. The key here is to make sure that critical aspects of the job are not ignored or that trivial aspects of the job are not given too much attention.
2. Results-oriented or behavioral rating systems are easier to defend than trait or person-centered systems. Since person-centered attributes must be inferred from the more observable aspects of the job, the standard for demonstrating job-relatedness is higher.
3. Appraisal results need to be reviewed with employees. The results of the evaluation process and the corresponding performance standards need to be communicated to ratees.
4. Evaluators should be trained in the use of the appraisal system. They should understand what the system was designed to accomplish and be trained in evaluation and feedback procedures.

In addition to these standards, others have suggested that, when possible, more than one rater should be used, a formal appeal process should be established, and documentation should be available to explain a given rating (e.g., notes regarding a critical work incident).[17]

In summary, certain steps can be taken to make performance appraisal systems legally defensible. These steps serve to increase the likelihood that major aspects of the job are appraised, reduce the likelihood that rater subjectivity and bias interfere with the rating process, and increase communication between rater and ratee. It is our view that these same steps will add to the effectiveness of the appraisal system. That is, the likelihood that the system will meet its objectives will be enhanced. This, of course, comes at a cost. However, given the centrality of performance measurement in the management process, this cost is usually justified.

---

[17] Bernardin and Beatty, *Ibid,* pp. 50–55.

Appraisal System Case Characteristic	N^b	Number of Legal Cases with Verdict for:		p		Standardized Discriminant Weights
		Plaintiff	Defendant			
Purpose of the appraisal system?	61			.22	$(x^2=1.47)$	.16
Promotion		18	15			
Other (layoffs, transfers, discharges)		10	18			
Job analysis used to develop appraisal system?	17			0.3^c		−.31
Yes		0	3			
No		11	3			
Type of appraisal system used?	48			.02	$(x^2=5.34)$	.38
Trait-oriented		17	8			
Behavior-oriented		7	16			
Presented validity information on appraisal system?	65			.99	$(x^2=.06)$	.01
Yes		10	10			
No		21	24			
Presented reliability information on appraisal system?	58			.99	$(x^2=.01)$	−.02
Yes		3	3			
No		28	24			
Frequency that appraisals were conducted?	19			.46	$(t=.075)^d$	.06
Mean		3.75	3.45			
SD		.71	.93			
Number of evaluators used?	32			.44	$(t=-0.79)^d$	.09
Mean		1.56	2.00			
SD		1.37	1.75			
Evaluators given formal training in appraising performance?	15			$.27^c$		−.16
Yes		0	1			
No		11	3			

Summary

The typical reader of this text will not be directly involved in the development of performance appraisal systems. The more common role will be to use existing procedures or to provide information to staff experts who are designing such systems. Irrespective of the procedures used in a particular company, users of the system should strive to make their decisions as job-related as possible and to communicate decision rules and outcomes to subordinates. When possible, raters should tailor their evaluations to the unique demands of the job. Some procedures allow for this by asking raters to eliminate rating dimensions that are not part of the target job and providing the opportunity to add job specific dimensions. Also, raters can supplement their evaluations by describing the behaviors or other relevant outcomes that were used in reaching conclusions. It may also be possible to develop informal strategies to accomplish a unique goal. The

Appraisal System Case Characteristic	N^b	Number of Legal Cases with Verdict for:		p	Standardized Discriminant Weights
		Plaintiff	Defendant		
Evaluators given specific written instructions?	27			.0001 $(x^2=16.22)$	−.47
Yes		1	11		
No		14	1		
Appraisal results reviewed with employees?	12			$.04^c$	−.20
Yes		2	7		
No		3	0		
Basis for employment discrimination charge?	55			.93 $(x^2=.01)$	−.02
Race		19	21		
Sex		8	7		
Type of organization (defendant)?	65			.005 $(x^2=7.44)$	.54
Industrial		14	4		
Nonindustrial		17	30		
Geographical location of organization (defendant)?	66			.20 $(x^2=2.22)$	−.23
Inside the Southeast		13	8		
Outside the Southeast		19	26		

[a]When the assumptions regarding the expected values could be met, chi-square tests (Yates' correction with one degree of freedom) were performed. Otherwise, the Fisher exact probability test was used.
[b]Differences among the sample sizes for each variable are due to missing data in the cases.
[c]Fisher exact probability test.
[d]t test.

Source: Hubert S. Feild and William H. Holley, "The relationship of performance appraisal system characteristics to verdicts in selected employment discrimination cases," *Academy of Management Journal*, 25, 1982, pp. 392–406. Reprinted by permission.

Table 16–1   **Distributions of Verdicts in Employment Discrimination Cases Involving Various Performance Appraisal System Case Characteristics**[a]

point being that individual initiative will likely enhance the usefulness of company-wide appraisal procedures. Well designed systems will not meet stated objectives unless raters understand the importance of their task, are rewarded appropriately for their appraisal efforts, and possess the required technical knowledge.

PROBLEMS

1. Assume that you manage 65 word processing technicians and the company recently installed an automated, results-oriented, performance appraisal system. Discuss some unintended and negative consequences that can be associated with such a system. What steps can you take to reduce the likelihood for such effects?

2. Describe the characteristics of a legally defensible performance appraisal system.
3. High quality performance appraisal systems can be very expensive. Describe a framework for calculating the costs per employee associated with a job-related, behavioral performance appraisal system.
4. Describe the ideal performance measurement system for assessing training needs.
5. Critique the Schmidt et al. procedure for estimating SD_y.
6. For what set of jobs will SD_y likely be large? For what set of jobs will SD_y likely be small? At the level of the individual firm, how can labor market characteristics affect SD_y?

REFERENCES

Cascio, W. F. Costing human resources: The financial impact of behavior in organizations (second edition—Chapter 8—Estimating the economic value of job performance), Boston, Kent Publishing Company, 1987.

Carroll, S. J., and Schneier, C. E., *Performance appraisal and review systems,* Glenview, Ill: Scott, Foresman and Company, 1982.

Rynes, S. L., and Milkovich, G. T. *Current issues in human resource management: Commentary and readings* (Chapter 6—Performance evaluation), Plano, Texas, Business Publications, Inc., 1987.

PREPARING FOR THE ECONOMICS OF COLLECTIVE BARGAINING

T|he previous section discussed methods of personnel practices that are more commonly used in nonunion environments. With the decline in union membership to below 19 percent of the labor force, many managers view collective bargaining with less interest than in previous years. However, unions and collective bargaining are still a fact of life for most human resource managers in both the private and public sectors. For example, Freeman and Medoff state that about half of private nonagricultural employment are in establishments where a majority of either production employees or nonproduction employees are unionized.[1] In a nonrandom study of 778 large firms Audrey Freedman found that 63 percent of the employees worked in companies with some unionized employees.[2] As was presented in Chapter 10, slightly less than half of all public sector employees are represented by labor organizations.[3] With these current levels of unionization, it is of major importance for managers to know how wages and benefits are determined and personnel practices established within these organizations.

One unique element that unions bring with them to organizations is wages, benefits, and terms and conditions of employment decided upon by both labor and management. This process is known as collective bargain-

---

[1] Richard Freeman and James Medoff, What Do Unions Do?, Basic Books, Inc., New York p. 34.

[2] Audrey Freedman, Managing Labor Relations, The Conference Board, 1979.

[3] Richard Freeman, "Unionization Comes to the Public Sector," Journal of Economic Literature, Vol. 24, No. 1, March 1986, pp. 41–134.

ing. In this chapter we will discuss methods of preparing for collective bargaining. It is the first of four chapters detailing the negotiations process and outcomes. Chapter 18 discusses the tactics and procedures of the negotiations process. Chapter 19 presents methods of administering a collective bargaining agreement. Finally, Chapter 20 analyzes the impact of collective bargaining and unions on management. In developing a strategy and information for bargaining, a number of issues will be raised and examined in this chapter that you should be aware of. First, how does the type of product market the firm is operating in influence wage and benefit objectives and outcomes in bargaining? Second, what is the type of information that is needed for collective bargaining? Third, how is this information used in determining these goals and objectives? Finally, how do you cost out labor agreements, and what is the potential impact of the agreement on the firm and labor organization?

Product Market, Corporate Strategy, and Collective Bargaining

During the past two decades there have been many changes in the structure of American business that have had major effects on how management and unions prepare for collective bargaining. For industries, like autos, steel, and apparel, foreign competition and recession have forced firms to reevaluate past practices and assumptions regarding wages and collective bargaining. In other sectors of the economy the deregulation of industries, like airlines and trucking, has opened these industries up to significant new levels of competition and they are no longer guaranteed "reasonable returns" through state or federal regulatory boards. Also, products and services which were once thought to be natural monopolies, like the telephone industry, have been divided creating more competition and uncertainty about pricing products and labor. All these changes have brought about a new look in employer collective bargaining and compensation policies.

As was discussed in Chapters 4 and 5, labor can be viewed as the derived demand for the product. Using this concept Alfred Marshall developed four rules for determining the elasticity of the demand for labor by an industry that are commonly known as Marshall's rules. These four factors are:

1. the degree of substituting other inputs for labor in the production process (i.e. elasticity of substitution),
2. elasticity of demand for final output,
3. importance of labor in the total costs of production, and
4. elasticity of supply of other inputs.[4]

---

[4] Alfred Marshall, *Elements of Economics,* 3rd ed. (London: Macmillan, 1899).

The basic idea for using these rules is that firms make adjustments in response to a change in the price of labor by substituting a relatively less costly factor for a relatively more expensive one. Also, firms can expand or contract labor as the level of output changes (i.e. scale effect).

You may want to apply these rules to tactics that unions sometimes use to make the demand for labor less elastic as shown in Example 17–1. Which of Marshall's rules may apply to each of these circumstances? For example, Case A in the Example shows that by setting higher standards, the ability to substitute other nonlicensed teachers in the production process is reduced. Now you and your classmates can apply these rules to the next two cases in the Example with the person not identifying the appropriate rules buying the pizza at your favorite spot.

For management involved in collective bargaining these rules can help formulate a strategy of developing priorities to use either more labor or capital in the production process based on anticipated future demand. Management would like to have as much flexibility as possible in allocating firm resources across both labor and capital. Therefore, managers in negotiations with labor would attempt to create a demand for labor that is

---

EXAMPLE 17.1   APPLICATIONS OF MARSHALL'S RULES

A. Teacher union chief Albert Shanker urged education leaders to join him in an effort to create a tough new national exam for entry to the profession. When he was asked if the test was really a way to help his members get higher pay and status, Shanker said: "I confess (it is). And you might also get the same quality and standards that go with it (professionalism)."

Source: Associated Press, January 15, 1985.

B. Western Union and the United Telegraph Workers had a labor contract whereby "any worker with at least five years experience can remain on the payroll for a period equal to the employee's tenure if the job is eliminated and if another job at the company can't be found."

Source: *Wall Street Journal,* July 29, 1985.

C. "A Union that staged a one-day strike because of a contract offer that included 'too much money' went back to work Thursday.

"The walkout by the 400-member Local 32 of the International Association of Heat and Frost Insulators and Asbestos Workers ended when management agreed to a union demand for substantially less in wages and fringe benefits in a contract aimed at preserving current and future employment levels."

Source: United Press International, 1985 provided by Steven Allen, North Carolina State University.

as elastic as possible. Labor is not assumed to be a completely variable input in production. Therefore the ability to maintain flexibility in the production process to both increases or decreases in demand is often a key policy issue for most managers.[5] Also, the impact of collective bargaining and the preparations may be developed along the lines suggested in Figure 17–1.

In the figure it is assumed that collective bargaining may raise wages to W_1 through the threat of a work stoppage by a union. If management does not agree to this higher wage, severe costs may ensue through lost sales revenue and customer good will. Management may find it cost-effective to accept W_1 to avoid or end a strike. However, the increase in the wage from W_0 to W_1 means a loss of jobs from L_0 to L_1. The situation presented in Figure 17–1 would also apply to the case of a monopoly. Under this market structure, there would also be a downward sloping labor demand curve. However, it would not necessarily apply to a labor market monopsony, where there is only one buyer of labor services.[6] In both of these cases the firm is assumed to be on the demand curve for labor.

Another policy for the firm in planning for collective bargaining is a competitive strategy that is consistent with the environment of the firm. Porter suggests that such a strategy should take into account both internal and external factors that influence the firm.[7] As part of such a strategy he states that the firm should consider the company's strengths and weaknesses, personal values of the implementers of a collective bargaining strategy, as well as the industry opportunities, and broader economic expectations. Therefore, many firms develop a collective bargaining approach using the firm's competitive strategy as well as the culture of the organization in formulating a bargaining strategy.

To illustrate how these corporate plans might be linked to a short-run bargaining strategy the following three examples can be useful. First, if the firm's strategy for input factors, such as labor, are based on an equality based personnel policy that is implemented through collective bargaining, less emphasis can be placed by management in attempting to implement a strong ability clause for promotion in a collective bargaining agreement. A second example involves a company that has the ability to easily speed up the production process. In this case, an increase in wages and benefits in collective bargaining are compensated for by increases in productivity. Third, a firm may have objectives as to the number of employees that will

---

[5] Walter W. Oi, "Labor as a Quasi-Fixed Factor," *Journal of Political Economy,* Vol. 70, No. 6, December, 1962, pp. 538–555.

[6] As was discussed in Chapter 6, a monopsony is the condition where there is only buyer of labor services. Under these circumstances, wages and employment can move up because of bargaining. The marginal cost and the supply curve are not the same. The movement is along the marginal cost curve and the result can be increases in wages and employment.

[7] Michael E. Porter, *Competitive Strategy: Techniques for Analyzing Industries and Competitors,* New York: The Free Press, 1980.

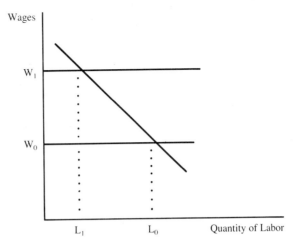

Figure 17-1   **Wage and Employment Assumptions of Management in Preparing for Collective Bargaining**

be employed at different wage ranges, and aim for that number in collective bargaining. Conversely, a firm may have an employment objective, using the scale effect in production, and will attempt to set a wage objective in bargaining to meet that employment level.

Given the changes that have occurred in the environment of bargaining, a number of firms and unions have announced reductions in benefits to employees called *concession bargaining.* An outline for planning under conditions of concession bargaining is presented in Table 17-1. The bargaining outline details key elements that employers may ask from unions in order to reduce the total wage bill or increase productivity. The Table details both the appropriate conditions for bargaining for concessions from the union and some mechanics for planning for concession bargaining. The mechanics of planning involve simple wage freezes or cuts in adjustments in current formulas of compensation determination. Productivity enhancement can be achieved by either conversions to new systems or the elimination of restrictive clauses.[8] If these concessions are not sufficient, attempts at subcontracting work out to potentially lower cost suppliers can be examined. Finally, management should attempt to anticipate what are the major issues that the union may ask for in bargaining, and attempt to cost out those provisions in advance. This can include potential profit-sharing plans to job security provisions during the life of the agreement.

---

[8] George Johnson, "Work Rules, Featherbedding and Partial Optimal Union-Management Bargaining," NBER Working Paper, 1985.

Table 17-1 can serve as a guide to issues that are likely to arise during the course of negotiations. To illustrate, concessions can have major effects on the value of the firm. For example, Becker finds that shareholders in large companies with bargaining settlements in 1982-83 that had concession bargaining agreements received increases of 8 to 10 percent in the value of their holdings.[9]

Impact of the Labor Market for Unionized Workers

In developing a strategy for bargaining an important consideration is the kind of market that is available to the members of the bargaining unit. If the labor market is tight for skilled workers, and there are opportunities elsewhere, higher wage offers are more likely to be presented than if there were loose labor markets. The composition of the market for labor is also an important consideration. If skilled workers are scarce, but unskilled workers are plentiful, the differential should be wider between the two groups of workers and planned in advance. Further changes in the demand and supply of skilled workers should be planned by using local or national forecasts. If changes occur which increase wages for skilled workers during the course of a contract, the union is often likely to demand increases in wages for both the skilled and unskilled workers. Example 17-2 shows how unanticipated changes in demand can lead to problems in bargaining. Therefore, careful analyses of the relevant labor market and supply factors may be of major importance in minimizing the total wage bill for the firm.

To the extent it is possible, management should attempt to obtain what union preferences are in negotiations. For example, some unions may attempt to maximize the earnings of the median union voter, known as the median voter rule. In this case the union will have greater preferences for higher wages at the expense of employment because the median union voter's job would not be affected. Other unions, such as the International Ladies Garment Workers Union, have traditionally emphasized work sharing among members at the expense of higher wages, during periods of economic concessions. Further, knowing the preferences of union members and leaders on issues such as wages versus fringe benefits are essential in developing ways of estimating the cost of a labor contract. Finally, personnel issues such as obtaining a formal grievance procedure, and implementing a seniority based internal labor market, are among the most valued union goals in bargaining, and management should estimate their potential costs and benefits prior to negotiations.

Although most negotiations end in a settlement, the process of planning for a potential strike suggests that local labor market characteris-

---

[9] Brian Becker, "Concession Bargaining: The Impact on Shareholders' Equity" *Industrial and Labor Relations Review,* January 1987, vol. 40, no. 2, pp. 268–79.

I. Conditions for Concession Bargaining
   A. Profitability Factors
   B. General Economic Factors
      1. Unemployment rate in the area.
      2. Lack of demand for product or excess inventory
      3. Competitive disadvantage with imports and productivity
      4. Competitive disadvantage with other company locations
      5. Consideration of shutting down or moving
   C. Strategic Considerations
      1. Mid-term versus end-of-contract bargaining
      2. General economic condition of industry and competitors' bargaining situations

II. Mechanics of Concession Bargaining
   A. Planning for Concession Bargaining
      1. Internal audit of company's economic condition
         a. Can profitability be achieved solely through labor-union concessions
         b. Are additional investment in capital, promotion or new-product development needed?
         c. How much savings must be realized in labor costs to turn around the company's economic condition? Is such a savings realistic as a goal?
         d. Does it make more economic sense to shut down plant and/or relocate than to bargain for concessions?
      2. Collective bargaining analysis: Where can economies be achieved in current agreement?
         a. Wages
            (1) Deferred increases—set time deferral versus increases triggered by specified events (i.e., achievement of defined profitability level)
            (2) Wage freezes
            (3) Foregoing increases
            (4) Rollbacks in wages—Differentials and shift preferences
         b. Cost-of-living allowances and adjustments
            (1) Readjustments of formulas
            (2) Deferral of adjustments
            (3) Removal of cost-of-living adjustment
         c. Productivity and incentive revisions
            (1) Revisions of standards
            (2) Conversions to new systems
            (3) Elimination of restrictive clauses
         d. Benefits
            (1) Holidays, vacations, paid leave
            (2) Benefit plans—funding mechanisms
         e. Subcontracting and technological change
         f. Union information requests
            (1) Extent of legal disclosure requirements
            (2) Format for compliance
         g. Mandatory subjects
         h. Impact of other Federal statutes
      3. Planning and anticipation of union strategies

Source: Audrey Freedman, "The New Look in Wage Policy and Employee Relations," The Conference Board, 1985. Reprinted by permission.

Table 17-1 **Bargaining Outline Under Concession Bargaining**

EXAMPLE 17.2

THE SKILLED/UNSKILLED LABOR DIFFERENTIAL AND THE COLLYER INSULATED WIRE COMPANY

The Collyer Wire Company negotiated a three-year labor contract in which unskilled production employees were compensated on an incentive basis, but skilled maintenance tradesmen were paid on a nonincentive basis. During the course of the contract the company found that wage rates for skilled tradesmen were not sufficient to attract and retain the numbers of skilled maintenance mechanics and electricians required for the efficient operation of the plant. In fact the skilled labor force had dropped from 40 to 30 in a year and a half, and the company had been unable to attract these types of employees. During the term of the contract the company requested that wages be increased for these workers, but the union refused. They would only allow the wage increase as part of a total plant job evaluation program in which all wages could be increased. The company followed by unilaterally increasing wages of skilled maintenance employees by 20 cents per hour. The union protested stating that this violated the collective bargaining agreement. They proceeded to file charges with the NLRB and later sought the services of an arbitrator to resolve this dispute.

Could this problem have been avoided by careful planning for bargaining?

Source: Collyer Insulated Wire, A Gulf and Western Systems Co. and Local Union 1098, IBEW, AFL-CIO, 192 NLRB No. 150, August 23, 1971.

tics also are significant. If unemployment is high in a local area and there are few opportunities, this obviously imposes costs on potential strikers causing them to accept a lower wage. Conversely, the ability to find alternative forms of employment may increase the resistance of the union members to the employer's offer.

Beyond factors that influence local labor markets, national factors also should be accounted for in developing strategies for collective bargaining. Among the most important trends has been the growth in union wages relative to other workers in the 1970s. During the 1980s intensified competition from domestic nonunion or foreign firms and the relaxation of barriers to entry under deregulation has resulted in reductions in the differential of union to nonunion wages. As Figure 17–2 shows throughout the latter half of the 1970s, the union percent change in wages was consistently above the nonunion change. However, from 1983 to 1984, as a result of union concessions at the bargaining table for approximately 3 million union members, union wage changes dropped below nonunion ones.[10] Additional changes have occurred in the union labor market that

---

[10] Robert S. Gay, "Union Settlements and Aggregate Wage Behavior in the 1980's," *Federal Reserve Bulletin,* December 1984, pp. 843–856.

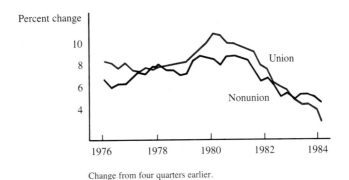

Change from four quarters earlier.

Source: Robert S. Gay, "Union Settlements and Aggregate Wage Behavior in the 1980's, *Federal Reserve Bulletin,* December, 1984, pp. 843–856.

Figure 17–2   **Union and Nonunion Wage Changes 1976–1984**

have resulted in the implementation of two-tier labor agreements. Under this type of provision, a dual pay plan is established in which new hires are paid less than incumbent employees for doing the same job. A survey by the Bureau of National Affairs found in 1983 and 1984 two-tier provisions covered 450,000 workers and in 1984 about 8 percent of all contracts contained this provision. During that same year 17 percent of service industry contracts had these provisions.

In industries that have become deregulated, like trucking and airlines, the major carriers like Yellow Freight and American Airlines have implemented these two-tier agreements. In American Airlines' case, they estimate this provision saved them $100 million in 1984. In these major agreements they allow new employees to progress to the top-tier or regular wage scales over a specified period of time. An example of a Two-Tier Wage Scale for flight attendants at American Airlines is presented in Figure 17–3. Those persons hired before December 6, 1983 received $1200 per month, but those hired after that date made $900 per month. Furthermore, for the first twelve years after the initial hire, these attendants were on a much lower wage growth pattern. However, after twelve years of employment, they switched to the higher wage pattern shown in the Figure. Union leaders argue that the two-tier system affects morale and reduces productivity. In addition, negotiators must be careful not to set wages too low or new workers will not be attracted to the firm or cause higher than average turnover resulting in potentially lower profits.[11]

A further result of the decline in the union labor market has been evidenced in the willingness of unions to relax work rules. One major type of change that has been prevalent in the 1980s leaves the organization of work intact, but makes it more efficient. Some examples of these types of

---

[11] William T. Dickens and Larry Katz, "Interindustry Wage Differences and Industry Characteristics," NBER, Working Paper, 2014, 1986.

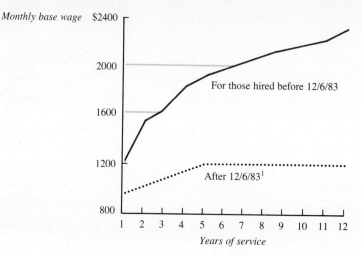

Monthly base wage

For those hired before 12/6/83

After 12/6/83[1]

Years of service

[1]*The scale for those hired after 12/6/83 stops after five years.*

Source: Reprinted by permission of the *Wall Street Journal,* © Dow Jones & Company, Inc. (1985). All Rights Reserved.

Figure 17–3   **An Example of a Two-Tier Wage Plan for Flight Attendants at American Airlines**

rules include greater management flexibility in scheduling work, relaxing seniority provisions in job assignments, and reducing the number of separate job classifications by combining duties and eliminating unnecessary jobs. These work-rule changes generally only give a one-time boost to the level of productivity, unless they signal an on-going effort to increase productivity at the workplace. Further changes have involved revamping the entire organization of work. For example, unionized workers can learn all of the jobs in a work area rather than a narrow job function.

Methods of pay and bonuses also have undergone changes. Rather than lump sum bonuses, many unions have accepted profit-sharing arrangements or have bargained over the share of output contributed by labor.[12] However, unions have been reluctant to abolish cost-of-living adjustments as a result of relatively long three-year labor contracts. Management also has been particularly resistant to changes in contract length due to the high cost of negotiations as well as increased strike costs.

Many of these changes in the unionized labor market have occurred as a result of more competitive product markets. In unionized markets, subject to foreign competition, domestic firms have incentives to move production abroad. In other unionized industries, nonunion firms have reduced the ability of unions to maintain wage premiums for their

---

[12] Martin Weitzman, *The Share Economy, Conquering Stagflation,* Harvard University Press, 1984.

members, and the ability of unions to win wage premiums has been reduced during the 1980s.[13] These economic factors influencing the union labor market and their future direction are important considerations in developing a bargaining plan.

Information For Bargaining

Goals and Objectives

As was suggested in the previous section, a key element in deciding what information is needed for collective bargaining is the strategy that is decided upon by the organization. The issues to be considered regarding strategic choice policies are presented in Table 17–2. This table presents a strategy matrix relating where decisions are made, the type of employers, the nature of the decisions, and the role of government in the development of a strategy.[14] The strategy used in large part determines the type of information needed in collective bargaining as well as the type of preparation needed for bargaining. For employers, the key issues include the role of human resources, and particularly the bargaining unit within the overall strategy of firm goals. This includes policies on unions, non-labor investments, plant location, new technology, and contracting out, also known as outsourcing of services, or products. In addition, bargaining preparations should be developed within the context of the employment relationship and the industrial relations system. This includes a variety of personnel policies as well as collective bargaining policies and negotiations strategies. Finally, the kind of information gathered is influenced by the conditions and organization of the workplace. If there are new policies or employee participation, the introduction of new technology, or a new organizational design of the workplace, information on the costs and benefits of these policies needs to be analyzed prior to negotiations. This strategy mix outlined in Table 17–2 can form the basis of firm and union goals in bargaining, and this is a way of deciding the type of information needed for bargaining based on these firm goals.

Although the table delineates general strategies, it does not present the kinds of information about specific topics in collective bargaining that are needed at the negotiations table. As a basis for determining which topics are often discussed, Table 17–3 presents items which the NLRB has determined are mandatory ones for bargaining. Two other groups of topics for bargaining which are "voluntary" or permissive items, that are neither mandatory nor illegal. Neither party can be compelled against its wishes to

---

[13] Richard B. Freeman and Morris M. Kleiner, "Union Organizing Drives Resulting N.L.R.B. Elections During a Period of Economic Concessions," I.R.R.A. *Proceedings,* December 1986, pp. 41–47.

[14] Thomas A. Kochan, Robert B. McKersie, and Peter Cappelli, "Strategic Choice and Industrial Relations Theory, *Industrial Relations,* Vol. 23, No. 1, (Winter 1984), pp. 23.

Decision level	Employers	Nature of decisions Unions	Government
I. Macro or global level for the key institutions	The strategic role of human resources; policies on unions; investments; plant location; new technology; and outsourcing	Political roles (e.g., relations with political parties and other interest groups); union organizing (e.g., neutrality and corporate campaigns); public policy objectives (e.g., labor law reform); and economic policies (e.g., full employment)	Macro economic and social policies; industrial policy (protection vs. free trade)
II. Employment relationship and industrial relations system	Personnel policies and negotiations and strategies	Collective bargaining policies and negotiations strategies (employment vs. income)	Labor and employment standards law; direct involvement via incomes policies or dispute settlement
III. Work place: individuals and groups	Contractual or bureaucratic; and individual employee/workgroup participation	Policies on employee participation; introduction of new technology; work organization design	Regulations of worker rights and/or employee participation

Source: Thomas A. Kochan, Robert B. McKersie, and Peter Cappelli, "Strategic Choice and Industrial Relations Theory," *Industrial Relations,* Vol. 23, No. 1 (Winter, 1984) pp. 23. Reprinted by permission.

Table 17–2   **Industrial Relations Strategy Matrix**

negotiate over voluntary items, nor can a contract be delayed over the signing of a voluntary item. In recent years several items have moved from the mandatory to the permissive list as a result of NLRB decisions. For example, a firm's policy to transfer or consolidate units of its operation or to provide information regarding its decision was changed from being mandatory to voluntary under the NLRB's *Otis Elevator Decision.*[15] Illegal bargaining items are those which are forbidden by law. Examples of illegal items include a closed shop agreement, a hot cargo clause (refusing to handle goods made by a company where the union is on strike), or a union shop security agreement in a state with a right-to-work law.

In developing goals and policies at the bargaining table the value of each of these items, mandatory and voluntary ones, should be assessed both in terms of the costs and savings of changing each one. Although a

---

[15] *Otis Elevator Company,* 269 N.L.R.B. No. 162, April 6, 1984.

Wages
Hours
Discharge
Arbitration
Holidays—paid
Vacations—paid
Duration of agreement
Grievance procedure
Layoff plan
Reinstatement of economic strikers
Change of payment from hourly base to salary base
Union security and checkoff
Work rules
Merit wage increase
Work schedule
Lunch periods
Rest periods
Pension plan
Retirement age
Bonus payments
Price of meals provided by company
Group insurance—health, accident, life
Promotions
Seniority
Layoffs
Transfers
Work assignments and transfers
No-strike clause
Piece rates
Stock purchase plan
Workloads
Change of employee status to independent contractors
Motor carrier—union agreement providing that carriers use own equipment before leasing outside equipment
Overtime pay
Agency shop
Sick leave

Employer's insistence on clause giving arbitrator right to enforce award
Management rights clause
Cancellation of seniority upon relocation of plant
Discounts on company products
Shift differentials
Contract clause providing for supervisors keeping seniority in unit
Procedures for income tax withholding
Severance pay
Nondiscriminatory hiring hall
Plant rules
Safety
Prohibition against supervisor doing unit work
Superseniority for union stewards
Checkoff
Hunting on employer forest reserve where previously granted
Change in operations resulting in reclassifying workers from incentive to straight time, or cut work force, or installation of cost-saving machine
Job posting procedures
Employee physical examination
Union security
Bargaining over "bar list"
Truck rentals—minimum rental to be paid by carriers to employee-owned vehicles
Musician price lists
Arrangement for negotiation
Change in insurance carrier and benefits
Profitsharing plan
Company houses
Subcontracting
Discriminatory racial policies
Production ceiling imposed by union

Table 17-3 **Items Mandatory for Bargaining**

negotiating team cannot assess with perfect foresight which items will become major ones in the bargaining process, some assessment of the cost of increasing or decreasing major items in the contract under varying scenarios often forms the basis of planning for bargaining and is used in major firms. The methods for costing the benefits and costs of provisions in the contract will be presented later in this chapter.

Obtaining and Evaluating Information for Bargaining

One of the basic requirements of the NLRA is that financial information on the firm be provided to the representatives of the employees.[16] Under court interpretation of the NLRA in *NLRB* v. *Truitt* (1956) the Supreme Court ruled:

> Good faith bargaining necessarily requires that claims made by either bargainer should be honest claims . . . If an argument is important enough to present in the give and take of bargaining, it is important enough to require some sort of proof of its accuracy.

The NLRB interpreted this action to require information be provided on wages paid to individuals and groups of employees, compensation of employees outside the bargaining unit, time study materials, productivity information, and all reasonable balance sheet information. If an employer pleads an inability to pay, the firm's financial information must be furnished.

Although the type of financial information available to persons in the company varies, the key negotiators for management should be aware of the potential impact of changes in the collective bargaining agreement on the market value of the firm and its cash flows.[17] However, when large unionized companies were asked how they determine wages, the vast majority listed the following in order of importance: industry patterns, local labor market conditions, expected company profits, and productivity or labor cost trends in the industry.[18]

In addition, the type of information that is made available to both management negotiators and unionized employees is often limited. As Table 17–4 shows, using data from a survey of 49 senior human resource managers from the Conference Board list of large companies, full financial data is only available to top human resource managers, and unionized employees generally do not have access to key strategic marketing or accounting information. Therefore, the range of a potential settlement may vary as a result of the lack of accurate or full financial information.

Firm financial data also is important in planning for strikes which occur once every eleven years for the typical union member.[19] The type of financial data needed for this type of analysis include establishing projec-

---

[16] Morris M. Kleiner, "Public Policy Implications of Financial Information Requirements Under the National Labor Relations Act," *Journal of Accounting and Public Policy,* Vol. 3, No. 4 Winter 1984, pp. 253–257; and Morris M. Kleiner and Marvin Bouillon, "Providing Business Information to Production Employees: Correlates of Compensation and Profitability," *Industrial & Labor Relations Review,* forthcoming, 1988.

[17] Eugene F. Fama, *Foundations of Finance* (New York: Basic Books, 1976).

[18] Freedman, *ibid.*

[19] Freeman and Medoff, *ibid,* p. 218.

	Availability at Plant or Facility Level to?			Available in Business Units to
	Top Human Resources Executive	Human Resources Manager	Unionized Employees	Unionized Employees
Strategic business plan	G	G	P	P
Capital investment:	G	G	P	P
new plants	G	G	P	P
new technology	G	G	G	G
Marketing:	G	P	P	P
new product development	G	P	P	G
R&D	G	P	P	P
competitor information	G	P	P	P
Costs of production	G	G	G	G
Detailed:	G	G	G	G
labor costs	G	G	G	G
material costs	G	G	G	G
equipment	G	G	P	G
overhead	G	G	P	P
Comparative with other				
facilities	G	G	P	G
with competitors	G	G	P	G
Accounting information				
Profitability—total aggregated	G	G	G	G
by strategic business unit	G	P	P	P
by product line	G	P	P	P
Depreciation method	G	P	P	P
Acquisition and divestiture plans	G	P	P	P
Work-force and divestiture plans	G	G	G	G
Hiring requirements, skill requirements	G	G	G	G

G = generally available
P = proprietary

Source: David Lewin, "Opening the Books: Corporate Information-Sharing with Employees," The Conference Board, New York, 1984. Reprinted by permission.

Table 17-4 **A Summary of Financial Information Sharing by Category of Information**

tions of revenue data, labor cost information, and nonlabor cost data. In addition, estimates need to be made of the changes in wages and benefits that are likely to occur following a strike by both labor and management, and the impact this is likely to have on the offers of both sides. Any estimate of the financial benefits or costs of a settlement should consider the present value of a settlement over the life of the agreement. Figure 17–4 illustrates how such an analysis can be estimated over the potential strike time. In this model it is assumed that current and potential future union wage demands are known to the company, and that these demands decline over time. The figure plots the present value of profits (PVP) as a function of the length of a strike. First, the employer loses profits due to lost sales. Second, long term profits may be higher if the firm refuses a union demand because the longer strike means that the employees will be willing to settle for smaller wage increases. In Figure 17–4 the second effect dominates the first one, and later on, lost profits through lost sales dominate. As the figure shows, the present value of profits increases and then decreases over strike time. (You may want to develop the same analysis for unions, assuming they attempt to maximize the total wage bill of their members.)

Another way of planning for potential strikes suggests that bargaining continues for both labor and management as long as the information that is gained from an additional round of negotiation outweighs the additional bargaining costs. Strikes tend to limit the length of negotiations by increasing the costs of continuing this learning process. In an analysis of large firms, the results show the uncertainty of the firm's profitability increases the likelihood of a strike as part of the learning process by unions attempting to find the best estimate of a firm's economic health.[20]

Costing Labor Agreements

In this section of the chapter we will present various methods of costing out two basic pieces of information: the average costs for the bargaining unit and the estimated value of increased demands made during negotiations. As part of this analysis we will present the potential impact of negotiations on the profit/loss statement of the firm and on the market valuation of the share price of the stock of the company. Therefore, it is important to trace bargaining and its potential outcomes through to the monetary bottom line value of the firm.

For employers, labor costs are viewed as total wages paid plus fringe benefits and payments to government. Total labor costs or the wage bill is equal to the number of employees times the total cost per employee. In calculating the average compensation for the bargaining unit the following information is necessary:

- salary steps and benefit programs
- the distribution of employees in the unit according to steps, shifts, and time of service
- each employee's coverage status and benefits.[21]

In addition to these items, overtime estimates should be made and costs allocated based on the information gathered in these areas.

An example of how a company might cost out a wage increase based on total labor cost per year or per hour is presented in Example 17–3 (see p. 370). In this case a determination is first made as to the number of hours

---

[20] Joseph S. Tracy, "Contract Negotiations and Strikes," NBER, 1985.

[21] Wayne F. Cascio, *Costing Human Resources: The Financial Impact of Behavior in Organizations,* Kent Publishing Co., Boston, MA 1982 p. 101.

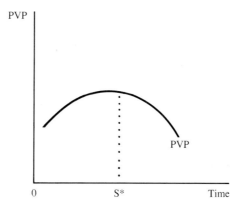

Source: *Wall Street Journal,* October 14, 1985.

Figure 17–4 **Employer Present Value of Profit (PVP) Function in a Model Strike Activity**

worked. This is done by reviewing company benefit programs, firm seniority to vacation plans, and itemizing the lost time during recent periods. Next, the firm can identify annual cost per employee, which is presented on the left side of the example. This rate represents the latest rate rather than an average rate over the length of the contract. Given a pay for time worked of 1896 hours at the site, the right side of the example shows the cost in dollars per hour of a potential 5 percent wage increase. The effect is determined by multiplying the base wage by 5 percent. This yields a cost per hour increase of $.325 and an annual base wage increase of $616.20 ($.325 × 1896 hours).

An important part of the wage package is fringe benefits. On average, fringe benefits are 37 percent of wages in major collective bargaining agreements.[22] In this illustration benefits are also 37 percent of labor cost per hour. Since these costs are such a high percent of total costs, it is important to estimate the impact of changes in wages on the fringe benefit packages and legally required benefits. For example, the 5 percent increase in wages would result in automatic increases in holidays, vacations, and other items that are paid off based on wages. Other benefits that would also go up by 5 percent include

	Base cost per hour	*5 percent effect*
Overtime premium	$.41	$.02
Social Security[23]	.47	.02
Pension plan	.83	.04
Total hourly increase		$.08

[22] *Facts for Bargaining,* Bureau of National Affairs, Inc. 1978.

[23] Social Security payments for the median worker would probably increase by less than the full 5 percent since some employees would reach the legal maximum level.

EXAMPLE 17.3   EVALUATING COMPANY COSTS PER YEAR
AND PER HOUR

Annual cost		Cost per hour
$12,324	Hours worked	$ 6.50
	Benefits	
777	Overtime premium	.41
133	Shift premium	.07
572	Holidays	.30
910	Vacation	.48
300	Accident and sickness	.16
330	Long-term disability	.17
312	Occasional absences	.16
52	Other absences	.03
597	Medical costs	.31
180	Dental insurance	.09
120	Life insurance	.06
150	Health insurance	.08
891	Social Security	.47
25	Federal unemployment	.01
84	State unemployment	.04
60	Workmen's Compensation	.03
1,568	Pension plans	.83
78	Christmas and other bonuses	.04
100	Miscellaneous benefits	.05
25	Retiree costs	.01
$ 7,264	Total benefits	$ 3.80
$19,588	Total cost	$10.30

Data from Walter A. Hazelton, "How to Cost
Labor Settlements," *Management Accounting,*
May 1979, p. 22. Reprinted by permission.

In this example, all of these items are directly tied to wages, and for a $.325 increase in direct wages, the other benefits listed increased by $.08. The ratio of $.08 to $.325 or 24.6 percent is called the *variable benefit ratio* or *roll-up provision* in labor relations. By developing a base like hours worked, benefit costs can be added together and provide a way of evaluating total costs. However, in making projections of the total costs of the contract, additional analysis requires that the examination of the workforce be made that addresses likely turnover, and the age and tenure of employees, as well as wage structure of the bargaining unit.

As was discussed in Chapter 2, a way of examining a potential three-year contract is through a discounted cash flow model. As we discussed in that chapter, the model focuses on the cash receipts and disbursements associated with a contract proposal and explicitly weighs the time value of money.[24] In applying this approach to a labor contract proposal, a labor relations specialist would first determine the incremental cash flows that would arise from each of the alternatives under consideration. This would involve not only direct receipts and disbursements associated with the contract changes, but also cash flows in all parts of the company's operations. An example of the present value of a labor contract and the annuity equivalent wage rate over the life of a collective bargaining agreement is presented in Table 17–5 for manufacturing, non-manufacturing, and overall. The estimate was constructed by calculating the present value of working one hour each month over the term of the contract (at 10 percent per year). The present value of working one hour each month was multiplied by the average weekly hours. The weekly earnings were multiplied by 4.35 to convert to monthly earnings. Monthly earnings were multiplied by average fringe benefits of 1.32. Finally, the estimate of the present value of full time employment over the life of the contract was multiplied by the number of workers in the bargaining unit. The annuity equivalent wage rate paid over the life of the contract also is presented in the table. This wage rate is the hourly base wage which, if paid over the life of the contract, has the same present value at 10 percent as the calculated hourly wage rates based on the contract terms and the expected cost-of-living adjustments. The averages presented in the table are taken over contracts. The annuity equivalent wage changes show some decline in the wage rate over the life of the collective bargaining agreement for the years 1979 through 1982 as inflation rates declined and greater competition occurred in product markets.

An illustration of this multi-time evaluation procedure may also include changes from a labor intensive mode of operation to one which uses more capital. One of the best examples of an application using an implicit discounted cash flow model to changing technology and policy related to changes in competition was in the implementation of containerization (i.e. a mechanical method of loading and unloading ships) in the Pacific Long Shore Industry.[25] In 1959, the International Longshoremen's and Warehousemen's Union and the Pacific Maritime Association signed a seven-year Mechanization and Modernization Agreement in which the union gave up highly restrictive work rules and accepted the implementation of containerization in exchange for a $29 million fund that was to be used to guarantee job security. Although this meant substantial up front costs for the employers association, the impact was to raise productivity by one-third from 1960 to 1964 after twenty-five years of virtually no change. A further

---

[24] Michael H. Granof, *How to Cost Your Labor Contract,* Bureau of National Affairs Inc., Washington, D.C. 1973.

[25] Paul T. Hartman, *Collective Bargaining and Productivity: The Longshore Mechanization Agreement,* (Berkeley: University of California Press, 1969).

Industry	1979		1980		1981		1982	
	NPV	WR	NPV	WR	NPV	WR	NPV	WR
Manufacturing	146	16.0	98	18.4	42	16.5	82	12.3
Non-manufacturing	179	17.1	174	18.7	180	17.4	181	11.6
Overall	157	16.4	128	18.5	92	16.9	122	12.0

All NPV estimates are in millions of dollars.
Estimates obtained from BNA, Collective Bargaining Negotiations and Contracts

Source: John M. Abowd, "Collective Bargaining and the Division of the Value of the Enterprise," NBER, 1985.

Table 17-5 **Average Net Present Value of Labor Costs (NPV), and Annuity Equivalent Wage Rate (WR) at 10% Per Year Over the Life of the Collective Bargaining Agreement**

impact was increased productivity through more shippers using these West Coast ports, and as a result, no claims were made against the $29 million fund. Although the buyout of costly work rules had positive results for employers in this case, it is important for employers as well as labor union negotiators to cost out over long time horizons expected returns from any long term change in the area of work rules to include productivity changes.

In recent years alternative methods of wage determination in collective bargaining have emerged particularly among the largest U.S. firms. Prior to the 1980s the method used among the largest U.S. firms was to examine industry patterns and use that as a basis for wage determination.[26] Table 17-6 shows the trend among the largest U.S. companies has been away from the use of industry patterns and local labor market conditions and toward factors internal to the firm. These factors, like expected company profits and productivity, have become more important in firm wage determination. Therefore, items on the firm's balance sheet, like productivity data and stock market performance, are viewed with greater care as a way of assessing the impact of alternative wage demands.

A further illustration of this issue can be found in the recent literature on the impact of labor relations phenomena such as high wage bargains and strikes on the market value of the firm.[27] A recent study found that for every unanticipated dollar given to workers in collective bargaining the shareholder lost a dollar in the total valuation of the firm. Further analysis of the impact of strike activity that involved 1000 or more workers on shareholder equity showed that the average strike resulted in a 4.1 percent drop in shareholder equity which represented a decline of $41 million in the

---

[26] David E. Shulenburger, "A Contour Theoretic Approach to the Determination of Negotiated Wage Change in the Building Construction Industry," *Economic Inquiry,* 16, July 1978, pp. 395–410.

[27] John Abowd, "Collective Bargaining and the Division of the Value of the Enterprise," NBER Working Paper, 1985 and Brian Becker and Craig Olson, "The Consequences of Strikes for Shareholder Equity," *Industrial and Labor Relations Review,* Vol. 39, No. 3, April 1986, pp. 425–438.

	Number of Companies	
Factor	1978	1983
Industry patterns	81	39
Local labor market conditions and wage rates	56	41
Expected company profits	26	37
Company productivity or labor cost trends	8	37

Source: Audrey Freedman, "The New Look in Wage Policy and Employee Relations," The Conference Board, 1985. Reprinted by permission.

Table 17–6　**Most Important Influence on Wage and Benefit Targets 1978 and 1983**

valuation of the firm.[28] Moreover, the results show that the stock market consistently underestimates the cost of a strike to shareholders, since they find that two-thirds of the decline in returns to shareholders occurs after the strike is announced. These empirical results suggest that in preparing for bargaining it is important to analyze the impact of alternative wage bargains, as well as strategies, that may lead to strikes, on the overall value of the firm.

To a much greater extent than before, preparing for bargaining has been delegated to a group with expertise from varying sectors of the firm. This function is becoming more concerned with the companies' economic performance, as management's wage objectives are most affected by internal factors. This reexamination of the firm in the process of collective bargaining has caused the human resources staff to become more knowledgeable about cost and profit structures and deal with the price of labor as one of the factors of production.[29] This priority placed on labor costs makes management ask the question, how, taken together, can the terms of a settlement reduce labor costs per unit of output. In reading and studying this material on preparing for bargaining, you should now be more aware of the environmental and internal firm specific issues that must be examined before your organization develops a strategy for bargaining, which the next chapter details.

PROBLEMS

1. The United Telephone Company of Golden Gopher Center has recently been informed that telephone service in its area is being deregulated. Firms and individuals can now be provided telephone service through a variety of sources including satellite equipment. In light of this change in their

---

[28] Becker and Olson, *ibid.*

[29] Audrey Freedman and William E. Fulmer, "Last Rites for Pattern Bargaining," *Harvard Business Review,* March-April 1982.

product market the firm is considering several changes in its human resource cost structure that you are to evaluate.

Bargaining Unit Wage Structure

    Base wage + fringe $ 8.50 per hour − 50 workers
    Base wage + fringe 10.50 per hour − 100 workers
    Base wage + fringe 12.50 per hour − 50 workers

Bargaining unit workers average an 8 hour day, five days a week, for 52 weeks per year.

	Current	Next Year Estimate without regulation	Next Year Estimate with regulation
Total revenue	$20,000,000	$20,000,000	
Operating costs	$16,000,000		
Nonlabor costs	$ 3,000,000	$ 3,000,000	$3,000,000

  a. If state regulators allows $.75 of each dollar wage increase to be passed on in the form of increased tolls what is the cost to United of a 10 percent across the board wage increase demanded by the union? Now estimate total revenue and operating costs with regulation, all else equal.

  b. With deregulation, there are now no controls on costs or revenue structure. Now estimate the impact on operating costs of a 10 percent increase in bargaining unit costs. Estimate the present value impact on profits for both the regulated and nonregulated cases assuming a 10 percent discount rate.

  c. If workers and shareholders are better off under regulation, who might be made worse off?

2. The Universal Football League and the Players Association have agreed to negotiate total player compensation based on the economic health of the league. Currently salaries for players are 60 percent of total revenue.

Universal Football League
Balance Sheet

	Current	Projected
Total revenue	$ 10,000,000	$ 13,000,000
Player compensation	6,000,000	
Market value of teams	$100,000,000	$150,000,000

  a. If the current linkage of player salaries to total revenue holds, what would total player compensation be in the projected period?

  b. The union negotiator now wants to link player compensation to the market value of the team, and maintain the same ratio of salary to market value for the projected period as in the past. He argues that economic benefits to football league communities have driven team values up, and that players should share in those benefits. Estimate total player compensation in this case, and the appropriateness of this measure of economic health. Discuss the extent to which the market value of the teams would decline if compensation levels increased.

  c. How likely would the union be to go along with wage decreases if revenues and the market value of the teams were declining?

3. The Freeman Screw and Bolt Manufacturing Company and the United Steel Workers union are preparing for negotiations, each using different criteria in attempting to establish wages. The union states that wages and fringe benefits in the company should be increased at 5 percent per year for the next three year contract life which is consistent with local labor market trends in the area for workers similar to those in the bargaining unit. The labor relations director says wages and fringes should only increase 2 percent per year, which is the recent growth in revenue for the company, due to increased foreign competition. You are to evaluate each proposal and its impact on the company profits, shareholders, and the union.

REFERENCES

Casio, Wayne L., *Costing Human Resources: The Financial Impact of Behavior in Organizations,* Kent Publishing Co., Boston, Ma. 1982.

Freedman, Audrey, *The New Look in Wage Policy and Employee Relations,* The Conference Board, New York 1985.

Granof, Michael H., *How to Cost Your Labor Contract,* BNA, Washington, 1973.

Kleiner, Morris M., Richard Block, Myron Roomkin and S. Salsburg, ed. *Human Resources and the Performance of the Firm,* Industrial Relations Research Association, Madison, Wisconsin, 1987.

Weitzman, Martin, *The Share Economy, Conquering Stagflation,* Harvard University Press, 1984.

CHAPTER 18

NEGOTIATING THE AGREEMENT

As the showdown nears, Hoffa impresses upon the employers that they must think "realistically" and meet his demands. If their "realistic" offer is well below his asking price, he reacts like an enraged bull, exploding in seemingly uncontrollable rage. Ripping the paper on which the offer was written, shouting cries of crude class warfare and personal vengeance, and threatening a massive strike, he storms out of the conference room.

from R. James and E. James, *Hoffa and the Teamsters,* D. Van Nostrand, Princeton, N.J., 1965.

A lthough many managers view the process of collective bargaining as being filled with theatrics, and apparent irrational behavior as the quote suggests, there is considerable evidence that collective bargaining is quite rational and makes sense from both the management and union's view. The purpose of this chapter is to enhance your understanding of the bargaining process within a structured framework. A number of examples are presented illustrating how this process and its outcomes fit into an overall model of bargaining behavior.

In studying this chapter you should be able to answer the following questions. How do positions on bargaining develop for both unions and management? What are the tactics and approaches that are used in negotiations? What are the sources of bargaining power, and how can they be used to obtain your goals? If a strike occurs, what causes the parties to settle, and when are settlements optimal? If time permits in this course, a case is presented in the Appendix of the chapter which allows you to test your bargaining skills with your fellow classmates. This application should allow you to put the discussion and framework in this chapter to a practical test in negotiations.

Positions of Labor and Management on Bargaining

A useful method of analyzing bargaining is to examine it from the position that the value of the firm can be allocated between union workers and shareholder claimants, and that this takes place as part of the negotiations process. This assumes that there are economic profits that can be allocated between the union members and shareholders with managers serving as the agents of shareholders. An illustration of how wages are determined in such a case is presented in Figure 18–1. For the firm, the demand curve, D, is the change in revenue for a change in an additional unit of labor. For the union, it would establish a wage that takes into account the employment effect of compensation in a manner that maximizes utility of the union. The idea of efficient contracts begins with the two parties to a transaction agreeing to terms that exploit the possibilities of joint gains. Accordingly, labor agreements negotiated under the labor demand model discussed in the previous chapters are inefficient, because the welfare of both parties could be increased if they could establish both wages and employment levels during negotiations.[1] The inefficiency of an agreement in the labor demand model is illustrated in Figure 18–1. In this figure isoprofit curves (See Chapter 4) describe different wage and employment combinations that produce the same profit levels. In this figure the isoprofit curves are superimposed on the labor demand curve, with more profitable curves nearer the origin, that is P_3 results in higher profits than P_1. At point X the wage/employment outcome predicted by the labor demand model is inefficient because both parties would be better off if they established a wage-employment combination to the right of the demand curve at a point of tangency between an isoprofit curve and a union utility or union preferences which are equal along any point on the curve, (U_1). In this example, any settlement along the line segment (Y, W_U, L_U) would make one or both sides better off without making the other party worse off.

The contract curve model creates an "enforcement" problem for the union because once the employer and the union have concluded the bargain, the employer has an incentive to not live up to the contract by providing less employment at the contract wage rate of W_U than the

---

[1] Brian E. Becker and Craig A. Olson, "Labor Relations and Firm Performance" in *Human Resources and the Performance of the Firm,* ed. Morris M. Kleiner, Richard Block, Myron Roomkin, and Sidney Salsburg, IRRA Research Volume, 1987.

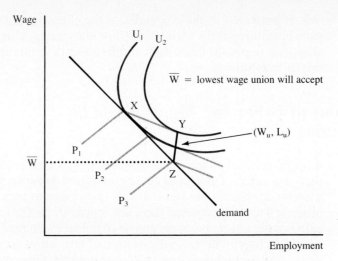

Figure 18-1 **Efficient Contract Curve Analysis of Bargaining**

implicitly agreed upon employment of L_U. For example, point X on the labor demand curve to the left of (W_U, L_U) yields higher profits to the employer if wages remain at W_U.[2] The enforcement problem is particularly hard because the contract curve changes as the demand shifts with changes in product demand. Therefore, the union should be able to differentiate between employer requests to reduce employment because of lower demand from the employer's desire to move off the contract curve. This is hard because of incomplete information about demand for the firm's product and the employer's incentive to portray a decline in demand as the source of all requests for reductions in employment. Recent empirical research on this model has been generally supportive of the model for a number of industries. Further, this evidence suggests that the tradeoff is close to a dollar of higher than expected wage increases for union members coming from shareholders' assets.[3]

When management was asked its goals in bargaining on wages and fringe benefits, its reply was generally to limit these increases.[4] During the 1980s management policy changed to requests for givebacks or concessions that were discussed in the previous chapter. More importantly, these requests from a status quo position to one of concessions has become more aggressive and has covered more issues. For example, management has taken the initiative in seeking changes in a variety of work rules to include assigning jobs, layoffs, transfers, and promotion decisions. These manageri-

[2] Barry T. Hirsch and John T. Addison, *The Economic Analysis of Unions,* Allen and Unwin, Boston, 1986.

[3] This model is the strongly efficient bargaining contract model solution in John Abowd, "Collective Bargaining and the Division of the Value of the Enterprise," NBER, 1985.

[4] Audrey Freedman, *Changes in Managing Employee Relations,* New York: The Conference Board, 1985.

al preferences reflect the greater pressures to improve productivity and thereby show better firm performance for shareholders. Unions have been asked to participate in quality of work life or productivity centers to enhance output per unit of labor and increase firm performance.[5]

To illustrate, some of the items that are at the top of management avoidance lists in negotiations are the following: joint union-management pension and health plans, automatic cost escalating provisions, more pay for unworked time, work jurisdiction limitations, and union representation on corporate boards.[6] Although this list may overlook some of the areas that management may wish to avoid, it does provide some potentially important costs and control variables that are typically cited as pitfalls in bargaining for management.

As was mentioned in Chapter 9, Samuel Gompers', first president of the AFL, reply to the question of what were the objectives of the union movement was "more." Beyond this simple statement of the objectives of unions, there are many goals that unions establish in bargaining, some of which were discussed in Chapter 17. When unions become the bargaining agent for a group of employees their first objective is to secure recognition and security for the union in the organization. Typically, a union security provision is the first item listed for unions that have just won bargaining rights. In states where a union shop provision is legal (i.e. one must be a union member or pay dues to maintain employment, see Chapter 10) this is the type of provision that unions try to obtain. In other cases, the recognition of the union as the sole bargaining agent for employees is negotiated. Following the attainment of these basic union rights, they are likely to try to obtain material benefits for their members.

Unlike the wealth maximization assumed for shareholders, union goals are often seen as being more complex. The union leadership may have one set of objectives such as job security, but the majority of the membership may want higher wages and better fringe benefits. The conflict between the leadership and membership can result in the rejection of the terms and conditions of employment agreed upon by the leadership and management. On nonwage issues, unions' general goals are those of equality at the workplace. This translates into trying to obtain the use of grievance procedures and seniority in making policy regarding the organized employees at the workplace. The attainment of these nonmonetary objectives is one of the major concessions employers are willing to make when faced with potential organizing.[7]

---

[5] Walter Gershenfeld, "Employee Involvement and Firm Performance" in *Human Resources and the Performance of the Firm,* ed. Morris M. Kleiner, Richard Block, Myron Roomkin, and Sidney Salsburg, IRRA Research Volume, 1987.

[6] Charles S. Loughran, *Negotiating a Labor Contract: A Management Handbook* (BNA Books, 1984).

[7] Richard B. Freeman and Morris M. Kleiner, "Union Organizing Drives Resulting in N.L.R.B. Elections During a Period of Economic Concessions," IRRA, Proceedings, 1986, pp. 41–47.

Tactics in Bargaining

Understanding the process of collective bargaining is particularly complex. The factors that determine the outcomes of bargaining are sufficiently varied, so that it is hard to devise models that are both appropriate and manageable. Nevertheless, one way of examining the process is the method used in commercial transactions. For example, Mr. Green walks into Orange Auto Sales Inc. and offers $14,000 for a new $15,000 sticker price car, but is willing to pay as much as $14,500. Similarly, Orange Auto Sales is willing to take as little as $14,250 for the car. The parties may then bargain over the difference. The exact terms of the transaction will depend on the skill and tactics of the negotiators. If there was no overlap in the offer and demand preferences, no transaction is made. The major differences between this commercial bargaining and ones made in labor negotiations is that in collective bargaining they meet on a regular and consistent basis to reach an agreement, and there is a longer bargaining relationship involving higher relative costs to both parties.

A behavioral description of the bargaining process has been developed by Walton and McKersie who suggest four alternative activities in the bargaining process.[8] The first is distributive bargaining and its function is to resolve conflicts of interest (one side gains and the other loses) between labor and management. The second activity is called integrative bargaining, which tries to find common ground among the parties and solve problems (both parties gain). The third is attitudinal structuring which influences the views of the participants toward each other and affects the ties that relate the two parties they represent (it creates an atmosphere where concessions are likely to be made). The fourth is intraorganizational bargaining whose purpose is achieving a consensus within each member of the group that interacts with one another (parties try to convince constituents in their own group to change positions). Tests of this model of negotiations on union and management negotiators found that distributive bargaining success was determined by bargaining power and the low probability of a strike.[9] Whereas success in integrative bargaining was dependent on trust, support, and friendliness by the opponent.

One of the better examples of the use of all four of the Walton and McKersie descriptions of the bargaining process was by former Teamster Union President, Jimmy Hoffa. In Example 18–1, a simple approach, called the six step method, is presented for the practice of collective bargaining. During the various stages of negotiations there are uses of distributive, integrative, attitudinal, and intraorganizational bargaining. For example, in Step 4 of the example, Hoffa uses an "I win, you lose"

---

[8] Richard E. Walton and Robert B. McKersie, *A Behavioral Theory of Labor Negotiations,* McGraw-Hill, New York, 1965.

[9] Richard B. Peterson and Lane Tracy, "Testing a Behavioral Theory Model of Labor Negotiations," *Industrial Relations,* February 1977, pp. 35–50.

EXAMPLE 18.1   HOFFA'S SIX-STEP BARGAINING PROCESS

Step 1 — He develops his bargaining demands far in advance of the formal negotiations.

Step 2 — He gives stern indignant lectures on the nature and ethical implications of his demands and how both sides can gain. He tells employers that he is reasonable, but that the passionate union members' feelings must be deferred to.

Step 3 — He portrays the employers as harsh and uncompromising to Teamster leaders and membership.

Step 4 — He tells the employer association that they must meet his demands now or surrender after a strike which will be costly to them but inexpensive to the union.

Step 5 — He uses his economic power and plays one employer off against another (whipsawing), and applying secondary pressure on other employers not involved in the dispute.

Step 6 — In the face of these diverse pressures, threats, and promises, the employers capitulate.

Source: R. James and E. James, *Hoffa and the Teamsters*, D. Van Nostrand, Princeton, N.J., 1965, pp. 26–29.

approach to employers. In Step 2 he suggests that both sides can win in negotiations. In Steps 2 and 5, Hoffa tries to create an atmosphere or appearance of reality in which concessions are likely to be made. Finally, in Step 3 he uses intraorganizational bargaining, by trying to influence the union membership to prepare for a potential strike by stating that the opponents are difficult and uncompromising. This illustrates the use of various approaches and tactics depending upon the stage of the negotiations and the goals of the parties.

Bargaining Power

As Example 18–1 suggests, the use of power enabled the Teamster Union negotiator to achieve the results he desired over a long period of time. Although the concept of bargaining power has been defined in various ways, we chose the definition presented by Chamberlain and Kuhn which states that it is "the ability to secure another's agreement on one's own terms."[10]

---

[10] Neil W. Chamberlain and James W. Kuhn, *Collective Bargaining*, McGraw-Hill, New York, 1986.

Therefore, a union's bargaining power at any point of time is management's willingness to agree to the union's terms. Similarly, management's willingness depends on the costs of agreeing with them. In the context of this definition of bargaining power, it is not developed as an absolute amount of power that never changes. Shifts in the economic environment or internal factors may cause the costs to change for both sides.[11] Costs in terms of this model include both pecuniary and nonpecuniary ones.

As part of this use of these bargaining models, negotiators may want to use the tactic of bluffing to influence the perceived costs to both sides. The use of bluffing and factual presentations may be useful for both sides in making proposals, offers, and counteroffers and sequentially providing information about the intent, settlement range, and preferences of the other side. Each new piece of information provides clues about the other that may lead to a greater likelihood of a settlement.

Perhaps the most visible tactic that unions use is the strike. With this approach the union withholds its services until an agreement is reached. Similarly, management can engage in a lockout, not allowing striking workers to enter the place of employment, or hire nonunion workers to replace the ones that are striking. When the union strikes, the employees' cost is lost wages, and union leaders may be voted out of office if the work stoppage is unsuccessful. If management must close part of its operation as a result of a strike, the losses will include present profits and potential future profits through the loss of customers. As Chamberlain and Kuhn suggest, "the union estimate of how long management can take a strike will affect its estimate of the cost to the management of refusing to agree to the union's terms."[12]

With setbacks in recent years by unions in bargaining, there have been new tactics that they have used to increase the costs of disagreement with them. For example, when there was an impasse at Standard Brands Inc., the United Food and Commercial Workers local obtained a $150,000 budget and obtained advertising in the local Los Angeles paper to announce a series of radio ads protesting the company's demand that the union agree to concessions before the negotiations could start. Shortly following the appearance of the advertising, the firm dropped its demands, negotiations began, and an agreement was reached. One of the first responses of the company following the agreement was to get the union to stop the advertising campaign.[13] The use of communications and pressure on potential customers, suppliers, and banks has been a tactic that unions have

---

[11] For an illustration of an application of this model with the inclusion of shifts over time see Morris M. Kleiner and Charles E. Krider, "Determinants of Negotiated Agreements for Public School Teachers," *Educational Administration Quarterly,* Vol. 15 (13), Fall 1979, pp. 66–82.

[12] Chamberlain and Kuhn, *Ibid,* p. 180.

[13] *Wall Street Journal,* February 22, 1985, p. 1.

used in addition to the more traditional strike weapon to increase the cost of disagreement to management.

For management there are often carefully structured procedures and guidelines that form the basics for developing tactics to bargain with a union. Typically, they call upon management to take the initiative in bargaining. This procedure suggests that they draft a written contract that serves as the basis for negotiations. This draft should contain existing working conditions plus whatever changes management would propose at the first stage of bargaining. The burden is then on the union to show that existing conditions need to be improved.[14] Within this procedure, management should ask the union for a full explanation of each of their proposals so that all of their demands are intelligible. In this way, some of their demands may be dropped, if they can not be supported by sound arguments. Once the union makes a counterproposal, management should determine the cost of the proposal, and then decide which package of benefits, that may include productivity improvements, the company is willing to provide. For management, this tactic is to make these objectives the key economic issues in a counterproposal to the union.

Management also perceives one of its key functions as the ability to allocate resources to their maximum efficient use. When a firm accepts union demands for a seniority-based layoff structure, the power of the union does not deprive management of the ability to lay off an individual when their services are no longer required. Management attempts to retain, as much as possible, the ability to allocate and commit the resources of the firm. Even when employees participate in managerial decision-making, the firm views its interests served if it performs these business functions. The specific provision that allows management the right to allocate resources is the management rights clause of the agreement. This provision reserves rights not directly specified in the contract to management.

A strategy for bargaining and the ways of using bargaining power involve not only pay, but also the effort put forth at the workplace. This relationship has been called the wage-effort bargain.[15] The components of the pay package using this approach are: 1) pay for time worked; 2) the effort bargain; 3) premium pay; 4) pay for time not worked; and 5) contingent benefits linked to either individual or business performance. In negotiations, the tactics and power relationship can be applied to each of these five components as part of a collective bargaining agreement. To illustrate, negotiating new pay and benefit levels for time worked for fixed time periods are part of the wage bargain. The standards and work load, like the size of a crew, are key elements of the effort bargain. Often there are

---

[14] James W. Hunt, *Employer's Guide to Labor Relations,* Bureau of National Affairs, Washington, D. C., 1979.

[15] James P. Begin, *The Practice of Collective Bargaining,* Richard D. Irwin, Homewood, Ill., 1985.

trade-offs made on these two elements of the pay package. For example, premium pay, which is paid for time worked on holidays or overtime, and its allocation among the workforce is a key element in the total wage-effort bargain. The number of days or hours and a specification of the conditions for pay for time not worked are considered key elements of an overall agreement.

In order to obtain their desired objectives in the wage-effort bargain, firms and unions sometimes attempt to use the economic environment of negotiations as key factors in order to impose additional costs of disagreeing. Some of the tactics include utilization of the local business cycle, selection of an appropriate timing of the contract, and the use of strike insurance.[16] To illustrate, if there is high unemployment in an area, management can suggest to the union leadership that during a strike, there would be substantial income losses to the membership. Unions like to pick an expiration date during a peak season, (e.g., Christmas shopping season for a retail establishment) in order to maximize potential short-term income losses for the firm. On the other hand, companies in manufacturing try to build up inventories prior to a strike, and in this way reduce the potential impact of a work stoppage. The union leadership sometimes suggests that although the wage-effort bargain is acceptable to them, the rank and file would never ratify a potential agreement. With recent mergers and acquisitions, management is now more likely to suggest that the shareholders should not accept a high final demand from a union. Finally, a number of firms and some industries have strike insurance, with the best known being the airline industry prior to deregulation. Under these insurance policies, the company is reimbursed for lost revenue, minus a usually large deductible if the union strikes. One of the most visible effects of strike insurance occurred in Major League Baseball. In 1981, when the owners had 60 days of strike insurance minus a deductible, a strike developed that lasted over two months. However, in 1985, when there was no strike insurance for Major League Baseball, the strike lasted only two days. Taken together, the use of these tactics can play a major role in shifting bargaining power within the range of potential settlements.

Bargaining as a Game

Another way of analyzing bargaining behavior, in a formal way, is through what economists and mathematicians call game theory. This method of analyzing bargaining behavior states that the outcome is determined by the participants' joint strategy selection. One commonly used strategy is known as minimax. Within this decision rule, the firm assumes that no matter

---

[16] Robert J. Flanagan, Robert S. Smith, and Ronald G. Ehrenberg, *Labor Economics and Labor Relations,* Scott, Foresman and Co., Glenview, Ill., 1984.

what strategy it may chose, the union's response will always be optimal from its perspective. Similarly, the union assumes the firm will choose to argue in a way leading to the lowest wage settlement for any given strategy that the union may choose.

An illustration of such a bargaining relationship can be seen in Figure 18–2. In this figure the curve r^u represents the risks that the union is willing to incur in advancing their wage effort bargain demands. Similarly, the curve r^m represents the risks that management, acting on behalf of the shareholders, is willing to incur in advancing a particular wage offer. Labor and management will advance an offer or demand that lowers the cost-benefit ratio (probability of a profitable conflict that it believes the other party faces.). If both sides can correctly estimate the opposing side's preferences with respective strike points of W_0 and W_n, then the point of equal risk of conflict is wage W^f.

The figure shows how a measure of bargaining power can be formulated, and how a point on the contract curve can be reached by each group exerting power. The equilibrium point has been derived mathematically and is referred to as the Nash point. Both parties are equally satisfied, and the point corresponds to that obtained by splitting the difference between the union's minimum wage-effort demand and management's maximum offer.

The situation presented in Figure 18–2 assumes that complete information about the other side is available to both parties. Once that assumption is dropped, there exists the possibility of a strike. The likelihood of miscalculation on both sides goes up, with the increase in real and potential misinformation. Further, strikes are the result of incorrect expectations due to the business cycle, technological change, or managerial changes. Any of these factors may lead to greater probabilities of industrial conflict.

A statistical analysis of splitting the difference bargaining for forty-three negotiations compared the initial offer to the final outcome in the late 1960s.[17] On average, the union wanted a 23 percent wage increase, and management initially made an 8 percent offer. The average final outcome was a 12 percent increase. In eleven cases out of forty-three, "the employer made no concession at all." On the other hand, somewhat more recent analysis by Farber found for 80 contract negotiations in 10 large manufacturing firms during the 1954–70 period, that the actual wage-settlements were quite close to the unions' most preferred wage outcome, when actual and potential strikes were accounted for.[18] The statistical evidence suggests that depending on the economic environment of negotiations, and the

---

[17] Daniel S. Hammermesh, "Who 'Wins' in Wage Bargaining?" *Industrial and Labor Relations Review,* 26 (1973) pp. 1146–1149.

[18] Henry S. Farber, "Bargaining Theory, Wage Outcomes, and the Occurrence of Strikes: An Econometric Analysis," *American Economic Review,* 68:3 (June 1978) pp. 262–71.

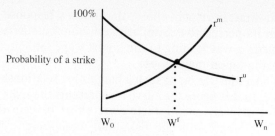

Figure 18-2 **Bargaining in a Nash Equilibrium**

period of time, management or the union can come closer to their objectives in bargaining.

One model of game theory that is often applied to collective bargaining is the *prisoners dilemma* approach, since it was first applied to whether or not a prisoner should confess to a crime. Table 18-1 presents a potential payoff matrix for an employer and union under alternative payoffs to various strategies. For example, if management is persuaded to concede by a promise of a union concession, but the unions do not follow through, the result is that shown in the lower left corner of the table. In this cell there is a high wage-effort bargain and the employer's profits are reduced. In the next round, the employer may not concede and neither may the union. This result is shown in the lower right corner; a strike in which both sides lose, but less than if a unilateral concession had been made. This game theory model suggests that by attempting to gain either a high wage-effort bargain or profits, both parties may lock themselves into a position where they may lose.[19]

Within this context, strikes are again associated with uncertainty. Changes in either the economic environment of bargaining, or in the leadership of either labor or management, can be a major factor in increasing the uncertainty of the environment of negotiations, thereby enhancing the likelihood of strikes.[20] You may want to go through Table 18-1 assuming you are the union or management and choose an appropriate strategy, assuming you know the approach the other side is taking.

The application of these game theory approaches has been in the development of strategy forms for bargaining. An example of a form that you can use in bargaining is presented in Example 18-2. This form requires the bargaining team to list objectives based on a strategy that the team determines. It also allows for an evaluation of the bargaining objectives following the determination of outcomes. The checklist serves as a guide in

---

[19] A. Rapaport and A. M. Chammak, *Prisoner's Dilemma* (Ann Arbor: University of Michigan), 1965.

[20] J. Zeuthen, *Problems of Monopoly and Economic Warfare* (London: Routlege and Kegan Paul), 1930.

		Management Strategy	
		Concede	*Not Concede*
	Concede	No strike, acceptable wage-effort bargain	management enforces a favorable wage-effort bargain, profits rise
Union Strategy	Not Concede	Union enforces a favorable wage-effort bargain, profits are reduced	work stoppage, both union and management lose, but less than if a unilateral concession was made

See Morton D. Davis, *Game Theory, A Nontechnical Introduction,* Basic Books, New York, 1970, for further treatment of this issue.

Table 18-1   **Game Theory Payoffs for the Management and Union**

developing alternative concession and resistence strategies for specific issues and overall objectives.

Strikes as a Tactic

Strikes in the private and public sectors are the tactics that typically receive the most attention in the media, and are the most visible outcome of collective bargaining. Yet, as was discussed in Chapter 9, in 1984 in the U.S., only .04 percent of total worktime involving 1000 or more workers was lost to strikes, and this is less than half the total days lost in countries like Italy, Sweden, and Canada.[21]

Table 18–2 shows that, although work stoppages in the U.S. are relatively low, this still means that strikes affect between 376,000 and 2.5 million workers and occur between 62 to 424 times every year at companies with at least 1000 workers during the 1970s and 80s. Unlike many other countries, bargaining in the U.S. is decentralized by firm or business line within a firm, which creates more bargaining situations and more opportunities for strikes. However, with the decline in the percent organized, and the high unemployment rates in the early 1980s, there has been a noticeable decline in strike activity. Unions often argue that strikes are the price that society pays for free collective bargaining. As was pointed out in Chapters 9 and 10, management has attempted to restrict this tactic over time in both the private and public sectors. Strikes have been viewed by unions, management, and scholars of the topic in varying ways. This ranges from the perspective that strikes are irrational or are mistakes, to the view that they make economic sense and are ways that unions use to find out how

---

[21] Estimates from International Labor Organization, *Year Book of Labor Statistics,* 1981, Tables 3 and 28.

EXAMPLE 18.2 STRATEGY AND EVALUATION OF BARGAINING OUTCOMES FORM

Bargaining* Items	Priorities**	Range of Bargaining Objectives			Initial*** Bargaining Position	Evaluation Results		
		Pessimistic (P)	Realistic (R)	Optimistic (O)		P	R	O

Source: Reprinted by permission from *ASPA Handbook of Personnel and Industrial Relations,* by Dale Yoder and Herbert Heneman, pps. 7-116; 7-120 to 7-121, copyright © 1979, by The Bureau of National Affairs, Inc., Washington, D.C.

much money firms can allocate toward labor. In this section, we will examine some of the ways that firms and unions can view strikes as a tool in collective bargaining.

Perhaps the most widely cited method of strike behavior was developed by Sir John Hicks. As presented in Figure 18–3, the increasing cost to an employer, as a result of lost revenue, suggests that as a strike progresses, an employer should be willing to increase the wage-effort offer, and this is shown by the upward sloping employer-concession schedule (ec).

For union members, as a result of intraorganizational bargaining, they may develop a feeling of solidarity during the first stages of a potential strike. At this point they may have high wage demands. As time passes, the loss in income that union members suffer has the effect of reducing their wage demands. This is shown in Figure 18–3 as (ur), the union-resistance curve, which has a downward slope.

During the course of the strike, the union's demands decrease and the employer's offer increases until at point s the two lines intersect. At this point a settlement is reached, and the parties agree upon a wage-effort bargain increase of w, and the strike is ended. Similar to our game theory approach, if both sides knew the other's approach and the shape of the curve of the opposition, the settlement of w could have been reached prior to the strike. This way both sides could have avoided the costs.

	Number of Stoppages	Workers Involved in thousands	Percent of Workdays Idle
1970	381	2,468	.29
1971	298	2,516	.19
1972	250	975	.09
1973	317	1,400	.08
1974	424	1,796	.16
1975	235	965	.09
1976	231	1,519	.12
1977	298	1,212	.10
1978	219	1,006	.11
1979	235	1,021	.09
1980	187	795	.09
1981	145	729	.07
1982	96	656	.04
1983	81	909	.08
1984	62	376	.04

Source: Bureau of Labor Statistics, *Monthly Labor Review*, November 1985, Vol. 108, No. 11, p. 107.

Table 18-2   **Work Stoppages Involving 1,000 Workers or More 1970-1984**

Although strikes are the most common manifestation of reductions in work, there have been other tactics that unions have been using to increase the costs of disagreeing on management when impasses are reached in negotiations. One of these other tactics used by unions is *working to rule.* Under this job action, the workers in the bargaining unit perform only the minimum work required of them in the job description or contract. As a result there is a slowdown of production or services, and the effect may be similar to a strike. Example 18-3 suggests that the impact of a work to rule policy for the nurses in the Boston union can be as effective as a strike.

In addition to these job actions, unions can also engage in boycotts, union label campaigns, and corporate campaigns. Boycotts are usually directed against specific producers and in recent years have included firms such as J. P. Stevens, Farrah Slacks, and Gallo Wines.[22] Union label campaigns tend to be more general, such as the Ladies Garment Workers' "Look for the Union Label" and "Buy American" programs. Corporate campaigns are usually more detailed and of greater length, and are aimed at isolating a company from the "corporate community." An example of this tactic was the Textile Workers campaign during the 1970s to put social pressure on J. P. Stevens through their lenders and their board of directors. These approaches usually are used when the strike weapon is thought by the union to be too weak because of the ability of the firm to find alternative sources of labor.

A method of analyzing the effect of a strike or work slowdown over

---

[22] Gene Daniels and Kenneth Gagola, *Labor Guide to Negotiating Wages and Benefits,* Reston Publishing Company, Inc., Reston, Va., 1985, pp. 33-34.

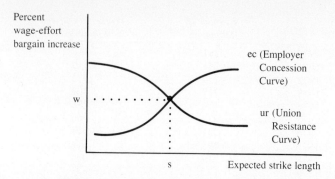

Figure 18-3 **Hick's Bargaining Model with Expected Strike Length**

time also can be analyzed using our cost-benefit approach in Table 18–3. Although some of this analysis may at first appear cryptic to you, a numerical example may help illuminate the kinds of decisions facing the firm when a strike begins and during its duration. In order to keep our analysis as simple as possible, a hypothetical firm is created with potential sales revenue of $10,000 per period and it has a discount rate of 10 percent. When production starts, 1500 units of labor are required. At the beginning of the impasse the union's wage demand is $10.00, and it follows the Hick's Model downward toward a minimum acceptable wage of $5. For simplicity, no hours per day or days per week are presented in the columns in Table 18–3. Columns 4 and 7 indicate the present values of total revenue and total labor cost, for a wage agreement occurring at the start of period t, where t can range from 1 to 5 where revenue and wages are paid at the end of the period. By examining the table you should be able to show that a profit-maximizing firm will hold off agreeing to a wage contract, and incur a strike or other job action until the beginning of period 5. At this period on the table the difference between the present value of total revenue and the present value of the wage bill is $1552 and is the largest of any of the five periods. Therefore, the profit-maximizing firm would be willing to settle at that point. Thus the firm is actually buying a lower wage by taking a strike.

Period (t)	Total Revenue If Produce	Discount Factor*	Present Value of Total Revenue if Agreement on Wage**	Wage Union Will Agree On	Units of Labor	Present Value of Wage Bill if Management Agrees on Wage**
(1)	$10,000	.909	$37,908	$10.00	1,500	$56,862
(2)	$10,000	.826	$28,817	$ 9.00	1,500	$38,903
(3)	$10,000	.751	$20,552	$ 7.00	1,500	$21,580
(4)	$10,000	.683	$13,039	$ 6.00	1,500	$11,735
(5)	$10,000	.621	$ 6,209	$ 5.00	1,500	$ 4,657

*Discount Factor = $1/(1 + .10)^n$
**All wages assumed paid at the end of the period

Table 18-3 **A Numerical Example of Revenue and Wage Bill for Alternative Strike Periods**

EXAMPLE 18.3   RULES ARE RULES

Registered nurses at Boston City Hospital and two chronic-disease hospitals, who were unable to secure a contract with the city, repeated this chant for two weeks: "Rules are Rules." They refused all non-nursing duties, like emptying the trash, moving beds, or washing floors. Overtime hours, that the three hospitals depend upon, were turned down.

"Historically the nurses did so many jobs that weren't in their contract that when they stopped doing them, they virtually crippled the hospital," said Roberta Golick, a federal mediator who helped in the talks. "It accelerated the negotiations process faster than any other union device could have."

Recently, the 700 nurses won a labor contract calling for solid pay raises. A victory, members of Local 285 of the Service Employees-International Union said was made possible by working-to-rule. A potential strike was avoided. By staying on the job and following their contracts to the rule, they can earn wages and pressure the company at the same time. John Zalusky, an AFL-CIO economist, stated, "job actions are a perfectly legal way to drive a company crazy."

Source: *Boston Globe,* 1985, Lynda Gorov.

In this example, the firm has advance knowledge of the changes in wage demands, and signs an agreement that maximizes the present value of its profits. This process, which is similar to our game theory approach, determines the length of the strike and the wage settlement.

Determinants and Effects of Strikes

Although the example presented in the previous section assumes that the employer has perfect knowledge, in most cases neither labor nor management knows what the response of the other side will be in bargaining. From an economic viewpoint, an important element of strike activity is uncertainty. This generally involves the size of profits, and the costs of agreeing or disagreeing with the other party. In this method of analysis, a strike is assumed to take place whenever bargaining continues beyond the expiration of the current contract.[23] However, in many cases bargaining takes

---

[23] Martin J. Mauro, "Strikes as a Result of Imperfect Information," *Industrial and Labor Relations Review,* Vol. 35, No. 4, July 1982, pp. 522–538.

place after a contract expires and the employees typically continue working under the old contract. As we have discussed earlier, prior to the strike, bargaining costs only involve the direct costs of bringing the two sides to the negotiating table. Once a strike begins, there are additional costs in the form of lost production and wages.

Empirical tests of this information gathering model of strike behavior by Tracy shows that a one-standard deviation increase in the variability of the firm's total stock market returns is associated with about a three percent increase in the probability of a strike. In addition, he finds that conditions in the firm are more important than general economic or labor market conditions. More specifically, the marginal effect from variability in the firm's stock market returns is more than twice the magnitude and more significant than the marginal effect from variations in the overall performance of all stocks.[24] Further statistical analysis of the informational value of strikes on management and labor finds that when strikes have occurred during a previous round of negotiations, that there is a significantly lower probability of a strike during the current round of negotiations.[25]

Additional analysis finds that there tends to be considerable variation in the occurrence and length of strike activity by large industry groups. As Table 18–4 shows, from 1973–77 strikes for establishments with 1000 or more workers occurred with much greater frequency and were of longer duration in the transportation industry than in paper products, due in part, to more rapid changes in technology and the industrial structure in that industry. As a result of the variations in the kinds of internal and external factors facing these industries, it is not surprising that strikes, which may be an attempt by the union to obtain information on what the firm can afford, should vary based on uncertainty across industries. Although the results from this table show some lengthy strikes, other research on industry strike activity suggest the net loss of output within an industry is small.[26] The reason lies in the ability of nonstruck firms to increase their output, and of the struck firms to draw on inventories.

For unions, a successful strike can have a major effect on enhancing its credibility with the membership. By demanding and obtaining increased wages, and other terms and conditions of employment, the attitudinal structuring of the group they represent is enhanced in bargaining, and the intraorganizational strength of the union is solidified. Some argue that strikes occur sometimes simply because unions do not want their primary economic weapon, the strike, to get rusty. The union can occasionally call a strike to show the firm that it is in a relatively strong position. Although the statistical evidence is sketchy and at an economy-wide level, the inability of

---

[24] Joseph S. Tracy, "Contracts and Strikes," NBER, 1985.

[25] Mauro, *Ibid.*

[26] George R. Neumann and Melvin W. Reder, "Output and Strikes in U.S. Manufacturing: How Large are the Losses?" *Industrial and Labor Relations Review,* Vol. 37, No. 2, January 1984, pp. 197–211.

	Number of Negotiations	Ratio of Strike Frequency	Average Strike Duration (Calendar Days)
Food (20)	261	.06	56.8
Apparel (23)	114	.02	16.0
Paper (26)	143	.07	30.0
Chemicals (28)	140	.09	67.3
Stone, Clay, Glass (32)	80	.08	32.2
Primary metals (33)	226	.11	37.4
Fabricated metals (34)	91	.20	45.5
Machinery (35)	203	.26	41.9
Electrical machinery (36)	221	.16	60.4
Transportation equipment (37)	207	.21	57.4

Source: Joseph S. Tracy, "Contracts and Strikes," NBER, 1985. Standard Industrial Classification Code in parenthesis.

Table 18-4 **Strike Activity and Duration by Industry for Occurrences with 1,000 or more Employees, 1973–77**

unions to enhance the wage-effort bargain as a result of a strike has led to their decline.[27]

Unlike the lack of information on the impact of strikes on unions, we know more about their effects on firms. For example, the major studies show that the stock market can predict the likelihood of a strike and that the impact is to reduce the market valuation of the firm.[28] However, whether those effects are large ones are still somewhat controversial. A recent study has found that the average cost of a strike to shareholders of large publicly-held companies is approximately $47 million, and that the average cost to each striking employee is almost $21,000. The strike costs are higher in steel and electrical products than in chemicals and utilities.[29] Like most other significant human resource policies, the occurrence, duration, and outcome of a strike influences the value of the firm.

Summary

The last two chapters have presented the approaches and methods that you can use in knowing about the bargaining process, or being a member of a collective bargaining team. To summarize, bargaining should first be planned as a strategic variable within the context of overall firm goals.

---

[27] Bruce E. Kaufman, "The Determinants of Strikes in the United States, 1900–1977," *Industrial and Labor Relations Review*, Vol. 35, No. 4, July 1982, pp. 473–490.

[28] George R. Neumann, "The Predictability of Strikes: Evidence from the Stock Market," *Industrial and Labor Relations Review*, Vol. 33, No. 4, July 1980, pp. 525–535.

[29] Brian E. Becker and Craig A. Olson, "The Impact of Strikes on Shareholder Equity" *Industrial and Labor Relations Review*, Vol. 39, No. 3, April 1986, pp. 425-438.

Second, in preparing for bargaining, "information is power," and both internally generated data and external economic factors should be obtained and analyzed. Third, goals and objectives in bargaining need to be formulated and strategies for obtaining them evaluated. Fourth, although impasses are not common, preparations should be made for dealing with them by both the union and management. Throughout the planning and implementation of a bargaining policy, the planners should be aware that the wages and conditions agreed upon, or the work stoppages that result, will have significant economic consequences on the monetary value and long-run position of the organization.

PROBLEMS

1. Develop a plan for Joy and Sons Mfg. Inc. who are faced with the following situation. For every dollar wage increase given by the company to the local union members, the stockholders lose an equivalent amount from the value of the company. What type of strategy should be developed to maximize shareholder wealth?

2. Develop a union bargaining strategy for the local machinists union, who are risk takers, and wish to maximize the amount of the total firm's assets going to the bargaining unit.

3. The Gottlieb Auto Parts Company, a profit maximizing firm, is faced with the following dilemma. Accept the union offer of $10 per hour which will result in a wage bill $500,000 for period 1 and 2 or take a strike through period 1 and the union will accept a wage of $8 per hour and a wage bill of $400,000. Wages are paid at the end of the period. Total revenue is expected to be $1 million in both periods if no strike occurs, and the discount rate is 8 percent. On a present value basis should the company take a strike or settle? What might be the long-term effects of the company taking a strike on labor relations?

REFERENCES

Daniels, Gene and Kenneth Gagola, *Labor Guide to Negotiating Wages and Benefits,* Reston Publishing Co., Inc., Reston, Va. 1985.

Edwards, P. K., *Strikes in the United States 1881–1974,* St. Martin's Press, New York, 1981.

Hirsch, Barry T. and John T. Addison, *The Economic Analysis of Unions: New Approaches and Evidence,* Allen and Unwin, Boston, 1986.

Loughran, Charles S., *Negotiating a Labor Contract: A Management Handbook* (BNA Books, Washington), 1984.

Walton, Richard and Robert B. McKersie, *A Behavioral Theory of Labor Negotiations,* McGraw-Hill, New York, 1965.

APPENDIX

COLLECTIVE BARGAINING CASE JayHawk Communications*

Introduction

"Jayhawk Communications" is a mock negotiations case designed to give you experience at the bargaining table. It provides you with an opportunity to (1) prepare for negotiations by establishing bargaining positions and arguments based on analysis of economic and financial data and (2) actually negotiate a contract. To negotiate the contract, you will have to identify and implement bargaining strategies designed to resolve differences between the parties, yet try to "win" the negotiations. The negotiating experience will provide you with an opportunity to identify and critique your own strengths and weaknesses at collective bargaining. It should be a learning experience for the inexperienced negotiator as well as the veteran.

Jayhawk Communications concerns the negotiations of a renewal agreement between Jayhawk Communications Company (JC Co.) and Local 1000 of the Communication Workers of America (CWA), representing JC's employees. The case includes information concerning the company and the union, recent relations between the parties, and the present contract which is due to expire. Five issues are highlighted because of their importance in recent negotiations in the telecommunications industry, and given time constraints in this course, you should limit yourself to a discussion of those items.

Each management and union team may use the information and data provided to justify its demands. Each team may also add relevant data (from "legitimate" sources!) to enhance its bargaining position, but the additional material may not contradict what is given. The teams must negotiate over the five highlighted issues. However, either team may make additional demands with respect to these provisions.

Each company and union team should keep in mind that strikes and lockouts, although sometimes unavoidable, can be extremely costly to both parties and sometimes the public. Each team should make a "good faith" effort to reach an agreement. This will require that conflicts *between* union and management teams and *within* each team be resolved. While your goal is peaceful resolution of the negotiations, you also want the best possible contract for your team—in other words, think twice before you give up the ship in the middle of the storm.

The mock negotiations proceed as follows:

1. Each of you will be assigned to a company or union team. As a group you will determine the role each team member will play.

2. Each team will establish a list of bargaining demands and formulate arguments supporting each demand.

3. Each team member should be familiar with the simulation materials and is expected to be involved in the negotiations.

4. The allocation of time for planning and preparation, recesses in negotiations, caucuses, etc., and the manner of conducting the negotiations will be determined by the teams themselves.

5. Each team should be aware that unexpected situations may arise which could affect the negotiations. This may be the result of actions by the other party. The facilitator will be available to answer questions, but will not be directly involved in the bargaining process over the five issues.

Background

The parties to this bargaining relationship are the Jayhawk Communications Company (JC Co.) and Local 1000 of the Communication Workers of America (CWA). The corporation is a leading regional telephone company. According to net income reported to the major industry association for 1986, the company's total net income was $13,955,000. It has 640,000 local connections and 2325 employees. The bargaining unit here has 555 members and the company expects this number to decline over the next several years.

The company operates in a four state region in the midwest with its headquarters in Capitol City. With a population of 70,000, Capitol City is the largest city within a radius of 200 miles. While many of the bargaining unit employees are located in small towns near Capitol City, some unit employees are scattered across the state. The company negotiates with four other smaller units in the state and one unit in each of the other three states.

Characteristics of the Industry

The telecommunications industry has experienced solid growth in recent years. The telephone industry experienced growth of 15 percent in operating revenues in 1986. A recent survey indicates that the six largest companies forecast a 13 percent increase in operating revenues for 1987. JC experienced a 12 percent increase in total revenues and sales in 1986 and forecasts a 1987 increase of approximately 8 percent in its operating revenues.

The entire telecommunications industry is going through a period of great change. In 1983 the companies successfully achieved substantial rate increases from numerous state regulatory commissions. These increases significantly helped to improve their cash flow positions. Also, the agreement to settle the government's antitrust suit against the American Telephone and Telegraph Company has had a major impact on the nature of the industry creating much uncertainty about the future cost structure of the industry.

The Company

Because the CWA, Local 1000 has represented JC Co. employees since 1947, the bargaining relationship between the company and the union is a very mature one. It has until last year been a very stable and strike-free relationship. However, last year's union elections were hotly contested and the new union president is young, militant, and out to show the members what he can do. Because of the closeness of the election results, he must "deliver the goods" to solidify his position. Consequently, the company is bracing for a very difficult and hard-fought negotiations.

JC Company's financial picture is good but the uncertainty of the current "post-break-up" period is making JC's top officials very cautious in their views on the future. Since the President of JC Company is personally opposed to any item that introduces uncertainty into total labor costs and places a high premium on maintaining managerial flexibility in making scheduling decisions, the labor relations staff predicts that the negotiations will be hard-fought from *both* sides of the bargaining table.

Issues For Mock Bargaining: JC Company and CWA, Local 1000

The Union

The local union president elected in last year's election has in recent weeks vowed to "turn JC Company on its ear to get a settlement that all union members can live with," because his election promises to be focused on providing job security for the members.

The relationship between the union and company has deteriorated in the past year. The number of grievances has increased 90 percent, and the general tone of many workers is hostile and militant. The union claims that its complaints are due largely to the fact that the company has become sloppy and inconsistent in its supervisory functions, but the company counters that the union leadership is merely trying to show off. Like the company's labor relations staff, the local union leadership predicts a very difficult round of negotiations.

(1) Wages, Job Security, and Contract Duration

The company would like to sign a three year contract with the union, provided that the costs of the contract are both reasonable and reasonably certain. Although the labor relations staff is satisfied with the two year cycle of contract negotiations, the president of the company has stated repeatedly that he is "sick and tired of constantly being in negotiations with those baboons," and he strongly believes that greater industrial relations stability will result from a longer negotiations cycle as "old wounds have longer to heal."

However, even with the longer contract duration, the president is adamantly opposed to any wage or fringe benefit provision that introduces uncertainty and unpredictability with respect to its labor costs. While the labor relations staff does not agree with the president's strong view on the contract duration issue, it sees it as a personal concern of the president that will have to be given some priority.

The union is less certain about the advantages of a long-term contract. It sees a longer negotiations cycle as "chaining" the employees to set wages in an economic period when inflation and unemployment have the potential to run rampant. In the deregulation period the union has learned the hard lesson of layoffs and lower wage gains for its members. Therefore, the union's willingness to agree to a long-term contract will depend partly on its ability to achieve substantial break-throughs on other high priority issues, most notably job security and its demand for company sponsored retraining for workers who may be laid off.

In addition, the union leadership and many younger workers are worried about contracting out work to nonunion firms, and the use of new technology which will result in layoffs. Given the use of seniority provisions in deciding who gets to work, the younger workers are pressuring the union leadership hard on this issue. Given high unemployment rates in recent years, and the lower wages in the nonunion sector, this issue has risen in importance in the current round of negotiations.

Wages will certainly be an important issue in this year's negotiations. Both sides will present carefully thought-out proposals that are based on the best available data pertaining to wages and costs. Such factors as (a) comparative wages and earnings, (b) the company's ability to pay, (c) the company's propsective earnings and profit picture, (d) the industry's prospects, (e) past and future changes in the cost of living, and (f) employee productivity, morale, and performance will play an important part in the parties' arguments on the wage issue.

(2) Two Tier Wage Plan

In order to reduce future labor costs, while maintaining current economic benefits to continuing employees, the company is proposing a two tier wage plan. Under this plan, current employees would maintain and advance under the current wage progression scheme. However, newly hired employees would be paid twenty-five percent below the current wage scale and would advance along this lower scale during the period of the contract. The union is opposed to this plan suggesting that it would create "second class citizens" at the workplace, and reduce productivity because the low paid "new workers" would resent being paid lower wages for doing "the same work" as continuing employees.

(3) Holidays

The present contract provides for 6 paid holidays: New Year's Day, Memorial Day, Independence Day, Labor Day, Thanksgiving Day, and Christmas Day. The union views this as way below the national average and is certain to present demands for more holidays and for language regulating work and pay on holidays. Presently the company has the unilateral right to schedule employees for holiday work. During union meetings, the employees have repeatedly stressed the unfairness of this situation. While it is not a major issue, the holiday provision could become a very heated debate.

The company views the holiday issue as primarily economic in nature. Holidays cost money and the company's position will be that anything it gives away in holidays will be subtracted from possible wage increases. While it might be willing to exchange an existing holiday for a "floating" holiday, the company will be very reluctant to add holidays or change the rate of pay. As for the scheduling of holiday work, the company will be adamantly opposed to any infringement on its right to determine holiday work schedules. It believes that the nature of its operation and service requirements make it necessary to retain substantial flexibility with respect to scheduling work on holidays.

(4) Successorship

With industry deregulation, the CWA has become very concerned that companies will be forced or will desire to set up new companies to handle certain aspects of their business, e.g., the sale of equipment. To insure that the union will represent the employees in this environment the union is asking that the following clause be included in the new contract:

> The provisions of this Agreement shall be binding upon the Union and the Company and its successors and assigns; and all of the terms contained herein shall not be changed in any respect by the consolidation, merger, sale, transfer, or assignment of the Company of any or all of its property, or affected or changed in any respect by any change in the legal status, ownership or management of the company.

The Union views this clause as a high priority item in this round of negotiations because rumor indicates that the company is well on its way to forming a new *union-free* subsidiary to handle the sale of certain types of equipment.

The company will be firm in its opposition to the clause and will take the position that existing laws protect the union in successorship situations. Further, the company thinks that having this provision would reduce the market value of Jayhawk because a new owner would have a union present.

(5) Technological Change and Job Security

Technological change has posed a constant threat to the job security of employees in the telecommunications industry. While other companies in the industry have provided programs to protect their employees from the impact of these changes, JC Co. has done little to insure the jobs and incomes of its workers. The present contract provides only that "where technological changes are made which reduce the earning opportunities of the employees covered herein, every reasonable effort shall be made to transfer displaced employees to other work of equal earning opportunities." The union views job security as a top priority issue in these negotiations.

The union will demand several significant contract provisions related to job security. They include:

- the elimination of sub-contracting of CWA bargaining unit work,
- the formation of a joint labor/management committee to develop a long-term plan for reducing the work year—through implementation of items such as longer vacations, a 32-hour work week, additional holidays, and excused work days, etc., and
- the development of a Supplemental Income Protection Plan that would provide an early retirement option for employees over 55 who are displaced by technological change.

For Employees in the Bargaining Unit

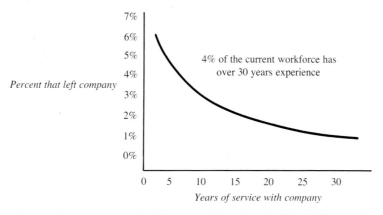

Percent that left company

4% of the current workforce has over 30 years experience

Years of service with company

***Figure 18–A1*   Normalized Turnover Curve for JayHawk Communications Inc. For Employees in the Bargaining Unit**

JC Company
Statement of Income
Year Ended December 31, 1986
(thousands of dollars)

	1986
Operating Revenues	
Access Rev.	45,193
Local Service	29,568
Toll Service	33,597
Miscellaneous	6,521
Less Uncollectible Revenue	(396)
Total	114,483
Operating Expenses	
Maintenance	21,513
Depreciation & Amortization	20,589
Other Operating Expenses	33,797
Federal Income Tax	9,975
State, Local, and Other Taxes	7,173
Total	93,047
Net Operating Income	21,436
Other Income	(1,711)
Total	19,725
Interest and Other Deductions	
Interest on Long-Term Debt	5,583
Interest on Short-Term Debt	17
Other fixed charges	170
Total	5,770
Net Income	13,955
Percent of Total Operating Revenue	12.2%

Balance Sheet

Assets	1986
	(thousands of dollars)
Investments	
Telephone Plant	286,156
Less: Depreciation	88,446
	197,710
Other Investments	16
Total Investments	197,726
Current Assets	
Cash	(2,108)
Temporary Cash Investments and Deposits	0
Accounts Receivable, Net	18,206
Materials and Supplies	1,120
All other	147
Total Current Assets	17,365
Prepaid Accounts and Deferred Charges	911
Total Assets	216,002

Liabilities and Owner's Equity	1986
	(thousands of dollars)
Capital Stock and Surplus	
Preferred Stock	0
Common Stock	27,089
Other Capital	14,747
Retained Earnings	43,965
Total Equity	85,801
Long-Term Debt	62,881
Non-Current Liabilities	73
Total Non-Current Liabilities	62,954
Current and Accrued Liabilities	
Current Maturities of Long-Term Debt	1,048
Notes Payable	5,000
Accounts Payable	14,342
Advance Billings	1,236
Accrued Taxes	(969)
Accrued Interest	1,650
Other	3,724
Total	26,031
Deferred Credits	
Accumulated Deferred Taxes on Income	29,122
Deferred Investment Tax Credit	11,943
Other	151
Total	41,216
Total Capitalization and Liabilities	216,002

The market value of the stock is $24 per share, and this price has not varied by more than 20 percent during the past year.

Data as of 12/10/86

	Title	Employees	Start	Average Hourly Wage	Payroll
	Cable Splicer Helper	0		—	—
A	Frame Attendant	4		10.81	89,939.20
	Line Worker	16	$6.35	10.81	359,756.80
	Appr. Equip. Tech.	0		—	—
	Sr. Line Worker	3		11.32	70,636.80
B	Station Worker	91		11.27	2,133,186.00
	Storekeeper	14		11.32	329,638.40
	Tech. I	0		—	—
	Cable Splicer	48	$6.35	11.78	1,176,115.20
	Combination A Worker	10		11.78	245,024.00
	Const. Foreman	12		11.78	249,028.80
C	Equipment Tech.	5		11.78	122,512.00
	Sr. Storekeeper	3		11.78	73,507.20
	Testboard Tech.	6		11.78	147,014.40
	C. O. Technician	44	$6.45	12.22	1,118,375.50
D	Combination B	14		12.22	355,846.40
	Installer	11		12.22	279,593.60
	Tech. II	0		—	—
	Chief Combination	4		12.88	107,161.60
E	Equip. Installer	9		12.88	241,113.60
	Toll Technician	15		12.88	401,856.00
	Plant Clerk	12	$5.04	8.00	199,638.40
	Total Plant	321		11.60	7,721,812.80
	Commercial Clerk	2		8.25	34,320.00
	Service Center Clerk	98	$5.04	6.97	1,420,286.40
	Service Rep.	39		8.29	672,152.00
	Total Commercial	139		7.36	2,126,758.40
	Traffic Clerk	1		8.25	17,160.00
	Operators	94	$4.85	7.97	1,558,356.80
	Total Traffic	95			1,575,516.80
	Company Total	555		9.914	11,424,088.00

*The authors want to thank Jean Baderschneider, Mobile Inc., for her help in the development of this bargaining simulation.

ADMINISTERING THE COLLECTIVE BARGAINING AGREEMENT

A fter reaching a collective bargaining agreement, the labor relations process is sometimes assumed to end. This is wrong. Practitioners and scholars generally agree that what is gained at the bargaining table can be lost in how the agreement is administered. For example, a union may have given up restrictions on job assignments, but workers refuse to cooperate. If management refuses to protect its perogatives by challenging this practice, then this potential management benefit is lost during the life of the contract. For both labor and management, the collective bargaining agreement is only as good as the persons on both sides who administer that agreement. A long standing labor relations adage is "what is won at the bargaining table should not be given up in how the contract is administered in the shop." It is the day-to-day administration of an agreement that determines how well the objectives of the contract are realized.[1]

In this chapter you will have an opportunity to learn how the collective bargaining agreement is administered. After reading this chapter you should be able to answer the following questions: What are the major areas of dispute during the life of a collective bargaining agreement? How does bargaining occur and proceed during the life of the agreement? What is a grievance procedure, and how are disputes handled between labor and management? Do different kinds of grievance procedures have an effect on

---

[1] Robert B. McKersie and William W. Shrophire Jr., "Avoiding Written Grievances: A Successful Program," *Journal of Business,* April 1962, pp. 135–52.

productivity and firm profits? Finally, what is the legal basis of the final step of the grievance procedure—arbitration, and when should firms or unions go to this step? If time permits in this course, two arbitration cases are presented in the Appendix at the end of the chapter that give you the opportunity to apply your knowledge of the grievance/arbitration process to these situations.

Disputes During the Collective Bargaining Agreement

Labor contracts are often agreed to in some haste with many details left vague. Some areas are intentionally unclear because neither side could reach an agreement on this particular issue. In other cases, in order to avoid a contract expiration deadline, the language that was agreed upon could be left open to varying interpretations. Finally, in long-standing collective bargaining relationships the agreement has often been added to, with varying provisions being in conflict with earlier ones. As Table 19-1 shows there are a wide variety of issues that are discussed and agreed upon in bargaining and many of these provisions can lend themselves to varying interpretations by two of the actors who are involved parties in collective bargaining—namely labor and management. As the table suggests, these issues vary from union recognition to layoffs, rehiring, and worksharing.

The Grievance Procedure

When there is a disagreement over the terms and conditions of the contract, the procedure that is used to adjudicate the dispute is the grievance procedure. A grievance is any complaint or dissatisfaction arising from the interpretation or application of the contract. The grievance procedure is the mechanism that is established for enforcing the agreement. Former Supreme Court Justice William O. Douglas stated in providing the decision that formed the legal basis of this process, "The grievance procedure is . . . part of the continuous collective bargaining process. It, rather than the strike, is the terminal point of a disagreement."[2]

Within the grievance procedure process, there are several individuals in the industrial relations system that play a major role in handling grievances. From managements' perspective the plant foreman or supervisor is the first individual involved in the grievance procedure. This person represents management in the initial stages of the grievance process. The union's initial representative in the grievance procedure is the union steward, who is either elected by the workers in a work area or appointed by

---

[2] William O. Douglas, *United Steelworkers of America* v. *Warrior and Gulf Navigation Company,* June 20, 1960.

Source: 1985-88 Agreement between United Telephone Company of Missouri and the Communications Workers of America.

Table 19-1 **Contents of a Collective Bargaining Agreement**

the union president. This person is usually the one who would file a claim on behalf of a union member who would be stating that a violation of the contract had been committed. The principal task of the foreman and steward in the grievance process is to decide whether there has been a violation of the agreement, if there has been an unjust act or hardship imposed on an employee, and if management or the employee is responsible.

Figure 19-1 shows the steps in a typical grievance procedure from both management's and labor's perspective. Although the number of steps and titles of representatives vary, this figure provides information about which union representative is likely to deal with their counterpart for the employer. You should be aware that each successive step of the procedure moves up the "chain of command" for both organizations, and assumes that as the grievance moves to each successive step no agreement or settlement of it has been reached at a lower level.

For the union the key actor in the grievance procedure, and in all of

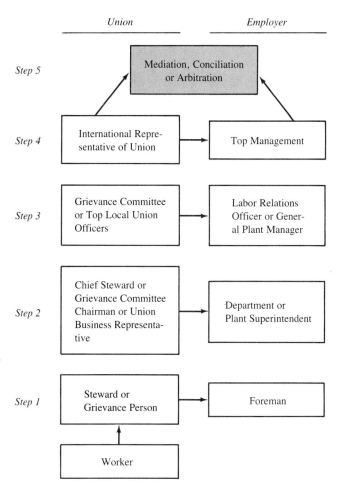

Source: Phillips L. Garman, *Handling Grievances,* University of Illinois, Institute of Labor and Industrial Relations, 1971. Reprinted by permission.

Figure 19-1   **Steps and Parties Involved in Various Stages of the Grievance Procedure**

contract administration is the union steward. Figure 19–2 shows the pivotal role the steward plays in representing the union organization to the union member as well as representing both the union member and organization to management. The steward's main job is to present grievances of workers within their jurisdiction to the proper management representatives in order to obtain a fair adjustment. As part of their responsibility, they attempt to remove potential causes of grievances and look out for contract violations. Example 19–1 shows the new frustrations that union stewards have faced in the 1980s as a result of increased product market competition.

One of the major criticisms of grievance procedures is that they are

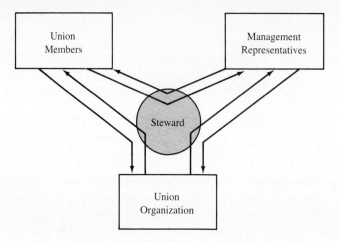

Source: Phillips L. Garman, *Handling Grievances,* University of Illinois, Institute of Labor and Industrial Relations, 1971. Reprinted by permission.

Figure 19-2 **Relationship of the Union Steward in Union-Management Relations**

too formal or legalistic. The result is that many grievances are filed, and there are logjams that result in many meritorious ones being disregarded and frivolous ones being pursued. One company that attempted to reduce the number of written grievances was International Harvester (I.H.) in the late 1950s. In response to the heavy use of the grievance procedure in the form of written grievances, I.H. instituted a clinical approach to the use of the grievance procedure.[3] In this approach, potential grievances were discussed with plant committees and company psychologists, who took a problem-solving approach to the grievance. If an agreement could not be reached at this informal problem solving session then a formal grievance was filed.

The goal of both labor and management is to settle a grievance at the lowest possible step of the process. Toward this end, firms other than International Harvester (now called Navistar Inc.) have also attempted to implement a problem solving approach to grievance procedures. Another illustration is that of the automotive division of General Motors during the early 1970s. During this period the division contained eighteen plants which included approximately 65,000 employees in the bargaining unit. The total number of grievances written and unwritten for 1973 was approximately 120,000. Table 19-2 (see p. 410) presents the percent of grievances settled at each step of the procedure for General Motors. Step one-half is the problem-solving, clinical approach similar to the one adopted by I.H., and most grievances are settled at this point. Of the ones that become written grievances, most are settled at the general foreman

---

[3] McKersie and Shrophire, *ibid.*

EXAMPLE 19.1   # THE UNION SHOP STEWARD IN AN ERA OF PAYROLL CUTS

Alan Moseley, a union shop steward for the United Steelworkers Local 1010 in East Chicago, Indiana, is frustrated. This time it is because of talks with Inland Steel over whether eight new jobs should go to union or salaried workers. Mr. Moseley is part of a battle for control of the shop floor. American business' drive to cut costs through layoffs and work-rule changes has fostered mistrust among union blue-collar workers.

As employment has declined at Inland Steel, workers complain of being worked too hard, and grievances have jumped 50% from last year. Many union members complain that although they accepted a 9% pay cut in 1983, they have lost 3100 jobs. As a result, union members do not trust the company.

An example of this frustration occurred when a supervisor caught two workers sleeping on workbenches and suspended them for a day, causing Mr. Moseley to file a grievance. Sympathetic workers caused production to drop in subsequent shifts. Furthermore, worker dissatisfaction caused two departments to drop out of joint committees with management, reducing Inland's joint labor-management committees to only two.

Source: Alex Kotlowitz, *Wall Street Journal,* April 1, 1987.

level. Although only .7 percent of all grievances reach an outside arbitrator, this represented approximately 252 cases that had to be decided upon by a third party during 1973.

The Grievance Procedure and Fractional Bargaining

In one of the first major volumes identifying the impact of collective bargaining on management, Slichter, Healy, and Livernash suggested that higher or lower numbers of grievances did not necessarily mean good or bad labor relations.[4] They suggested that in some cases, grievances were low because management had the upper hand at the work site, and the union was too weak to file grievances. In other cases, where grievances were high, they suggested that this may mean the absence of an informal, unwritten grievance procedure, but in these cases the written grievance is the first step of the process. Therefore, this type of firm only has more formal grievances.

There also is much bargaining that takes place under the scope of the grievance procedure. At times groups of workers and their representatives

---

[4] Sumner H. Slichter, James J. Healy, and E. Richard Livernash, *The Impact of Collective Bargaining on Management,* The Brookings Institution, Washington, D. C., 1960.

	Percent of grievances settled
Step one-half: Foreman - Verbal	70% of total
	Percent of written
Step One: Foreman - written	14
Step one and one-half: General Foreman	75
Step Two: Appeal to shop committee	6.5
Step Three: Appeal to Corporation and International Union	3.8
Step Four: Arbitration	.7

Table 19-2   **Grievance Settlement at General Motors: 1973**

engage in grievance bargaining. When small groups of workers exert pressure on supervisors to bargain over these grievances it is called fractional bargaining.[5] The grievances of the group of workers is sometimes as likely to be considered on the merits of the group's bargaining power as on the merits of the grievance. Since management is often more concerned with meeting a production or quota deadline, they may settle a grievance with a group of workers who threaten a walkout or slowdown. By using their power in small groups, unions may gain workrule provisions in fractional bargaining that they could never obtain at the negotiation table.

Usually union officials and industrial relations representatives are opposed to fractional bargaining.[6] For union leaders, granting autonomy in bargaining to small groups during the life of a contract can result in charges of favoritism and disorganization within the union hierarchy. For industrial relations representatives there exists the potential for work disruptions and confusion and conflict in company policy, if supervisors in different parts of the company handle grievances in different ways. If this is the case, the value of the written bargaining agreement can be reduced to the harm of both unions, management, and the organization.

The Grievance Procedure, Productivity, and Profits

Since almost all collective bargaining agreements have grievance procedures of varying kinds, this has led a number of scholars and practitioners to ask whether cooperative labor relations practices which generally means a low number of grievances, results in greater firm productivity and profitability. The reason why a lower number of grievances may result in higher productivity are that fewer hours need to be displaced from the production process to the handling of potential grievances. Second, in organizations with lots of grievances, behavioral or psychological reactions

---

[5] James W. Kuhn, *Bargaining in Grievance Settlement,* New York, Columbia University Press, 1961.

[6] Neil W. Chamberlain and James W. Kuhn, *Collective Bargaining,* McGraw Hill Inc., New York, 1986.

of employees to perceived inequitable treatment may result in a reduction of work effort.[7]

Three statistically based analyses have examined the relationship between grievances and industrial relations, productivity, and profits. The basic finding of all three studies was that there is strong support for the proposition that good industrial relations in the plant leads to higher productivity and profits. In a study of eighteen General Motors plants, the results found that there was higher productivity where labor relations practices were rated good, and where grievances were low.[8] In a second study of nine manufacturing plants over five years, a cooperative union management program resulted in increased productivity in six of eight plants where it could be measured.[9]

In a third study whose production results are presented in Figure 19–3, Professor Casey Ichniowski found a significant inverse relationship between plant production and grievance rates when other factors were held constant. His empirical results can be summarized by comparing a plant operating at the average grievance rate to one operating without grievances. For a given plant, a move from no grievances to the average among the paper mills studied would correspond to a 1.2 percent drop in output, and up to a 14.6 percent drop in profits.[10] Further, increases in the grievance rate corresponded to even greater decreases in productivity.

In nonunion plants the same relationship between grievances and productivity was found. By simulating the expected number of grievances in a nonunion plant, Ichniowski found that higher "estimated" grievances corresponded with reduced economic performance. He suggests that the same effects of good labor relations policies and practices on productivity exist in the nonunion environment.

Nonunion Grievance Policies and Practices

A book by two Harvard professors, Richard Freeman and James Medoff, states that having a voice in the employment relationship through the grievance procedure and the final step of arbitration, where an impartial outside party decides the grievance, results in less turnover and consequently higher productivity.[11] If this is the case, then why do not more firms in the

---

[7] Casey Ichniowski, "The Effects of Grievance Activity on Productivity," *Industrial and Labor Relations Review,* October, 1986, pp. 75–89.

[8] Harry Katz, Thomas Kochan, and Kenneth Gobeille, "Industrial Relations Performance, Economic Performance and the Effects of Quality of Working Life Efforts: An Inter-Plant Analysis," M.I.T. Sloan Working Paper 1329–82, July 1982.

[9] Michael Shuster, "The Impact of Union-Management Cooperation on Productivity and Employment," *Industrial and Labor Relations Review,* 36 No. 3, April 1983, pp. 415–30.

[10] Ichniowski, ibid.

[11] Richard Freeman and James Medoff, *What Do Unions Do?* Basic Books, New York, 1984.

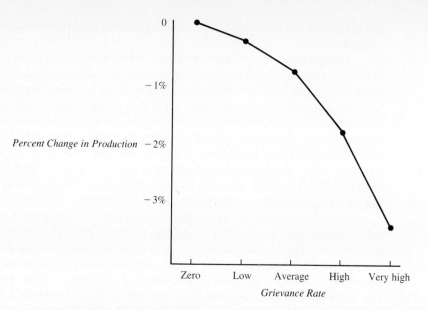

From C. Ichniowski, "Industrial Relations and Economic Performance: Grievances, Arbitrations, and Productivity," NBER, Working Paper, 1985.

Figure 19-3   **Grievance Rates and Changes in Production**

nonunion sector have grievance procedures ending in arbitration? They suggest that nonunion firms respond more to the preferences of young workers who tend to be more mobile, and have a lesser desire for a voice mechanism through the grievance/arbitration system. Further, as long as these firms are aware and act on potential areas of grievances for these young workers, they are not likely to ask for a system of grievances and arbitration.

A Bureau of National Affairs study of personnel policies in nonunion firms found that firms with "good labor relations" policies had some form of a formal grievance system.[12] However, even though a grievance policy was in existence, most employees feel intimidated by potential reprisals if they file a grievance against management. Further, firms that had recent union organizing drives increased the existence of a formal grievance procedure from 49 to almost 66 percent even when the union lost the election.[13] Further, the existence of a formal grievance procedure reduces managerial flexibility. In spite of the apparent lack of muscle of nonunion grievance procedures, at least one study, by Daniel Spencer, has found that

[12] "Policies for Unorganized Employees": Personnel Policies Forum Survey No. 125 (Washington, D. C.: B.N.A., April 1979).

[13] Richard B. Freeman and Morris M. Kleiner, "Management Responses to Union Organizing Drives," NBER, 1987.

voluntary turnover by employees is reduced with more voice mechanisms, even in nonunion environments.[14]

One common feature of nonunion grievance procedures is that the final step concludes with a company official making the final decision. Also, recent empirical results show that the percentage of the final decisions that upheld the original action by management is very high.[15] Moreover, about half of the nonunion companies supported the supervisor in every case. In less than a third of the companies there were outside arbitrators, as opposed to supervisors, who were allowed to decide the grievance issue. For most companies it was viewed that if management loses, it would be perceived as getting a "black eye" with employees. In cases that might otherwise require adjudication by an outside arbitrator, a management imposed decision would be less likely to eliminate the perception of inequitable treatment and then potentially could restore greater work effort. Although grievance procedures may reduce turnover for the organization, recent studies by Lewin and Peterson suggest that persons who file grievances have higher turnover rates than persons who do not file them in both union and nonunion enterprises.[16]

An illustration of one type of nonunion grievance procedure is shown in Example 19–2. As this shows, many large firms are turning to this form of "industrial law" at the workplace in order to avoid unions and avoid wrongful discharge lawsuits in the courts with the reduction in the "employment at will" doctrine in many states. However, the loss of flexibility appears to be a concern for many managers.

The Arbitration Process

The Legal Basis of Labor Arbitration

The use of labor arbitration began to grow dramatically following World War II. This was due in part to the success of the War Labor Board which attempted to maintain industrial peace during the U.S. struggle against Nazi Germany and Japan. There are two major kinds of disputes that occur and are potential candidates for arbitration. First, there are rights disputes, which are typically found in grievance arbitration. Under this process, the resolution of disputes arises from different interpretations of the terms of an existing agreement. The second kind is interest or contract arbitration, where a third party resolves a dispute between the parties over a contract.

---

[14] Daniel G. Spencer, "Employee Voice and Employee Retention," *Academy of Management Journal,* Vol. 29, No. 3, 1986 pp. 488–502.

[15] Ronald Berenbeim, *Nonunion Complaint Systems: A Corporate Approach,* Report No. 770, (New York: The Conference Board, 1980).

[16] David Lewin and Richard B. Peterson, "Behavioral Outcomes of Grievance Activity," Working Paper, Columbia University Graduate School of Business, April 1987.

EXAMPLE 19.2   INTERNAL REVIEW PANELS IN NONUNION BUSINESSES

Recently, a manager at Control Data Corp. was fired because, his boss claimed, he refused to cooperate in a plan to improve his performance. The manager disagreed and contended that his boss's idea of feedback consisted of verbal abuse and threats. The employee appealed his dismissal to a grievance panel of three peers and two managers. After taking testimony from both sides, the panel overruled the boss, and recommended reinstatement with back pay.

For a growing number of companies that are dissatisfied with little-used "open-door" grievance policies, they are instituting peer-review boards to resolve disputes over firings, promotions, and disciplinary actions. Most consist of peer and management representatives, and their decisions are most often binding on both sides.

The trend represents an effort by some companies to broaden employees' rights in disciplinary matters. Companies also say the grievance panels build a better relationship, help deter union organizing, and perhaps most importantly, stem the rising number of costly lawsuits claiming wrongful discharge and discrimination.

Approximately 100 companies now use peer boards, including Federal Express Corp., Digital Equipment Corp., General Electric Co., Citicorp, and Borg-Warner Corp., but such panels can be time-consuming and costly to run. For example, Federal Express says it has spent up to $10,000 on a single case—transporting workers and managers to an off-site hotel, compiling documents and reviewing the testimony.

Perhaps not surprisingly, many managers think the money could be used for other purposes. The programs may have sapped managers' morale company executives acknowledge. Managers often consider the boards an intrusion on their rights and say the panels are incapable of deciding subtle personnel issues. "Many supervisors bristle, 'I'm the supervisor, and I feel this is the way to go,'" says Gene Salas, a manager at Borg-Warner's Sterling Heights, Michigan plant.

Source: Larry Reibstein, *Wall Street Journal,* December 3, 1986.

The third party sets the terms and conditions of the agreement. This procedure is rarely used in the private sector, but is used extensively in the public sector as was explained in Chapter 10.

Example 19–3 shows how arbitration of individual worker/player salaries within the context of an overall contract for Major League Baseball is determined. In baseball, the arbitrator is involved in elements of both rights and interest disputes. That is, the dispute arose out of the contract (rights dispute) between management (baseball owners) and the players' union. However, the arbitrator must decide on the appropriate compensation level for the following season (an interest dispute item). Therefore,

EXAMPLE 19.3   ARBITRATION IN PROFESSIONAL SPORTS: THE CASE OF BASEBALL

Tal Smith's baseball season is a grueling, three-week road trip filled with statistics, agents, and money. Every winter Mr. Smith is active in baseball's fastest-growing game: arbitration. In the game, players with two to six years in the majors can file for binding salary arbitration if contract negotiations do not result in a settlement.

Both sides—the player and the team representative—submit salary figures in sealed envelopes to the arbitrator. Both present their cases, comparing the salary of the player with that of players of comparable performance. When the arbitrator makes his decision, there's no compromise and either the player wins or the team wins. The winner matters greatly to baseball's money-losing owners, who are eager to slow the growth of players' salaries. Owners took a cost-cutting step recently by refusing to join in a bidding war for some high-priced players (players with six years of major league service who are permitted to jump to the highest bidder). Now, the owners say that players are retaliating by submitting higher salary demands in arbitration. Should players win in arbitration, the owners add, salaries will continue to grow higher.

This is where Mr. Smith steps into action. Using simple box scores as well as computer analyses of statistics and salaries, he builds a case against the player's salary bid. Arbitrators are required to use comparisons with players of similar performance and salary levels. Last year, for instance, Boston third-baseman Wade Boggs stated that he was as important to his team as George Brett, generally considered the league's best third baseman, was to the Kansas City Royals. Mr. Smith, arguing for Boston, pointed out that Mr. Boggs, then a three-year veteran, did not hit many home runs, while Mr. Brett was an 11-year man with home-run power. Boggs won and has filed again this year for a record $1.85 million (which would put him ahead of Mr. Brett's $1.35 million, and some analysts worry that a Boggs victory would boost salaries even higher).

Owners suggest that the mere threat of salary arbitration causes them to give players higher salaries than they deserve. And when an owner is called into arbitration, he may bid higher just to avoid losing the case. "So even when the agent loses, he wins," says Mr. Gould. "He's gotten more than was on the table before and what's it cost him? Half the arbitrator's salary." In 10 years of arbitration only once has a player left the process with a salary lower than he had the previous year, and that was in the case of a player who had simply left the team during the season.

Players see things differently. They say arbitration provides them with needed negotiating leverage against cheap owners. Indeed, about 95 percent of those eligible for arbitration this year, filed for it. They dismiss the length-of-service argument that so many owners emphasize. If they perform as well as an established veteran, they argue, why shouldn't they be paid as well?

Is professional baseball engaging in rights or interest arbitration?

Source: Hal Lancaster, *Wall Street Journal,* February 19, 1986, p. 33.

there are elements of both interest and rights disputes in Major League Baseball arbitration procedures.

There were a series of Supreme Court and NLRB cases decided since the 1950s that established the role of arbitration as a major method of deciding labor disputes between unions and management. These decisions established the right of the arbitrator to be the final adjudicator of disputes between labor and management on issues involving the interpretation of the collective bargaining agreement. The first Supreme Court case to establish arbitration as the appropriate arena for disputes was the Lincoln Mills case.[17] In this dispute the Supreme Court stated that Section 301 of the Taft-Hartley Act meant that the federal court system can enforce collective bargaining agreements between labor and management, including those that provided for the arbitration of future grievances. If an agreement has an arbitration provision and the courts agree with it, the award is enforced by the courts if either party fails to comply with it.

However, the most significant set of Supreme Court cases establishing rights arbitration was decided by the Court in 1960.[18] The key issue facing the Supreme Court was whether the arbitrator's decisions could be reviewed by the courts. The response of the Court was usually no. The court established three important protections for arbitration in three separate cases called the Steelworkers Trilogy. In all three cases the Steelworkers Union was the party challenging the company. In the first case involving American Manufacturing Company, the basic issue was the role of the federal courts, when called upon to enforce a collective-bargaining contract containing an agreement to arbitrate future questions of contract interpretation. The facts involved an employee who had been disabled and accepted worker's compensation. After a doctor had certified his ability to return to work, the company refused to reinstate him. The company claimed that the grievance was a frivolous one. The Court ordered arbitration of the dispute.

The second case involved Warrior and Gulf Navigation Company; the issue was the permissible scope of federal judicial inquiry into a labor agreement containing an arbitration clause, when there is doubt about the arbitration clause's coverage of the particular dispute. The facts of the case were that the employer subcontracted work when the company's employees were on a partial layoff. The lower court upheld management's subcontracting right, but the Supreme Court stated that the arbitration agreement and no strike clause meant that arbitration was the appropriate arena for the dispute.

In the third case involving the Enterprise Wheel Corporation the key

---

[17] *Textile Workers Union* v. *Lincoln Mills,* 355 U.S. 448 (1957).

[18] *United Steelworkers of America* v. *Warrior and Gulf Navigation Co.,* 363 U.S. 574; *United Steelworkers of America* v. *Enterprise Wheel and Car Corp.,* 363 U.S. 593; and *United Steelworkers of America* v. *American Manufacturing Co.,* 363 U.S. 564 (1960).

issue was the role of the federal courts in enforcing an arbitration award. The facts of the case were that several employees were discharged for walking out in protest of the firing of another employee. The company refused to arbitrate the grievance, but the lower court ordered it. The arbitrator then reduced the discharge to disciplinary suspension and ordered reinstatement with back pay for all time lost except for a ten day suspension minus earnings from other employment. The company refused to comply, contending that the ruling occurred after the expiration of the contract. The Supreme Court ruled that the federal courts should enforce the award as long as the arbitrator stays within the scope of the bargaining agreement and the award is based on his construction of the agreement.

As a result of the Steelworkers Trilogy, four key principles were established.[19] First, the arbitrator has the authority to determine whether an issue is arbitrable. Second, the courts should not review the merits of a grievance or substitute its judgment for that of an arbitrator. Third, the arbitrator must confine him/herself to the interpretation and application of the agreement. Fourth, although questions of arbitrability should be resolved in favor of coverage by the arbitration process, the courts should refuse to order arbitration if it is clear on the face of the contract language that the claim has been excluded from the process.

Since the Court's decision in the Trilogy cases, there have been several cases that have established the role of arbitration as first, the trade-off for a no-strike provision involving the union in a contract, and second determined the relationships of the NLRB to arbitration. A second set of three cases decided in 1962 related the requirement for arbitration of damages for violation of a no-strike clause rather than taking the disputes directly to the federal courts.[20] The most significant case linking arbitration to a no-strike promise was decided by the Supreme Court in 1970 in the *Boys Market* case. The Court ruled that an injunction could be issued when a strike occurred in violation of a no-strike clause prior to arbitration of an issue, and that the company could sue the union for income lost during the strike.[21]

A second issue for the arbitration process has been the potential conflict between the NLRA coverage of unfair labor practices and good faith bargaining (which was covered in Chapter 10), and the same issues being covered in the arbitration clause of the contract. The issue was partially resolved in the 1971 Collyer case.[22] In this situation the company unilaterally raised wages for one group of workers, but the union wanted

[19] Paul Prasow and Edward Peters, *Arbitration and Collective Bargaining: Conflict Resolution in Labor Relations,* McGraw-Hill, New York, 1970.

[20] *Sinclair Refining Co.* v. *Atkinson,* 370 U.S. 195 (1962); *Atkinson* v. *Sinclair Refining Co.,* 370 U.S. 238 (1962); and *Drake Bakeries* v. *Local 50,* 370 U.S. 254 (1962).

[21] *Boys Markets, Inc.* v. *Retail Clerks Union Local 770,* 398 U.S. 235 (1970).

[22] Collyer Insulated Wire Co., 192 NLRB 150 (1971).

wages increased for all workers claiming this was both a failure to bargain issue and a violation of the contract. The Board stated that it would defer hearing for a potential unfair labor practice case until the arbitration process had been completed. This decision affirmed a long standing policy of voluntarism, which is allowing the private means of adjudication to take precedence over the process involving government regulation.

However, in 1977 the NLRB reconsidered the Collyer decision and did not allow the arbitration process full reign over the arena of unfair labor practices.[23] Specifically, they ruled that if there was a potential violation of individual employee rights guaranteed under Section 7 of the NLRA, the appropriate arena for a settlement would be the NLRB. This gave individuals protection under federal regulations, but left unions and management, who felt discriminated against, the private means of arbitration for the adjudication of grievances.

Another area of legal conflict has occurred between the Courts and Title VII of the 1964 Civil Rights Act (which was covered in Chapter 8), and the grievance arbitration process.[24] In 1974 the Supreme Court in *Alexander-Gardner Denver* stated that an arbitrator's decision could not keep an employee from utilizing the courts in matters involving possible discrimination even though this prospect is not open in most other grievance issues. The Court did provide that substantial weight be given the arbitrators decision, and that Title VII should supplement rather than replace the arbitration process. In these types of cases the employer must prove that any disciplinary penalty was applied legitimately and in a nondiscriminatory manner.

One issue raised by the *Gardner-Denver* case was that when arbitrators make their decision the loser would take their grievances to the courts to get a "second bite of the apple."[25] However, a recent study has shown that when employees lose at arbitration, they have a 90 percent chance of losing at trial, even assuming they survive employer attempts to have their case thrown out of court. Furthermore, there has been little evidence of employees increasing their use of this potential second chance at a hearing when they lose in the arbitration arena.

Costs and Benefits of the Arbitration Process

The legal foundations developed by the courts have fostered the growth of grievance arbitration as the dominant form of settling disputes over the interpretation of labor agreements in the private sector, and recent trends

---

[23] Roy Robinson Chevrolet, 228 NLRB 103 (1977); General American Transportation Corporation, 228 NLRB 102 (1977).

[24] *Alexander* v. *Gardner-Denver Co.,* 415 U.S. 35 (1974).

[25] Karen Elwell and Peter Feuille, "Arbitration Awards and *Gardner-Denver* Lawsuits: One Bite or Two," *Industrial Relations,* Vol. 23, No. 2 (Spring 1984) pp. 287–297.

suggest that it will hold a similar position in the public sector. For example in 1944, 73 percent of all collective bargaining agreements had third party arbitration, but by the early 1980s over 99 percent of all contracts had this procedure in the private sector.[26] By encouraging the use of arbitration and upholding the ability to enforce decisions in the courts, firms with unions significantly increased their use of this process. For example, about 15,000 grievance arbitrations are conducted annually through the American Arbitration Association (AAA), a private nonprofit organization, and another 12,000 are directed by the Federal Mediation and Conciliation Service (FMCS).[27] With this widespread use of the arbitration process, it has become increasingly important for management and unions to analyze the costs and benefits of using this procedure.

The costs of arbitration can be developed in two segments, first the direct costs of the process, and second, the indirect costs that may include losses in output. With regard to the direct costs of arbitration, they have doubled from $566.59 in the early 1970s to $1132 in the early 1980s. As Table 19–3 shows, there are substantial costs to management and unions in using arbitration, to include both the time and funds allocated to the process. Within the context of our present value cost-benefit approach, the long time delays of arbitration also are a major factor in deciding whether to use the process. For example, the Federal Mediation and Conciliation Service noted in a study that examined the number of days from the filing of a grievance to the final award was 242 days, or approximately eight months. That is, it took almost half a year to get to the arbitration hearing. It took another month and a half in appointing an arbitrator, and more than two months before the arbitrator could hear the case. After the hearing, it took the arbitrator an average of 46 days before an award was issued.[28] These delays usually favor management, since unions are typically the party filing the grievance.

Table 19–3 also presents some of the indirect costs of going to arbitration, that include lost employee time at the workplace, which would typically include the employee and the union steward, who are paid approximately $10 per hour. Further costs include using a lawyer at approximately $75 per hour, and filing fees with the private sector groups that coordinate arbitration hearings like the American Arbitration Association. Other potential costs are making transcripts of the hearings. In many cases these costs total over $2500 to each side. Given these direct and indirect costs of over $5000 per hearing, which are typically shared equally

---

[26] Frank Elkouri and Edna A. Elkouri, *How Arbitration Works,* ed. (Washington, D.C., Bureau of National Affairs, 1973), and Federal Mediation and Conciliation Service, Thirty-fourth Annual Report Fiscal Year 1981, Washington, D.C., U.S. Government Printing Office, 1982.

[27] Steven S. Briggs and John C. Anderson, "An Empirical Investigation of Arbitrator Acceptability," *Industrial Relations,* Vol. 19, No. 2 (Spring 1980) pp. 163–174.

[28] Federal Mediation and Conciliation Service, *ibid.,* p. 39

	1981[1]
Days charged by arbitrator	
Total	3.3
Travel	.3
Post-hearing study	2.0
Per diem rates	$ 299.62
Total charged	$1,132.31
Management's estimated cost of arbitration expenses for a one-day hearing.[2]	
Prehearing	
Lost time: Grievant and witnesses	
@ $10/32 hours	$ 320.00
Lawyer research @ $15/4 hours	60.00
Interview witness @ $75/4 hours	300.00
Filing fee	50.00
Lawyer presentation of case	
@ $75/hour/6 hours	$ 450.00
Lost time: Grievant and witnesses	
@ $10/32 hours	$ 160.00
Hearing room: Shared equally	50.00
Total hearing	$1,390.00
Post hearing expense	
Lawyer: Preparation of posthearing	
brief @ $75/8 hours	600.00
Total posthearing	$ 600.00
One half of arbitrator's expenses	
and fees	$ 566.16
Total cost to management	$2,556.16

[1]Federal Mediation and Conciliation Service, Thirty-Fourth Annual Report Fiscal Year 1981 (Washington, D.C.: U.S. Government Printing Office, 1982) p. 39.
[2]Estimates derived from John Zalusky, "Arbitration: Updating a Vital Process," *American Federationist*, November 1976, p. 6.

Table 19-3   **Direct and Indirect Costs of Arbitration, 1981**

by both labor and management, both sides are careful not to enter the arbitration process unless they view the potential benefits as being significant.

Although the costs of going to the arbitration process can be expensive, there are many potential benefits to the parties. First, and perhaps most important, is that arbitration is used to settle differences between labor and management without the parties resorting to a strike or lockout. Although the costs of arbitration are high, they may be small in comparison to a work stoppage (see Chapter 17). Second, a benefit of using arbitration is the perception by workers that they have a voice in the final determination on issues affecting their worklife. The use of this process may, as Justice Douglas suggested, have "certain therapeutic value" at the workplace, and reduce turnover as Freeman and Medoff find.[29] Third, since the arbitration process is entered into in a voluntary manner by both sides, there is

---

[29] Douglas, *ibid* and Freeman and Medoff, *ibid.*

generally greater acceptance of the award as being fair. Further, the process may be used to quiet a constituency of the union, who may not accept union or management authority, but will accept the decision of an outside arbitrator.

A further issue in assessing the arbitration process is the selection of an arbitrator. Most private sector arbitrators are selected from lists provided by the Federal Mediation and Conciliation Service (FMCS) or the American Arbitration Association (AAA). Recent analysis of arbitrator demographic characteristics showed that the average age of arbitrators was 57.6 years. Forty-five percent have law degrees, and 23 percent have Ph.Ds, and the average education level is 6.5 years of college attendance. Only a small percent of all the arbitrators are called upon to settle disputes.[30] In fact, in 1970 only 31 percent of arbitrators on the total AAA list were used during the year, and less than 2 percent of the arbitrators on the list had more than 30 cases in that year. The dominant factor in getting arbitration cases was experience, which the parties viewed as having acceptability in labor disputes for both unions and management.[31]

Mediation and Fact-Finding

Although arbitration is the dominant form of dispute resolution during the course of a contract, other forms of third party dispute resolution are used, but generally in resolving interest disputes. The weakest form of dispute resolution is *conciliation* or *mediation.* In this form, the mediator attempts to get both parties to reach a compromise. The mediator does not make a decision, but rather tries to persuade the negotiators to come to a voluntary agreement. The Federal Mediation and Conciliation Service provides federal mediators in potential labor disputes under provisions of the Taft-Hartley Act (see Chapter 10), and in disputes in the public sector.

A second and somewhat stronger form of third party resolution of disputes is *fact-finding.* The purpose of fact-finders is to investigate and assemble all the facts surrounding a dispute. After hearings at which both parties can make their cases, a report is presented which often includes recommendations. Unlike arbitration, the parties have the choice of either accepting or rejecting the recommendations. Much like the arbitration of rights disputes, fact-finders are usually chosen by the parties and there are large elements of voluntarism in the process. The procedure has many of the same monetary costs and benefits associated with the grievance arbitration process. However, in fact-finding, the parties may reject the decision of the third party with no recourse to the Courts.

The strongest form of third party intervention is arbitration. By

---

[30] Briggs and Anderson, *ibid.*

[31] Walter J. Primeaux and Dalton Brannen, "Why Few Arbitrators are Deemed Acceptable," *Monthly Labor Review,* September 1975, pp. 27–30.

definition, the decision of an arbitrator is final and binding. The objective of arbitration, by contrast to most forms of mediation and fact-finding is adjudication. Usually, the use of arbitration in either interest or rights disputes occurs after efforts at mediation or fact-finding have failed.[32]

Summary

This chapter has identified the major issues involved in administering a collective bargaining agreement. Grievances involve both the union steward as well as the company foreman. Typically, these disputes are settled by a foreman and union steward following a meeting. However, most private sector collective bargaining agreements in the U.S. have a grievance procedure with binding arbitration as the final step. The U.S. Supreme Court, through the trilogy decisions, affirmed the role of the arbitrator in settling private sector labor disputes. Recent studies have linked the existence and functioning of grievance procedures to lower turnover and higher productivity in the firm. Finally, the arbitration process, which is the final and most expensive part of the grievance procedure, can serve as both a check and balance and as a quality control mechanism for managing human resource decisions.

PROBLEMS

1. Describe the role of the foreman and the union steward in adjudicating grievance disputes between labor and management.
2. **a.** As a result of rulings by the Supreme Court, what criteria determines whether a grievance is arbitrable?
   b. What criteria determines whether a case should go before an arbitrator or the NLRB, if both have potential jurisdiction?
   c. What rights do individuals have under arbitration and the courts, if there is a charge of racial discrimination?
3. What effect do increases in grievances have on firm output and profitability? Is the effect the same for nonunion firms?
4. The Krider Cub Corporation is facing the decision of whether to pursue a case which the union has filed to go to arbitration in the current quarter. Certain union members, at the beginning of the final year of a contract, are refusing to perform certain maintenance functions on their equipment in potential violation of the contract. The company has suspended the workers for not performing these tasks. The grievance has gone through all four lower steps of the grievance procedure and you must decide whether to go to arbitration. The company will provide backpay if they do not go to arbitration.

---

[32] Elkouri and Elkouri, *ibid.*

Current Cost Data for Krider Cub Corporation

Maintenance costs if performed by union members	$10,000 current year
Maintenance costs if performed under sub-contract to mechanics	$15,000 current year
Backpay to workers if company loses or backpay if the company settles at this point	$ 5,000
Probability of winning arbitration case	.5
Total management costs of going to arbitration, direct and indirect	$ 2,500
Expected time to chose arbitrator and receive decision	3 months

Should Krider Cub go to arbitration based on current costs and benefits? Should they go to arbitration based on the impact of the arbitration procedure on the future labor relations climate?

REFERENCES

Berenbeim, Ronald, *Nonunion Complaint Systems: A Corporate Approach.* New York: The Conference Board, 1980.

Elkouri, Frank and Edna A. Elkouri, *How Arbitration Works,* BNA, Washington, D.C., 1981.

Ichniowski, Casey and David Lewin, "Grievance Procedures and Firm Performance," *Human Resources and the Performance of the Firm,* ed. M. Kleiner, R. Block, M. Roomkin, and S. Salsburg, I.R.R.A., 1987.

Slichter, Sumner, James Healy, and E. Richard Livernash, *The Impact of Collective Bargaining on Management,* Brookings Institution, Washington, D.C., 1960.

CASE I
DISCIPLINE AND
THE VETERAN
EMPLOYEE

Federal Mediation & Conciliation Service, Administrator
In the Matter of the Arbitration between Jayhawk Communications
Company and International Brotherhood of Electrical Workers (IBEW)
FMCS Case #1000, G. Fitch, Arbitrator
Appearances:
For the Company: Attorney, Personnel Director, Personnel Administra-
tor, Division Plant Supervisor, Division Manager,
and Central Office Supervisor
For the Union: International Representative, IBEW, Asst. Business
Mgr., Local Union 723, Steward, Witness, Grievant,
Grievant, and Grievant

The Hearing was held on Thursday, June 21, 1987, in Capital City before
the undersigned arbitrator, G. Fitch. All witnesses were sworn. No transcript was taken. Both sides had full opportunity to present evidence and to
question the witnesses. Both parties filed post-hearing briefs which were
received by the arbitrator.

The Issue

Did the Company have just cause for the 15 working day suspension imposed on the grievants, under the facts and circumstances of this case? If not, what shall be the remedy?

The Facts

The Company is a public telephone utility employing approximately 1500 persons in its operations. Of these 1500, about 600 are represented by the IBEW, and about 160 are represented by another union; the remainder are supervisory or other non-bargaining unit personnel.

This case involves three long-service employees represented by the IBEW: Employee A, a Transmission Technician, seniority date April 6, 1974; Employee B, Installation and Repair Worker, seniority date September 9, 1964; and Employee C, Central Office Technician, seniority date April 2, 1957.

On Friday, December 5, 1986, at about 3:30 p.m. supervisor Blanc, who was on his day off drove by the American Legion and noticed two Company vehicles parked in front. He recognized one as being the vehicle of Employee A. Taking the keys from the ignition, he took them on to Capital City where Employee A normally returns his vehicle at the end of the day.

Since no one had been dispatched to the Legion, the supervisory personnel in Capital City awaited Employee A's return or word from him about the missing keys.

About 6 p.m. Employee A returned, having used a spare set of keys to start his Company vehicle. He was questioned by the supervisors on arrival and admitted to having been at the Legion and having had a beer while he was there. He declined to identify other employees who were with him, so the supervisors, through a process of elimination and several phone calls, discovered on their own that he had been in the company of Employee B and Employee C. In each of the various separate inquiries the employees were told not to lie, that it would go easier on them if they told the truth. All three have long and unblemished service records and there seems to be no question that each was truthful in volunteering the extent of his participation in the Legion episode.

All three were suspended pending investigation and a meeting was held the following Monday, December 8, 1986. At the Monday meeting the story unfolded which was later repeated in greater detail for the arbitrator.

Employee B had been asked by the Legion secretary to stop over and repair the phone when he had time. On minor jobs he often does not report the trouble to the central office, but just works it into his schedule. He noted that if he reported each such instance it would be centrally indexed and might reflect poorly upon the quality of his workmanship—that is, if it turned out that the customer had merely left the phone off the hook it would still be noted as a need for service, and if the same customer did it again, it might look as though he had not properly repaired the trouble the first time. Thus, over the years he has simply investigated problems reported directly to him, as his schedule permitted, *before* reporting any servicing to the central office.

In this particular instance a new heat exchanger had been recently installed at the Legion and he mentioned this to Employee A at lunch. Employee A was interested and Employee B suggested that if both completed their work by mid-afternoon they go over and fix the phone and Employee B would show Employee A the new heat exchanger. Both had returned to the office having completed their various assignments at about 3:30 p.m. and decided to go on over to the Legion. Although there was no one at the Legion when they got there, Employee B was a member and had a key.

They fixed the phone and then Employee B called in to the Central Office to make sure they had no further assignments for him. The dispatcher noted on his time sheet that from 4 to 5 p.m. he he was cleaning and restocking his truck, and this is presumably what Employee B indicated in the phone call. In addition to calling in to make sure they were not needed, they left the radio on in Employee A's vehicle in case the office tried to reach them that way.

After fixing the phone and calling the dispatcher, they then called over to Employee B's brother who was working and suggested that he stop on his way home. Employee A and Employee B then played a game of pool and Employee C (Employee B's brother) showed up around 4:30 p.m. All three had a beer from the cooler and went to see the new heat exchanger. They left for their various homes and reporting locations around 5:15. (Their normal quitting time is 5 p.m.). Employee B and Employee C left first and when Employee A discovered his keys were missing, he thought Employee B and Employee C had taken them as a practical joke. He used his spare set to drive his Company vehicle back to Capital City.

At the conclusion of the Monday (December 8, 1986) meeting, the Company indicated that it would investigate further before determining what discipline to impose. All three were returned to work and told that any suspension would be assessed after the first of the year so as not to affect them before the Christmas holidays. Two days later supervisors Blanc and Space went out to the American Legion and ascertained that there was indeed a new cord on the telephone. They also noted that the Legion had installed a unique heat exchanger on the heating system.

It was subsequently determined that each of the three would be given a 15 working day suspension beginning January 2, 1987, for:

> "Drinking alcoholic beverages during working hours [and] driving a Company vehicle after drinking an alcoholic beverage." (Joint Exhibit 3)

The suspensions were grieved as excessively harsh in view of the grievants' long service, unblemished records, truthful response to questioning, and also by comparison with penalties given out in other cases involving alcohol. The Company, in its written attachment to the suspension notices, noted that it initially set the suspensions at 30 days due to the seriousness of the offense, but had reduced the time by half (15 days) in view of the grievants' good service records and their truthfulness during the investigation.

Application of the Rules and Contentions

The applicable rules were entered in evidence as Joint Exhibit 4. There are rules of conduct followed by a section on safety. The rules of conduct are distinguished as either: "minor incidents" (subject to progressive discipline starting with a warning), "major incidents" (where discipline starts with suspension), and "intolerable incidents" (which subject the offender to immediate discharge). Under the safety section penalties are not indicated, although deliberate or repeated violation of the safety rules is shown as a "major incident" under #7 of that section.

While there is really no argument that the grievants' conduct was improper, the Union points out that they did not specifically violate the rules on alcohol:

Major Incident #4. Reporting to work, or working under the influence of intoxicants and/or drugs.

Intolerable Incident #2. Possession, or use, of intoxicants on Company premises during working hours.

The driving of Company vehicles in combination with consumption of intoxicants (including beer) is prohibited under the safety rules, but the Union claims this has been enforced, with a single exception, only in the case of arrest or accident.

The Company admits that up to 1986 its enforcement of the rule against intoxicants in the context of the use of Company vehicles was lax. It offered a November 1985 memo to supervisors and a July 1986 notice to employees indicating that from that time on it no longer intended to tolerate drinking, even at meals, when using Company vehicles. At this time the Company also withdrew the use of Company vehicles for driving to and from Christmas parties (Company Exhibit 2, November 1986).

The Union raised some question as to proof that the notice was actually posted or the memo communicated by supervisors to employees. A further notice containing guidelines on the use of Company vehicles and the prohibition on drinking went out after the October 1985 arbitration award which had involved discipline for after hours use of a Company car after having a few beers.

Although the Company contends that its change in policy with regard to stricter enforcement of the drinking prohibition when using Company vehicles has been adequately communicated, whatever the grievants may have thought on that score, the Company has never tolerated drinking *on the job* under any circumstances similar to this case. In 1984 Employee D was discharged after a customer reported alcohol on his breath. Although he was eventually reinstated after treatment for alcoholism, he was terminated two years later for a repetition of the offense (Company Exhibit 1). In 1986 Employee E was given a two week suspension for stopping at a tavern during working hours. The length of suspension in his case had been modified because of the extenuating circumstance of the recent death of his child.

The only other incidents of drinking during working hours were: the incident in the aftermath of a major fire in 1985 when supervisors brought back beer for the clean-up crew after dinner. It has been tradition that when a central office is converted ("cut-over") from one type of equipment to another—the last phase involving up to 40 people—upon completion of the task the employees and supervisors go to a nearby tavern for whatever remains of the shift to celebrate. Before the November 26, 1986 memo, Company trucks and vans were normally driven to and from these parties. There has only been one cut-over since 1985. The Company approved the party, but disallowed use of Company vehicles.

DECIDE THIS CASE AS IF YOU WERE THE ARBITRATOR AND PRESENT YOUR REASONING.

CASE II
Subcontracting Bargaining Unit Work

DECIDE THE FOLLOWING SUBCONTRACTING CASE AS IF YOU WERE THE ARBITRATOR.

Facts

The Public Utilities Board (PUB) ordered all state telephone companies to upgrade their service by reducing all eight-party telephone lines to five-party lines by December 31, 1986. This order, which has been submitted as Company Exhibit 1, had statewide applicability and gave telephone companies three (3) years to upgrade their service throughout the state in conformity with such order.

The "Company" began to comply with the PUB order immediately upon its publication. The Company had many exchanges throughout the state wherein eight-party lines had to be cut-over to five-party lines. As a practical matter, because of required engineering input and scheduling of work, all the Company's exchanges with eight-party lines could not be cut-over simultaneously. Indeed, the Company complied with the PUB order on a "company by company" basis in accordance with the completion of the necessary engineering analysis and the availability of engineering supervision and work scheduling for each exchange.

Inevitably, one company had to be the final one for which the engineering input was available. This was the Lawrence Area, the territory of IBEW Local (the "Union"). Throughout the state the Company has many geographical divisions. Different unions represent the different divisions. Some divisions are represented by the International Brotherhood of Electrical Workers (IBEW) and some by the Communication's Workers of America (CWA).

Upon the completion of the engineering work for the Lawrence Exchange, the Company had three (3) months remaining to cut-over the eight-party lines within this exchange to five-party lines by the December 31, 1986 PUB deadline. Therefore, as a practical matter the Company had three (3) months and not three (3) years to complete the required cut-overs with the Lawrence Area.

At the outset of this three (3) month period, the Company utilized only workers who were members of IBEW Local (the Union) to perform the mandated cut-over work within the Lawrence Area. At this time, the Company estimated that the Lawrence Area would require approximately 2800 hours to be fully upgraded with five-party lines. After the first 33 days of this three (3) month period had elapsed, only 1200 hours of work on the Lawrence Area upgrade project had been completed by all the IBEW Local workers, including substantial overtime. And, only 38 working days remained until the expiration of the PUB deadline.

At this point, the Company had to reevaluate the Lawrence Exchange upgrade project. The Company concluded: (1) that using all available IBEW Local workers during the final 38 days, assuming that the workers would perform at the same rate over the final 38 days as they did over the first 33 (which period had included significant overtime), would not provide sufficient hours to meet the PUB deadline; (2) that the PUB deadline was an absolute mandate; (3) that the weather during November and December could reduce the number of working days from 38; (4) that the Company should endeavor to complete the upgrade project at least several days before the final PUB deadline to account for negative contingencies and the Holidays; and (5) that approximately 550 to 600 additional hours beyond what all the IBEW Local workers could provide, even with overtime, were needed to meet the PUB deadline.

Because the Company needed 550 to 600 skilled hours which represented about ¼ to ⅓ of a year, in the space of two months, it had only two alternatives. One alternative was outside contract labor, and the second alternative was temporarily transferring some of its Communications

Workers of America (CWA) employees from one of its other adjacent locations, to the Lawrence Area. For reasons of quality, efficiency and to minimize conflicts with the Union, the Company chose to utilize its own trained CWA cut-over workers from another location in the state. The Company concluded that in fact the quality of the cut-over work would be superior if it were performed by its experienced CWA workers rather than by an outside contractor. And, in any event, the PUB deadline precluded extensive negotiations with outside contractors in order to select one and to establish a reliable quality control procedure.

The Company had already complied with the subject PUB order at all its other exchanges. Therefore, other divisions of the Company were able to temporarily "loan" trained cut-over workers to the division encompassing the Lawrence Area.

After the Company determined that it needed to transfer some 600 hours of CWA cut-over workers into the Lawrence Area to meet the PUB deadline, it contracted the Union to so inform them. This was done by the Company to prevent a misunderstanding. The Company's temporary transfer plan did not have and was not intended to have, any adverse effect on the Union's cut-over workers: no lay-offs were caused, working hours were not curtailed, there were no workers on lay-off to call back first, no downgrading, etc. Therefore, there was no supplanting of any kind and no adverse impact on the bargaining unit.

The temporary CWA employees joined the Lawrence Area upgrade project and the work continued. The Exchange eight-party line to five-party line cut-over work was completed December 26, 1986—just before the PUB deadline. Approximately 550 hours of CWA workers' time were expended on the subject Lawrence Exchange upgrade as projected by the Company. This 550 hours equals only about ¼ of a person-year. The transfer of ¼ of a person-year was only necessitated because of the PUB order and the fact that the upgrade project had to be pursued on an area by area basis. The Company did not arbitrarily transfer its CWA employees into the Lawrence Area, nor did the transfer adversely affect the Union or its members. The fact is, that the Company faced legitimate business operational needs and business emergencies and addressed them in a manner designed to insure quality workmanship for its customers without negative impact on any of its employees. This statement is added to the stipulation that during the period of time involved, both CWA and IBEW members worked overtime.

Application of the Rules and Contentions

The Union grieved complaining that the Company violated the contract by acting as it did in using CWA members to perform bargaining unit work within the Districts specified in the Recognition clause of the Contract. Two sections of it follow:

"Section 2.1. The Company hereby recognizes the Union as the exclusive bargaining representative for all Plan and Traffic Department employees within the Company's operations designated as the Districts of the Division with respect to wages, hours, and working conditions.

Section 2.2. The term 'Employee' or 'Employees' wherever used in this Agreement shall refer to an employee or employees in the unit described in Section 2.1 and shall include both sexes except as otherwise specifically provided herein. The term 'Plant,' 'Plant Employees,' 'Traffic,' or 'Traffic Employees' whenever used in the job classifications specified in Appendix 'A'.

In its post-hearing brief, the Union lays the greatest stress on the recognition clause, and along with the brief submitted with three arbitration decisions each holding in favor of this International's Locals and that the employers therein had violated contracts under much the same circumstances as those present here. Each decision held that the recognition clause had been violated. One arbitrator said that the recognition clause in his case, which identified certain facilities of the employer in specified localities, was a bestowal of work to the unit employee working at those localities, not subject to invasion by others. He said: "To have employees from outside the bargaining unit come into the unit was an infringement on the bargaining unit recognized as under the jurisdiction of Local 1912." That was his sole basis for the award to the Local.

In this case there was no claim made by this Union that: the Company committed an unfair practice; that the Company acted in bad faith by concealment, misrepresentation, or otherwise; that seniority was ignored or violated; that the Company's actions resulted in a layoff or failure to recall; or that the Company's actions were motivated or caused by any but business considerations compelled by circumstances stemming from the mandatory PUB order and its time limit.

CHAPTER 20

IMPACT OF UNIONS ON MANAGEMENT

The controversy surrounding the impact of unions on management can be exemplified by the following.

> "As a small company I would close the company down before I would put up with a union."

> "In our industry once a plant becomes unionized it takes seven years before that plant becomes able to compete with a nonunion one."

> anonymous employer responses to union organizing study[1]

In North Carolina, for example, where few workers are organized, the average weekly wage of a production worker in manufacturing is about $175 a week less than in the state of Washington, where nearly half of the workforce is organized. . . . Not to mention a lower standard of living and a less profitable level of economic activity for merchants and businessmen.

> "Why Unions?" AFL-CIO, 1982, p. 11.

---

[1] Richard B. Freeman and Morris M. Kleiner, "Employer Responses to Union Organizing Drives," NBER, 1987.

T hese comments by both management and unions show that they view the impact of unions quite differently. For management responding to potential union organizing, unions are seen as creating inefficiencies in the production process that make the enterprise not as competitive, perhaps even to the shutdown point. The union perspective is quite different. They suggest that unions are able to raise wages, increase the standard of living, and increase profits for merchants. In this chapter you will have an opportunity to assess to what extent each of these statements stands up to economic analysis and empirical results of the impact of unions on management.

After reading this chapter you should be able to answer the following questions: Do unions really raise wages, and if so, by how much over nonunion enterprises? What impact do unions have on management as a result of a union organizing campaign? Do unions enhance or reduce productivity in firms? Finally, what impact do unions have on the balance sheet of an organization? In answering these questions you should also refer to Chapters 17–19 and examine how knowing answers to these issues may help you in the negotiation and administration of a collective bargaining agreement.

Union Impacts on Wages and Fringe Benefits

In many public arenas, such as newspapers, television, and radio, the headlines regarding industrial relations often read that "Unions win pay raises." In this section we will examine the extent to which unions are responsible for these pay raises, and to the degree other factors in the economic environment influence these wage and benefit changes. There are varying ways of defining and analyzing the impacts of unions on compensation and employment. The most often used concept is that of relative wages, which for economists means the amount by which unions have increased the wages of their members in comparison to the wages of comparable nonunion workers.

As was presented in Chapters 9 and 17, one of the major goals of trade unions is to take "wages out of competition," and not have employers compete based on lower total compensation to workers. However, through the bargaining process, backed by the threat of a strike, unions may be able to raise wages and thereby cause potential variations in wages across firms. If two groups of workers had the same characteristics in every way, except one group of workers was organized and the other was not, the data on wages paid to the two groups of workers could be calculated in the following manner. Let W_u be the wage paid to union members and W_n the wage paid to nonunion ones. If the difference between the two could be attributed to only the presence of unions, then the relative wage effect (E_1) that unions achieve for their members would be given as follows:

$$E_1 = (W_u - W_n / W_n) \times 100 \qquad (1)$$

However, equation (1) does not measure the true effect of the union's impact on earnings because there is no estimate of what earnings of unionized workers would be if they were not in a union, or if unions did not exist.

Two factors, called the threat and spillover effects, may cause further inaccuracies in measuring union and nonunion wage differences. The threat effect results in a positive relationship of unions on nonunion earnings. This suggests that wages are kept higher in the nonunion sector as a result of the existence of unions. The implications of the threat effect are illustrated in Figure 20–1.[2] As a result of higher wages in the union sector, workers from that sector lose employment and move to the nonunion sector causing the supply curve to shift outward from S_0 to S_1 (for a detailed explanation see Chapters 4, 5, and 17 relating to the elasticity of the demand curve). However, as a response to the potential threat of union entry, nonunion employers increase their workers' wages to W_n, which lies between W_0, the equilibrium wage without unions and W_u, the union wage. This results in employment falling to E_n. As a result there is unemployment equal to $L_n - E_n$. As a result, the nonunion wage is now higher than W_0, and the estimated union-relative wage advantage is smaller than in equation (1).

This is shown in Equation (2).

$$E_2 = (W_u - W_n)/W_n \times 100 \qquad (2)$$

However, an empirical analysis by Kahn and Morimune found that there is a "wait unemployment effect" in which nonunion workers leave their jobs and wait for union jobs, indirectly raising nonunion wages.[3]

The second factor called the spillover effect causes lower wages in the nonunion sector which results in the union/nonunion wage differential being overstated. The spillover effect is presented graphically in Figure 20–2. In graph (1) the unionized sector is modeled, and in graph (2) the non-unionized sector is depicted. At first, let us assume that workers can move between the two sectors with no costs until wages in both sectors are equalized. Prior to unionization, the equilibrium wage will be W_1 and employment will be E_u^1 and E_n^1 in both sectors.

---

[2] For a detailed graphical representation of the threat and spillover effects and unemployment impact, see Robert J. Flanagan, Robert S. Smith, and Ronald G. Ehrenberg, *Labor Economics and Labor Relations,* Scott, Foresman and Co., Glenview, Ill., 1984.

[3] Lawrence M. Kahn and Kimio Morimune, "Unions and Employment Stability: A Sequential Logit Approach," *International Economic Review,* February 1979, pp. 217–236.

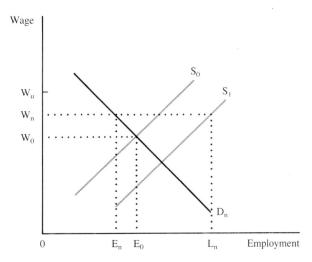

Figure 20-1   **Impact of Threat Effect of Unions on the Nonunion Sector**

If a union organizes workers in graph (1) and raises wages to W_u^2, employment will decline to E_u^2. These workers can then seek employment in the nonunion sector. The supply curves in these two sectors will shift to S_2 in both cases. In the nonunion sector the wage rate will decline to W_2^n at a larger employment level of E_n^2.

In this analysis, the union has increased the wages of those members who managed to keep their jobs. However, they have accomplished this at the expense of lowering the wage rate that was initially paid in the nonunionized sector. Consequently, the "real" relative wage effect E_3 is computed as

$$E_3 = (W_u^2 - W_1)/W_1 \times 100 \qquad (3)$$

Estimates of the Impact of Unions on Wages and Fringes

During the past several years there have been many analyses attempting to estimate the extent to which unions raised the wages of their members relative to wages of comparable nonunion workers. Many of these studies have used information on large samples of individuals, and have attempted to separate wage differentials as a result of unionization from differences that are due to personal characteristics and variations in the occupation and industry of employment. These studies have estimated how much more union members get paid than nonunion workers, after controlling for any differences between the two groups as a result of other factors that might be expected to affect wages.

Table 20–1 presents a summary of estimates of the union/nonunion

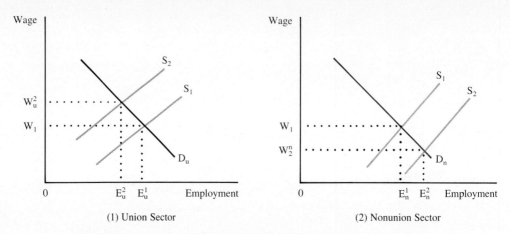

(1) Union Sector   (2) Nonunion Sector

Figure 20-2   **Impact of Spillover Effect of Unions on the Nonunion Sector**

wage differences by different worker, firm, and regional characteristics in a now classic work by H. Gregg Lewis.[4] The results show that the largest differences between union and nonunion wages are as a result of industry variations, and the extent of union organization. However, many demographic characteristics such as sex, race, and marital status have little impact on the wage differences between union and nonunion workers. The wage gap referred to in the table represents the differences in union and nonunion wages for the characteristics.

Although the results presented in Table 20-1 represent the finding of mainly cross-sectional studies, there have been major differences in the impact of unions based on the conditions of the aggregate economic environment during different time periods. Table 20-2 presents estimates of the relative impact of unions during various time periods from 1923 through 1982. For example, during the 1930s, the depression contributed to the union relative wage advantage of over 20 percent. In part, this was due to the inability of firms to cut wages because they had long term contractual obligations during much of the early 1930s. During and following World War II, as a result of greatly increased demand for all labor, the relative wage differential decreased. During the 1950s and 60s, at the height of union density in this country, the relative wage effect was between 15 to 20 percent. During the late 1970s and early 1980s, partially as a result of union and management negotiating cost of living agreements (COLAs) and labor strongholds in many high wage industries, the relative wage effect of unions was over 25 percent. This unusually high wage differential between union and nonunion workers may have caused employers to further resist

[4] H. Gregg Lewis, *Union Relative Wage Effects: A Survey,* University of Chicago Press, Chicago, 1986.

Characteristic	Results	Conclusions
1. Sex (male − female)	41 studies, mean is −.005	Male/female wage gap is ambiguous
2. Race (black − white)	CPS data suggests difference equal to zero: other sources show difference between .05–.10	overall results murky
3. Marital status (Married-other)	overall mean for 11 studies about: −0.1	overall effect is −0.1
4. Major industry		
a. (nonmanufacturing - manufacturing)	a. positive: range .08 − .24	a. excess of nonmanufacturing over manufacturing: about .10
b. (construction-other nonmanufacturing)	b. more than .10 difference in 11 of 13 studies	b. mean wage gap in construction is high compared to manufacturing or nonmanufacturing
5. Occupation	Results refer to studies of both sexes	Wage gap for white collar workers is less than for blue collar
a. (white-blue collar)	a. W-B collar negative mean is −.10	
b. (within blue collar)	b. craft−operatives −.01 service workers−operatives −.05 laborers−operatives .04	
6. Region: city size (excess over South)	range is −.08 to .02 wage gap higher in South	Gap is bigger for the South Gap is smaller in SMSA's
7. Schooling (years)	CPS estimates about −.015 per year other data sources about −.03 per year	Wage gap falls as schooling increases
8. Age, Experience, Seniority	Wage-gap/experience profile is U-shaped, with a minimum at 26-31 years for CPS and 20-32 for other data sets Wage-gap/age profile also U-shaped Seniority/wage-gap profile is less clear	Wage gap/experience and wage-gap/age profiles are U-shaped

The profile for wage gap for seniority is unclear |
| 9. Extent of unionism | unclear | unclear |

Source: *Union Relative Wage Effects: A Survey*, by H. Gregg Lewis, University of Chicago Press, pp. 115–156. Copyright © 1986 by University of Chicago Press. Reprinted by permission.

Table 20–1   **Union/Nonunion Wage Gap Differences by Worker, Firm and Regional Characteristic**

trade unions, and contributed to the further decline in union density in the U.S.[5]

---

[5] Richard B. Freeman, "The Simple Economics of Declining Union Density," National Bureau of Economic Research, 1984.

	Relative Wage (U-NU) x 100
1923 - 1929	17.5%
1930 - 1933	25
1934 - 1939	22
1940 - 1941	15
1942 - 1944	6
1945 - 1949	2.5
1950 - 1954	12
1955 - 1959	17
1960 - 1964	17
1965 - 1969	11
1970 - 1974	14
1975 - 1979	23
1980 - 1982	27

Sources: C. J. Parsley, "Labor Union Effects on Wage Gains: A Survey of Recent Literature," *Journal of Economic Literature,* Vol. XVIII March 1980, pp. 1–31, H. Gregg Lewis, *ibid,* and Daniel Hamermesh and Albert Rees, *The Economics of Work and Pay,* Harper and Row Publishers, New York, 1984.

Table 20-2 **Estimates of the Effect of Unions on Relative Wages 1923–1982**

Another area of employee compensaton that unions can have a major impact upon is fringe benefits. In 1951 about 17 percent of compensation of U.S. blue-collar workers consisted of fringe benefits, but by 1981 that figure had gone up to over 35 percent in union establishments. One major question has been whether unions influence this portion of the compensation package in the same way as wages. The results of various statistical analyses suggest that in establishments having the same characteristics and paying the same wages, fringe expenditures are 30 percent higher under unionism.[6] These results show that unionization is a major determinant of fringe-benefit programs and expenditures that have come to constitute such a large share of compensation. Further, not taking fringe benefits into account understates the real effect of unions on total compensation.

In contrast to these analyses, which state that unions dramatically increase compensation to nonunion workers, some recent findings suggest that this increased compensation is partially a differential for a more structured work setting, less flexible hours, faster work pace, and more hazardous jobs.[7] In fact, one study estimated that two-fifths of the estimated union/nonunion total compensation differential reflects such compensation for unfavorable working conditions. Further, the decision to vote for a union may be influenced by these nonpecuniary terms and conditions of employment.

---

[6] Richard B. Freeman, "The Effect of Trade Unions on Fringe Benefits," *Industrial and Labor Relations Review,* 34 (July 1981) pp. 489–509.

[7] Greg Duncan and Frank Stafford, "Do Union Members Receive Compensating Wage Differentials?" *American Economic Review* 70 (June 1980) pp. 355–71.

Union Organizing Impacts on Management

As the statements at the beginning of this chapter suggest, managers are often opposed to the potential organization of their employees. In this section, we will examine first the extent to which managers are directly affected by an organizing drive. Second, an examination of what managers do during and after an organizing drive in terms of basic personnel practices and wages and benefits will be presented. Third, we will examine managerial strategies during an organizing drive to include wage policies and the use of consultants.[8]

Perhaps the most important question for a manager acting in their own interest is, "What happens to me as a result of an organizing drive?" The information in Table 20–3 shows that in approximately three-fourths of the companies replying to this survey, no changes occurred to the manager of the enterprise following the organizing drive. However, in those cases where some action was taken, it was likely to have a negative effect on the career of the manager. Table 20–3 lists three types of potential outcomes of a union organizing campaign. First, in row one are the results of an election where the union lost the NLRB conducted election (see Chapter 10 for the procedure for these referendums). In row two are the cases where the union won the election, but no collective bargaining agreement was reached. In row three are the cases where the union won the election and a collective bargaining agreement was reached. For example, in no case was the manager promoted if the union won a contract following an organizing drive, but in 23 percent of the cases the manager was either sent off for further training, reassigned, demoted, or fired. In only three percent of the cases was the manager promoted following a campaign where the union lost, but in 20 percent of the cases the fact that an election occurred had a potentially negative effect on the careers of the manager involved. Based on these results, it is not surprising that managers are so opposed to union organizing drives.

A second major issue to be addressed is the responses that management undertakes during the course of a union organizing drive. Specifically, what are the changes in personnel practices and wages that occur during and after a union organizing campaign? Table 20–4 presents the ratios of personnel policies before and after an organizing drive for three potential outcomes of an organizing drive that resulted in an NLRB conducted election. In addition, comparisons of personnel practices are made with a control group of establishments (4) in the same industry for similar kinds of workers that did not have an organizing drive. The results show numerous

---

[8] Much of this section is based on a National Science Foundation study of approximately 400 establishment responses to questions related to potential, and past organizing drives, Freeman and Kleiner, *ibid.*

	Total Percent Promoted	Percent Promoted	Percent No Effect	Percent Sent for Retraining	Percent Reassigned	Percent Demoted	Percent Fired
1) Union lost Election	64	3	76	3	7	7	4
2) Union won but no contract	11	5	70	5	5	15	0
3) Union won and a contract	25	0	77	2	11	2	8

*200 Union organizing drives with 20 or more workers in the potential bargaining unit in New England and
the Midwest.
Source: R. Freeman and M. Kleiner, "Employer responses to union organizing drives," NSF, 1987.

Table 20-3   **Impact of a Union Organizing Drive on Affected Managers***

changes in the type of policies firms provide employees after an organizing
drive. More specifically, the largest changes take place in group 1, where a
negotiated agreement was reached. Within personnel policy areas, the
largest changes for group 1 occurred in the grievance procedure policy, as
well as in the written seniority provisions. There were no major differences
in the policies affecting the written posting of promotions. Finally, it
appears that where contracts are negotiated there is a decline in provisions
affording profit-sharing as part of the employee benefit plan, because unions
often perceive that this may introduce greater uncertainty into compensation, and management may control the way it is allocated.

In contrast to the relatively large changes in personnel policies that
resulted from a union organizing drive during the 1980s, there were
relatively small changes in wages and fringe benefits. Table 20-5 (p. 442)
shows the levels and changes in wages and benefits adjusted by the business
wage index for firms in the various categories. Unlike the results of 15 to 25
percent for the relative wage effect shown earlier in the chapter, newly
organized unions during the 1980s were unable to increase wages much
above firms in which the union lost the organizing drive election. As a result
of deregulation, increased foreign competition, and nonunion wage competition, unions did not appear to be able to increase the wage and benefit
differential, at least during the first round of negotiations, following a
collective bargaining agreement.

Example 20-1 shows that even in firms that are already organized,
companies may be asking for concessions as a result of the changes in the
product market. Attempts at reducing labor costs during the 1980s has been
a major agenda of management. However, even where unions have not been
able to increase wages, they do have the effect of being able to obtain "voice
benefits" like a grievance procedure and the use of seniority in promotions
and layoffs.

During an organizing drive there are varying strategies that management uses. Some of these methods of attempting to halt an organizing drive
may include the following tactics. First, management can use actual wage or

Companies with Drives	(1) Union wins election gains contract		(2) Union wins drive but does not obtain contract		(3) Union loses election		(4) Control group (no election or union)	
	Before	After	Before	After	Before	After	Before	After
Grievance procedure	.38	.86	.46	.64	.49	.66	.44	.52
Written seniority	.42	.70	.39	.71	.53	.63	.33	.39
Written posting promotion	.40	.66	.61	.75	.67	.76	.49	.58
Profit sharing	.36	.24	.57	.68	.55	.63	.47	.55

From: Richard B. Freeman and Morris M. Kleiner, "Union Organizing Drives Resulting in N.L.R.B. Elections During a Period of Economic Concessions," I.R.R.A. Proceedings, 1986, p. 46. Reprinted by permission.

Table 20–4 **Contrasts of Personnel Practices in the Face of an Organizing Drive Leading to an NLRB Election**

benefit increases or promises of wage increases during the course of an organizing drive. These tactics are illegal, and using them would flaunt stated public policies, but for some managers the expected benefits may outweigh the costs of a fine (see Chapter 10 for a fuller explanation of these issues). Second, in other cases firing of a union organizer and sympathizers are used, as well as failing to negotiate a contract in good faith after a union has won an NLRB election. Both of these tactics also are generally considered illegal. Third, management may hire a consultant to assist them in attempts at winning an election during an organizing drive.[9] The purpose of the consultant is to help management in formulating a strategy to convince the workers to vote against the union, or to assist in contract negotiations.

These three tactics are not mutually exclusive ones and may be used in combination. For example, the use of consultants in these elections may signal that the firm appears to be willing to spend a substantial amount of money fighting potential unionization. The use of this procedure is of particular interest, since the average fee is between $800 to $1500 per day and total costs for an election average over $30,000. An additional question is the extent of consultant effectiveness in defeating a union in NLRB sponsored elections or in stopping a negotiated contract. A recent study found that firms that extensively used consultants in NLRB elections,

[9] John Lawler, "The Influence of Management Consultants on the Outcomes of Union Certification Elections," *Industrial and Labor Relations Review,* Volume 38, No. 1, October 1984, pp. 38–51.

	Current wages and benefits (1977 dollars)	Changes in wages and benefits 1 year before elections to current (percent)
Union wins election gains a contract (1)	$5.83 (2.37)	3.3
Union wins election loses contract (2)	$5.48 (2.09)	-1.0
Union loses election (3)	$5.82 (1.66)	2.4
No organizing drive (4)	$5.39 (1.68)	-1.1

Standard deviations are in parentheses.

*Based on 200 Union Organizing Drives with 20 or more workers in the unit in New England and the Midwest.

From: Richard B. Freeman and Morris M. Kleiner, "Union Organizing Drives Resulting in N.L.R.B. Elections During a Period of Economic Concessions," I.R.R.A. Proceedings, 1986, p. 43. Reprinted by permission.

Table 20-5   **Mean Wages and Benefits and Changes in Wages and Benefits by Organizing Category 1980–86***

which appeared close at the beginning of the election, was one-third more likely to defeat the union either through the election process or in no contract being reached. Further, in these enterprises in which the firm defeated the union, companies which used consultants increased wages three percent less in the year following an election than firms that defeated the union and did not use a consultant. For the average firm in this large sample, this was equivalent to approximately $45,000 difference in total wage increases given by firms who did not use consultants versus those that did use them. Firms that used consultants extensively, were somewhat more likely to commit unfair labor practices than those that did not use them at all. Overall, firms that hired consultants extensively were more likely to defeat the union in close elections and give lower wage increases to workers following the election.[10]

Unions and Productivity

One of the more controversial areas in the study of union-management relations is the impact of unions on the productivity of the enterprise. As the statement at the beginning of this chapter suggests, management often thinks that their firm would be less productive with a union than without one. Often management examines the restrictive work rules that are granted in bargaining and concludes that the enterprise is less productive as

---

[10] Richard B. Freeman and Morris M. Kleiner, *ibid.* The authors definition of an extensive use of a consultant was using a consultant 23 days or more during an organizing drive.

EXAMPLE 20.1 EVEN PROFITABLE FIRMS PRESS UNION
WORKERS TO TAKE PERMANENT PAY CUTS

An example of workers taking pay cuts can be shown by Ernest Arzberger who used to earn $12.37 an hour. He figures that whoever replaces him will get about $6 an hour.

Mr. Arzberger is a meatcutter who worked 37 years for Kroger Co., and was dismissed after the company decided to sell its 43 Pittsburgh-area supermarkets because their 2850 employees refused to accept wage and benefit changes. Wetterau Inc., a grocery wholesaler based in St. Louis, is buying the stores and plans to sell these Kroger stores to independent operators, who will run them with lower-paid help and buy supplies from a Wetterau subsidiary.

"I made a good living," says Mr. Arzberger, who at age 62 will take early retirement. "I bought my own house, sent my boy through college and gave the girl a nice wedding. But it won't be that way for the younger people who get our jobs."

All across the country in a variety of industries, employers are fighting to cut payroll costs. Their campaign resembles the "give-backs" of the early 1980s, when many companies who were losing money and seeking temporary concessions to help during the recession. However, in many cases, the current battle is quite different.

Now, despite an economic recovery, many profitable companies—Kroger, Greyhound, and Goodyear Tire & Rubber, to name a few—are saying to their workers: Your wages are just too high for us to maintain profits in the future. We need wage and benefit cutbacks.

"We could stagger along and then go belly-up in the next recession," says an executive at a Midwestern capital-goods concern, "or we can deal with the pay issue now and give ourselves a chance for a future." His company has negotiated some concessions from its unions and expects more. It also reduced pay scales for nonunion salaried employees.

"The rationalization of high, noncompetitive labor costs is moving forward with a vengeance," says A. Gary Shilling, a New York economic consultant. "Major economic and political changes, such as deregulation and intense world-wide and domestic competition, are forcing wage cuts in important areas of the economy."

Source: *Wall Street Journal*, Ralph E. Winter, March 6, 1984.

a result of these provisions. Often items in contracts have made work rules and policies that include limiting daily or weekly output per worker, requiring that unnecessary work be done, having unnecessary workers employed, requiring crews of excessive size, and requiring that work be done only by a particular craft or occupational group. Perhaps the most often cited example is the use of firemen on modern diesel locomotives. Although firemen were needed during the day of the coal fired locomotive, their job disappeared with the widespread use of the diesel engine. However, the union contract protects these positions from elimination, and the individuals who currently hold these jobs are usually on the train "only for the ride." Recent negotiations in the railroad industry have gradually reduced the firemen positions through attrition.

Another line of analysis summarized in Freeman and Medoff's book states that in most cases productivity is much higher at a given point in time under unionism.[11] They state that this is the case because of lower turnover in unionized settings as a result of higher pay and the "voice effect" of the grievance procedure. In addition, there is better training and improved communication in unionized settings. Finally, there is the "shock effect" on specified contractual obligations and long term increases in wages and benefits. Therefore, management is likely to be much more efficient in using and allocating labor at the workplace (see Chapter 5).

A number of statistical studies have attempted to examine the relationship between unionism and productivity levels and changes in productivity. For the most part these studies have been static ones, that is, they examine firms at a point in time. The results on productivity levels show that in more cases than not, there is a positive effect of unions on levels of productivity. These impacts of unions on levels of productivity are summarized in Table 20–6. These results suggest that there is a positive effect. However, you should not think that because productivity is higher that firms would welcome unions with open arms. Firms are evaluated on their profitability and potential growth in output or market share, not only productivity. We now turn our attention to the impact of unions on productivity growth and later to profits.

One of the major objections of management to unions is that they reduce technological change. This occurs because unions are sometimes said to be afraid that technology will result in a reduction of jobs for the organized workforce. On the other hand, unions may speed up the rate of technology and productivity growth by inducing management to substitute new capital for labor as the price of labor goes up, or to pay for the development of new technologies. In the case of the impact of unions on changing technology, the potential impact is not always clear. However, there have been a number of studies which have attempted to estimate the effect of unions on changes in productivity. Several of these studies are summarized in Table 20–7 (p.446). These results, compiled by Professor Steven Allen, suggest that the overall impact is to reduce productivity growth, although the impact is often not statistically significant.[12] Therefore, it appears from these results that labor unions reduce the growth in productivity, although their impact does not appear to be a large one.

Within the context of having a union present are there any policies or

---

[11] Richard B. Freeman and James L. Medoff, *What Do Unions Do?* Basic Books, New York, 1984.

[12] Steven G. Allen, "Productivity Levels and Productivity Change Under Unionism," mimeo, North Carolina State University, 1986.

Studies Using Value Added or Shipments (Sector, Unit of Comparison, Year)	Approximate Percentage Difference in Productivity (with Amount of Capital per Worker and Other Factors Held Fixed) Between Union and Nonunion Units
1. Manufacturing Industries, States	
1972A	20 to 25; 10 to 15
1972B	10
1977	31
Changes between 1972 and 1977	9
2. Wooden Household Furniture, Plants, 1975-1976	15
3. Construction (Revenue Deflated by Area Price Index), States, 1972-1975	21 to 28
4. Office Building Construction (Revenue Deflated by Area Price Index), General Contractors, 1974	39
5. Manufacturing, Individual Businesses, 1980	−2
Studies Using Physical Units of Output (Sector, Unit of Comparison, Year)	
6. Cement (Tons), Plants, 1974	6 to 8
7. Cement (changes in tons), Plants that Went from Nonunion to Union, 1953–1976	1953-1976 6
8. Underground Bituminous Coal (tons), Mines	
1965	33 to 38
1970	−4 to 8
1975	−20 to −17
1980	−18 to −14
9. Construction (Square Feet), Projects, 1974	36

Sources: (1) 1972A: C. Brown and J. Medoff, "Trade Unions in the Production Process," *Journal of Political Economy* 86, no. 3 (June 1978): 355-78; 1972B and 1977: Estimated with Jonathan Leonard from data based on Census of Manufacturers. (2) J. Frantz, "The Impact of Trade Unions on Productivity in the Wood Household Furniture Industry" (Undergraduate thesis, Harvard University, 1976). (3) S. Allen, "Unionized Construction Workers Are More Productive," (North Carolina State University, 1981, mimeographed). (4) and (9) S. Allen, "Unionization and Productivity in Office Building and School Construction" (North Carolina State University, 1983, mimeographed), 27-30. (5) K. Clark, "Unionization and Firm Performance: The Impact on Profits, Growth, and Productivity," Harvard Business School HBS 83-16 (1983). (6) and (7) K. Clark, "The Impact of Unionization on Productivity: A Case Study," *Industrial and Labor Relations Review* 34 (July 1980): 466. (8) M. Connerton, R. B. Freeman, and J. L. Medoff, "Industrial Relations and Productivity: A Study of the U.S. Bituminous Coal Industry" (Harvard University, 1983 revision, mimeographed). Approximate percentage differences were calculated as antilogs of estimated union coefficients in semi-log regression models.
Source: from *What Do Unions Do?* by Richard B. Freeman and James L. Medoff. Copyright© 1984 by Basic Books, Inc. Reprinted by permission of the publisher.

Table 20-6 **Estimates of the Union Productivity Effect**

Studies Using Industry Data	*Impact of Unionization on Annual Productivity Growth*
1. Kendrick and Grossman (1980)	3.6 percent slower under unionism; 1.8 percent faster where union share rises by 10 percentage points
2. Mansfield (1980)	5.4 to 6.1 percent slower under unionism
3. Hirsch and Link (1984)	3.6 to 4.4 percent slower under unionism and 0.5 to 0.7 percent slower where union share rises by 10 percentage points
4. Terleckyj (1980)	a. 4 percent slower under unionism b. insignificant 3 percent slower under unionism c. 3 percent slower under unionism d. insignificant 2 percent slower under unionism
5. Terleckyj (1984)	a. insignificant 0.5 percent slower under unionism b. 1.0 percent slower under unionism c. insignificant 0.5 percent slower under unionism
6. Sveikauskas and Sveikauskas (1982)	insignificant .44 percent slower to .01 percent faster under unionism
7. Freeman and Medoff (1984)	a. insignificant .4 percent slower under unionism b. insignificant .3 percent slower under unionism c. insignificant .3 percent slower under unionism

Studies Using Firm Data	
8. Link (1981)	2.5 percent slower under unionism
9. Link (1982)	a. 10.3 percent slower under unionism b. 9.2 percent slower under unionism
10. Clark and Griliches	insignificant 1 percent higher under unionism

Source: from "Productivity Levels and Productivity Change Under Unionism," by Steven G. Allen. National Bureau of Economic Research Working Paper No. 2304, July 1987. Reprinted by permission.

Table 20-7 **Studies of Unionization and Productivity Change in Manufacturing**

procedures which enhance productivity? A number of studies have found that a good industrial relations climate relating to discipline, absenteeism, and grievances is positively related to productivity. However, in studies thus far, quality-of-worklife policies at the plant had little impact on measures of overall plant performance.[13]

Unions and the Balance Sheet

One of the major concerns for managers and shareholders of a firm related to human resources is the impact of unions on profits and the market value of the firm. In earlier chapters (Chapters 2, 17, and 18) we related the impact of union elections, bargaining, and strikes on market reaction. In this section you will have an opportunity to examine further the impact of unions on profits and compare them to firms that do not have unions. Also, we will review some of the other studies of impacts of unions on the bottom line of the firm that have been presented in other sections of this text.

The impact of unions on firm profitability has been the subject of several studies during the last few years. Some studies use the term *quasi-rent* or return on capital, which is business receipts less variable costs divided by a measure of the value of capital as a measure of profits. A second measure that is used is the *price-cost margin* defined as the excess of prices over variable costs. Third, and perhaps the most accurate measure of firm value is the stock market value of the enterprise (see Chapter 2 for a further description of this approach).

Calculations of the union impacts on these three measures—return on capital, price-cost margin, or market value of the firm—show clear negative impacts.[14] Estimates for price-cost margin and quasi-rents divided by capital are presented in Table 20–8. The profitability differences range from a statistically insignificant 4 percent to a −37 percent using the price cost margin estimates. Similarly, the quasi-rent results show that unions reduce profits from a low of −9 percent to a maximum of −32 percent. Finally, evidence from capital markets show that new unionization results in some decline in shareholder wealth.[15] The results from these estimates provide evidence for the potential reasons why management is so opposed to union organizing and the potential presence of a union. Another key question has been under what economic conditions do unions have a greater impact on reducing profits? That is, do unions reduce the profits to a greater extent in firms that are in highly concentrated industries or in ones which are

[13] Harry C. Katz, Thomas A. Kochan, and Kenneth R. Gobeille, "Industrial Relations Performance, Economic Performance, and QWL Programs: An Interplant Analysis," *Industrial and Labor Relations Review,* October 1983, Vol. 37, No. 1, pp. 3–17.

[14] Freeman and Medoff, ibid.

[15] Richard Ruback and Martin B. Zimmerman, "Unionization and Profitability: Evidence from the Capital Market," *Journal of Political Economy,* Vol. 92, No. 6, December 1984, pp. 1134–57.

Sample	*Approximate Percentage Difference in Profitability Due to Unionism*	
	Price-Cost Margin	Quasi-Rents Divided by Capital
Industries		
1. 139 Manufacturing Industries, 1958-76	−17	−12
2. 168 Internal Revenue Service Major Industries, 1965-76	−37	−32
3. State by Industry,		
1972, 400 observations	4[2]	−27
1977, 360 observations	−14	−9
Companies		
4. 902 Individual Businesses, 1970-80	−16	−19

Sources: (1) and (2): R. B. Freeman, "Unionism, Price-Cost Margins, and the Return to Capital": National Bureau of Economic Research Working Paper No. 1164 (1983). (3): Calculated in conjunction with Jonathan Leonard from 2-digit Standard Industrial Classification by state data. (4): Kim B. Clark, "Unionization and Firm Performance: The Impact on Profits, Growth, and Productivity," Harvard Business School HBS 83-16 (1983). Approximate percentage differences were calculated as antilogs of estimated union coefficients in semi-log regression models.
[a] Not statistically significant.
Source: from *What Do Unions Do?* by Richard B. Freeman and James L. Medoff. Copyright © 1984 by Basic Books, Inc. Reprinted by permission of the publisher.

Table 20-8   **Effects of Unions on Profits**

more competitive? A study by Kim Clark states that firms in highly concentrated industries are able to pass increases in labor costs on to consumers with no effect on profits. Using regression analysis on a private data set, he finds that unions reduce profits more in less concentrated industries and in lower profit businesses.[16] Another analysis on a data set using publically available information from the Survey of Manufacturers and Internal Revenue Service finds results consistent with the hypothesis that, unions capture a sizable fraction of monopoly profits in concentrated industries, but have little effect on profits when markets are more competitive.[17]

As pointed out in other sections of this textbook, studies of the impact of new unionization, strikes, and abnormally large wage settlements reduce the value of the firm to shareholders. This result is consistent with the other studies reviewing the impact of unions on measures of profits.[18] In spite of

---

[16] Kim B. Clark, "Unionization and Firm Performance: The Impact on Profits, Growth, and Productivity," *American Economic Review,* December 1984, pp. 893–919 uses the PIMS database, a privately collected data set from the Harvard Business School.

[17] Thomas Karier, "Unions and Monopoly Profits," *The Review of Economic and Statistics,* February 1985, Vol. 58, No. 1, pp. 34–42.

[18] Paula B. Voos and Lawrence R. Mishel, "The Union Impact on Profits: Evidence from Industry Price-Cost Margin Data," *Journal of Labor Economics,* Vol. 4, No. 1, 1986, pp. 105–132.

these negative estimates of effects on profits, Freeman and Medoff argue that the net effects of unions on the aggregate economy is positive. The basic argument is that unions reduce turnover through higher wages and greater voice at the workforce. This, in turn, leads to lower turnover in the union sector. Consequently, this potentially lower overall turnover results in a lowering of the loss to firms of current workers or specific human capital (see Chapter 11). According to Freeman and Medoff, this gain is greater than the losses to the economy as a result of the inefficiencies that unions produce. Needless to say, these conclusions have been the source of much controversy among students of industrial relations, managers, and unionists.

Summary

This chapter has developed the role that unions have on management behavior and on the performance of private sector organizations. There is substantial empirical evidence to suggest that unions increase wages and benefits for their members, but that the impact varies substantially by industry, occupation, region, and demographic group. Given these increased costs, it is not surprising that mangers oppose new union organizing drives, and that their future in the organization is impacted by unionism. Finally, sections in the chapter reported on the controversy surrounding the impact of unions on private sector firm productivity, and noted that there are conflicting results. However, most analytical studies show that the impact of unions on profitability and stockholder returns are negative.

PROBLEMS

1. **a.** Explain why unionized firms would pay more for workers than nonunion firms.
   b. In estimating the wage differential between union and nonunion firms, what factors might cause you to overestimate the impact of unions?
   c. Under what conditions might you underestimate the union/nonunion wage differential?
2. As a manager seeking advancement within your organization, would you be likely to accept or resist a union organizing drive in your enterprise? Why? What methods would you use to resist union organization, and what are the implications of those methods in maintaining the reputation of the firm in the area?
3. Assume you are a clerical employee at the Lewin National Bank, and you are considering joining a union organizing drive at your branch office. You are faced with the following set of circumstances assuming an imminent election, with wages paid at the beginning of each period, and your vote will determine the outcome.

Wage and benefits per hour

Current
$5.50

A. Projected if no organizing after		B. Projected if drive and union loses election after	
one year	two years	one year	two years
$5.78	$6.06	$5.94	$6.24

C. Projected if union wins election and no contract is reached after		D. Projected if union wins and contract is reached after	
one year	two years	one year	two years
$5.50	$5.50	$5.80	$6.44

a. If you want to maximize earnings, rank the set of outcomes and show the present values (A through D) under which you would be better off after one year with a personal discount rate of 8 percent.

b. Using the same 8 percent rate, rank the scenarios and show present values (A through D) that would maximize hourly earnings after the two year period?

c. Should you vote for the union if you are limited to choices B through D with a two year time horizon, and the expected probability of scenario C is .3 if you vote for the union?

4. In what ways can unions result in increased productivity within an enterprise? The empirical evidence shows that unions reduce profits. How can unions increase productivity yet the net effect is a reduction in profits?

REFERENCES

Abowd, John, "Collective Bargaining and the Division of the Value of the Enterprise," National Bureau of Economic Research, 1986.

Becker, Brian and Craig A. Olson, "The Impact of Strikes on Shareholder Equity," *Industrial and Labor Relations Review,* Volume 39, No. 3, April 1986, pp. 425–438.

Clark, Kim B., "Unionization and Firm Performance: The Impact on Profits, Growth, and Productivity," *American Economic Review,* (December 1984) pp. 893–919.

Karier, Thomas, "Unions and Monopoly Profits," *Review of Economics and Statistics,* Vol. 57, No. 1, February 1985, pp. 34–42.

Lewin, David, "Industrial Relations as a Strategic Variable," *Human Resources and the Performance of the Firm,* ed. Morris M. Kleiner, Richard Block, Myron Roomkin, and Sidney Salsburg, I.R.R.A., 1987.

Slichter, Sumner, James J. Healy, and E. Robert Livernash, *The Impact of Collective Bargaining on Management,* The Brookings Institution, Washington, D. C., 1960.

CHAPTER 21

HUMAN RESOURCES ISSUES IN THE ECONOMY

The role of employees in the organization has been summarized as follows:

"Treating people—not money, machines, or minds—as the natural resource may be the key to it all. ... in Japan organization and people (in the organization) are synonymous. Moreover, the people orientation encourages love of product and requires risk taking and innovation by the average worker."

in Thomas J. Peters and Robert H. Waterman, Jr.
In Search of Excellence: Lessons from America's Best-Run Companies, Warner Books, New York, 1984, p. 39.

I n the highly popular book cited for this quotation, the authors present the idea that using only a cost/benefit technique or present value analysis can lead to short-sighted approaches and often wrong decisions by management. One of the most important tasks of management, they argue is to also make "seat of the pants" decisions and ones based on the quality of the product, as opposed to only "rational" ones based on numbers. However, even Peters and Waterman acknowledge that important decisions must also be based on facts and some underlying quantitative assumptions about the future. In this text we have emphasized the facts and methods of analyzing decisions on the most important input of production—people. By examining this aspect of production, we have linked the personnel function to the bottom line of the organization and to the other functional parts of an enterprise—namely finance, operations, marketing, and accounting.

In this concluding chapter, we first plan to show the significance of human resources in the aggregate economy and how the U.S. labor market has been internationalized. Second, we will identify an important policy and practices of using temporary workers that managers are utilizing in human resource management. Finally, we offer some conclusions regarding the approach we have taken in this textbook, and other courses that you may be interested in enrolling in this field during your tenure as a student.

After reading this concluding chapter you should be able to answer the following questions: Is there a relationship between wages and unemployment? What are the alternative types of unemployment in the aggregate economy? How may the current wage system contribute to unemployment and the lack of economic growth? How has the internationalization of the U.S. economy affected labor markets? What are the costs and benefits of using temporary workers?

Human Resources in the Economy

Thus far, we have emphasized the importance of human resources mainly from the perspective of the enterprise. However, from society's perspective what happens in the organization and aggregate labor market will have major impacts on the national economy. In this section we will discuss two different perspectives of the way human resources may impact on the larger economic environment and how public and firm policies may be used to influence aggregate performance.

During much of the 1950s, 1960s, and early 1970s, the idea was held among a majority of economists and policymakers that inflation would diminish if unemployment rose. This implied that government fiscal or monetary policy could be used skillfully to maneuver the aggregate economy to acceptable levels of both inflation and unemployment. However, during the late 1970s and early 1980s the U.S. was faced with both relatively high rates of wage changes and high unemployment rates. In order to discuss these issues in more detail, some basic concepts need to be developed.

First, the overall rate of wage inflation in the economy is the annual percentage rate of increase in a composite measure of hourly earnings in the economy. Second, the unemployment rate, as defined in Chapter 3, is an overall measure of labor market vacancies in the economy. In the context of the aggregate economy there are generally three different types of unemployment experience based on their underlying economic causes. First, frictional unemployment is generally referred to as unemployment that occurs during a full employment situation because some people are "between jobs." Since labor markets are dynamic and information is imperfect, it takes time for unemployed workers and employers with openings to find one another causing this temporary unemployment to occur. Second, structural unemployment occurs when there is a mismatch between the skills demanded and supplied in a given area or an imbalance for workers across geographic areas.[1] In the early 1960s and 1970s the federal government was heavily involved in policies to reduce structural unemployment. These policies involved provisions of both classroom and on-the-job training. More recently, the *Job Training Partnership Act of 1982* has put an emphasis on public/private cooperation in providing training and jobs to reduce structural unemployment. Finally, cyclical unemployment refers to the economy's periodic reductions in the rate of growth of aggregate demand or output and its derived demand—labor. These fluctuations in the business cycle result in parallel movements in the national unemployment rate.

The early relationship that was examined between the unemployment rate and wage inflation was called the Phillips Curve, and is briefly discussed in Chapter 3.[2] Figure 21–1 develops a map of potential curves noting the basic trade-offs. For example, along curve *a*, a 5.5 percent unemployment rate is associated with a 2.5 percent rate of wage inflation. Further, a movement up the curve *a* results in a 3 percent unemployment rate which is associated with a 7 percent rate of wage inflation. Along this curve, the policymakers can choose alternative points based on their own values and the political consequences.[3] For example, a high unemployment choice might lead voters who were fearful of losing their jobs to vote against a particular politician. Alternatively, persons on fixed incomes would be opposed to high rates of wage inflation if their incomes were not somehow linked to inflation directly through a cost-of-living adjustment.

However, during the 1970s higher rates of unemployment began to be associated with higher rates of wage inflation. This suggested to some that the stable negative trade-off between wage inflation and unemployment was unwarranted. The counter argument was that while this trade-off between wage inflation exists at a point in time, the position of the trade-off is determined by a number of factors that change over time. The impact of these factors is to shift the curve upward and to the right as shown by curves

[1] Ronald Ehrenberg and Robert Smith, *Modern Labor Economics,* Scott, Foresman and Co., Glenview, Ill., 1985.

[2] A.W. Phillips, "The Relation Between Unemployment and the Rates of Change of Money Wage Rates in the United Kingdom, 1862–1957," *Economica* 25 (November 1958) pp. 283–99.

[3] Paul A. Samuelson and Robert M. Solow, "Our Menu of Policy Choices," *The Battle Against Unemployment,* ed. Arthur M. Okun (New York: W. W. Norton, 1965) pp. 71–76.

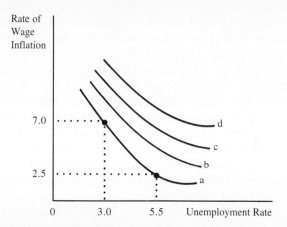

Figure 21-1 **The Relationship Between the Rate of Wage Inflation and the Level of the Unemployment Rate**

b through *d* in Figure 21–1. This suggests that higher rates of wage inflation have become associated with a given level of unemployment. Still another position has argued that the long run trade-off curve is vertical and that trying to keep the unemployment rate low through monetary stimulus will lead mainly to growing rates of inflation.[4]

The economists that suggested the Phillips Curves shifted outward stated that there were labor market rigidities in the system such as shifts in the structure of employment (e.g., increase in the labor force participation of teenagers or women), that may have kept unemployment rates high.[5] Others argued that the growth in the union/nonunion wage differential caused wages to increase (see Chapter 20). Further, the existence of multi-year labor contracts and the spread of cost-of-living escalator clauses may have been partially responsible for the insensitivity of wage inflation to the unemployment rate in the 1970s and early 80s.[6] Further, numerous macroeconomic policies such as federal deficits can have major impacts on both a movement along the curve as well as enhancing shifts of the curve.[7]

A number of economists have called these high levels of unemploy-

---

[4] Milton Friedman, "The Role of Monetary Policy," *American Economic Review,* 58 (March 1968) pp. 1–17.

[5] Katherine G. Abraham, "Structural/Frictional vs. Demand Deficient Unemployment," *American Economic Review,* 73 (September 1983) pp. 708–24.

[6] Daniel Mitchell, *Unions, Wages, and Inflation* (Washington, D.C.: Brookings Institution, 1980).

[7] Lawrence A. Gordon, Morris M. Kleiner, and R. Natarajan, "Capital Budgets and Government Deficits: Implications for GNP and Labor," *Journal of Accounting and Public Policy,* Vol. 5, No. 4, December 1986, pp. 217–32.

ment, increasing wage changes, and lack of economic growth, *stagflation.* According to Professor Martin Weitzman of M.I.T., one of the major causes of stagflation is that the wage system is not tied to productivity.[8] To illustrate, Figure 21–2 shows the growth in compensation and hourly output of the U.S. economy from 1977 to 1985. Hourly compensation or unit labor costs have grown by approximately 70 percent whereas output has grown about 5 percent. The result, he argues, is unwarranted growth in wages which leads to growth in wage inflation and lack of real economic growth in the economy.

As a partial cure for stagflation Dr. Weitzman offers the following diagnosis and prescription. He suggests that these ills of the economy are caused by the way labor is compensated. Namely, tying the compensation of a firm's employees to an outside unit of account (typically a cost-of-living index) whose value is independent of the firm's well-being is not appropriate. He suggests alternative payment schemes in which a worker's pay is tied to an appropriate index of the firm's performance—namely a share of its revenues or profits. To illustrate, a union at American Telephone and Telegraph (AT&T) would negotiate over the share of total revenue going to labor rather than average wages per hour. The incentives, he argues, are to increase employment, expand output, and lower prices. A more realistic "mixed" system consisting of a base wage plus a profit-sharing component will have basically the same results.

An empirical test of the impact of this type of system on the aggregate economy has been implemented for Japan.[9] Many Japanese workers receive approximately 25 percent of their pay in the form of semi-annual bonuses. One question has been whether part of Japan's remarkable ability to stabilize unemployment at low steady rates that are at or below 3 percent during the 1970s and 80s is due to the automatic pay flexibility that comes with profit or revenue sharing. Bonuses also are important quantitatively relative to reported company profits, ranging from 42–76 percent of operating profits before taxes from 1965–83, and constitute about 10 percent of net domestic product or aggregate output. Using standard econometric models of the economy, the estimated employment effect of this method of bonuses in Japan is to increase the level of employment in that country to between 1.25 to 2.50 percent. Although not a panacea by itself, the bonus system in Japan helps maintain relatively tight labor markets, but so do other complementary aspects of the Japanese system.

If similar results are obtainable in the U.S. as a result of the implementation of a bonus compensation system for a large part of the labor force, the impact would probably be some reduction in the unemploy-

[8] Martin L. Weitzman, *The Share Economy: Conquering Stagflation* (Harvard University Press, 1984).

[9] Richard B. Freeman and Martin L. Weitzman, "Bonuses and Employment in Japan," NBER Working Paper Series, 1978, 1986.

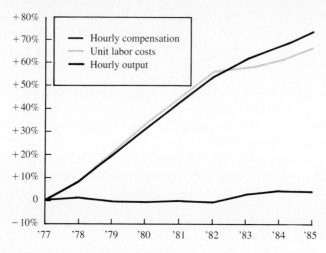

Source: Bureau of Labor Statistics, 1986.

Figure 21-2 **Pay in Perspective: Private Nonfarm Businesses**

ment rate. However, the likelihood of such a proposal being implemented in the U.S. is probably slim, in part, as a result of union leadership opposition and because unions often attempt to reduce profit sharing as a fringe benefit.[10] They argue that workers should not bear downside wage risks during economic downturns and that business revenue outcomes are generally beyond their control. However, variable compensation has been adopted in some areas of professional sports, like the National Basketball Association, and in certain manufacturing establishments, as well as limited profit-sharing programs in a wider variety of other firms.[11]

Internationalization of the U.S. Labor Market

Besides being able to learn from the labor market policies of other countries, like Japan, that may apply to the U.S., there are also important elements of competition on an international scale. For example, countries in the Far East, such as Korea and Taiwan, whose wage rates are less than one-half those in the U.S., are luring American firms particularly in light manufacturing where skill levels and pay are relatively lower than in this country. This increased competition internationally is resulting in some reassessment of the appropriate geographic market for labor. The implications for the U.S. labor market are significant. Rather than competing only

[10] Rudy Oswald, "Comments on The Share Economy," *Industrial and Labor Relations Review*, Vol. 39, No. 2, January 1986, pp. 287–88.

[11] George Strauss, "Participation and Gainsharing Systems: History and Hopes," University of California, Berkeley, 1986.

against firms in this country, companies are looking abroad for sight selections based in large part on labor costs. Although an increasing amount of competition on wage rates and output is from less developed countries, the majority of both trade and competition is based on labor compensation and productivity from industrialized countries. Table 21–1 shows comparisons of changes in manufacturing output and annual percent changes in hourly compensation in manufacturing for 12 developed countries from 1979 to 1985. The U.S. ranked ninth of these countries in changes in manufacturing output and fifth in holding down unit labor costs. However, when you take into account the increasing value of the U.S. dollar relative to the currencies of the other countries in the Table, U.S. labor costs grew relatively even more rapidly.[12] This shows that the U.S. is not as competitive as many of the other industrial countries on wage issues, and that manufacturing jobs and output may be lost as a consequence.

For unions who seek to take wages out of competition, this is an unwelcome additional source of wage competition. Even though a particular industry may be highly organized in the U.S., with nonunion firms paying approximately similar wages, non-U.S. firms may be able to offer lower wages and produce similar products at a lower price. As a result of this internationalization of the labor market, unions have discussed ways of narrowing these wage differentials across countries. However, at this time there has been very limited success in this process of international union cooperation in narrowing this wage gap.

In a recent study by John Abowd and Richard Freeman, they find the "trade content" of the U.S. economy, measured by exports plus imports relative to Gross National Product (i.e., the summation of all goods and services produced in a year) has increased. However, the share of labor in non-traded sectors, notably services, has risen, so that we have a smaller fraction of workers directly affected by trade than in the past.[13] However, production workers in these industries are more closely tied to world markets than in the past. This relationship is shown in Table 21–2, where traded goods are defined as those products in manufacturing, mining, and agriculture.

Another important development has been the growth in employment in the U.S. of foreign-owned companies. For example, there has been a more than doubling of U.S. employees working for U.S. affiliates of foreign companies from 1974 to 1983. Currently, over 2.5 million U.S. employees work for a U.S. affiliate of a foreign company. Surprisingly, foreign-owned enterprises have a comparable unionization rate to domestically-owned enterprises, are concentrated in the traded goods sector, and have higher wages and productivity than domestic producers.[14]

---

[12] Arthur Neef, "International Trends in Productivity and Unit Labor Costs in Manufacturing," *Monthly Labor Review,* Vol. 19, No. 12, December 1986, pp. 12–17.

[13] John Abowd and Richard B. Freeman, "The Internationalization of the U.S. Labor Market," NBER, 1986.

[14] *Ibid.*

Country	Annual Percent Change in Manufacturing Output	Annual Percent Change in Unit Labor Costs (U.S. Dollars)
U.S.	3.1	3.7
Canada	1.7	6.6
Japan	5.7	−1.1
France	3.8	8.3
Germany	3.2	2.8
Italy	3.7	12.0
U.K.	4.2	6.7
Belgium	5.7	1.7
Denmark	1.9	5.9
Netherlands	4.4	.8
Norway	2.0	7.6
Sweden	3.3	6.2

Source: Arthur Neef, "International Trends in Productivity and Unit Labor Costs in Manufacturing," *Monthly Labor Review,* Vol. 109, No. 12, December 1986, pp. 12–17.

Table 21-1 **Annual Percent Changes in Unit Labor Costs (U.S. Dollars) and Manufacturing, 1979–85**

Temporary Workers in the U.S. Economy

Another policy that has been growing in the U.S. labor market is the contracting out of certain types of work. During the 1982–85 period personnel supply services grew in employment by 71.5 percent in comparison to an 11.9 percent growth in employment in all private nonagricultural industries.[15] For example, Kelly Services, Inc., the largest supplier of temporary office services, doubled its sales to over 1 billion dollars in 1986 over a three year period. Further, the growth of contingent workers, who are defined as leased employees from other companies, temporary workers, involuntary part-timers, employees of subcontractors, and homeworkers who work in their residence, has grown from 8 million workers in 1980 to over 18 million in 1985.[16] Since they are marginal workers in the firm they are extremely sensitive to changes in cyclical aggregate demand. A major reason for this growth is the ability of companies to respond quickly to peaks and downturns in the demand for labor by hiring personnel for short periods of time.[17] Further, fewer commitments need to be made on behalf of the company to long term benefits like vacation time, pensions, and insurance. Further, the main part of the workforce becomes more insulated from the upturns or downturns in the economy, and the employer has a

[15] Wayne J. Howe, "The Business Services Industry Sets Pace in Employment Growth," *Monthly Labor Review,* Vol. 109, No. 4, April 1986, pp. 29–36.

[16] *Business Week,* December 15, 1986, p. 53.

[17] Katherine G. Abraham, "Flexible Staffing Arrangements: Models and Some New Evidence," NBER, 1986.

Total Traded Goods*	1970	1980	1983
1. Exports and Imports as a percent of GNP	27.1%	59.7%	49.5%
2. Percent of GNP	30.1%	28.7%	26.3%
3. Percent Employment	31.6%	26.7%	24.2%

*Traded goods sector consists of manufacturing, mining, and agriculture.
Source: John Abowd M. and Richard B. Freeman, "The Internationalization of the U.S. Labor Market,"
    NBER, 1986.

Table 21–2   **Changing Trade Content of the U.S. Labor Market**

better image as a reliable employer. In contrast to pay being linked to overall performance as in our share economy discussion, in this case employment is the variable that is tied to the performance of the firm. The level of employment becomes a highly variable input in the production process.

An example of the use of temporary help in major industries is provided in Example 21–1. However, the cost of using such a policy includes the lack of loyalty that these persons have toward the company and its objectives. Further, individuals that work for these short periods of time often receive wage premiums to compensate for the relatively high turnover involved in being a temporary employee, as well as not receiving forms of deferred compensation such as pensions.

An additional area of concern during the decade of the 1980s has been the changes in the business cycle as well as the effects of deregulation on the economy. During the recession of the early 1980s when unemployment reached 10.5 percent, firms became more concerned about having too many workers. This reassessment over the costs and availability of labor has continued throughout the decade as unemployment rates have continued to be over 6 percent into the latter part of the 1980s. The huge swings in the business cycle from recession to recovery and its impact on hiring decisions continues to be a major source of uncertainty for employers. Generally, a major concern of enterprises is having too many workers in recessions, and too few in an economic expansion, and the additional cost is particularly felt in many highly cyclical industries such as autos, housing, and other durable goods, like refrigerators.

Decisions on pay and employment have also become more uncertain as a result of the deregulation of numerous industries that include airlines, trucking, telecommunications, and banking. In previous decades, decisions on employment and pay could be made under the assumptions of constant or growing revenues. With more competition and a greater efficiency-orientation, these industries are more concerned with cost-cutting and obtaining higher levels of productivity. In making hiring, layoffs, and promotion decisions, the elimination of the assumptions of a fixed or growing source of revenue means adjusting human resource requirements based on firm product demand. Attempting to resolve short-run cost-benefit approaches to human resource management with long term people-

EXAMPLE 21.1 ARE TEMPORARY EMPLOYEES WORTH IT?

When Grumman Corp. needed 20 software engineers, they could have spent several months hiring those people, only to face dismissing them after the one-year contract ended. Instead the Bethpage, N.Y. company hired free-lance engineers to fill the positions. "When you have a layoff, you have less of a layoff in the public-relations sense of the word," say Robert Farrell, a purchasing manager at Grumman, which has about 700 temporary workers in all.

Companies that are reducing their permanent workforce are making greater use of free-lancers for such professional positions as engineers, programmers, and project managers. When business turns sour, the temporary workers are the first to go, thereby avoiding the costs of laying off permanent employees.

The trend toward the use of temporary employees is especially noticeable at companies with no-layoff policies, says Jerome M. Rosow, president of Work in American Institute, a research center in Scarsdale, N.Y. "In more sophisticated companies you see tighter staffing margins that are below 100 percent to avoid lay-offs, so they use temporary workers for unexpected peak loads," he says.

Although there are benefits, using temporary workers raises troubling management issues. "While contract employees make financial sense (because of costs to hire permanent workers), there are questions about the potential disruptive effect on the organization," say Jerrold Bratkovich, senior vice–president of the Hay Group, a Philadelphia consulting firm.

Temporary workers usually have no stake in the company and therefore little loyalty. They are often paid more per hour than permanent employees doing the same work, sometimes causing internal bickering. Furthermore, says Mr. Bratkovich, constantly changing the size of the workforce and quality may hurt productivity. "It focuses people's attention on the fluctuation and what it will do to them," diverting them from doing their job, he says.

About 140 temporary workers —programmers, engineers, and technical writers—now work at Hewlett-Packard's computer divisions. A freelancer's wages and benefits (about $45 an hour for an experienced software programmer) can range from 50 percent to 100 percent higher than a permanent employee's. After figuring the cost of benefits for a permanent worker, a contract worker's pay averages about 20 percent higher, says Mr. Prather, manager of software engineering. "It's worth that 20 percent if you're looking to hire people quickly and who are already experienced; you don't have to train them and that saves you money," he says.

Source: *Wall Street Journal,* Larry Reibstein, April 18, 1986.

oriented goals and objectives mentioned by Peters and Waterman at the beginning of the chapter is one of the most important issues any manager must address. Moreover, treating workers in a fair and equitable manner, and providing them with the physical tools and incentives to do their job can result in significant long run payoffs.

Summary

This textbook has attempted to provide you with a general knowledge of labor market and human resource management concepts, practices, and policies within the context of a decision-oriented approach. By the nature of this book we have had to be brief in covering the wide range of topics which are necessary for any general manager to know about employment issues. However, for those of you who want to take additional courses on this topic, most universities or colleges offer some or all of the following courses which expand upon the material covered in this introduction to the human resources area. These courses include:

- Collective Bargaining
- Compensation Management
- Dispute Resolution and Arbitration
- Labor Economics
- Labor History
- Labor Relations
- Performance Appraisal
- Personnel Management
- Public Sector Labor Relations
- Public Policy and Labor
- Staffing, Selection, and Training

The approach we have taken in this text will hopefully allow you to make better overall decisions regarding human resource costs and benefits. The real test of your mastery of these concepts will be their application in a work environment. As this field progresses through more thorough research and skilled practical applications, the human resource profession will be able to provide better answers to make the workplace both a more efficient and equitable place to spend your worklife.

PROBLEMS

1. As a government policymaker what are the benefits or consequences of moving along the Phillips Curve from a high unemployment low wage inflation point to a low unemployment high wage inflation point? What might cause this trade-off to not be feasible?

2. As a Chief Executive Officer of your firm develop verbally the costs and benefits of having total compensation tied to the economic performance of your firm. Why do you think a union in such a firm might object to in this type of linkage?

3. Ahlburg Bicycle Manufacturing Inc. is faced with the following scenario. The demand for bicycles has gone up temporarily (1 year), but is expected to return to former levels. The company would like to capitalize on this fortunate turn of events, and must make some key human resource decisions. Quantitatively and verbally analyze their planning strategy.
Current Cost of Workforce
   100 employees
   $10.50 per hour (no overtime)
   40 hours per week
   50 weeks per year
   Training and recruitment cost per worker $7000
   Overtime is paid at 1.5 base rate
   Contracting out pay for Kochan Temps. Inc. is $12.00 per hour
The temporary increase in demand will result in a 20 percent increase in total labor demand. Which policy should Ahlburg Inc. follow?
(a) require overtime of current workers
(b) hire more workers
(c) subcontract labor
Why?

4. What are the problems in using only a cost/benefit approach in analyzing human resource management issues?

REFERENCES

Abowd, John M. and Richard B. Freeman, "Internationalization of the U.S. Labor Market," NBER, 1986.

Gordon, Robert J., "Why U.S. Wage and Employment Behavior Differs from that in Britain and Japan," *Economic Journal,* 92 (March 1982) pp. 13–44.

Mitchell, Daniel., *Unions, Wages, and Inflation,* Washington, D.C.: The Brookings Institution, 1980.

Wachter, Michael L., "The Changing Cyclical Responsiveness of Wage Inflation Over the Postwar Period," *Brooking Papers on Economic Activity,* No. 1, 1976, pp. 115–67.

Weitzman, Martin L., *The Share Economy: Conquering Stagflation,* Harvard University Press, Cambridge, MA, 1984.

Name Index

Subject Index